CLASSIC READINGS IN URBAN PLANNING

AN INTRODUCTION

CLASSIC READINGS IN URBAN PLANNING

AN INTRODUCTION

EDITED BY

Jay M. Stein

Department of Urban and Regional Planning
University of Florida

McGRAW-HILL, INC.

New York   St. Louis   San Francisco   Auckland   Bogotá
Caracas   Lisbon   London   Madrid   Mexico City   Milan
Montreal   New Delhi   San Juan   Singapore   Sydney   Tokyo   Toronto

This book was set in Times Roman by Better Graphics, Inc.
The editors were Meredith Hart and David Dunham;
the production supervisor was Leroy A. Young.
The cover was designed by Carla Bauer.
The photo editor was Anne Manning.
R. R. Donnelley & Sons Company was printer and binder.

CLASSIC READINGS IN URBAN PLANNING
An Introduction

This book is printed on recycled, acid-free paper containing 10% postconsumer waste.

1 2 3 4 5 6 7 8 9 0 DOH DOH 9 0 9 8 7 6 5 4

ISBN 0-07-061138-6

Library of Congress Cataloging-in-Publication Data

Classic readings in urban planning: an introduction / edited by Jay
    M. Stein.
        p.   cm.
    Includes bibliographical references.
    ISBN 0-07-061138-6
    1. City planning—United States.   I. Stein, Jay M.
HT167.C565   1995
307.1'216'0973—dc20   94-4273

ABOUT
THE EDITOR

JAY M. STEIN is professor and chairman of the Department of Urban and Regional Planning, College of Architecture, University of Florida. He previously served as chairman of the Department of Planning and Design, SUNY, Buffalo; as acting dean, School of Architecture and Planning, SUNY, Buffalo; and as visiting professor of Infrastructure Planning and Management, Stanford University. His research interests are in growth management, infrastructure planning, and economic development. The author of numerous articles and books, his most recent writings include *Growth Management: The Planning Challenge of the 1990s* and *Public Infrastructure Planning and Management.*

ABOUT
THE AUTHORS

ALAN A. ALTSHULER is professor of urban policy and planning at the Kennedy School of Government and Graduate School of Design at Harvard University. He was formerly with the Department of Government at Cornell; associate professor at Massachusetts Institute of Technology; and Dean of the Graduate School of Public Administration at New York University. In addition to *The City Planning Process*, his numerous other writings include *The Urban Transportation System: Politics and Policy Innovation*.

SHERRY R. ARNSTEIN has served as a director of Community Development Studies for The Commons, a nonprofit research institute in Washington, D.C., and Chicago. She was the chief citizen participation advisor for Model Cities Administration with the Department of Housing and Urban Development from 1967–1968. She has served as Staff Consultant to the President's Committee on Juvenile Delinquency, Special Assistant to the Assistant Secretary of HEW, and Washington Editor of *Current Magazine*.

RICHARD BABCOCK has been a consultant to the Chicago firm of Ross & Hardies since 1981. He was a governor's appointee to the Northeastern Illinois Planning Commission from 1965–1972 and Chairman of the Governor's Commission on Clean Air Act. He was formerly the President of the American Planning Association and a member of the American Bar Association Advisory Commission on Housing and Urban Growth. He was an adjunct professor at the University of Illinois, Chicago, and a lecturer at several universities, including Harvard, Northwestern, Georgia Tech, UCLA, and the University of Wisconsin. He has taught at the University of Michigan Law School, Northern Illinois University, and at Florida State Law School. He is the author of numerous books, including *Billboards, Glass Houses and the Law*, and *The Zoning Game Revisited*, and co-author of *City Zoning: The Once and Future Frontier* and *Special Districts: The Ultimate in Neighborhood Zoning*.

MICHAEL P. BROOKS is a professor in the Department of Urban Studies and Planning in the School of Community and Public Affairs at Virginia Commonwealth University. He is the former dean of the College of Design at Iowa State, of the School of Architecture and Environmental Design at the State

University of New York at Buffalo, and of School of Community and Public Affairs at Virginia Commonwealth. From 1979–1980 he served as the president of the American Planning Association.

RACHEL CARSON pioneered in calling worldwide attention to the risks of herbicides and chemicals in the environment to our health. Her extensive knowledge and writings stirred a controversy that resulted in increased research on the impacts of pesticides. She was a graduate of the Pennsylvania College for Women and received her master's degree from Johns Hopkins. She worked as an aquatic biologist for the United States Bureau of Fisheries in 1936 and became editor in chief of the Publications of the U.S. Fish and Wildlife Services in 1947. Other works include *Under the Sea-Wind, The Sea Around Us*, and *The Edge of the Sea*.

HENRY G. CISNEROS is the former mayor of San Antonio, Texas, and the current Secretary of the Department of Housing and Urban Development. He has a master's degree in urban and regional planning from Texas A & M University and a doctorate in public administration from George Washington University.

PAUL DAVIDOFF was a pioneer in the field of advocacy planning. While serving as a member of the faculty of City Planning at the University of Pennsylvania and then at Hunter College of the City University of New York, he worked tirelessly for the rights of the poor and the powerless. He also founded and served as executive director of the Suburban Action Institute, New York. Davidoff held a law degree and a master's degree in planning from the University of Pennsylvania. The Association of Collegiate Schools of Planning has created the Paul Davidoff Award in his memory.

JOHN M. DeGROVE is the director of the Florida Atlantic University/Florida International University Joint Center for Environmental and Urban Problems. Generally regarded as a pioneer and national authority in growth management, he was instrumental in the conception and passage of Florida's landmark 1985 Growth Management Act. DeGrove is the author of numerous publications, including *Land, Growth and Politics*, published by the American Planning Association. He also serves as consultant to the state/regional/local planning and growth management systems in several states.

SABINA DEITRICK recently received her Ph.D. degree from the Department of City and Regional Planning at the University of California, Berkeley. She is currently an Assistant Professor of Public and International Affairs at the University of Pittsburgh.

ANTHONY B. DOWNS is a senior fellow in the Economic Studies program at the Brookings Institution. He has previously served as an assistant professor of economics and political science at the University of Chicago; as a member of the Real Estate Research Corporation; and as director of the Urban Institute Manpower

Demonstrations Research Corporation. Dr. Downs has also served on several national commissions and advisory boards including the National Commission on Urban Problems and the Advisory Commission on Regulatory Barriers to Affordable Housing. His numerous publications include *Racism in America, Neighborhoods and Urban Development*, and (coauthor) *Urban Decline and the Future of American Cities*.

JOHN W. DYCKMAN was professor of geography and environmental engineering at Johns Hopkins University where he also served as director of the Johns Hopkins European Center for Regional Planning and Research in Nord-Pas de Calais. He previously served as the James Irvine Professor of Planning, School of Urban and Regional Planning, University of Southern California.

WALTER C. FARRELL, JR. is a professor of educational policy and community studies at the University of Wisconsin, Milwaukee, and a research affiliate in the Center for the Study of Urban Poverty at the University of California, Los Angeles. His research focuses on the race and class underpinnings of the urban underclass, urban education, and social issues.

JOHN FORESTER is a professor in the Department of City and Regional Planning at Cornell University. He has written extensively on planning theory and critical social theory. *Making Equity Planning Work* (with Norman Krumholz) received the Association of Collegiate Schools of Planning Paul Davidoff Award.

JOHN FRIEDMANN is a professor in the Urban Planning Program at the University of California, Los Angeles. Dr. Friedmann has written widely on regional planning and planning theory, including *Planning in the Public Domain: From Knowledge to Action*. The Association of Collegiate Schools of Planning presented Dr. Friedmann with the Distinguished Planning Educator Award in Buffalo, New York (1988).

JOEL GARREAU has spent four years exploring America's Edge Cities from coast to coast. He is regarded as a keen observer of American urban life. A senior writer for the *Washington Post*, his publications include *The Nine Nations of North America*.

DAVID R. GODSCHALK is a professor in the Department of Urban and Regional Planning at the University of North Carolina at Chapel Hill. He is the former editor of the *Journal of the American Institute of Planners* and has served on the editorial boards of *Journal of the American Planning Association* and the *Journal of Planning Education and Research*. His recent research has focused on land use policy, dispute resolution, growth management, and hazard mitigation. His writings include *Constitutional Issues of Growth Management* (coauthor) and *Understanding Growth Management: The Planner as Dispute Resolver*.

WILLIAM W. GOLDSMITH is a professor of city and regional planning at Cornell University where he also serves as director of the Program on International Studies in Regional Planning. He has worked with the Puerto Rico Planning Board and taught in the Graduate Planning Program in San Juan, as well as at the Universidad de Los Andes and the Universidad de Javeriana in Bogotá, Colombia. His research is on local institutions as generators of social and economic development. He is the coeditor of *Urban and Regional Planning in an Age of Austerity* (with Piere Clavel and John Forester) and *Separate Societies: Poverty and Inequality in U.S. Cities* (with Edward J. Blakely).

CHARLES M. HAAR is the Louis D. Brandeis Professor of Law at Harvard University. He has also served as chairman of the Joint Center for Urban Studies at the Massachusetts Institute of Technology and Harvard University. He has served as a member or chairman of several national task forces and committees including Preservation of Natural Beauty, Model Cities, and on Suburban Problems. He was a member of the United States delegation to the UN Conference on Habitat in 1976.

PETER HALL has been a professor in the Department of City and Regional Planning and director of the Institute of Urban and Regional Development at the University of California, Berkeley. His publications include, *Cities of Tomorrow: An Intellectual History of Urban Planning and Design in the Twentieth Century.*

CATHERINE HILL is currently a Ph.D. candidate in the Department of Urban Planning and Policy Development at Rutgers University. She recently coauthored (with Ann Markusen) an Economic Policy Institute study, *Converting the Cold War Economy: Investing in Industries, Workers and Communities.* Hill's current work focuses on the impact of military base closures on local communities.

ALLEN B. JACOBS is professor and chairman of the Department of City and Regional Planning at the University of California, Berkeley. He served as director of city planning in San Francisco from 1967–1974. He came to San Francisco from the faculty of the University of Pennsylvania after working as a planner in Cleveland, Pittsburgh, and Calcutta.

HARVEY M. JACOBS is a professor in the Department of Urban and Regional Planning and the Institute for Environmental Studies, University of Wisconsin-Madison. His areas of interest include land use, growth management, and land planning theory.

JANE JACOBS challenged conventional ideas about physical planning and argued the virtues of big, diverse, crowded, and dense cities. Her writings include *The Death and Life of Great American Cities*, *The Economy of Cities*, *Cities and the*

Wealth of Nations, and from her Toronto vantage point, *The Question of Separatism*.

JAMES H. JOHNSON, JR. is a professor of geography and director of the Center for the Study of Urban Poverty at the University of California, Los Angeles. His research interests include the study of interregional black migration, minority conflict in advanced industrial societies, and urban poverty and social welfare policy.

CLOYZELLE K. JONES is a professor of education at the University of Michigan, Dearborn. His research interests focus on the education of the urban poor, affirmative action issues in higher education, and urban poverty.

NORMAN KRUMHOLZ is a professor in the Department of Urban Planning, Design, and Development, College of Urban Affairs at Cleveland State University. His writings have focused on neighborhood and equity planning. He is a former director of planning for Cleveland and the former president of the American Planning Association.

GILL-CHIN LIM is dean of International Studies and Programs at Michigan State University. He was previously a faculty member in the Department of Urban and Regional Planning at the University of Illinois, Urbana-Champaign. His area of interest includes comparative urban development and complex decision making.

CHARLES LINDBLOM was a professor in both the departments of Economics and Political Science at the Institute for Social and Policy Sciences at Yale University until his retirement in June, 1987. He has held multiple administrative and academic positions including a directorship of the Institute for Social and Policy Studies. For his 1985 study of "Social Science and Problem Solving" he was awarded a Guggenheim Fellowship. His extensive writings on public policy issues include *Inquiry and Change: The Troubled Attempt to Understand and Shape Society*, *The Intelligence of Democracy: Decision-Making Through Mutual Adjustment*, and *Politics and Markets: The World's Political Economic Systems*.

KEVIN LYNCH was formerly a professor in the Urban Studies and Planning Program at the Massachusetts Institute of Technology. Lynch's numerous writings, including *Images of the City*, *A Theory of Good City Form*, *What Time Is This Place?*, and *Site Planning*, all emphasized the importance of people's perceptions in designing the environment. Lynch was also a partner in the environmental design firm of Carr, Lynch Associates, which was involved in many important projects including site planning for the new town of Columbia, Maryland.

PETER MARCUSE is a professor in the Urban Planning Program at Columbia University. His areas of interest include planning theory and housing and community development.

ANN MARKUSEN is a professor of urban planning at Rutgers University. Her writings include *Dismantling the Cold War Economy*, *Profit Cycles, Oligopoly, and Regional Development*, *Regions: The Economics and Politics of Territory*, and *Silicon Landscapes*.

PATRICIA M. METZGER is a research associate with the Florida Atlantic University/Florida International University Joint Center for Economic and Urban Problems. Her research interests include local and regional governance and intergovernmental systems. Metzger's articles have appeared in *Land Use Policy* and *Environmental and Urban Issues*.

LEWIS MUMFORD is probably the foremost urban historian of our era. He is the author of numerous articles and over thirty books, including *The Culture of Cities*, *Sketches from Life*, and *The Ecological Basis of Planning*. Over a long and highly productive career, Mumford received numerous awards, including honorary membership in the American Institute of Certified Planners.

RICHARD P. NATHAN is the director of the Nelson A. Rockefeller Institute of Government and provost of the Nelson A. Rockefeller College of Public Affairs and Policy at the State University of New York at Albany. Nathan previously served as a professor of public and international affairs at the Woodrow Wilson School at Princeton University and as senior fellow at the Brookings Institution. His writings include *Jobs and Civil Rights* and *The Role of the Federal Government in Promoting Equal Opportunity in Employment and Training*.

OSCAR NEWMAN is currently a principal in the Institute for Community Design Analysis, Inc., in Great Neck, New York. He has served as a professor and director of the Institute of Planning and Housing at New York University. He has been a consultant for the U.S. Department of Housing and Urban Development, the New York City Housing Authority, and housing development agencies throughout the country.

MELVIN L. OLIVER is an associate professor of sociology and associate director of the Center for the Study of Urban Poverty at the University of California, Los Angeles. His research has focused on minority conflicts in advanced industrial societies and black social networks in cities.

FRANCIS H. PARKER is a professor of urban planning at Ball State University and was department chair from 1984–1993. His teaching and research interests include land use law and policy, transportation planning, and planning theory. His most recent publication is *Indiana Railroad Depots: A Threatened Heritage*.

LISA PEATTIE is a senior lecturer and emeritus faculty member in the Department of Urban Studies and Planning at Massachusetts Institute of Technology. Her research and publications, which have focused on social anthropology and developing areas, include, *Thinking About Development* and *Women's Claims.* Her book *Planning: Rethinking Ciudad Guayana* received the Association of Collegiate Schools of Planning's Paul Davidoff Award.

FRANK J. POPPER is the former chair of the Department of Urban Studies at Rutgers University, where he currently teaches in the Urban Planning and Geography departments. From 1984–1987 he was a member of the American Planning Association's Board of Directors. His areas of interest include land-use planning and the politics of land use. His "Understanding American Land Use Regulation Since 1970" received the 1989 Award for the Best Article in the *Journal of the American Planning Association.*

JOHN RAWLS is a professor of philosophy at Harvard University. He has written widely on issues of justice, fairness, and equity.

MARTIN REIN is a professor in the Department of Urban Studies and Planning at Massachusetts Institute of Technology. His research interests include social policy planning, program administration, and evaluation. He is the coauthor (with Peter Marris) of *Dilemmas of Social Reform.*

JOHN W. REPS is a professor emeritus in the Department of City and Regional Planning of Cornell University. Known as "Mr. Maps," he has written extensively on the history of American city planning, including *The Making of Urban America.*

ANNE WHISTON SPIRN is a professor of landscape architecture at the University of Pennsylvania and is the author of *The Granite Garden: Urban Nature and Human Design.*

GEORGE STERNLIEB is formerly the director of the Rutgers University Center for Urban Policy Research. He is the author of numerous articles and books, including (with Robert W. Burchell) *Planning Theory in the 1980s.*

MICHAEL B. TEITZ is a professor in the Department of City and Regional Planning at the University of California, Berkeley. His areas of interest include social programs and policy, urban economics, and spatial structures.

WILBUR R. THOMPSON is professor emeritus of economics at Wayne State University, now living in Albuquerque, N.M. He received his Ph.D. in economics from the University of Michigan (1953) and is the author of numerous articles on regional and urban economics, including, *An Econometric Model of Postwar State Industrial Development* and *A Preface to Urban Economics.* Thompson has been a visiting professor at several major universities as well as a lecturer for the Brookings Institution's Urban Policy Program. Most recently, he held the Albert A. Levin Chair of Urban Studies and Public Service at Cleveland State University.

MARTIN WACHS has been a professor of urban planning at the University of California, Los Angeles since 1976. His extensive writings on transportation issues include *Transportation for the Elderly: Changing Lifestyles, Changing Needs, Ethics in Planning,* and *The Car and the City.* He is the recipient of the Pike Johnson Award for Transportation Research, and the Distinguished Planning Educator Award. He has also received a Guggenheim Foundation Fellowship and has twice won research fellowships from the Rockefeller Foundation.

ROBERT C. WEAVER is distinguished professor emeritus of Urban Affairs at Hunter College, City University of New York. He has received approximately thirty honorary degrees from such universities as Amherst, Boston College, Rutgers, Columbia, Harvard, the University of Michigan, and Temple. Weaver served previously as administrator of the Department of Housing and Urban Development. His publications include *Negro Labor: A National Problem*, *The Negro Ghetto*, *The Urban Complex*, and *Dilemmas of Urban America*. He is a fellow of the Academy of Arts and Sciences (emeritus) and was named to the National Association of Homebuilders Hall of Fame in 1982.

MARC A. WEISS is a professor in the Urban Planning Program at Columbia University. His areas of interest include planning history and real estate development. He is the author of *The Rise of the Community Builders*.

WILLIAM H. WHYTE has been a prolific writer, activist, and consultant who has always challenged conventional wisdom. His *Organization Man* (1956) questioned suburban utopia, and his *The Exploding Metropolis* argued the disamenities of sprawl and urban renewal. His more recent work has focused on how people interact with urban spaces. In this area, his publications include *Is Anybody Listening? Open Space Action*, *Cluster Development*, and *The Social Life of Small Urban Spaces*. He is the recipient of numerous awards, including the Benjamin Franklin Magazine Writing Award, the Liberty and Justice Book Award, the American Institute of Architects Award, the Natural Resources Council Award, and honorary membership in the American Institute of Certified Planners.

CONTENTS

PREFACE

Classic Readings in Urban Planning is intended to be a main or supplementary textbook for advanced undergraduate or beginning graduate-level introductory courses in urban and regional planning. Planning commissioners, professional planners, lawyers, architects, and governmental officials should also find the book useful as a general overview of the field of urban planning.

The book is designed to be used easily by both faculty and students in an introductory urban planning course. *Classic Readings in Urban Planning* contains thirty-nine classic readings organized into thirteen sections or planning subfields. Each reading is introduced with an abstract, and each section includes a list of recommended supplementary readings. This list contains current works in the subfield, as well as classic readings that could not be included as main selections. Both instructors and students should find these lists to be useful for more extensive study of an area. The complete collection of readings contained in this book should serve as a comprehensive introduction to urban planning.

The Classic Concept

In preparing *Classic Readings in Urban Planning*, I have assumed that the best way to be introduced to our field is to read a carefully chosen group of major works, the classics. Webster's (1979: 334) defines classic as: "of the highest class; most representative of the excellence of its kind; having recognized worth." Classic readings are of superior quality, represent outstanding scholarship, and may have significantly influenced or changed the field.

My assumption is that it is far more interesting and exciting to *directly* experience ideas and read—even struggle—with original writings, than it is to review someone else's synopsis *about* those ideas. I have never read a summary or description of the work of Jane Jacobs, Lewis Mumford, Kevin Lynch, or Paul Davidoff, for example, that adequately captures the eloquence of their writings and the passion of their convictions. I believe that there is no better way to excite students about planning than to have them read the classics written by some of the leading authorities in our field.

Selecting the Classics

In a field as broad based as planning, selecting a small group of classics from a rich literature is a formidable task. As the recent valiant attempt by Johnson and Silver (*Journal of the American Planning Association*, Winter 1990: 101–102) to name the classics in planning shows, a consensus simply does not exist on what are *the* books in urban planning. Nevertheless, I have attempted to use a systematic approach for identifying the classics included in this book.

Even though I have used a very thorough process for screening the classics, the selections included in *Classic Readings in Urban Planning* cannot be viewed as representing *the* works in urban planning. Designing a textbook has required several compromises with the concept of classics. These compromises include consideration of the level and complexity of writings for an introductory course; a need to represent several different voices and views on issues; an attempt to sufficiently cover the major fields of planning; and a desire also to address some of the current and compelling issues of the day. Finally, an unfortunate but real constraint has been the difficulty and sometimes prohibitive cost involved in obtaining reprint permissions from publishers.

Thirty-nine selections covering thirteen planning subfields do not allow any area to be covered in great depth. It does, however, make for a rather lengthy textbook. Given the diversity, long history, and intellectual traditions of the planning field, the size of this text could easily be increased threefold and still not cover all the significant, major writings that truly deserve to be called classic. Such an increase in size, however, would be impractical for one volume and make the price unaffordable to students.

Yet the issues I faced in organizing this book are similar to those experienced by every instructor when preparing a course. Instructors must select materials from a large universe of possibilities. There is never enough time or space to cover all that students need to learn. Choices must be made. The question in designing a course or a textbook is the same. In the very limited time or space available, what *must* absolutely be covered, what is *essential*, what *must* students be exposed to, what *must* they read?

I designed a four-step process to answer this question, to select the materials, and to provide the organizational framework for *Classic Readings in Urban Planning*. These steps include:

1. A survey and analysis of introductory course syllabi
2. A survey of experts

3. An identification of award-winning writings

4. A review of planning literature

ACSP Course Survey

As part of an effort to review the introductory urban planning course offered by my department at the University of Florida, I conducted a survey in the summer of 1992 of all introductory courses offered by corresponding and members schools of the Association of Collegiate Schools of Planning (ACSP). The forty-four universities that responded to the survey are listed at the end of the Preface.

The survey of introductory courses served two major purposes. First, it provided the basis for organizing the book into its thirteen sections. These are the subfields of planning that the survey identified as most frequently covered in introductory courses. Most instructors in introductory courses have apparently decided that other important areas of planning—such as research methods, regional planning, and historic preservation—are more appropriately covered in other parts of the curriculum. I nevertheless regret that our own space limitations have caused us to omit these subfields.

The surveys served a second purpose of providing input for selection of readings included in the book. The course syllabi were analyzed by subfields, and a list was compiled of the most frequently assigned readings. Readings from this list have been chosen either as main selections in the text or as recommended supplementary readings.

Panel of Experts Survey

In fall 1992 I conducted a survey of planning faculty experts representing the thirteen fields of planning to be covered in the book. The experts were chosen on the basis of their fields of interest as listed in the *Guide to Graduate Education in Urban and Regional Planning*, seventh edition (Association of Collegiate Schools of Planning, September 1990). The experts were not selected in a "scientific" manner, but rather were chosen on the basis of my own knowledge of their work and an interest in having diverse representation. The experts were sent a questionnaire which asked:

1. "Please list below the three articles or books (including your own) that you consider to be *essential* reading *in the above field* for an introductory/survey course in urban planning. . ."

2. "Also please list three books or articles, *regardless of field*, that you think are *absolutely essential*—that a student *must* read—in an introductory/survey course in urban planning. . ."

These survey results were a major influence in selecting the readings for the book. The experts who were consulted and who also agreed to the publication of their names are listed in the Acknowledgments.

Writings and Authors Receiving Special Recognition

A third input to the classics selection process involved identifying writings, and authors, that had received awards or special recognitions. Award designations included: the Association of Collegiate Schools of Planning's Distinguished Planning Educator Award, the Paul Davidoff Award, and the Chester Rapkin Award for the best article published in *The Journal of Planning Education and Research*; Society of American City and Regional Planning History Awards— Lewis Mumford Prize for Best Book and Catherine Bauer Wurster Prize for Best Article; honorary membership in the American Institute of Certified Planners; and outstanding journal articles selected by the editors and editorial board of the *Journal of the American Planning Association*.

Review of the Literature

As a final input to the selection process, I conducted my own review of the planning literature. This involved reviewing *Urban Affairs Abstracts* and extensive reading of the book review sections and articles in the *Journal of the American Planning Association*, *Journal of Planning Education and Research*, and the *Journal of Planning Literature*. I also engaged in many informal conversations with colleagues in my own department and around the country regarding their suggestions for the book.

Conclusion

Although the classics selected for this text have been chosen by a thorough, systematic process, the book is not intended to be a compilation of *the* writings in planning. Instead, the thirty-nine selections included in *Classic Readings in Urban Planning* are an attempt to balance the multiple needs of an introductory textbook with the concept of classic readings.

This collection of readings should serve as an excellent introduction to the field of planning. It is a treasure chest of outstanding writing by some of the most important contributors to the planning field. I hope that the reader will enjoy the adventure of studying these selections, capture the excitement and commitment of the authors, and be encouraged to pursue additional work in urban planning.

Jay M. Stein

ACKNOWLEDGMENTS

I am greatly indebted to my students and colleagues in the Department of Urban and Regional Planning, College of Architecture, at the University of Florida for their ideas and support. Research assistants Pamela Herhold, Betsy Kane, and Scott Lagueux, as well as my secretaries Joan Hartley and Juanita Pelham, provided valuable assistance and much of the leg work in the preparation of the manuscript. Margaret Giery, also a research assistant, deserves special recognition for always managing to have a cheerful disposition despite the pressures of long hours and tight deadlines. Robert E. Burns, Kansas State University, and Ernest Sternberg, SUNY–Buffalo, provided valuable suggestions in reviewing the manuscript. I also appreciate the support and professionalism of B. J. Clark, David Dunham, and Meredith Hart of McGraw-Hill, Inc.

I especially wish to thank my friends and colleagues in the member schools of the Association of Collegiate Schools of Planning who generously shared their introductory urban planning course syllabi and also served as a panel of experts in helping to select the classics that are this book. Without their contributions, this book would not have been possible. Responsibility for any and all errors is, of course, mine. Finally, I am most grateful to Sylvia Lewis for her assistance in securing permission rights to the American Planning Association publications included in this volume.

I am most indebted, however, to my wife, Karen, and to my two daughters, Danielle and Melissa, for their patience, understanding, and cheerfulness. They are always a source of inspiration for me.

LIST OF PROGRAMS PARTICIPATING IN COURSE SURVEY

The University of Akron
Department of Geography and Planning

University of Alabama
Department of Geography

Appalachian State University
Department of Geography and Planning

Arizona State University
Department of Planning

Auburn University
Graduate Program in Planning

Ball State University
Department of Urban Planning

California State University
City and Regional Planning Program
Department of Political Science

University of California, Berkeley
Department of City and Regional Planning

University of California, Los Angeles
Urban Planning Program

Clemson University
Department of Planning Studies

Cleveland State University
Department of Urban Studies

University of Florida
Department of Urban and Regional Planning

Florida State University
Department of Urban and Regional Planning

The George Washington University
Department of Urban Planning and Real Estate Development.

University of Guelph
University School of Rural Planning and Development

Hunter College of The City University of New York
Department of Urban Affairs & Planning

Indiana University of Pennsylvania
Department of Geography and Regional Planning

Iowa State University
Department of Community and Regional Planning

The University of Iowa
Graduate Program in Urban and Regional Planning

Kansas State University
Department of Regional and Community Planning

University of Kansas
Graduate Program in Urban Planning

McGill University
School of Urban Planning

Mankato State University
Urban and Regional Studies

University of Maryland at College Park
Department of Urban Studies and Planning

Memphis State University
Graduate Program in City & Regional Planning

Morgan State University
City and Regional Planning

State University of New York at Albany
Department of Geography and Planning

State University of New York at Buffalo
Department of Planning and Design

The Ohio State University
Department of City and Regional Planning

University of Oregon
Department of Planning, Public Policy, and Management

University of Pittsburgh
Urban and Regional Planning

Portland State University
Department of Urban Studies and Planning

Rutgers University
Department of Urban Planning and Policy Development

Ryerson Polytechnical Institute
Department of Urban and Regional Planning

San Jose State University
Department of Urban and Regional Planning

University of Saskatchewan
Regional and Urban Development Program

Sonoma State University
Department of Environmental Studies and Planning

University of Southern California
School of Urban and Regional Planning

Technical University of Nova Scotia
Department of Urban and Rural Planning

Technion—Israel Institute of Technology
Faculty of Architecture and Town Planning

The University of Tennessee
The School of Planning

Texas A&M University
Master of Urban Planning Degree Program

The University of Wisconsin, Madison
Department of Urban and Regional Planning

The University of Wisconsin, Milwaukee
Department of Urban Planning

"PANEL OF EXPERTS"

Ivonne Audirac
Howell R. Baum
Eugenie L. Birch
Edward J. Blakely
Richard Bolan
Scott A. Bollens
Michael P. Brooks
John Bryson
Robert B. Cervero
Susan Christopherson
Charles E. Connerly
Cheryl K. Constant
Linda C. Dalton
John DeGrove
Joseph F. DiMento
Timothy P. Duane
Carl Feiss
Peter S. Fisher
Joan Fitzgerald

Bernard J. Freiden
Gary Gappert
Margot W. Garcia
David R. Godschalk
William W. Goldsmith
Genevieve Giuliano
Penelope Gurstein
Edward W. Hill
Marie Howland
Allen B. Jacobs
Harvey M. Jacobs
Ibrahim Jammal
Edward J. Kaiser
Jerome L. Kaufman
W. Dennis Keating
Richard E. Klosterman
Donald A. Krueckeberg
Norman Krumholz
Richard T. Lai

Jacqueline Leavitt
Melvin R. Levin
Gill-Chin Lim
Riad G. Mahayni
Peter Marcuse
Jerry V. Mitchell
Raffaella Y. Nanetti
Kenneth Pearlman
Martin Rein
William M. Rohe
Catherine L. Ross
Robert D. Rugg
Mitchell J. Rycus

Peter V. Schaeffer
Robert G. Shibley
Christopher Silver
Stanley M. Stein
Ann L. Strong
Lawrence E. Susskind
June M. Thomas
David P. Varady
Martin Wachs
Orjan Wetterqvist
Robert K. Whelan
Margaret Wilder

Jay M. Stein

Association of Collegiate Schools of Planning. 1990. *Guide to Graduate Education in Urban and Regional Planning,* Seventh Edition.

Gary T. Johnson and Christopher Silver. 1990. "From the Book Review Editors." *Journal of the American Planning Association* 56, 1: 101–102.

Webster's New Twentieth Century Dictionary of the English Language, Unabridged, 2d edition, 1979. New York: Simon and Schuster.

1

HISTORY

Towns, Time, and Tradition: The Legacy of Planning in Frontier America

John W. Reps
Professor Emeritus of City and Regional Planning, Cornell University

Town Planning in Frontier America is a shortened version of John Reps's longer and more detailed book, *The Making of Urban America* (1965). In these books, Reps covers city plans from the first European settlement at St. Augustine in 1565 to the frontier planning experiences of the middle of the nineteenth century. In this section, Reps examines nineteenth-century frontier planning and discusses the obstacles involved in transferring planning knowledge from England to her former colony. Finally, he summarizes the planning failures and achievements of the era. He focuses on the lessons that can be learned from our frontier development-planning experiences and applied to the challenges of modern urbanization.

By the middle of the 19th century the basic pattern of urban settlement east of the Mississippi had been established. Virtually all of what were to become the major cities of an increasingly urban nation had begun as planned communities: Boston, New York, Philadelphia, Baltimore, Washington, Pittsburgh, Buffalo, Cleveland, Detroit, Chicago, Cincinnati, Indianapolis, St. Louis, and New Orleans. Not all had been planned with skill, and in every case the explosive growth of these urban centers was soon to outrun the bounds of their original borders. In each of these, as well as in dozens of planned cities of smaller size, something of the heritage of its planned beginnings remains. In many, indeed most, the character and quality of the first settlement forms prescribed by their founders exceeds in merit the accretions of the later 19th century and of our own era.

We are now entering a new period of American urbanization. By the year 2000 current projections indicate that we will develop as much additional land for urban purposes as we did in the first 400 years of city building from 1565 to 1965. In addition, we are setting about the complex task of reconstructing the blighted and congested centers of our existing cities. Increasingly the effort to create a better life will focus on the issues of city growth and control of the urban environment, along with attempts to grapple with the nagging social problems of poverty and racial segregation.

The American philosopher George Santayana once observed that those who are ignorant of history are condemned to re-live it. What are the lessons to be learned from our planning experience during the first period of frontier development as we approach the new frontier of making our cities habitable for ourselves and succeeding generations? Let us try to sum up our failures and our achievements during that remarkable era of our history when we laid the foundation for an urban civilization.

We must not let national pride warp our perspective. The North Atlantic proved a major barrier to the transplanting of town planning techniques and concepts which were highly developed in Europe at the beginning of colonization and which continued to advance and change in the centuries to follow. The resources of colonial settlers pitted against the difficulties of a harsh and often hostile environment permitted little more than the minimum requirements of town life let alone the amenities or embellishments which were commonplace in 17th- and 18th-century Europe.

Compare, for example, the Quebec of Champlain with the Charleville of its founder, Duke Charles III. Both date from 1608. Quebec consisted of Champlain's crude "Habitation" and a tiny grid of streets hugging the banks of the St. Lawrence River. Charleville embodied all the theories of Renaissance formal planning, with its elaborate hierarchy of streets and open squares on which fronted carefully scaled buildings all making up a sophisticated composition in civic design. Not until 1791, with L'Enfant's Baroque plan for Washington, did American urban planners produce a large-scale example of what had long been established as a standard plan form in Europe.

Or, contrast the development pattern of the West End of London in the mid-18th century with the plan of Savannah and its multiple squares. While the plan forms are essentially similar, the differences between them in the third dimension were striking. Fronting the London squares stood elegant and restrained terrace houses of urbane dignity and harmonious proportions. Lining the squares of frontier Savannah were the simplest of huts and cabins. Not for nearly a century did Savannah attain something of the character of even the least imposing of Georgian London's squares. The lag between city planning practice in Europe and what occurred in the colonial empires of North America was thus substantial.

The reasons for these differences between colony and mother country are readily understandable. The strangeness of the environment, the slowness of communications, the absence of traditions, the lack of institutional patterns, and the necessity to create anew even the most elementary of urban services and facilities—all contributed to prevent the speedy and complete transfer to the New World of what had been learned about city planning in the old. Today these inhibiting factors have vanished, yet one can argue that in comparison with such remarkably well-ordered European cities as Stockholm and Amsterdam we still lag far behind European practice in urban planning. No longer do we have the excuse of limited physical resources; indeed, their very abundance may contribute to our urban physical disarray. Yet in a sense we still act like primitive colonials, helpless to put into practice the latest lessons of how to arrange cities in patterns which are both functional and beautiful.

Our failure to achieve an urban order fitting for the time and within our capabilities may well stem from attitudes toward the city developed in our swaddling years. America was peopled by Europeans who were hungry for land. In a seemingly limitless continent the most insatiable appetites could be satisfied. For a time fear of Indian attack combined with old habits of settlement to promote the development of compact agricultural villages. But when the natives were overcome and when the boundless extent of the land became apparent, the old associations of village and town life gave way to a quite different agricultural settlement pattern of isolated farmsteads. As early as 1623 in Plymouth Governor Bradford regretfully described these events:

"For now as their stocks increased . . . there was no longer any holding them together, but now they must of necessitie goe to their great lots; they could not other wise keep their katle; and having oxen growne, they must have land for plowing and tillage. And no man now thought he could live, except he had catle and a great deale of ground to keep them; all striving to increase their stocks. By which means they were scatered all over the bay, quickly, and the town, in which they lived compactly till now, was left very thine, and in a short time allmost desolate. . . . And this, I fear, will be the ruine of New-England."[1]

For a good many Americans it was rural life which represented the ideal. The town was something from which to escape. The Jeffersonian notion of an agrarian democracy represents an old and deep feeling in American culture which has its manifestation today in the attempt to find in endless suburbia the freedoms which our ancestors sought on the western frontier of settlement. It is perhaps a permissible exaggeration to state that today's urban sprawl began in 17th-century Plymouth.

One feature of American planning in the frontier era is the almost total absence of three-dimensional design. This is not to say that effective bits of townscape were unknown—countless New England villages testify to the care taken by early settlers in the siting of individual buildings. For the most part, however, towns were conceived of in only two dimensions. The example of Williamsburg is virtually unique. Here was a town in which the plan of streets and building sites was developed as part of a larger vision of the future which included the location, size, and elevational treatment of its major structures. This approach to total urban design is the great lesson which Williamsburg has to teach—not the plan itself, the architectural style of its buildings, or the layout of its gardens. These belong to another era, and mere imitation of their dimensions and appearance is an insult to the integrity of colonial designers. Many of the shortcomings of the nation's cities today have resulted from earlier failures to realize that the third dimension of architecture is a vital ingredient of urban planning.

Another characteristic of American town planning was the widespread use of the gridiron or checkerboard pattern. As in virtually all other periods of wholesale colonization in world history, early colonial and later frontier towns were planned mainly on a geometric pattern of rectangular blocks, straight streets, and right-angle intersections. As the plan form most economical to survey, quickest to build, and easiest to understand, it is not surprising that the orthogonal system prevailed. For European visitors this feature of the American scene was novel and, at first impression, desirable. Thus, Francis Baily, noting the "perfect regularity" of

Philadelphia and Baltimore was moved to comment, "This is a plan of which the Americans are very fond, and I think with reason, as it is by far the best way of laying out a city. All the modern-built towns in America are on this principle." However, what may have at first seemed like a vision of a new world urban rationality all too quickly blurred into an impression of sterile dullness. By the time Baily reached Cincinnati his infatuation with the grid had given way to disenchantment:

"I have taken occasion to express my approbation of the American mode of laying out their new towns, in a general way, in straight lines; but I think that oftentimes it is a sacrifice of beauty to prejudice, particularly when they persevere in making all their streets cross each other at right angles, *without any regard to the situation of the ground,* or the face of the surrounding country: whereas, these ought certainly to be taken into consideration, in order that a town may unite both utility and beauty; and, with a little attention to this, a town might still preserve the straight line, and yet avoid that disgusting appearance which many of the new towns in America make."[2]

The seeds of senseless mechanized and unimaginative town planning which was to characterize much of the 19th century were sown in colonial soil. Yet not all gridiron plans of the frontier era of American urban development were of this quality. One thinks of New Haven, with a generous one-ninth of the original town left as an open green; or of Savannah, with its multiple squares breaking the monotony of the grid; or of Jeffersonville, with its alternating pattern of open squares and building blocks. Even Philadelphia's original plan contained the five squares laid out by Penn, the largest intended as a town center and the four smaller as recreation grounds. And Williamsburg demonstrates that the orthogonal plan is not incompatible with an atmosphere of formality and dignity.

It was less the first gridiron plans, which, in most cases were too modest in size to be offensively dull, than the later extensions of cities that violated good sense in community planning. Without regard to topography or, more importantly, failing to include in the additions to the city some of the open spaces of the original design, these new areas mechanically repeated almost endlessly the grid street system without any relieving features. Savannah stands almost alone as an exception to this dreary tradition.

The reasons are not difficult to identify. Planning of towns and development of land, in the beginning a community enterprise, fell into the hands of individuals and corporations whose almost sole aim was private profit. Even if the proper skills and sensibilities had been present, there was little incentive to plan well when mediocre planning, or worse, yielded generous financial returns. Moreover, as most communities abandoned responsibility for town planning to individuals they failed to create adequate legal and administrative institutions for the public control of private land development.

Our present urban land policy has scarcely departed from this position. Most important decisions about the timing of development, its location, and its design remain in private hands, tempered only mildly by regulations supposedly intended to protect the public interest. Because memories are short and historical perspective lacking, our generation regards this as the American tradition. So it is, but it is not the only tradition of our town planning history, nor has it proved the most effective.

The examples of Annapolis, Williamsburg, Savannah, Washington, and many of the 19th-century planned state capital cities remind us that public initiative and investment for the planning of cities once served to create an urban environment superior in quality to that of the present when measured against available financial and intellectual resources. The history of modern American city planning since the turn of the century can be read as an attempt, faltering and so far largely ineffective, to recapture that earlier tradition which placed the planning of towns as a responsibility of the community at large.

If American urban history has anything to contribute to the modern world aside from mere antiquarian enjoyment it is that good cities—beautiful, as well as safe and efficient—will arise only when it is the city itself that assumes the obligation for its own destiny.

NOTES

1 William Bradford, *History of Plymouth Plantation*, W. T. David, ed., New York, 1908, pp. 293–94.
2 Francis Baily, *Journal of a Tour in Unsettled Parts of North America in 1796 & 1797*, London, 1856, pp. 105, 226–27.

The First Urban Transformation

Lewis Mumford

In the introduction to *The City in History*, Lewis Mumford observes that the book begins "with a city that was, symbolically, a world; it closes with a world that has become, in many practical aspects, a city" (p. *xi*). Although it took many decades to realize this transformation, it is nevertheless a remarkable one. The selection included here, "The First Urban Transformation," is the opening section of the chapter, "The Crystallization of the City." Here, Mumford describes the "implosion" that led to the first great expansion of civilization: the creation of cities. Under the leadership of the new "institution of Kingship," the diverse and scattered elements of a civilization were compressed into the boundaries of cities. This contrasts to the explosion of our own era, as boundaries disappear and we become more of a global community. Mumford argues that to understand this process—and to understand the city in our own age—we must study its origins, form, functions, and historical development.

In view of its satisfying rituals but limited capabilities, no mere increase in numbers would, in all probability, suffice to turn a village into a city. This change needed an outer challenge to pull the community sharply away from the central concerns of nutrition and reproduction: a purpose beyond mere survival. The larger part of the world's population never in fact responded to this challenge: until the present period of urbanization, cities contained only a small fraction of mankind.

The city came as a definite emergent in the paleo-neolithic community: an emergent in the definite sense that Lloyd Morgan and William Morton Wheeler used that concept. In emergent evolution, the introduction of a new factor does not just add to the existing mass, but produces an over-all change, a new configuration, which alters its properties. Potentialities that could not be recognized in the pre-emergent stage, like the possibility of organic life developing from relatively stable and unorganized 'dead' matter, then for the first time become visible. So with the leap from village culture. On the new plane, the old components of the village were carried along and incorporated in the new urban unit; but through the action of new factors, they were recomposed in a more complex and unstable pattern than that of the village—yet in a fashion that promoted further transformations and developments. The human composition of the new unit likewise became more complex: in addition to the hunter, the peasant, and the shepherd, other primitive types entered the city and made their contribution to its existence: the miner, the woodman, the fisherman, each bringing with him the tools and skills and habits of life formed under other pressures. The engineer, the boatman, the sailor arise from this more generalized primitive background, at one point or another in the valley section: from all these original types still other occupation groups develop, the soldier, the banker, the merchant, the priest. Out of this complexity the city created a higher unity.

This new urban mixture resulted in an enormous expansion of human capabilities in every direction. The city effected a mobilization of manpower, a command over long distance transportation, an intensification of communication over long distances in space and time, an outburst of invention along with a large scale development of civil engineering, and, not least, it promoted a tremendous further rise in agricultural productivity.

That urban transformation was accompanied, perhaps preceded, by similar outpourings from the collective unconscious. At some moment, it would seem, the local familiar gods, close to the hearth fire, were overpowered and partly replaced, certainly outranked, by the distant sky gods or earth gods, identified with the sun, the moon, the waters of life, the thunderstorm, the desert. The local chieftain turned into the towering king, and became likewise the chief priestly guardian of the shrine, now endowed with divine or almost divine attributes. The village neighbors would now be kept at a distance: no longer familiars and equals, they were reduced to subjects, whose lives were supervised and directed by military and civil officers, governors, viziers, tax-gatherers, soldiers, directly accountable to the king.

Even the ancient village habits and customs might be altered in obedience to divine command. No longer was it sufficient for the village farmer to produce enough to feed his family or his village: he must now work harder and practice self-denial to support a royal and priestly officialdom with a large surplus. For the new rulers were greedy feeders, and openly measured their power not only in arms, but in loaves of bread and jugs of beer. In the new urban society, the wisdom of the aged no longer carried authority: it was the young men of Uruk, who, against the advice of the Elders, supported Gilgamesh when he proposed to attack Kish instead of surrendering to the demands of the ruler of Kish. Though family connections still counted in urban society, vocational ability and youthful audacity counted even more, if it gained the support of the King.

When all this happened, the archaic village culture yielded to urban 'civilization,' that peculiar combination of creativity and control, of expression and repression, of tension and release, whose outward manifestation has been the historic city. From its origins onward, indeed, the city may be described as a structure specially equipped to store and transmit the goods of civilization, sufficiently condensed to afford the maximum amount of facilities in a minimum space, but also capable of structural enlargement to enable it to find a place for the changing needs and the more complex forms of a growing society and its cumulative social heritage. The invention of such forms as the written record, the library, the archive, the school, and the university is one of the earliest and most characteristic achievements of the city.

The transformation I now seek to describe was first called by Childe the Urban Revolution. This term does justice to the active and critically important role of the city; but it does not accurately indicate the process; for a revolution implies a turning things upside down, and a progressive movement away from outworn institutions that have been left behind. Seen from the vantage point of our own age, it seems to indicate something like the same general shift that occurred with our own industrial revolution, with the same sort of emphasis on economic activities. This obscures rather than clarifies what actually occurred. The rise of the city, so far from wiping out earlier elements in the culture, actually brought them together and increased their efficacy and scope. Even the fostering of non-agricultural occupations heightened the demand for food and probably caused villages to multiply, and still more land to be brought under cultivation. Within the city, very little of the old order was at first excluded: agriculture itself in Sumer, for example, continued to be practiced on a large scale by those who lived permanently within the new walled towns.

What happened rather with the rise of cities, was that many functions that had heretofore been scattered and unorganized were brought together within a limited area, and the components of the community were kept in a state of dynamic tension and interaction. In this union, made almost compulsory by the strict enclosure of the city wall, the already well-established parts of the proto-city—shrine, spring, village, market, stronghold—participated in the general enlargement and concentration of numbers, and underwent a structural differentiation that gave them forms recognizable in every subsequent phase of urban culture. The city proved not merely a means of expressing in concrete terms the magnification of sacred and secular power, but in a manner that went far beyond any conscious intention it also enlarged all the dimensions of life. Beginning as a representation of the cosmos, a means of bringing heaven down to earth, the city became a symbol of the possible. Utopia was an integral part of its original constitution, and precisely because it first took form as an ideal projection, it brought into existence realities that might have remained latent for an indefinite time in more soberly governed small communities, pitched to lower expectations and unwilling to make exertions that transcended both their workaday habits and their mundane hopes.

In this emergence of the city, the dynamic element came, as we have seen, from outside the village. Here one must give the new rulers their due, for their hunting practices had accustomed them to a wider horizon than village culture habitually viewed. Archaeologists have pointed out that there is even the possibility that the earliest grain-gatherers, in the uplands of the Near East, may have been hunters who gathered the seeds in their pouch, for current rations, long before they knew how to plant them. The hunter's exploratory mobility, his willingness to gamble and take risks, his need to make prompt decisions, his readiness to undergo bitter deprivation and intense fatigue in pursuit of his game, his willingness to face death in coming to grips with fierce animals—either to kill or be killed—all gave him special qualifications for confident leadership. These traits were the foundations of aristocratic dominance. Faced with the complexities of large-scale community life, individualistic audacity was more viable than the slow communal responses that the agricultural village fostered.

In a society confronting numerous social changes brought on by its own mechanical and agricultural improvements, which provoked serious crises that called for prompt action, under unified command, the hoarded folk wisdom born solely of past experience in long-familiar situations was impotent. Only the self-confident and adventurous could in some degree control these new forces and have sufficient imagination to use them for hitherto unimaginable purposes. Neolithic 'togetherness' was not enough. Many a village, baffled and beset by flooded fields or ruined crops, must have turned away from its slow-moving, overcautious council of elders to a single figure who spoke with authority and promptly gave commands as if he expected instantly to be obeyed.

Doubtless the hunter's imagination, no less than his prowess, was there from the beginning, long before either flowed into political channels: for surely there is a more commanding esthetic sense in the paleolithic hunter's cave than there is in any early neolithic pottery or sculpture. Nothing like the same superb esthetic flair as we find in the Aurignacian caves came back till the stone-and-copper age. But now heroic exertions, once confined mainly to the hunt, were applied to the entire physical environment. Nothing the mind projected seemed impossible. What one singularly self-assured man dared to dream of, under favor of the gods, a whole city obedient to his will might do. No longer would wild animals alone be subdued: rivers, mountains, swamps, masses of men, would be attacked collectively at the King's command and reduced to order. Backbreaking exertions that no little community would impose on itself, so long as nature met its customary needs, were now undertaken: the hunter-hero, from Gilgamesh to Herakles, set the example in his superhuman acts of strength. In conquering hard physical tasks every man became a bit of a hero, surpassing his own natural limits—if only to escape the overseer's lash.

The expansion of human energies, the enlargements of the human ego, perhaps for the first time detached from its immediate communal envelope the differentiation of common human activities into specialized vocations, and the expression of this expansion and differentiation at many points in the structure of the city, were all aspects of a single transformation: the rise of civilization. We cannot follow this change at the moment it occurred, for, as Teilhard de Chardin notes of other evolutionary changes, it is the unstable and fluid emerging forms that leave no record behind. But later crystallizations clearly point to the nature of the earlier evolution.

To interpret what happened in the city, one must deal equally with technics, politics, and religion, above all with the religious side of the transformation. If at the beginning all these aspects of life were inseparably mingled, it was religion that took precedence and claimed primacy, probably because unconscious imagery and subjective projections dominated every aspect of reality, allowing nature to become visible only in so far as it could be worked into the tissue of desire and dream. Surviving monuments and records show that this general magnification of power was accompanied by equally exorbitant images, issuing from the unconscious, transposed into the 'eternal' forms of art.

As we have seen, the formative stages of this process possibly took many thousands of years: even the last steps in the transition from the neolithic country town, little more than an overgrown village, to the full-blown city, the home of new institutional forms, may have taken centuries, even millennia; so long that many institutions that we have definite historic record of in other parts of the world—such as ceremonial human sacrifice—may have had time both to flourish and to be largely cut down in Egypt or Mesopotamia.

The enormous time gap between the earliest foundations in the Valley of the Jordan, if their latest datings are correct, and those of the Sumerian cities allows of many profound if unrecorded changes. But the final outbreak of inventions that attended the birth of the city probably happened within a few centuries, or even, as Frankfort suggested of kingship, within a few generations. Pretty surely it took place within a span of years no greater than the seven centuries between the invention of the mechanical clock and the unlocking of atomic power.

As far as the present record stands, grain cultivation, the plow, the potter's wheel, the sailboat, the draw loom, copper metallurgy, abstract mathematics, exact astronomical observation, the calendar, writing and other modes of intelligible discourse in permanent form, all came into existence at roughly the same time, around 3000 B.C. give or take a few centuries. The most ancient urban remains now known, except Jericho, date from this period. This constituted a singular technological expansion of human power whose only parallel is the change that has taken place in our own time. In both cases men, suddenly exalted, behaved like gods: but with little sense of their latent human limitations and infirmities, or of the neurotic and criminal natures often freely projected upon their deities.

There is nevertheless one outstanding difference between the first urban epoch and our own. Ours is an age of a multitude of socially undirected technical advances, divorced from any other ends than the advancement of science and technology. We live in fact in an exploding universe of mechanical and electronic invention, whose parts are moving at a rapid pace ever further and further away from their human center, and from any rational, autonomous human purposes. This technological explosion has produced a similar explosion of the city itself: the city has burst open and scattered its complex organs and organizations over the entire landscape. The walled urban container indeed has not merely been broken open: it has also been largely demagnetized, with the result that we are witnessing a sort of devolution of urban power into a state of randomness and unpredictability. In short, our civilization is running out of control, overwhelmed by its own resources and opportunities, as well as its superabundant fecundity. The totalitarian states that see ruthlessly to impose control are as much the victim of their clumsy brakes as the seemingly freer economies coasting downhill are at the mercy of their runaway vehicles.

Just the opposite happened with the first great expansion of civilization: instead of an explosion of power, there was rather an *implosion*. The many diverse elements of the community hitherto scattered over a great valley system and occasionally into regions far beyond, were mobilized and packed together under pressure, behind the massive walls of the city. Even the gigantic forces of nature were brought under conscious human direction: tens of thousands of men moved into action as one machine under centralized command, building irrigation ditches, canals, urban mounds, ziggurats, temples, palaces, pyramids, on a scale hitherto inconceivable. As an immediate outcome of the new power mythology, the machine itself had been invented: long invisible to archaeologists because the substance of which it was composed—human bodies—had been dismantled and decomposed. The city was the container that brought about this implosion, and through its very form held together the new forces, intensified their internal reactions, and raised the whole level of achievement.

This implosion happened at the very moment that the area of intercourse was greatly enlarged, through raidings and tradings, through seizures and commandeerings, through migrations and enslavements, through tax-gatherings and the wholesale conscription of labor. Under pressure of one master institution, that of kingship, a multitude of diverse social particles, long separate and self-centered, if not mutually antagonistic, were brought together in a concentrated urban area. As with a gas, the very pressure of the molecules within that limited space produced more social collisions and interactions within a generation than would have occurred in many centuries if still isolated in their native habitats, without boundaries. Or to put it in more organic terms, little communal village cells, undifferentiated and uncomplicated, every part performing equally every function, turned into complex structures organized on an axiate principle, with differentiated tissues and specialized organs, and with one part, the central nervous system, thinking for and directing the whole.

What made this concentration and mobilization of power possible? What gave it the special form it took in the city, with a central religious and political nucleus, the citadel, dominating the entire social structure and giving centralized direction to activities that had once been dispersed and undirected, or at least locally self governed? What I am going to suggest as the key development here had already been presaged, at a much earlier stage, by the apparent evolution of the protective hunter into the tribute-gathering chief: a figure repeatedly attested in similar developments in many later cycles of civilization. Suddenly this figure assumed superhuman proportions: all his powers and prerogatives became immensely magnified, while those of his subjects, who no longer had a will of their own or could claim any life apart from that of the ruler, were correspondingly diminished.

Now I would hardly be bold enough to advance this explanation if one of the most brilliant of modern archaeologists, the late Henri Frankfort, had not provided most of the necessary data, and unconsciously foreshadowed if not foreseen this conclusion. What I would suggest is that the most important agent in effecting the change from a decentralized village economy to a highly organized urban economy, was the king, or rather, the institution of Kingship. The industrialization and commercialization we now associate with urban growth was for centuries a subordinate phenomenon, probably even emerging later in time: the very word merchant does not appear in Mesopotamian writing till the second millennium, "when it designates the official of a temple privileged to trade abroad." Going beyond Frankfort, I suggest that one of the attributes of the ancient Egyptian god, Ptah, as revealed in a document derived from the third millennium B.C.—*that he founded cities*—is the special and all but universal function of kings. In the urban implosion, the king stands at the center: he is the polar magnet that draws to the heart of the city and brings under the control of the palace and temple all the new forces of civilization. Sometimes the king founded new cities; sometimes he transformed old country towns that had long been a-building, placing them under the authority of his governors: in either case his rule made a decisive change in their form and contents.

The Turbulent Eighth Decade: Challenges to American City Planning

Peter Hall
Professor of City and Regional Planning, University of California

In this essay, Peter Hall presents a brief analysis of ten distinct stages in modern American planning history. The article is valuable as a sketch of planning history in this century.[1] However, as the accompanying letters to the editor indicate, Hall's historical interpretation has provoked considerable comment and criticism.[2]

City planning in America has no official certificate of birth. But, if a date has to be chosen, it is surely 1909: the year of the First National Conference on City Planning and Congestion and the publication of Burnham's Chicago Plan. American planning is 80 years old this summer. It celebrates other anniversaries too: it is 60 years since the appearance of the New York Regional Plan, 50 years since the Futurama Exhibit and the screening of *The City* at the New York World's Fair, and 40 years since the passage of the Housing and Slum Clearance Act. It is surely a year for celebration.

And also for reflection. In these eight decades, city planning in America has come a long way. It has established itself as an institutional force across the nation, as a part of the social and political fabric. And never was the need for planning so evident, as witness the stream of media reports that tell on the one hand of crack wars tearing the last remaining life out of inner city areas, of an urban underclass becoming ever more economically, socially, and geographically separated from the mainstream and, on the other, of unparalleled suburban growth pressures, of spreading freeway traffic gridlock, of resulting NIMBY-style conflicts. Thus, the problems that brought planning forth have not gone away. Some of them, indeed, show a frightening persistence. And planning—even using that term in the widest possible sense, to embrace a whole range of economic and social planning initiatives—has not yet come close to solving them.

The history of planning shows that these problems, and these responses, are not unique to the United States—though often, America is the bellwether that warns the rest of the world of coming urban storms. To an extraordinary degree, the international planning movement was born in reaction to a set of common problems in the world's great cities at the close of the nineteenth century. Early in the new century, the movement evolved to grapple with market forces that were transforming that city into a different kind of urban entity. Later, faced with the decline of the central city, it evolved yet new responses to that problem. There are intriguing parallels between one country and another, as there are between one historical period

[1] Reprinted by permission of the *Journal of the American Planning Association*, 55, 3, Summer 1989.
[2] Reprinted by permission of the *Journal of the American Planning Association*, 56, 1, Winter 1990.

and another: the urban underclass is perceived as a central problem today, as it was at the turn of the century.

But the historical comparisons are not precise, and neither are the geographical ones. The underclass of 1989 is not the same phenomenon as the underclass of 1890. Urban renewal in 1989 is again a major issue, but it is not the same as renewal in 1949. And planning in the United States has evolved differently from planning in Great Britain, France, Germany, and Scandinavia. The reasons for these differences, both over time and across place, are a mixture of economic forces, political traditions, and cultural ideologies. Issues recycle and come uppermost again, but the responses are subtly different in every era and every country. Why that should be is a central topic for the planning historian.

Without too much historic-poetic license, we can distinguish ten periods in the brief history of planning, both here in the United States and elsewhere in the world.

THE CITY PATHOLOGICAL, 1890–1901

Quite suddenly, between 1880 and 1890, the respectable bourgeois urban world discovered the slum city that festered underneath it. Two remarkable pieces of journalism—Andrew Mearns' *The Bitter Cry of Outcast London*, in 1883, and Jacob Riis' *How the Other Half Lives*, in New York in 1890—provided the trigger. The reaction was a mixture of fear and guilt. In London, Beatrice Webb wrote of "a new consciousness of sin . . . a collective or class consciousness, amounting to a conviction, that the industrial organism, which had yielded rent, interest and profit on a stupendous scale, had failed to provide a decent livelihood and tolerable conditions for a majority of the inhabitants"; while H. M. Hyndman, leader of the Social Democratic Foundation, wrote that "[e]ven among the useless men and women who dub themselves 'society' . . . [t]he dread word 'Revolution' is sometimes spoken aloud in jest." And in New York, Jacob Riis evoked the same fear: the tenement dwellers, he wrote, "hold within their clutch the wealth and business of New York, hold them at their mercy in the day of mob-rule and wrath. The bullet-proof shelters, the stacks of hand-grenades, and the Gatling guns of the sub-Treasury are tacit admissions of the fact and of the quality of the mercy expected."

The origin, then, was precisely the same: it was the discovery of the urban underclass, numbering—according to both Riis and the Tenement House Commission of 1894—three in five of the New York population. The motive, in the words of the commission, was "[t]he redemption of the tenement classes," which lay "partly in the redemption of family, the most conservative unit in civilization, to its proper share of space, natural light and air, and the cultivation of the domestic arts, one of which is cleanliness." And, in New York and Chicago and a dozen other cities, it was the socialization of the new immigrants who were so overrepresented in the tenement population. That was the principal motive behind Jane Addams' settlement house movement at Hull House in Chicago, itself modeled faithfully on Toynbee Hall in London's East End; it was likewise the major concern of the sociologist-planner Clarence Perry, who devised the concept of neighborhood unit at the Russell Sage Foundation between 1909 and 1929; it was also the obsessional subject-matter of Robert E. Park and his co-researchers in the Chicago School of Sociology during the 1920s. But neither Addams, nor Perry, nor Park found an effective answer: an immigrant later confessed that he went to Hull House "for an occasional shower, that was all"; Park, in 1925, concluded a paper on community organization and juvenile delinquency by apologizing that his paper lacked a moral, confessing that "the problem of juvenile delinquency seems to have its sources in conditions over which, in our present knowledge, we have very little control."

There was, however, one key feature of the American response that sharply marked it off from that of the Europeans. There, in Britain, France, and Germany alike, the answer was government support for social housing programs. Here, the New York Tenement House Commission report of 1900, principally authored by Lawrence Veiller, decisively rejected public intervention; private benevolence could do the job, the commission held, provided a framework of physical regulation was put in place. As Catherine Bauer bemoaned in the 1930s, that one report put back the cause of public housing in America for decades. Peter Marcuse has suggested that this unique divorce occurred because of the three issues that then emerged—fire and disease dangers, fear of disorder, protection of real estate values. The first two issues soon faded, leaving the infant art of planning to an alliance of real estate interests and middle class home-buyers.

THE CITY BEAUTIFUL, 1901–1915

Whatever the explanation, the fact is that almost from the start, and for at least two decades, American city planning was almost entirely removed from the kind of social concern that drove the movement in Europe. In the first decade of the new century, the City Beautiful movement represented a deliberate and conscious attempt to impose on America's greatest cities the kind of heavily formalistic urban reconstruction that Haussmann had carried through in Paris, and Cerda in Barcelona, between 1850 and 1870. The irony was that virtually all those attempts were made by patrons of an autocratic regal or imperial regime, while here—in Cleveland, in San Francisco, in Chicago above all—the agency was an alliance of downtown merchants. Burnham shamelessly appealed to their base motives: "No one has estimated the number of millions of money made in Chicago and expended elsewhere," he suggested, "but the sum must be a large one. What would be the effect upon our retail business at home if this money were circulated here? What would be the effect upon our prosperity if the town were so delightful that most men who grow independent financially in the Mississippi Valley, or west of it, were to come to Chicago to live?" Pericles' investment in ancient Athens, he argued, was still paying for itself in tourist revenue. He may, of course, have had tongue in cheek. But he knew his audience; rather remarkably, most of the plan got completed.

Not elsewhere, though. The plan contained a built-in contradiction, in that it favored centralization but then tried to control it. Already, at that crucial first National Conference on City Planning and Congestion in 1909, other planners and their business backers were seeing that this solution—a kind of aristocratic city for merchant princes, as Mel Scott once put it—was going to cost more than the backers were willing to pay. The result, hastened perhaps by Burnham's death in 1912, was an abrupt switch from the City Beautiful to the City Functional.

THE CITY FUNCTIONAL, 1916–1939

The new solution was far more down-to-earth. It included zoning of land uses accompanied by advisory city planning commissions. It proved instantly and hugely successful. Starting with New York City's historic Zoning Ordinance of 1916, zoning had been adopted by more than 750 communities by the end of the 1920s. The reason was that everyone could see that it was good for business. So, of course, was the City Beautiful, or so its proponents had claimed; but everyone could see that zoning came much cheaper.

What was good for business was the right kind of people: the right customers downtown, the right neighbors in the new streetcar suburbs. In New York, the Fifth Avenue merchants backed zoning because they were concerned that floods of immigrant garment workers would compromise their exclusive stores. Edward Bassett, father of the New York scheme, later wrote that one of the major purposes of zoning was to prevent the "premature depreciation of settled localities." Out in the suburbs, it was the same story: the first-known use of zoning, in Modesto, California, in the 1880s, was to keep Chinese laundries out of residential areas. In the historic 1926 Supreme Court case of *Euclid v. Ambler*, the great planner-lawyer Alfred Bettman argued that zoning served the public welfare by enhancing the community's property values: the Court's decision gave the inhabitants of Euclid, a middle class bedroom community next door to Cleveland, a guarantee that their investments would not be compromised by industrial development.

In practice, as one later observer succinctly put it, the notion was to preserve real estate values in settled neighborhoods, while imposing only nominal restrictions in areas that held out the possibility of profit. One of the basic city planning texts of the 1920s, from the husband-and-wife team Hubbard and Hubbard, italicized the point: *"Zoning and plat control divide honors in being reported the most profitable results of city planning."* As the Hubbards succinctly put it in a chapter heading: "IT PAYS TO PLAN." Thus, far from being a device to speed the transition of the immigrant poor from the tenements to the streetcar suburbs, zoning in practice became a way of keeping them where they were. And, despite rare exceptions like Bettman's Cincinnati, zoning was usually divorced from city planning: the first was legally based, mandatory, and invariable, the second voluntary, advisory, nonmandatory, and irregular. In practical terms, the City Functional was—and is—without doubt the dominant American contribution to the planning movement; but it is a curiously low-key, unidealistic one. It is driven hard by the demands of profit from land development. And it is almost totally bereft of vision.

THE CITY VISIONARY, 1923–1936

There was a massive exception to all this, of course: the small band of visionaries—including Lewis Mumford, Henry Wright, Clarence Stein, Stuart Chase, Benton MacKaye, and Catherine Bauer—who constituted the Regional Planning Association of America from 1923 on. Dedicated followers and interpreters of Ebenezer Howard and Patrick Geddes, they blended the ideas of their British masters with skeins of distinctively American thought—Harvard physiography, Thoreau's ideas on self-sufficiency, and southern regionalism—to produce something much more than the sum of its parts. The basis, for both Howard and Geddes, was a Kropotkinesque anarchism: a vision of small, largely self-sufficient rural communities in ecological balance with their rich natural resources. Because of this, they went far beyond even Howard's blueprint for garden cities as the solution for the ills of the congested metropolis: they wanted nothing less than a reconstruction of the whole foundation of American life, based on what they saw as the liberating effect of the automobile and the electric power plant.

It did not, and perhaps could not ever, come to pass; the vision was too utopian, the forces lined up against them were too strong. Their main practical experiment, the garden city of Radburn, soon came to grief in the Depression and is today swallowed up in the amorphous suburban sprawl of northern New Jersey. What might have been the truest realizations of their vision, the greenbelt towns of Rexford Tugwell's Resettlement Administration and the regional plan for the Tennessee Valley, alike foundered, as Congress halted the first, and as personal feuding and ideological differences drained the second of meaning.

The New Deal represented a unique chance for American planning to go a European road, a decade before Europe itself did so; but by 1936, with FDR in political retreat, the battle was lost and it fell to Britain, Sweden, and France to implement the RPAA's ideas. Writing to Frederic Osborn after publication of Abercrombie's 1944 Greater London Plan, Mumford said that it was "the best single document on planning, in every respect, that has come out since Howard's book itself. . . . The original job of making the idea credible has been performed," he went on, "and the main task now is to master the political methods that will most effectively translate it into a reality. We have not yet reached that stage here," he prophetically concluded, "and I fear the results of our immaturity will show once the post-war building boom . . . gets under way."

He proved right: the British Labour government of 1945 essentially did what Tugwell had failed to do, and what Howard had thought no government anywhere would ever do, successfully launching a national program that eventually resulted in 30 new towns; America had to rest content with a series of isolated commercial initiatives, some of which, such as James Rouse's Columbia, had superficial similarities to their British cousins, but none of which represented the core of the Howard-Mumford-Osborn vision.

There was a rare paradox here, as Mumford would have been the first to emphasize. Because the United States was so far ahead of Europe in technological diffu-
sion, in the 1920s and 1930s it was already possible to see the implications in a
way that would have been impossible elsewhere. Clarence Stein's contribution to
the 1925 RPAA manifesto, *Dinosaur Cities*, uncannily predicts the outmovement
of industry from the cities and the resulting inner city problem that would actually take place more than 40 years later. Benton MacKaye's essay of 1930, *The
Townless Highway*, similarly anticipates the freeway and the dispersed settlement
form of the 1950s and 1960s. So, in a different way, did Frank Lloyd Wright's personal manifesto *Broadacre City*, a few years later, though he always held aloof
from the RPAA group. After World War II, the irony was that they all lived to see
their vision, but as a shell without the substance: bedroom suburbs instead of garden cities, white-collar commuters instead of farmer-artisans. All of these planners
were visionaries, and the forces of reality—embodied in the City Functional tradition—proved too strong.

The tragic irony was already evident, for those who could foresee what was
coming, in the epic intellectual battle of 1930–1931 between Lewis Mumford and
Thomas Adams, author of the Regional Plan of New York, over what the RPAA
saw as the failings of that plan. For Mumford, it was a pernicious document, whose
implementation would result in a multiplication of the failings it purported to con-
demn: congestion, overcentralization, uncontrolled growth. The plan, in essence,
was the City Functional at the regional scale. For Adams, who had begun his career
as Howard's lieutenant at Letchworth, the issue was "whether we stand still and
talk ideals or move forward and get as much realization of our idea as possible in
a necessarily imperfect society, capable only of imperfect solutions to its problems." They parted ways; and much of the plan became reality, largely because of
the energies of Robert Moses, who provided the needed arterial connections, while
the remarkable vision of the RPAA remained forever on paper.

THE CITY RENEWABLE, 1937–1964

There was but one historical thread connecting the RPAA with postwar America,
and a curious one at that: it was the role that Catherine Bauer, perhaps the group's
most effective political advocate, played as proponent of affordable housing. Her
first attempt to achieve this, which culminated in the creation of the Federal
Housing Association in 1934, had perverse effects: very soon, the agency was
redlining the inner cities and effectively denying mortgages in predominantly
black areas. The second attempt, which resulted in the historic Wagner Act of
1937, represented an uneasy compromise between Bauer and the construction
unions, who wanted public housing, and the real estate interests who had backed
the 1934 Act, and who wanted anything but. Public housing was to be seen as a
temporary expedient for the deserving poor, who would soon be out of it and into
FHA-supported mortgages; it would exclude the predominantly black urban underclass. The means to that end was the federal government's support of the construction but not the subsequent running costs. When at the end of the 1940s that

barrier was reached, and poor welfare families at last entered the projects, the resulting financial contradictions proved catastrophic: they were symbolized, a quarter-century later, by the demolition of the Pruitt-Igoe apartments in St. Louis, which had been allowed to deteriorate until they became uninhabitable.

But in 1949 and 1954, Congress again grappled with the issue. And this time, as Catherine Bauer memorably put it, "seldom had such a diverse group of would-be angels tried to dance on the same small pin." Once again, though, it was the real estate lobby that emerged right in the center. They wanted, not public housing, but federally aided commercial development at the edge of downtown. The public housers went along with them in the hope of getting something, but were largely thwarted; in city after city—Philadelphia, Pittsburgh, Hartford, New Haven, Boston, San Francisco—the developers sought "the blight that's right," as Charles Abrams inimitably put it. So it was the low-income black sections close to the CBD that went, while the promised public housing failed to materialize.

The truly amazing feature of those years, in retrospect, is the way in which it happened. True, the real estate interests proved as powerful as they had before. But they marshaled wide-ranging growth coalitions that embraced liberal-technocratic mayors like New Haven's Lee and Chicago's Daley, labor councils, construction-trade representatives, good-government groups, professional planners and others; at first, even the public housing lobby. It took a long time to appreciate that, as in Boston's West End, they were actually destroying entire stable neighborhoods.

That was because of the prevailing intellectual ethos. The fashionable buzz-words of the late 1950s and early 1960s were comprehensive renewal, systems analysis in planning, and integrated land use-transportation planning. Planning was invaded by a battery of computer-based techniques derived from the transportation engineers, and by a related philosophy derived from the aerospace program and ultimately embodied in Robert McNamara's Pentagon. Planning, it was argued, could be based on rational choice among alternatives, using quantified techniques. Anything that could not be expressed in numbers was inherently suspect. The result was a heavy bias in favor of efficiency, which could be measured in terms of time and money, and against equity and intangibles, which could not: the City Functional approach, plus computer models. Given that bias, the destruction of old neighborhoods for new freeways and new commercial development was not merely inevitable; it came to have a scientific validity.

Finally, the break came. To appreciate the force of the change, it is only necessary to compare the content of the *Journal* in, say, 1959 and in 1969. The furor broke in the early 1960s, with publication of devastating criticisms like Herbert Gans's *The Urban Villagers* and Martin Anderson's *The Federal Bulldozer*. It happened also to be the time of the first revolt against urban freeways, which stopped San Francisco's Embarcadero freeway in mid-air. Within an astonishingly short time, it caused an almost complete inversion of almost every basic value in American planning practice and planning education. And not merely in the United States: the same revolution stopped freeways in London, the Covent Garden redevelopment, and renewal in central Stockholm, as well as producing paralysis over the Les Halles redevelopment in Paris.

THE CITY GRASSROOTED, 1965–1980

By the end of the 1960s, all was changed. The civil rights movement had been followed by the free speech movement; the riots had torn through the newly renewed cities, revealing just how little the process had done for the underclass; opposition to Vietnam, and with it the whole Pentagon style of planning, was at its peak. Almost every value that planners had cherished was now stood on its head. Instead of a belief in top-down planning by benign value-free experts, there was now a deep distrust of professional expertise and a demand for advocacy planning based on grassroots involvement. But, paradoxically, in one vital respect there was little change: the planners would now perform many of the functions of the elected officials and it was by no means clear how they could avoid the charge that they were still controlling and manipulating the action.

Within a few years, the new skein of radical planning unraveled into a number of incompatible threads: the social learning or new humanist school, the neo-anarchism of Friedmann, and finally the ascendant Marxists, who made common cause for only a very short while until they too splintered in debate. They were however united on one point: their agreement that the planner had not got much power, and deserved to have less. Planners, in the version that came to dominate in the late 1970s, were mere agents of the capitalist local state, seeking palliatives to stave off crisis in the system; but in the process, they would sidestep one problem only to face another. Because traditional theories of planning had ignored this essential fact, the Marxists argued, they were essentially vacuous, and worse: in seeking to define an ideal mode of planning, devoid of social and political content, they aimed to depoliticize planning and thus to legitimate it and better serve the system.

THE CITY THEORETICAL, 1975–1989

It was the most disturbing critique of planning that had emerged in the profession's seven decades of life, particularly since so much of it was coming from within the nation's—and the world's—most prestigious planning schools. But it was more notable for what it destroyed than for what it put in its place. If planning had been a mere tool of the system, how then to create something that was not? At this point, many of the radical critics fell silent. Some flatly denied that, given continuance of the system, any positive theory of planning action was necessary or desirable. Others retreated to bold but largely vacuous rhetoric. By the end of the 1970s, planning theory had become divorced from planning practice. And the top products of the nation's top planning schools were becoming increasingly uninterested in the day-to-day activity of planning.

In the 1980s, some continued to argue at these rarified levels of theory. In a revealing special issue of *Society* (November/December 1988), eight professors from the nation's top schools debate the question of planning, power, and politics. The truly amazing point about this discussion is that hardly anywhere, in nearly 40 pages of close print, is there any mention of the kinds of things planners actually do, the kinds of issues they confront in their working lives. (To be fair, Charles Hoch devotes two paragraphs to homelessness.) Now, no one would deny that it is vitally important for student planners to understand why planners do what they do, particularly if and when they act irrationally. But one would have thought it also vital to relate this to the subject of what they do.

Other top theorists have sought various ways out of the impasse. Some, like Allen Scott and Manuel Castells, have moved away from questions of the relation between theory and action, and into heavily empirical investigations of changing economic and social structures—a movement, in other words, from urban planning to urban political economy. Others, like Ann Markusen, Barry Bluestone and Bennett Harrison, have sought to combine this style of analysis with active regional policy prescription for older industrial regions. Yet others, like John Friedmann and John Forester, have continued to grapple with the problem of connecting theory with action—in Forester's case, by drawing on German critical theory. But, stripped of the dense Teutonic undergrowth, the resulting prescriptions sound uncannily like those of the advocacy planners of 15 years earlier: cultivate community networks, listen carefully to the people, go out to those who are least well organized, educate the citizenry, supply plenty of information, and ensure that people know how to use it. It is essentially a theory of practice.

Numerous other members of academe, both faculty and students, seem to have tired of the debate, preferring to get back to hands-on planning. The big growth areas of the 1980s have included economic development planning for distressed regions and communities, the understanding of project finance as the key to urban development and redevelopment, the achievement of affordable housing, and the use of the personal computer, coupled with geographic information systems, to help solve these and other problems.

The result, not unique to the United States, but exceptionally evident here, has been the emergence of several kinds of disjunctures: between planning theory and planning practice; between what is taught in the top schools and in the more run-of-the-mill institutions; and, within the former, between theoretical and practical streams. As a result, these top schools now turn out two types of students. One type flourishes in a great variety of special situations: research for distressed cities and regions, community leadership, heroic efforts with slum-dwellers in third-world cities. The other are academic theorists—professorial clones. The more mundane institutions still turn out conventional planners, that is, land use planners, the people the outside world still recognizes by the term.

THE CITY ENTERPRISING, 1980–1989

Meanwhile, outside the ivory tower, life goes on. Planning practice, as ever, relates to the challenges and opportunities before it. The most distinctive feature of the 1980s is what could be called planning-as-project, or planning-as-real-estate-development. The models are Baltimore's Inner Harbor, Boston's Quincy Market and Waterfront, San Diego's Horton Plaza, and a score of imitators. (In Europe, the same phenomenon is visible on an even grander scale, in London's Docklands and in the Parisian Eurodisneyland.) Each consists of the megadevelopment of a huge site, through the cooperation of public and private capital, and involving major injections of money from government—huge public works, subsidies linked to private leverage, and tax exemptions in the form of enterprise zones—as well as new institutional forms. Some might say that this is urban renewal all over again. Indeed, in Boston and Baltimore the development follows a straight line, but the scale is grander and the stakes are bigger—no less than the transformation of decayed industrial and port cities into leading centers of the new nodal-service economy, through a new combination of producer services, theme-park entertainment, leisure shopping and street theater. No wonder the students in the schools are studying project finance.

The radical critics can, of course, have a field day once again. As has occurred so often in twentieth-century American urban history, public planning and public money are being harnessed to the pursuit of private profit: the City Functional lives. As in the era of urban renewal, powerful growth coalitions back the enterprise. While the new service jobs may be dead-end and low-paying—no adequate substitute for the lost opportunities in the steel mills and the docks—the fact is that, in many cities of the industrial heartland, this is the only game in town.

The service sector may also be the most potent source of jobs, perhaps the only source of jobs, to bring the unemployed, unskilled underclass of the surrounding inner city back into the mainstream economy. That particular bundle of concerns— the transition to a service economy, the sharp division within that economy between the white collar providers of producer services and the pink collar providers of consumer services (and, within the white collars, between top managers/professionals and keyboard punchers), the mismatch between demand and supply in the job market, the increasing marginalization of the underclass—constitutes one of the great challenges to American city planning at the end of the 1980s. Do you join in meeting it, or catcall from the sidelines? This is the dilemma that faces many in the profession and the schools today.

THE CITY OF ECOLOGICALLY CONSCIOUS NIMBYISM, 1980–1989

In yet other places, there is a different set of challenges: the growth of the suburbs, the development within them of entirely new service nodes (Tyson's Corner, I-680, Irvine) and the transformation of older rural centers, the rapid spread of suburban gridlock as the infrastructure of the 1960s is overwhelmed, the problems of water supply and waste management and air quality, the loss of open space and rural qualities in huge swathes of land around the major metropolitan areas. Hand in hand with these trends, inevitably, goes the multiplication of special interest groups devoted to maintaining and enhancing the quality of environment, but also to stopping further development—the arrival of NIMBYism as the populist political philosophy of the 1980s. Everywhere from New Hampshire and Virginia to the San Francisco Bay and the Central Valley, these problems of growth and spread now dominate the lives of many, perhaps most, Americans. And planning, as yet, has no clear and consistent set of answers.

Further, the two bundles of concerns may have a common basis. The Rousification of the cities really represents a desperate attempt to find an answer to a question that many cannot bring themselves to say out loud: in the new urban landscape of technology-led deconcentration, what exactly is the role of the traditional city? Even if some places manage to survive on the basis of their special qualities—New York, Chicago, and Los Angeles as major world centers; Boston and San Francisco, as centers of education, technology, culture, and tourism; and Atlanta, Dallas, and Denver as regional nodes—can all of America's cities survive? Or do they represent some historic anomaly, destined to disappear like the ghost towns of the West? Or will they be reconstructed as Disney-style parodies of the places they once were, living museums of the urban past? Is it possible again to create *integrated* downtowns, as Jonathan Barnett suggests in the Spring 1989 *Journal*?

THE CITY PATHOLOGICAL REVISITED, 1890–1989

Tied to these concerns is another: the rediscovery of the original obsession, the one that gave rise to planning's birth. To tell the truth, the urban underclass never went away; that much is clear from a succession of fine empirical studies, from DuBois at the end of the nineteenth century, through Park and his colleagues in the 1920s, Frazier in the 1930s and again in the 1950s, Myrdal in the 1940s and Moynihan in the 1960s, to Wilson in the 1970s and 1980s. What is uncanny is that all tell essentially the same story: of traditional preindustrial cultures overwhelmed by the transition to urban life, of the particular stress on the first urban-born generation, of the collapse of the family and the destruction of traditional parental authority, of the resulting problems in the schools and the courts.

There is perhaps one difference, underlined by Wilson: the sharp division of the black community, since the 1960s, into a middle class mainstream group and an ever-more-segregated underclass. But, as DuBois clearly shows, the same division was present in Philadelphia in 1899; it was just not as sharply etched in the geography of the city. Because the black community was always so ghettoized—a fact missed by the Chicago pioneers, and only discovered through recent research—mainstream and underclass lived cheek by jowl. Now they do not, and the child of the underclass grows up in a community where only very poor people live, where only very poor children go to school. Donna Shalala and Julia Vitullo-Martin gave us the figures in the Winter 1989 *Journal*: nearly two-thirds of all poor blacks, in 1980, lived in areas where the great majority of people are poor. The possibility of escape is virtually zero, and the clear threat is the one broached by Park as long ago as 1924: "In the great city the poor, the vicious, and the delinquent, crushed in an unhealthful and contagious intimacy, breed in and in, soul and body." As the media report the horrendous trends—three out of five black births are illegitimate, three in five poor black families are female-headed, the leading cause of death for black teenage males is homicide—what is clearly at stake, as Park long ago foresaw and has now come true, is nothing less than the future of urban life in America.

Given a challenge of that order, there is not much justification for continuing to stand on the academic sidelines. America needs its best brains, its most fertile imaginations, in its urban planning profession. It needs a new generation of Mumfords, Steins, Bauers, Tugwells, Perloffs. And its planning schools need to focus their efforts on feasible solutions. To be sure, they will not be achieved by unaided local action; they will need policy initiatives in state capitols and in HUD, backed by the planning profession.

Shalala and Vitullo-Martin provide a preliminary six-part list: a federal borrowing authority to rebuild urban capital stocks; a regenerated HUD to grapple with the housing problems of the poor; a national rescue corporation for distressed cities; powerful education training job programs targeted at children and teenagers; criminalization of addictive drugs; and a national campaign to deal with AIDS. Others may have different lists; they should be debated through successive issues of this *Journal*. Once the debating and the lobbying is over, and a program is adopted, it will need dedicated and imaginative application. In planning's 80 years, there never was a more vital job to do.

Author's note: I wish to thank Michael Teitz for valuable comments on a first draft of this essay.

'The Turbulent Eighth Decade' Reviewed

Charles Hoch
University of Illinois at Chicago

Peter Hall, in "The Turbulent Eighth Decade: Challenges to American City Planning" in the Summer 1989 issue of the *Journal* (55, 3: 275–82), celebrates the institutional establishment of planning in the United States and urges a revival of the "problem-solving" practice that allegedly informed planning practice before the mid-1960s. Attacks on conventional planning practice by the advocate planners and their radical descendants have, according to Hall, triggered several decades of academic criticism in the "top schools," stripping practical "hands-on" learning of its respectability. In Hall's view the "mid-level" schools escaped such professorial obfuscation and continued turning out the "how-to" practitioners, while the "top schools" produced two separate types of graduates: flourishing practitioners doing good things and nay-saying theorists catcalling from the sidelines. Hall wants academic "theorists" at the "top" schools to enter the fray and struggle as "hands-on" planners to remedy contemporary physical and social problems.

First, Hall offers a sketch of planning history to legitimize his call for practical reform. The story goes like this. Efforts to cure the pathological city at the turn of the century (1890–1901) using social housing and other socialist schemes failed. Formal physical improvements were tried instead. However, plans for the city beautiful (1901–1915) were too expensive for commercial/business elites who opted for the city functional (1916–1939). The visionary new town (1923–1936) and renewal (1937–1964) schemes over the next 40 years proved no match for the imperatives of the city functional. When radical planners pointed out that these schemes failed because they contradicted the imperatives of the capitalist land economy in the 1960s (1965–1980), a crisis emerged among planning academics. Some planners intensified their efforts to innovate and reform in the midst of the formidable obstacles (1980–1989), while others pursued abstract discussions avoiding the pressing problems of the day (1975–1989). The city functional continues to dominate in the 1980s with Rousification of older cities and the NIMBYism of the suburbs. Radical critics may dismiss these development trends as simply another version of profit making at public expense, but since this is "the only game in town" they would do well to join in or be left out.

Hall conducts a radical analysis of planning history up to the 1960s. After this point Hall shifts his attention from a radical assessment of what planners did, to focus on what leftist planning theorists have said or are saying about planning. The Marxists, anarchists, and humanists all agreed in the 1970s, he contends, "that the planner had not got much power, and deserved to have less." Clearly, what disturbs Hall is not the left-wing orientation of the academics he criticizes. He uses such concepts to make his historical argument. What bothers Hall, I think, is the fact that the theorists discredit the use of power by planners. Hall wants planners to possess sufficient power to solve the major problems of our time—problems that he admits have been with us for over a century.

Perhaps Hall hopes to shame the critics of power by framing them as marginal and abstract purists who have nothing useful to say. In his eyes they offer up "bold but vacuous rhetoric" analyzing *why* planners do what they do, but not relating such analyses to *what* planners do. Theory and practice have been separated. The critical theorists are to blame.

What America needs, urges Hall, is "a new generation of Mumfords, Steins, Bauers, Tugwells, Perloffs. And its planning schools need to focus their efforts on feasible solutions." Planners should offer solutions, Hall continues, backed by the power of the state and the profession. Ironically, Hall misses the crucial message uncovered by his own critical review of the work of these famous planners in his historical sketch. Not only did each fail to solve the problem(s) they worked on, but the solutions they proposed were adapted in ways that generated perverse effects, often worse than the problems they initially had tried to solve.

Like the Pardoner in Chaucer's *Canterbury Tales*, who failed to con his fellow travelers after amusing them with stories illustrating his prowess as a con artist, Hall's critique of the "City Functional" and the works of Mumford, Stein, and the others betrays an attachment to the theoretical criticism he would banish as unfeasible. I do not believe that reviving the spirit that animated the efforts of the famous planners he mentions to foster the development of "feasible" state-sponsored projects will avoid the perverse effects Hall himself has pointed out.

It is really not the fault of the academic theorists that planners are relatively powerless to eliminate the inner city underclass or to stop exclusionary zoning. The very institutionalization of planning that Hall celebrates has led to the specialization, fragmentation, and bureaucratization of the work planners do, including the work of academics. The theorists Hall mentions in his article have undertaken considerable empirical research exploring how these conditions (as well as others) enhance the vulnerability of planning and frustrate planners' efforts to offer useful and effective advice. For instance, all the contributors to the recent symposium on planning theory in *Society* (November/December 1988) have conducted recent empirical analyses of planning. Consider Ernest Alexander's studies of plan evaluation and implementation, John Friedmann's studies of Latin American urban settler movements, Howell Baum's several books on the psychology of planners in organizational settings, Seymour Mandelbaum's review of Philadelphia plans, and my own research on planners and political conflict. Certainly, the critical and useful observational case work of John Forester does more than offer up advocacy planning in "Teutonic" clothing.

These theorists do not separate theory and practice, as Hall concludes. They recognize the intellectual futility of the distinction. They are busy trying to understand the moral and technical dimensions of planning in the context of particular organizational settings, community histories, political relations, and psychological dispositions. Hall might not like what these planning theorists are doing, but then he should take issue with the substance of their work rather than dispatch rhetorical caricatures of his own creation.

Howell S. Baum
University of Maryland

I was puzzled by Peter Hall's interpretation of planning history in the Summer 1989 *Journal*. His descriptions of the early decades of professional planning are reasonable, but I do not recognize much of what he sees in recent years. I was particularly struck by the captious description of "The City Theoretical, 1975–1989." Unlike any of the other sections of the essay, this one characterizes planning through the activities of academics, rather than practitioners.

The flattering implication is that academics have, at last, had an impact on practice. However, Hall really means to use this focus as a handle for nastily attacking a few selected individuals. In fact, it soon seems that Hall really has had an intellectual disagreement (or worse) with some of his colleagues, and he means to let them have it. Note what he says about disjunctions "between what is taught in the top schools and in the more run-of-the-mill institutions, and, within the former, between theoretical and practical streams. . . . [T]hese top schools now turn out two types of students. One type flourishes in a great variety of special situations. . . . The other are academic theorists—professorial clones [ouch!]. The more mundane institutions still turn out conventional planners." Apparently, at Berkeley, a "top school," where Hall teaches, certain "academic theorists" seem to have thought differently about planning from Hall. Such disagreement is an understandable source of annoyance, but certainly no basis for generalizing about the history of American city planning.

As an occasional theorist (this is not what I call myself first, but it is not a shameful occupation) and a faculty member at what may be a "run-of-the-mill institution" (but see later), I want to comment on several specific points Hall makes.

First, Hall is unclear about the nature of "the day-to-day activity of planning." What planners do from day to day is think, talk, write, draw, and interact while trying to understand physical or social conditions and trying to improve them some small bit. Yet Hall seems somewhat contemptuous of people who do these things. Only the "mundane," "run-of-the-mill" institutions, rather than those at the "top," educate them.

But, snobbism aside, despite Hall's professions of concern for "practice," he really says little about these everyday activities. In his concluding section, which sets forth what "America's best brains" should be interested in, he talks about policy issues and programs. Planners should think about policy issues and programs, he says, but the practical work of planning also involves trying to influence the thinking of others, trying to develop reasonable but at least minimally feasible proposals, and accepting modest forward movement as a measure of progress toward making broader needed changes.

I want also to defend myself against a counterfactual characterization. Hall refers to "eight professors from the nation's *top schools* [emphasis added by me out of gratitude]" who contributed to a *Society* symposium on planning, power, and politics. He finds the "truly amazing point" that these essays include hardly "any mention of the kinds of things planners actually do, the kinds of issues they confront in their working lives." First, I was one of only six contributors to the symposium. More important, in the symposium there is certainly more discussion of, not to mention sympathy for, planners' practical concerns than in Hall's essay. The issue is available for (re-)reading.

A number of us are part of a growing network of researchers on planning practice. (We come from both "top" and "run-of-the-mill" institutions.) Hall charily acknowledges Charles Hoch's work on homelessness but does not mention his research on planners in conflict. He dismisses John Forester with unsuccessful cuteness and does not acknowledge his work on mediation and planners' use of language in their work. Hall altogether neglects Sy Adler, who has looked at how information technologies affect planning practice and the political uses of consultants; Linda Dalton, who recently surveyed the entire empirical literature on planning practice and has studied planners' roles in implementation; Patsy Healey, who has studied land use planners and their ideas in practice; Beth Howe, who has done considerable research on planners' ethics; Jerry Kaufman, who has looked at ethics with Howe and has studied planners' use of negotiation; and Seymour Mandelbaum, who is analyzing how planners write and read plans. I have done research on planners' perceptions of their practice and their cognitive maps, the influence of bureaucratic organizations on planners' problem-solving efforts, and planners' socialization into agencies. I mention these people as examples, without meaning to exclude many others working in the field. Much of their work has been published, and all would be pleased to send reprints of chapters, articles, or papers on request.

Finally, as a Baltimorean, I would, unhappily, dissent from Hall's characterization of Baltimore as a developmental success. Unfortunately, the city has suffered the problems of all cities losing manufacturing employment and the middle class, and the very poor, who are disproportionately black, suffer from all the problems Hall categorizes at the end of his essay. The development of Harborplace does not balance the utter breakdown of the public school system. The meaning of this educational catastrophe is that Baltimore, like most other large cities, cannot reproduce itself intellectually or socially. With each year, the city's population is less and less capable of managing everyday problems.

Certainly, as Hall would concede, these are issues planners should take on. But the "day-to-day activity" of planning involves more than good "brains"; it requires being able to think and work with other people. Come to think of it, these problems of practice might be something Professor Hall could direct the staff of his research institute to study.

Seymour J. Mandelbaum
University of Pennsylvania

Peter Hall has always had a flair for the big ideas that bridge the differences between diverse elements in the community of planners. I fear, however, that his essay in the Summer 1989 issue of the *Journal* alienates rather than integrates.

The essay is flawed in its inception by confounding "planning" with the "planning movement." All cities are planned: not more, not less, just differently. Planning, therefore, can have no birthday. In contrast, a starting point may reasonably be ascribed to the "movement." Indeed, the first organizers reconstructed history in order to emphasize their newness: "We are planners not architects, political economists, engineers, landscape architects, public health officers." If, however, we treat these late nineteenth and early twentieth century distinctions skeptically, we should imagine " our" history as structured by several different movements and several beginnings. Failure to accept multiple histories writes some of us out of the community of planners.

Hall "without too much historic-poetic license" insists that "we can distinguish" a set of ten periods in the history of planning. All schemes of periodization are, of course, licensed or warranted by a measure of their cogency. It makes sense to construct the past in this or so way (and even to pretend that what we are doing is simply seeing what is obviously before all of our eyes) because it serves a useful purpose. If we did not create a story of change in context, structure, or program we would not understand the dynamics or meaning of events.

I am not sure whether Hall's history deals with planning or the self-images of the leaders of the movement. In either case, however, he provides no warrant for his particular sequence of ten periods. Would I be badly mistaken if I guessed, for example, that he is demonstrating a dismal and demobilizing lesson? The rapid succession of periods suggests to me that urban policy communities have a very short collective attention span and, therefore, may be persuaded of new initiatives though they are not likely to show much persistence. Today's "vital task" will be relegated to the back burner—if not tomorrow, then in the next decade.

Finally (and here, I confess, my ox has been gored) he indicts the several authors of the papers on planning theory published in the November/December 1988 issue of *Society*. They largely ignore, he argues, the "subject of what [planners] do."

The *Society* papers are part of a larger set to be published as *Planning Theory in the 1990s*. Reviewers will, I am sure, be quick to compare this volume with its predecessor on theory in the 1980s and they will have a good deal to say about the emphasis on process and the "interpretive turn." It would be a mistake, however, to ignore the deep responsiveness of the papers to the way practitioners structure their worlds. I am not sure what Hall means by the "subject" of planners' activity. If "subject" means "substance" then certainly the emphasis upon communication in the *Society* papers is appropriate. Planners spend most of their days "talking" and sensible observers may suspect that they act in order to talk, rather than the other way 'round.

Hall argues that the community of planning theoreticians works from the "sidelines" and that much of its talk is self-referenced. He warns that, given the intense challenge of the "underclass," we cannot any longer afford academic detachment. I think his characterization of the community of theoreticians is badly distorted (it is small, part-time, and very committed to repairing the world) but more significantly, his sensibilities are mistaken. You cannot maintain a community of theorizers as part of the planning movement unless you allow them a free space and a substantial measure of internalized shop talk. One shouldn't imagine that the conversation in the community of theorizers is a "debate" that will conclude with a "program"; there is no end to this sort of talk. Far from being attenuated, the "justification for continuing to stand on the academic sidelines" is strengthened when phenomena are defined with great passion as compelling "challenges" and when we are asked to focus on "feasible solutions."

Floyd Lapp
Past Chairman (1982–1984), American Institute of Certified Planners, Former Member, Board of Directors, American Planning Association

Peter Hall's "The Turbulent Eighth Decade" is accompanied by a collage of 28 people and events going back to the World's Columbian Exposition in Chicago in 1893. Only four of these—a BART subway train, Constitution Plaza in Hartford, the Pruitt-Igoe housing project, and New Jersey's State Development and Redevelopment Plan—clearly had origins after 1960, and half of these are viewed negatively by the author. The implication is obvious, and so he concludes his article by advising us that planning "needs a new generation of Mumfords, Steins, Bauers, Tugwells, and Perloffs."

Michael Brooks, in an appeal for a return to the utopian visionary, reformist spirit, which appeared in the Spring 1988 issue of the *Journal* (54, 3: 241–48), cited some of Hall's heroes, as well as Olmsted, Burnham, Wright, and Perry. On the page adjoining Brooks's article is an ad for Mel Levin's *Planning in Government* with a headline that reads, "Make No Big Plans." The ad goes on to say that Daniel Burnham's admonition "is an albatross that hangs on the neck of the planning profession."

All of this is part of the ongoing debate between comprehensive and incrementalist planners, short- and long-term plans, and claims of too much processing and not enough planning.

The 1980s have been a turbulent decade as a result of several factors or images:

- The regulatory review process has grown expensive, time consuming, and litigious as a result of a buildup of community participation from the 1960s and environmental reviews initiated in the 1970s. The pace has frustrated the people by conveying a sense that nothing ever gets done. After emerging from this frustration, personalities, communities, and city halls often become alienated and end up competing rather than cooperating in doing planning.
- Public funding cutbacks in many places have reduced our ability to adequately do both the planning and the processing.
- Negative views of government, encouraged by Washington, have accompanied the rise of the private sector development project as the "plan." The public sector is put in the position of reacting rather than initiating.
- Crumbling infrastructure calls for "quick-fix," functional plans rather than long-term, comprehensive solutions.
- Social problems, statistically worse than in the 1960s, and now more life-threatening with AIDS, crack, and other drugs, are calling for the right questions even before answers can begin to be formulated. One feels humbled by this awesome collection of tragedies. The textbooks covering how to do planning in this environment have not yet been written.
- A perceived mediocre track record of programs and buzz words has evoked skepticism and limited faith in tomorrow.

One can only wonder how Hall's and Brooks's heroes would be doing in this changed environment and if we would even know who they are.

More than a quarter-century ago, when I entered planning, Ed Bacon was on the cover of *Time, Scientific American* devoted an entire issue to cities, and Constantinos Doxiadis was on "Meet the Press." Cynically one might view the scene in the 1970s and 1980s as composed of festival marketplaces and Disneyworld. Indeed, James Rouse was on the cover of *Time* a few years ago.

Although the national attention has shifted, this doesn't mean that good planning work isn't going on in many communities. Today's heroes are not national and international figures but local planners and projects that are part of an incredibly more complex and uncertain environment. We don't know their names or their projects, but we meet them from time to time at conferences. The really good leaders know the human dimension of management, so they are also building the next generation of nameless planning heroes. . . . and so it goes.

Peter Hall replies: I have long thought it a good academic principle not to respond to well-founded critiques of one's work; but I must defend myself against charges of personal animus. I have none; on the contrary, I have the greatest personal regard for the individual work of the six (sorry!) authors of the *Society* symposium, which I have often used and cited. But I stick to my point, which is the divorce of high-level planning theory from the subject matter of planning practice—a point I think central, and of great importance to our profession. *Journal* readers can doubtless access the articles, and judge for themselves.

ONE. HISTORY—SUGGESTED READINGS

Boyer, Christine. 1983. *Dreaming the Rational City*. Cambridge: M.I.T.

Hall, Peter. 1975. *Urban and Regional Planning*. New York: Wiley.

Hall, Peter. 1988. *Cities of Tomorrow: An Intellectual History of City Planning in the Twentieth Century*. Oxford, UK: Blackwell.

Krueckeberg, Donald A. 1983. *Introduction to Planning History in the United States*. New Brunswick, NJ: Center for Urban Policy Research.

Mandelbaum, Seymour J. 1985. 'Historians and Planners: The Construction of Pasts and Futures." *Journal of the American Planning Association* 51, 2: 185–88.

Mumford, Lewis. 1938. *The Culture of Cities*. New York: Harcourt, Brace.

Mumford, Lewis. 1945. *City Development*. New York: Harcourt, Brace.

Mumford, Lewis. 1967. *The Myth of the Machine: The Penetration of Power*. New York: Harcourt, Brace.

Mumford, Lewis. 1968. *The Urban Prospect*. New York: Harcourt, Brace.

Reps, John W. 1965. *The Making of Urban America: A History of City Planning in the United States*. Princeton, NJ: Princeton.

Schuyler, David. 1986. *The New Urban Landscape*. Baltimore: Johns Hopkins.

Scott, Mel. 1969. *American City Planning*. Berkeley: University of California Press.

Warner, Sam Bass. 1976. *Street Car Suburbs: The Process of Growth in Boston*. New York: Atheneum.

2

PLANNING THEORY
AND ETHICS

The Science of "Muddling Through"

Charles E. Lindblom
Former Professor of Economics, Yale University

In this article, Charles Lindblom presents a compelling critique of the rational planning model. The author argues that the formalized planning approach to decision making—the rational-comprehensive method—can be practiced only on very simple problems. For complex problems, it is not feasible to conduct a systematic comparison of a multitude of values. Thus, according to Lindblom, most decision makers rely on a method of "successive limited comparisons," or "muddling through," rather than on the rational-comprehensive method.

Suppose an administrator is given responsibility for formulating policy with respect to inflation. He might start by trying to list all related values in order of importance, e.g., full employment, reasonable business profit, protection of small savings, prevention of a stock market crash. Then all possible policy outcomes could be rated as more or less efficient in attaining a maximum of these values. This would of course require a prodigious inquiry into values held by members of society and an equally prodigious set of calculations on how much of each value is equal to how much of each other value. He could then proceed to outline all possible policy alternatives. In a third step, he would undertake systematic comparison of his multitude of alternatives to determine which attains the greatest amount of values.

In comparing policies, he would take advantage of any theory available that generalized about classes of policies. In considering inflation, for example, he would compare all policies in the light of the theory of prices. Since no alternatives are beyond his investigation, he would consider strict central control and the abolition of all prices and markets on the one hand and elimination of all public controls with reliance completely on the free market on the other, both in the light of whatever theoretical generalizations he could find on such hypothetical economies.

Finally, he would try to make the choice that would in fact maximize his values.

An alternative line of attack would be to set as his principal objective, either explicitly or without conscious thought, the relatively simple goal of keeping prices level. This objective might be compromised or complicated by only a few other goals, such as full employment. He would in fact disregard most other social values as beyond his present interest, and he would for the moment not even attempt to rank the few values that he regarded as immediately relevant. Were he pressed, he would quickly admit that he was ignoring many related values and many possible important consequences of his policies.

As a second step, he would outline those relatively few policy alternatives that occurred to him. He would then compare them. In comparing his limited number of alternatives, most of them familiar from past controversies, he would not ordinarily find a body of theory precise enough to carry him through a comparison of their respective consequences. Instead he would rely heavily on the record of past experience with small policy steps to predict the consequences of similar steps extended into the future.

Moreover, he would find that the policy alternatives combined objectives or values in different ways. For example, one policy might offer price level stability at the cost of some risk of unemployment; another might offer less price stability but also less risk of unemployment. Hence, the next step in his approach—the final selection—would combine into one the choice among values and the choice among instruments for reaching values. It would not, as in the first method of policy-making, approximate a more mechanical process of choosing the means that best satisfied goals that were previously clarified and ranked. Because practitioners of the second approach expect to achieve their goals only partially, they would expect to repeat endlessly the sequence just described, as conditions and aspirations changed and as accuracy of prediction improved.

BY ROOT OR BY BRANCH

For complex problems, the first of these two approaches is of course impossible. Although such an approach can be described, it cannot be practiced except for relatively simple problems and even then only in a somewhat modified form. It assumes intellectual capacities and sources of information that men simply do not possess, and it is even more absurd as an approach to policy when the time and money that can be allocated to a policy problem is limited, as is always the case. Of particular importance to public administrators is the fact that public agencies are in effect usually instructed not to practice the first method. That is to say, their prescribed functions and constraints—the politically or legally possible—restrict their attention to relatively few values and relatively few alternative policies among the countless alternatives that might be imagined. It is the second method that is practiced.

Curiously, however, the literatures of decision-making, policy formulation, planning, and public administration formalize the first approach rather than the second, leaving public administrators who handle complex decisions in the position of practicing what few preach. For emphasis I run some risk of overstatement. True enough, the literature is well aware of limits on man's capacities and of the inevitability that policies will be approached in some such style as the second. But attempts to formalize rational policy formulation—to lay out explicitly the necessary steps in the process—usually describe the first approach and not the second.[1]

The common tendency to describe policy formulation even for complex problems as though it followed the first approach has been strengthened by the attention given to, and successes enjoyed by, operations research, statistical decision theory, and systems analysis. The hallmarks of these procedures, typical of the first approach, are clarity of objective, explicitness of evaluation, a high degree of comprehensiveness of overview, and, wherever possible, quantification of values for mathematical analysis. But these advanced procedures remain largely the appropriate techniques of relatively small-scale problem-solving where the total number of variables to be considered is small and value problems restricted. Charles Hitch, head of the Economics Division of RAND Corporation, one of the leading centers for application of these techniques, has written:

> I would make the empirical generalization from my experience at RAND and elsewhere that operations research is the art of sub-optimizing, i.e., of solving some lower-level problems, and that difficulties increase and our special competence diminishes by an order of magnitude with every level of decision making we attempt to ascend. The sort of simple explicit model which operations researchers are so proficient in using can certainly reflect most of the significant factors influencing traffic control on the George Washington Bridge, but the proportion of the relevant reality which we can represent by any such model or models in studying, say, a major foreign-policy decision, appears to be almost trivial.[2]

Accordingly, I propose in this paper to clarify and formalize the second method, much neglected in the literature. This might be described as the method of *successive limited comparisons*. I will contrast it with the first approach, which might be called the rational-comprehensive method.[3] More impressionistically and briefly—and therefore generally used in this article—they could be characterized as the branch method and root method, the former continually building out from the current situation, step-by-step and by small degrees; the latter starting from fundamentals anew each time, building on the past only as experience is embodied in a theory, and always prepared to start completely from the ground up.

Let us put the characteristics of the two methods side by side in simplest terms.

Rational-comprehensive (root)

1a Clarification of values or objectives distinct from and usually prerequisite to empirical analysis of alternative policies.

2a Policy-formulation is therefore approached through means-end analysis: First the ends are isolated, then the means to achieve them are sought.

3a The test of a "good" policy is that it can be shown to be the most appropriate means to desired ends.

4a Analysis is comprehensive; every important relevant factor is taken into account.

5a Theory is often heavily relied upon.

Successive limited comparisons (branch)

1b Selection of value goals and empirical analysis of the needed action are not distinct from one another but are closely intertwined.

2b Since means and ends are not distinct, means-end analysis is often inappropriate or limited.

3b The test of a "good" policy is typically that various analysts find themselves directly agreeing on a policy (without their agreeing that it is the most appropriate means to an agreed objective).

4b Analysis is drastically limited:
  i) Important possible outcomes are neglected.
  ii) Important alternative potential policies are neglected.
  iii) Important affected values are neglected.

5b A succession of comparisons greatly reduces or eliminates reliance on theory.

Assuming that the root method is familiar and understandable, we proceed directly to clarification of its alternative by contrast. In explaining the second, we shall be describing how most administrators do in fact approach complex questions, for the root method, the "best" way as a blueprint or model, is in fact not workable for complex policy questions, and administrators are forced to use the method of successive limited comparisons.

Intertwining Evaluation and Empirical Analysis (1b)

The quickest way to understand how values are handled in the method of successive limited comparisons is to see how the root method often breaks down in *its* handling of values or objectives. The idea that values should be clarified, and in advance of the examination of alternative policies, is appealing. But what happens when we attempt it for complex social problems? The first difficulty is that on many critical values or objectives, citizens disagree, congressmen disagree, and public administrators disagree. Even where a fairly specific objective is prescribed for the administrator, there remains considerable room for disagreement on sub-objectives. Consider, for example, the conflict with respect to locating public housing, described in Meyerson and Banfield's study of the Chicago Housing Authority[4]—disagreement which occurred despite the clear objective of providing a certain number of public housing units in the city. Similarly conflicting are objectives in highway location, traffic control, minimum wage administration, development of tourist facilities in national parks, or insect control.

Administrators cannot escape these conflicts by ascertaining the majority's preference, for preferences have not been registered on most issues; indeed, there often *are* no preferences in the absence of public discussion sufficient to bring an issue to the attention of the electorate. Furthermore, there is a question of whether intensity of feeling should be considered as well as the number of persons preferring each alternative. By the impossibility of doing otherwise, administrators often are reduced to deciding policy without clarifying objectives first.

Even when an administrator resolves to follow his own values as a criterion for decisions, he often will not know how to rank them when they conflict with one another, as they usually do. Suppose, for example, that an administrator must relocate tenants living in tenements scheduled for destruction. One objective is to empty the buildings fairly promptly, another is to find suitable accommodation for persons displaced, another is to avoid friction with residents in other areas in which a large influx would be unwelcome, another is to deal with all concerned through persuasion if possible, and so on.

How does one state even to himself the relative importance of these partially conflicting values? A simple ranking of them is not enough; one needs ideally to know how much of one value is worth sacrificing for some of another value. The answer is that typically the administrator chooses—and must choose—directly among policies in which these values are combined in different ways. He cannot first clarify his values and then choose among policies.

A more subtle third point underlies both the first two. Social objectives do not always have the same relative values. One objective may be highly prized in one circumstance, another in another circumstance. If, for example, an administrator values highly both the dispatch with which his agency can carry through its projects *and* good public relations, it matters little which of the two possibly conflicting values he favors in some abstract or general sense. Policy questions arise in forms which put to administrators such a question as: Given the degree to which we are or are not already achieving the values of dispatch and the values of good public relations, is it worth sacrificing a little speed for a happier clientele, or is it better to risk offending the clientele so that we can get on with our work? The answer to such a question varies with circumstances.

The value problem is, as the example shows, always a problem of adjustments at a margin. But there is no practicable way to state marginal objectives or values except in terms of particular policies. That one value is preferred to another in one decision situation does not mean that it will be preferred in another decision situation in which it can be had only at great sacrifice of another value. Attempts to rank or order values in general and abstract terms so that they do not shift from decision to decision end up by ignoring the relevant marginal preferences. The significance of this third point thus goes very far. Even if all administrators had at hand an agreed set of values, objectives, and constraints, and an agreed ranking of these values, objectives, and constraints, their marginal values in actual choice situations would be impossible to formulate.

Unable consequently to formulate the relevant values first and then choose among policies to achieve them, administrators must choose directly among alternative policies that offer different marginal combinations of values. Somewhat paradoxically, the only practicable way to disclose one's relevant marginal values even to oneself is to describe the policy one chooses to achieve them. Except roughly and vaguely, I know of no way to describe—or even to understand—what my relative evaluations are for, say, freedom and security, speed and accuracy in governmental decisions, or low taxes and better schools than to describe my preferences among specific policy choices that might be made between the alternatives in each of the pairs.

In summary, two aspects of the process by which values are actually handled can be distinguished. The first is clear: evaluation and empirical analysis are intertwined; that is, one chooses among values and among policies at one and the same time. Put a little more elaborately, one simultaneously chooses a policy to attain certain objectives and chooses the objectives themselves. The second aspect is related but distinct: the administrator focuses his attention on marginal or incremental values. Whether he is aware of it or not, he does not find general formulations of objectives very helpful and in fact makes specific marginal or incremental comparisons. Two policies, X and Y, confront him. Both promise the same degree of attainment of objectives *a, b, c, d,* and *e.* But X promises him somewhat more of *f* than does Y, while Y promises him somewhat more of *g* than does X. In choosing between them, he is in fact offered the alternative of a marginal or incremental amount of *f* at the expense of a marginal or incremental amount of *g.* The only values that are relevant to his choice are these increments by which the two policies differ; and, when he finally chooses between the two marginal values, he does so by making a choice between policies.[5]

As to whether the attempt to clarify objectives in advance of policy selection is more or less rational than the close intertwining of marginal evaluation and empirical analysis, the principal difference established is that for complex problems the first is impossible and irrelevant, and the second is both possible and relevant. The second is possible because the administrator need not try to analyze any values except the values by which alternative policies differ and need not be concerned with them except as they differ marginally. His need for information on values or objectives is drastically reduced as compared with the root method; and his capacity for grasping, comprehending, and relating values to one another is not strained beyond the breaking point.

Relations Between Means and Ends (2b)

Decision-making is ordinarily formalized as a means-end relationship: means are conceived to be evaluated and chosen in the light of ends finally selected independently of and prior to the choice of means. This is the means-ends relationship of the root method. But it follows from all that has just been said that such a means-ends relationship is possible only to the extent that values are agreed upon, are reconcilable, and are stable at the margin. Typically, therefore, such a means-ends relationship is absent from the branch method, where means and ends are simultaneously chosen.

Yet any departure from the means-ends relationship of the root method will strike some readers as inconceivable. For it will appear to them that only in such a relationship is it possible to determine whether one policy choice is better or worse than another. How can an administrator know whether he has made a wise or foolish decision if he is without prior values or objectives by which to judge his decisions? The answer to this question calls up the third distinctive difference between root and branch methods: how to describe the best policy.

The Test of "Good" Policy (3b)

In the root method, a decision is "correct," "good," or "rational" if it can be shown to attain some specified objective, where the objective can be specified without simply describing the decision itself. Where objectives are defined only through the marginal or incremental approach to values described above, it is still sometimes possible to test whether a policy does in fact attain the desired objectives; but a precise statement of the objectives takes the form of a description of the policy chosen or some alternative to it. To show that a policy is mistaken one cannot offer an abstract argument that important objectives are not achieved; one must instead argue that another policy is more to be preferred.

So far, the departure from customary ways of looking at problem-solving is not troublesome, for many administrators will be quick to agree that the most effective discussion of the correctness of policy does take the form of comparison with other policies that might have been chosen. But what of the situation in which administrators cannot agree on values or objectives, either abstractly or in marginal terms? What then is the test of "good" policy? For the root method, there is no test.

Agreement on objectives failing, there is no standard or "correctness." For the method of successive limited comparisons, the test is agreement on policy itself, which remains possible even when agreement on values is not.

It has been suggested that continuing agreement in Congress on the desirability of extending old age insurance stems from liberal desires to strengthen the welfare programs of the federal government and from conservative desires to reduce union demands for private pension plans. If so, this is an excellent demonstration of the ease with which individuals of different ideologies often can agree on concrete policy. Labor mediators report a similar phenomenon: the contestants cannot agree on criteria for settling their disputes but can agree on specific proposals. Similarly, when one administrator's objective turns out to be another's means, they often can agree on policy.

Agreement on policy thus becomes the only practicable test of the policy's correctness. And for one administrator to seek to win the other over to agreement on ends as well would accomplish nothing and create quite unnecessary controversy.

If agreement directly on policy as a test for "best" policy seems a poor substitute for testing the policy against its objectives, it ought to be remembered that objectives themselves have no ultimate validity other than they are agreed upon. Hence agreement is the test of "best" policy in both methods. But where the root method requires agreement on what elements in the decision constitute objectives and on which of these objectives should be sought, the branch method falls back on agreement wherever it can be found.

In an important sense, therefore, it is not irrational for an administrator to defend a policy as good without being able to specify what it is good for.

Non-Comprehensive Analysis (4b)

Ideally, rational-comprehensive analysis leaves out nothing important. But it is impossible to take everything important into consideration unless "important" is so narrowly defined that analysis is in fact quite limited. Limits on human intellectual capacities and on available information set definite limits to man's capacity to be comprehensive. In actual fact, therefore, no one can practice the rational-comprehensive method for really complex problems, and every administrator faced with a sufficiently complex problem must find ways drastically to simplify.

An administrator assisting in the formulation of agricultural economic policy cannot in the first place be competent on all possible policies. He cannot even comprehend one policy entirely. In planning a soil bank program, he cannot successfully anticipate the impact of higher or lower farm income on, say, urbanization—the possible consequent loosening of family ties, possible consequent eventual need for revisions in social security and further implications for tax problems arising out of new federal responsibilities for social security and municipal responsibilities for urban services. Nor, to follow another line of repercussions, can he work through the soil bank program's effects on prices for agricultural products in foreign markets and consequent implications for foreign relations, including those arising out of economic rivalry between the United States and the U.S.S.R.

In the method of successive limited comparisons, simplification is systematically achieved in two principal ways. First, it is achieved through limitation of policy comparisons to those policies that differ in relatively small degree from policies presently in effect. Such a limitation immediately reduces the number of alternatives to be investigated and also drastically simplifies the character of the investigation of each. For it is not necessary to undertake fundamental inquiry into an alternative and its consequences; it is necessary only to study those respects in which the proposed alternative and its consequences differ from the status quo. The empirical comparison of marginal differences among alternative policies that differ only marginally is, of course, a counterpart to the incremental or marginal comparison of values discussed above.[6]

Relevance as Well as Realism   It is a matter of common observation that in Western democracies public administrators and policy analysts in general do largely limit their analyses to incremental or marginal differences in policies that are chosen to differ only incrementally. They do not do so, however, solely because they desperately need some way to simplify their problems; they also do so in order to be relevant. Democracies change their policies almost entirely through incremental adjustments. Policy does not move in leaps and bounds.

The incremental character of political change in the United States has often been remarked. The two major political parties agree on fundamentals; they offer alternative policies to the voters only on relatively small points of difference. Both parties favor full employment, but they define it somewhat differently; both favor the development of water power resources, but in slightly different ways; and both favor unemployment compensation, but not the same level of benefits. Similarly, shifts of policy within a party take place largely through a series of relatively small changes, as can be seen in their only gradual acceptance of the idea of governmental responsibility for support of the unemployed, a change in party positions beginning in the early 30's and culminating in a sense in the Employment Act of 1946.

Party behavior is in turn rooted in public attitudes, and political theorists cannot conceive of democracy's surviving in the United States in the absence of fundamental agreement on potentially disruptive issues, with consequent limitation of policy debates to relatively small differences in policy.

Since the policies ignored by the administrator are politically impossible and so irrelevant, the simplification of analysis achieved by concentrating on policies that differ only incrementally is not a capricious kind of simplification. In addition, it can be argued that, given the limits on knowledge within which policy-makers are confined, simplifying by limiting the focus to small variations from present policy makes the most of available knowledge. Because policies being considered are like present and past policies, the administrator can obtain information and claim some insight. Non-incremental policy proposals are therefore typically not only politically irrelevant but also unpredictable in their consequences.

The second method of simplification of analysis is the practice of ignoring important possible consequences of possible policies, as well as the values attached to the neglected consequences. If this appears to disclose a shocking shortcoming of successive limited comparisons, it can be replied that, even if the exclusions are random, policies may nevertheless be more intelligently formulated than through futile attempts to achieve a comprehensiveness beyond human capacity. Actually, however, the exclusions, seeming arbitrary or random from one point of view, need be neither.

Achieving a Degree of Comprehensiveness   Suppose that each value neglected by one policy-making agency were a major concern of at least one other agency. In that case, a helpful division of labor would be achieved, and no agency need find its task beyond its capacities. The shortcomings of such a system would be that one agency might destroy a value either before another agency could be activated to safeguard it or in spite of another agency's efforts. But the possibility that important values may be lost is present in any form of organization, even where agencies attempt to comprehend in planning more than is humanly possible.

The virtue of such a hypothetical division of labor is that every important interest or value has its watchdog. And these watchdogs can protect the interests in their jurisdiction in two quite different ways: first, by redressing damages done by other agencies; and, second, by anticipating and heading off injury before it occurs.

In a society like that of the United States in which individuals are free to combine to pursue almost any possible common interest they might have and in which government agencies are sensitive to the pressures of these groups, the system described is approximated. Almost every interest has its watchdog. Without claiming that every interest has a sufficiently powerful watchdog, it can be argued that our system often can assure a more comprehensive regard for the values of the whole society than any attempt at intellectual comprehensiveness.

In the United States, for example, no part of government attempts a comprehensive overview of policy on income distribution. A policy nevertheless evolves, and one responding to a wide variety of interests. A process of mutual adjustment among farm groups, labor unions, municipalities and school boards, tax authorities, and government agencies with responsibilities in the fields of housing, health, highways, national parks, fire, and police accomplishes a distribution of income in which particular income problems neglected at one point in the decision processes become central at another point.

Mutual adjustment is more pervasive than the explicit forms it takes in negotiation between groups; it persists through the mutual impacts of groups upon each other even where they are not in communication. For all the imperfections and latent dangers in this ubiquitous process of mutual adjustment, it will often accomplish an adaptation of policies to a wider range of interests than could be done by one group centrally.

Note, too, how the incremental pattern of policy-making fits with the multiple pressure pattern. For when decisions are only incremental—closely related to known policies, it is easier for one group to anticipate the kind of moves another might make and easier too for it to make correction for injury already accomplished.[7]

Even partisanship and narrowness, to use pejorative terms, will sometimes be assets to rational decision-making, for they can doubly insure that what one agency neglects, another will not; they specialize personnel to distinct points of view. The claim is valid that effective rational coordination of the federal administration, if possible to achieve at all, would require an agreed set of values[8]—if "rational" is defined as the practice of the root method of decision-making. But a high degree of administrative coordination occurs as each agency adjusts its policies to the concerns of the other agencies in the process of fragmented decision-making I have just described.

For all the apparent shortcomings of the incremental approach to policy alternatives with its arbitrary exclusion coupled with fragmentation, when compared to the root method, the branch method often looks far superior. In the root method, the inevitable exclusion of factors is accidental, unsystematic, and not defensible by any argument so far developed, while in the branch method the exclusions are deliberate, systematic, and defensible. Ideally, of course, the root method does not exclude; in practice it must.

Nor does the branch method necessarily neglect long-run considerations and objectives. It is clear that important values must be omitted in considering policy, and sometimes the only way long-run objectives can be given adequate attention is through the neglect of short-run considerations. But the values omitted can be either long-run or short-run.

Succession of Comparisons (5b)

The final distinctive element in the branch method is that the comparisons, together with the policy choice, proceed in a chronological series. Policy is not made once and for all; it is made and re-made endlessly. Policy-making is a process of successive approximation to some desired objectives in which what is desired itself continues to change under reconsideration.

Making policy is at best a very rough process. Neither social scientists, nor politicians, nor public administrators yet know enough about the social world to avoid repeated error in predicting the consequences of policy moves. A wise policy-maker consequently expects that his policies will achieve only part of what he hopes and at the same time will produce unanticipated consequences he would have preferred to avoid. If he proceeds through a *succession* of incremental changes, he avoids serious lasting mistakes in several ways.

In the first place, past sequences of policy steps have given him knowledge about the probable consequences of further similar steps. Second, he need not attempt big jumps toward his goals that would require predictions beyond his or anyone else's knowledge, because he never expects his policy to be a final resolution of a problem. His decision is only one step, one that if successful can quickly be followed by another. Third, he is in effect able to test his previous predictions as he moves on to each further step. Lastly, he often can remedy a past error fairly quickly—more quickly than if policy proceeded through more distinct steps widely spaced in time.

Compare this comparative analysis of incremental changes with the aspiration to employ theory in the root method. Man cannot think without classifying, without subsuming one experience under a more general category of experiences. The attempt to push categorization as far as possible and to find general propositions which can be applied to specific situations is what I refer to with the word "theory." Where root analysis often leans heavily on theory in this sense, the branch method does not.

The assumption of root analysts is that theory is the most systematic and economical way to bring relevant knowledge to bear on a specific problem. Granting the assumption, an unhappy fact is that we do not have adequate theory to apply to problems in any policy area, although theory is more adequate in some areas—monetary policy, for example—than in some others. Comparative analysis, as in the branch method, is sometimes a systematic alternative to theory.

Suppose an administrator must choose among a small group of policies that differ only incrementally from each other and from present policy. He might aspire to "understand" each of the alternatives—for example, to know all the consequences of each aspect of each policy. If so, he would indeed require theory. In fact, however, he would usually decide that, *for policy-making purposes*, he need know, as explained above, only the consequences of each of those aspects of the policies in which they differed from one another. For this much more modest aspiration, he requires no theory (although it might be helpful, if available), for he can proceed to isolate probable differences by examining the differences in consequences associated with past differences in policies, a feasible program because he can take his observations from a long sequence of incremental changes.

For example, without a more comprehensive social theory about juvenile delinquency than scholars have yet produced, one cannot possibly understand the ways in which a variety of public policies—say on education, housing, recreation, employment, race relations, and policing—might encourage or discourage delinquency. And one needs such an understanding if he undertakes the comprehensive overview of the problem prescribed in the models of the root method. If, however, one merely wants to mobilize knowledge sufficient to assist in a choice among a small group of similar policies—alternative policies on juvenile court procedures, for example—he can do so by comparative analysis of the results of similar past policy moves.

THEORISTS AND PRACTITIONERS

This difference explains—in some cases at least—why the administrator often feels that the outside expert or academic problem-solver is sometimes not helpful and why they in turn often urge more theory on him. And it explains why an administrator often feels more confident when "flying by the seat of his pants" than when following the advice of theorists. Theorists often ask the administrator to go the long way round to the solution of his problems, in effect ask him to follow the best canons of the scientific method, when the administrator knows that the best available theory will work less well than more modest incremental comparisons.

Theorists do not realize that the administrator is often in fact practicing a systematic method. It would be foolish to push this explanation too far, for sometimes practical decision-makers are pursuing neither a theoretical approach nor successive comparisons, nor any other systematic method.

It may be worth emphasizing that theory is sometimes of extremely limited helpfulness in policy-making for at least two rather different reasons. It is greedy for facts; it can be constructed only through a great collection of observations. And it is typically insufficiently precise for application to a policy process that moves through small changes. In contrast, the comparative method both economizes on the need for facts and directs the analyst's attention to just those facts that are relevant to the fine choices faced by the decision-maker.

With respect to precision of theory, economic theory serves as an example. It predicts that an economy without money or prices would in certain specified ways misallocate resources, but this finding pertains to an alternative far removed from the kind of policies on which administrators need help. On the other hand, it is not precise enough to predict the consequences of policies restricting business mergers, and this is the kind of issue on which the administrators need help. Only in relatively restricted areas does economic theory achieve sufficient precision to go far in resolving policy questions; its helpfulness in policy-making is always so limited that it requires supplementation through comparative analysis.

SUCCESSIVE COMPARISON AS A SYSTEM

Successive limited comparisons is, then, indeed a method or system; it is not a failure of method for which administrators ought to apologize. None the less, its imperfections, which have not been explored in this paper, are many. For example, the method is without a built-in safeguard for all relevant values, and it also may lead the decision-maker to overlook excellent policies for no other reason than that they are not suggested by the chain of successive policy steps leading up to the present. Hence, it ought to be said that under this method, as well as under some of the most sophisticated variants of the root method—operations research, for example—policies will continue to be as foolish as they are wise.

Why then bother to describe the method in all the above detail? Because it is in fact a common method of policy formulation, and is, for complex problems, the principal reliance of administrators as well as of other policy analysts.[9] And because it will be superior to any other decision-making method available for complex problems in many circumstances, certainly superior to a futile attempt at superhuman comprehensiveness. The reaction of the public administrator to the exposition of method doubtless will be less a discovery of a new method than a better acquaintance with an old. But by becoming more conscious of their practice of this method, administrators might practice it with more skill and know when to extend or constrict its use. (That they sometimes practice it effectively and sometimes not may explain the extremes of opinion on "muddling through," which is both praised as a highly sophisticated form of problem-solving and denounced as no method at all. For I suspect that in so far as there is a system in what is known as "muddling through," this method is it.)

One of the noteworthy incidental consequences of clarification of the method is the light it throws on the suspicion an administrator sometimes entertains that a consultant or adviser is not speaking relevantly and responsibly when in fact by all ordinary objective evidence he is. The trouble lies in the fact that most of us approach policy problems within a framework given by our view of a chain of successive policy choices made up to the present. One's thinking about appropriate policies with respect, say, to urban traffic control is greatly influenced by one's knowledge of the incremental steps taken up to the present. An administrator enjoys an intimate knowledge of his past sequences that "outsiders" do not share, and his thinking and that of the "outsider" will consequently be different in ways that may puzzle both. Both may appear to be talking intelligently, yet each may find the other unsatisfactory. The relevance of the policy chain of succession is even more clear when an American tries to discuss, say, antitrust policy with a Swiss, for the chains of policy in the two countries are strikingly different and the two individuals consequently have organized their knowledge in quite different ways.

If this phenomenon is a barrier to communication, an understanding of it promises an enrichment of intellectual interaction in policy formulation. Once the source of difference is understood, it will sometimes be stimulating for an administrator to seek out a policy analyst whose recent experience is with a policy chain different from his own.

This raises again a question only briefly discussed above on the merits of like-mindedness among government administrators. While much of organization theory argues the virtues of common values and agreed organizational objectives, for complex problems in which the root method is inapplicable, agencies will want among their own personnel two types of diversification: administrators whose thinking is organized by reference to policy chains other than those familiar to most members of the organization and, even more commonly, administrators whose professional or personal values or interests create diversity of view (perhaps coming from different specialties, social classes, geographical areas) so that, even within a single agency, decision-making can be fragmented and parts of the agency can serve as watchdogs for other parts.

NOTES

1 James G. March and Herbert A. Simon similarly characterize the literature. They also take some important steps, as have Simon's recent articles, to describe a less heroic model of policy-making. See *Organizations* (John Wiley and Sons, 1958), p. 137.

2 "Operations Research and National Planning—A Dissent," 5 *Operations Research* 718 (October, 1957). Hitch's dissent is from particular points made in the article to which his paper is a reply; his claim that operations research is for low-level problems is widely accepted.

For examples of the kind of problems to which operations research is applied, see C. W. Churchman, R. L. Ackoff and E. L. Arnoff, *Introduction to Operations Research*

(John Wiley and Sons, 1957); and J. F. McCloskey and J. M. Coppinger (eds.), *Operations Research for Management*, Vol. II, (The Johns Hopkins Press, 1956).

3 I am assuming that administrators often make policy and advise in the making of policy and am treating decision-making and policy-making as synonymous for purposes of this paper.

4 Martin Meyerson and Edward C. Banfield, *Politics, Planning and the Public Interest* (The Free Press, 1955).

5 The line of argument is, of course, an extension of the theory of market choice, especially the theory of consumer choice, to public policy choices.

6 A more precise definition of incremental policies and a discussion of whether a change that appears "small" to one observer might be seen differently by another is to be found in my "Policy Analysis," 48 *American Economic Review* 298 (June, 1958).

7 The link between the practice of the method of successive limited comparisons and mutual adjustment of interests in a highly fragmented decision-making process adds a new facet to pluralist theories of government and administration.

8 Herbert Simon, Donald W. Smithburg, and Victor A. Thompson, *Public Administration* (Alfred A. Knopf, 1950), p. 434.

9 Elsewhere I have explored this same method of policy formulation as practiced by academic analysts of policy ("Policy Analysis," 48 *American Economic Review* 298 [June, 1958]). Although it has been here presented as a method for public administrators, it is no less necessary to analysts more removed from immediate policy questions, despite their tendencies to describe their own analytical efforts as though they were the rational-comprehensive method with an especially heavy use of theory. Similarly, this same method is inevitably resorted to in personal problem-solving, where means and ends are sometimes impossible to separate, where aspirations or objectives undergo constant development, and where drastic simplification of the complexity of the real world is urgent if problems are to be solved in the time that can be given to them. To an economist accustomed to dealing with the marginal or incremental concept in market processes, the central idea in the method is that both evaluation and empirical analysis are incremental. Accordingly I have referred to the method elsewhere as "the incremental method."

Advocacy and Pluralism in Planning

Paul Davidoff

Former Professor of City Planning, Hunter College and the University of Pennsylvania

In this article, Paul Davidoff challenges the planning profession with a call for a new type of planner: the comprehensive city planner, who will be an advocate for the poor, broadly educated, and concerned as much with social and economic issues as with physical planning. Davidoff argues the importance of planners who are advocates rather than dispassionate professionals, and deeply involved in the politics of planning. According to Davidoff, for an effective urban democ-

Reprinted by permission of the *Journal of the American Institute of Planners* 31, 4, November 1965.

racy, planners should encourage pluralism by giving voice, power, and representation to the concerns of many interest groups, especially the poor.

The present can become an epoch in which the dreams of the past for an enlightened and just democracy are turned into a reality. The massing of voices protesting racial discrimination have roused this nation to the need to rectify racial and
other social injustices. The adoption by Congress of a host of welfare measures and
the Supreme Court's specification of the meaning of equal protection by law both
reveal the response to protest and open the way for the vast changes still required.

The just demand for political and social equality on the part of the Negro and
the impoverished requires the public to establish the bases for a society affording
equal opportunity to all citizens. The compelling need for intelligent planning, for
specification of new social goals and the means for achieving them, is manifest.
The society of the future will be an urban one, and city planners will help to give
it shape and content.

The prospect for future planning is that of a practice which openly invites political and social values to be examined and debated. Acceptance of this position
means rejection of prescriptions for planning which would have the planner act
solely as a technician. It has been argued that technical studies to enlarge the information available to decision makers must take precedence over statements of goals
and ideals:

> We have suggested that, at least in part, the city planner is better advised to start from
> research into the functional aspects of cities than from his own estimation of the values
> which he is attempting to maximize. This suggestion springs from a conviction that at
> this juncture the implications of many planning decisions are poorly understood, and
> that no certain means are at hand by which values can be measured, ranked, and trans-
> lated into the design of a metropolitan system.[1]

While acknowledging the need for humility and openness in the adoption of
social goals, this statement amounts to an attempt to eliminate, or sharply reduce,
the unique contribution planning can make: understanding the functional aspects
of the city and recommending appropriate future action to improve the urban condition.

Another argument that attempts to reduce the importance of attitudes and values in planning and other policy sciences is that the major public questions are
themselves matters of choice between technical methods of solution. Dahl and
Lindblom put forth this position at the beginning of their important textbook,
Politics, Economics, and Welfare:[2]

> In economic organization and reform, the "great issues" are no longer the great issues,
> if they ever were. It has become increasingly difficult for thoughtful men to find mean-
> ingful alternatives posed in the traditional choices between socialism and capitalism,
> planning and the free market, regulation and laissez faire, for they find their actual
> choices neither so simple nor so grand. Not so simple, because economic organization
> poses knotty problems that can only be solved by painstaking attention to technical
> details—how else, for example, can inflation be controlled? Nor so grand, because, at

least in the Western world, most people neither can nor wish to experiment with the whole pattern of socio-economic organization to attain goals more easily won. If for example, taxation will serve the purpose, why "abolish the wages system" to ameliorate income inequality?

These words were written in the early 1950's and express the spirit of that decade more than that of the 1960's. They suggest that the major battles have been fought. But the "great issues" in economic organization, those revolving around the central issue of the nature of distributive justice, have yet to be settled. The world is still in turmoil over the way in which the resources of nations are to be distributed. The justice of the present social allocation of wealth, knowledge, skill, and other social goods is clearly in debate. Solutions to questions about the share of wealth and other social commodities that should go to different classes cannot be technically derived; they must arise from social attitudes.

Appropriate planning action cannot be prescribed from a position of value neutrality, for prescriptions are based on desired objectives. One conclusion drawn from this assertion is that "values are inescapable elements of any rational decision-making process"[3] and that values held by the planner should be made clear. The implications of that conclusion for planning have been described elsewhere and will not be considered in this article.[4] Here I will say that the planner should do more than explicate the values underlying his prescriptions for courses of action; he should affirm them; he should be an advocate for what he deems proper.

Determinations of what serves the public interest, in a society containing many diverse interest groups, are almost always of a highly contentious nature. In performing its role of prescribing courses of action leading to future desired states, the planning profession must engage itself thoroughly and openly in the contention surrounding political determination. Moreover, planners should be able to engage in the political process as advocates of the interests both of government and of such other groups, organizations, or individuals who are concerned with proposing policies for the future development of the community.

The recommendation that city planners represent and plead the plans of many interest groups is founded upon the need to establish an effective urban democracy, one in which citizens may be able to play an active role in the process of deciding public policy. Appropriate policy in a democracy is determined through a process of political debate. The right course of action is always a matter of choice, never of fact. In a bureaucratic age great care must be taken that choices remain in the area of public view and participation.

Urban politics, in an era of increasing government activity in planning and welfare, must balance the demands for ever-increasing central bureaucratic control against the demands for increased concern for the unique requirements of local, specialized interests. The welfare of all and the welfare of minorities are both deserving of support; planning must be so structured and so practiced as to account for this unavoidable bifurcation of the public interest.

The idealized political process in a democracy serves the search for truth in much the same manner as due process in law. Fair notice and hearings, production of supporting evidence, cross examination, reasoned decision are all means employed to arrive at relative truth: a just decision. Due process and two- (or more) party political contention both rely heavily upon strong advocacy by a professional. The advocate represents an individual, group, or organization. He affirms their position in language understandable to his client and to the decision makers he seeks to convince.

If the planning process is to encourage democratic urban government then it must operate so as to include rather than exclude citizens from participating in the process. "Inclusion" means not only permitting the citizen to be heard. It also means that he be able to become well informed about the underlying reasons for planning proposals, and be able to respond to them in the technical language of professional planners.

A practice that has discouraged full participation by citizens in plan making in the past has been based on what might be called the "*unitary plan.*" This is the idea that only one agency in a community should prepare a comprehensive plan; that agency is the city planning commission or department. Why is it that no other organization within a community prepares a plan? Why is only one agency concerned with establishing both general and specific goals for community development, and with proposing the strategies and costs required to effect the goals? Why are there not plural plans?

If the social, economic, and political ramifications of a plan are politically contentious, then why is it that those in opposition to the agency plan do not prepare one of their own? It is interesting to observe that "rational" theories of planning have called for consideration of alternative courses of action by planning agencies. As a matter of rationality it has been argued that all of the alternative choices open as means to the ends ought to be examined.[5] But those, including myself, who have recommended agency consideration of alternatives have placed upon the agency planner the burden of inventing "a few representative alternatives."[6] The agency planner has been given the duty of constructing a model of the political spectrum, and charged with sorting out what he conceives to be worthy alternatives. This duty has placed too great a burden on the agency planner, and has failed to provide for the formulation of alternatives by the interest groups who will eventually be affected by the completed plans.

Whereas in a large part of our national and local political practice contention is viewed as healthy, in city planning where a large proportion of the professionals are public employees, contentious criticism has not always been viewed as legitimate. Further, where only government prepares plans, and no minority plans are developed, pressure is often applied to bring all professionals to work for the ends espoused by a public agency. For example, last year a Federal official complained to a meeting of planning professors that the academic planners were not giving enough support to Federal programs. He assumed that every planner should be on the side of the Federal renewal program. Of course government administrators will seek to gain the support of professionals outside of government, but such support should not be expected as a matter of loyalty. In a democratic system opposition to a public agency should be just as normal and appropriate as support. The agency, despite the fact that it is concerned with planning, may be serving undesired ends.

In presenting a plea for plural planning I do not mean to minimize the importance of the obligation of the public planning agency. It must decide upon appropriate future courses of action for the community. But being isolated as the only plan maker in the community, public agencies as well as the public itself may have suffered from incomplete and shallow analysis of potential directions. Lively political dispute aided by plural plans could do much to improve the level of rationality in the process of preparing the public plan.

The advocacy of alternative plans by interest groups outside of government would stimulate city planning in a number of ways. First, it would serve as a means of better informing the public of the alternative choices open, *alternatives strongly supported by their proponents.* In current practice those few agencies which have portrayed alternatives have not been equally enthusiastic about each.[7] A standard reaction to rationalists' prescription for consideration of alternative courses of action has been "it can't be done; how can you expect planners to present alternatives which they don't approve?" The appropriate answer to that question has been that planners like lawyers may have a professional obligation to defend positions they oppose. However, in a system of plural planning, the public agency would be relieved of at least some of the burden of presenting alternatives. In plural planning the alternatives would be presented by interest groups differing with the public agency's plan. Such alternatives would represent the deep-seated convictions of their proponents and not just the mental exercises of rational planners seeking to portray the range of choice.

A second way in which advocacy and plural planning would improve planning practice would be in forcing the public agency to compete with other planning groups to win political support. In the absence of opposition or alternative plans presented by interest groups the public agencies have had little incentive to improve the quality of their work or the rate of production of plans. The political consumer has been offered a yes—no ballot in regard to the comprehensive plan; either the public agency's plan was to be adopted or no plan would be adopted.

A third improvement in planning practice which might follow from plural planning would be to force those who have been critical of "establishment" plans to produce superior plans, rather than only to carry out the very essential obligation of criticizing plans deemed improper.

THE PLANNER AS ADVOCATE

Where plural planning is practiced, advocacy becomes the means of professional support for competing claims about how the community should develop. Pluralism in support of political contention describes the process; advocacy describes the role performed by the professional in the process. Where unitary planning prevails, advocacy is not of paramount importance, for there is little or no competition for the plan prepared by the public agency. The concept of advocacy as taken from legal practice implies the opposition of at least two contending viewpoints in an adversary proceeding.

The legal advocate must plead for his own and his client's sense of legal propriety or justice. The planner as advocate would plead for his own and his client's view of the good society. The advocate planner would be more than a provider of information, an analyst of current trends, a simulator of future conditions, and a detailer of means. In addition to carrying out these necessary parts of planning, he would be a *proponent* of specific substantive solutions.

The advocate planner would be responsible to his client and would seek to express his client's views. This does not mean that the planner could not seek to persuade his client. In some situations persuasion might not be necessary, for the planner would have sought out an employer with whom he shared common views about desired social conditions and the means toward them. In fact one of the benefits of advocate planning is the possibility it creates for a planner to find employment with agencies holding values close to his own. Today the agency planner may be dismayed by the positions affirmed by his agency, but there may be no alternative employer.

The advocate planner would be above all a planner. He would be responsible to his client for preparing plans and for all of the other elements comprising the planning process. Whether working for the public agency or for some private organization, the planner would have to prepare plans that take account of the arguments made in other plans. Thus the advocate's plan might have some of the characteristics of a legal brief. It would be a document presenting the facts and reasons for supporting one set of proposals, and facts and reasons indicating the inferiority of counter-proposals. The adversary nature of plural planning might, then, have the beneficial effect of upsetting the tradition of writing plan proposals in terminology which makes them appear self-evident.

A troublesome issue in contemporary planning is that of finding techniques for evaluating alternative plans. Technical devices such as cost-benefit analysis by themselves are of little assistance without the use of means for appraising the values underlying plans. Advocate planning, by making more apparent the values underlying plans, and by making definitions of social costs and benefits more explicit, should greatly assist the process of plan evaluation. Further, it would become clear (as it is not at present) that there are no neutral grounds for evaluating a plan; there are as many evaluative systems as there are value systems.

The adversary nature of plural planning might also have a good effect on the uses of information and research in planning. One of the tasks of the advocate planner in discussing the plans prepared in opposition to his would be to point out the nature of the bias underlying information presented in other plans. In this way, as critic of opposition plans, he would be performing a task similar to the legal technique of cross-examination. While painful to the planner whose bias is exposed (and no planner can be entirely free of bias) the net effect of confrontation between advocates of alternative plans would be more careful and precise research.

Not all the work of an advocate planner would be of an adversary nature. Much of it would be educational. The advocate would have the job of informing other groups, including public agencies, of the conditions, problems, and outlook of the group he represented. Another major educational job would be that of informing his clients of their rights under planning and renewal laws, about the general operations of city government, and of particular programs likely to affect them.

The advocate planner would devote much attention to assisting the client organization to clarify its ideas and to give expression to them. In order to make his client more powerful politically the advocate might also become engaged in expanding the size and scope of his client organization. But the advocate's most important function would be to carry out the planning process for the organization and to argue persuasively in favor of its planning proposals.

Advocacy in planning has already begun to emerge as planning and renewal affect the lives of more and more people. The critics of urban renewal[8] have forced response from the renewal agencies, and the ongoing debate[9] has stimulated needed self-evaluation by public agencies. Much work along the lines of advocate planning has already taken place, but little of it by professional planners. More often the work has been conducted by trained community organizers or by student groups. In at least one instance, however, a planner's professional aid led to the development of an alternative renewal approach, one which will result in the dislocation of far fewer families than originally contemplated.[10]

Pluralism and advocacy are means for stimulating consideration of future conditions by all groups in society. But there is one social group which at present is particularly in need of the assistance of planners. This group includes organizations representing low-income families. At a time when concern for the condition of the poor finds institutionalization in community action programs, it would be appropriate for planners concerned with such groups to find means to plan with them. The plans prepared for these groups would seek to combat poverty and would propose programs affording new and better opportunities to the members of the organization and to families similarly situated.[11]

The difficulty in providing adequate planning assistance to organizations representing low-income families may in part be overcome by funds allocated to local anti-poverty councils. But these councils are not the only representatives of the poor; other organizations exist and seek help. How can this type of assistance be financed? This question will be examined below, when attention is turned to the means for institutionalizing plural planning.

THE STRUCTURE OF PLANNING

Planning by Special Interest Groups

The local planning process typically includes one or more "citizens" organizations concerned with the nature of planning in the community. The Workable Program requirement for "citizen participation"[12] has enforced this tradition and brought it to most large communities. The difficulty with current citizen participation programs is that citizens are more often *reacting* to agency programs than *proposing* their concepts of appropriate goals and future action.

The fact that citizens' organizations have not played a positive role in formulating plans is to some extent a result of both the enlarged role in society played by government bureaucracies and the historic weakness of municipal party politics. There is something very shameful to our society in the necessity to have organized "citizen participation." Such participation should be the norm in an enlightened democracy. The formalization of citizen participation as a required practice in localities is similar in many respects to totalitarian shows of loyalty to the state by citizen parades.

Will a private group interested in preparing a recommendation for community development be required to carry out its own survey and analysis of the community? The answer would depend upon the quality of the work prepared by the public agency, work which should be public information. In some instances the public agency may not have surveyed or analyzed aspects the private group thinks important; or the public agency's work may reveal strong biases unacceptable to the private group. In any event, the production of a useful plan proposal will require much information concerning the present and predicted conditions in the community. There will be some costs associated with gathering that information, even if it is taken from the public agency. The major cost involved in the preparation of a plan by a private agency would probably be the employment of one or more professional planners.

What organizations might be expected to engage in the plural planning process? The first type that comes to mind are the political parties; but this is clearly an aspirational thought. There is very little evidence that local political organizations have the interest, ability, or concern to establish well developed programs for their communities. Not all the fault, though, should be placed upon the professional politicians, for the registered members of political parties have not demanded very much, if anything, from them as agents.

Despite the unreality of the wish, the desirability for active participation in the process of planning by the political parties is strong. In an ideal situation local parties would establish political platforms which would contain master plans for community growth and both the majority and minority parties in the legislative branch of government would use such plans as one basis for appraising individual legislative proposals. Further, the local administration would use its planning agency to carry out the plans it proposed to the electorate. This dream will not turn to reality for a long time. In the interim other interest groups must be sought to fill the gap caused by the present inability of political organizations.

The second set of organizations which might be interested in preparing plans for community development are those that represent special interest groups having established views in regard to proper public policy. Such organizations as chambers of commerce, real estate boards, labor organizations, pro- and anti-civil rights groups, and anti-poverty councils come to mind. Groups of this nature have often played parts in the development of community plans, but only in a very few instances have they proposed their own plans.

It must be recognized that there is strong reason operating against commitment to a plan by these organizations. In fact it is the same reason that in part limits the interests of politicians and which limits the potential for planning in our society.

The expressed commitment to a particular plan may make it difficult for groups to find means for accommodating their various interests. In other terms, it may be simpler for professionals, politicians, or lobbyists to make deals if they have not laid their cards on the table.

There is a third set of organizations that might be looked to as proponents of plans and to whom the foregoing comments might not apply. These are the ad hoc protest associations which may form in opposition to some proposed policy. An example of such a group is a neighborhood association formed to combat a renewal plan, a zoning change, or the proposed location of a public facility. Such organizations may seek to develop alternative plans, plans which would, if effected, better serve their interests.

From the point of view of effective and rational planning it might be desirable to commence plural planning at the level of city-wide organizations, but a more realistic view is that it will start at the neighborhood level. Certain advantages of this outcome should be noted. Mention was made earlier of tension in government between centralizing and decentralizing forces. The contention aroused by conflict between the central planning agency and the neighborhood organization may indeed be healthy, leading to clearer definition of welfare policies and their relation to the rights of individuals or minority groups.

Who will pay for plural planning? Some organizations have the resources to sponsor the development of a plan. Many groups lack the means. The plight of the relatively indigent association seeking to propose a plan might be analogous to that of the indigent client in search of legal aid. If the idea of plural planning makes sense, then support may be found from foundations or from government. In the beginning it is more likely that some foundation might be willing to experiment with plural planning as a means of making city planning more effective and more democratic. Or the Federal Government might see plural planning, if carried out by local anti-poverty councils, as a strong means of generating local interest in community affairs.

Federal sponsorship of plural planning might be seen as a more effective tool for stimulating involvement of the citizen in the future of his community than are the present types of citizen participation programs. Federal support could only be expected if plural planning were seen, not as a means of combating renewal plans, but as an incentive to local renewal agencies to prepare better plans.

The Public Planning Agency

A major drawback to effective democratic planning practice is the continuation of that non-responsible vestigial institution, the planning commission. If it is agreed that the establishment of both general policies and implementation policies are questions affecting the public interest and that public interest questions should be decided in accord with established democratic practices for decision making, then it is indeed difficult to find convincing reasons for continuing to permit independent commissions to make planning decisions. At an earlier stage in planning the strong arguments of John T. Howard[13] and others in support of commissions may have been persuasive. But it is now more than a decade since Howard made his defense against Robert Walker's position favoring planning as a staff function under the mayor. With the increasing effect planning decisions have upon the lives of citizens the Walker proposal assumes great urgency.[14]

Aside from important questions regarding the propriety of independent agencies which are far removed from public control determining public policy, the failure to place planning decision choices in the hands of elected officials has weakened the ability of professional planners to have their proposals effected. Separating planning from local politics has made it difficult for independent commissions to garner influential political support. The commissions are not responsible directly to the electorate and in turn the electorate is, at best, often indifferent to the planning commission.

During the last decade in many cities power to alter community development has slipped out of the hands of city planning commissions, assuming they ever held it, and has been transferred to development coordinators. This has weakened the professional planner. Perhaps planners unknowingly contributed to this by their refusal to take concerted action in opposition to the perpetuation of commissions.

Planning commissions are products of the conservative reform movement of the early part of this century. The movement was essentially anti-populist and pro-aristocracy. Politics was viewed as dirty business. The commissions are relics of a not-too-distant past when it was believed that if men of good will discussed a problem thoroughly, certainly the right solution would be forthcoming. We know today, and perhaps it was always known, that there are no right solutions. Proper policy is that which the decision-making unit declares to be proper.

Planning commissions are responsible to no constituency. The members of the commissions, except for their chairman, are seldom known to the public. In general the individual members fail to expose their personal views about policy and prefer to immerse them in group decision. If the members wrote concurring and dissenting opinions, then at least the commissions might stimulate thought about planning issues. It is difficult to comprehend why this aristocratic and undemocratic form of decision making should be continued. The public planning function should be carried out in the executive or legislative office and perhaps in both. There has been some question about which of these branches of government would provide the best home, but there is much reason to believe that both branches would be made more cognizant of planning issues if they were each informed by their own planning staffs. To carry this division further, it would probably be advisable to establish minority and majority planning staffs in the legislative branch.

At the root of my last suggestion is the belief that there is or should be a Republican and Democratic way of viewing city development; that there should be conservative and liberal plans, plans to support the private market and plans to support greater government control. There are many possible roads for a community to travel and many plans should show them. Explication is required of many alternative futures presented by those sympathetic to the construction of each such future. As indicated earlier, such alternatives are not presented to the public now. Those few reports which do include alternative futures do not speak in terms of interest to the average citizen. They are filled with professional jargon and present sham alternatives. These plans have expressed technical land use alternatives rather than social, economic, or political value alternatives. Both the traditional unitary plans and the new ones that present technical alternatives have limited the public's exposure to the future states that might be achieved. Instead of arousing healthy political contention as diverse comprehensive plans might, these plans have deflated interest.

The independent planning commission and unitary plan practice certainly should not co-exist. Separately they dull the possibility for enlightened political debate; in combination they have made it yet more difficult. But when still another hoary concept of city planning is added to them, such debate becomes practically impossible. This third of a trinity of worn-out notions is that city planning should focus only upon the physical aspects of city development.

AN INCLUSIVE DEFINITION OF THE SCOPE OF PLANNING

The view that equates physical planning with city planning is myopic. It may have had some historic justification, but it is clearly out of place at a time when it is necessary to integrate knowledge and techniques in order to wrestle effectively with the myriad of problems afflicting urban populations.

The city planning profession's historic concern with the physical environment has warped its ability to see physical structures and land as servants to those who use them.[15] Physical relations and conditions have no meaning or quality apart from the way they serve their users. But this is forgotten every time a physical condition is described as good or bad without relation to a specified group of users. High density, low density, green belts, mixed uses, cluster developments, centralized or decentralized business centers are per se neither good nor bad. They describe physical relations or conditions, but take on value only when seen in terms of their social, economic, psychological, physiological, or aesthetic effects upon different users.

The profession's experience with renewal over the past decade has shown the high costs of exclusive concern with physical conditions. It has been found that the allocation of funds for removal of physical blight may not necessarily improve the over-all physical condition of a community and may engender such harsh social repercussions as to severely damage both social and economic institutions. Another example of the deficiencies of the physical bias is the assumption of city planners that they could deal with the capital budget as if the physical attributes of a facility could be understood apart from the philosophy and practice of the service conducted within the physical structure. This assumption is open to question. The size, shape, and location of a facility greatly interact with the purpose of the activity the facility houses. Clear examples of this can be seen in public education and in the provision of low cost housing. The racial and other socio-economic consequences of "physical decisions" such as location of schools and housing projects have been immense, but city planners, while acknowledging the existence of such consequences, have not sought or trained themselves to understand socio-economic problems, their causes or solutions.

The city planning profession's limited scope has tended to bias strongly many of its recommendations toward perpetuation of existing social and economic practices. Here I am not opposing the outcomes, but the way in which they are developed. Relative ignorance of social and economic methods of analysis have caused planners to propose solutions in the absence of sufficient knowledge of the costs and benefits of proposals upon different sections of the population.

Large expenditures have been made on planning studies of regional transportation needs, for example, but these studies have been conducted in a manner suggesting that different social and economic classes of the population did not have different needs and different abilities to meet them. In the field of housing, to take another example, planners have been hesitant to question the consequences of locating public housing in slum areas. In the field of industrial development, planners have seldom examined the types of jobs the community needed; it has been assumed that one job was about as useful as another. But this may not be the case where a significant sector of the population finds it difficult to get employment.

"Who gets what, when, where, why, and how" are the basic political questions which need to be raised about every allocation of public resources. The questions must be answered adequately if land use criteria are the sole or major standards for judgment.

The need to see an element of city development, land use, in broad perspective applies equally well to every other element, such as health, welfare, and recreation. The governing of a city requires an adequate plan for its future. Such a plan loses guiding force and rational basis to the degree that it deals with less than the whole that is of concern to the public.

The implications of the foregoing comments for the practice of city planning are these. First, state planning enabling legislation should be amended to permit planning departments to study and to prepare plans related to any area of public concern. Second, planning education must be redirected so as to provide channels of specialization in different parts of public planning and a core focussed upon the planning process. Third, the professional planning association should enlarge its scope so as to not exclude city planners not specializing in physical planning.

A year ago at the AIP convention it was suggested that the AIP Constitution be amended to permit city planning to enlarge its scope to all matters of public concern.[16] Members of the Institute in agreement with this proposal should seek to develop support for it at both the chapter and national level. The Constitution at present states that the Institute's "particular sphere of activity shall be the planning of the unified development of urban communities and their environs and of states, regions and the nations as *expressed through determination of the comprehensive arrangement of land and land occupancy and regulation thereof.*"[17]

It is time that the AIP delete the words in my italics from its Constitution. The planner limited to such concerns is not a city planner, he is a land planner or a physical planner. A city is its people, their practices, and their political, social, cultural and economic institutions as well as other things. The city planner must comprehend and deal with all these factors.

The new city planner will be concerned with physical planning, economic planning, and social planning. The scope of his work will be no wider than that presently demanded of a mayor or a city councilman. Thus, we cannot argue against an enlarged planning function on grounds that it is too large to handle. The mayor needs assistance; in particular he needs the assistance of a planner, one trained to examine needs and aspirations in terms of both short and long term perspectives. In observing the early stages of development of Community Action Programs, it is apparent that our cities are in desperate need of the type of assistance trained planners could offer. Our cities require for their social and economic programs the type of long range thought and information that have been brought forward in the realm of physical planning. Potential resources must be examined and priorities set.

What I have just proposed does not imply the termination of physical planning, but it does mean that physical planning be seen as part of city planning. Uninhibited by limitations on his work, the city planner will be able to add his expertise to the task of coordinating the operating and capital budgets and to the job of relating effects of each city program upon the others and upon the social, political, and economic resources of the community.

An expanded scope reaching all matters of public concern will make planning not only a more effective administrative tool of local government but it will also bring planning practice closer to the issues of real concern to the citizens. A system of plural city planning probably has a much greater chance for operational success where the focus is on live social and economic questions instead of rather esoteric issues relating to physical norms.

THE EDUCATION OF PLANNERS

Widening the scope of planning to include all areas of concern to government would suggest that city planners must possess a broader knowledge of the structure and forces affecting urban development. In general this would be true. But at present many city planners are specialists in only one or more of the functions of city government. Broadening the scope of planning would require some additional planners who specialize in one or more of the services entailed by the new focus.

A prime purpose of city planning is the coordination of many separate functions. This coordination calls for men holding general knowledge of the many elements comprising the urban community. Educating a man for performing the coordinative role is a difficult job, one not well satisfied by the present tradition of two years of graduate study. Training of urban planners with the skills called for in this article may require both longer graduate study and development of a liberal arts undergraduate program affording an opportunity for holistic understanding of both urban conditions and techniques for analyzing and solving urban problems.

The practice of plural planning requires educating planners who would be able to engage as professional advocates in the contentious work of forming social policy. The person able to do this would be one deeply committed to both the process of planning and to particular substantive ideas. Recognizing that ideological commitments will separate planners, there is tremendous need to train professionals who are competent to express their social objectives.

The great advances in analytic skills, demonstrated in the recent May issue of this *Journal* dedicated to techniques of simulating urban growth processes, portend a time when planners and the public will be better able to predict the consequences of proposed courses of action. But these advances will be of little social advantage if the proposals themselves do not have substance. The contemporary thoughts of planners about the nature of man in society are often mundane, unexciting or gimmicky. When asked to point out to students the planners who have a developed sense of history and philosophy concerning man's situation in the urban world one is hard put to come up with a name. Sometimes Goodman or Mumford might be mentioned. But planners seldom go deeper than acknowledging the goodness of green space and the soundness of proximity of linked activities. We cope with the problems of the alienated man with a recommendation for reducing the time of the journey to work.

CONCLUSION

The urban community is a system comprised of interrelated elements, but little is known about how the elements do, will, or should interrelate. The type of knowledge required by the new comprehensive city planner demands that the planning profession be comprised of groups of men well versed in contemporary philosophy, social work, law, the social sciences, and civic design. Not every planner must be knowledgeable in all these areas, but each planner must have a deep understanding of one or more of these areas and he must be able to give persuasive expression to his understanding.

As a profession charged with making urban life more beautiful, exciting, and creative, and more just, we have had little to say. Our task is to train a future generation of planners to go well beyond us in its ability to prescribe the future urban life.

NOTES

1 Britton Harris, "Plan or Projection," *Journal of the American Institute of Planners,* XXVI (November 1960) 265–272.

2 Robert Dahl and Charles Lindblom, *Politics, Economics, and Welfare* (New York: Harper and Brothers, 1953) p. 3.

3 Paul Davidoff and Thomas Reiner, "A Choice Theory of Planning," *Journal of the American Institute of Planners,* XXVIII (May 1962) 103–115.

4 *Ibid.*

5 See, for example, Martin Meyerson and Edward Banfield, *Politics, Planning and the Public Interest* (Glencoe: The Free Press, 1955) p. 314 ff. The authors state "By a *rational* decision, we mean one made in the following manner: 1. the decision-maker considers all of the alternatives (courses of action) open to him; . . . 2. he identifies and evaluates all of the consequences which would follow from the adoption of each alternative;

. . . 3. he selects that alternative the probable consequences of which would be preferable in terms of his most valued ends."

6 Davidoff and Reiner, *Op. cit.*

7 National Capital Planning Commission, *The Nation's Capital; a Policies Plan for the Year 2000* (Washington, D.C.: The Commission, 1961).

8 The most important critical studies are: Jane Jacobs, *The Life and Death of Great American Cities* (New York: Random House, 1961); Martin Anderson, *The Federal Bulldozer* (Cambridge: M.I.T. Press, 1964); Herbert J. Gans, "The Human Implications of Current Redevelopment and Relocation Planning," *Journal of the American Institute of Planners*, XXV (February 1959), 15–26.

9 A recent example of heated debate appears in the following set of articles: Herbert J. Gans, "The Failure of Urban Renewal," *Commentary* 39 (April 1965) p. 29; George Raymond "Controversy," *Commentary* 40 (July 1965) p. 72; and Herbert J. Gans, "Controversy," *Commentary* 40 (July 1965) p. 77.

10 Walter Thabit, *An Alternate Plan for Cooper Square* (New York: Walter Thabit, July 1961).

11 The first conscious effort to employ the advocacy method was carried out by a graduate student of city planning as an independent research project. The author acted as both a participant and an observer of a local housing organization. See Linda Davidoff, "The Bluffs: Advocate Planning," *Comment*, Dept. of City Planning, University of Pennsylvania, (Spring 1965) p. 59.

12 See Section 101(c) of the United States Housing Act of 1949, as amended.

13 John T. Howard, "In Defense of Planning Commissions," *Journal of the American Institute of Planners,* XVII (Spring 1951).

14 Robert Walker, *The Planning Function in Urban Government;* Second Edition (Chicago: University of Chicago Press, 1950). Walker drew the following conclusions from his examination of planning and planning commissions. "Another conclusion to be drawn from the existing composition of city planning boards is that they are not representative of the population as a whole." p. 153. "In summary the writer is of the opinion that the claim that planning commissions are more objective than elected officials must be rejected." p. 155. "From his observations the writer feels justified in saying that very seldom does a majority of any commission have any well-rounded understanding of the purposes and ramifications of planning." p. 157. "In summary, then, it was found that the average commission member does not comprehend planning nor is he particularly interested even in the range of customary physical planning." p. 158. "Looking at the planning commission at the present time, however, one is forced to conclude that, despite some examples of successful operations, the unpaid board is not proving satisfactory as a planning agency," p. 165. ". . . (it) is believed that the most fruitful line of development for the future would be replacement of these commissions by a department or bureau attached to the office of mayor or city manager. This department might be headed by a board or by a single director, but the members or the director would in any case hold office at the pleasure of the executive on the same basis as other department heads." p. 177.

15 An excellent and complete study of the bias resulting from reliance upon physical or land use criteria appears in David Farbman, *A Description, Analysis and Critique of the Master Plan*, an unpublished mimeographed study prepared for the Univ. of Pennsylvania's Institute for Urban Studies, 1959–1960. After studying more than 100 master plans Farbman wrote:

"As a result of the predominantly physical orientation of the planning profession many planners have fallen victims to a malaise which I suggest calling the "Physical Bias." This bias is not the physical orientation of the planner itself but is the result of it. . . . "The physical bias is an attitude on the part of the planner which leads him to conceive of the principles and techniques of *his profession* as the key factors in determining the particular recommendations to be embodied in his plans. . ."

"The physically biased planner plans on the assumption (conviction) that the physical problems of a city can be solved within the framework of physical desiderata; in other words, that physical problems can be adequately stated, solved and remedied according to physical criteria and expertise. The physical bias produces both an inability and an unwillingness on the part of the planner to 'get behind' the physical recommendations of the plan, to isolate, examine or discuss more basic criteria. . . ."

". . . There is room, then, in plan thinking, for physical principles, i.e., theories of structural inter-relationships of the physical city; but this is only a part of the story, for the structural impacts of the plan are only a part of the total impact. This total impact must be conceived as a web of physical, economic and social causes and effects." pp. 22–26.

16 Paul Davidoff, "The Role of the City Planner in Social Planning," *Proceedings of the 1964 Annual Conference,* American Institute of Planners (Washington, D.C.: The Institute, 1964) 125–131.

17 Constitution of AIP, Article II "Purposes," in *AIP Handbook & Roster—1965,* p. 8.

Author's note: The author wishes to thank Melvin H. Webber for his insightful criticism and Linda Davidoff for her many helpful suggestions and for her analysis of advocate planning. Special acknowledgment is made of the penetrating and brilliant social insights offered by the eminent legal scholar and practitioner, Michael Brodie, of the Philadelphia Bar.

Justice as Fairness

John Rawls
Professor of Philosophy, Harvard University

All planners must be concerned with ethics, justice, and fairness. There is no better treatment of these issues than that in John Rawls's *A Theory of Justice.* In this introductory chapter, Rawls sketches his main ideas, which are in the social-contract tradition of Locke, Rousseau, and Kant. Like other contract approaches, this one stresses that justice as fairness has two elements: "(1) an interpretation of the initial situation and of the problem of choice posed there, and (2) a set of principles which, it is argued, would be agreed to" (p. 69). According to Rawls, the principles of justice that form the original social contract then determine all of society's further agreements and institutional arrangements.

Reprinted by permission of the publishers from *A Theory of Justice* by John Rawls, Cambridge, Mass.: The Belknap Press of Harvard University Press, Copyright © 1971 by the President and Fellows of Harvard College.

THE ROLE OF JUSTICE

Justice is the first virtue of social institutions, as truth is of systems of thought. A theory however elegant and economical must be rejected or revised if it is untrue; likewise laws and institutions no matter how efficient and well-arranged must be reformed or abolished if they are unjust. Each person possesses an inviolability founded on justice that even the welfare of society as a whole cannot override. For this reason justice denies that the loss of freedom for some is made right by a greater good shared by others. It does not allow that the sacrifices imposed on a few are outweighed by the larger sum of advantages enjoyed by many. Therefore in a just society the liberties of equal citizenship are taken as settled; the rights secured by justice are not subject to political bargaining or to the calculus of social interests. The only thing that permits us to acquiesce in an erroneous theory is the lack of a better one; analogously, an injustice is tolerable only when it is necessary to avoid an even greater injustice. Being first virtues of human activities, truth and justice are uncompromising.

These propositions seem to express our intuitive conviction of the primacy of justice. No doubt they are expressed too strongly. In any event I wish to inquire whether these contentions or others similar to them are sound, and if so how they can be accounted for. To this end it is necessary to work out a theory of justice in the light of which these assertions can be interpreted and assessed. I shall begin by considering the role of the principles of justice. Let us assume, to fix ideas, that a society is a more or less self-sufficient association of persons who in their relations to one another recognize certain rules of conduct as binding and who for the most part act in accordance with them. Suppose further that these rules specify a system of cooperation designed to advance the good of those taking part in it. Then, although a society is a cooperative venture for mutual advantage, it is typically marked by a conflict as well as by an identity of interests. There is an identity of interests since social cooperation makes possible a better life for all than any would have if each were to live solely by his own efforts. There is a conflict of interests since persons are not indifferent as to how the greater benefits produced by their collaboration are distributed, for in order to pursue their ends they each prefer a larger to a lesser share. A set of principles is required for choosing among the various social arrangements which determine this division of advantages and for underwriting an agreement on the proper distributive shares. These principles are the principles of social justice: they provide a way of assigning rights and duties in the basic institutions of society and they define the appropriate distribution of the benefits and burdens of social cooperation.

Now let us say that a society is well-ordered when it is not only designed to advance the good of its members but when it is also effectively regulated by a public conception of justice. That is, it is a society in which (1) everyone accepts and knows that the others accept the same principles of justice, and (2) the basic social institutions generally satisfy and are generally known to satisfy these principles. In this case while men may put forth excessive demands on one another, they nevertheless acknowledge a common point of view from which their claims may be adjudicated. If men's inclination to self-interest makes their vigilance against one another necessary, their public sense of justice makes their secure association together possible. Among individuals with disparate aims and purposes a shared conception of justice establishes the bonds of civic friendship; the general desire for justice limits the pursuit of other ends. One may think of a public conception of justice as constituting the fundamental charter of a well-ordered human association.

Existing societies are of course seldom well-ordered in this sense, for what is just and unjust is usually in dispute. Men disagree about which principles should define the basic terms of their association. Yet we may still say, despite this disagreement, that they each have a conception of justice. That is, they understand the need for, and they are prepared to affirm, a characteristic set of principles for assigning basic rights and duties and for determining what they take to be the proper distribution of the benefits and burdens of social cooperation. Thus it seems natural to think of the concept of justice as distinct from the various conceptions of justice and as being specified by the role which these different sets of principles, these different conceptions, have in common.[1] Those who hold different conceptions of justice can, then, still agree that institutions are just when no arbitrary distinctions are made between persons in the assigning of basic rights and duties and when the rules determine a proper balance between competing claims to the advantages of social life. Men can agree to this description of just institutions since the notions of an arbitrary distinction and of a proper balance, which are included in the concept of justice, are left open for each to interpret according to the principles of justice that he accepts. These principles single out which similarities and differences among persons are relevant in determining rights and duties and they specify which division of advantages is appropriate. Clearly this distinction between the concept and the various conceptions of justice settles no important questions. It simply helps to identify the role of the principles of social justice.

Some measure of agreement in conceptions of justice is, however, not the only prerequisite for a viable human community. There are other fundamental social problems, in particular those of coordination, efficiency, and stability. Thus the plans of individuals need to be fitted together so that their activities are compatible with one another and they can all be carried through without anyone's legitimate expectations being severely disappointed. Moreover, the execution of these plans should lead to the achievement of social ends in ways that are efficient and consistent with justice. And finally, the scheme of social cooperation must be stable: it must be more or less regularly complied with and its basic rules willingly acted upon; and when infractions occur, stabilizing forces should exist that prevent further violations and tend to restore the arrangement. Now it is evident that these three problems are connected with that of justice. In the absence of a certain measure of agreement on what is just and unjust, it is clearly more difficult for individuals to coordinate their plans efficiently in order to insure that mutually beneficial arrangements are maintained. Distrust and resentment corrode the ties of civility, and suspicion and hostility tempt men to act in ways they would otherwise avoid. So while the distinctive role of conceptions of justice is to specify basic rights and duties and to determine the appropriate distributive shares, the way in which a conception does this is bound to affect the problems of efficiency, coordination, and stability. We cannot, in general, assess a conception of justice by its distributive role alone, however useful this role may be in identifying the concept of justice. We must take into account its wider connections; for even though justice has a certain priority, being the most important virtue of institutions, it is still true that, other things equal, one conception of justice is preferable to another when its broader consequences are more desirable.

THE SUBJECT OF JUSTICE

Many different kinds of things are said to be just and unjust: not only laws, institutions, and social systems, but also particular actions of many kinds, including decisions, judgments, and imputations. We also call the attitudes and dispositions of persons, and persons themselves, just and unjust. Our topic, however, is that of social justice. For us the primary subject of justice is the basic structure of society, or more exactly, the way in which the major social institutions distribute fundamental rights and duties and determine the division of advantages from social cooperation. By major institutions I understand the political constitution and the principal economic and social arrangements. Thus the legal protection of freedom of thought and liberty of conscience, competitive markets, private property in the means of production, and the monogamous family are examples of major social institutions. Taken together as one scheme, the major institutions define men's rights and duties and influence their life-prospects, what they can expect to be and how well they can hope to do. The basic structure is the primary subject of justice because its effects are so profound and present from the start. The intuitive notion here is that this structure contains various social positions and that men born into different positions have different expectations of life determined, in part, by the political system as well as by economic and social circumstances. In this way the institutions of society favor certain starting places over others. These are especially deep inequalities. Not only are they pervasive, but they affect men's initial chances in life; yet they cannot possibly be justified by an appeal to the notions of merit or desert. It is these inequalities, presumably inevitable in the basic structure of any society, to which the principles of social justice must in the first instance apply. These principles, then, regulate the choice of a political constitution and the main elements of the economic and social system. The justice of a social scheme depends essentially on how fundamental rights and duties are assigned and on the economic opportunities and social conditions in the various sectors of society.

The scope of our inquiry is limited in two ways. First of all, I am concerned with a special case of the problem of justice. I shall not consider the justice of institutions and social practices generally, nor except in passing the justice of the law of nations and of relations between states. Therefore, if one supposes that the concept of justice applies whenever there is an allotment of something rationally regarded as advantageous or disadvantageous, then we are interested in only one instance of its application. There is no reason to suppose ahead of time that the principles satisfactory for the basic structure hold for all cases. These principles may not work for the rules and practices of private associations or for those of less comprehensive social groups. They may be irrelevant for the various informal conventions and customs of everyday life; they may not elucidate the justice, or perhaps better, the fairness of voluntary cooperative arrangements or procedures for making contractual agreements. The conditions for the law of nations may require different principles arrived at in a somewhat different way. I shall be satisfied if it is possible to formulate a reasonable conception of justice for the basic structure of society conceived for the time being as a closed system isolated from other societies. The significance of this special case is obvious and needs no explanation. It is natural to conjecture that once we have a sound theory for this case, the remaining problems of justice will prove more tractable in the light of it. With suitable modifications such a theory should provide the key for some of these other questions.

The other limitation on our discussion is that for the most part I examine the principles of justice that would regulate a well-ordered society. Everyone is presumed to act justly and to do his part in upholding just institutions. Though justice may be, as Hume remarked, the cautious, jealous virtue, we can still ask what a perfectly just society would be like.[2] Thus I consider primarily what I call strict compliance as opposed to partial compliance theory. The latter studies the principles that govern how we are to deal with injustice. It comprises such topics as the theory of punishment, the doctrine of just war, and the justification of the various ways of opposing unjust regimes, ranging from civil disobedience and militant resistance to revolution and rebellion. Also included here are questions of compensatory justice and of weighing one form of institutional injustice against another. Obviously the problems of partial compliance theory are the pressing and urgent matters. These are the things that we are faced with in everyday life. The reason for beginning with ideal theory is that it provides, I believe, the only basis for the systematic grasp of these more pressing problems. The discussion of civil disobedience, for example, depends upon it. At least, I shall assume that a deeper understanding can be gained in no other way, and that the nature and aims of a perfectly just society is the fundamental part of the theory of justice.

Now admittedly the concept of the basic structure is somewhat vague. It is not always clear which institutions or features thereof should be included. But it would be premature to worry about this matter here. I shall proceed by discussing principles which do apply to what is certainly a part of the basic structure as intuitively understood; I shall then try to extend the application of these principles so that they cover what would appear to be the main elements of this structure. Perhaps these principles will turn out to be perfectly general, although this is unlikely. It is sufficient that they apply to the most important cases of social justice. The point to keep in mind is that a conception of justice for the basic structure is worth having for its own sake. It should not be dismissed because its principles are not everywhere satisfactory.

A conception of social justice, then, is to be regarded as providing in the first instance a standard whereby the distributive aspects of the basic structure of society are to be assessed. This standard, however, is not to be confused with the principles defining the other virtues, for the basic structure, and social arrangements generally, may be efficient or inefficient, liberal or illiberal, and many other things, as well as just or unjust. A complete conception defining principles for all the virtues of the basic structure, together with their respective weights when they conflict, is more than a conception of justice; it is a social ideal. The principles of justice are but a part, although perhaps the most important part, of such a conception. A social ideal in turn is connected with a conception of society, a vision of the way in which the aims and purposes of social cooperation are to be understood. The various conceptions of justice are the outgrowth of different notions of society against the background of opposing views of the natural necessities and opportunities of human life. Fully to understand a conception of justice we must explicit the conception of social cooperation from which it derives. But in doing this we should not lose sight of the special role of the principles of justice or of the primary subject to which they apply.

In these preliminary remarks I have distinguished the concept of justice as meaning a proper balance between competing claims from a conception of justice as a set of related principles for identifying the relevant considerations which determine this balance. I have also characterized justice as but one part of a social ideal, although the theory I shall propose no doubt extends its everyday sense. This theory is not offered as a description of ordinary meanings but as an account of certain distributive principles for the basic structure of society. I assume that any reasonably complete ethical theory must include principles for this fundamental problem and that these principles, whatever they are, constitute its doctrine of justice. The concept of justice I take to be defined, then, by the role of its principles in assigning rights and duties and in defining the appropriate division of social advantages. A conception of justice is an interpretation of this role.

Now this approach may not seem to tally with tradition. I believe, though, that it does. The more specific sense that Aristotle gives to justice, and from which the most familiar formulations derive, is that of refraining from *pleonexia,* that is, from gaining some advantage for oneself by seizing what belongs to another, his property, his reward, his office, and the like, or by denying a person that which is due to him, the fulfillment of a promise, the repayment of a debt, the showing of proper respect, and so on.[3] It is evident that this definition is framed to apply to actions, and persons are thought to be just insofar as they have, as one of the permanent elements of their character, a steady and effective desire to act justly. Aristotle's definition clearly presupposes, however, an account of what properly belongs to a person and of what is due to him. Now such entitlements are, I believe, very often derived from social institutions and the legitimate expectations to which they give rise. There is no reason to think that Aristotle would disagree with this, and certainly he has a conception of social justice to account for these claims. The definition I adopt is designed to apply directly to the most important case, the justice of the basic structure. There is no conflict with the traditional notion.

THE MAIN IDEA OF THE THEORY OF JUSTICE

My aim is to present a conception of justice which generalizes and carries to a higher level of abstraction the familiar theory of the social contract as found, say, in Locke, Rousseau, and Kant.[4] In order to do this we are not to think of the original contract as one to enter a particular society or to set up a particular form of government. Rather, the guiding idea is that the principles of justice for the basic structure of society are the object of the original agreement. They are the principles that free and rational persons concerned to further their own interests would accept in an initial position of equality as defining the fundamental terms of their association. These principles are to regulate all further agreements; they specify the kinds of social cooperation that can be entered into and the forms of government that can be established. This way of regarding the principles of justice I shall call justice as fairness.

Thus we are to imagine that those who engage in social cooperation choose together, in one joint act, the principles which are to assign basic rights and duties and to determine the division of social benefits. Men are to decide in advance how they are to regulate their claims against one another and what is to be the foundation charter of their society. Just as each person must decide by rational reflection what constitutes his good, that is, the system of ends which it is rational for him to pursue, so a group of persons must decide once and for all what is to count among them as just and injust. The choice which rational men would make in this hypothetical situation of equal liberty, assuming for the present that this choice problem has a solution, determines the principles of justice.

In justice as fairness the original position of equality corresponds to the state of nature in the traditional theory of the social contract. This original position is not, of course, thought of as an actual historical state of affairs, much less as a primitive condition of culture. It is understood as a purely hypothetical situation characterized so as to lead to a certain conception of justice.[5] Among the essential features of this situation is that no one knows his place in society, his class position or social status, nor does any one know his fortune in the distribution of natural assets and abilities, his intelligence, strength, and the like. I shall even assume that the parties do not know their conceptions of the good or their special psychological propensities. The principles of justice are chosen behind a veil of ignorance. This ensures that no one is advantaged or disadvantaged in the choice of principles by the outcome of natural chance or the contingency of social circumstances. Since all are similarly situated and no one is able to design principles to favor his particular condition, the principles of justice are the result of a fair agreement or bargain. For given the circumstances of the original position, the symmetry of everyone's relations to each other, this initial situation is fair between individuals as moral persons, that is, as rational beings with their own ends and capable, I shall assume, of a sense of justice. The original position is, one might say, the appropriate initial status quo, and thus the fundamental agreements reached in it are fair. This explains the propriety of the name "justice as fairness": it conveys the idea that the principles of justice are agreed to in an initial situation that is fair. The name does not mean that the concepts of justice and fairness are the same, any more than the phrase "poetry as metaphor" means that the concepts of poetry and metaphor are the same.

Justice as fairness begins, as I have said, with one of the most general of all choices which persons might make together, namely, with the choice of the first principles of a conception of justice which is to regulate all subsequent criticism and reform of institutions. Then, having chosen a conception of justice, we can suppose that they are to choose a constitution and a legislature to enact laws, and so on, all in accordance with the principles of justice initially agreed upon. Our social situation is just if it is such that by this sequence of hypothetical agreements we would have contracted into the general system of rules which defines it. Moreover, assuming that the original position does determine a set of principles (that is, that a particular conception of justice would be chosen), it will then be true that whenever social institutions satisfy these principles those engaged in them can say to one another that they are cooperating on terms to which they would agree if they were free and equal persons whose relations with respect to one another were fair. They could all view their arrangements as meeting the stipulations which they would acknowledge in an initial situation that embodies widely accepted and reasonable constraints on the choice of principles. The general recognition of this fact would provide the basis for a public acceptance of the corresponding principles of justice. No society can, of course, be a scheme of cooperation which men enter voluntarily in a literal sense; each person finds himself placed at birth in some particular position in some particular society, and the nature of this position materially affects his life prospects. Yet a society satisfying the principles of justice as fairness comes as close as a society can to being a voluntary scheme, for it meets the principles which free and equal persons would assent to under circumstances that are fair. In this sense its members are autonomous and the obligations they recognize self-imposed.

One feature of justice as fairness is to think of the parties in the initial situation as rational and mutually disinterested. This does not mean that the parties are egoists, that is, individuals with only certain kinds of interests, say in wealth, prestige, and domination. But they are conceived as not taking an interest in one another's interests. They are to presume that even their spiritual aims may be opposed, in the way that the aims of those of different religions may be opposed. Moreover, the concept of rationality must be interpreted as far as possible in the narrow sense, standard in economic theory, of taking the most effective means to given ends. I shall modify this concept to some extent, as explained later, but one must try to avoid introducing into it any controversial ethical elements. The initial situation must be characterized by stipulations that are widely accepted.

In working out the conception of justice as fairness one main task clearly is to determine which principles of justice would be chosen in the original position. To do this we must describe this situation in some detail and formulate with care the problem of choice which it presents. These matters I shall take up in the immediately succeeding chapters. It may be observed, however, that once the principles of justice are thought of as arising from an original agreement in a situation of equality, it is an open question whether the principle of utility would be acknowledged. Offhand it hardly seems likely that persons who view themselves as equals, entitled to press their claims upon one another, would agree to a principle which may require lesser life prospects for some simply for the sake of a greater sum of advantages enjoyed by others. Since each desires to protect his interests, his capacity to advance his conception of the good, no one has a reason to acquiesce in an enduring loss for himself in order to bring about a greater net balance of satisfaction. In the absence of strong and lasting benevolent impulses, a rational man would not accept a basic structure merely because it maximized the algebraic sum of advantages irrespective of its permanent effects on his own basic rights and interests. Thus it seems that the principle of utility is incompatible with the conception of social cooperation among equals for mutual advantage. It appears to be inconsistent with the idea of reciprocity implicit in the notion of a well-ordered society. Or, at any rate, so I shall argue.

I shall maintain instead that the person in the initial situation would choose two rather different principles: the first requires equality in the assignment of basic rights and duties, while the second holds that social and economic inequalities, for example inequalities of wealth and authority, are just only if they result in compensating benefits for everyone, and in particular for the least advantaged members of society. These principles rule out justifying institutions on the grounds that the hardships of some are offset by a greater good in the aggregate. It may be expedient but it is not just that some should have less in order that others may prosper. But there is no injustice in the greater benefits earned by a few provided that the situation of persons not so fortunate is thereby improved. The intuitive idea is that since everyone's well-being depends upon a scheme of cooperation without which no one could have a satisfactory life, the division of advantages should be such as to draw forth the willing cooperation of everyone taking part in it, including those less well situated. Yet this can be expected only if reasonable terms are proposed. The two principles mentioned seem to be a fair agreement on the basis of which those better endowed, or more fortunate in their social position, neither of which we can be said to deserve, could expect the willing cooperation of others when some workable scheme is a necessary condition of the welfare of all.[6] Once we decide to look for a conception of justice that nullifies the accidents of natural endowment and the contingencies of social circumstance as counters in quest for political and economic advantage, we are led to these principles. They express the result of leaving aside those aspects of the social world that seem arbitrary from a moral point of view.

The problem of the choice of principles, however, is extremely difficult. I do not expect the answer I shall suggest to be convincing to everyone. It is, therefore, worth noting from the outset that justice as fairness, like other contract views, consists of two parts: (1) an interpretation of the initial situation and of the problem of choice posed there, and (2) a set of principles which, it is argued, would be agreed to. One may accept the first part of the theory (or some variant thereof), but not the other, and conversely. The concept of the initial contractual situation may seem reasonable although the particular principles proposed are rejected. To be sure, I want to maintain that the most appropriate conception of this situation does lead to principles of justice contrary to utilitarianism and perfectionism, and therefore that the contract doctrine provides an alternative to these views. Still, one may dispute this contention even though one grants that the contractarian method is a useful way of studying ethical theories and of setting forth their underlying assumptions.

Justice as fairness is an example of what I have called a contract theory. Now there may be an objection to the term "contract" and related expressions, but I think it will serve reasonably well. Many words have misleading connotations which at first are likely to confuse. The terms "utility" and "utilitarianism" are surely no exception. They too have unfortunate suggestions which hostile critics have been willing to exploit; yet they are clear enough for those prepared to study utilitarian doctrine. The same should be true of the term "contract" applied to moral theories. As I have mentioned, to understand it one has to keep in mind that it implies a certain level of abstraction. In particular, the content of the relevant agreement is not to enter a given society or to adopt a given form of government, but to accept certain moral principles. Moreover, the undertakings referred to are purely hypothetical: a contract view holds that certain principles would be accepted in a well-defined initial situation.

The merit of the contract terminology is that it conveys the idea that principles of justice may be conceived as principles that would be chosen by rational persons, and that in this way conceptions of justice may be explained and justified. The theory of justice is a part, perhaps the most significant part, of the theory of rational choice. Furthermore, principles of justice deal with conflicting claims upon the advantages won by social cooperation; they apply to the relations among several persons or groups. The word "contract" suggests this plurality as well as the condition that the appropriate division of advantages must be in accordance with principles acceptable to all parties. The condition of publicity for principles of justice is also connoted by the contract phraseology. Thus, if these principles are the outcome of an agreement, citizens have a knowledge of the principles that others follow. It is characteristic of contract theories to stress the public nature of political principles. Finally there is the long tradition of the contract doctrine. Expressing the tie with this line of thought helps to define ideas and accords with natural piety. There are then several advantages in the use of the term "contract." With due precautions taken, it should not be misleading.

A final remark. Justice as fairness is not a complete contract theory. For it is clear that the contractarian idea can be extended to the choice of more or less an entire ethical system, that is, to a system including principles for all the virtues and not only for justice. Now for the most part I shall consider only principles of justice and others closely related to them; I make no attempt to discuss the virtues in a systematic way. Obviously if justice as fairness succeeds reasonably well, a next step would be to study the more general view suggested by the name "rightness as fairness." But even this wider theory fails to embrace all moral relationships, since it would seem to include only our relations with other persons and to leave out of account how we are to conduct ourselves toward animals and the rest of nature. I do not contend that the contract notion offers a way to approach these questions which are certainly of the first importance; and I shall have to put them aside. We must recognize the limited scope of justice as fairness and of the general type of view that it exemplifies. How far its conclusions must be revised once these other matters are understood cannot be decided in advance.

NOTES

1 Here I follow H. L. A. Hart, *The Concept of Law* (Oxford, The Clarendon Press, 1961), pp. 155–159.

2 *An Enquiry Concerning the Principles of Morals*, sec. III, pt. I, par. 3, ed. L. A. Selby-Bigge, 2nd edition (Oxford, 1902), p. 184.

3 *Nicomachean Ethics*, 1129b–1130b5. I have followed the interpretation of Gregory Vlastos, "Justice and Happiness in *The Republic*," in *Plato: A Collection of Critical Essays*, edited by Vlastos (Garden City, N.Y., Doubleday and Company, 1971), vol. 2, pp. 70f. For a discussion of Aristotle on justice, see W. F. R. Hardie, *Aristotle's Ethical Theory* (Oxford, The Clarendon Press, 1968), ch. X.

4 As the text suggests, I shall regard Locke's *Second Treatise of Government*, Rousseau's *The Social Contract*, and Kant's ethical works beginning with *The Foundations of the Metaphysics of Morals* as definitive of the contract tradition. For all of its greatness, Hobbes's *Leviathan* raises special problems. A general historical survey is provided by J. W. Gough, *The Social Contract*, 2nd ed. (Oxford, The Clarendon Press, 1957), and Otto Gierke, *Natural Law and the Theory of Society*, trans. with an introduction by Ernest Barker (Cambridge, The University Press, 1934). A presentation of the contract view as primarily an ethical theory is to be found in G. R. Grice, *The Grounds of Moral Judgment* (Cambridge, The University Press, 1967).

5 Kant is clear that the original agreement is hypothetical. See *The Metaphysics of Morals*, pt. I (*Rechtslehre*), especially §§ 47, 52; and pt. II of the essay "Concerning the Common Saying: This May Be True in Theory but It Does Not Apply in Practice," in *Kant's Political Writings*, ed. Hans Reiss and trans. by H. B. Nisbet (Cambridge, The University Press, 1970), pp. 73–87. See Georges Vlachos, *La Pensée politique de Kant* (Paris, Presses Universitaires de France, 1962), pp. 326–335; and J. G. Murphy, *Kant: The Philosophy of Right* (London, Macmillan, 1970), pp. 109–112, 133–136, for a further discussion.

6 For the formulation of this intuitive idea I am indebted to Allan Gibbard.

Planning in the Public Domain: Discourse and Praxis

John Friedmann
Professor of Urban Planning, University of California

This selection is a reprint of a speech delivered by John Friedmann upon receiving the Distinguished Planning Educator Award of the Association of Collegiate Schools of Planning. In his comments, Friedmann contends that planning is inherently moral practice. In the absence of absolutes, what is morally defensible practice? Friedmann's answer is that the planner must "make common cause" with the excluded and disaffected and join the people's struggle for "collective self-empowerment and participation" (pp. 77–78).

It has become commonplace to say that we are living in postmodern times. And the postmodern temper tells us: anything goes! The end of philosophy has been proclaimed (by philosophers) as a misguided search for absolutes in metaphysics and epistemology. The fashionable term today is hermeneutics, which is a way of knowing that is said to be post-empirical. We borrow freely from the past, recombining fragmented memories in ways that seem arbitrary and playful. Aesthetic standards have gone by the board. At best, we have kaleidoscopic vision. At worst, we are lost in a house of mirrors, with ever-shifting perspectives. Imposter and genuine value are hard to distinguish from one another. The fake is real, and the real is fake.

Unless you want to be a public laughingstock, it is quite impossible, in the face of this explosion of certainties, to expound old dogmas and verities. All standards, all absolutes, have been relativized. It is therefore not surprising that a vulgar pragmatism has moved to center stage: what works, works. And what works is money, technology, brute power, the magic of the media to create believable worlds. But that road leads to nihilism and, ultimately, self-destruction. There is another "higher" pragmatism, however, which may show us a way out. Its most lucid exponent is Richard Bernstein, who, in a series of luminous books, has been attempting to rescue for contemporary usage the Aristotelian distinctions among *techne, episteme, praxis,* and *phronesis* (technical knowledge, theoretical knowledge, moral public action, and everyday judgment or practical knowledge).

The "higher" pragmatism of Bernstein—who draws on Pierce, Dewey, and Habermas—does away with Truth writ large, focusing our attention instead on how human beings create a sense of community, on that which makes possible human speech—dialogue—and thus underlies the very essence of our humanity: the need to share, to communicate, to reach out to other human beings and touch them deeply. The term community, however, suggests a misleading homogeneity

Reprinted by permission of the *Journal of Planning Education and Research*, 8 (1989), copyright owned and published by the Association of Collegiate Schools of Planning.

and solidarity. The essence of communication is to begin with difference, with nonconcordance searching for concordance or agreement. And that is also what brings a public space into existence. For it is only by appearing in public space, as Hannah Arendt reminds us, that we acquire a truly human face.

I want to focus on praxis, or moral public action, because it is here that I see a direct link to planning. Planning, I shall argue, is an inherently moral practice—a praxis—in the sense that it affects the way we live—relations among people and their institutions. The question immediately arises: if planning is a moral praxis, how shall we ensure a morally defensible practice *in the absence of absolutes?* As planners, we are concerned with social change, more specifically with willed or intended social change (measured from whatever may be the status quo). But we also want this change to be morally defensible; we want it to be "good."

There was a time when planners' lode star was a notion of the common good. That notion turned out to be deceptive. What we imagined as the common good of the *polis* was always contested terrain. The common good cannot be assumed a priori, nor can it be determined by research. It is not a given. The public good is a notion of process; *it emerges in the course of planning itself, and its concrete meaning is constantly evolving.*

In what I have just said, there is a basic assumption that the *polis,* what I have called the public domain, actually exists. But this is by no means a certainty. It presupposes a territorially organized society (neighborhood, city, province, or national state), a sense of citizenship (rightful belonging), and legitimate voice. It presupposes democratic freedoms and rights. Not all societies are so organized. For a sense of public to exist, there has to be a measure of sharing: cultural predispositions, a common past, cherished institutions, a legitimate authority. But where these conditions exist, there too exists a public domain and the possibility of reaching a shared understanding of what, in particular instances, may be called "the common good." Issues rise to public attention. For a period of time, they become the talk of the political community. And it is in relation to issues that perplex the polity that planning comes into its own.

Planners have a certain knowledge of things without which they would not have a moral praxis at all, but would be like ordinary citizens, searching for answers without knowing where to look. It is this special knowledge that distinguishes planners from other professionals and gives them whatever authority they may have. Let me begin, in talking about what planners know, by suggesting that planning discourse—which is the intellectual tradition into which we fit, which colors our vocabulary, the way we think, and the community of discourse to which we relate ourselves—is nourished by three streams, separate yet stemming from a common source. The central stream is *moral discourse* and is concerned with ethical choice, or how we shall live with one another; the second stream is *technical discourse*, or how we may effectively (and efficiently) relate means to ends; and the third stream is *utopian discourse*, which is concerned with visionary images of the "good life."

Although these streams or traditions of discourse are interconnected, they sometimes seem to have an existence of their own, each pre-empting the space of the others. But how shall we judge technique that is deprived of vision and ethical judgment? We can admire its virtuosity but ultimately must reject it, because pure technique means to slash blindly into the life of living communities. At the other extreme, utopian vision divorced from technical discourse and ethical judgment is but a harmless play of the imagination with no practical consequences. In between them, moral discourse by itself quickly degenerates into Sunday morning sermonizing. It is priggish and judgmental. In planning, the three separate streams of discourse must be brought together. That is the special virtue of the praxis of planning.

Let me clarify what I mean by the centrality of moral discourse in planning. Gone are the times when planners thought that making choices for others is simply the privilege of those having technical knowledge. The sentence, "I am technically competent; therefore, I can tell you how to live," simply lacks the power to persuade. Since there are no technicians of life (either individual or social), we must assume a vast multiplicity of skills that bear on what we call "life." But even if we could imagine a situation in which 1,000 "doctors of life" were to tell us how to live "correctly" (according to the technical norms of efficacy and efficiency), and they could do so with each doctor's own special "know-how" without running into contradictions, and without the uncertainty that is constitutive of life, they would still not be able to make a complete prescription, for there are no experts on human subjectivity. Even psychologists cannot climb into the ego as the source of human choice.

These sorts of considerations bear directly on the uncomfortable questions familiar to all planners: planning for whom, with whom, and against whom? An imbalance of power is a condition of life. And planners often find themselves on the side of those with power, specifically the powers of the state. (There are other planners who opt for the side of the weak, and I shall return to them later.) So we know that planners have an ability to impose their plans (assuming they can get them by the politicians). But that is not the whole of the story, because moral discourse raises for us the unavoidable question of citizen participation. Unfortunately, to turn planning over to the people in a sort of self-management euphoria does not work either, because again, self-management is not an absolute and has its limitations, too. Like it or not, the state is inevitably a player, but only one among several. And the stage, we must confess, is getting more and more crowded with a consequent dilution of state power.

All effective planning is therefore a negotiated process among affected parties who have different values, concerns, and interests at stake. What do planners bring to this process? What special knowledge is theirs? I want to become a little more specific now than merely to assert that they bring moral, technical, and utopian knowledge into the negotiated process we call planning. What special skills do planners have?

- Planners know, or ought to know, how to facilitate the process we call negotiated planning so that people can resolve their differences and move forward.
- Planners know, or ought to know, how to define problems in the public domain

(i.e., problems that have risen to the surface of public discussion and concern) in ways that make them tractable. Of course, some problems are so deeply rooted that it would be foolish to think they can be dealt with successfully without major political changes, or even changes in public attitudes and opinion. To point this out and perhaps search for second-best solutions is a planning skill, too. In defining what the problem is, planners typically use comprehensive criteria: historical, spatial, economic, cultural, and political, among others. In their description of the problem, however, planners will seize upon those dimensions of the problem which are critical from a viewpoint of action.

• Planners know, or ought to know, about the efficacy (and relative efficiency) of the intervention strategies potentially available.

• Planners know, or ought to know, about the political dynamics that bear on a solution of the problem.

• Planners know, or ought to know, how to get new and pertinent knowledge. For example, they know how to research the possible impacts of proposed intervention strategies on the interests and values of the relevant authors, on the environment, and on other concerns people may have.

• Planners know, or ought to know, how problem dynamics and intervention strategies relate to images of the good society. Will they move us closer to or further from utopian visions?

To say that planners know how to do these many things (or even that they ought to have this kind of knowledge) is to employ "know" in the weak sense, for planners' knowledge is never absolute, nor does it carry the authority of the True Word. Planners' knowledge necessarily involves a great deal of experience, guesswork, intuition, and risk-taking (hence, also a knowledge of what the risks are). Above all, it involves a willingness to engage the other players in the planning game in a common discourse and to be guided by their wisdom as well. Planners must be radically open to new facts, new insights, new understandings. If this renders problem solutions more complex, so be it. Nothing will be gained by simple formulations when the reality is not simple.

And so, when we ask for whom planners plan, the answer is not the traditional one of the public interest, or the "common people," or some such convenient phrase. In any planning game we are likely to find many players, and each player is likely to bring along a crew of planners that will see the world from their own perspective. Planners in America do not occupy a monopoly position of power (not even so-called central planners) and they never did; they are moving instead in a field of rapidly shifting forces that reflects the fluid power positions (and different configurations) of the players in the game. The public interest, or the common good, is an emergent. It is that toward which the game, or process, is oriented, which gives it meaning, and which makes it, indeed, the central process of a democratic polity.

This formulation, of course, presupposes that all the interested players are allowed to play. And this, we know, is not typically the case. A good part of what we call planning has therefore to do with people's struggle for collective self-empowerment and participation. It is a struggle for a change in the political configuration, for a change in the rules that govern the game, for new understandings and reinterpretations of familiar shibboleths. Planners alone cannot change the rules of the game that are changed only under massive public pressure. But they can make common cause with the excluded and disaffected groups in the society, working with them in ways that lead to their greater access to the bases of social power and the conversion of that power into power that is also politically effective.

With the planning game a multiple dialog, what is it that prevents the game from degenerating into a free-for-all in which the most powerful, the most ruthless, inevitably get their way? There are several possible answers to this, including (and not least importantly) the formal constraints of a strong democratic tradition. But part of the appropriate answer is also, I believe, that all the planners in the game, regardless of the players they work for, participate in the three streams of common planning discourse: the technical, moral, and utopian. Although they will not necessarily see things the same way, planners share a common language and approach which can help hold chaos at bay. This is another way of saying that planners are professionals.

Rational planning was one of the triumphs of the modern age. It prided itself in being the scientific way to guide society's future course of progress. But in the end, like so many myths of modernity, planning, too, had to bite the dust. Science, it turned out, was not the One True Way; and neither was planning. If we begin to see planning (now with different eyes) as a form of praxis in Aristotle's sense, as "free" moral and political action informed by knowledge and understanding, we shall discover that planning is as alive as ever and, perhaps for the first time, true to itself as one of the healing disciplines, like medicine and teaching. A teacher does not teach but educate—that is, bring out whatever is best in the student in a process of gradual self-discovery. Nor does a physician heal except as he (or she) cooperates with the natural processes of healing where they exist. In this image, then, the planner does not plan but works with the special skills and knowledge planners have to bring us closer to the utopias of our imagination. Planning discourse ties us back into old traditions of philosophy and practice, of which we are the contemporary embodiment. Planning discourse is the ground on which we stand.

REFERENCES

Arendt, H. 1958. *The Human Condition.* Chicago: The University of Chicago Press.
Bernstein, R. J. 1971. *Praxis and Action: Contemporary Philosophies of Human Activity.* Philadelphia: University of Pennsylvania Press.
Bernstein, R. J. 1985. *Beyond Objectivism and Relativism: Science, Hermeneutics, and Praxis.* Philadelphia: University of Pennsylvania Press.
Friedmann, J. 1987. *Planning in the Public Domain: From Knowledge to Action.* Princeton, NJ: Princeton.
Habermas, J. 1981 and 1984. *The Theory of Communicative Action*, 2 vols. Boston: Beacon Press.

TWO. PLANNING THEORY AND ETHICS—SUGGESTED READINGS

American Institute of Certified Planners. *AICP Code of Ethics and Professional Conduct* (Adopted April 29, 1989), and *Procedures Under the Code of Ethics and Professional Conduct.* Washington, DC: American Institute of Certified Planners.

Burchell, Robert W., and George Sternlieb. 1978. *Planning Theory in the 1980s.* New Brunswick, NJ: Center for Urban Policy Research.

Dyckman, John W. 1969. "The Practical Uses of Planning Theory." *Journal of the American Institute of Planners* 35, 5:298–301.

Faludi, Andreas, ed. 1973. *A Reader in Planning Theory.* New York: Pergamon.

Friedmann, John. 1987. *Planning in the Public Domain: From Knowledge to Action.* Princeton, NJ: Princeton.

Galloway, Thomas D., and Riad C. Mahayni. 1977. "Planning Theory in Retrospect: The Process of Paradigm Change." *Journal of the American Institute of Planners* 43, 1:62–71.

Hall, Peter. 1988. *Cities of Tomorrow: An Intellectual History of City Planning in the Twentieth Century.* Oxford, UK: Blackwell.

Howe, Elizabeth, and Jerome Kaufman. 1979. "The Ethics of Contemporary American Planners." *Journal of the American Institute of Planners* 45.

Klosterman, Richard E. 1985. "Arguments for and against Planning." *Town Planning Review* 56, 1:5–20.

Krieger, Martin H. 1974. "Some New Directions for Planning Theories." *Journal of the American Institute of Planners* 40, 3:156–63.

Rittel, Horst W. J., and Melvin M. Webber. 1973. "Dilemmas in a General Theory of Planning." *Policy Sciences* 4:155–69.

So, Frank S., and Judith Getzels, eds. 1988. *The Practice of Local Government Planning*, 2d ed. Washington, DC: International City Management Association.

Wachs, Martin, ed. 1985. *Ethics in Planning.* New Brunswick, NJ: Center for Urban Policy Research.

Wildavsky, Aaron. 1973. "If Planning Is Everything, Maybe It's Nothing." *Policy Sciences* 4:127–53.

3

COMPREHENSIVE PLANNING

The Goals of Comprehensive Planning

Alan Altshuler

Professor of Urban Policy and Planning, Harvard University

Alan Altshuler is interested in examining the political and administrative issues inherent in planning and land-use decisions in American cities. He focuses on how planners make difficult professional and value choices. Based on case studies of planning in Minneapolis and St. Paul, Minnesota, this selection is concerned with how planners define the public interest and engage in community goal conception. Altshuler argues that for planning to be successful, goal premises must be established in a politically compelling manner.

THE IDEAL OF COMPREHENSIVE PLANNING

Those who consider themselves comprehensive planners typically claim that their most important functions are (1) to create a master plan to guide the deliberations of specialist planners, (2) to evaluate the proposals of specialist planners in the light of the master plan, and (3) to coordinate the planning of specialist agencies so as to ensure that their proposals reinforce each other to further the public interest. Each of these functions requires for ideal performance that the comprehensive planners (a) understand the overall public interest, at least in connection with the subject matter of their plans, and (b) that they possess causal knowledge which enables them to gauge the approximate net effect of proposed actions on the public interest.

This chapter is concerned with some ways in which city planners have approached the former of these two requirements, which—contrary to most students of planning—I consider the more interesting one. If comprehensive planners deal with a great many more areas of public policies than specialists, their factual and causal knowledge in each area is bound to appear shallow—at least by comparison with that of the specialists in it. Hence their claims to comprehensiveness, if they are to be persuasive, must refer primarily to a special knowledge of the public interest.

Every government planner of integrity, no matter how specialized, must be guided by some conception of the public interest. And since plans are proposals of concerted action to achieve goals, each must express his conception as a goal or series of goals for his community. He will probably conceive these goals, of course, as constantly shifting rather than highly stable, as always intermediate rather than final, and as more in the nature of criteria than of concrete destinations. Community goal conceptions are likely to have these characteristics because of the limitations on collective human foresight and imagination. Nonetheless it is impossible to plan without some sense of community goals, call them what you will.[1] Moreover, for the planning process in any community to be democratic—and I assume in these pages that it should be—the goals must win approval from a democratic political process; they must not be goals simply prescribed for the community by planners.

In this chapter we shall examine a few of the difficulties that face planners as they strive to determine community goals democratically. In the next two chapters we shall deal with the difficulties they face as they try to concert action.

IMPLICATIONS OF THE IDEAL

The comprehensive planner must assume that his community's various collective goals can somehow be measured at least roughly as to importance and welded into a single hierarchy of community objectives. In addition, he must argue that technicians like himself can prescribe courses of action to achieve these objectives without great distortion or harmful side-effects of a magnitude sufficient to outweigh the gains achieved through planning. We may conceive a continuum of faith in the feasibility and desirability of comprehensive planning. The "ideal type" defender of comprehensive planning would contend that a serious effort should be made to plan in detail the future evolution of all important economic and social patterns. Others would limit their support to the planning-in-general-outline of change in particular strategic variables.

Those who contend that comprehensive planning should play a large role in the future evolution of societies must argue that the common interests of society's members are their most important interests and constitute a large proportion of all their interests. They must assert that conflicts of interest in society are illusory, that they are about minor matters, or that they can be foreseen and resolved in advance by just arbiters (planners) who understand the total interests of all parties. Those who claim that comprehensive planning should play a large part in the future evolution of any particular economic or societal feature have to assume similar propositions with regard to conflicts of interest likely to arise in connection with it.

To the extent, then, that comprehensive planning is possible, the correct law for a society is something to be discovered, rather than willed, by public officials. The role of the politician who ignores consistency or obstructs grand schemes to placate interest groups is hard to defend. So is the concept of majority will, and the idea that party conflict is desirable. It is in this sense that the claims of planners often seem to be in conflict with those of politicians. Both claim a unique ability to judge the overall public interest. The politicians's claim rests on his popular election, his knowledge of the community, his sensitivity to human needs, and his personal wisdom. The planner's claim is one of professionalism and research. If it seems somewhat devoid of human warmth, it also sounds more authoritative, more precise, more modern. As will be seen shortly, I have no wish to imply that city planners and politicians must (or, indeed, invariably do) defend their work on the basis of conflicting assumptions. It may well be that the capacities of planners and politicians are, for many purposes, suited to complement each other. Here we are not discussing everything that men called planners do, but rather some implications of the concept "comprehensiveness" in planning.

Few sophisticated American defenders of planning, certainly, believe that any group of planners can achieve a total comprehensiveness of perspective on any issue. Many do believe, however, that professional planners can come closer to achieving it on numerous vital issues than other participants in the urban decision process. The primary purpose of this chapter is to explore the theoretical foundations of this belief. It should be noted, however, that the explicit claims of practicing planners often seem to suggest that a fair approximation of genuine comprehensiveness is currently attainable. The case studies in this volume provide a number of illustrations.

CASE STUDY ILLUSTRATIONS

In his introduction to the *St. Paul Land Use Plan*, for example, Herbert Weiland, the St. Paul planning director, described his conception of the planning function in these words:

> The total city planning process, of which land-use planning is but one part, involves a continuing program of deriving, organizing, and presenting a comprehensive plan for the development and renewal of [the city] . . . The plans must be economically feasible, and must promote the common good, and at the same time [must] preserve the rights and interests of the individual.

Long discussions with every planner involved in the preparation of the St. Paul plan persuaded me that these words were meant literally. City planning was comprehensive and for the common good, not for any lesser objectives.

Several members of the St. Paul planning staff were highly critical of C. David Locks, Weiland's predecessor, for having offered advice freely to operating agencies without first developing a comprehensive plan. Locks himself, however, had also conceived his responsibilities broadly, though he had not considered the time ripe for explicitly comprehensive planning during most of his tenure. He had written in the Planning Board's 1957 publication, *The Proposed Freeways for St. Paul*, for example, that while others had considered the cost of freeways and their effect on traffic, the Planning Board had "special responsibilities posed by virtue of its function and status as an advisory representative citizen's group concerned with the development of all facets of the community's life."[2]

In considering the development of Ancker Hospital, politicians turned finally to city planners to interpret the overall public interest. First the city planners in the St. Paul Housing and Redevelopment Authority, and eventually those in the City Planning Bureau as well, accepted the challenge with confidence. When interviewed, both groups of planners stated without hesitation that they were better equipped to interpret the public interest than the consultant hospital architect, whose primary concern was how best to build a hospital. They believed that because their perspective was broader, their recommendation was highly likely to be wiser, or more rational.[3]

In formulating the *Central Minneapolis Plan*, Rodney Engelen, with the full support of Planning Director Irvin, cast his arguments in the broadest possible terms. The operational goal of the *Plan* was clearly a limited one: economic growth. Engelen, however, felt that he had to justify the goal itself. He stressed the functions of downtown as bearer of culture, disseminator of news and ideas, haven for unique activities, supplier of taxes to support all public services, and so on. When interviewed, he emphasized that his concern was to enrich the lives of all citizens, not to line the pockets of downtown businessmen. It was merely fortuitous, he believed, that in this case the interests of property owners and those of society coincided. He realized that on many subjects this coincidence did not exist, or was not perceived, and that in such cases the political implementation of the public interest might be impossible.

Engelen admitted freely that no plan or evaluation could be entirely comprehensive, as did all the planners interviewed for this study when pressed. His (and their) disclaimer was perfunctory, however, as if only a minor detail were at stake. Engelen wrote, for example, that the *Central Minneapolis Plan* could not truly be termed comprehensive because "there are and will always be elements—new aspects—yet to be studied and yet to be decided upon." He thus rejected a conception of comprehensiveness that I have suggested is useless: i.e., that the comprehensive plan should deal with everything. In short, he admitted that the object of any decision is necessarily limited, at very least in time, but he preserved the implication that the planner's approach—i.e., his goal orientation—to the object may be comprehensive.

THE SEARCH FOR PLANNING GOALS

All Twin Cities planners agreed that community goals could in the final analysis be discovered only through public discussion. Planners might propose alternative articulations, but goal statements could have no claim to represent community thought unless the community or its legitimate representatives ratified them after serious discussion and deliberation. In theory the primary problem was to guide the discussion and to decide when it had gone on long enough. The primary problem in practice, it developed, was to get a discussion going.

St. Paul's planners hoped, for example, that vigorous discussion would follow publication of their *Land Use Plan.* No one showed any interest in discussing it, however. The reason seemed to be that the *Plan*'s stated goals were too general. No one knew how the application of these goals would affect him in practice. Those who were not completely uninterested in the *Plan* had learned long ago to be suspicious of high-sounding generalities. The planners had not succeeded in showing opinion leaders the relationship between the *Plan*'s stated general goals and its great mass of "standards," or more specific goals. As a result, nonplanners decided with uncoordinated unanimity to ignore the *Plan* until someone proposed specific applications of it. Only at this point, they felt, would there by anything comprehensible—whether or not comprehensive—to argue about.

Minneapolis planners argued that the St. Paul planners' premises were wrong, and would have been wrong even if discussion of their plan had developed. For a discussion truly to influence the planning process, they said, it had to begin before detailed planning got under way. In their view, no one could effectively interpolate changes into a plan after it was complete without upsetting its internal harmony. If one of the goals of a plan were changed, then in theory every specific recommendation should be altered to some extent. No one had the time or intellectual energy to do this when a plan had already taken definite shape, however. The crucial phase in the evolution of any plan, then, was the development of its first draft. Goals should be determined before this phase moved far along.

Minneapolis planners themselves tried to obtain approval for planning goals before developing their central area plan. They decided at the start that they needed a goal statement which would be both "operational" and acceptable to all "reasonable" citizens of the city. By "operational," they meant that progress toward the goal could be objectively measured, and that the broad costs, both tangible and spiritual, of striving toward it could be foreseen. Comprehensive goals, they judged, could not be operational. Therefore, reasonable men could not pass on them intelligently. It followed that goals could win intelligent public approval only if they were partial. The question was: *how* partial? Perhaps it was possible to articulate, and plan to achieve, highly general goals even if not truly comprehensive ones.

They endeavored to bring about a public discussion of essential goal options before preparing the detailed plan. Fortunately, planners and planning consultants throughout the nation had applied themselves to downtown problems in recent years, and had developed a more or less integrated theory explaining characteristic downtown problems. Consequently, Minneapolis planners were able to present their preferred goals with tightly reasoned arguments behind them. The parts were related and mutually reinforcing. The man of affairs with a limited amount of time could quickly grasp the objectives and the main lines of reasoning on which the recommendations were based. The most general operational goal that the planners proposed was "the economic growth of downtown." They recognized that this goal was itself deceptive, however, in that although it sounded noncontroversial the steps necessary to its accomplishment could not keep from being controversial. In their publications on downtown planning goals, therefore, they chose to emphasize what they termed "design goals." These were in fact *types* of projects—rather than project proposals for specific streets and blocks in Minneapolis—that had been tried in other cities. The planners tried to explain the relationship between these types of proposals and the economic problems facing urban downtowns in the current period. It was possible to discuss the types of dislocation that might be expected, and so on, without bringing in specific project proposals. The discussion was really a model of comprehensible argument in favor of middle-range (i.e., operational but still general) planning goals. I strongly doubt that existing theory was sufficiently developed to support comparable justifications of goal recommendations in any other area of city planning activity.[4]

Even in this area, however, the specific financial costs and unintended side-effects that would arise on application in Minneapolis were difficult to foresee. Any intelligent discussion of planning goals had to take these (or their unpredictability) into account. For the discussion to be fully useful, the planners judged, its participants had to be willing to inform themselves about planning detail at some significant expenditure of time and effort. The discussion had to continue throughout the planning process, which itself would have peaks of activity but no final termination. Since the overall goal was partial, the discussants had to be urged to consider the full complexity of its side-effects. This they could not do if they confined themselves to examination of the central economic reasoning behind the "design goals."

The first problem was how to find discussants. The comprehensive planner's search is more complicated than that of any specialist. He cannot be satisfied to consult a narrow constituency. Presumably he should understand every important goal of each of society's members. If he must deal with groups rather than individuals he should not limit himself to constellations of interest that maintain permanent formal organizations. But the planners knew of no way to approach the city's "potential" groups. These would not become actual groups unless some immediate threats activated their potential members; some potential groupings of interests that the observer might identify would not become actual even then. Even those in the first category, however, had no leaders to speak for them. The abstract discussion of goals could seldom seem sufficiently immediate to spur them to organize and choose representatives. It seemed that in no other public endeavor than general goal determination was the disproportion greater between the number of groups that *might* reasonably become involved and the number that *would*.

The planners soon found that they could carry on a continuing discussion only with men whose jobs required them to spend time on the study and discussion of civic affairs. Only a few organizations in the city had such men on their payrolls. All of these fit into a few categories. Most were large downtown business firms or organizations of businessmen. A few good government groups (supported mainly by the contributions of businesses or businessmen) had representatives who took an interest in city planning, but for the most part they were in the same position as planners: they could talk abstractly about the public interest but they could not claim any special qualifications to represent particular interests. The other permanent organizations in the city did not bother to have representatives spending the bulk of their time observing civic affairs. Each had a few continuing interests (racial issues, taxes, city hiring policy, etc.) and became politically active only when immediate threats to these arose.

Making the best of this situation, the planners tried to carry on a discussion of goals with the professional "civic affairs" representatives of downtown business. These professional discussants, however, lacked the power to commit their firms to anything; consequently, as the discussion became more specific they became more and more noncommittal. The businessmen who had the power to commit their firms to specific courses of action had neither the time nor interest to engage in almost endless discussion with the city planners. In a short while, even the professional discussants found that they had no time to study each tentative planning formulation with care. Thus, a major difficulty was revealed. Even had the planners been able to handle all the complexity of life, they would not have found laymen willing or able to evaluate their work.[5]

If it can be so difficult to spur well-informed discussion even of such limited goals as those of the *Central Minneapolis Plan*, the question necessarily arises: what should be considered an adequate discussion of planning goals? Was the discussion in this case adequate although its only participants were businessmen whose interest in the discussion was mild and who were concerned only with direct economic costs and consequences? One might say that it was, because other groups could have entered the discussion to raise additional points had they wished. I did not find any elected officials in Minneapolis, however, who accepted this reasoning. Most were rather inarticulate about their objections, but a few were able to state their views quite precisely.

Downtown businesses are, according to these objectors, "organizations in being." Their owners are accustomed to watching the civic scene and searching for issues likely to affect their interests. They enter the discussion of any proposal at a very early stage and understand its potential impact on their interests relatively early. Other members of the public, however, tend to became aware that something is afoot and then to conceptualize their interests more slowly. After the perception begins to dawn, most take quite some time to organize. The range in the amount of time, and in the degree of immediacy of a threat or opportunity, that it takes to move different types of people with potential interest in a proposal to the threshold of organizational expression is enormous. Government never moves slowly enough or poses issues clearly enough to give everyone his say. It is fair to assume, however, that only when government moves at a snail's pace and deals with issues of rather direct and immediate impact can a significant proportion of the great multitude of interests express themselves. Therefore comprehensive democratic planning is virtually impossible. No legislature or committee of interest group leaders can rationally evaluate a statement of comprehensive goals. Its members cannot, in the absence of specific project proposals and citizen reactions to them, predict how the countless measures needed to accomplish the goals will affect the overall quality of community life or the interests of their own constituents and organizations. Consequently, they are likely to prefer operating on levels where comprehension and prediction are most feasible, even if this means fragmenting policy choices rather than integrating them. In practice, this means that they will rarely commit themselves to let general and long-range goal statements guide their consideration of lower-level alternatives.

There are no doubt many local politicians in America who would not find the preceding argument a compelling one. In localities lacking a coherent "power elite" firmly committed to a plan, however, it has a high degree of plausibility as a prescription for political survival. Its specific dictates are bound to be, at a minimum, a "project" rather than a "general planning" orientation and a disinclination to deal with controversial issues.

SYSTEMATIC CRITICISMS OF THE COMPREHENSIVE PLANNING IDEAL

The crucial assumptions of those who claim that comprehensive democratic planning is possible and desirable have of course been challenged more systematically than this. Martin Meyerson argued in a 1954 article that the major attacks could be divided into two types.[6] The first is that planning limits the range of individual choice by imposing centrally made decisions. The second is that planning requires "vastly more knowledge . . . about a huge variety of factors" than can be obtained or grasped by any individual or closely integrated group. Meyerson asserted that the few who had tried to answer these criticisms had been more successful in answering the first than the second. They had answered the first by saying that freedom is opportunity, not just the absence of restraint; and that planning agencies are created because people sense a failure of the market and of politics to satisfy their desires. As for the second question: unfortunately, wrote Meyerson, "we all know" that the assertion that planning can provide a rational basis for substantive policy decisions is just a goal today. The danger, he went on, is that planners will become content for it to remain a goal. He left the problem with a call for research.

It is questionable, however, whether planners have answered even the first objection successfully. Though it is certainly true that freedom consists of opportunity as well as the absence of restraint, there is little agreement as to whether planning to date has anywhere in the world produced more opportunity *in toto* than restraint. Only "commonsense" estimates are possible, as any more precise balance sheet would have to be based on determinations of the significance of particular opportunities and restraints. Neither the philosophic (assuming values to be objective) nor the scientific (assuming them to be subjective) foundations for such determinations exist. Second, the fact that people sense a failure of the market and the political process to meet their needs hardly forces one to conclude that they are better satisfied with the planning process. A reading of American city planning publications, not to mention conversations with numerous practicing planners, reveals a preoccupation among city planners with the failure of their work to win popular approval. Moreover, the winning of popular approval would itself prove very little. Planners themselves do not hesitate to bemoan the unwisdom of many popular governmental programs. They emphasize that the public must be educated by its leaders to favor comprehensive planning. They admit that the unguided public is likely to prefer an alderman who does petty favors for constituents to one who studies the city's overall needs.

Those who have made this first objection to comprehensive planning have generally emphasized that ambitious plans can only be realized through the generous exercise of public power. They have contended that every grant of power to government increases the chance of its abuse, increases the pervading influence of bureaucracy and red tape in the lives of citizens, decreases the self-reliance of citizens, and, as the habit of delegating tasks to government becomes prevalent, undermines their healthy suspicion of those who wield power. They have said that those charged with taking a comprehensive view of political problems are necessarily charged with safeguarding the complex requisites of the social and political system entrusted to their care. In the case of American society, this means a system in which the rights of individuals to wide spheres of personal freedom are recognized.

If the planner is truly to think comprehensively, in this view, he must consider not only the goals of society, but also the framework within which these goals can be pursued. If all proposals to enlarge governmental power threaten the framework of individual liberty to some degree, the planner must share society's initial bias against them. Those who oppose planning have generally asserted that planners have a professional bias in favor of bigger and bigger government, less and less subject to pressures from interest groups. Planners, they say, are in the business of creating new proposals which call for governmental activity. The planner's own interest is in the success of his plans: that is, in additional governmental activity *ad infinitum.* Most grants of power to government are long-term ones, because the electoral process is ponderous and inflexible. To reverse a major decision once ratified is extremely difficult, though it happens occasionally, as with Prohibition. The general pattern is for public interest to focus on an issue for a short while, and then move on. The planner's bias in favor of ever-larger government should therefore disqualify him from evaluating either his own proposals or those of others. Demands for public action in modern society are so numerous that only by subjecting each to the most searching criticism, based on an initial negative bias, can the trend toward concentration of power (which admittedly cannot be stopped) be slowed to a moderate rate. When government must act to deal with some pressing issue, every effort should be made to define the problem narrowly and to deal with it specifically. The approach should be one dealing with bottlenecks, not planning the whole production line. In other words, it should be piecemeal, not comprehensive.

If these are some of the views intelligent people still can hold regarding the issue that Meyerson says planning defenders have dealt with rather successfully, we may expect to have considerable difficulty in dealing with the one he says planners have been unable to handle. In part the problem is, as Meyerson says, the inability of planners to know about the interrelations of a huge variety of factors. But every profession deals with matters of incredible complexity. No profession can bring order to the mass of facts until it knows what it hopes to accomplish. From its goals, the members of a profession can derive criteria for judging the importance of facts. Using these criteria, they can develop theories about which consequences of specific types of proposals are the most important to control. The next step is to develop techniques for controlling these consequences. All specialists have lists of techniques for dealing with the characteristic problems they encounter. Planners too have some when they act as specialists. The floor-area ratio, for example, is a characteristic device used to resolve an aesthetic problem: the fact that rigid height and bulk building regulations yield unvaried architectural patterns.

This need for criteria, however, returns comprehensive planners to their basic problem. To develop theories about what they should know when creating comprehensive plans or evaluating specialist plans comprehensively, they need to know society's goals. Unless society has goals that can be discovered and applied, the task of theory building cannot begin. The difficulty of dealing with factual complexity will always seem insuperable, though the truly insuperable difficulty may be that of defining the aims of the theory-building endeavor. The market and political bargaining processes depend on the assumptions that only individuals have goals,[7] that these normally conflict, and that the mysteries of bargaining yield the best results possible for men. The planner cannot rely on a hypothetical invisible hand; he must validate his claim to arbitrate, whereas the bargainer must only validate his claim to negotiate. Planners cannot claim to arbitrate on the basis of their own views of the public interest. If there are important conflicts of interest in a society that cannot be resolved to the advantage of all parties, then planners require the guidance of a strong political arbitrator. The alternative is a conception that essential harmony underlies all apparent clashes of interest.

The view that clashes of interest are only apparent has always appealed to one element of the American intellect. It is assumed by most conservative defenders of laissez-faire no less than by progressive attackers of "politics." Marver Bernstein reminds us, for example, that almost all American movements for regulatory legislation have had to adjust their arguments to this conception. In order to have any chance of success, they have had to protest their general disapproval of public action, even while saying that in this particular case it was needed to stop flagrant abuses by a few unscrupulous individuals. The ostensible purpose, always, has had to be restoration of the natural harmony of interests.[8] We may conceive a progression of steps in "natural harmony" thinking from support of laissez-faire, to regulation of specific abuses, to comprehensive planning. Laissez-faire theorists, of course assume that the interests of mankind are best served with no conscious coordination of effort. Theorists of regulation assume that just as healthy human organisms often require treatment for specific ills, so with healthy economic and social systems. The next step is to say that social and economic systems are not very good self-regulators, but rather require constant, carefully planned direction and care if they are to perform adequately. In this view, suitable to an age which accepts positive government, nature provides the common ends but human intelligence and elaborately coordinated effort are required to choose and implement the proper means of achieving them.

Those who reject comprehensive planning meet this reasoning in a variety of ways. Let us consider two of those which seem most plausible.

First, many writers, including the authors of *The Federalist*, have contended that conflict of interest is an invariable feature of all societies, and that the worst conflicts of interest are between those who manipulate governmental power and those who do not. By this view, whenever all those who possess governmental power are able, let alone encouraged, to synthesize their interests into a comprehensive goal, the rest of society had better watch out. A corollary of this position is that the few goals shared by all the members of society are not the goals most important to individuals. Thus, the primary function of government should be to provide an ordered framework in which civilization can prosper. The framework may be indispensable, because freedom is meaningful only within civilized society, but from the individual's viewpoint it is still only a precondition, not a preeminent goal in itself. Except during moments of supreme crisis for a society, in this view, the normal thing is for its members to differ, for each to want to seek happiness in his own way with a minimum of organized societal interference. This argument leads naturally into the argument against planning outlined above on pages 88–89.

Second, there are those who say that even if human interests harmonize and "big government" must be tolerated in modern life, the goal of comprehensiveness in decision-making should be viewed with the utmost suspicion. These critics do not, any more than those whose views are outlined above, recommend the banishment of intelligence from the handling of human affairs. They say only that the ways of the world are often contrary to logic. Logically, the wisest decisions should be those made at the highest level, where the widest range of arguments can be considered. But in fact, because the human mind can grasp only a limited number of considerations at any time, decision-makers at the highest level can act only by drastically over-simplifying their choice problems. According to this view, any comprehensive scheme is a Procrustes bed. The decision-maker does better to recognize the unforeseen and the unique in every situation without rigid preconceptions. He can, when "other things are equal," endeavor to harmonize each day's decisions with those taken previously, but he should recognize that other things often are *not* equal. What is lost in administrative unity when the piecemeal approach is employed is made up in superior contact with public opinion and the special needs of each situation.

The greatest virtue of the piecemeal approach, in this view, is that it poses a large number of policy questions. The comprehensive approach implies that politicians need only approve general policy statements periodically, leaving the rest to be deduced by experts. Politicians not unnaturally react to this idea with hostility. They recognize that if they are to be the actual deciders of policy, they must exercise their influence continuously, at levels of generality sufficiently low so that their decisions may affect the matters of interest to their constituents. They may forego interference with administration below certain levels of generality, but they must never let administrators persuade them to set the cutoff point too high. The question of where it should be is always debatable, of course. Highway engineers tend to think that the setting of highway routes should be a technical endeavor. Others, including city planners, often complain that highway engineers are inclined to handle the side-effects of route location—which may be as important as the intended effects—as peripheral matters. In a democracy, the administrators can advise but they cannot determine finally which side-effects are too important for them to handle themselves, or to ignore.

Pressure groups have a similar interest to politicians in the piecemeal approach. Their members typically are interested in direct and immediate consequences to themselves, not in the overall public interest. It is a value of the piecemeal approach that interest groups can deal with questions their members care about. They need not feel that by the time their members become aware of any threat or opportunity the issue will have been foreclosed by prior community approval of generalities. Interest groups depend for their survival on issues which move their members and on at least occasional partial successes.[9] A vigorous public opinion in turn cannot survive without vigorous interest groups, whose leaders articulate issues, command attention in the mass media, and assure supporters in dissent that they are not alone. In the absence of strong evidence to the contrary in any particular society, therefore, it should be assumed that whatever saps the vigor of interest groups saps the vigor of democracy. The ideal of comprehensive planning seems ultimately antagonistic to the level of group conflict which typically characterizes stable democratic societies. It casts doubt on the very value of public discussion, at least after the stage of determining general goals. If a group of planners can comprehend the overall public interest, then any challenge to their specific proposals must be attributable either to their own incompetence or lack of integrity, or to the selfishness and shortsightedness of their critics. Faced with such polar explanations, those who take the side of the planners are apt to conclude that competition among parties and interest groups is alien to the public interest. Dictators frequently employ this very logic to defend their systems.

Defenders of planning may meet these criticisms in part by saying that they do not rely on the idea of a comprehensive harmony of human interests. They may contend merely that maintenance of a framework in which civilization can flourish is an enormous task, requiring all of man's ingenuity and foresight. Pressure groups are currently so vigorous, they may continue, and comprehensive planning is so weak, that concern for maintaining the divisive forces in our society at adequate strength is misplaced. Even if ideal comprehensive planning is impossible and in theory "big government" threatens democracy, they may conclude, democratic societies must strive toward the first and tolerate large doses of the second if they are to meet the challenge of modern welfare expectations and rapid technological change. This argument is highly plausible, but here as elsewhere serious debates center around location of the cutoff points, and planners suffer from lack of a theory to justify their positions in these debates.

To critics of planning there is an essential difference between public actions to meet crisis threats to crucial societal values and actions to ameliorate the effects of every societal dislocation. The passionate proponents of economic reform in the 1930's and of foreign aid in the postwar decade were able to argue that American democracy was in clear and mortal peril. Proponents of strong public action to bring about desegregation in the 1960's can cite highly serious injustices and threats to domestic tranquility as the justifications for intervention. Few defenders of city planning cite such serious or immediate crises. They say instead that planning is desirable to help minimize the pains of adaptation to change, and to develop cities in which everyone's opportunity for fulfillment will be enhanced. They generally fail, however, to confront certain obvious questions squarely. How, for example, should one judge whether the alleviation of a specific social pain warrants the amount of growth in governmental power over the lives of individuals which it will require? Is it possible to achieve a high level of intelligent consensus about the substance of personal fulfillment, and the kinds of environment most conducive to it? The final judge of proposed answers to such questions must be the political process. And here is where planners' troubles have usually begun.

POLITICAL RESTRAINTS ON THE GOAL DEVELOPMENT PROCESS

Speaking broadly, there are two ways to win political acceptance for new ideas in a stable democratic system. The first is to challenge the theoretical foundations of popular beliefs with which they conflict. This way is slow at best. Moreover, it requires a highly persuasive theory. Such theories are never easily come by, nor, if they challenge older persuasive theories, do they win acceptance quickly. In the United States, the other theories with which a thoroughgoing defense of comprehensive planning would have to contend are not even perceived as theories, but rather as part of the American tradition. Perhaps in consequence, American planners have generally eschewed full-scale defense of social planning, preferring to conciliate the powerful reasoning of American conservatism rather than to challenge it directly. The only theoretical defense of public planning which planners have frequently asserted has been based on a conception of planning as businesslike foresight. The simple theories required to defend this idea of planning have won fairly easy political acceptance, but they have not dealt with the inevitable political and social implications of serious efforts to plan generally or comprehensively. It has remained necessary, therefore, to deal with these implications *ad hoc* when such efforts have been made.

One way, then, to win political acceptance for new ideas is to challenge the theoretical foundations of older ideas with which they conflict. The other way is to adapt one's own arguments and objectives to the beliefs, attitudes, and political customs already prevalent. The latter way is more likely to yield immediate results, and it minimizes the risk that no results at all will be produced. American planners almost invariably have chosen it, no doubt in part because they are influenced even more by American culture than by international planning theory. It has certainly contributed to the political security of planners and the planning function. It has perhaps obscured, however, the problem of maintaining a clear professional viewpoint.

There is no need to search far for an explanation. It is extremely difficult for any agency whose explicit function is to propose new ideas to avoid coming into frequent conflict with established ways of thinking and doing things. Even if general strategy is articulated in the most conventional possible terms, this tactical dilemma is bound to remain. With respect to planning, it is bound to be most apparent when the planning is general and community goals must be determined. Given the importance of such a determination—if it is in fact to provide a guide for future public action—and the infinite varieties of emphasis possible, one would expect that the officials making it would run the risk of offending everyone. Even if they are oblivious of their own safety, the problem of winning political approval for their proposed goal statements remains.

Two methods of dealing with this problem at the level of general goals may be outlined.[10] The first is to state goals on which all reasonable men can agree. Unfortunately, goals of this type tend not to provide any basis for evaluating concrete alternatives. Thus, the St. Paul *Land Use Plan* stated as its most general goal the "evolution of St. Paul as a better place to live and work," and the *Plan* constantly justified its more specific proposals in terms of increasing "liveability." The second alternative is to propose somewhat more controversial goals in the expectation that the community's elective policy-makers will consider, if necessary amend, and ultimately approve them. Conceivably, planners might offer elected officials several choices of goals in each area of concern, though to the extent that they did so they would reduce the possibility of all the goals finally chosen being consistent with each other. Inconsistency might be turned to positive advantage, however. Part of using this approach successfully would be to deal in "packages," so that those in the minority when one goal was approved might hope to be in the majority when others were. The objective, of course, would be to win all or almost all reasonable politicians to support of the package.

This method is tried frequently in the American system, but it seldom succeeds where the package is a set of general goals. Part of the reason, we have seen, is that many "reasonable" politicians in the system oppose general planning and the articulation of general goals on principle. Even more important is the fact that American politicians typically depend on public discussion to inform them of the interest and values affected by any proposal. If planners cannot spur adequate discussion of their goal statements, politicians cannot, and know they cannot, make informed choices among them. Even when discussion is achieved, the dictates of prudence and democratic ethics impel politicians to wait for consensus to form before acting. The upshot is that very few proposals emerge as law from American legislative processes until and unless the vast majority of articulate groups interested in them favors some version of them. In the case of novel proposals, virtual unanimity seems generally to be required unless the need for decision is seen by the vast majority to be inescapable.[10]

In the national sphere, these "rules" may be waived when survival seems to be the stake. In most areas of urban life, however, people with money can escape the worst consequences of any change. Thus, Scott Greer has characterized the American city as one of "limited liability" from the viewpoint of the individual.[11] To illustrate: if a middle-class neighborhood becomes a slum, the original residents can move out, and though this has a price it is generally easier and cheaper than fighting the trend. So long as the general standard of living is rising, most of the newcomers are taking a step upward; they are likely to be apathetic toward efforts to resist the transition, and positively hostile to programs which might "improve" the neighborhood's prospects sufficiently to drive rents up. The immediate threats in urban life, then, are of individual dislocation rather than of societal survival, or even decline.

Politicians in American society occasionally alert their constituents to specific ills and dangers, and champion specific programs for dealing with them. It has recently become fashionable, moreover, for some politicians to conduct well-publicized quests for consensual, nonoperational general goals. It is a rare politician indeed, however, who leads his constituents in formulating positive operational social goals. The quest itself would be likely to stir antagonism among those who did not believe societies should have positive goals, and it would almost certainly stir new demands against the politician's limited resources. Moreover, those few citizens who long for positive planning rarely approach unanimity in any meaningful detail on what its substance should be. The obstacles to positive political leadership are such that even those who emphasize the potential educative role of the American Presidency usually admit that the President can be effective only so long as he confines his efforts to a very few widely perceived social ills and foreign dangers. The President who obtains authority to set up general planning agencies in moments of national crisis is likely, once the crisis begins to abate, to see them scuttled by Congress while he himself is charged with Caesarism. Consider the fate of the National Resources Planning Board, abolished by Congress in 1943 though its functions had been advisory only and it had carefully avoided direct confrontations with other agencies.[12] The incomparably more significant Office of War Mobilization and Reconversion achieved immense powers of coordination in the course of its brief life, but only during total war and at the expense of adopting a highly judicialized bottleneck—as opposed to policy-oriented comprehensive—planning approach.[13] The Bureau of the Budget has nurtured its far more limited influence similarly. Few chief executives at the local level have formal powers comparable to those of the President in his, and of course none have comparable prestige.[14] In general, the American distrust of executive power has found more forceful legal expression at the local level than at the national, perhaps because of the need for foreign and military policies nationally, and because opponents of executive power since the brief Federalist interregnum have found the constitution which it produced too difficult to change.

The opponents of planning have recognized the difference by focusing their attention on national rather than local planning efforts. Businessmen have been the primary patrons of the urban planning movement in America since its beginnings. As the planning movement has matured, moreover, fewer and fewer large property owners and executives have seen anything ironical about their providing the primary base of political support for local land-use planning while continuing bitterly to oppose anything remotely resembling national economic planning. The major reason for the survival of this apparent inconsistency has probably been that leaders of property-oriented groups have lacked confidence that they could control planning at the federal level under the President. If this view is correct, the critics have spared local planning from their attacks just *because* local politicians have had insufficient power to defy the veto groups of their political system.

THE IDEAL OF MIDDLE-RANGE PLANNING

The point has been made in previous sections that truly comprehensive goals tend not to provide any basis for evaluating concrete alternatives. It is thus difficult to stir political interest in them and impossible to plan rationally in their service. Recognizing this, at least implicitly, many contemporary planners claim to practice middle-range planning—which they define as planning for the achievement of goals that are general, but still operational. It is not very fruitful to strive for greater definitional precision than this, because the image is one of balance between the contradictory ideals of comprehensiveness and specialization. Experienced planners have a "feel" for the conception, however, and explain it to neophytes by citing illustrations. For our purpose, the *Central Minneapolis Plan* may be cited as clearly falling in the "middle range."

The middle-range planning ideal has much to recommend it, despite its imprecision. It permits the promise of meaningful political discussion and approval of planning goals, even if the achievement may in practice be highly elusive. In addition, criticisms of comprehensive planning rooted in liberal democratic theory are much less forceful when applied to middle-range planning. From the viewpoint of the general planner, however, the middle-range planning ideal has one crucial flaw. It provides no basis for the planner to claim to understand the overall public interest. Men who plan to achieve operational—even though relatively general—goals are specialist, not comprehensive, planners. Consequently, they have no obvious theoretical basis for claiming to know better than other specialists how far each specialist goal should be pursued, and with what priority.

SPECIALIZATION VS. COMPREHENSIVENESS: THE UNEASY BALANCE

The case for efforts at genuinely comprehensive planning has generally rested heavily on the thought that planners can resolve conflicts among goals in expert fashion. If they cannot, if they can only articulate specialist goals, then elected officials would seem required to act as the comprehensive arbiters of conflict. If it is assumed that arbiters operate most successfully when all important considerations are presented vigorously to them, one might argue reasonably that each important cluster of operational goals should be defended by a separate agency. Philip Selznick, for instance, has contended that leaders who wish to maximize their influence should structure their organizations so that the lines of jurisdiction dividing subunits are those along which important issues are likely to arise. His reasoning is that if issues arise within subunits they are likely to be decided by the subunit head, without the chief executive becoming aware of them. It is when subunits themselves come into conflict that arbiters at the next higher level are most likely to learn of issues.[15] Delegation of overall authority to arbitrate, in this view, even within the framework of highly general goal statements, is bound to transfer the substance of power from the delegator to the delegatee. If the delegator retains appellate jurisdiction he may dilute this effect. The more that he is committed to uphold the comprehensive policy vision of the delegatee, however, the less he will be able to do so. In trying to persuade politicians to make this delegation and to commit themselves to comprehensive policy visions, defenders of comprehensive planning must contend that the politicians will further the welfare of their constituents by doing so. To the extent that planning agencies lack truly comprehensive perspectives, this contention becomes less and less plausible.

Beyond this, even in pursuit of their own specialist goals, planners operate in a world of whole objects, not of analytical aspects. They cannot conceive means that will further the operational goals of primary interest to them without affecting innumerable others in uncontrolled fashion. Sophisticated planners recognize this, and try not to serve their stated goals exclusively. The operational goal of the *Central Minneapolis Plan*, for example, was downtown economic growth. Its authors realized, however, that they could not reasonably ignore other goals. They wrote and spoke as though the cultural, political, spiritual, recreational, and other functions of downtown could never conflict with each other or with the economic function. In practice, they were saved by their common sense; they did not press their pursuit of economic goals sufficiently far to spur public awareness of potential serious conflicts. Conceivably, they might have listed all the significant operational goals they hoped to serve, but they would still have been left with the problem of balancing them. In short, every concrete object of planner attention is a miniature of the whole. The important analytical problems that arise in planning for an entire urban area arise in planning any section of it.[16] Perhaps the only escape is frankly to adopt a specialist orientation, even while remaining willing to adjust specific proposals as highly distasteful side-effects become apparent. It may still be plausible to maintain, however, that planners are custodians of values that somehow deserve to take precedence over the values propounded by other specialists. Let us consider the most persuasive lines of reasoning frequently advanced in support of this view.

One of the simplest was stated by Allison Dunham in a well-known article several years ago.[17] He claimed to have found after a survey of the planning literature that planners almost invariably believed that, at the very least, they were the officials best qualified to evaluate site proposals for every kind of facility. They based their position on the premise that planners were experts in the impacts of land uses on each other. The argument, in other words, was not that planners were "wiser" than operating agency officials but that on certain types of issues their specialty deserved first place in the pecking order of specialities.

Two queries come immediately to mind. First, are the impacts of uses on each other regularly more important in site decisions than the intended purposes of each use? Second, can locational problems be separated meaningfully from all other problems? For illustrative purposes, consider a central issue of the Ancker Hospital site controversy: how should the potential health benefits of a contiguous medical center be balanced against the traffic congestion it would produce? Was it possible to say in the abstract which variable deserved greater weight? Was traffic congestion more a locational problem than building the medical center? The proponents of the medical center, it will be recalled, said that it could come into being only if Ancker Hospital were built on the one available site adjacent to the city's two largest existing hospitals. The only way to argue that planners should normally be given the benefit of the doubt in disputes of this kind is to say, as Dunham did, that specialists think of the needs of their constituents, while planners think of the impact of specialist proposals on others. In this case, the constituents were sick people and hospital staff personnel, while the "others" included many of the same people, but in their other capacities—as drivers and investors, for instance. The key question is whether the "others" should have had any more presumptive right to prevail than the recognized constituents.[18]

Another objection to this definition of planner competence is that it provides only the haziest indication of the legitimate jurisdiction of planners and of government. Just what is a locational decision? It is hardly enough to say, as planners generally have, that locational decisions are those that have an impact on surrounding property or people. Almost anything I do to my property affects my neighbor in some way. For instance, if I rent out rooms in my one-family home, I have changed the use of my land and therefore made a locational decision, by a common planner definition. Should government therefore control everything, as it already controls my right to rent out rooms? Planners deny that it should, but they have rarely asked where the cutoff point should be. They have typically been satisfied to say that government should intervene only in cases of "substantial" harm, and that common sense will prevail in interpreting the word "substantial." They may be right, but this formulation gives the citizen no theoretical guidance as to whose common sense should prevail in cases of disagreement between other decision-makers and planners.

A second persuasive line of reasoning to support the view that planners should generally prevail in such disputes is that they alone among city officials spend their days analyzing city problems from an overall point of view. Operating agency officials cannot rise above their day-to-day administrative chores, and in any event their perspectives are conditioned by the narrow responsibilities of their departments. Even politicians typically devote most of their time to maintaining contacts with, and to performing errand boy services for, their constituents. In dealing with legislative proposals, they generally focus on details of immediate interest to local groups rather than on the overall picture. In most cities, moreover, councilmen are elected from wards; in many they work only part time at their jobs; and in some each councilman heads a city department. Only planners can devote all their time to thought about city problems at the most general level.

The most obvious criticism of this position is that freedom from operating responsibility may not be the best condition in which to make high-level decisions. Some prominent decision-makers have argued that it is a poor one. Winston Churchill, for example, has written that Stafford Cripps became restive and hypercritical of his colleagues while serving as parliamentary whip during World War II. What he needed, according to Churchill's diagnosis, was responsibility which would absorb his energies and give him a sense of the concrete issues. Those who are free from operating responsibility, concluded Churchill, tend to develop an unhelpful watchdog mentality. It is unhelpful because they usually think too abstractly to be cogent critics of complex choices among policies.[19] Similarly, Chester Barnard has written that study and reflectiveness without operating responsibility tend to lead to the treatment of things by aspects rather than wholes, to a disregard of factors which cannot be expressed precisely, and to an underestimation of the need for artistry in making concrete decisions. Because so many crucial factors cannot find expression in words, Barnard concluded, the interdependencies of social life can only be grasped intuitively. Only men of long and responsible experience are likely to acquire very much of this intuitive grasp, and therefore only such men—who will also grasp the supreme difficulty of planning in this "world of unknowns"—are qualified to plan.[20] This is unquestionably a rather mystical position, but for all that it is no less a respectable and forceful one.

Barnard and Churchill agree, then, that freedom from responsibility for operating decisions is anything but fit training for planning.[21] Those who accept their view are likely to believe that any one of a number of city officials may qualify better than the planning director to serve as the wise chief advisor of politicians on broad policy issues. The Minneapolis and St. Paul city councils consistently acted on this belief. To the extent that they desired coordination of public works, they normally relied on their city engineers to achieve it. When the Minneapolis City Council decided in 1953 to separate capital budgeting from ordinary budgeting, it set up a committee composed of politicians and civic leaders. The committee was given a small staff headed by a former city councilman. Planners were shut out of the capital budgeting process entirely. When the St. Paul City Council decided that it needed a special advisor on the interstate freeway program, it appointed City Engineer George Shepard, who had been about to retire. When Minneapolis City Engineer Hugo Erickson left the city government for private employ in the late 1950's, his successor proved inadequate (in the City Council's view) for the unofficial task of city public works coordinator. Within a year, the Council lured Erickson back into government, giving him the title of Development Coordinator. Minneapolis planners believed that they should have been given the job, but they could offer no strong arguments to support their view that Erickson was less able to take the overview than they. The politician most responsible for bringing Erickson back told me that the planners thought too abstractly and with insufficient regard to cost, whereas Erickson, though less articulate, understood the infinite, inexpressible complexity of governmental choice. In fairness to the planners, it should be added that Erickson had made his entire career in Minneapolis, looking to the City Council for his raises, perquisites, and promotions. He had risen primarily because of his technical competence, to be sure, but also because the councilmen felt confident that he would not embarrass them politically and that his overriding loyalty was to themselves. Planning Director Irvin, needless to say, could not claim similar qualifications.

A third defense that planners frequently make of their aspiration to be more than "mere" specialists is that governmental efficiency is served by having one agency keep track of everything that every city agency does, calling attention to conflicts and to means of coordinating effort for the benefit of all. The distinction between coordination and planning, however, is of practical importance only so long as planners have no power. Without power, they can as coordinators simply try to persuade groups of specialists that their respective interests will be served by improved coordination. As soon as planners begin to impose solutions or advise politicians to impose them, however, they have entered the substantive planning field. That is, they have set their perception of the public interest on substantive matters against those of the specialists who have rejected their advice. Similarly, when planners request authority to prepare a city's capital budget, they cannot justify the request on grounds of "simple efficiency," which would have to be established by the criteria of all the specialists' own goals. They must assert, at least implicitly, that they have some means of choosing among the values entrusted to each operating agency. In other words, they must claim to have goals. And the coordination of action in pursuit of substantive goals, is, if it is anything, substantive planning.

One might say that the planner needs coordinative power only because some specialists stupidly or obstinately refuse to cooperate with others in the interests of "simple efficiency," even though no significant values are threatened. The answer is that no one can determine that this is the case in any particular controversy without examining it in detail. Philip Selznick has illustrated this point clearly in his analysis of the history of the Communist party.[22] The party refused to cooperate with other leftist parties in the decade before the Popular Front, despite the obvious threat of fascism. Yet this period of isolation, Selznick contends, made the party a much more valuable tool to its masters during and after the Popular Front period. During the isolation period, the "character" of the party developed and became incorruptible. This extreme example illustrates a simple point: that cooperation and isolation in themselves have important effects on organizations. If an agency head claims that a measure advanced in the name of efficiency actually threatens important values—and any agency head who refuses the advice of the planning director will say this—no outsider can refute him until he examines the bases of his arguments in detail. If we assume that most agency heads are men of good conscience, we can likewise assume that they will have some reasons that seem genuinely sufficient to them, and that they will seem so as well to at least some reasonable outsiders. In the end, no act of coordination is without its effect on other values than efficiency.

Some planners reading this chapter will no doubt judge that the issues raised in it are "ivory tower stuff," and in the immediate sense perhaps they are—though to me they appeared quite close to the surface in the Twin Cities. The purpose of this chapter, however, has been to challenge the planning profession to reinforce its most fundamental arsenal. In the long run, I suspect, general planning and evaluation will have little effect on American cities unless their goal premises can be established in sufficiently compelling fashion (both politically and intellectually) to make politicians take notice.

NOTES

1 A few planners, mainly in the universities, have recently come to doubt this. They are taken with Herbert Simon's model of "satisficing" administrative man, which I believe they fail to understand thoroughly. Several have suggested to me that this model shows up all talk about the need for planning goals as irrelevant. The satisficing model is set forth in Herbert Simon and James G. March, *Organizations* (New York: John Wiley and Sons, 1958), esp. pp. 140–141, 163, 175; Herbert Simon, *Models of Man* (New York: John Wiley and Sons, 1957), Chaps. 10, 14, 16; and Herbert Simon, "Theories of Decision-Making in Economics and Behavioral Science," *American Economic Review*, LXIX, No. 2 (June 1959), p. 253–283.

According to Simon, most theorists until recently accepted the model of "maximizing" (economic) man. Maximizing man was assumed to have all the alternatives that he needed before him and to be able to rank them all with reference to the desirability of their consequences. His ranking ability rested on his possession of a "utility function," which amounted to his values or goals. For purposes of simplicity, I am leaving out here the issue of his ability to forecast consequences. Let us deal in this discussion only with the evaluation of foreseeable consequences.

Satisficing (administrative) man, on the other hand, is moved by stimuli ("e.g.," writes Simon, "a customer order or a fire gong") to search for alternatives. When he finds one that is "good enough," he intelligently avoids spending time, energy, and resources on further search.

Simon himself tends to be indifferent to high-level goal determining processes, so it is understandable that some planners should have concluded that satisficing man does not need goals. According to their interpretation, the determinants of satisficing man's choices are largely, perhaps mainly, subconscious. He knows that in any case most of the consequences of any choice are incomparable on any single operational scale of value. Consequently, being a practical man rather than a utopian intellectual, he reconciles himself to the fact that his choices are bound to be essentially intuitive. From the standpoint of an outsider, the evidence that an alternative is satisfactory is bound to be no more than that it has been chosen.

The above is a misinterpretation of Simon. In his sustained discussions of satisficing Simon always makes clear that one can only speak of an alternative's being satisfactory if it meets standards set prior to its selection. Standards, however, are neither more nor less than goals. If they are not ultimate goals, they must ultimately be evaluated on the basis of their relation to ultimate goals. The very notion of formulating precise standards of adequacy at the beginning of a search for alternatives is, it strikes me, a more literal application of means-ends language than is normally feasible at the higher levels of politics and administration. The processes of balancing ideals, estimates of feasibility, and probable costs of further search are generally far more subtle than this language suggests. The phrase that Chester Barnard frequently used, "successive approximations," seems more appropriate here. This does not mean, however, that general discussions of goals and priorities can be dispensed with in any meaningful planning exercise.

More generally, it may be noted that the satisficing model, even correctly understood, hardly represents a major advance in our understanding of human psychology. The maximizing model has long been recognized as an ideal type, a useful measuring rod against which to compare optimal aspirations with achievements, rather than as a descriptive model of human choice. It has been most useful in economics, where it has been feasible to hypothesize a single substantive goal for actors other than ultimate consumers. Use of the satisficing model, on the other hand, requires that we have substantive knowledge of such variables as the values of actors, the costs of search, and the obstacles to implementation of particular proposals. Unless observers have such knowledge, the satisficing model approaches the conception of it held by the planners mentioned above. It tells us nothing about why any particular actor considered any particular standard "good enough."

One other point worth stressing is that Simon's actors typically assess values, and consequently the significance of obstacles and costs, in purely subjective fashion. Consequently, Simon's theories are essentially theories of irresponsible choice. This may not seem terribly significant when decision-makers are choosing for themselves alone—as in the market—or for hierarchical organizations that have no pretensions of democracy or of responsibility to non-members. Such theories make both criticism and justification of choices on the basis of value considerations impossible, however, and this does matter in a democratic polity.

In *Organizations* Simon and March discuss the satisficing model in their chapter entitled "Cognitive Limits on Rationality." By contrast, my concern is with social and political obstacles to rationality. My purpose in these pages is political, not psychological, analysis. The approach taken here is that of the politician or citizen confronted with conflicting expert arguments, and anxious to decide wisely. Either may decide whimsically in the end, but it seems both nihilistic and paralyzing to assume in the beginning that no more is possible. It is also untrue, except in a number of rather obvious senses. The goodness of ultimate goals may not be demonstrable, but they are generally not the controversial ones. All the others can be analyzed and compared in terms of the consequences, unintended as well as intended, likely to flow from pursuing them. Simon specifically admits this, but he relegates scholarly consideration of such analyses and comparisons to the Siberia of "philosophy." His followers, whether "practical men" or self-conscious "scientists," are thus led to ignore these matters. I consider this unfortunate. (This viewpoint is elaborated in my introduction to a forthcoming reader that I have edited, entitled *The Politics of American Public Administration* [New York: Dodd, Mead & Co., 1966].)

Moreover, most planners themselves consider it essential for them to be able to demonstrate the nonarbitrary nature of their recommendations. I believe that Paul Davidoff and Thomas Reiner, in their recent article, "A Choice Theory of Planning," have articulated a major preoccupation of the profession in writing: "We are concerned with the problem, so trenchantly posed by Haar, that a major task confronting the planner is to see that he acts in a nonarbitrary manner, administratively as well as conceptually. We develop in these pages a theory of nonarbitrary planning." (*Journal of the American Institute of Planners*, XXVIII, No. 2 [May 1962], 103–115. The quotation is at p. 103. The piece by Charles Haar referred to is: "The Master Plan: An Inquiry in Dialogue Form," *Journal of the American Institute of Planners*, XXV, No. 3 [August 1959], 133–142.) It is clearly impossible to plan nonarbitrarily without knowledge of the proper goals for the planning endeavor.

2 *The Proposed Freeways for St. Paul*, Community Plan Report 4, June 1957, p. 30.

3 Planners tend to use the words "rational" and "wise" interchangeably in evaluating public choices. This is in accord with the usage of natural law philosophers, but not with that of contemporary economic and social theorists. For the latter, the term "ra-

tional" refers to the efficiency of means where ends are known. "Wisdom" refers to deep understanding and the ability to make what are considered "good" judgments on complex human issues, when goals and efficient means are not generally known.

Consequently, the planners use of the word "rational" in the classic sense to defend their distinctly modern "expert" recommendations makes for some confusion of thought. This confusion has a political function, however. It conveys the impression that expert logic or technique can produce "good" decisions on complex human issues.

4 A major reason for this was probably that in no urban section but downtown did simple economic goals appear entirely plausible. Outside the United States, planners rarely considered them so even for downtown. See, for example, the British Town and Country Planning Association's analysis of central London problems: *The Paper Economy* (London: Town and Country Planning Association, 1962).

5 From their viewpoint as political administrators, on the other hand, Minneapolis planners and their consultants won a major, and far from inevitable, victory in persuading the professional discussants that the general lines of economic reasoning in the *Central Minneapolis Plan* were valid, and that a plan based on them would quite probably benefit downtown business. After all, even the contribution of a plan to economic growth— let alone to the public interest—was impossible to predict and difficult to identify after the fact. Trend changes after specific actions were taken were possible to measure, but no one could prove that the actions studied had caused the result. Only comparative analysis of many cities could begin to test the efficacy of particular methods, and reliable comparative data were rare.

Still, the arguments of city planners in their role as economic planners had a hardheaded quality seldom present in their other work. They wrote as though from having defined their goal clearly they could identify the major bars to progress toward it without much trouble. Knowing the enemy, they could conceive tightly reasoned, even if untested, lines of attack.

6 "Research and City Planning," *Journal of the American Institute of Planners*, XX, No. 4 (Autumn 1954), 201–205.

7 Readers will note that I say the political *bargaining* process depends on this assumption, not the political *discussion* process.

8 Marver Bernstein, *Regulating Business by Independent Commission* (Princeton: Princeton University Press, 1955), Chaps. 1, 2.

9 Not all interest groups need *political* successes, of course, because not all are primarily political in their orientation. Business firms, labor unions, and churches, for example, can retain their memberships without engaging in politics. They tend to retreat from politics, however, and thus to disappear as *politically significant* interest groups, when their members perceive public discussion as invariably fruitless.

10 The phrases "vast majority" and "virtual unanimity" must be taken to mean proportions of those interested in each issue. Charles Merriam wrote thirty-five years ago in his classic description of Chicago politics that while virtually any group in the city could veto proposals affecting it, even the weakest group could get its proposals approved if no other group rose to object (*Chicago: A More Intimate View* [Chicago: University of Chicago Press, 1929]). Edward Banfield reports that Chicago's political system, run by the most powerful machine in the nation, operates still in roughly the same manner (*Political Influence* [New York: The Free Press of Glencoe, 1961]). According to Banfield, the "bosses" have few or no policy objectives of their own, and therefore decide issues in response to the electoral interests of their organization (i.e., the

"machine"). They seem to accept the view that electoral benefits are probable only when what we have termed the "vast majority" and "virtual unanimity" rules are followed, and when ample time is given potential interests to recognize their concern and express it.

No political machines operated in either of the two cities I studied, but the professional politicians who ran each acted similarly to the Chicago "bosses" in committing their prestige and influence.

Some members of the planning profession have themselves publicly approved the politicians' instinct. The President of the American Institute of Planners wrote in 1955, for example, that at a minimum policies adopted by government should be acceptable on a voluntary basis to 80 or 90 per cent of the public (John T. Howard, "The Planner in a Democratic Society—A Credo," *Journal of the American Institute of Planners*, XXI, No. 3 [Spring-Summer 1955], 62–65). If he meant, which I doubt he did, that it was all right for 10 or 20 per cent to be strongly opposed, he was a radical by the standards of most local politicians.

11 *The Emerging City* (New York: The Free Press of Glencoe, 1962).

12 See Edward H. Hobbs, *Behind the President* (Washington, D.C.: Public Affairs Press, 1954), Chap. 3; A. E. Holmans, *United States Fiscal Policy 1945–1959* (London: Oxford University Press, 1961), pp. 33–36; and Charles E. Merriam, "The National Resources Planning Board: A Chapter in American Planning Experience," *American Political Science Review*, XXXVIII, No. 6 (December 1944), 1075–1088.

13 See Herman Somers, *Presidential Agency* (Cambridge: Harvard University Press, 1950), Chap. 2; and V. O. Key, Jr., "The Reconversion Phase of Demobilization," *American Political Science Review*, XXXVIII, No. 6 (December 1944), 1137–1153.

14 Both of the Twin Cities had very "weak" mayors, even by local standards.

15 Philip Selznick, *Leadership in Administration* (Evanston: Row, Peterson, and Company, 1957).

16 The more limited objects (e.g., neighborhoods instead of whole cities) do present somewhat different, if not lesser, problems to the comprehensive planner. Cause and effect are easier to trace on the small scene, and important differences of interest are likely to be fewer. On the other hand, if planners emphasize the common interest of each homogeneous unit, they may well accentuate the differences between units.

17 A Legal and Economic Basis for City Planning," *Columbia Law Review*, LVIII (May 1958), 650–671.

18 This distinction recalls John Dewey's definition of the public interest (in *The Public and Its Problems* [New York: Henry Holt and Co., 1927]) as the interest in a decision of all those not directly party to it. Critics have pointed out that the parties to the decision have some claim to be considered part of the public too, in most cases the most clearly affected part. Those who dispute over definitions of the public interest are not mere academic quibblers. The phrase "public interest" has inescapable normative, and therefore political, significance. Those whose interest is opposed to it by a proposed definition therefore have ample reason to quibble.

19 *The Second World War*, Vol. IV: *The Hinge of Fate* (Boston: Houghton-Mifflin Co., 1950), p. 560.

Churchill was not arguing against the making of large decisions by generalists, of course. He himself was Prime Minister. Nor was he criticizing the British practice of concentrating authority within the civil service in the hands of generalists. Several points may be noted. The generalists in a British ministry exercise all formal power of decision not exercised by the minister himself. They bear responsibility as well for deciding which issues, and which specialist analyses of them, are important enough for the minister to consider. The elite corps of the generalists, the Administrative Class, are expected on entry only to think, write, and speak clearly, and to have done well in their subjects of undergraduate concentration. Any subject will do, although subjects fit for "gentlemen" (i.e., men devoted to culture rather than to making a living), notably the classics, have traditionally predominated. British administrators have no formal technical training for their work at all. They are platonic rather than functional leaders, but matured on responsibility rather than study. Those at the higher levels are notably unsympathetic to the ideal of general planning. They take well-known pride in deciding "each case on its merits."

Parenthetically, where city planners are employed in British ministries they are considered technicians, capable of contributing useful advice on specialized aspects of issues, but not of being entrusted with the power to make decisions.

20 Chester Barnard, *Organization and Management* (Cambridge: Harvard University Press, 1948), Chap. 4.

21 It should be clear that when I speak of "planning" in this chapter, I mean the work of determining overall policy guidelines for public activity, and means of implementing them. No single individual or agency makes such determinations alone in an American community. The recommendations of some, however, are bound to carry more weight than those of others. The crucial questions at issue here are (1) whether the views of planning agencies on controversial policy issues should normally be granted presumptive validity in the absence of strong evidence discrediting them; and (2) whether the training and career patterns of professional city planners equip them well for planning at the higher levels.

22 *The Organizational Weapon* (Glencoe: The Free Press, 1960).

The Master Plan: An Impermanent Constitution*

Charles M. Haar
Professor of Law, Harvard University

In this selection, Charles M. Haar discusses "The Master Plan" from a lawyer's perspective. He examines the concept, purpose, and nature of the *master plan*—an impermanent constitution—its potential influence on development, and its relationship to the law. Haar is concerned that enabling acts and plans tend to be too vague for measurable realization in the courts. The ultimate concern, however, of a lawyer and his client with the master plan is its impact on private property. Haar states (p. 117): "Where the brush strokes are so broad that no one knows what they mean, city planners cannot register surprise when their own private interpretation does not become the accepted one."

General ideas are no proof of the strength, but rather of the insufficiency of the human

Reprinted with permission from *Law and Contemporary Problems*, copyright 1955, Duke University School of Law.

* I wish to acknowledge the assistance given by conversations with Professors Ayres Brinser, John M. Gaus, and Louis Wettmore, and by the collaboration of Emanuel L. Gordon, Esq., and of Ramond L. Posel, of the Harvard Law School Class of 1953.

intellect; for there are in nature no beings exactly alike, no things precisely identical, no rules indiscriminately and alike applicable to several objects at once. The chief merit of general ideas is that they enable the human mind to pass a rapid judgment on a great many objects at once; but, on the other hand, the notions they convey are never other than incomplete, and they always cause the mind to lose as much in accuracy as it gains in comprehensiveness.

II Alexis de Tocqueville
Democracy in America 13 (Bradley ed. 1946)

. . . The plan shall be made with the general purpose of guiding and accomplishing a coordinated, adjusted, and harmonious development of the municipality and its environs which will, in accordance with present and future needs, best promote health, safety, morals, order, convenience, prosperity, and general welfare, as well as efficiency and economy in the process of development; including, among other things, adequate provision for traffic, the promotion of safety from fire and other dangers, adequate provision for light and air, the promotion of the healthful and convenient distribution of population, the promotion of good civic design and arrangement, wise and efficient expenditure of public funds, and the adequate provision of public utilities and other public requirements.

U.S. Dep't of Commerce
A Standard City Planning Enabling Act §7 (1928)

City planning in this country has witnessed a combination of professions and talents rare in any reform movement. From the outset sound legislation was recognized as essential for the development programs of the "new city." Great impetus was lent to erecting a legal framework for land planning by the United States Department of Commerce, which, through its Advisory Committees, promulgated and popularized standard enabling legislation for city planning and zoning.[1] Consequently, the theory of city planning[2] has had a decisive imprint in at least one area—state enabling legislation permitting municipalities to plan for and control the uses of land within their corporate areas.

Today enabling legislation for urban planning exists in all states but three.[3] Within this legal matrix the master plan[4] concept is an established element. Since it has arrived at such status, one may assume that it is legislative policy to encourage, or enjoin, recognition of the master plan's significance in the process leading from planning to reality. But, as is the case with most statutes (plus the need for allowing wide discretion and experimentation in so novel a proposal as city planning), planning enabling laws are cast in broad, amorphous terms. Hence, the enabling acts indicate a general area of purpose which forms the basis for more detailed elaboration, initially by local legislatures and administrators, and finally by courts. To perform this task of elaboration it is necessary to grasp the motivations and uses of city planning. Accordingly, this paper is directed towards an examination of the function and nature of the master plan in order to appraise the appropriateness of the legal accommodation it has received.

I. THE CONCEPT OF THE MASTER PLAN

What is the master plan? This is one of those ultimates which any serious profession—especially in periods of crises—will ponder long and hard. It is racking the professional city planners. As such, it may be a valuable exercise for pedagogic purposes. Occasionally, a discussion framed in such terms may even lead to pertinent observations on the planning process. And it may contribute that advantage of defining any general term—a convenient short-hand to facilitate communication.

Under the strong conviction, however, that "master plan" has a variety of meanings, dependent both upon the context in which it is employed, and the purposes for which it is invoked, this paper attempts to view the problem solely as one of the uses of a plan. What precisely is the legislature shooting for by prescribing the writing of a plan? What are the "strategic points of decision making" sought to be influenced by the plan? Master plan may mean one thing when used to advise on the timing of construction of New York City schools, and quite another in the allocation of lands for recreational uses in a rural setting. Again, when utilized by a federal agency for ensuring that a locality is beginning a serious and coordinated attack on slums so that the granting of federal funds is warranted, its contents and scope must differ from the case of a court scrutinizing a zoning ordinance under attack as not consonant with the master plan. And, of course, whether viewed historically over time within one nation, or across-the-board between a country dominated by the institution of private property and one where nationalization of development rights—or of land itself—has become the accepted way of dealing with land-use problems, the master plan concept cannot be said to have a universal meaning. Nor is there any one way of formulating or administering it.

This is not to deny the necessity of paying close attention to the master plan concept in and of itself. Even though there are disagreements at the periphery, there is a core meaning that is fairly well agreed upon. Moreover, the empiric situation remains: the concept is constantly used. If its employment were confined to the planning profession alone, there would be small incentive to join in the fray, painful and so often fruitless are the awards of dictionary definition disputes. But the inescapable dilemma persists: the word "master plan" is used in enabling legislation, local ordinances, and judicial decisions. In the field of law this rather ethereal concept may have major practical importance: not only may the individual client's rights in his property be drastically affected; but—as is often the guise such issues take—constitutional questions dealing with fundamental relations between the state and the individual are at stake. Accordingly, with this switch in interest from the master plan as a technical exercise, the point of inquiry resolves itself into: what are the possible contributions of the master plan in formulating decisions concerning land use; what control should the plan exercise over the implementary regulations; to achieve this desired degree of relation between theory and practice, what criteria should be enumerated for the use of administrators, reviewing courts, and private developers?

With this orientation, the initial question is rephrased, so that it becomes: what, as envisioned by the enabling laws, are the uses of the master plan? Unfortunately the functions of the master plan are often beclouded in the enabling acts. There is also diversity of purpose in the acts of the different states. Still worse, there is often inconsistency of purpose even within the same statute. For these reasons, even a limited attempt at classification and precipitating out the various functions served by the master plan may be useful for purposes of clarification. While there is overlapping, it is believed each category underscores a sufficiently distinct consideration.

An approach to the master plan from the lawyer's perspective is necessarily dominated by the question of impact—what part does the plan play in men's affairs? An analysis of the planning enabling laws discloses a dichotomy in the ends sought to be achieved through a master plan: one part is largely didactic and deals with the virtues of planning; another—and quite distinct—portion moves away from speculation and is concerned with directing the application of human energies in land development. Recognition of this split may lead to understanding the difficulties of making any practical application of the pure theory of the master plan. Again, it may help reshape the enabling acts to emphasize the processes by which the master plan manages to get itself realized.

The larger share of the typical enabling act concerns itself with the making of plans. The uses to society of this mechanism are envisioned as six broad types: (1) a source of information; (2) a program for correction; (3) an estimate of the future; (4) an indicator of goals; (5) a technique for coordination; and (6) a device for stimulating public interest and responsibility.

With respect to these values, the planning enabling laws are largely in the nature of an exhortation to the planners concerning theories and techniques of planning. As presently drafted, this part of the planning enabling acts constitutes a rudimentary text for the construction of a plan. It does limn the ethical and moral base of planning so as to make it an acceptable part of community institutions. To the professional planners, this part of the legislation may be of large significance; the proper contents and scope of the plan may cause much soul-searching and debate. It may also, in addition to setting up an internal ideal, serve the very practical purpose of strengthening the planning commission within the whole range of activities of local agencies competing for appropriations from the local budget. But so far as the other agencies of local government, the citizen of the city, the property owner and his lawyer, and the reviewing state courts are concerned, it is couched as a private dialogue between the state legislature and the local planning commissions.

A second set of functions allotted to the plan by most of the planning enabling laws deals with the plan's effects upon local legislative controls of land-use. It is this second broad group of uses of the plan which concerns the interest groups affected by planning. These uses seem to divide into five broad types: (1) a prophesy of public reaction; (2) a tool for the planning commission in making reports; (3) a guide to effectuating procedures and measures; (4) an ordinance regulating the use of land; and (5) a guard against the arbitrary.

This second major portion of the enabling act deals with the effectuation of the master plan: it concentrates on the impact, potential and actual, of the plan on the growth and decay of a city as these processes take shape–how the physical environment is modified by law. Only to the extent that the uses of the first type are incorporated into those of the second type, or influence the actual shape of their enactment, are they of any consequence in land-use activities. Only to this extent are planning theories and techniques given a role in the structure of local government.

II. WHAT THE MASTER PLAN MEANS TO THE PLANNER

The following are conceived to be the uses of the master plan relating primarily to the formulation of plans.

1. A Source of Information

The acknowledged initial step of the master plan procedure is what the British Town and Country Planning Act designates as the "survey."[5] It furnishes a picture of the present state of conditions in the city. Most state statutes direct the planning commission, in the preparation of the plan, "to make careful and comprehensive surveys and studies of present conditions and probable future growth" of the community.[6] These include, we are advised by professional planners—although they are rarely specified in the enabling acts—studies of economic activity, population composition and growth, land uses, channels of movement, systems of public facilities, and physical resources and liabilities.[7]

Gathering and analysis of information is essential; it is the explanation and the buttress of the various conclusions embodied in the master plan. Further, the inventory process has value in itself. For even if the plan becomes a dust gatherer after it is set on its way,[8] this information can prove of use in injecting some light into the operations of such haphazard physical developments as do occur in the future. Thus, a formal attempt to abide by the master plan idea leaves at least this trace.

Of course, if it is to have meaning, the plan itself sets goals, embodies decisions; if it is to have practical effect, procedures must be established to see that these decisions have effect on land. The data itself is not necessarily part of the plan, but a necessary antecedent and, occasionally, a supporting reference. Thus, this category relates to the value of making a plan, and not properly to the plan itself. This thrusts back to a basic precept—planning as a process rather than a rigid blueprint, so that for purpose of analysis master-plan-in-progress would be a more accurate though cumbersome title.[9] An accounting analogy may be useful here: the master plan is the balance sheet of the planning process, a snapshot of conditions and goals as they exist at one particular moment in time; a new balance sheet must be drawn up periodically over time for the use of the analyst, at any given point of time, to sum up the changes in standards, ideas, and facts over the interval of time elapsed since the last balance sheet; the moving picture is momentarily forced out of the free flow of life and time into the static balance sheet or printed master plan for the sake of convenience of analysis and discussion. But the plan itself is basically a flexible point of departure.

2. A Program for Correction

By hypothesis the plan serves to indicate the area's sore spots and functional deficiencies. The enabling acts are necessarily couched in general welfare terms.[10] Hence, the stress on safety from fire and other dangers, provision for light and air, promotion of proper distribution of population, adequate supply of "public requirements." By asking the right questions, it helps answer the fundamental query, where do we begin? It probes for community needs not obvious at a given time. By comparing these sore spots in relation to their effects upon other aspects of the area's physical development and the magnitude of their repercussion upon the people, as well as inadequacies in the rendering of any municipal services to which people aspire, some priority of action can be recommended. In making determination of priority, of the city's "resources, possibilities and needs,"[11] the planners have stressed that financial ability and community predilections must be weighed.

3. An Estimate of the Future

The Standard Planning Act directs the planning commission to survey present conditions "and future growth" of the municipality, and directs that the plan shall be made with the general purpose of guiding a development of the municipality which will, "in accordance with present and future needs" best promote the community welfare.[12] In determining goals some attempt must be made to grapple with the changes of the morrow, for obviously, as the term "planning" readily implies, the planner should be concerned with emerging conditions. Thus, we are again advised by professional planners—and by some indefinite provisions in the acts—plans must be premised upon estimates of industrial growth, of the future age and group compositions of the population, and the other variables affecting the physical development of the community.

Thereby master planning puts a brake on the natural tendency to plan only for the immediate. It is the long-range point of view that is put forth as a unique contribution of the planning perspective. Alfred Bettman with characteristic cogent simplicity put it this way: "One of the personal difficulties of planners is that they itch to plan something they will live long enough to see, which is a bad itch from the point of view of good planning."[13] A mid-way view, perhaps, of this relation (although closer to the Bettman view than a first glance might warrant) is expressed by the California Planning Act's injunction that the master plan shall be "for a reasonable period of time next ensuing" after the adoption thereof as may practically be covered thereby.[14] Of course, only approximations of the city's future can be made. Consequently, to realize the full potentialities of the use of the plan, periodic modifications of the general plan should be required. This is outrightly recognized in the British legislation, which requires a five-yearly review of the development plan in the light of the then existing conditions.[15] The American acts more generally provide that the master plan may be amended "from time to time." Despite the inherent limitations on foreseeability, some awareness of prevailing direction will be attained; upon this basis anachronistic development can be curbed–that is, provided this potential use of the long-range view is allowed some play in the actualities of land development, and controls over such development.

4. An Indicator of Goals

The master plan should not merely incorporate ascertained or probable trends of development. Otherwise, only an incomplete job would ensue. Objectives should be set in terms of what kind of city the community wants. After the alternative courses of conduct have been presented, debated, and a selection made, the plan represents the decisions and judgments of a community concerning its desirable physical form and character. In this respect it is a blueprint of values—although once more it evolving nature must be emphasized. The plan can never be a total solution, for it exists over time, just as it is a statement of values at one moment in time. In providing this value scheme it brings to bear upon debate of current physical development long term considerations founded on basic assumptions. And while predicating goals, the problems that may impede their achievement, as well as the means for circumventing the obstacles, thrust themselves forward for analyses and solution. Hence, its educative force on the planners and the planned is again apparent—and its potentiality in the sphere of land development if these goals are allotted a role in the land-use field. Again, if the plan is backed by sanction, it itself becomes a factor in forcing the direction of the future.

5. A Technique for Coordination

The planning commission is conceived of by the planning enabling laws as an integrating agency. It is directed to study and crystallize the inter-relationships of the various land-uses and structures within the city. With different bodies concentrating on streets, parks, school sites, zoning, etc. (and with the increasing tendency to delegate new measures such as public housing or urban redevelopment to newly created authorities), there is a danger that each specific activity affecting the physical environment will lack coordination with the others, and that maladjustments, inefficiencies, and waste will ensue. It is the special task of city planning—comprehensive planning—to supply this coordination and mutual adjustment. The master plan is the instrument used to fulfill this function, in the words of the Pennsylvania statute, of "guiding and accomplishing a coordinated, adjusted, and harmonious development of the city and its environs. . . ."[16] The various land-uses and physical installations—the physical expression of the myriad of human activities in the city—are combined into a coordinated system. In so far as possible, each piece of property is to be in the right location for its particular use. This will guide the planning activities to achieve greatest efficiency of the whole.

By embodying information and standards concerning these inter-relationships, the plan can provide a pattern against which specific proposals for use or building may be viewed. As such, it "represents a recognition . . . of the fact that the value of each specific thing is determined only in relation to things outside itself, and that therefore one must have a guide to things outside in order to make intelligent decisions about the specific thing."[17] Through its use as a check-list, a more accurate realization of the consequences of any specific planning action may be acquired. And to the degree that the plan carries weight, a touchstone upon which to judge the merit of a proposed action is provided.

The coordination is not only horizontally with other activities affecting the physical environment, but also over time. It is the long-range point of view and the phasing of the program for reaching the ultimate objectives that emphasize the potential contribution of the master plan.

6. A Device for Stimulating Public Interest and Responsibility

What the previous categories of the values served by the master plan may very well add up to is simply this: the chief purpose of the master plan is that of mutual education. In the process of making a master plan, the planner may learn which issues are the relevant ones so far as the people are concerned, what terms are meaningful to them, and which alternatives make sense as they view them. This education of the planning board and staff is crucial for any plan to survive. Concomitantly, mustering public interest and participation in city planning is one of the most serious problems faced by the profession:[18] preparing the plan can be an effective channel of communication. It is generally understood that today full use must be made of the democratic process to achieve understanding and acceptance by the people who are affected by planning, and who must undertake the responsibility of enacting and maintaining it.

Whether the full implications of this view, and the two-way nature of the educative program, are grasped by the planning enabling laws is somewhat doubtful. Again, the intense concentration on the making of the plan rather than "doing something" with the plan, has weakened any salutary effects the state acts could have achieved. Most acts speak in terms of "making and adopting" *the* plan. The decision-making process as a presentation of alternatives to the citizens, with an evolution by debate and consideration of other alternatives, before a plan is chosen by community acceptance is not the activating assumption of the acts. While this is not precluded by the typical enabling law, its orientation is not towards that full public participation advocated by certain political scientists. Most enabling statutes do require the planning commission "to promote public interest in and understanding of the master plan." But it is primarily a case of the planning commission selling a plan it itself has conceived and formulated. True, many acts require public hearings prior to the adoption of the master plan;[19] but the positive potentialities are ignored.[20] Nevertheless, as occasionally used today by progressive planning commissions, even without express legislative authorization, the use of a series of plans has helped infuse life into the planning process.[21]

Evaluation: The Master Plan Is Hortatory

It should be evident from the foregoing uses of the master plan—if these were the sole values derived therefrom–that the statutory mandate to make and adopt a master plan is really synonymous with a mandate to plan. The master plan embodies recommendations for an area's development based on predictions of needs and resources for an estimated period of time. Comprehensiveness (a concern with the interaction of the elements of physical development), projection (a concern with the indicia of change), and policy (a commitment to desired goals) are its major premises.

Considered in this light, the generalized statutory emphasis of the master plan concept as it has thus far been limitedly articulated, is purely hortatory. So perceived, the property owner—and the lawyer in his professional capacity—can remain indifferent to this intellectual exercise of the planning profession. Hence, also, the difficulty of defining more precisely what the master plan is—for it becomes another way of asking what is physical planning.[22]

III. WHAT THE MASTER PLAN MEANS TO PROPERTY INTERESTS

Planning law is directed towards (a) having a plan made; and (b) having it influence development. Given the requisite skill and energy, goal (a) may present little difficulty. The core-problem, however, rests in achieving goal (b): how to get the plan, a process of ideas, to touch and concern controls, the process of doing. Here is the area where the property owner's interest, and that of the lawyer he hires to represent it, comes into play; it is also the sphere of activity which concerns the other agencies of local and state government.

Thus far there have developed four primary ways in which local governments exert impact on physical development—public works, zoning, subdivision controls, and protection of mapped streets. To the city planner, the relation of the master plan to such regulatory ordinances is simple and clear. The plan is a long-term general guide for the development of the city; the regulatory laws are tools to bring the plan's goals into realization. Warnings have constantly emanated from the planners that the two must not be confused. "Instead of being itself the city plan, for which unfortunately it is often mistaken," says one of the early standard works in the field,[23] "zoning is but one of the devices for giving effect to it." To select another example, in an unpublished note to his model County Planning Enabling Act, Bettman wrote:[24]

> There has been some discussion as to whether the zoning plan is to be conceived of as a part of the master plan. But when the arguments are analyzed, there will be found to be some confusion as to the difference between the planning and the execution. The zoning ordinance is, of course, execution and the planning precedes it. . . . It may be that to

some extent a land classification and utilization program, and a zoning plan are synonymous. But the mention of both is desirable so as to make perfectly clear that the zoning plan is a part of a precising of the plan for land classification and utilization.

In this translation into results in the physical form and character of the community, what are the advantages attributable to the existence of a master plan? More specifically, what has led to the theoretical desideratum of a two-step process—first the master plan, second the implementary legislation—which is to be found in planning literature and in most planning acts? And what is the bridge between them?

1. A Prophesy of Public Reaction

The first use that may be listed, viewing the master plan from the vantage of the impact it has on men's affairs, flows from the previous categories of Part II, especially number 6. At least one practical event of great importance emerges for the perspicacious developer of land. The master plan is at the very minimum an intelligent prophesy as to the probable reaction of the local governmental authorities to a given proposal for development. Notice is thereby served on parties (public as well as private, it should be noted) dealing in decisions affecting urban conditions as to the probable outcome of their proposals, where these are dependent upon planning approval, or even where the less direct but often more important sanction of needed public cooperation is involved. And, as is the case with the administering of many regulatory devices, more important in final tally than the impact of sanction is the educational influence of the regulatory program. In the light of the master plan, the private land owner may shape his own plans in the plastic stage when they have not yet crystallized; collision with the public interest can in some instances be deflected. Hence, the inclusion of the public interest in programs of land development may be effected without controversy.

2. A Tool for the Planning Commission in Making Reports

The previous category of prevision of the future on behalf of the private land developer merges into this one—a basis for internal coordination of government actions and programs. Public action—streets, schools, public buildings, housing—vitally affects community development. Yet different programs may vary widely in objective and timing. As the Housing and Home Finance Agency recently put it: "What is important is that there be a means whereby the program of any agency can be reviewed and adopted as may be desirable in relation to other programs in the community and in relation to one over-all plan."[25]

This potentially vital review function has been assigned to the planning commission. The usual procedure requires that before taking action necessitating expenditure of public funds, incidental to the location, character, or extent of a government building, the proposal shall be referred to the planning commission for review and recommendations. The effect of such recommendation varies widely among the states. In some instances it has no consequence; only the moral and publicity preventives are available. In others, an overriding vote by the local legislature is necessary. Sometimes this is a unique veto power, where more than a majority—as much as three-fourths—is required to override the commission's disapproval.[26] And, in some instances, two steps are required: it must be overruled by the sponsoring municipal agency, and then by the local legislature.[27]

This coordination not only is between various governmental agencies, but may also be extended by the enabling act to include these activities and those of private developers. An example is the recent spate of legislation setting up public housing and urban redevelopment authorities. Nearly all of these require the new social welfare programs to accord with a master plan of land use for the community. Again, where referral of subdivision applications for a report by the commission is required before the plat may be filed, the master plan may influence the commission's decision.[28] In some instances, it is conclusive.

To Bassett, the author of the standard work on the master plan,[29] the use of the plan was strictly as a private guide for the planning commission. This is borne out by the Standard Planning Act, which makes no provision that the municipal legislature shall approve or adopt a master plan. Although not considering it quite as bad as legislative adoption, Bassett was dubious even of that Act's requirement that the plan must be adopted by the commission in whole or in part.[30] The fetish of plasticity and ease of change made him question even this relatively minor type of finalization. This attitude is flatly embodied in his Model Planning Law: "It [the master plan] shall be a public record, but its purposes and effect shall be solely to aid the planning board in the performance of its duties."[31]

The paradoxical conclusion emerging from the Bassett position is that it makes discussion of the legal aspects of the master plan superfluous.[32] In his Model Law, its existence is not a condition of referral to the commission. Indeed, the municipality has the option not to refer at all. Subdivision control is not dependent on the prior formulation of a plan, nor are any of the planning controls. The master plan becomes solely an engineering technique which the commission is encouraged to use.[33] As such, any effect the statutory direction to make plan has, must operate through the route of moral suasion. And, *a fortiori*, since the plan does not affect private conduct, there is no job for courts which the general guide can assist.

3. A Guide to Effectuating Procedures and Measures

The key-role of the master plan in the coordination of diverse activities affecting the city's land has been noted. This, too, is the role that it can provide for the whole series of legislative acts dealing with the whole series of such activities. The master plan can be most useful in establishing the framework within which to set the legal regulatory devices. Without such coordination, one regulatory device affecting one parcel of land, like zoning regulations, may undo the efforts of other controls over the same parcel, like subdivision regulations. Special regulation of tenement buildings may be rendered wholly ineffective by other laws taking a different approach to the control of the general environment.

Here there has been some confusion in the existing legislation. In the exercise of subdivision controls, the plan is sometimes made a guide for the regulations to be issued by the commission, the regulations having the direct contact upon the private land owner. The term "guide" is too weak in the case of zoning, where the zoning enabling statutes require that zoning regulations be made "in accordance with the master plan"; under other enabling acts, the master plan is supposed to erect the general policy framework within which to set the zoning regulation.

4. An Ordinance Regulating the Use of Land

The guide may become the ruler. Sometimes, enabling acts lend immediate binding effect to certain aspects of the master plan. The Pennsylvania Planning Act,[34] for example, makes the master plan itself the regulatory measure for the laying out of streets and parks. It is not a criterion by which to weigh implementary legislation; in itself it regulates and has direct impact on property rights.

It should be noted that this is contrary to the theory of the master plan—at least as understood by many planners. "It [master plan] is in no way legally binding upon private property," to select one example of this thought, "until or unless its recommendations are translated into official changes of the zoning map."[35] But in many spheres this binding effect is accorded the master plan by the enabling acts. Here, its function becomes the simple and familiar one of a government control on private activity. Consequently planning and enforcement may become undesirably confused.

5. A Guard Against the Arbitrary

A basic legal consequence of the master plan follows from its "comprehensiveness." This can be broken down into two aspects: by its requirements of information gathering and analysis, controls are based on facts, not haphazard surmises—hence their moral and consequent legal basis; by its comprehensiveness, diminished are the problems of discrimination, granting of special privileges, and the denial of equal protection of the laws. Hence, the two most frequent sorts of attack upon government regulation become less available to the private landowner. If the local community has gone to the point of preparing a master plan, his chances of success in attacking an ordinance, based on the plan, are considerably diminished.

Evaluation: Diversity of Legal Impacts

Statutory directives characteristically are buttressed by sanctions. There arises therefore a presumption that master plan provisions are not mere exhortations. This is reinforced by the prominence, both in sequence and length, which these provisions occupy. But while the statutory references are cast in large and hopeful terms, they assign no clear legal position to the plan. The legal impact of planning is significant only as it imports governmental control of physical development; therefore, it follows that the master plan portions of planning law are legally significant only in relation to such control. And in the four broad areas—public works, zoning, subdivision, and streets—thus far traditionally assigned for impact by the master plan, no consistent pattern of interpretation of the effect of the plan on the real world has yet emerged in the legislation or judicial opinions. The whole gambit of possible effects of the plan on land-use controls is run. In some acts there is a tacit recognition that the official map, even though it must be submitted to the planning commission for its recommendation, need not comply with the master plan.[36] The requirement in the Zoning Enabling Act that the zoning ordinance shall be made "in accordance with a comprehensive plan" has apparently carried the courts no further than requiring that the ordinance be reasonable and impartial so as to satisfy the *constitutional* conditions for the exercise of a state's police power.[37] In others, the adoption of the master street plan is necessary before the planning commission can become the platting authority, but no further mention is made of tying the commission's activities to the plan.[38] And still others give the master plan itself the direct effect of a detailed land-use ordinance. Some acts do not even require the adoption of the master plan in order to exercise subdivision controls.[39]

IV. THE CRITERIA FOR A STATUTORY CHECK-LIST

An appraisal of existing planning legislation in the light of these two categories of potential uses of the master plan reveals striking inadequacies which require amendments. The importance of mutual education of the planner and the citizen needs to be stressed—right from the initial stage of survey where citizens' groups and associations, by the sheer process of gathering information, can learn of the adjustment of values. Secondly, the inevitably restrictive impact of the master plan—if it is to have any meaning—must be given effect by a general control, at crucial points, over implementary legislation regulating private use of land, as well as over land development by government agencies; here, the regulatory and planning aspects of the plan itself should be dissociated.

Why the master plan has not developed in the United States, and, more particularly, has never received full recognition from the courts, is subject to a simple explanation. The acts are vague as to what constitutes a master plan. Plans, even where adopted, are so indefinite as to what the city should be that they are incapable of measurable realization in the courts. The basic postulate of this paper, therefore, is that the planner's job is to rewrite the enabling acts so as to give them more concreteness. So far as possible the act should require the preparation of a minimum check-list for the people dealing with the plan—other city agencies, land developers, lawyers, and courts. Where the brush strokes are so broad that no one knows what they mean, city planners cannot register surprise when their own private interpretation does not become the accepted one. If the act can clearly state the type of policies and goals that should be covered by the plan, the master plan can be given substance, for any implementing legislation that does not accord with such statement would be *ultra vires* the enabling act.

The current formulation of the master plan, as directed by the typical enabling act, falls short of this desideratum. Usually, such acts content themselves with repeating the language of the Standard Act:[40]

> Such plan . . . shall show the commission's recommendations for the development of said territory, including, among other things, the general location, character, and extent of streets, viaducts, subways, bridges, waterways, water fronts, boulevards, parkways, playgrounds, squares, parks, aviation fields, and other public ways, grounds and open spaces, the general location of public buildings and other public property, and the general location and extent of public utilities and terminals, whether publicly or privately owned or operated, for water, light, sanitation, transportation, communication, power, and other purposes; also the removal, relocation, widening, narrowing, vacating, abandonment, change of use or extension of any of the foregoing ways, grounds, open spaces, buildings, property, utilities, or terminals; as well as a zoning plan for the control of the height, area, bulk, location, and use of buildings and premises. . . .

If the enabling law is to help the master plan play an important part in the formulation and administration of government controls affecting land, it needs to be far more specific in its focus on objective and means than the above enumeration. And if the coordinative and the long-run perspectives of the plan are its unique contributions to making land-controls through the intervention of the state more scientific, the act should help clarify these roles. Thus, the makers of a plan should be directed to study and reach conclusions for presentation to the citizenry on certain underlying factors affecting a city's growth. This requirement should be mandatory. The findings and objectives to be covered by the plan should be full enough to guide the legislature in enacting ordinances which bite on property rights, and to give content to a judicial scrutiny as to whether the ordinance corresponds with the plan.

The stress, it is submitted, should be away from the physical and building aspects of development, and from, also, the public or municipal part of such development. Emphasis on the one factor reflects overconcern not only with the physical but also with the execution rather than the planning phase; stress on the latter factor flows from the view of the plan as a tool for the commission to be used primarily to check on land-use activities of other municipal departments, an interfamily arrangement, so to speak, rather than a use of the plan's criteria in the regulation of the private land developer. It does not seem too unfair a characterization of the enabling acts to say that the master plan in the past has really been thought of as a preliminary or sketchy zoning ordinance, street layout, etc.

Obviously it would be impertinent to attempt to list all such factors here, but a glimpse at the type of specifications can be attempted. The master plan should be required to state conclusions as to anticipated future population; anticipated employment opportunities; the goals for housing; transportation objectives; industrial, commercial, and residential needs; the over-all space requirements for each of these needs; and the relationship which shall exist between the spaces allotted for the different uses. The master plan should be asked to specify in general terms the amount and type of community facilities which shall be provided, and their interaction with the various land use areas; desirable standards of population density, of light, air, and open space; methods of transportation and communication and their inter-relation with the various land use areas. This is simply a starting suggestion as to the types of things the statutes should require the master plan to contain.

This sort of formulation, it should be noted, can give the assistance the court was seeking in the *Fairlawns* case.[41] The validity of the zoning ordinance turned, in the court's mind, upon its being "expressive of a plan which is comprehensive." This it defined as a relation "to the reasonable needs of the community, both at present and in the foreseeable future." And, with no further specifications as to what considerations of "reasonable needs" and the "foreseeable future" are, the court was compelled to strike out on its own.[42]

> The zoning regulations in question are clearly expressive of a plan to maintain the predominantly residential character of the town but still permit the less objectionable forms of business. The plan is not applied to a narrowly restricted area or for a limited time. In terms, the regulations cover nearly the whole town of Bethel and are in effect for an indefinite time. They leave some districts of the town open for uses other than business and residential. They therefore satisfy the requirement of the statute that such regulations be in accordance with a comprehensive plan.

This may or may not have been the proper planning tests to apply; but in the absence of other legislative guidance there is little room for complaint.

Ayres v. City Council of Los Angeles,[43] a notable decision, is a difficult one to understand against any theory of the master plan. It, too, perhaps indicates how amorphous phrasing may mislead the court. That case refused to compel the city council to approve a proposed subdivision. The city wished to impose conditions, mainly relating to dedication of land for highway widening. Petitioner urged that the planning commission could not act since a master plan had not yet been adopted by ordinance of the city council. The court rejected the relevance of this contention, stressing the great amount of time required to draw a complete plan. It also noted that the city charter provided for adoption of *portions* of the plan (though it is not indicated whether relevant geographical portions had been here adopted). The court concluded:

> . . . subdivision design and improvement obviously include conformance to neighborhood planning and zoning, and it may properly be said that the formulation and acceptance of the uniform conditions in the development of the district constitute the practical adoption of a master plan and zoning requirements therefor.

The dissent thought this an "amazing statement" because it permitted "practical adoption" to supplant the necessity of observing an apparently forthright statutory directive to enact a master plan. Planners *must* think it amazing because it completely ignores the purpose of requiring a plan, *viz.*, (a) as a check on the commission's competence to pass upon plats; (b) as a base for decision; and (c) as a base for review of that decision.

The court seems to attribute to the plan the sole function of achieving equal protection since it is by the following of what has been done in one part of an area that its "practically adopted" plan is made. The plan then is not a goal but a mirror of what has been done in the past!

In discharging this basic reason for the master plan's existence, the statute should require the publishing of supporting studies for these general assumptions and goals. This has the normal advantages of requiring administrative findings of fact. Not only is the body devising the plan thereby apprised of what it is to do, thereby obtaining a background of information necessary for sound regulation, but the studies will permit the community to analyze the alternative goals presented and to come to an intelligent decision. Through the obtaining of data, and its analysis, an awareness of the need for planning (and that its alternative is limitation by course of events of freedom of alternative), and the responsibility it carries, does emerge in the electorate. Furthermore, property owners and the reviewing courts are helped in deciding whether the recommendations make sense or not.

This type of statutory guidance is also fruitful concerning the uses of a plan for the planner listed in Part II. No effort is made at a complete listing of the contents of a plan, nor a stratification as to methods of composition. What is attempted is an instruction to the commission as to the type of goals the citizens should decide about. These are largely generalized relationships of land-use over time which, if established by the master plan, can best carry out the plan's use as an aid for decision-makers.

In the constant struggle of choice between the over-general and the over-detailed, all kinds of gradations are possible. Not only have the present acts been far too generalized, but where they have touched earth, they have tended to be far too concrete. The plan should state the goals—the desirable maximum density of people per area; the question of how to arrange them should be left to the implementing regulation. The singling out by the present acts of *location* of uses seems mistaken. The use of the master plan in some areas of subdivision and street control as a vehicle of legislation should be discouraged. The need for isolating the regulatory from the planning function is overlooked. Unless the two are separated, the broad view will tend to be lost in the day-to-day handling of details. Different types of education and different kinds of people are needed in the different areas of planning and details. And, from the sheer mass of work, bearing in mind the limited resources of staff and time, energies will be devoted to the more immediate, usually more pressing task of the regulating of the land-use activities rather than to the broad, future aspects of such activities.

The stress in the enabling acts on the *location* of the various facilities also appears undesirable. It is the *relation* of airport sites to residential, industrial, and commercial areas that is the long-range planning function. It is not the function of a master plan to examine the territory and pinpoint in detail the sites and locations of the various activities; its job is that of goals and relationships. Blush as one may, it is primarily, as pointed out in Part II, a philosophic guide to a way of life; the pin-pointing of lots, unavoidably necessary in the transmission of planning ideas, is not the optimal use of the plan.

For this reason, the enabling acts should be amended to make clear that the master plan consists of statements of objectives and illustrative materials. The identification of the plan with maps is undesirable, for maps import location. Perhaps the term "diagrams" should be substituted.

Again, if the master plan is to include a zone plan—as is almost universally prescribed by the enabling acts—why not a subdivision plan, street plan, urban redevelopment plan, etc.? This inclusion of the zone plan was probably not thought through. Rather, it is a reflection of the time and conditions surrounding the adoption of the Standard Planning Act when the zoning instrument was regarded not only as the pack-horse but also the only domesticated animal on the planning team. The logic of the Standard Act would lead to the absurd position of a subsuming of all a municipal government's functions to "city planning"—and under the aegis of the planning commission.

Lordship Park Association v. Board of Zoning Appeals[44] is a particularly interesting case for illustrating the serious problem raised if the plan is permitted to assume the function of an official map. The planning board denied approval of a proposed subdivision on the ground that it did not take into account the future construction of an extensive road along the Long Island Sound, a project contemplated in the master plan.[45] On appeal, the court reversed, ordering the town to approve the plaintiff's application. The court stated that the sole ground for disapproving the application was the adoption of the master plan, and the non-conformity with it of the proposed subdivision plat. This, it ruled, was an improper ground. For the master plan's provisions could not be consulted since

  a the Council intended it to be only a "preliminary plan" not definitive of town policy;

  b no regulations were ever adopted compelling compliance with the plan; and

  c no public hearing had been held upon adoption of the plan.

Ground (a) is of course conclusive, if it can be determined that the town council did not intend the plan at all to influence the commission. The court here, however, shows ignorance of the nature of a master plan, at least as it has been propounded by the planning profession:[45a] "The vote of the town council at that time was not to adopt a definitive town plan. It was that the 'preliminary plan' be *adopted and used as a guide for future development subject to future changes*" (emphasis supplied). How else can a master plan operate? Is not the underscored part of the court's statement the traditional definition of the use of a master plan?

Ground (b) is not explained in the opinion and would seem to be another way of stating the court's objection that the plan was not intended by council to be a measure of decision, one that bites into the property rights of a landowner. The court itself must have felt some doubt as to the adequacy of its position for it went on to find a constitutional basis for holding the plan ineffective, a practice usually avoided where adequate non-constitutional grounds for decision are available.[46]

The point of singular interest in the case is that it shows the master plan being used as a device to acquire the kind of restrictive option that legislation respecting the official map usually bestows. In order for the plan to serve this purpose it must partake of the characteristics of the official map. It is entirely possible to have such a "mixed" master plan (precise and definitive of decision in one respect, general and tentative in others), but—especially here where the plan is adopted by the local legislature—the union of function may lead to confusions.

Practically the most important reason for separating out the two functions is to prevent the allotting of the function of a zoning commission or of the formulation of subdivision regulations to the planning commission. This is, perhaps, the worst manifestation of the overloading detail which may warp the planning function. There is the important consideration, in addition, that the planning commission should be immunized, so far as possible, from the dissatisfactions and pressures where an individual owner is hurt by the land-use regulations.

This practical problem inspired the creation of the independent planning commission. To render it immune from the advances of interest groups, present enabling acts provide that the commission shall be composed primarily of private citizens of high standing in the community; their terms of office are staggered, usually made longer than the executive and the legislature. It is important to note that in those cities where it is the planning commission which is put in charge of drawing the zoning ordinance, or of making and enforcing subdivision regulations, this advantage of insulation does not even exist. For the commission can as effectively—or as ineffectively—ward off the interest groups seeking to change the zoning as it can attacks upon the master plan. If this be the premise of the enabling act, the argument for a two-step process of planning and regulating is weakened. It is true, on the other hand, that the composition of the commission may at least tend in the direction of supporting the zoning or other ordinance.

The basic premise of the master plan is that it is long-range: hence, proper planning of land uses will not be distorted by immediate pressures and short-range considerations. This is the recognized contribution of planning to the running of the ordinary affairs of local government. For example, the granting of a variance to run a grocery store may seem unimportant when focussing on the immediate neighborhood. But long-range planning may show that this will result in a flood of such demands, or be inconsistent with the desirable allocation of land uses for commercial purposes in the entire municipality, or hinder the proposed future evolution of the area into a fine residential one. The expressed aim is to make the master plan play a greater part in men's affairs through its control of executory legislation. The relevant inquiry in formulating a planning enabling act then becomes: if the master plan is to have too definite effect upon zoning or subdivision controls, as would follow from invalidating any implementary legislation in conflict with its provisions, will not those same pressures that are said to distort the implementary controls be brought to bear on the master plan? In fact, the end-result may be worse, for the long-range plan may be distorted in the process. Keeping the plan out of vexatious details may reduce the imminence of this threat.

But planning, in an important sense, cannot afford to withstand "pressures"; if it is to have a chance of success, it must attempt to accommodate them. One crucial function of the master plan is to obtain a basis of consent. The act should require the preparation by the experts of a series of alternative plans, on which hearings are held, with the legislature selecting one. Only by continued discussions of alternative courses of action (not in the sense of a legal hearing in which a definite proposal is submitted for argument) can the objectives be formulated, and the goals stated in a way which makes sense to the people. Planning is a leading to understanding and the possibility of community acceptance of the master plan, not, as it has often tended to be, a holier-than-thou attitude with respect to *the* plan. The idea of experts who prepare *the* plan is a static one. Those who are affected by the plan must participate in its making and in carrying it out. And as it changes, as it must, to cope with new conditions and to introduce new concepts, the different interest groups must be won over, or reconciled.

Overloading of detail may also impair public acceptance. This is critical where the plan is regarded as a statement of goals, isolated and illuminated by experts, but selected by the representatives of the community. Once the master plan is limited to findings, principles, and relations, and is prevented from containing detail, it will be more understandable and arouse greater interest. Proposals concerning mass transportation as opposed to the use of private automobiles, or the separation of industries from residences are exciting issues which can command the attention of the voter. The technical details of whether a setback should be ten or twenty feet, or the differences between floor area ratios and other bulk controls are not subjects which can stimulate such debate, nor receive definition and redefinition by the ordinary public. The plan will help achieve the goal of stimulating the people, focussing their interest on planning, and induce them to undertake the responsibility of enacting the planning measures necessary to achieve these goals. Bearing this proposal in mind, a broad statement as to how much daylight shall be provided in each room—not the details of a zoning plan which require much spelling out in scientific terms of angles of elevation—is the proper concern of the master plan. The comprehensive scope of the master plan gives it great imaginative appeal, and is therefore a peculiarly appropriate way of stimulating public interest in the whole city. Indeed, this is an overwhelming reason for the two-step process. The plan should be adopted and amended only after public hearings by the planning commission with further public hearings by the legislature.[47]

V. THE WRITTEN MASTER PLAN

The master plan is an ever changing recordation of the city planner's *end-result thinking*, embodied in a series of diagrams, charts, standards, and policies. Theoretically there is no need for the recordation of these results. The fact that a planning jurisdiction has no deliberately produced "master plan" in progress does not conclusively indicate its absence. Given an individual who (1) is engaged in city planning and (2) has the capacity to retain mentally all the ingredients that make up that process, there would be no need for that body of materials called the master plan. The improbability of such a mnemonic freak[48] indicates, however, that the failure to engage in the task of producing a tangible master plan shows a failure to engage in city planning. In short, the need for the master plan manifests nothing more than the need for city planning itself.

Nor is it a self-proving proposition that the existence of a master plan affects the constitutional validity of specific land-use controls. The injury alleged in each case of land-use regulation must be pitted against the measure's relation to the health, safety, morals, and welfare of the community.[49] Production of facts and arguments to substantiate the relation would not seem to be dependent upon evidence of a master plan: facts and arguments do or do not have strength independent of their embodiment in a tangible plan. It might very well be that the validity of a land-use control would depend upon whether a particular design of development was being pursued; but the existence of such a design can be argued without producing a tangible master plan.[50] (Indeed, the latter is no assurance that the design will be followed for, according to orthodox planning theory, the master plan gives no legal status to its constituent recommendations.) But the fact nevertheless remains that zoning and subdivision litigation gives rise to questions with respect to which courts might well feel the lack of touchstone of decision [and] lends considerable psychological sway to guiding policies which are presented in tangible form. Courts inevitably do lend weight to expertise. True, the same effect can be achieved (as, say, in the proposed New York City Zoning Regulation) by a direct expression in the zoning ordinance of the policy reasons for the insertion of the various provisions, and of how the whole has been shaped to achieve a more efficient and attractive city. Yet the existence of a master plan (assuming the measure in issue conforms thereto) indicates in a more satisfactory fashion that this expertise has really been put to work on the particular problem before the court. Thus the deference it commands is more likely to be brought into play.[51] In this oblique manner the master plan principle may affect planning litigation. Hence, the value of making a master plan both as a basis for winning community consent to any proposed regulations, as well as enhancing the chances for judicial approval of a particular regulation. Hence, also, its importance for the property owner.

This may be the major significance of the master plan today in terms of impact on the property owner, as listed before in Part III. If the plan is regarded not as the vest-pocket tool of the planning commission, but as a broad statement to be adopted by the most representative municipal body—the local legislature—then the plan becomes a law through such adoption. A unique type of law, it should be noted, in that it purports to bind future legislatures when they enact implementary materials. So far as impact is concerned, the law purports to control the enactment of other laws (the so-called implementary legislation) solely. It thus has the cardinal characteristic of a constitution. But unlike that legal form it is subject to amendatory procedures not significantly different from the course followed in enacting ordinary legislation. To enact a nonconforming measure amounts merely to passing the law twice.

At the present stage of development, however, it is on so slender a reed that the touchstone values of the master plan must hang. This may prove disappointing to planners. As Mr. Justice Holmes pointed out,[51a] "there is in all men a demand for the superlative." The yearning for an absolute principle, and a master plan that truly answers all questions is understandable.

Yet this seems the limited function to which the master plan can withdraw in order to perform most effectively in the grand effort to improve American cities: a reminder of the myriad of activities affecting land, their inter-relation, their long-run effects which the day-to-day administrator is too busy to consider. The implementing legislation, on pain of being outside the statute, must conform to its generalized propositions. True, to remove any conflict, the local legislature need but repass the master plan, changed so as to permit the regulation presently desired. But the need of the formal step of amending the plan insures to some degree that the expert's long-range and coordinative contributions are given play in the real world. It may also be desirable—along the lines of the greater than majority vote required by some statutes if the local legislature desires to reverse the planning commission's recommendation concerning a proposed municipal construction—to require that for this purpose the legislature can amend the plan only by a two-thirds or three-quarters vote. This will highlight the master plan's primary role as a constitution. It is a point of view which should be introduced in a courtroom when a particular measure is being assayed.

Existing planning enabling legislation is in large measure based on assumptions of the role of the master plan which have not been clarified, nor established by experience; not enough thought has been given in the planning profession to the crucial phase of planning implementation in the planning process; the proper contents of the plan, as determined by the needs of the particular decision-makers for which it is to serve as a guide, have not been analyzed; on the local government level, indifference is the general reaction to the master plan, largely attributable, it is suggested, to its failure to develop as an authoritative, legally enforceable device. No detailed plan should be adopted except as authorized by and pursuant to the master plan. From the perspective of the lawyer and his client,[52] it is the ultimate impact of the plan on property that determines the vital uses of the master plan, and, therefore, its proper contents. To the degree that machinery is not created for implementing the master plan in the existing world of real property development, society is denied the very real values of the planning process.

Only recently have theory and practice begun to converge in the administration of cities. The search for certainty has warped the function of the master plan; similarly, and paradoxically, the polar principle of flexibility has obviated its usefulness as a standard. An analogy to the field of law is not inappropriate. To the layman, there are clear rules of law that speedily resolve disputes and give ready answers; to the layman, too, the master plan can, with precision, solve all future land-use problems. To the professional, in both instances, life is far more complicated and in too much a state of flux to be handled in so slide-rule a fashion. The lawyer, of all people, should be sympathetic to the planner as he grapples with this heavenly kingdom of the master plan.

NOTES

1 U.S. Department of Commerce, A Standard City Zoning Enabling Act (rev. ed. 1926) [hereinafter cited as Standard Zoning Act]; U.S. Department of Commerce, A Standard City Planning Enabling Act (rev. ed. 1928) [hereinafter cited as Standard Planning Act]. *Cf.* National Municipal League, Model City Charter (5th ed. 1941) (first planning provision, 1925).

2 Since the planning movement is most developed on the municipal level, the phrase city planning is used throughout to indicate over-all physical planning. No functional distinction is intended to be made between the city and other governmental units or regions as respects the need for master planning.

3 Florida, Mississippi, and Wyoming. There are others which are only thin sketches. For a digest of planning enabling legislation see Housing and Home Finance Agency, Comparative Digest of the Principal Provisions of State Planning Laws Relating to Housing, Slum Clearance and Urban Redevelopment (1952).

4 This is the term most frequently employed. "Comprehensive plan," "general plan," "municipal plan," "city plan," "long range plan," or just plain "plan" are also used. But the differing nomenclature appears to have no functional significance. According to Bassett, the term master plan was first used in a report, Recent New York Legislation for the Planning of Unbuilt Areas, Regional Plan of New York and Environs (1926). Its incorporation in the highly influential Standard Planning Act accounts for its presence in most enabling statutes. Heeding the message of Stuart Chase, planners have hotly decried the misdescriptive character of the term master plan; *e.g.,* Stanberry, *Is the Term Master Plan Obsolete?*, American Society of Planning Officials News Letter, June 15, 1949, p. 49, and following discussions elicited in *id.*, Aug. 15, 1949, p. 66, and Oct. 15, 1949, p. 84; Urban Land, Feb. 6, 1947, p. 1; N.Y.-Phila. Chapter, American Institute of Planners, Excerpts from Paknikar Thesis 3 and *passim* (1954) (mimeographed). Essentially the objections have been that the term connotes (1) a single perfectly interrelated plan while in fact it is a series of plans, (2) a rigid design or blueprint rather than a flexible working guide, (3) "slavery and comprehensive authority," (4) a concern with purely physical arrangements and facilities thus leading planners to minimize basic social and economic purposes. "Development plan" (the term used in the British Town and Country Planning Act, 1947, 10 & 11 Geo. 6, c. 51) or "long range comprehensive plan" or "general community plan," the term used by the Housing and Home Finance Agency, are more favored terms. While it is easy enough to recognize a term of art, the relatively uncharted position of the planner may well justify this desire for a more accurate terminology.

5 1947, 10 & 11 Geo. 6, c. 51, §5. For a comparison of the British and American techniques, see Charles M. Haar, Land Planning Law in a Free Society 67–70 (1951).

6 *E.g.*, Pa. Stat. Ann. tit. 53, §9166 (1938); Mass. Ann. Laws c. 41, §81C (1953 Supp.).

7 Ladislas Segoe (with the collaboration of Walter H. Blucher, F. P. Best, F. Stuart Chapin, Jr., and Others), Local Planning Administration (Int'l City Managers' Ass'n, Chicago, 1941).

8 The blame for this is sometimes laid at the door of roving planning consultants. The usually lay composition of the planning commission has dictated the wide use of consultant directed plans. See, *e.g., The Consultant and the City Plan*, American Institute of Planners, Proceedings at Joint Conference 6–10 (1950).

9 There is no more clearly marked area of agreement among commentators than that the master plan is not a static blueprint, *e.g.*, Segoe and Others, *op. cit. supra* note 7, at

29; Edward M. Bassett, The Master Plan 61–64 (1938). Typical of prefatory statements to master plans is the following: "Thus, it should be added that these plans and again the 'best thoughts' applied. If it is recognized that cities are things in the process, then, any planning to be of value must be flexible to a degree and certainly continuing. In this respect, to amplify on a thought of John Dewey, it is not sufficient to achieve a planned City of Fairbanks, but far more . . . a planning City of Fairbanks." R. W. Beck and Associates, Wolf, I Comprehensive Plan, Fairbanks, Alaska (1954).

10 The restatement of the judicial definition of the police power is almost universal.

11 To use the words of the Massachusetts Enabling Act, Mass. Ann. Laws c. 41, §81C (1953 Supp.).

12 Standard Planning Act, *op. cit. supra* note 1, §7.

13 Alfred Bettman, City and Regional Planning Papers (13 Harvard City Planning Studies) 8 (1946).

14 Cal. Gov't Code §65271; see also §65201.

15 Town and Country Planning Act, 1947, 10 & 11 Geo. 6, c. 51, §6.

16 Pa. Stat. Ann. tit. 53, §9166 (1953); *cf.* Ohio Rev. Code §713.02 (1953) ("with a view to the systematic planning of the municipal corporation").

17 Alfred Bettman, in American Society of Planning Officials, Conference on Planning Problems and Administration 60 (1940).

18 See, *e.g.*, Pomeroy, *The Planning Process and Public Participation*, in An Approach to Urban Planning 9–37 (Breese and Whiteman ed. 1953). Since the plan embodies basic goals and policies, an estimate of popular values is a primary necessity. A broad base of public participation is, therefore, to be encouraged.

The enabling acts contain oblique recognitions of this factor. A typical provision is that of Colorado: "The commission shall have power to promote public interest in and understanding of the plan and to that end may publish and distribute copies of the plan or any report and may employ such other means of publicity and education as it may determine." Colo. Stat. Ann. c. 163, §169 (1949). See also Pa. Stat. Ann. tit. 53, §9168.

19 *E.g.*, N.Y. City Charter §197b (adopted by referendum Nov. 3, 1936) (1943); Md. Ann. Code Gen. Laws art. 66B, §17 (1951).

20 The master plan is usually open for public inspection, and may be distributed in summary form. The commission often has the duty to consult and advise with public officials and agencies, educational, professional, and other organizations, and individual citizens, concerning the carrying out of plans.

21 The public relations of planning has of course always been precarious and has elicited varying stratagems. The charge that planning is collectivist regimentation probably caused the following kind of appeal: "Don't think for a minute that you can escape these problems by running away to a new location. . . . You will find that the areas you leave behind breed communism and socialism and increasing dependence on state and federal aid. The only solution is to attack and change these conditions through proper planning." Passaic-Bergen County Planning Ass'n, Let's Face the Facts About the Passaic-Bergen County Area 4 (undated pamphlet).

22 "Master planning seems to me . . . to be absolutely essential for city planning. Indeed I am inclined to believe that on analysis the two will be found to be synonymous, or very nearly synonymous, terms. I am not talking about the application of planning in the current administration, but planning as a guide to be used in current administration on spe cific projects and specific problems." Bettman, *supra* note 17. That planners generally in effect recognize this synonymity, see the collection of remarks on the master plan in EXCERPTS FROM PAKNIKAR THESIS, N.Y.-PHILA. CHAPTER, AMERICAN INSTITUTE OF PLANNERS (1954) (mimeographed) in which one could substitute the word planning for that of master plan, wherever the latter term occurs, and be left with a series of generalized statements on the aims and methods of planning.

23 SEGOE AND OTHERS, *op. cit. supra* note 7, at 44.

24 Note 14 of Bettman's notes on *A Model County Planning Enabling Act*, in NATIONAL RESOURCES COMMITTEE ARCHIVES (Box 159).

25 HOUSING AND HOME FINANCE AGENCY, SLUM CLEARANCE AND URBAN REDEVELOPMENT PROGRAM, THE GENERAL COMMUNITY PLAN: A PRELIMINARY STATEMENT 2 (1950). For the enthusiastic reaction of one planner, see Agle, *Housing and Urban Redevelopment,* in AN APPROACH TO URBAN PLANNING, *op. cit. supra* note 18, at 54–76.

26 *E.g.*, PA. STAT. ANN. tit. 53, §9188 (1953); OHIO REV. CODE §713.12 (1953). *Cf.* ME. REV. STAT. c. 80, §87 (1953) (apparently a 4/5 vote is required for reversal). The provision for an extraordinary majority to overrule the commission is apparently unique in our governmental structure. Yet the planning commission in the exercise of this power is continually referred to merely as a recommendatory or advisory body. Gratton v. Conte, 364 Pa. 578, 73 A.2d 381 (1950) is interesting for the contention there made that even with this increased percentage, the commission could be overruled only when the council specifically found the recommendation to be wholly arbitrary.

27 N.J. STAT. ANN. §40: 55-1.13 (1953 Supp.).

28 N.J. STAT. ANN. §40: 55-1.14 (1953 Supp.). Section 40: 55-1.20 provides that when the master plan for streets has been adopted the board may require that the streets shown on the plat conform in design and in work to the proposals shown on the master plan.

29 THE MASTER PLAN (1938).

30 "It ought to be a plastic plan kept within the confines of the commission." *Id.* at 67–68. "A master plan is nothing more than the easily changed instrumentality which will show a commission from day to day the progress it has made." *Id.* at 5.

31 EDWARD M. BASSETT, FRANK B. WILLIAMS, ALFRED BETTMAN, AND ROBERT WHITTEN, MODEL LAWS FOR PLANNING CITIES, COUNTIES, AND STATES (7 HARVARD CITY PLANNING STUDIES) 40 (1935).

32 See THE MASTER PLAN, *op. cit. supra* note 29, at 118, where Bassett strongly opposes the requirements of a 2/3 or 3/4 vote by the local legislature to override the commission's recommendation. Contrast section 6 of his Model Planning Act with that of Bettman. See page 33 of MODEL LAWS FOR PLANNING CITIES, COUNTIES, AND STATES, *supra.* See also *id.* at 18 and 41.

33 "The writer's view has been that a master plan should not be adopted by any official body except by a planning commission . . . . [otherwise] when the commission desires to alter certain features in it the legislative body must first be persuaded to authorize the change. This is certain to work disastrously because as soon as a plan ceases to be plastic it becomes a quasi-official map which has not been prepared and executed with the care and precision that the law requires in the case of official maps." THE MASTER PLAN, *op. cit. supra* note 29, at 61–62.

34 PA. STAT. ANN. tit. 53, c. 48 (1953).

35 AM. INST. OF ARCHITECTS, REPORT ON ZONING AND THE MASTER PLAN 9 (1944).

36 N.J. STAT. ANN. §40: 55-1.3 (1953 Supp.). The New Jersey act clearly distinguishes between the "master plan" and the "official map"; indeed, it takes the form of two separate acts. The Municipal Planning Act (§§40:55-1.1 to 40:55-1.29) deals with the master plan adopted by the planning commission; the Official Map and Building Permit Act (§§40:55-1.30 to 40:55-1.42) deals with the official map adopted by the local legislature. There is no close nexus between the two, however. True, if the relevant portion of the master plan has been adopted, the legislature must refer the proposed official map (or amendment thereof) to the planning board for its recommendation (§40:55-1.35). But no further statement is made in the act as to the consequences of disapproval by the commission because of conflict with the master plan.

37 *E.g.*, Parsons v. Town of Weatherford, 135 Conn. 24, 60 A.2d 771 (1948); Kuehne v. East Hartford, 136 Conn. 452, 72 A.2d 474 (1950).

38 *E.g.*, TENN. CODE ANN. §3407.10 (Michie Supp. 1943).

39 *E.g.*, TEX. REV. CIV. STAT. ANN. art. 974a (1954). Washington, which has the famous duty to "inquire into the public use and public interest proposed to be served by the establishment" of the subdivision (WASH. REV. CODE §58.16.060 (1951)) nowhere mentions the applicability of the master plan in making such or other determinations.

40 STANDARD PLANNING ACT §6.

41 Fairlawns Cemetery Ass'n v. Zoning Comm'n of Bethel, 138 Conn. 434, 86 A.2d 74 (1952).

42 138 Conn. at 440, 86 A.2d at 77.

43 34 Cal.2d 31, 41–42, 207 P.2d 1, 7 (1949). Specifically, the court upheld the requirement that petitioner dedicate ten feet of land, and set aside an additional ten feet for shrubbery for a boulevard contiguous to his subdivision, but apparently independent of it. *Cf.* Newton v. American Society Co., 201 Ark. 493, 148 S.W.2d 311 (1941).

44 137 Conn. 84, 75 A.2d 379 (1950).

45 The plan had been enacted by the Town Council pursuant to special legislation. This state act provided that the town council of Stratford should have "the power to provide a master plan or plans for the entire town or for any part thereof, which plan or plans may provide for the future layout and location of all highways . . . and, if such plan or plans be adopted, may prescribe by ordinance, rules and regulations, determining the manner in which such plan or plans shall be made, filed, recorded, changed, altered or amended . . . and may by rule and regulation compel compliance with such plan or plans." 137 Conn. at 88, 75 A.2d at 380–381.

45a 137 Conn. at 89–90, 75 A.2d at 381.

46 In holding that a public hearing was constitutionally required the court cited no apposite authority. While most enabling acts require such a hearing upon adoption of a master plan it has never been suggested that a constitutional requirement is present. For comment on this aspect of the decision, see Note, 49 MICH. L. REV. 909 (1950).

47 The New Jersey courts in a series of cases involving actions by municipalities to set aside or enjoin conveyances of lots for failure to obtain plat approval, mentioned as ground for the denial of relief that it had either not been alleged or proved that a master plan had been previously adopted by the planning board. City of Rahway v. Raritan Homes, 21 N.J. Super. 541, 91 A.2d 409 (1952); Borough of Oakland v. Roth, 25 N.J. Super. 32, 95 A.2d 422 (1953); City of Newark v. Padula, 26 N.J. Super, 251, 97 A.2d 735 (1953). In all of these cases, however, it was similarly either not alleged or proved that a planning board had been created by the local governing body. Conclusive weight cannot therefore be attached to the language respecting the plan. The subdivision statute (N.J. STAT. ANN. §40:55-12), however, as regards the master plan was the same as that involved in the *Ayres* case, *supra* note 43. There the court seemed to read the statute as requiring the prior formulation of the master plan.

Fred G. Stickel speaking before a Bergen and Passaic Counties Planning Seminar (reproduced in 62 REGIONAL PLAN ASS'N BULL. 4 (1952)) argued, prior to these cases, that regardless of any specific section of the statute, when read as a whole "you cannot help but see that all actions and powers of the board are based on the premise that its first function and duty, *i.e.*, the preparation and adoption of a master plan, has been done. . . . I realize full well that many boards are exercising their functions without having prepared and adopted some sort of master plan, and they are getting away with it. Why, therefore, should I demur? Because if I am right, and the courts agree with me, planning will receive a definite setback at a very inopportune time."

The newly enacted New Jersey planning statutes effective January 1, 1954 (N.J. STAT. ANN. §40:55-1.1–40:55-1.1.42) remove any doubt and make clear that there is no such requirement. In this respect the new Act follows its evident design throughout to reduce the power of the commission and thereby the status of the plan.

48 Formal embodiment is essential to lend it requisite status, as concerns public relations, and to impress its existence and significance on the lawmaker. Most important, however, is that there be in existence definite evidence of the substantive elements of the plan.

49 The classic statement in the zoning field is, of course, Village of Euclid v. Ambler Realty Co., 272 U.S. 365 (1926). A nearly exhaustive list of zoning cases is contained in 117 A.L.R. 1117–1148 (1938).

50 This may be what the majority was driving at in Ayres v. City Council of Los Angeles, *supra* note 43.

51 See, *e.g.*, Berkfield Realty Co. v. City of Orange, 12 N.J. Super. 192, 79 A.2d 326 (1951).

51a Holmes, *Natural Law*, 32 HARV. L. REV. 40 (1918).

52 The famous "bad man" suggested by Mr. Justice Holmes as the focus for understanding the meaning of law? See Holmes, *The Path of the Law*, 10 HARV. L. REV. 457, 459 (1897).

THREE. COMPREHENSIVE PLANNING—SUGGESTED READINGS

Branch, Melville C. 1985. *Comprehensive City Planning, Introduction & Explanation.* Chicago: American Planning Association.

Bryson, John. 1988. "A Strategic Planning Process for Public and Non-Profit Organizations." *Long Range Planning* 21, 1.

Chapin, F. Stuart, and Edward J. Kaiser. 1979. *Urban Land Use Planning*, 3d ed. Urbana: The University of Illinois Press.

Howard, Ebenezer. 1946. *Garden Cities of Tomorrow.* London: Faber.

Kent, T. J. 1964. *The Urban General Plan.* San Francisco: Chandler.

So, Frank S., and Judith Getzels, eds. 1988. *The Practice of Local Government Planning*, 2d ed. Washington, DC: International City Management Association.

4

LAND USE, ZONING, AND GROWTH MANAGEMENT

The Purpose of Zoning

Richard Babcock

Since the publication of this book, significant changes have occurred in both the purposes and the techniques of zoning and land-use regulation. The increase in the importance of centralized authorities at the regional, state, and federal levels is especially noteworthy. Nevertheless, "The Purpose of Zoning" is valuable for its clear, cogent discussion of the planning theory and the property-value theory of zoning. Richard Babcock observes that from its early days in the 1920s, zoning has been used primarily as a tool for protecting homogeneous, single-family residences from incursions. Yet, according to Babcock, zoning is, first and foremost, a "process," whose principles must be consistent with goals determined by the political process.

"In the perfect market, natural zoning would result."

Ratcliff

"The witness, I have inferred, takes the position that good zoning requires that this property-holder . . . should be protected against himself."

Record on Appeal. Corthouts v. Town of Newington, 140 Conn. 284 (1953)

The most fun as well as the safest path for the amateur commentator is to keep things anecdotal. But even the practicing attorney, faced with the duty to discharge immediate assignments, is not free from the impulse to point the way. Hence my intention in this and the following chapters to consider a few of the issues underlying most disputes involving public regulation of private land.

Why do we have zoning anyway?

It is indicative of the chaotic nature of the subject that there is no generally accepted answer to this question. At the start I suggested that zoning caught on as an effective technique to further an eminently conservative purpose: the protection of the single-family house neighborhood. In spite of all the subsequent embellishments that objective remains paramount. As might be expected, such a motive is rarely articulated as a rationale for this popular device, either by the supporters or critics of zoning.

There are, however, some plausible theories offered in support of zoning. I am not concerned here with the deeper psychological motivations which drive many of the backers of zoning. These may vary from a fear of Negro infiltration to a vague identification of zoning with "good government." While they cannot be ignored by anyone practicing in this field, I am concerned here with more rational purposes of zoning.

We can dismiss the early legal fictions which were created to validate zoning under the jurisprudence of the 1920's. The early proponents of zoning claimed that the single-family district was insulated to prevent the spread of fires. Minimum house size requirements were supposedly related to public health. Billboards were said to endanger public morals because of the promiscuous activities which took place behind them. No one really believed these fictions in 1920 and no one believes them today. And today our courts have progressed beyond the need for this type of shibboleth.

I have found in circulation two relatively rational theories of the purpose of zoning which I refer to as the "property value" theory and the "planning" theory. For the purpose of clarifying the issues let me state these theories in a generalized fashion.

THE PROPERTY VALUE THEORY

To most real estate brokers and promoters, and to some land economists, lawyers, and judges, zoning is a means of maximizing the value of property. The use of property, under this theory, is basically determined by the dynamics of the market. Denver attorney George Creamer speaks for this view:

> The dynamics of a community, so long as that community remains economically free, dictate the uses to which land will inevitably gravitate, whatever expedient of zoning be employed. Zoning otherwise employed than as a braking mechanism is probably misapplied, and, historically, is probably futile.[1]

Although the exponents of this theory purport to believe in the dominance of free market forces, they are strong supporters of zoning. This paradox can be understood only by the realization that under this theory the "proper" zoning of property is determined by market forces. Zoning is merely an adjunct to the market mechanism.

The basic axiom of this theory is that each piece of property should be used in the manner that will insure that the sum of all pieces of property will have maximum value, as determined by market forces. In other words, every piece of property should be used in the manner that will give it the greatest value (i.e., its "highest and best use") without causing a corresponding decrease in the value of other property. The zoning ordinance can achieve this goal by prohibiting the construction of "nuisances," provided the common-law concept of nuisance is extended to include any use which detracts from the value of other property to a degree significantly greater than it adds to the value of the property on which it is located.

In the Property Value theory, for every piece of land there is a "proper" zoning classification. Above every town there exists a Platonic ideal zoning map, waiting to be dropped into place. This map shows for each piece of property the use or uses which will give to the sum of all property the greatest total value. This theory is what enables many judges to determine the proper zoning classification for property based solely on the estimates of appraisers of the value of the property and surrounding property under various zoning classifications. The Property Value theory requires only ordinary arithmetic, and has the appeal of all simple solutions to complex problems.

A corollary of the Property Value theory is that the planners tend to be meddlers who, by their tinkering, upset the natural market forces. Zoning, properly concerned, does no more than protect the market from "imperfections" in the natural operation of supply and demand. Professor Richard Ratcliff, economist at the University of Wisconsin, is an outspoken proponent of this view:

> We start with the premise that the arrangement of community land uses should be the product of social preferences; and that, but for the imperfections of the real estate market, the market interactions of demand and supply would create a city so organized. Thus we view city planning as a device for releasing the basic forces of demand rather than inhibiting them.[2]

If Professor Ratcliff's outlook had too much the appearance of economic determinism, it remained for Allison Dunham, University of Chicago law professor, to soften Ratcliff's dictum and to provide a rationale by which all local control over private development could be justified: public control in all events is justified, but in some cases there must be compensation to the landowner.

Dunham, the lawyer, sensed the social flaw in economist Ratcliff's theory. "With respect to private land use decisions," he said, "considerations of economy and efficiency are reflected in the market price, but no beneficial or detrimental impact of a land use upon other lands is reflected in the market for a particular land use."[3] The public may take (regulate) says Dunham but "[t]he public need not compensate an owner when it takes (restricts) his privileges of ownership in order to prevent him from imposing a cost upon others; but when the state takes (uses or restricts) his property rights in order to obtain a public benefit it must compensate him."

As for the role of the planner, Dunham decrees: "The city planner may interfere with and supervise the land use decisions of a private developer only because of the interaction of one land use upon another and only then where the private developer's land use adversely affects others."

I am not sure I understand what he means by "interaction" but I suspect Professor Dunham is saying that any control by a municipality over private land use is justified by that municipality's goals, but that development cannot be forbidden or regulated without compensation unless it has a direct and demonstrably adverse impact on neighboring land. The community may without compensation stop X from developing a subdivision of half-acre lots if the consequence would be overflowing septic tanks ("a cost upon others"); but the community cannot, without compensation require Y to build only on three-acre lots if three-acre lots are required not for reasons of public health but simply because a majority happen to prefer that kind of living.

There are two difficulties with this market-oriented theory, even with Dunham's cash sweetener.

In the first place, under this theory any land use which unduly lowers the value of neighboring property has to be a "nuisance." Whether the municipality, in order to regulate, should pay or need not pay depends on the degree of adverse impact. But the blind concentration on property values can hide less savory values that may not be entitled to protection, whether by uncompensated regulation or by cash payment. The Property Value theory does not ask why a particular development has an adverse impact on values of neighboring property.

New Jersey lawyer-planner Norman Williams illustrates:

> When the argument is made that property values will be affected what is meant is simply that some factor is present which some people may dislike, and which may therefore tend to result in a net reduction in the number of people interested in buying property in the area affected—thus tending to push values down. The real question is always a simple one—what is the factor which is involved? Some factors which affect property values (or which are thought to do so) are legitimate subjects for public regulation, by zoning or otherwise; others are not. For example, the invasion of factories and the movement of Negroes into a residential neighborhood both may be thought to affect property values. Yet one is obviously a proper subject for zoning protection, while the other is not. The fact that property values may be affected gives reason to look into the situation, but by itself tells nothing about whether governmental protection is appropriate.[4]

To use zoning as a tool solely for protecting the values of neighboring property is an extreme form of parochialism our society cannot afford in the twentieth century. As Finley Peter Dunne pointed out, it is possible to cheer too loudly for the rights of property:

> But I'm with th' rights iv property, d'ye mind. Th' sacred rights an' th' divine rights. A man is lucky to have five dollars; if it is ten, it is his dooty to keep it if he can; if it's a hundred, his right to it is th' right iv silf-dayfinse; if it's a millyon, it's a sacred right; if it's twinty millyon, it's a divine right; if it's more thin that, it becomes ridickilous. In anny case, it mus' be proticted. Nobody mus' intherfere with it or down comes th' constichoochion, th' army, a letther fr'm Baer an' th' wrath iv Hivin.[5]

I am disturbed for another reason by the Ratcliff–Dunham apology for zoning. Both spokesmen do not define the scope of the "public" whose interest justifies some public limitation on the free market forces. There appears in their thinking a view that private development can be limited by regulation (or compensation) only where there is a direct and adverse impact upon a neighbor's land, or upon the municipality in which the land happens to be located. Both views assume a parochial definition of the "public" that will be affected by land development. Ratcliff sees the "imperfections of the real estate market" as equivalent to essentially local forces and Dunham obviously is concerned with impact upon land uses in the immediate neighborhood. In the former case, I suspect the emphasis is explained by a lack of interest in regional consequences of local land-use development; the Dunham amendment suggests not indifference but a firm rejection of the idea that metropolitan or regional interests have any place in the municipal regulation or, indeed, the taking of private land.

I believe that in many cases the reasonableness of zoning should be determined by reference to factors far more complex than a simple balancing of values of neighboring property, whether or not cash boot is tossed on to the scales. This doubt leads to my disenchantment with the other doctrinal justification for zoning.

THE PLANNING THEORY

I suppose that every city planning student is required to write on the blackboard a hundred times the Planner's Oath: "Zoning is merely a tool of planning." Walter Blucher asked some years ago if the zoning tail was wagging the planning dog. The question points up the view of the planner that zoning is only a minor appendage to the essential body, city planning.

Standard planning dogma requires that a planner invited to prepare a municipal zoning ordinance go through the following ritual: First, a very junior planner makes a survey of the municipality and prepares a map showing the land uses. On the basis of this and reams of other data, and of consultations with community leaders, a very senior planner prepares a "comprehensive plan" for the community, which indicates the community's idea of what it wishes its future to be. The planner then sets forth a number of means for "implementing" the plan, including, typically, a capital improvements program, a subdivision control law, and a zoning ordinance. In the planner's view, understandably, the zoning ordinance is merely one of a number of methods of effectuating an overall municipal plan.

I do not suggest that this exercise should be abandoned. It is a laudable if not legally essential exercise for a community to analyze and articulate its communal goals and objectives before it enacts controls over the use of private land. This discipline, required by law if not in fact in England, has not achieved the responsible status it should have in this country. This is Harvard Professor Haar's "impermanent constitution," the comprehensive municipal plan. It is said that only when the community has, in its plan, set forth and exposed to public scrutiny its goals and desires can the arbiter, required to settle land use disputes, measure the reasonableness of the implementing ordinances. Professor Haar explains:

> To the professional planner, the dependence of zoning upon planning is relatively simple and clear. The city master plan is a long-term general outline of projected development; zoning is but one of the many tools which may be used to implement the plan. Warnings have constantly emanated from the planners that the two must not be confused. . . .
>
> The legal implications of this theory seem manifest. A city undertaking to exercise the land regulatory powers granted to it by state enabling legislation should be required initially to formulate a master plan, upon which regulatory ordinances, of which the zoning ordinance is but one, would then be based. Such ordinances could be judicially tested not only by constitutional standards of due process and equal protection, but also by their fidelity to the specific criteria of the master plan.[6]

Thereby is born the "principle" that a zoning ordinance must (should) be based upon a plan.

What, then, is a Plan? Hugh Pomeroy defined it this way:

Well—what do we mean by comprehensive plan? The nearest I can come to defining it is this: it is a plan that makes provision for all the uses that the legislative body of that municipality decides are appropriate for location somewhere in that municipality. That's Number 1. Number 2, it makes provision for them at the intensities of use that the legislative body deems to be appropriate. In Number 3—the locations that the legislative body deems to be appropriate. That is the mechanical concept. Beyond that the plan should consistently represent developmental objectives for the community. And if you can have a good enough statement of developmental objectives, then I don't think that a deviation from a particular mechanical device such as regulations by districts—the departure from that—violates the attribute of comprehensiveness that consists of endeavoring to carry out these objectives.

Perhaps what troubles me about this definition is not what it says but what it implies. The corollary to this precept, accepted by many lawyers (though not Professor Haar), and by most planners and laymen is that the validity of local land-use laws should be measured *only* by their consistency with the municipal plan. This is no more of a valid purpose for zoning than is the concept of the use district. The public disclosure of municipal objectives may be a necessary first step by which equal treatment of similarly situated individuals within the municipality can be determined. To this extent the municipal plan serves as a useful intramural yard-stick for the municipal regulations. The local plan in this sense is imperative as a device to bring some consistency and impartiality in local administrative decisions among residents of the same municipality.

It is an error, however, to dignify the municipal plan with more authority than this limited function. But to measure the validity of zoning by the degree to which it is consistent with a municipal plan does just that. The municipal plan may be just as arbitrary and irresponsible as the municipal zoning ordinance if that plan reflects no more than the municipality's arbitrary desires. If the plan ignores the responsibility of the municipality to its municipal neighbors and to landowners and taxpayers who happen to reside outside the municipal boundaries, and if that irresponsibility results in added burdens to other public agencies and to outsiders, whether residents or landowners, then a zoning ordinance bottomed on such a plan should be as vulnerable to attack as a zoning ordinance based upon no municipal plan.

The trouble, then, with the Planning Theory of zoning is that by deifying the municipal plan it enshrines the municipality at a moment in our history when every social and economic consideration demands that past emphasis on the municipality as the repository of the "general welfare" be rejected.

It has to be conceded, however, that zoning has been a huge success in most of our suburbs if the Planning Theory of zoning means doing with land what the municipality alone wants done, provided it announces its intentions in advance. If planning is designed to provide that environment which a majority of the voters within the boundaries of a particular municipality believe they want, then zoning has been remarkably successful and I predict it will prosper. Indeed, if planning is intended to achieve not only physical amenities but also to accomplish some unstated or whispered social and political objectives, zoning has been far more effective than its originators dared expect. In this sense, far from being a "negative tool" zoning has been a positive force shaping the character of the municipality to fit its frequently vague but nevertheless powerful preconceptions.

If, when we speak of planning, we postulate objective standards for physical environment and let the social chips fall where they may, then zoning as an implement of planning has not merely failed but has been instrumental in the failure of planning. This failure is pernicious. Like another Noble Experiment with about the same birthdate as zoning, it erodes the civic conscience by permitting us to wrap our selfish anti-democratic aims in a garment of public interest.

I suppose what really disturbs me is that because zoning is the most universal of all the legal tools for shaping the character of the municipality, any unwise use of the process has a far greater impact upon our national character than does the abuse of a less widely employed device for control of land use. The zoning power is so fragmented that its abuse does not have a dramatic impact. Dollar venality in the execution of one urban redevelopment project will receive strident and outraged attention from the metropolitan press, while daily evidence of intellectual dishonesty and moral corruption in the application of zoning in our suburban areas is accepted as a civic norm. If you are of the school which has as its premise that each of the hundreds of municipal units in a politically fragmented system of local government may regulate as it pleases and exclude whom and what it chooses to exclude, then you should embrace the present state of affairs and the existence of a municipal plan is sufficient. If, however, you suspect, as I do, that the current practice impinges not merely upon property rights but upon some less tangible values which are important in a democratic society, then it is time to redefine our goals and to restate the Planning Theory of zoning in the hope that this exercise may lead us to reshape our implements for land-use control.

In my opinion there can never be any single foreordained purpose of zoning. Both the Planning Theory and the Property Value Theory of zoning set forth valid goals for some people in some situations. Their proponents err only when they set up their hypothesis as the one valid purpose of zoning. They err when they try to turn zoning into a tool to implement only their own local purposes.

Zoning needs no purposes of its own. Zoning is no longer a "movement" like the Single Tax or Prohibition; zoning is a process. It is that part of the political technique through which the use of private land is regulated. When zoning is thought of as a part of the governmental process it is obvious that it can have no inherent principles separate from the goals which each person chooses to ascribe to the political process as a whole.

While we should not insist that zoning have "purposes" we can insist that the zoning process be exercised in accord with certain principles, that the "means" if not the "ends" of zoning be governed by neutral principles. This necessitates an inquiry into (a) whether zoning has spawned its own indigenous set of principles, or whether it is subject merely to the principles applicable to other forms of governmental action; and (b) whether it makes sense to restrict the zoning debate to only two parties: the landowner and the local municipality.

NOTES

1 George L. Creamer, "The Social Paradox of Zoning and Land Controls in an Expandiing Urban Economy," 39 *Dicta* 269, 290 (1962).

2 Ratcliff, *Real Estate Analysis*, p. 328.

3 Allison Dunham, "A Legal and Economic Basis for City Planning," 58 *Colum. L. Rev.* 650, 658–59 (1958).

4 Norman Williams, "Planning Law and Democratic Living," 20 *Law & Contemp. Prob.* 317, 334 (1955).

5 Finley Peter Dunne, "On Property Rights," in *Mr. Dooley on the Choice of Law,* ed. by Edward J. Bander (Charlotteville, Va.: Michie Co., 1963), p. 74

6 Charles M. Haar, "In Accordance with a Comprehensive Plan," 20 *Law & Contemp. Prob.* 317, 334 (1955).

Understanding American Land Use Regulation Since 1970

Frank J. Popper

Professor of Urban Planning and Geography, Rutgers University

Frank J. Popper examines the recent emergence of centralized, as opposed to local, land-use regulations at the regional, state, and federal levels in the United States. After analyzing and disputing two prevailing explanations for this centralization, Popper offers an alternate interpretation for the trend, one involving practical adaptiveness and political staying power. He concludes that "the right to make particular regulatory decisions shifts unpredictably over time from one level of government to another. No principle of administrative rationality, constitutional entitlement, economic efficiency, or even ideological predisposition truly determines the governmental locus of decisions" (p. 154). This article received the 1989 Award for the Best Article in the *Journal of the American Planning Association*.

Land use regulation has probably changed more since 1970 than in any comparable period in the nation's history. Two decades ago American land use regulation consisted almost entirely of local zoning; it no longer does. Instead, it has become increasingly centralized—that is, more likely to originate with regional, state, and federal agencies rather than with local ones (Healy and Rosenberg 1979; Popper 1981; DeGrove 1984). The changes in regulation have transformed American planning: its practice, its aims, its role in American government, even its attractiveness as a career. But planners have not grasped the extent of the regulatory changes, their political meaning, or their professional consequences.

Reprinted by permission of the *Journal of the American Planning Association* 54, 3, Summer 1988.

Two competing interpretations—one liberal, the other conservative—now attempt to explain the recent history of American land use regulation. The liberal view maintains that the environmental shortcomings of local land use regulation, especially zoning, led to the creation in the early 1970s of new regional, state, and federal regulatory powers. Those policies, liberals contend, were largely unable to withstand the conservative onslaught—against centralized regulation, against bureaucracy, against environmentalism—that began in the middle 1970s and crested with the Reagan administration. Thus the liberals maintain that the new centralized regulatory programs never got a chance to prove themselves. Like the local controls they were intended to supplement, they amounted to insufficient land use regulation.

The conservative perspective, on the other hand, argues that the new initiatives, far from being insufficient, created so many and such potent centralized regulatory mechanisms that the nation in effect had serious federal regulation of land use by the late 1970s and still has it in the late 1980s. The conservatives, however, maintain that the public reacted against what it rightly saw as bureaucratic overreaching: it brought conservatives to power to try to restrain the new programs, and the battle to neutralize them continues to this day. The conservatives argue that the programs in fact got a chance to prove themselves and did so too well. The conservatives believe that the centralized initiatives' key political difficulty was not that they constituted too little land use regulation as the liberals maintain, but that they constituted too much.

In this article I first examine the emergence of centralized land use regulation in America. Then I present the two existing interpretations of the overall experience of centralized regulation.[1] Next I suggest a way to reconcile the interpretations through an alternative explanation that fits the facts and explains events since 1970 better than the other two. I take a less ideological, more pragmatic approach: I argue that centralized regulation has unobtrusively succeeded in ways neither liberals nor conservatives appreciate. In particular, it has overcome its initial practical disadvantage of unfamiliarity, achieved wide (though often specialized) application, received substantial public acceptance, and even attained a measure of acquiescence from land use conservatives, including those in the Reagan administration. I conclude by exploring this revisionist interpretation's surprisingly optimistic implications for the future of American land use regulation. Much of the interpretation draws on but differs from my previous work (Popper 1981), which is to say that I changed my mind. I used to subscribe to the liberals' interpretation, but now I find the revisionist one more persuasive.

THE RISE OF CENTRALIZED REGULATION

There may never have been a time when it was as good to be an American city planner or land use lawyer as the late 1960s and early 1970s. Planning was coming alive; huge segments of the public were interested in it and its possible contributions, probably for the first time in American history. The post-World War II building boom, culminating in the record-high development rates of the late 1960s, had produced a professionally exhilarating set of environmental problems. Even more exciting, planners, land use lawyers, and their political allies had new and apparently practical solutions to those problems, which the public would accept.

There was no denying the magnitude of the country's land use difficulties. Development projects of all kinds—commercial, residential, industrial, and governmental—were getting bigger and polluting more. The interstate highway system, begun in 1956 and reaching completion from the middle 1960s on, had created vast new stretches of urban or potentially urban land. Too much of it seemed to be succumbing to formless sprawl and strip development, or to shoddily built leisure home projects, ruinous strip mines, and polluting power plants. The nation's countryside was urbanizing rapidly and unattractively.

Under the pressures that such developments caused, long-standing deficiencies in local land use regulation became clear. Zoning, the action arm of local planning and the nation's most prevalent mechanism for land use control, seemed especially fallible. Most zoning agencies and ordinances had originated in the 1920s and 1930s, and were often inadequate to cope with the 1960s' development. They could not handle huge suburban residential projects that might affect dozens of rapidly growing localities beyond the boundaries of the regulating one. They could not deal with big energy facilities that might have regional, state, or even national impacts. They could not deal with large, complicated public works projects. In all such cases lone communities were dealing with land use questions of regional or state impacts but were making their decisions without consideration of surrounding communities and often causing harm.

Another reason local planning and zoning did not work well was that in most of the country, particularly in the small, rural communities now in the path of urban expansion, relevant laws had never really existed in the first place. Such communities espoused the American ideal of rugged individualism; many of their residents thought zoning verged on socialism. Some excellent examples of that viewpoint come from the Appalachian part of New York (Robbins 1974) and from the Missouri and Arkansas Ozarks (Lewis 1976).

In 1971 George Hartzog, director of the National Park Service, became concerned about the proliferation of commercial development on the edge of Mammoth Cave National Park in Kentucky. "I talked to those people down there about zoning," he told writer John McPhee. "'Zoning?' they said. 'Zoning?' I had the impression that I was in a foreign land" (McPhee 1977: 258). In 1971 only 30 percent of Kentucky's cities and 20 percent of its counties had zoning. Even in seemingly more urban New York state, only 40 percent of the cities had zoning, and the counties had no zoning powers at all (RuBino and Wagner 1972: 9, 16). In many rural places where zoning laws did exist, they were undemanding, unenforced, or ignored (Williams 1975).

To counter that ragged local performance, a loose coalition of environmentalists, city planners, land use lawyers, state and federal officials, progressive business people and developers, and citizen activists of all kinds emerged, bearing an alternative—more precisely, a supplement—to local land use regulation: centralized land use regulation. The coalition's goal was new regulation that would operate at higher levels of government and would apply mainly to projects that were large or in environmentally sensitive areas.

The Rockefeller Brothers Fund Task Force on Land Use and Urban Growth produced a report, *The Use of Land*, which became one of the best-known documents of the movement for higher-level regulation (Reilly 1973). It declared, "Important developments should be regulated by governments that represent all the people whose lives are likely to be affected by it, including those who could benefit from it as well as those who would be harmed by it. Where a regulatory decision significantly affects people in more than one locality, state, regional, or even federal action is necessary" (Reilly 1973: 27). From the late 1960s well into the 1970s, that approach received the imprimaturs of the nation's leading land use lawyer, Chicago's Richard Babcock (1966), the National Commission on Urban Problems (1968), the American Society of Planning Officials (Heeter 1969), Ralph Nader's Study Group on Land Use in California (Fellmeth 1973), the American Bar Association (Fishman 1977), and the American Law Institute (1977). In yet another of the period's authoritative-influential documents, sponsored by the Council on Environmental Quality, Babcock's law partners Fred Bosselman and David Callies called the rising movement "The Quiet Revolution in Land Use Control" (Bosselman and Callies 1972).

As an exercise in intellectual advocacy, interest-group politics, and the self-advancement of the planning profession, the Quiet Revolution was remarkably effective. In 1969 only Hawaii—a state whose development patterns, land market, and local government structure differed deeply from those of the rest of the country—had a state law regulating land use, and it had been passed in 1961, another era entirely. By 1975 the Quiet Revolution had achieved at least 20 new environmentally-oriented state land use laws, mostly in the northeast, the upper midwest, and the far west. Those laws variously regulated the siting and operation of all large development projects, particular kinds of large projects such as power plants or strip mines, or projects in environmentally sensitive places such as coasts, mountains, wetlands, and farmlands (Rosenbaum 1976; Healy and Rosenberg 1979; Popper 1981; DeGrove 1984). Thirty-seven states had new programs of statewide planning or statewide review of local regulatory decisions (Council of State Governments 1976: 23–26).

At the federal level the Quiet Revolution succeeded in obtaining programs where the federal government funded state ones. Through the 1972 Coastal Zone Management Act, the U.S. Department of Commerce gave the 30 Atlantic, Pacific, Gulf, and Great Lakes states grants totalling about $16 million a year to plan for and regulate coastal development. The 1977 Surface Mine Control and Reclamation Act gave the states $110 million annually in Interior Department grants to regulate strip mining. The 1970 Clean Air Act, the 1972 Clean Water Act, and the 1974 Safe Drinking Water Act gave the states a total of nearly $3 billion yearly in Environmental Protection Agency grants to carry out regulatory and construction programs with complex but definite land use implications, including controls on the location of new projects (Natural Resources Defense Council 1977: 40–97). The 1973 Flood Disaster Protection Act required that states and localities regulate development in flood plains before they (and their residents) could buy federal flood insurance or receive federal flood disaster aid (Natural Resources Defense Council 1977: 121–32).

It is hard now to recall the euphoric excitement of the land use community in the early 1970s, but it was wonderful while it lasted. Congress even came close to passing the ultimate Quiet Revolution legislation, the National Land Use Policy Act—which amounted to an extension of the Coastal Zone Management Act to all noncoastal areas of the country or, from another perspective, a national expansion of the state comprehensive laws regulating all large developments, such as those in Florida, Oregon, and Vermont (Plotkin 1987: 149–200).

The National Land Use Policy Act, as the epitome of the Quiet Revolution, would have given federal grants ($100 million annually in the 1975 bill, probably coming from the Interior Department) to draw up statewide land use plans, devise procedures to protect environmentally sensitive areas, and regulate big private developments and public works. The legislation was introduced under varying forms (and names) every year from 1968 to 1975 by liberal Democrats such as Arizona Representative Morris Udall and the late Washington Senator Henry Jackson. It reached its high tide in 1974, when the Senate passed it by a wide margin, as it had in 1972 and 1973. But the House rejected it by seven votes when President Nixon withdrew his support, reputedly in a bid for conservative votes to prevent impeachment (Lyday 1976: 40).

Planning, legal, and environmental organizations closely watched the act's progress. As a low-ranking staff member at the Chicago headquarters of the American Society of Planning Officials (ASPO) in the early 1970s, I knew that high-ranking ASPO staff members made nearly daily telephone calls to Washington to check on the bill. I assumed that much more was done at the American Institute of Planners (now merged with ASPO to form the American Planning Association), which was in Washington and, unlike ASPO, had a lobbying operation. An ASPO deputy executive director believed the act's passage would increase planners' average income by $2,000. Land use lawyers would get even more. Yet the planners, lawyers, and environmentalists were also animated by a truly public-spirited desire to show how well they would perform if given the opportunity. In 1974 the act's narrow defeat seemed to them an annoyance that would soon be rectified. Their chance would come again.

THE LIBERAL POINT: TOO LITTLE CENTRALIZED REGULATION

Land use liberals now interpret the 1974 defeat of the National Land Use Policy Act as a near miss, after which the cause of centralized land use regulation went into decline. The liberals argue that there never was enough centralized regulation, never had been, probably never would be. They believe the years since 1974 have not been good to the Quiet Revolution; in a noisy counterrevolution, the political climate has turned hostile. The reasons are familiar: a more difficult and a volatile economy (for instance, in the energy and agricultural sectors), a resurgent conservatism, strained government finances, growing public distrust of such devices as regulation and federal grants in all fields of policy, a disenchantment with government itself.

The liberal perspective emphasizes that in recent years states have passed few new land use laws and most states still lack genuinely strong ones. Moreover, in the states that have them, the regulations have often been weakened in scope, budgets, staffing, and enforcement (Popper 1981: 116–53, 165–68; DeGrove 1984: 217–31, 308–31). Throughout the 1970s, for instance, the Florida comprehensive and California coastal programs had no enforcement staff whatever (Popper 1981: 119). Sometimes the state regulatory bodies deliberately effaced themselves, lowered their bureaucratic profile. Beginning in the late 1970s, for example, the Florida and Vermont land use programs shortened their applications and combined them with those of other state environmental agencies. They also began to hold joint hearings with state, local, and federal agencies.

By the early 1980s it was distinctly more possible in many places than it had been five years earlier for conservative state and local politicians to successfully take positions against centralized land use regulation. In 1972 Governor Ronald Reagan opposed a voters' initiative to create state commissions that would regulate development along the California coast. But when the initiative passed, he made predominantly environmentalist appointments to the commissions that were in regions where such sentiment was powerful—for instance, the areas centered around San Francisco and Santa Cruz. By contrast, in his 1982 gubernatorial race California Republican George Deukmejian made the coastal commissions a special target. Once in office, he substantially reduced their personnel and funding. In 1987, for instance, he cut $400,000 out of a budget of $5 million and closed the Santa Cruz and Santa Barbara offices.

At the federal level, there was a comparable deterioration of early 1970s planning hopes and of the federal support of state regulatory programs. At the urging of many developers and localities, the Reagan administration in effect abandoned, for example, the Coastal Zone Management Act. The administration never asked for funding for it in any of its annual budget proposals; Congress had to supply the funding every year. The Reagan-era directors of the program were always publicly committed to terminating it. Many talented staffers left and their jobs went unfilled. Some operations, such as those that supplied special regulatory funds for states whose coasts were experiencing intense energy development, have been terminated (Mitchell 1986: 325–26). The Clean Air, Clean Water, Safe Drinking Water, Flood Disaster Protection, and Surface Mine Control and Reclamation acts have suffered similar neglect (Hays 1987: 501–4).

Some planners, lawyers, and environmentalists experienced a nostalgia for the National Land Use Policy Act (for example, Strong 1981). The feeling was irrational, but understandable. The legislation seemed the great might-have-been of American land use planning and the Quiet Revolution, the missed opportunity that would have convinced the public that centralized regulation could deliver something it wanted. In 1978, three years after the bill had lost any chance of passage, a group of land use professionals established the American Land Forum (I later joined its board), in large part to keep alive the impulses that animated the National Land Use Policy Act.

Thus in 1983 the forum (which by then had become the American Land Resource Association) held an open meeting at its Bethesda, Maryland, headquarters on the topic "Toward a Land Resource Policy Agenda." Charles Little, founder of the forum, suggested, "I'd like to reopen something that really interested me. Is there a piece of overarching legislation that isn't like the National Land Use Planning and Policy Act of 1974 but is something we can concoct here that would provide the policy context for all of these locally wonderful things to happen? . . . I don't want to lose sight of our need to have a single, consensus-building kind of approach that would be something we would take to the doorstep of Congress and say, 'Look, here's exactly what you ought to do.'" Neil Sampson, head of the National Association of Conservation Districts, then observed, "There is some virtue in reconceptualizing the land use bill, in tearing it apart and seeing what it was and wasn't." It was left to me to be "bothered by the continual returning to the idea of a National Land Use Policy Act or redoing it or in fact reconceptualizing it. That strikes me as the political equivalent of never getting over whomever it was you had a crush on when you were seventeen. There's a lack of consensus here about what overarching idea would replace the 1974-style approach" (American Land Forum 1983: 21–22). That was a minority opinion. The clear sense of the meeting was that the country needed more centralized land use regulation.

THE CONSERVATIVE COUNTERPOINT: TOO MUCH CENTRALIZED REGULATION

Land use conservatives—most developers, many local officials, nearly all libertarians, and certainly political figures such as Ronald Reagan and James Watt—see the matter differently. They emphasize the vast amount of centralized land use legislation that has passed since 1970, as well as the bureaucratic toils in which the laws have enmeshed unsuspecting homeowners, developers, and localities. The conservatives like to count up numbers of laws, the contradictions between them, and the resulting long application-processing times that lead to regulatory horror stories. Conservatives then tell the stories to embarrass and cow the agencies administering the laws (Porter 1986; Pacific Legal Foundation 1985).[2]

The conservatives can clearly produce strong evidence of excessive regulation, often out of the mouths of liberals. Chicago lawyer Fred Bosselman, shortly after the last defeat of the National Land Use Policy Act (which he helped draft), wrote that "Congress has already passed so many federal land use regulations that in a few years only a rare development project of any size will get by without two and probably more federal approvals" (Bosselman 1975: 136–37). His prediction came true. By 1979 Lance Marston, the Interior Department official who might well have directed the implementation of the National Land Use Policy Act had it passed, estimated that there had been "at least—*at least*—a 20 percent growth in federal land use programs in the last three years" (Meyer 1979: 58, emphasis in the original). He was referring to such legislation as the Surface Mine Control and Reclamation Act and the amendments to the Clean Air, Clean Water, and Safe Drinking Water acts—all of which, like the National Land Use Policy Act, relied primarily on federal grants to states. In that light, the failure of the more lightly funded Land Use Act became almost immaterial to conservatives: far too much legislation like it (and worse, because better funded) sprang up in its wake.

At the state level the growth of land use legislation was equally impressive and equally objectionable to conservatives. By the early 1980s California had 41 state agencies besides the coastal commissions with overlapping regulatory responsibilities for the coastal zone—the Energy Commission, the Forestry Board, the State Lands Commission, the Public Utilities Commission, and so on. Six Minnesota agencies exercised 679 regulatory (and nonregulatory) powers (Popper 1981: 161; see also Bosselman, Fuerer, and Siemon 1976). These clear-it-with-yet-another-regulator programs inevitably antagonized the regulated. The theme of runaway regulation—with its subthemes of delay, expense, paperwork, inconsistent rules, disappointment, and injustice for applicants—figured strongly in the important 1987 Supreme Court case, *Nollan v. California Coastal Commission*, which at a minimum invalidated much of the commission's regulation concerning beach access for the public. The counsel for the victorious plaintiffs—a family that had sought to demolish a dilapidated beach house in Ventura but was overruled by the commission, which wanted plans for more public access to the beach portion of the property—was the Pacific Legal Foundation in Sacramento, probably the nation's leading conservative public-interest law firm. When one counts both state and federal agencies, most of the private land in America and all the biggest projects on it have been subject throughout the late 1970s and the entire 1980s to large amounts of centralized regulation—multiple, frustrating layers of it. Private land is now one of the most centrally regulated sectors of the American economy.

Just as centrally regulated, unbeknownst to most land use liberals, are America's *public* lands—the third of the nation, primarily in the deep-rural, intermountain west and Alaska, which the federal government owns. Those are the lands of the Interior Department's Bureau of Land Management (the largest federal land agency, which holds a fifth of the entire United States), the Interior Department's National Park Service and its Fish and Wildlife Service, and the Agriculture Department's Forest Service: the country's national parks, forests, wildlife refuges, public grazing areas, and the federally designated wildernesses within those lands. California, the nation's most populous and in many ways most urban state, nonetheless is 45 percent public land, primarily away from the coast and especially east of the Central Valley. Arizona is 44 percent public land, Wyoming 48 percent. Alaska, Idaho, Nevada, Oregon, and Utah are over half public land; Nevada is an astonishing 86 percent public land. The federal holdings comprise much of America's fabled wide open spaces and its surviving frontier (Popper 1986). They are the source, through federal leasing to private contractors, of half the nation's timber, a third of its known coal and uranium reserves, four-fifths of its oil shale, and similarly large proportions of its copper, silver, lead, natural gas, phosphate, potash, and grazing grass. The holdings amount to a second land tenure system in the United States, almost a sore-thumb outpost of federal-*rentier* socialism in the American economy. They are governed by federal land use laws entirely separate from those that apply to private land.

After 1970 that body of federal public-land law expanded rapidly, just like other forms of centralized land use regulation. The prime federal statute regulating the public lands is the 1976 Federal Land Policy and Management Act, which even sounds like the unpassed National Land Use Policy Act. Under the 1976 National Forest Management Act, the Forest Service is conducting what may be the largest, most detailed planning-and-regulation exercise in American history on the service's 298,000 square miles, an area more than a tenth larger than Texas (see Hunt 1987; Wilkinson and Anderson 1987). The 1980 Alaska National Interest Lands Conservation Act created ten new national parks, most bigger than any in the Lower 48. At least ten other major pieces of legislation to preserve the federal lands passed between 1970 and 1980 (Nelson 1982: 27).

All those federal-land laws greatly resemble the post-1970 private-land laws that the federal government passed. Not only do both sets of laws centralize and regulate, but they also deal with impacts that cross local and state boundaries, have a strong environmental-planning focus, and are aimed at managing growth (in the public-land case, for example, by establishing a moratorium on new coal leasing on the land in 1971 through 1981 and again in 1983 through 1985). In addition, both sets of laws try to blend conservation and development (on the public lands, through the doctrine of multiple use) and seek to preserve environmentally sensitive areas (on the public lands, national parks, wildernesses, wildlife refuges, and trails). As with the private lands, the liberal centralized regulatory efforts on the public lands provoked a conservative counterreaction that Ronald Reagan symbolized. Other potent symbols of revitalized conservatism on the public lands were James Watt, Reagan's first Interior Secretary, and the Sagebrush Rebellion, the grassroots western attempt to shrink the public-land holdings and loosen the laws regulating them. Reagan, Watt, and the Sagebrush Rebellion were highly successful, at least at the latter task: oil, gas, mineral, and timber leasing accelerated, and the government opened more land to those efforts (Popper 1984). The same pattern played itself out in the many states, both western and eastern, with large holdings in state parks and forests. (Eleven states, including such eastern ones as Connecticut, Florida, Louisiana, Michigan, Minnesota, New York, and Pennsylvania, are more than one-tenth state lands [Pekkanen 1983: 178].)

The conservatives maintain that the new programs, whether on public or private land, have overreached, gone too far. They also argue, more tellingly because less ideologically, that the programs have fallen short of many of their stated objectives even when sympathetic liberals rather than hostile conservatives administer them. It can be difficult, for instance, to show any direct, indisputable environmental results from the programs (Popper 1981: 193–94). Moreover, if the previous, solely local regulation was often unenforced or ignored, so is the new centralized regulation; a recent and generally positive study of seven state land use programs found that "the lack of an effective monitoring and enforcement component in the system has emerged as the Achilles heel in implementation" (DeGrove 1984: 391).

The centralized programs' attempts to compel, stimulate, or provide incentives for stronger local land use regulation have often proved ineffectual in the face of local resistance. Many rural localities still have weak zoning or lack it entirely (Rudel 1984), and are comfortable with the situation. Almost 30 percent of New York's municipalities, for instance, still lack zoning (McGuinness 1987: 1)—an improvement over the 60 percent figure of the early 1970s, but not huge progress.[3] And most localities are years behind in their attempts to comply with the local-planning requirements of the Florida comprehensive and California coastal laws.

More revealing, after nearly two decades of centralized programs, some planners and land use lawyers—the professional groups with the most to gain—are beginning to lose patience with the programs' deficiencies. Much of the criticism is reminiscent of the late 1960s liberal criticism of zoning (for instance, McGuinness 1987) or—most strikingly—it adopts the conservative position that almost any regulation at any level of government is objectionable excess, doomed to frustration, and also harmful to the public (for instance, Bikales 1987). By the middle 1980s, conservatives could find ample confirmation for their consistent 1970s contention that the failings of the centralized programs would turn out to be much the same as those of the local programs they were supposed to supplement or improve on. Adding more programs at higher levels of government would merely spread and amplify the defects of too much regulation.

THE PRAGMATIC RESOLUTION: INCREASINGLY FAMILIAR CENTRALIZED REGULATION

There is a simpler explanation for the events since 1970. Centralized land use regulation did not collapse from insufficiency, as the liberals maintain. Nor did it collapse from overextension, as the conservatives argue. Instead it did not collapse at all: it continues to expand, but more slowly than liberals hope and conservatives fear. Its fortunes ebb and flow, depending mainly on the politics of the individual states, federal agencies, or land use fields that apply it; but on the whole it is quietly thriving. It is more tempered, more narrowly focused than it was in the early 1970s, less a subject of extravagant ideological claims (or even attention) from either liberals or conservatives. The basic problem of centralized regulation then was that the two groups—as well as the public at large—had little practical experience with it. Nearly two decades later, its unfamiliarity has diminished, and it is becoming utterly acceptable, even ordinary, to much of the political spectrum, including many of its former enemies. The agencies and laws embodying it are melting into almost boring respectability. But the price of achieving familiarity is that centralized regulation evolves in directions its friends and enemies alike might not expect or even recognize.

Given that perspective, a number of important features of the American land use scene of the late 1980s fall into place. There is, for example, more centralized regulation now than there ever has been, but that regulation is also less likely to be comprehensive, more likely to be specialized, oriented to particular purposes (Brower and Carol 1987). The trend already was visible in the late 1970s, when the executive director of the California League of Cities, Don Benninghoven, said, "There is no interest in statewide land use planning in California. None. Not by cities, not by counties, not by the state. . . . We've given up on the grand scheme of doing anything statewide. Instead, we concentrate on legislation on specific problems, such as coastal protection, prime agricultural land, and preserving Lake Tahoe" (*Planning* 1977: 7). The sentiment, provocative then, is now near-conventional wisdom, for the state level has seen many new centralized regulatory efforts of specialized kinds in the 1980s: programs for hazardous waste facilities, farmland protection, wetland and floodplain regulation, groundwater protection, industrial- and energy-facility siting, sensitive-area preservation (for example, along the Maryland shore of Chesapeake Bay [Powers 1986]), state parks and forests (Fund for Renewable Energy and the Environment 1988). Every state, for example, now has some form of protective legislation for farmland (National Association of State Departments of Agriculture Research Foundation Farmland Project 1987). State parks are a newly exciting land use field (Myers and Reid 1986).

The new acceptability of centralized regulation also means that the combination of even a few single-purpose laws can easily be as effective as a comprehensive land use law of the Florida–Oregon–Vermont sort. In the late 1980s New Jersey has unobtrusively made itself a leader in combining single-purpose laws. It has state-required and state-reviewed local regulations; regional regulations for the rural fifth of the state in the Pinelands near Philadelphia and Atlantic City and for the urban 30-square-mile, high-growth Hackensack Meadowlands near New York City and Newark; state hazardous waste, coastal zone, wetland, and farmland protection laws that are among the strongest in the country (Duerksen 1983: 218–29); and the nationally unique *Mount Laurel* legislation governing the local placement and amount of new low income housing. Several of those programs only came into being after 1980. The state is seriously considering a demanding state land use plan, regional regulation of the land use impacts of transportation facilities, and a state shore-and-ocean agency with powers that would surpass those of any existing state coastal zone program.

Many of the state land use programs that dated back to the 1970s have made significant midcourse administrative corrections as centralized regulation has become more familiar in the 1980s. Most programs have tried to simplify and coordinate their bureaucratic procedures so as to defuse conservative resistance without actually undoing their regulation (Popper 1981: 165–68; Duerksen 1983: 150–68). Some programs have undergone formal self-evaluations that led to tighter regulation. The Vermont program, for instance, made two such studies (Vermont Environmental Board 1981; Byers and Wilson 1983), which finally resulted in a 1987 law that extended state regulation to developments with fewer than ten lots, thus closing a loophole builders had previously used to escape regulation.

In some states the 1970s' centralized programs have found especially high public acceptance and made hefty political gains in the 1980s. Florida passed a package of legislation in 1984, 1985, and 1986 that amounted to an entire second-generation effort at centralized regulation, a revamping and expansion of the state's

1972 comprehensive land use law (Rhodes 1986; deHaven-Smith and Paterson 1986). Many programs tried to consolidate their political support, often by at least partially winning over such former enemies as developers and local governments—for instance, by persuading developers that the programs could improve their product and so help them charge higher prices for it (DeGrove 1984: 383–84; Popper 1981: 205–6; Wilson 1987b: 34A). The Oregon program, to take the most impressive case of political consolidation, first had to survive a series of developer-inspired voters' initiatives that would have abolished it. The challenges, in 1976, 1978, and 1982, became progressively weaker; by the middle 1980s many of Oregon's builders and some of its local governments occasionally found themselves siding with and participating in the state's key land-and-environment citizens' watchdog group, 1000 Friends of Oregon. In 1986 Florida's program was buttressed by the formation of 1000 Friends of Florida, which was modeled on the Oregon group and expected to elicit similar support from the program's previous opponents. A review of the recent experience of the 1970s state programs concluded that "it is clear that the movement to strengthen the state's role in growth management is winning new support in the 1980s" (DeGrove and Stroud 1987: 8).

At the federal level, the Reagan administration always claimed that it opposed centralized land use regulation. But when forced or embarrassed by Congress, it still undertook such measures, albeit specialized, hedged, and relatively unpublicized ones. In 1981 it agreed to the Farmland Protection Policy Act, intended to prevent federal agencies' actions from contributing to agricultural land loss; then it used the law mainly as a way to defer to state farmland protection programs (Dunford 1984). In 1982 it actively promoted the Coastal Barrier Resources Act, intended to restrain growth in selected barrier areas, such as islands and exposed mainland beaches, that are vulnerable to damage from hurricanes, erosion, and other natural hazards (and which thus often necessitate large federal flood insurance payments). In 1987 the administration proposed to triple the size of the protected area—but it would even so have totalled barely 2,000 square miles (an area about the size of Delaware) and would still have been only on the Atlantic and Gulf coasts, a relatively small proportion of the area that might have been protected (Mitchell 1986: 320–22). In 1987 the administration agreed to an expansion of the 1977 Surface Mine Control and Reclamation Act to cover strip mines of less than two acres, a heretofore-serious loophole for coal operators. It put over 7,000 square miles of river banks into the federally protected wild and scenic river system. On the public lands it has added nearly 11,000 square miles of federally designated wilderness since 1981. The Reagan administration was not greatly enamored of centralized land use regulation but did not prove as uniformly hostile to it as its liberal critics assumed.

Because the administration *was* perceived as hostile (and not just by liberals), an interesting spillover effect appeared: the long-ignored local level of land use regulation revived in many places in the 1980s. Most planners know from experience that zoning, especially in big cities, is now more pervasive, sophisticated, and effective than it ever has been. Chicago's Richard Babcock, still the nation's leading land use lawyer just as he was over 20 years ago when he endorsed centralized regulation as a supplement to zoning (Babcock 1966; 166–84), has more recently argued that zoning has a large continuing usefulness even in the absence of centralized regulation (Weaver and Babcock 1980; Babcock and Siemon 1985). In a 1986 interview he admitted zoning's defects, then said, "But what would you substitute for it? Do you want no control over development at all? That would be turning back the clock" (Knack 1987: 23). He never mentioned centralized regulation.

Zoning and local regulation, in fact, have shown a practical adaptiveness and political feasibility that no one anticipated in 1970. By the late 1980s local regulation's surprise liveliness is particularly evident in a series of stringent (and technical) growth-management initiatives in the Sun Belt. In 1986 Los Angeles voters approved a proposition to limit the floor area ratio of new buildings in many neighborhoods to 1.5, a ballot-box downzoning from the planning department's previous ratio of 3.0. The same year San Francisco voters approved a proposition tightly controlling the height, size, and number of downtown buildings (*Zoning News* 1986a: 2). In 1987 San Diego became the largest city in the nation to try to limit its population when it passed an ordinance capping the permitted number of new residential housing units at 8,000 a year, about half the number built in 1986. Even Houston, famous as the nation's largest city without zoning, was reconsidering its stance (*Zoning News* 1986b: 2–3). Meanwhile, local planners throughout the country were exploiting the many new real-world opportunities for linkage policies (Merriam, Brower, and Tegeler 1985), impact fees (Frank and Rhodes 1987), aesthetic regulation (Duerksen 1986), controls on office, commercial, and industrial growth (Fulton 1986), development moratoria (Wilson 1987b), agricultural zoning (Toner 1984), and innovative variants on permitting systems (Gordon 1984) and master plans (Lorenzen 1987).

Liberals looking at American land use in the late 1980s might easily take comfort in the acceptance of centralized regulation; conservatives might well be pleased with the limitations on it. But neither group actually is satisfied; liberals bemoan centralized regulation's shortfall, conservatives fear its overreach. Both groups misunderstand their situation. At the federal level populist conservatives preside over a nation that has more of the centralized regulation they loathe than it has had at any point in its history. In addition, while conservatives prefer local government to the federal government, they distrust all government and regulation intensely and so cannot be truly happy about the explosion of local regulation. (That was a theme in the 1987 Supreme Court case, *First English Evangelical Lutheran Church of Glendale v. County of Los Angeles*, where the Court ruled that a property owner can be compensated for an economic loss resulting from a land use regulatory decision such as a downzoning—a major conservative victory.) At the same time liberals keep wishing, mostly in vain, for more federal regulation. They do not realize that their political possibilities are now better at the state, regional, and local levels than they have ever been.

THE PRAGMATIC RESOLUTION'S IMPLICATIONS

The interpretation I have suggested has intriguing political and professional consequences that in large measure are encouraging for planners. There is now more land use regulation—centralized and local, for big projects and small, on private and public land—than ever before. The future probably will see even more regulation. Membership in environmental organizations keeps climbing steadily. The public's support for land use and environmental regulation has remained high and constant throughout the 1970s and 1980s, and shows no signs of wavering (Dunlap 1987). The Reagan administration was not able to alter that consensus, and sometimes had to accommodate to it. The liberal impulses that drove the Quiet Revolution and the National Land Use Policy Act did not decline or disappear. They won out, and nobody noticed.

Yet in one respect the Reagan-conservative approach to land use regulation achieved an odd triumph: no one expects major federal initiatives anymore. No one, including state and local governments and planners and environmentalists, relies on such initiatives (or the prospect of them) as they did in 1972 or 1975. The federal government has become dissociated from the other parties, decoupled from them. Under Reagan federalism, each level of government and each individual government goes its own way, develops and manages and finances its own programs that spring from its own circumstances; free administrative enterprise prevails. Thus regulation can bubble up from local government and simultaneously trickle down from the state (or even federal) level. Alternatively, it need not appear at all, at any level. Or it may appear at one level and then be resisted at another, as when the federal government tries to cut back funding for state surface mine regulation or opposes state coastal zone regulation intended to restrain oil and gas drilling on the federal Outer Continental Shelf. In all such cases the rules are those of *laissez faire* bureaucratic democracy, and no outcome is foreordained (Peterson and Lewis 1986; Nathan, Doolittle, and Associates 1987).

The result can be remarkable variation across governments—here a sign of true, flexible responsiveness to the wishes of the relevant constituencies: the population gets the regulation it wants. Thus state land use regulation flourishes in Florida, New Jersey, and Oregon, but languishes in Colorado (DeGrove 1984: 291–333). Local regulation booms in California as it busts in Kansas (Rudel 1984: 494). State regulation thrives in Vermont while local regulation falters; just across the Connecticut River in New Hampshire, the situation is reversed (Merrill 1987). State and local regulators work together poorly in Maine, well in Florida and North Carolina (DeGrove 1984: 99–176, 335–70). Federally funded state coastal zone regulation performs nicely in Washington state, does not exist at all in Georgia or Illinois (Mitchell 1986; 327). The job market has adjusted accordingly; planners have gravitated to politically congenial settings. In early 1987 California counted for 11 percent of the nation's population, but 17 percent of the members of the American Planning Association. Florida had 5 percent of the American population, 8 percent of APA's members. By contrast, New York state had 7.3 percent of the population, but only 5 percent of the APA's membership.[4]

In the late 1980s American planners have plenty to do. The development boom that began in 1982 now dwarfs the late-1960s one that led to centralized regulation. But the new boom is more geographically uneven, leaves a big hole in the center of the country. The northeast and the far west, particularly in urban and suburban areas, experience near-boomtown capitalism while much of the Great Plains

(Popper and Popper 1987), the south, the midwest, and the intermountain west, especially their rural areas, undergo near depression. Moreover, planners across the nation face a daunting menu of new land use issues: acid rain, the cutoff of low income housing construction, hazardous waste, foreign land ownership, suburban traffic gridlock, deindustrialization, high-tech growth corridors, affordable housing for the middle class, the greenhouse effect, LULU blockage, aging strip developments, the disappearance of small- and mid-scale farming and ranching, gentrification that displaces the poor, homelessness, and—most extensively—the simple ugliness, inconvenience, indistinctiveness, and sterility of much new 1980s development. Large areas of New Jersey, Los Angeles' San Fernando Valley, or urban and suburban Florida can be highly affluent, boast an impressive array of land use controls, and still look vile. Improving the regulations will provide work for planners at all levels of government, including federal. In truth, the professional opportunities for planners—and the chances for genuine power—have never been greater.

But it would help if planners grasped the real nature of the American federalist system of land use controls. It is so loose, so deliberately disjointed and open ended, that it is barely a system in the sense that European elite civil service bureaucracies understand the term. The right to make particular regulatory decisions shifts unpredictably over time from one level of government to another. No principle of administrative rationality, constitutional entitlement, economic efficiency, or even ideological predisposition truly determines the governmental locus of decisions. It is more often a matter of the inevitably uncertain catch-as-catch-can pluralism of democratic power politics.

Thus in 1964 American land use regulation was totally local and appeared likely to stay that way. By 1974 it seemed likely to become more federal. In 1984 it had again confounded prophecy and become more state-level and local. By 1994 it may have shifted again, and our previous conceptions of it will once more look foolish. A future, more liberal administration might, for instance, heavily promote federal regulation, revitalize some of the mechanisms the Reagan administration has neglected (say, the Clean Water Act), perhaps even support a 1990s version of the National Land Use Policy Act. Yet over decades spanning several national political and ideological cycles, late-twentieth-century American society has consistently acquired more regulation, centralized and local, and more tolerance for it. The cycles have come and almost completely gone, often revealing themselves as ephemera, birds of political passage. Regulation has grown throughout and shown true political staying power. In much of the country and certainly in the large population centers, there seems to be more land use regulation every year, regardless of who is in power in Washington, the state capitals, or city hall. American planners should take heart from those trends. They can feel proud of their accomplishments since 1970.

Author's note: This paper was originally presented at an international seminar on Urban Land Management Under Different Political Systems, in Warsaw and Lodz, Poland, September 20–23, 1987. The seminar was sponsored by the Regional Economy Department of the Polish Academy of Sciences, the Urban Development Economics Department of the University of Lodz, and the Polish Town Planners Society. Michael Greenberg, Michael Heiman, Harvey Jacobs, Janet Lynn, Robert Mason, James Mitchell, Deborah Epstein Popper, Jerzy Regulski, Neil Smith, William Toner, and three anonymous *JAPA* reviewers offered valuable comments on successive drafts.

NOTES

1 A third, less widely held but more radical interpretation argues that centralized regulation sprang primarily from large development corporations more concerned with protecting their profits than promoting environmental quality. This interpretation disagrees with those of both the liberals and conservatives; it maintains that centralized regulation is objectionable not because in practice it is ineffective or excessively effective, but because it is ideologically regressive and socially inequitable. The interpretation agrees with the liberals that centralized regulation has faded since the middle 1970s. For examples of the interpretation, see Plotkin (1987) and Walker and Heiman (1981). The interpretation, however trenchant, has come solely from a small number of academics and has had no influence beyond academe.

2 McClaughry (1975) presents an early prediction of those kinds of difficulties. He is a Republican conservative who in 1982 ran for the Senate from Vermont on a platform opposing the state's land use law.

3 For a similar example from Maine, see Wilson (1987a).

4 I received this information in a computer printout from the American Planning Association, dated April 7, 1987; at the time, I was a member of the APA board and received the printout in that capacity.

REFERENCES

American Land Forum. 1983. Toward a Land Resource Policy Agenda. *American Land Forum* 4, 3: 11–30.

American Law Institute. 1977. *A Model Land Development Code: Official Draft.* Philadelphia: American Law Institute.

Babcock, R. 1966. *The Zoning Game: Municipal Practices and Policies.* Madison: University of Wisconsin Press.

Babcock, R., and C. Siemon. 1985. *The Zoning Game Revisited.* Cambridge, MA: Lincoln Institute of Land Policy.

Bikales, E. 1987. Ten Reasons to Dump Vermont's Act 250. *The Yankee Planner* 4, 1: 6–7.

Bosselman, F. 1975. Commentary. Pp. 136–37 in *Agenda for the New Urban Era*, edited by H. Perloff. Chicago: American Society of Planning Officials.

——— and D. Callies. 1972. *The Quiet Revolution in Land Use Control.* Washington: Government Printing Office.

Bosselman, F., D. Feurer, and C. Siemon. 1976. *The Permit Explosion: Coordination of the Proliferation.* Washington: Urban Land Institute.

Brower, D., and D. Carol, editors. 1987. *Managing Land-use Conflicts: Case Studies in Special Area Management.* Durham, NC: Duke University Press.

Byers, G., and L. Wilson. 1983. *Managing Rural Growth: The Vermont Development Review Process.* Montpelier: Vermont Environmental Board.

Council of State Governments. 1976. *State Growth Management*. Lexington, KY: Council of State Governments.

DeGrove, J. 1984. *Land, Growth and Politics*. Chicago: American Planning Association.

DeGrove, J., and N. Stroud. 1987. State Land Planning and Regulation: Innovative Roles in the 1980s and Beyond. *Land Use Law & Zoning Digest* 39, 3: 3–8.

deHaven-Smith, W., and R. Paterson. 1986. The 1986 Glitch Bill—Missing Links in Growth Management. *Florida Environmental and Urban Issues* 14, 1: 4–9.

Duerksen, C. 1983. *Environmental Regulation of Industrial Plant Siting: How to Make it Work Better*. Washington: Conservation Foundation.

———. 1986. *Aesthetics and Land-Use Controls: Beyond Ecology and Economics*. Chicago: American Planning Association.

Dunford, R. 1984. Feds Drag Their Feet on Three-Year-Old Farmland Conversion Law. *Planning* 50, 12: 24–25.

Dunlap, R. 1987. Polls, Pollution, and Politics Revisited: Public Opinion on the Environment in the Reagan Era. *Environment* 29, 4: 6–11, 32–37.

Fellmeth, R. 1973. *Politics of Land: Ralph Nader's Study Group Report on Land Use in California*. New York: Grossman.

Fishman, R., editor. 1977. *Housing for All Under Law: New Directions in Housing, Planning, and Land-Use Law*. Cambridge, MA: Ballinger.

Frank, J., and R. Rhodes, editors. 1987. *Development Exactions*. Chicago: American Planning Association.

Fulton, W. 1986. Office in the Dell. *Planning* 52, 7: 13–17.

Fund for Renewable Energy and the Environment. 1988. *The State of the States*. Washington: Fund for Renewable Energy and the Environment.

Gordon, D. 1984. The Power of the Point System. *Planning* 50, 12:15–17.

Hays, S. 1987. *Beauty, Health, and Permanence: Environmental Politics in the United States, 1955–1985*. New York: Cambridge University Press.

Healy, R., and J. Rosenberg. 1979. *Land Use and the States*, second edition. Baltimore: Johns Hopkins University Press.

Heeter, D., editor. 1969. *Toward a More Effective Land-Use Guidance System: A Summary and Analysis of Five Major Reports*. Chicago: American Society of Planning Officials.

Hunt, F. 1987. National Forest Planning: Charting the Future for 191 Million Acres of Trees and Grass. *American Land Forum* 7, 3: 18–23.

Knack, R. 1987. Troubador Babcock. *Planning* 53, 8: 21–27.

Lewis, S. 1976. Antiplanners Are Coming, Antiplanners Are Coming. *Planning* 42, 2: 11–13.

Lorenzen, L. 1987. Old Faithful. *Planning* 53, 9: 11–14.

Lyday, N. 1976. *The Law of the Land: Debating National Land Use Legislation 1970–1975*. Washington: Urban Institute.

McClaughry, J. 1975. The New Feudalism—State Land Use Controls. Pp. 37–57 in *No Land Is An Island: Individual Rights and Government Control of Land Use*, edited by Institute for Contemporary Studies. San Francisco: Institute for Contemporary Studies.

McGuinness, D. 1986. Fixing What's Broke. *NY Planner* 5, 6: 7.

———. 1987. Planning Shortfalls in New York's Towns and Villages. *Small Town & Rural Planning* 7, 1: 1.

McPhee, J. 1977. *Pieces of the Frame*. New York: Farrar, Straus, and Giroux.

Merriam, D., D. Brower, and P. Tegeler, editors. 1985. *Inclusionary Zoning Moves Downtown*. Chicago: American Planning Association.

Merrill, L. 1987. The Road Not Taken. *Planning* 53, 11: 22–24.

Meyer, P. 1979. Land Rush. *Harper's* 265, 1: 45–60.

Mitchell, J. 1986. Coastal Management Since 1980: The U.S. Experience and Its Relevance for Other Countries. Pp. 319–45 in *Ocean Yearbook 6*, edited by E. Borgese and N. Ginsburg. Chicago: University of Chicago Press.

Myers, P., and A. Reid. 1986. *State Parks in a New Era: A Survey of Issues and Innovations.* Washington: Conservation Foundation.

Nathan, R., F. Doolittle, and Associates. 1987. *Reagan and the States.* Princeton, NJ: Princeton University Press.

National Association of State Departments of Agriculture Research Foundation Farmland Project. 1987. *Farmland Notes* 6, 1: 1–4.

National Commission on Urban Problems. 1968. *Building the American City.* Washington: U.S. Government Printing Office.

Natural Resources Defense Council. 1977. *Land Use Controls in the United States: A Handbook on the Legal Rights of Citizens.* New York: Dial Press/James Wade.

Nelson, R. 1982. The Public Lands. Pp. 14–73 in *Current Issues in Natural Resource Policy,* edited by P. Portney. Baltimore: Johns Hopkins University Press.

Pacific Legal Foundation. 1985. *The California Coastal Commission in the '80s: Disquieting Continuities and Suggestions for Reform.* Sacramento: Pacific Legal Foundation.

Pekkanen, J. 1983. The Land: Who Owns America? Part I. *Town & Country* 137, 5036: 175–86.

Peterson, G., and C. Lewis, editors. 1986. *Reagan and the Cities.* Washington: Urban Institute.

Planning. 1977. California Flirts with Growth Control. *Planning* 43, 8: 7–8.

Plotkin, S. 1987. *Keep Out: The Struggle for Land Use Control.* Berkeley: University of California Press.

Popper, D., and F. Popper. 1987. The Great Plains: From Dust to Dust. *Planning* 53, 12: 12–18.

Popper, F. 1981. *The Politics of Land-use Reform.* Madison: University of Wisconsin Press.

———. 1984. The Timely End of the Sagebrush Rebellion. *The Public Interest* 76: 61–73.

———. 1986. The Strange Case of the Contemporary American Frontier. *The Yale Review* 76, 1: 101–21.

Porter, D., editor. 1986. *Growth Management: Keeping on Target?* Washington: Urban Land Institute.

Powers, A. 1986. Protecting the Chesapeake Bay: Maryland's Critical Area Program. *Environment* 28, 4: 5, 44–45.

Reilly, W., editor. 1973. *The Use of Land: A Citizen's Policy Guide to Urban Growth.* New York: Crowell.

Rhodes, R. 1986. Growth Management in Florida: 1985 and Beyond. *Florida Environmental and Urban Issues* 13, 2: 1–3, 24–25.

Robbins, D. 1974. New York Towns Squelch Local Zoning Laws. *Planning* 40, 8: 6.

Rosenbaum, N. 1976. *Land Use and the Legislatures: The Politics of State Innovation.* Washington: Urban Institute.

RuBino, R., and Wagner, W. 1972. *Supplement* to *The States' Role in Land Resource Management.* Lexington, KY: Council of State Governments.

Rudel, T. 1984. The Human Ecology of Rural Land Use Planning. *Rural Sociology* 49, 4: 491–504.

Strong, A. 1981. Land as a Public Good: An Idea Whose Time Has Come Again. Pp.

217–32 in *The Land Use Policy Debate in the United States*, edited by J. de Neufville. New York: Plenum Press.

Toner, W. 1984. Ag Zoning Gets Serious. *Planning* 50, 12: 19–24.

Vermont Environmental Board. 1981. *Act 250: A Performance Evaluation.* Montpelier: Vermont Environmental Board.

Walker, R., and M. Heiman. 1981. Quiet Revolution for Whom? *Annals of the Association of American Geographers* 71, 1: 67–83.

Weaver, C., and R. Babcock. 1980. *City Zoning: The Once and Future Frontier.* Chicago: American Planning Association.

Wilkinson, C., and H. Anderson. 1987. *Land and Resource Planning in the National Forests.* Covelo, CA: Island Press.

Williams, N. 1975. The Future of Land Use Controls. Pp. 27–42 in *Future Land Use: Energy, Environmental, and Legal Constraints*, edited by R. Burchell and D. Listokin. New Brunswick, NJ: Rutgers University Center for Urban Policy Research.

Wilson, R. 1987a. Dire Straits. *Maine Times* 19, 28: 16–20.

———. 1987b. Managing Maine's Growth. *Maine Times* 20, 10: 34A–35A.

Zoning News. 1986a. Is Growth Management Really Alphabet Soup? *Zoning News.* December: 2.

———. 1986b. Houston Plan Raises "Specter of Zoning." *Zoning News.* December: 2–3.

Planning the Use of Land for the 21st Century

Harvey M. Jacobs

Professor of Urban and Regional Planning, University of Wisconsin

Harvey M. Jacobs presents a postmodern challenge to the scientific, rational land-use planning model that has prevailed in this century. He states that "in general, the mission of the postmodern land use planning professional is to acknowledge that land use planning is not and cannot be a technocratic, scientific exercise" (p. 163). Instead, Jacobs asserts that postmodern land-use planning should focus, not just on the ecological concerns of land but also on serving as a stage to resolve complex social and political issues.

One scholar-policy analyst has declared, to much dissent, an end to history (5). The basis for his call is the incredible transformations we have witnessed around the

Reprinted by permission of the *Journal of Soil and Water Conservation*, 47 (1992), Soil and Water Conservation Society.

globe in recent years: the end of communism in Eastern Europe, the Soviet Union, and even China; the introduction of market capitalism in these places; the seeming end of the cold war; the balkanization of Eastern Europe and the Soviet Union; the unification of Germany; and the prospect of a united Europe.

This expression of transformation in the political and social world is mirrored in other fields and goes by another name, postmodernism. Postmodernism arose in architecture as a way to design; it seemed to reflect an eclectic, "anything goes" style. Postmodernism has spread to literary criticism, cultural criticism, and the social sciences as a theoretical framework for examining and commenting upon the world we live in (*4, 8, 16, 20*). The concern of postmodernism is the whole project of modernism/modernity—that multicentury project we have collectively engaged in to create a modern world.

Postmodernism seeks to observe, critique, and reframe this project. It does this by looking to unearth the project's unspoken assumptions, airing them for debate and causing us to pause, on our way to the 21st century, to be certain that where we will arrive is where we wish to be going. Most importantly, postmodernism is a critique of our paradigm for understanding, organizing, and acting upon the world (*14*).

My assertion here is threefold:

1 That land use planning, as we know it and practice it, is largely a modernist conceptualization.

2 The most salient challenges to land use planning practice and doctrine are postmodern in character.

3 We are thus suspended between modernism and postmodernism in our thinking about how to best engage in land use planning, and this provides us with a unique opportunity to reframe what we do, in what I believe to be a more relevant, though more ambiguous, professional practice (*1*).

A MODERNIST CONCEPTUALIZATION

As we know it and practice it, land use planning was invented at the turn of the century; science, rationalism, and scientific management were prominent. We invented a way to do land use planning that can be summed up in six points. It presumed that:

1 We could perform a complete physical and social analysis of the capacities of and demands on the land.

2 Our analysis would yield information that would lead to better individual and social decision-making.

3 This process of analysis and information generation would rely heavily on professionals and experts.

4 What would result from this analysis would be a single best pattern of land use (this is best expressed in zoning with its single-use districts).

5 While there was a cultural inclination to local control, there was a professional orientation toward centralization in administrative authority for land at the regional, state, and national levels.

6 Urban society was at the height of the social hierarchy, and other land use concerns needed to be subsumed to it. So we invented and practiced a land use planning that, for the most part, for much of the twentieth century did not challenge the presumed inevitability of rural land abandonment, rural land restructuring, rapid urban growth, and pervasive urban sprawl (*11*).

THE POSTMODERN CHALLENGE

So what has been the postmodern challenge to this model? Rather than responding on a point-by-point basis, let me simplify and suggest that it has one main theme—the rise of a diverse, populist citizens' movement in land use planning. This citizens' movement challenges:

- The presumption of experts' preeminent knowledge.
- The need for perfect knowledge and information to plan for land.
- The use of rationality and the scientific method as the only means of informing land use planning decisions.
- The inevitable need to centralize resource management to achieve sound resource objectives.
- This movement makes clear that land use is a social and political resource, as well as an ecological one.

Rather than leaving all of this in the abstract, though, let me cite some specific examples. The context for these examples will be the land use issues of the urban fringe in the United States.

One of the things that will be confirmed by the 1990 census is that America's urban fringe, suburbia, finally has become the dominant demographic place of the United States. While America's rural places have not been primary since 1920, in the intervening 70 years we have come to think of ourselves as an urban nation—even though this reflected our population base, rather than our land use pattern. For the immediate future, this will need to change again as we acknowledge that the land use and social pattern that has endeared itself to America's masses and been the subject of long-standing lampoons is now the paramount one.

Readers of the *JSWC* are aware of a number of prominent land use issues that have arisen in the last 20 years as this demographic transformation was taking its present shape. Among these, for example, are agricultural land protection, sustainable agriculture, wetland protection and management, so-called LULU (locally unwanted land uses) or NIMBY (not in my backyard) land uses, and the so-called quiet revolution in land use control. I would assert that in each case the issue came to prominence largely because citizens seeking the good life in the urban fringe challenged the prevailing wisdom of professionals—their paradigms, methods, assumptions, and values.

Let me explore three of the issues in some detail to make my case.

Agricultural Land Protection

We are all aware of the figures about the rate of conversion of agricultural land to nonagricultural uses in the post-World War II period and the debates about these figures (*7, 17, 22*). Regardless of the "correct" figure, agricultural land protection continues to be the most prominent urban fringe/rural land use planning issue in the United States (*15*). It came to prominence by citizens challenging the conventional wisdom of agricultural economics and agricultural economists over the disappearance of prime agricultural land to shopping malls and housing developments. The conventional wisdom of these professionals suggested that there was no problem with the conversion of this land because land as a resource was being substituted by technological and managerial innovations.

Historically, this analysis is, in fact, correct. The decline in the farm population and the shifting pattern of agricultural land use has not resulted in a decline in farm output—just the opposite. Fewer farmers are producing more food products more "efficiently." But for many citizens, particularly those in the ex-urban fringe, the protection of agricultural land is not an issue to be assessed solely on the basis of economic theory, through the lens of such concepts as efficiency. Rather, agricultural land protection is an issue to be assessed on its landscape, aesthetic, and quality-of-life attributes. The enduring and wide-ranging existence of agricultural land protection as an urban fringe land use planning issue represents a poignant example of the conflict between the judgments of professionals and citizens.

Sustainable Agriculture

A similar story exists with the issue of sustainable agriculture. This is a subject that was largely brought to the public policy agenda by citizens concerned with elements other than classic economic efficiency as the basis for agricultural production. Instead, what was asserted was a set of quality-of-life and hidden-cost issues relative to those who live in rural America, an enduring rural land resource base, and, importantly, the caliber of food produced from the agricultural system. We find that this debate takes particular form around the question of biotechnology and biotechnological innovation. Groups of citizens are asking a postmodern question: Just because we can do it, should we? Within the story of sustainable agriculture, we see citizens challenging the conventional wisdom about what constitutes costs and benefits and what values are important in planning and policy.

The Quiet Revolution

My last example has to do with the so-called quiet revolution in land use control. The quiet revolution is a movement begun in the 1960s, much supported by land use professionals, to remove land use planning authority from local governments and transfer it to more central regional or state agencies (*2, 19*). To some extent this can be seen as the next step in what first occurred in the early part of the century when modern land use planning was invented and through policy instruments, such as zoning, land use authority was removed from the individual to the local goverment.

The classical examples of the quiet revolution include the creation of the Adirondack Park Agency in New York State; similar kinds of agencies for the California coast and the Lake Tahoe area in California and Nevada; and statewide planning acts in Florida, Vermont, and Oregon. There has been a recent resurgence of activity in Florida and Vermont, with revisions of their previous legislation, as well as substantive explorations of similar activities and agencies in Maine, Georgia, Rhode Island, Maryland, and New Jersey and substate activities in New Jersey, around the New Jersey Pinelands, and in Wisconsin, around the Lower Wisconsin River (*3, 6, 21*).

In all of these instances, the argument was the same—local people and local governments (where authority initially rested) will always be elitist, discriminatory, parochial, and antiecological in their approach to planning and policy. The presumption of these acts and agencies is that the new central authority will be none of these things—it will act in the greater public interest.

Affected citizens, the public, aren't so sure. Why? Because affected citizens often find themselves concerned with the removal of local control over their land and their neighborhoods to the authority of distant, hard-to-access professional bureaucrats. So, concurrent with the rise of a new regionalism is a new localism, again largely citizen-driven (*9, 12*).

THE UPSHOT

What does all this mean for land use planning? As I suggested, we are suspended between modernism and postmodernism. I see three trends shaping the future of land use planning.

1 Land use planning, particularly on the urban fringe, will become evermore plural. More individuals and more groups will assert more interest in land use planning. And all of them will argue, with evermore sophistication, that their perspective on the public interest is the appropriate one.

2 Land use planning will become evermore conflictual, among these individuals and groups and among the groups and land professionals.

3 Land use planning will become evermore political. The era of land use planning dominated by professionals is over, if it was ever really here.

So what is the function of the land professional in this postmodern world?

The cutting edge of professional practice will be in recognizing the limited perspective that most participants bring to the land use planning debate and working to broaden it to assure that all legitimate concerns and interests are taken into account. Only in this way will we be able to construct and implement an enduring land use planning process.

Let me offer two examples of postmodern land practice. With regard to agricultural land protection, I suggested that much of the citizen interest is in the landscape and the aesthetic qualities of agricultural land. These exist and are legitimate; farmers and farmland owners need to acknowledge this. At the same time, citizens need to understand the real economics of farming and how they fit into a program of farmland protection. An unworked, unproductive, deteriorating farm landscape is in no one's interest; yet, a program of farmland protection that does not deal with the real economics of farming could yield just such a result. Farmland needs farmers who can farm for a living; farmland protection needs to be a part of a larger program directed at the health of the local/regional farm economy. And farmland protection advocates and detractors also need to acknowledge that efforts to protect farmland will have impacts on the long-term economic and social security of family farmland owners, the land use options available for future generations of users, the viability of farming for the next generation of farmers, and, especially at the urban fringe, the availability of moderate-priced housing (*13*).

The case of wetlands is similar. Wetlands also are lands in which society has developed environmental values; they are no longer regarded as "wastelands." In so doing, society, in the form of protection and management statutes, has begun to assert social rights in these lands (*10, 18*). But as the owners of these lands know, there are real equity issues when social values in land preservation are placed on the shoulders of those for whom the land may represent a "banked" source of economic value. The inequity served upon these landowners needs to be made clear and explicitly addressed in land use planning. Conversely, like with the case of farmlands, the owners of these lands need to recognize the diverse, legitimate social rights of present and future society in "their" land.

What this means for professional practice is that the analysis that gets performed in land use planning needs to change. This analysis needs to reflect not just the ecological characteristics of land but also its social characteristics. As analysts, we need to ask not just "what is the ecological carrying capacity of the land" and "what is the economically efficient use of the land" but "what is a socially equitable way to plan for the land's use."

In general, the mission of the postmodern land use planning professional is to acknowledge that land use planning is not and cannot be a technocratic, scientific exercise. Land is a unique ecological resource, but it is also a unique social resource. Land use planning often acts as the stage for fundamental and complex social debate about individual and social rights and the articulation of ideals about democracy and social justice.

More than 200 years ago, in the late 18th century, Thomas Jefferson enunciated a position about the social component of land in an emerging democratic society. As we begin to plan for the 21st century, the democratic, social, and equity issues in land are no less and, in fact, are more pronounced.

Land use planning at the urban fringe is an exercise in social planning masked as technical planning. To be truly successful, we must recognize it as such and act accordingly.

At the same time, though, we must remember that the land needs to endure. As we plan, we must be certain that its interests also are accounted for.

REFERENCES CITED

1 Beauregard, Robert A. 1989. *Between modernity and postmodernity: The ambiguous position of U.S. planning.* Environ. and Planning D: Society and Space 7(4): 381–395.

2 Bosselman, Fred, and David Callies. 1971. *The quiet revolution in land use control.* U.S. Govt. Printing Office, Washington, D.C.

3 Collins, Beryl R., and Emily W. B. Russell, eds. 1988. *Protecting the New Jersey Pinelands.* Rutgers Univ. Press, New Brunswick, N.J.

4 Dear, Michael. 1986. *Postmodernism and planning.* Environ. and Planning D: Society and Space 4(3): 367–384.

5 Fukuyama, Francis. 1989. *The end of history?* The National Interest (16): 3–18.

6 Fulton, William. 1989. *In land use planning, a second revolution shifts control to the states.* Governing 2(6): 40–45.

7 Gustafson, G. C., and Nelson L. Bills. 1984. *U.S. cropland, urbanization and landownership patterns.* Agr. Econ. Rpt. No. 520. Econ. Res. Serv., U.S. Dept. Agr., Washington, D.C.

8 Harvey, David. 1989. *The condition of postmodernity.* Basil Blackwell, Oxford, Eng.

9 Heiman, Michael. 1990. *From "Not in my backyard!" to "not in anybody's backyard!": Grassroots challenge to hazardous waste facility siting.* J. Am. Planning Assoc. 56(3): 359–362.

10 Hunter, David B. 1988. *An ecological perspective on property: A call for judicial protection of the public's interest in environmentally critical resources.* Harvard Environmental Law Rev. 12(2): 311–383.

11 Jacobs, Harvey M. 1989. *Debates in rural land planning policy: A twentieth century history from New York State.* J. Rural Studies 5(2): 137–148.

12 Jacobs, Harvey M. 1989. *Localism and land use planning.* J. Arch. and Planning Res. 6(1): 1–17.

13 Jacobs, Harvey M. 1989. *Social equity in agricultural land protection.* Landscape and Urban Planning 17(1): 21–33.

14 Kuhn, Thomas S. 1962. *The structure of scientific resolutions.* Univ. Chicago Press, Chicago, Ill.

15 Lapping, Mark B., and Julia Moser. 1992. *1990 in review.* In A. Gilg [ed.] *Progress in Rural Policy and Planning* (vol. 2). Bellhaven, London, Eng.

16 Milroy, Beth Moore. 1991. *Into postmodern weightlessness.* J. Planning Educ. and Res. 10(3): 181–187.

17 National Agricultural Lands Study. 1981. *Final report.* U.S. Dept. Agr., Washington, D.C.

18 Owen, Catherine R., and Harvey M. Jacobs. 1992. *Wetland protection as land use planning: The impact of Section 404 in Wisconsin.* Environmental Manage. (in press).

19 Popper, Frank J. 1988. *Understanding American land use planning since 1970: A revisionist interpretation.* J. Am. Planning Assoc. 54(3): 291–301.

20 Punter, John. 1988. *Post-modernism.* Planning Practice and Res. 4: 22–28.

21 Sinclair, Susan. 1988. *Expectations and opportunities: Growth management in the late eighties.* Task Force on Rural Development, Nat. Governors' Assoc., Washington, D.C.

22 Soil Conservation Society of America. 1981. *The National Agricultural Lands Study, an interview with Robert Gray.* J. Soil and Water Cons. 36(2): 62–68.

Growth Management and the Integrated Roles of State, Regional, and Local Governments

John M. DeGrove

Patricia M. Metzger

John M. DeGrove and Patricia M. Metzger sketch the history of growth management planning in the United States and show how the approaches to it have evolved over the past twenty years. DeGrove and Metzger conclude that although growth management systems have expanded the roles and responsibilities of state and regional governments, local "home rule" still remains strong.

Growth management focuses on the need to plan rationally to accommodate the impacts of growth. It assumes that, even if a single jurisdiction succeeds in managing its growth in a responsible fashion, it may well experience the negative impacts of unmanaged growth by neighboring jurisdictions. Properly defined and understood, growth management is a comprehensive concept, concerned not only with the physical impacts of growth but with the economic and social impacts as well. Thus state, regional, and local governments can and should adopt growth management systems to manage growth better, whether their areas are experiencing strong population and economic growth pressures or are experiencing unwanted decline and need a growth strategy to revive a weak economy.

This chapter explores the necessary roles of government—state, regional, and local—to manage the impacts of growth and change. Growth management will only occur in a comprehensive or coordinated fashion if government takes the lead in establishing an integrated framework. Government, however, should not be the only actor in growth management. The private sector, citizens, and civic and special interest groups also have important roles to play.

THE NEED FOR INTERGOVERNMENTAL COORDINATION IN GROWTH MANAGEMENT

In eight statewide growth management systems—Florida, Hawaii, Oregon, Georgia, Vermont, Maine, New Jersey, and Rhode Island—each level of government has distinct but integral roles. While these governance systems vary as to their "top-down" or "bottom-up" character, ultimately they all rely on coordination of individual but interrelated roles and responsibilities.

Successful growth management also requires coordination among local governments (horizontal consistency) and between state and regional agencies and local governments (vertical consistency). As growth problems, such as pollution, mass transit, and siting locally unwanted land uses ("LULUs"), spill over municipal boundaries into suburban and even exurban areas, local governments must cooperate to resolve these issues and also involve higher (regional and state) levels of government.

This chapter examines the role each level of government plays in statewide growth management systems and discusses the difficulties each level of government faces in fulfilling and coordinating these roles.

STATE APPROACHES TO GROWTH MANAGEMENT PLANNING

Oregon's legislature approved its landmark growth management legislation in 1973. Its comprehensive, integrated approach has made it the most powerful of any state's in influencing the development and implementation of growth management systems. Vermont's growth program, adopted in 1970 as Act 250, with subsequent implementing legislation approved in 1971 and 1972, was in effect a permitting system akin to Florida's development of regional impact (DRI) process approved in 1972. The state land use planning framework that was meant to form the policy framework for the system failed to clear the legislature in the 1970s. Under Vermont's Act 250, developers proposing projects that exceeded certain thresholds were required to receive approval from district (regional) environmental commissions, with appeals possible to a state environmental board. Act 250 affected about one third of all development in Vermont.

Florida's land use, water resources, and planning laws adopted in 1972 and 1975 were either limited in scope (only developments of greater-than-local impacts subject to a special regional review) or, as with the Local Government Comprehensive Planning Act of 1975, had few enforceable standards and even less funding. California's coastal legislation, adopted by an initiative of the voters in 1972 (Proposition 20) and revised in 1976, has had a long, painful and only partially successful implementation history. Colorado's brave start in developing a state role in managing growth in 1970 and 1974 has been crippled by adverse court decisions and legislative hostility. North Carolina's Coastal Area Management Act has been successful within the narrow scope of its mandate, while Hawaii's effort to move from a limited land use law to a broader growth management system has suffered a series of setbacks. Hawaii is now experiencing a stalemate over the appropriate roles of the state and the four main islands, each a separate local government.

The growth management systems of the 1970s emerged out of public concern for environmental and natural resources (typically farm and forest lands), while the systems of the 1980s and the 1990s have broadened their scope to include a "quality of life" focus. From the late 1970s through the 1980s, this concern has been associated most closely with transportation planning in an attempt to avoid problems such as freeways functioning more as parking lots than as efficient traffic movers.

Public frustration with traffic congestion, however, has not been the only driving force in the second wave of state growth strategies that emerged in the 1980s and continue to develop in the 1990s. Environmental concerns broadened to include protection of farm and forest lands, natural areas such as unique upland habitat, wetlands, water recharge areas, and the separation of urban development and the rural countryside. In addition, concern for providing an adequate supply of affordable housing and economic development policies that promote growth where needed, and not just attempts to manage it, has resulted in different growth strategies than those of the 1970s. Balance of the equally legitimate needs of economic development and job creation with the need to protect natural systems has become the challenge in the 1990s.

In the 1970s, no state except Oregon came close to embracing the broad scope of growth strategies developed in the 1980s and 1990s. Oregon has been a leader in the areas of land use, comprehensive planning, and growth management. Oregon's influence is the product of at least two factors: (a) the relatively broad scope of Oregon's Senate Bill 100, which enacted the statewide growth management system, and (b) the substantial experience and relative success of the Oregon growth management system by the time other states began to develop the "second wave" of growth management strategies in the mid-1980s. Senate Bill 100 contained all of the key procedural and substantive components, except concurrency, that were adopted in the state growth systems of the 1980s. Concurrency is only now being addressed in the Oregon system.

To understand what was learned during the implementation period of early programs from 1973 to 1985, we will look at a series of state growth management systems that began with Florida's revised system in 1985 and continued in quick succession to New Jersey (1986), Maine, Vermont, and Rhode Island (1988), Georgia (1989), Washington (1990), and other states (Maryland, Virginia, California) now actively considering legislation. An overview of their systems reveals a number of concepts that arose out of the years of implementation experience since 1973. The thread that links and defines the new state/regional/local roles in each of these systems is *consistency*, usually defined as a requirement that a set of goals and policies adopted by the state legislature form the framework for the system and that mandated state, regional, and local plans be consistent with the goals and policies defined by the new system and with each other.

In Oregon, every city and county must prepare a plan with implementing regulations that is "acknowledged" as consistent by the state's Land Conservation and Development Commission. In Florida, local government plans are deemed consistent once they are "in compliance with" the goals and policies of the state and relevant regional plans as well as with the state's minimum criteria rule that details the policies and data that local plans must include to be in compliance. In New Jersey, consistency is achieved, at least in theory, through a complex negotiation process led by the counties called "cross-acceptance." Its goal is to bring all municipal plans and the state plan into consistency with each other. In Maine, full consistency is technically not mandated, but the incentives for taking the final step to "certification" are substantial. Similarly, in Georgia, the final step in the consistency process occurs when the regional agency "qualifies" the plan as consistent. The incentive/disincentive system is such that local governments almost certainly will take this final step. Rhode Island has a clear mandate for consistency. The penalty for noncompliance is to have the state prepare the plan for the local government. In Vermont, if local governments choose to plan at all, the plan must be consistent with state and regional goals and policies. Finally, in Washington State, the mandate for consistency exists and the means to achieve it were provided through a "second phase" law passed in the 1991 legislative session.

Florida has the strongest concurrency requirement. No other state says flatly that, after a local government has adopted its comprehensive plan and land development regulations, no new development may be permitted unless the concurrency requirement has been met.[1] This "pay as you grow" policy is a major challenge for Florida, a state that has engaged in deficit financing of growth for decades.[2] As Florida's initial round of adopting plan and development regulations under the 1985 Growth Management Act nears its completion, funding concurrency requirements is assuming crisis proportions.

Increasingly strong mandates in recent state growth management systems have precipitated compact urban development strategies designed to discourage urban sprawl. Oregon again pioneered in this area. Goals 3 and 14 of its 1973 statewide plan mandated the development of "urban growth boundaries" and decreed that all urban development would take place within those boundaries (with certain limited and well-defined exceptions). The rural countryside would be reserved for agricultural and forestry uses.

While no other state has achieved anything close to Oregon's record in separating rural and urban uses, all state growth management strategies adopted between 1985 and 1991 include a more or less mandatory set of policies to combat urban sprawl and to promote more compact urban development patterns. In Florida, local governments are establishing urban service boundaries designed to contain urban sprawl. It is likely that growth patterns will change dramatically as these policies aimed at separating rural and urban uses mature. Washington state passed a "phase two" law strengthening the initial 1990 statute, which has very strong urban sprawl policies.

Oregon has also been the leader in terms of affordable housing strategies. Goal 10 of Oregon's statewide plan, as developed through case law and legislative actions, mandates that local governments define the need for affordable housing and provide a mix of housing densities to achieve such a goal. In the Portland region, mandated densities are 6, 8, and 10 dwelling units per acre, resulting in a drastic increase in land zoned for multifamily use. As a result, Oregon has the most aggressive planning and regulatory framework for affordable housing in the nation, and other states have followed its lead in making policies and in implementing strategies, including the key component of funding.

New Jersey is a separate case in that the development of its State Development and Redevelopment Plan was driven by the New Jersey Supreme Court's "Mt. Laurel" decisions defining the responsibility of the state and its municipalities in providing affordable housing (*Southern Burlington Co. NAACP v. The Township of Mt. Laurel*, 1975—"Mt. Laurel I"; *Southern Burlington Co. NAACP v. The Township of Mt. Laurel*, 1983—"Mt. Laurel II").

Vermont's commitment of substantial resources to a Housing and Conservation Trust Fund set up in 1987 is an outstanding example of strong housing legislation.

Recurring real estate transfer tax revenues as well as special legislative appropriations and bond issue funds were earmarked to support the effort. These have provided some $30 million in "one-time" sources along with several million annually from the transfer tax. More than half of the funds expended so far have been for housing. This result contradicts accusations often made against local growth control initiatives that they are hostile to the provision of affordable housing and economic development.

The protection of the rural landscape, including farm and forest lands, wetlands, water recharge lands, and uplands that protect endangered species, is another major component of state growth strategies. Earmarked funding sources,[3] special programs to acquire environmentally important lands,[4] and additional regulatory programs to better protect land, water, and air resources are being adopted as elements of these growth strategies.[5]

Clearly, the adoption and implementation of state growth management systems, which began in the 1970s, evolved through the 1980s, and continue into the 1990s, have established new roles and objectives for state governments. These laws have also assigned new roles to regional agencies and local governments to create a partnership for growth management, with authority and responsibility shared by all three levels of government.

REGIONAL GOVERNANCE ROLES IN RECENT GROWTH MANAGEMENT SYSTEMS

Substate regional agencies generally suffered a decline in funding and program significance from the mid-1970s through the years of the Reagan administration. The exception was regional agencies established or reempowered as part of new state roles in planning and growth management. Although the regional coastal commissions in California and regional planning councils in Florida were both established in the 1970s, it has been the state planning and growth management strategies of the 1980s that have created a true resurgence of regionalism.

Typically, the improvement of regional agencies has taken place through building on existing councils of governments (COGs) that previously were unimportant actors in growth management systems (Florida Advisory Council on Inter-governmental Relations, 1991). Increased state funding has greatly strengthened these regional governance systems, as have the state laws establishing the new systems and assigning to regional agencies a range of roles and responsibilities. These include (a) the identification of important regional resources and facilities, (b) the development of regional plans and programs with which local plans must be consistent, (c) review of local plans for consistency with regional goals and policies, (d) conflict resolution procedures to bring about horizontal consistency between and among local plans, and (e) technical assistance to local governments.

Growth management at the regional level probably has progressed the furthest in Florida. Its 11 regional planning councils (RPCs) were established largely to review developments of regional impact (DRIs), but they played no other significant role until the 1984 State and Regional Planning Act directed the adoption of regional plans and the 1985 Growth Management Act mandated regional review of local plans for consistency and compatibility with the relevant regional plan. Florida's growth management system has a "top-down" policy framework. RPCs develop regional plans based on the state's comprehensive plan, then review local plans for consistency with the regional plan and for compatibility with neighboring local plans.

Governing boards at the regional level comprise varying combinations of local elected and appointed officials in each state. Florida statutes require that local government officials account for two thirds of the RPC's board membership. Representation of all municipalities in the region is not mandatory but is required for each county. The remaining membership is appointed by the governor, typically nonelected citizens of the region. Members pay dues that constitute approximately 40% of the RPCs' funding. Georgia law requires each county and municipality to be a member of the regional development centers (RDCs) and that each member pay dues. In fact, Georgia's growth management legislation describes RDC membership and dues payment as a specific role of local governments. In addition, each county and the municipalities within that county must jointly elect a county resident to serve as the "nonpublic" representative of the county. Each regional agency has a 15-member executive committee, one third of whose membership is composed of nonelected citizens of the region.

Vermont law also includes all local governments as dues-paying members of Regional Planning Commissions. Towns do, however, have the option of switching from one regional commission to another and several have done so. In Maine, local elected officials from towns in the area the regional council represents must constitute 50% of the board's representation. Member towns may appoint nonelected officials to make up the remainder.

Perhaps the foremost role of regional governments in an integrated growth management system is the development of plans that establish regional goals and policies and identify regionally significant resources—natural, man made, economic, and institutional. These plans address growth-related issues and impacts that often transcend jurisdictional boundaries and lack a mechanism for their management and resolution. Historically, cities and counties in metropolitan regions have formed extrajurisdictional boards and councils, usually Councils of Government, to provide forums for discussion. Such councils, however, typically have no statutory authority or roles, and their plans and policies exist outside of any governing framework. Although regional councils in Florida, Georgia, Vermont, and Maine are not true governments with directly elected officials and regulatory and taxing authority, through their regional plans and policies, they do have statutory authority over local plans.

Regional governments review local plans for a variety of reasons. For the most part, the purpose of regional review is to ensure local consideration of greater-than-local issues and to maintain a comprehensive and integrated growth policy framework. Regional councils review local plans for their compatibility with other local plans and for their consistency with regional goals. Georgia's RDCs and Vermont's regional commissions, however, have an additional role in plan review, which is determining local plan compliance with the state's planning goals and minimum standards.

Florida and Georgia differ from Vermont and Maine in that their regional governments also review the effects of DRIs on regional resources and facilities. DRI review in Florida provides an additional source of funding via processing fees for the regional government—approximately 20% of the RPC's revenues. Although regional reviews of DRIs in Florida and Georgia are not binding on the local government's final approval for development, the DRI process serves an important regional role in local land use decisions that have greater-than-local impacts.

Regional governments in Florida, Georgia, and Vermont are also responsible for mediating interlocal conflicts. In Georgia's legislation, the mediation role of RDCs is intended to assist the DRI process and obviate formal resolution at the state level, and local governments must participate in region-led mediation to resolve conflicts within and among local plans. With the implementation of growth management systems under way in Georgia and also in Vermont, however, neither of their regional governments has yet attempted formal conflict mediation. Florida's RPCs are assigned a mediation role by statute to resolve conflicts within and among local plans, but to date they have not been strongly active in this role.

Technical assistance to local governments is another regional role in Florida, Georgia, Vermont, and Maine. Regional governments in Georgia and Vermont aid in creating a statewide geographic information system to serve local governments and state agencies. Local governments in Florida and Georgia may contract with the regional governments to prepare their comprehensive plans. The RPCs in Florida's more rural areas tend to perform this role more frequently than the urban RPCs, due to the small or nonexistent planning staffs of rural local governments.

Florida's growth management system has had the longest history of the four case states. All of Florida's RPCs adopted regional plans by 1987 and now are undertaking their required 3-year review. Some, such as the South Florida and the Southwest Florida RPCs, are beginning to assume nontraditional regional roles in examining social and economic issues. In Georgia, although the RDCs originally existed as area planning and development commissions (APDCs) since the early 1970s, their major new roles within the growth management system are just beginning to be implemented. The state appears committed to funding at the regional level, despite a long tradition of local home rule.

Vermont and Maine, also strong home rule states, have shown mixed results. Many towns in Vermont have resisted regional involvement and some are reluctant to participate in the regional planning commissions or in the growth management system. Even here, substantial funding increases by the state are allowing regional agencies to enlarge their staff, and many towns are taking advantage of this funding. In Maine, towns depend greatly on the regional planning councils for technical assistance and intergovernmental coordination. State funding has improved the capacity of regional agencies to provide services.

In all four states, full implementation of regional roles and responsibilities, particularly technical assistance, regional plan development, and local plan review, will require consistent and adequate funding for staff and facilities. Failure to function effectively at the regional level could diminish coordination between the state and local levels. In Florida, legislative funding for RPCs has been barely sufficient to meet their numerous and diverse responsibilities. As a result, some RPCs have sought funding alternatives, such as grant monies. For example, both the Tampa Bay and the East Central Florida RPCs serve as the Area Agencies on Aging, and RPCs in urban areas of the state staff metropolitan planning organizations. RPCs in the state's heavily populated areas argue that state funding should be based more on population (currently 30% of funding is population based) due to the larger number of local governments and broader array of regional problems. Increased funding is associated with increased powers, however, and neither the state nor the local governments appear interested in granting broader authority to the regional level.

State funding of regional councils in Georgia has been reduced 3% for FY 1991 and 1992 due to the economic slowdown. State officials are confident, however, that funding will increase within the next few years.[6] Georgia's RDCs receive base funding of $75,000 each, per year. The funds, however, are earmarked for state program tasks, such as assisting in statewide surveys. RDCs also receive discretionary funding for unique regional needs and supplemental funding, distributed on a population-based formula, for growth management responsibilities. To receive both base funding and supplemental funding, however, RDCs must collect a minimum of $0.25 per capita from local governments, and, while most RDCs average $0.50 to $0.75 per capita, the state and the RDCs are encouraging greater local contributions. Furthermore, the state is requiring greater accountability from the RDCs and plans to use $50,000 of funding initially slated for regional projects to develop an accounting system for the RDCs. Future funding to the RDCs will be contingent upon their compliance in submitting financial reports and participation in audits.

Maine's regional councils in 1990 received $600,000, cut to $532,000 in 1991. Future shortfalls are predicted for the state's general fund, which supports the regional councils.[7] In Vermont, funding of regional commissions has remained steady, given that a percentage of the property transfer tax is earmarked for regional funding. It was, however, necessary to appropriate from the state's general fund $230,000 of the regions' total funding of $1.31 million to mitigate a recent shortfall.[8] Vermont's regional commissions currently also rely on municipal dues for part of their budgets. Membership dues are voluntary and it appears that future shortfalls at the state level might require increased contributions from municipalities.

ROLES OF LOCAL GOVERNMENTS IN INTEGRATED GROWTH MANAGEMENT SYSTEMS

Even the most "intrusive" regional and state roles in these new growth management systems leave the major tasks of implementing the system to local governments. Local governments are discovering that, once these new systems are adopted, home rule powers are strengthened in three important ways: (a) protection from a neighboring government's spillover impacts through the horizontal consistency requirement; (b) protection from state agencies who may not, except in carefully defined circumstances, carry out programs that are inconsistent with local plans; and (c) direct state support for the plan adoption and plan implementation system.

The growth management systems in Oregon (1973), Florida (1985), and Georgia (1989) have come on line over a 19-year period. They have variously been described as top down (Oregon, Florida) and bottom up (Georgia) in their attempts to develop an intergovernmental strategy featuring the concepts of consistency, concurrency, compact urban growth patterns, affordable housing, economic development, and the protection of natural systems.

In these states, each local government is responsible for adopting and implementing plans consistent with state planning goals and standards. This role is demanding and requires months of staff time to prepare and implement a plan. Unfortunately, many local governments, often rural, do not possess the expertise or resources to conduct in-depth facilities assessments and other required studies. These governments must depend on regional governments for technical assistance and on state governments for financial assistance.

Oregon and Florida have assisted local governments in appropriating funds for plan development.[9] Florida's Department of Community Affairs has also appropriated funds (more than $3 million) for preparation of local land development regulations and for special projects related to plan development and implementation. Despite initial complaints from local governments over the financial burdens of mandated planning, all of Oregon's local plans have been "acknowledged," and more than half of Florida's local plans have been found "in compliance" or are pending compliance.[10] The plan adoption phase in Florida should end in 1992—four years from the submission of the first local plan in April 1988. In Georgia, local governments are required to prepare plans consistent with the state's minimum standards and criteria. Full consistency involves a process in which plans become "qualified," with strict penalties for not taking the final step toward qualification.

While Oregon is now considering a concurrency policy to meet the infrastructure demands of new development, many of Florida's local governments with adopted plans are struggling to maintain service levels and catch up with infrastructure backlogs. Limited fiscal home rule in Florida further complicates the implementation of local plans and the management of concurrency. Local governments have relatively few options in raising revenue because they may not levy income taxes, and the state constitution caps property taxes and exempts from assessment the first $25,000 of property value. Counties may levy a one-cent local option sales tax for infrastructure, but it must be approved by referendum,[11] and the six-cent local option gasoline tax falls short of the needed revenues.

Implementation of plans not only creates fiscal burdens for local governments but also heightens tension about different approaches to policy. Rural local governments in Oregon and Florida object to the "urban" focus of state growth management policies and seem to resent the role of the state in directing the use and development of their lands, especially farm and forest lands.[12] Florida's Department of Community Affairs (DCA) has upheld in its review of local plans the applicability of state growth policies to rural areas and has developed strategies for rural local governments for complying with these policies other than by simply lowering allowable densities. In Georgia's "bottom-up" system, local plans have more flexibility in terms of setting policy but ultimately will have to comply with state and regional standards to be qualified.

Public participation is an important part of the planning process. In fact, Goal 1 of Oregon's statewide planning goals is "citizen involvement" to "ensure" the involvement of citizens in all phases of the planning process. Similarly, Florida's "plan implementation" goal is to "encourage" citizen participation at all levels of the planning process. Moreover, Oregon, Florida, and Georgia require public hearings prior to local plan adoption, but ensuring adequate public input demands more than several hours of formal hearings. Florida law also provides for citizens to formally enter the plan adoption process and challenge the DCA's compliance determinations. Furthermore, an "aggrieved or adversely affected" person may challenge the consistency of local regulations or a development order, with the adopted local plan (Fla. Stat., sec. 163.3184).

Growth management watchdog groups have also greatly affected the plan adoption and implementation process. For example, 1000 Friends of Oregon and 1000 Friends of Florida monitor closely their respective local and state actions in implementing the law. Both groups have intervened in administrative hearings and the appeals process, often arguing that a local plan will not uphold certain growth management policies. These organizations have proved to be major actors and have played a key role in assuring full implementation of the growth management systems.

CONCLUSION

Growth management systems have had a major impact on intergovernmental relations and have expanded the roles and responsibilities of local, regional, and state levels of government. Experience with these systems to date provides clear evidence that local government home rule is strengthened, even though states have taken a lead role in defining the parameters of the new systems, assigning roles and responsibilities to each level, and providing the funds needed to make the systems work. While funding growth management has proved to be difficult, especially in recessions, the record so far is impressive.

There is a need to bring all the stakeholders, public and private, to the negotiating table to hammer out a consensus on the necessary elements of an effective growth management system. Georgia has created a remarkable consensus-building effort through its Growth Strategies Commission, and Florida and Oregon have achieved similar results. The most effective state systems have managed to sustain the broad-based consensus that supported their adoption in the first place. With additional states, such as Maryland and Virginia, likely to adopt growth management plans in the future, there appears to be a growing national consensus in support of this approach to balancing economic growth with a high quality of environmental life.

NOTES

1 *Concurrency*, as defined in Florida's growth management system, means simply that an absolute "pay as you grow" policy will be in effect for six facilities (recreation, transportation, sewer, solid waste, drainage, and potable water) that require the setting of levels of service by local governments. Local governments may not approve new development that would lower these established levels of service. Furthermore, infrastructure backlogs must be made up over a negotiated period of time.

2 In 1987, Florida's State Comprehensive Plan Committee—more commonly referred to as the "Zwick" Committee because of its chair, Charles Zwick—estimated the cost of resolving infrastructure backlogs at the state and local levels to be over $52 billion, including an $18 billion deficit in funding local infrastructure and service needs.

3 The Vermont Housing and Conservation Trust Fund, adopted in 1987, also serves as a key instrument in protecting natural resources as well as assuring affordable housing in the state. A nine-member trust fund board governs the appropriation of monies from the fund, which is supported by a $5 million annual earmarked funding source. The fund may be used for purchasing farm or forest lands in the interest of containing urban sprawl.

4 Florida's Preservation 2000 program, adopted by the 1990 legislature, will provide $3 billion in additional funding to an already aggressive public lands acquisition program.

5 For example, the Georgia legislature in 1991 passed a new mountain and river corridors protection law, and Florida in 1987 passed legislation creating its Surface Water Improvement and Management program.

6 This information came from telephone interviews with the following state Department of Community Affairs officials: Mike Gleaton, Assistant Director, Office of Comprehensive Planning; Griff Doyle, Director, Office of Coordinated Planning; and Patty Schmidt, Chief of Planning Section, Office of Comprehensive Planning.

7 Funding information for Maine's regional councils was provided by the state Office of Community Development and Planning.

8 Funding information for Vermont's regional commissions was provided by Greg Brown, Director, Local and Regional Planning Office of the state Department of Housing and Community Affairs.

9 Through the Local Government Planning Assistance Program, Florida's Department of Community Affairs awarded $22.6 million to local governments to revise or develop plans in compliance with state guidelines. During its 10-year plan adoption phase, Oregon's Land Conservation and Development Commission appropriated nearly the same amount to local governments for plan development. See Florida Department of Community Affairs (1989) and John M. DeGrove, *Land, Growth and Politics* (1984) for discussions of state planning assistance to local governments in Florida and Oregon, respectively.

10 As of May 1991, Florida's Department of Community Affairs had found 121 local plans "originally in compliance" and 49 "not in compliance"; however, 64 plans were brought into compliance through agreements with DCA and 55 have pending compliance agreements (1000 Friends of Florida, Executive Committee meeting notes, May 24, 1991).

11 As of June 1991, only 26 of Florida's 67 counties had successfully adopted this additional sales tax for local infrastructure; 15 counties have held local option sales tax referenda, some of them more than once, but they failed.

12 See the spring 1989 issue of *Landmark*, the quarterly journal of 1000 Friends of Oregon, for a more complete discussion of this issue.

REFERENCES

DeGrove J. M. (1984). *Land, growth and politics*. Chicago: APA.

Florida Advisory Council on Intergovernmental Relations. (1991). *Substate regional governance* (Interim Report). Tallahassee, FL: ACIR.

Florida Department of Community Affairs. (1989). DCA assists locals in all phases of planning process. *Technical Memo, 4*, 1–2.

Florida Department of Community Affairs. (1990). The truth about growth management in rural areas. *Technical Memo, 5*, 1–2, 6.

Howe, D. A. (1991). *Review of growth management strategies used in other states* (prepared for Oregon Department of Land Conservation and Redevelopment, Portland, OR).

Liberty, R. R. (1988, June). *The Oregon planning experience: Repeating the success and avoiding the mistakes.* Paper presented at the Conference on the Chesapeake Bay Critical Area Protection Program, University of Maryland, School of Public Affairs.

Nelson, A. C. (1990, August). Blazing new planning trails in Oregon. *Planning*, pp. 32–35.

Pelham, T. (1991, March). The state of Florida's growth management program. *Florida Planning, 2*, 1, 8.

Southern Burlington Co. NAACP v. the Township of Mt. Laurel [Mt. Laurel I], 67 N.J. 151, 336 A.2d 713, appeal dismissed and cert. denied, 423 U.S. 808 (1975).

Southern Burlington Co. NAACP v. the Township of Mt. Laurel [Mt. Laurel II], 92 N.J. 158, 456 A.2d 390 (1983).

Author's note: This chapter is based in part on research conducted by Dr. John M. DeGrove and funded by a grant from the Lincoln Institute of Land Policy, Cambridge, MA. We wish to thank Christine Moore, Florida Atlantic University, for her assistance in preparing this chapter.

FOUR. LAND USE, ZONING, AND GROWTH MANAGEMENT—SUGGESTED READINGS

Babcock, Richard, and C. Siemon. 1985. *The Zoning Game Revisited*. Cambridge, MA: Lincoln Institute of Land Policy.

Bosselman, Fred, David Callies, and John Banta. 1973. *The Taking Issue*. Washington, DC: U.S. Government Printing Office.

DeGrove, John. 1984. *Land Growth and Politics*. Chicago: American Planning Association.

DeGrove, John. 1992. *Planning and Growth Management in the States: The New Frontier for Land Policy*. Cambridge, MA: Lincoln Institute of Land Policy.

Godschalk, David R., David J. Brower, Larry D. McBennett, Barbara A. Vestal, and Daniel C. Herr. 1979. *Constitutional Issues of Growth Management*. Chicago: American Planning Association.

Haar, Charles M., and Michael Allan Wolf. 1989. *Land Use Planning*. Boston: Little, Brown.

Hagman, Donald G. 1971. *Urban Planning and Land Development Control Law*. St. Paul, MN: West.

Phillips, E. Barbara, and R. T. LeGates. 1981. *City Lights: An Introduction to Urban Studies*. New York: Oxford University Press.

Popper, Frank. 1981. *The Politics of Land-use Reform*. Madison: The University of Wisconsin Press.

Reilly, William K. 1973. *The Use of Land: A Citizen's Policy Guide to Urban Growth*. New York: Crowell.

Scott, Randall W., ed. 1971. *Management and Control of Growth*. Washington, DC: Urban Land Institute.

Stein, Jay M., ed. 1993. *Growth Management: The Planning Challenge of the 1990s*. Newbury Park, CA: Sage Publications.

5

DESIGN AND URBAN FORM

What Is the Form of a City, and How Is It Made?

Kevin Lynch

Kevin Lynch pioneered in investigating and measuring people's perceptions about the quality of their environment in relation to the spatial, physical city. Lynch's *A Theory of Good City Form* summarizes his more theoretical work. In this particular selection, the author moves toward building a full theory of city form by reviewing planning, functional, and normative theory. He states that "building a full theory will be a long-range effort, if it is to be a theory which deals with form and process, and which is an understanding, an evaluation, a prediction, and a prescription, all in one" (p. 187). It is in this combination that all three branches of theory should merge.

Three branches of theory endeavor to explain the city as a spatial phenomenon. One, called "planning theory," asserts how complex public decisions about city development are or should be made. Since these understandings apply to all complex political and economic enterprises, the domain of this theory extends far beyond the realm of city planning, and it has been well developed in those other fields. So it has a more general name: "decision theory."

The second branch, which I call "functional theory," is more particularly focussed on cities, since it attempts to explain why they take the form they do and how that form functions. This is a reasonably thick theoretical limb—if not as robust as decision theory—and engages renewed interest today.

The third branch, spindly and starved for light, but on which so many actions are hung, is what I would call "normative theory." It deals with the generalizable connections between human values and settlement form, or how to know a good city when you see one. This is our concern.

As on any healthy tree, the three branches should spring securely from a common trunk. Unlike the branches of trees we know, they should not diverge. They should interconnect and support each other at many points. A comprehensive theory of cities would be a mat of vegetation, and some day the branches will no longer exist in separate form. While working perilously far out on the weakest branch, we must be aware of the other two and look for favorable places to insert a graft.

So this chapter scans planning theory and functional theory, the two companion branches to our own. It also sets forth what I mean by the "form" of the city. Otherwise, what are we talking about?

Almost all recent theories about the spatial form of urban settlements have been theories of urban function. They ask: "How did the city get to be the way it is?"

and that closely related question, "how does it work?" One cannot ask, "What is a good city?" without some convictions about answers to those previous questions. Theories of function, in their turn, cannot be constructed without some sense of "goodness," which allows one to focus on the essential elements. All functional theories contain value assumptions—most often hidden ones—just as all normative theories contain assumptions about structure and function. Theoretical developments in one arena impose themselves on the other. A developed theory of cities will be simultaneously normative and explanatory.

As yet, there is no single theory of city genesis and function that brings together all the significant aspects of city life. These theories look at the city from quite different points of view, and some particular viewpoints are much more fully developed than others.

The city may be looked on as a story, a pattern of relations between human groups, a production and distribution space, a field of physical force, a set of linked decisions, or an arena of conflict. Values are embedded in these metaphors: historic continuity, stable equilibrium, productive efficiency, capable decision and management, maximum interaction, or the progress of political struggle. Certain actors become the decisive elements of transformation in each view: political leaders, families and ethnic groups, major investors, the technicians of transport, the decision elite, the revolutionary classes.

From the standpoint of normative theory, these functional theories have some common deficiencies. Perhaps it is these very deficiencies which allow me (or is it the pervading dullness which motivates me?) to compress this extensive literature into a single appendix. If we had a compelling functional theory, no book on city values could be written without it. As it is, these theories depend on values which are unexamined and incomplete. Second, most of them are essentially static in nature, dealing with small shifts, balancings, or external changes which will be damped out, or lead to final explosions, or, at most, cause radical jumps that reach some new and endless plateau. None deals successfully with continuous change, with incremental actions that lead in some progressive direction.

Third, none of these formulations (except the historical, or "antitheoretical," view) deals with environmental quality, that is, with the rich texture of city form and meaning. Space is abstracted in a way that impoverishes it, reducing it to a neutral container, a costly distance, or a way of recording a distribution which is the residue of some other, nonspatial, process. Most of what we feel to be the real experience of the city has simply vanished. Fourth, few of the theories consider that the city is the result of the purposeful behavior of individuals and small groups, and that human beings can learn. The city is the manifestation of some iron law or other, rather than the result of changing human aspirations.

It surprises no one to hear that it is impossible to explain how a city should be, without understanding how it is. Perhaps it *is* surprising to encounter the reverse: that an understanding of how a city is depends on a valuing of what it should be. But values and explanations seem to me inextricable. In the absence of valid theory in either branch, concepts elaborated in the one must employ provisional assumptions from the other, while making that dependence explicit and maintaining as much independence as is possible.

In distinction to functional and normative theory, planning theory deals with the nature of the environmental decision process—how it is and should be conducted. This is a subject treated at length in many other sources. Since normative theory is intended to be useful in creating better cities, clearly it must be aware of the situations in which it is likely to be used.

Cities are built and maintained by a host of agents: families, industrial firms, city bureaus, developers, investors, regulatory and subsidizing agencies, utility companies, and the like. Each has its own interests, and the process of decision is fragmented, plural, and marked by bargaining. Some of these agents are dominant, leading; others will follow those leaders. In this country, the leading agents tend to be the great financial institutions, which establish the conditions for investment; the major corporations, whose decisions as to the location and nature of productive investment set the rate and quality of city growth; and the large developers, who create extensive pieces of the city itself. On the public side, we must add the major federal agencies, whose policies of taxation, subsidy, and regulation merge with the actions of private finance to set the investment conditions, and the large, single-purpose, state or regional agencies which are charged with creating highways, ports, water and disposal systems, large reservations, and similar major chunks of city infrastructure. The basic patterns set by these form givers (to appropriate an egotistical term from architecture) are filled in by the actions of many others, in particular the location decisions of individual families and of firms of modest size, the preparatory activities of real estate speculators, small developers, and builders, and the regulatory and supporting functions of local government. The latter agencies, although unable to control the main currents, do much to set the quality of a settlement, through their fire, building, and zoning codes, by the way they service development with schools and roads and open space, and by the quality of those services: education, policing, and sanitation.

This process has certain marked characteristics. The leading agents, who have such a tremendous influence, do not control city development in any directed, central fashion. Typically, they are single-purpose actors, whose aim is to increase their profit margin, complete a sewer system, support the real estate market, or maintain a taxation system which generates sufficient revenue (and yet provides sufficient loopholes). These purposes are usually remote from the city form that they shape. No one takes anything like a comprehensive view of the evolving spatial structure, except perhaps the local planning agency, which is one of the weaker actors. When this is added to the great number of agencies who have *some* role to play in the game, and whose acts, however passively responsive, have great cumulative power, then we have a city-building process which is complex and plural, marked by conflict, cross-purpose, and bargaining, and whose outcome, while often inequitable or even unwanted, seems as uncontrollable as a glacier.

Yet it is controlled, if not with conscious purpose, by the leading actors we have named, and it can also be modified consciously by public effort, although with only partial (and sometimes with surprising) effect. Most purposeful public actions, beyond the single-minded decisions of public works agencies, are reactions to pressing difficulties, which are carried out with haste, poor information, and no theory, and which are designed to return the system to some previous condition.

Comprehensive theory might seem of remote value in such restrictive situations, and yet it is just here that a coherent theory is so badly needed. It is needed to make restricted actions effective, as well as to enlighten the inevitable political bargaining, or even to point to needed changes in the decision process itself. Thus structural theory guides the quasi-intuitional actions of a trained engineer in some emergency, and military theory illuminates the confused art of war. But theory must be of a certain kind, if it is to be useful. It must speak to purposes, and not about inevitable forces. It must not be esoteric, but be clear enough to be useful to all sorts of actors. It must be usable in rapid, partial decisions and in the constant "steering" of policy as the complex settlement changes. Indeed, as we shall see, various normative theories of the city have been used in just that way, however misguided they might have been.

Creating cities can be quite different in other societies. The power to decide may be highly decentralized but also egalitarian, instead of decentralized but unequal, in the United States. More often, it is more highly centralized. The motives of power may differ. The basic values of the society may not only be different from our own, but also more homogeneous and stable. Decisions may be made according to tradition, without explicit rational analysis. The level of material resources, of skill and technology, can be substantially lower, which changes the constraints and shifts the priorities. The rate of change may be faster or slower. All these variations in the dimensions of the decision process make varying demands on any normative theory. A general theory must be able to respond to those differences. At the same time, there do seem to be certain regularities in the contemporary decision process, at least within the large urban settlements which dominate our landscape today. We find plurality, complexity, and rapid change everywhere.

Whenever any significant actor, public or private, engages to make an important decision in this complex environment, that effort to decide has typical features. The first question is: "What is the problem?" The consciousness of a problem is always an integrated perception, however vague, that is simultaneously an image of the situation and its constraints, of the goals to be achieved, of who the clients are, and what kinds of resources and solutions are available. Problems do not exist without some inkling of all of these features, and the decision process is no more than a progressive clarification of this set, until a firm basis for action is found—one in which solution, aims, clients, resources to be used, and perceived situation all seem to match one another. To achieve this mutual fit may require modifying any or all of these separate features. But the initial concept of the problem is crucial. Often enough, it is wrong to begin with—the situation so poorly understood, the clients so restricted, the aims or the solution envisaged so inappropriate, that nothing can be done except to make things worse.

Some of the preconceptions that accompany initial problem definition are fundamental. One is the view of the basic type of response that is appropriate. For example: seeing a difficulty, one may not try to remove it, but simply seek to understand it and to predict its future course, so that one can adapt, survive, and prosper if possible. Grass bends to the wind, but the "street-wise" person does more: he takes advantage of the wind's momentary course and power.

At the other end of the scale, one may be convinced that a fundamental change in the rules of the game is essential. Society must make a radical shift. An environmental problem is the occasion for motivating others to that radical change. Nothing less than this great leap will do, and so a housing shortage is best converted into a confrontation and a revolutionary lesson. Or, following another alternative, one makes a persuasive model of a habitat or society which is radically better than the present one, but which can be realized gradually.

Between passive response and great leaps lies the strategy of making repeated changes in selected factors, in order to improve the whole piecemeal. One such gradualist approach is to change persons so that they can function better in an existing context. People's lives are enriched by learning to observe and understand their own city neighborhoods, and they begin to come to grips with their own life situations. Teaching children or the handicapped how to get about the city, or homeowners how to make a garden or repair a house, are other examples of this mode of intervention.

Alternatively, one may focus on modifying the environment, the better to fit the intentions of the person, which is the typical planning approach. The normative theory we have in mind is designed for use in this environment-modifying, piecemeal, and gradualist mode. However, it can also supply educative information, or the fuel for a more radical change. Changing minds, changing society, or even changing nothing at all, may in many situations be a more appropriate response than changing the environment. Most people are convinced of the eternal rightness of their own favorite mode. On the contrary, a well-formulated problem always entails prior consideration of the proper scope and mode of intervention.

It is also crucial to decide who the clients are. Who should make the decisions? In whose interests should those decisions be made? Are deciders and decided-for the same? The clients identified at the beginning of a decision effort usually exclude certain vital interests. Bringing in a new client, in the course of the decision, is delicate work, sure to be resisted by those already at the table and likely to impede any decisive action.

A highly decentralized decision process, in which the immediate users of a place make the decisions about its form, is a powerful ideal. It reinforces their sense of competence, and seems more likely to result in a well-fitted environment, than if they are excluded. The basic view is philosophical anarchism. But there are users whom we judge incompetent to decide: too young, too ill, or under coercion. There are indivisible goods, like clean air, that affect millions of users simultaneously. There are places used by numerous transient clients, such as a subway. There are conflicting interests, users who succeed each other, and distant persons whose interests are partially affected by some local use. There are unknown clients, people who are not there yet, or who have not yet been born. There are clients who are unaware of their own requirements, or of what they might value if they had the opportunity. All these difficulties, plus the political troubles inherent in any effort to shift control to new clients as a problem develops, give planning decisions their characteristic tone of ambiguity, conflict, and fluidity.

Other professionals hold a contrary view: all crucial decisions are inevitably, or even preferably, made by a powerful few. Since dominant interests cannot be suppressed, and since some professionals are uniquely endowed by their marvelous training and ability to solve environmental problems, those gifted ones should stand beside the seats of power. Problems are complex, values subtle, and solutions specialized and delicate. Find an expert who can grasp the situation, and give him room to work. Some of our more remarkable environments arose from heroic leadership of that kind, but few are well fitted to the purpose of their users. This model performs best when values are clear and common, and problems largely technical.

Professional planners take on many different roles in this complicated decision landscape. Most of them, perhaps, are project planners, working for some definite client, such as a corporation or government agency, and preparing a solution to some limited, well-defined problem, according to an explicit set of purposes. Here they are sheltered from most of the debates about the client or the mode of intervention. Those crucial decisions have been made for them.

Other planners consider themselves to be working in the public interest. Since they must work near some center of power in order to be effective, they are beset by the issues I have sketched out above: who is the client? who should make the decisions? how should goals be determined? are there in fact any common interests? how can I know them? how can power be effective without overriding those common interests with its own aims? At times, planners in this public interest role may try to avoid some of these dilemmas by attending primarily to the decision *process*—keeping it as open and equitable as possible—without attempting to set goals or to recommend solutions.

Retreating still further from decision, and in despair of discovering the public interest, many planners take on the primary role of informers (not spies!). They create accurate and timely information for public use: descriptions of the present state and how it is changing, predictions about coming events, and analyses of the results to be expected from this or that line of action. Actual plans and decisions are left to others, but presumably they will be better decisions because better informed. If these planners have strong beliefs about the decision process, they may shape their information especially for the use of certain groups: for decentralized users, for radical reformers, or for central decision makers. Alternatively, as I have mentioned above, they may think of themselves primarily as teachers, involved in educating, and so in changing, the public.

Lastly, some professionals are primarily advocates. They may be the advocates of some idea—such as new towns or bicycle paths or houseboats—in which case they must organize their own client base. These are pattern makers, who hope to be effective through the persuasiveness of their ideas. If sufficiently radical, they create utopias: patent models for a new society.

More frequently, they will be advocates of some interest group—a social class, a corporation, a neighborhood—and press that interest vigorously, in competition with other contenders. Many professionals, of course, are advocates without being aware of it, while others take a more conscious position. They look on society as highly connected but irredeemably plural and contradictory. All decisions are made by struggle and compromise; few values are held in common. Inevitably, any professional works for one group or another. Some will add: but this system is unjust, since some groups have little power and no hired advocate. Therefore, a professional of conscience works for those poorly represented groups, advocating their interests as forcefully and as narrowly as a planner hired by a real estate developer.

Advocates, informers, project designers, and public planners—these are perhaps the predominant professional roles today. Their theories and models, usually implicit and unexamined, play an important part in environmental decision, amid all the customary confusion of that process. Unmanageable problems are made manageable by restricting the clients to be attended to, by taking a model of change and thus a type of solution for granted, by assuming a narrow set of operative values, and by controlling the supply of information. Information of a fairly broad range is often gathered while initiating planning studies. In the press of decision, only a small portion of that information is used, and that is the portion which accords with the models already in the decider's head. Developing a theory that is sufficiently concise and flexible to be used under pressure is one way of directing the attention of decision makers to one set of issues rather than another.

The process of decision (and of design, which is a subset of decision) is one of managing the progressive development and definition of a problem, to the point where situation, client, aim, and solution are sufficiently well-fitted to take action. This process, when applied to large environments at least, has difficulties which seem to be common throughout the world. It likewise poses some common issues: such as those about the nature of the client, the model of change and its management, and the nature of the professional role. It has consequences for the ethics of planning, as well. Planning, to my mind, has its own special interest in any public debate. I would characterize that special interest as one which is prejudiced in favor of five things (besides its focus on spatial form and form-associated institutions): the long-term effects, the interests of an absent client, the construction of new possibilities, the explicit use of values, and the ways of informing and opening up the decision process. These are professional counterweights to the de-emphasis of those considerations by other actors.

But what is this city, that we dare to call good or bad? How can we describe it in ways that different observers will confirm, and which can be related to values and performance? This simple step conceals unseemly difficulties.

Settlement form, usually referred to by the term "physical environment," is normally taken to be the spatial pattern of the large, inert, permanent physical objects in a city: buildings, streets, utilities, hills, rivers, perhaps the trees. To these objects are attached a miscellany of modifying terms, referring to their typical use, or their quality, or who owns them: single-family residence, public housing project, cornfield, rocky hill, ten-inch sewer, busy street, abandoned church, and so on. The spatial distribution of these things is shown on two-dimensional maps: topographic maps, land use maps, street maps with notations, utility networks, maps of housing condition. These maps are accompanied by population counts (divided into classes of age, sex, income, race, and occupation), and usually by maps showing the spatial distribution of population (by which is meant where people sleep). Then there are descriptions of the quantity of traffic on the various main arteries, and statistics on the principal economic activities (that is, only those human activities which are part of the system of monetary exchange), and data on the location, capacity, and condition of particular public or semi-public buildings or areas, such as schools, churches, parks, and the like. These descriptions are familiar, and they are infected with difficulties, which are also familiar to anyone who has handled them. Lay citizens are baffled by these maps, graphs and tables. This might be taken as a sign of the scientific sophistication of the field, except that professionals have the same troubles.

The fundamental problem is to decide what the form of a human settlement consists of: solely the inert physical things? or the living organisms too? the actions people engage in? the social structure? the economic system? the ecological system? the control of the space and its meaning? the way it presents itself to the senses? its daily and seasonal rhythms? its secular changes? Like any important phenomenon, the city extends out into every other phenomenon, and the choice of where to make the cut is not an easy one.

I will take the view that settlement form is the spatial arrangement of persons doing things, the resulting spatial flows of persons, goods, and information, and the physical features which modify space in some way significant to those actions, including enclosures, surfaces, channels, ambiences, and objects. Further, the description must include the cyclical and secular changes in those spatial distributions, the control of space, and the perception of it. The last two, of course, are raids into the domains of social institutions and of mental life.

The cut is not trivial, however, since most social institutional patterns are excluded, as well as the larger part of the realms of biology and psychology, the chemical and physical structure of matter, etc. The chosen ground is the spatiotemporal distribution of human actions and the physical things which are the context of those actions, plus just so much about social institutions and mental attitudes as is most directly linked to that spatiotemporal distribution, and which is significant at the scale of whole settlements.

No one would claim that to describe these things is to grasp a human settlement in its fullness. We must see any place as a social, biological, and physical whole, if we mean to understand it completely. But an important preliminary (or at least a necessary accompaniment) to seeing things whole is to define and understand their parts. Moreover, social and spatial structure are only partially related to each other—loose coupled, as it were—since both affect the other only through an intervening variable (the human actor), and both are complex things of great inertia. For me, the acts and thoughts of human beings are the final ground for judging quality. These apparently ephemeral phenomena become repetitive and significant in at least three situations: in the persistent structure of ideas which is a culture, in the enduring relationships between people which are social institutions, and in the standing relations of people with place. I deal with the last. While the social, or economic, or political aspects of settlements are rather well-defined—and often too narrowly defined—the physical aspect is put so uncertainly that it is difficult to see whether it plays any role at all.

The cut I suggest seems to be the closest one that can be taken, that still permits us to comment on the contribution of spatial pattern to human aims. Moreover, it is a coherent view, since its common core is the spatial distribution, at a given scale, of tangible, physical persons, objects, and actions. It has the advantage of growing out of the commonsense view of the environment, while regularizing and expanding it.

Building a full theory will be a long-range effort, if it is to be a theory which deals with form and process, and which is an understanding, an evaluation, a prediction, and a prescription, all in one. It will hinge on purposeful human behavior and the images and feelings that accompany it. This is the joint at which all three branches of theory should grow together. Our particular subject, which is normative theory, must be considered with that possibility in mind. Such normative theory as exists today is disconnected from the other theoretical realms, but carries hidden assumptions about function and process.

There are certain requirements, then, for any useful normative theory of city form:

1 It should start from purposeful behavior and the images and feelings which accompany it.

2 It should deal directly with settlement form and its qualities, and not be an eclectic application of concepts from other fields.

3 It should connect values of very general and long-range importance to that form, and to immediate, practical actions about it.

4 It should be able to deal with plural and conflicting interests and to speak for absent and future clients.

5 It should be appropriate to diverse cultures and to variations in the decision situation (variations in the centralization of power, the stability and homogeneity of values, the level of resources, and the rate of change).

6 It should be sufficiently simple, flexible, and divisible that it can be used in rapid, partial decisions, with imperfect information, by lay persons who are the direct users of the places in question.

7 It should be able to evaluate the quality of state and process together, as it varies over a moderate span of time.

8 While at root a way of evaluating settlement form, the concepts should suggest new possibilities of form. In general, it should be a possible theory: not an iron law of development, but one that emphasizes the active purposes of participants and their capacity for learning.

Where shall we look for the material for such a theory?

The Social Life of the Street

William H. Whyte

For nearly two decades, William H. Whyte has been observing how people use streets and public spaces. Although *City* is about the design and management of urban spaces, Whyte's true fascination is with the life and rituals of people out on the streets. In this chapter selection, Whyte acts as our guide for "seeing" the street. Whether describing the importance of street corners or extolling the virtues of "schmoozers," Whyte is a treat to read. For him, the street is a stage.

It was a dandy hypothesis. How far, I had wondered, would people move out of the pedestrian flow to have a conversation? My hypothesis was that they would gravitate to the unused foot or so of buffer space along the building walls. It was a matter of simple common sense.

We focused time-lapse cameras on several street corners and recorded the activity for two weeks. On maps of the corners we plotted the location of each conversation and how long it lasted. To screen out people who were only waiting for the light to change, we noted only those conversations lasting a minute or longer.

The activity was not as expected. To our surprise, the people who stopped to talk did not move out of the main pedestrian flow; and if they had been out of it, they moved into it. The great bulk of the conversations were smack in the middle of the pedestrian flow—the 100 percent location, to borrow the real estate term. In subsequent studies we were to find the same impulse to the center in traveling conversations—the kind in which two people move about a lot but don't go very far. There is much apparent motion, but if you plot the orbits, you will find that they are centered around the 100 percent location.

Observers in other countries have also noted the tendency to self-congestion. In his study of pedestrians in Copenhagen, Jan Gehl mapped bunching patterns almost identical to those observable here. Matthew Ciolek studies an Australian shopping center with similar results. "Contrary to 'common sense' expectations," Ciolek notes, "the great majority of people were found to select their sites for social interaction right on or very close to the traffic lines intersecting the plaza. Relatively few people formed their gatherings away from the spaces used for navigation."

Just why people behave like this I have never been able to determine. It is understandable that conversations should originate in the main flow. Where there are the most people, the likelihood of a meeting or of a leave-taking is highest. What is less explainable is the inclination to remain in the main flow, blocking traffic, and being jostled by it. This seems to be a matter not of inertia but of choice—instinctive per-

Location of street conversations lasting two minutes or more at Saks Fifth Avenue and Fiftieth Street. Cumulative for five days in June. Note main concentration at corner, secondary one outside entrance.

haps, but by no means illogical. In the center of the crowd, you have maximum choice—to break off, to switch, to continue. It is much like being in the middle of a crowded cocktail party, which is itself a moving conversation growing ever denser and denser, occasionally ending up with everyone squeezed into a corner. It is a behavior universally deplored and practiced.

What attracts people most, in sum, is other people. If I labor the point, it is because many urban spaces are being designed as though the opposite were true and as though what people like best are the places they stay away from. People themselves often talk along such lines, and that is why their responses to questionnaires can be so misleading. How many people would say they like to sit in the middle of a crowd? Instead, they speak of getting away from it all, and they use terms like "oasis," "retreat," and "escape." I am very glad my hypothesis blew up in my face. It has forced me to look at what people do.

The best places to look are street corners. As a general rule, 100 percent conversations are spotted most often at the busiest crossroads locations. Fifth Avenue at Fiftieth Street is one such. The heaviest pedestrian flows are at the entrance to Saks department store and at the street corner. It is at these two places that the greatest number of conversations are clustered, with relatively few in the space between the corner and the entrance. Of 133 conversations we mapped over several days, 57 percent were concentrated in the highest-traffic locations. While there were no significant differences between men and women, men did tend to talk somewhat longer than women: 50 percent of male groups talked five minutes or longer, compared to 45 percent of female groups.

Lexington Avenue is more crowded yet—almost to the point of travesty between Fifty-seventh and Fifty-eighth streets. What with signs, floral displays, street vendors, its narrow, twelve-and-a-half-foot sidewalks are reduced to an effective walkway of five or six feet. At the peak of the lunchtime traffic, pedestrians have to walk single file. And it is then that the sidewalk is likely to be further blocked by conversation.

Pedestrians are surprisingly tolerant of the blockers. As an experiment, two of our researchers engaged in marathon conversation in the middle of the block. "Almost all of the pedestrians," one reported, "made an effort to avoid brushing against us even though this involved squeezing close to the displays or to the cars at the curbs. One woman did jostle me on purpose. A few made remarks under their breaths. But if the others felt resentful, they didn't show it. They were so polite that when they couldn't avoid brushing against us, they murmured apologies as they passed."

People waiting for people are interesting to observe, particularly so a few minutes after the hour. But most interesting of all are people who meet people they did not expect to. When I started observing street behavior, it was the high incidence of these chance meetings that struck me. But when you come to think of it, it is not chance at all. With about three thousand people an hour streaming past a spot, there is an actuarial probability that someone will see a friend, an acquaintance, or the familiar stranger you can almost place but not quite. The probability may be higher yet when you take shifts into account.

The postlunch groups heading back to the office around one o'clock look like junior and middle management people. The people you see around two are older, more expensively dressed, and apparently not in a hurry.

Of the street conversations we tracked, about 30 percent appear to have been unplanned. Some encounters were too brief to develop into a conversation—a quick hello and a wave of the hand. Some were awkwardly tentative, with neither party quite sure whether it would be right to pass on or stop. But many went on for three minutes or more. If one of the persons was with a group, the encounter sometimes involved a full round of introductions and handshakes.

It is difficult to gauge the value of chance encounters. Did the old friends meet for lunch as they said they would? Did the trade gossip turn out to be right? Possibly. But one thing is certain: it is at the crossroads that the chances are best. As we will see in the chapter on the outward move of corporate headquarters, chance is what they forfeit.

Most goodbyes are brief: a fast "ciao," "take care," a wave, and they're off. But a number are protracted, particularly so when they are an extension of a failed goodbye. It's a little like the people who hover in office doorways, forever on the verge of leaving, but never doing so. If people go through the motions of a goodbye and stop short at the point of consummation, a momentum is set up that can lead to progressively more emphatic goodbyes, up to the final resolving goodbye. It is fascinating to watch these three- and four-wave goodbyes and try to distinguish the real goodbye from the false ones. Don't be fooled by the glance at the watch. It is only premonitory. I have a wonderful film record of two men gripped

Kiss, kiss.

in indecision in front of Saks Fifth Avenue. They just can't bring themselves to part. There are several rounds of goodbyes and looks at the watch, but it's not until a third party comes along that they finally break out of their impasse.

Best to watch are the postlunch goodbyes of the senior executives. Sometimes there is a note of irresolution about the leave-taking, as if the real business the lunch was supposed to have been about has not yet been broached. Finally, someone brings it up. The deal? The contract? Yes, yes, of course. How could they have forgotten? They now proceed to the business and as they do, their foot and arm movements tend to become reciprocal. This is an indication of people obliging one another, and soon the matter will be completed.

One of the most notable social rituals is schmoozing. In New York's garment district on Seventh Avenue, you will see groups of men lined up along the curb, facing inward. There are often so many of them that you have to go out into the street along with the handcart pushers if you want to make any headway. Sometimes the vehicular traffic slows to a near halt for all the gabbing.

"Schmoozing" is a Yiddish term for which there is no precise definition. But basically it means "nothing talk"—idle gossip, political opinions, sports talk, but not, so they say, business talk. But groups do tend to form up along occupational lines; salesmen, for example, tend to schmooze with other salesmen, and patternmakers, with other patternmakers. Some of the schmoozers are retirees who like to come back around midday to keep in touch. Almost all garment district schmoozers are men.

Schmoozing on
Seventh Avenue.

Physically, it's an awful place. It is without trees or graces, it is noisy and fume-ridden, and the traffic is so bad even cyclists try to give the place a wide berth. If you ask the schmoozers if they wouldn't prefer the plazas and open spaces further uptown, they will look at you as though you are crazy. Those other places: people don't *work* there. Kid stuff. This is the center of things.

In one respect, it most certainly is: in few places will you see such a clear demonstration of the relation between centrality and word of mouth communication. The schmoozing groups are anything but static. Some will last only ten minutes or so, dissolve, and then be replaced by a new group. Other groups will constantly renew themselves, with newcomers joining as others leave. Then there are the people who roam. These are often senior men, to judge by the deference paid them. They work the block, stopping friends to chat for a moment or so, checking in briefly with the standing group. One man that we tracked talked with eighteen separate groups. He accosted them with a look of urgency, and they listened with interest. Whatever it was he was communicating, it was multiplied almost geometrically—and it wasn't "nothing talk" either.

Another great place for schmoozing is the diamond district, the single block on Forty-seventh Street between Fifth and Sixth avenues. Here Hasidic Jews play a large role. Schmoozing here is very much business, and many key transactions are carried out on the street. But there is a great deal of social schmoozing as well, and it carries on throughout the winter months.

Here there are ethnic factors to consider. You see a rich vocabulary of gestures rooted in the culture of the Orthodox Jews. In his remarkable study of gestures, David Efron compared those of the Eastern Jews in New York with southern Italians. The Italian gestures, Efron found, had a very specific meaning, and have had for generations. Reading old books on gestures (such as Andrea di Jorio's 1832 work on Neapolitan gestures), Efron found that gestures were the same as they were a century ago, for, indeed, in ancient Rome and Greece. Then as now, the gestures so well portrayed a particular meaning that one could tell a story with them that others could follow and understand.

But this was not the case with the European Jews. When Efron compared their gestures with what they were saying, he found that the gestures emphasized and punctuated what was being said but had no symbolic meaning in themselves. Writes Efron, "To use an analogy, the Jew very rarely employs his arm in the guise

of a pencil to depict the things he is referring to, but uses it often as a pointer to link one proposition to another, or to trace the itinerary of a logical journey; or else as a baton to beat the tempo of his mental locomotion." Efron found it to be especially characteristic of the Yeshiva type of Jew, who was accustomed to argumentation and syllogistic reasoning.

This is very observable on Forty-seventh Street. If you watch two men in a colloquy, you won't know what they are saying, but you will get a very clear impression of the *process* they are going through. It is the exercise of logic by reasonable, fair-minded men. The gestures sometimes indicate a dismay at the weak argument of the other, but generally these exchanges end up on an obviously friendly, or at least resolving, note.

Schmoozing is now to be seen all over, uptown and downtown, and while the intensity cannot match that of the garment district, the basic patterns are similar. Banks and corporations with large clerical staffs tend to have lots of schmoozers. These are also the kind of places that provide in-house cafeterias, recreation facilities, TV rooms, hobby clubs, and the like. But schmoozers want to get outside. They won't do much when they get there; generally they will form up abreast in a line. This is the most functional way to watch people go by. The schmoozers will sometimes exchange remarks on the passersby, but sometimes simply watch, bound in an amiable silence.

Schmoozers are fairly consistent in choosing locations. They show a liking for well-defined places—the edge of the curb, for example, or a ledge. They are also very pillar-tropic, obeying perhaps a primeval instinct for something at their backs. Rarely will they stand for long in the middle of large spaces.

Schmoozers are also consistent in the duration of their sessions, which will be either fairly brief or fairly long—fifteen minutes or even more. Some groups, as on Seventh Avenue, are of the semipermanent floating kind, and many last the whole lunch hour. The stayers dominate. If you add up the minutes spent by each schmoozer over an hour's time, you will find that the great majority of the total schmoozing minutes will be accounted for by the long-term schmoozers.

The most common form that street conversation takes is that of straight man and principal. For a while, one man dominates, while the other cooperates by remaining still and listening. Then there will be a shift—the onlooker can sense it coming—and the active man becomes the passive one.

Or should. Sometimes people will violate the tacit compact and keep on talking and gesturing beyond their time. Conversely, the straight man may fail to respect the pause during the principal's turn and jump in prematurely. When there are such failures of accommodation, there is a lack of symmetry in their movements. I have a film sequence of a long conversation on Fifty-seventh Street that is a catalog of discords. A cigar-smoking man has been long overextending his turn. This begins to be reflected in the gestures of the listener. He begins to look this way and that, as if for help and brushes lint off his lapels. He rocks up and down on his heels and then stops abruptly. He wheels to leave. The other man, still talking, grabs him by the sleeve and then finally releases him.

Soapboxers display cooperative antagonism in heightened form. About 1 P.M. they gather at Broad and Wall streets. Most are regulars; some are Henry George single-tax people, some specialize in world affairs, many concentrate on religion, interpretation of the Bible in particular. The proceedings will be highly adversarial, and that is why the soapboxers come—to dispute and be disputed. Some structure their discourse to be heckled and may be discomfited if they are not.

The classic form of their encounters is thrust and counterthrust. With a jabbing finger punctuating each point, one man advances on his adversary, who gives way at the same pace. After a climactic flourish, the first man stops, and his hands go limp. What more could possibly be said? The other man jabs out his finger. How could that be squared with Genesis? He advances on the other man, who gives way. The whole preceding scene is now acted out in reverse. Other soapboxers may egg them on. A man who is known as the Logician, a man with a spade beard and an incongruous tweed hat, may top off the session. Both men have missed the point.

The back-and-forth movements of street encounters have their parallel in speech. The pause is the crucial element. Professor Frieda Goldman-Eisler of the University College of London has found that in spontaneous speech 40 percent to 50 percent is silence and that the speed of speech is almost entirely a function of *not* speaking. Pauses have meaning: frequent ones indicate new thoughts, and few pauses, standard expression. When two people are talking, they show a tendency to match the rhythms of each other's pauses.

In their book *Rhythms of Dialogue*, Joseph Jaffe and Stanley Feldstein note the same phenomenon. Speakers tend to match the duration of each other's pauses and to space them at the same intervals. In this study of conversation, James M. Dabbs, Jr., of Georgia State University notes that each "turn" contained a number of pauses. These were of a continuation variety, not for interruption. The pause that concludes a turn, however, is a "switching" pause and is a clear signal to the other that he can take over. Distinguishing one kind of pause from the other takes art, and if one lingers on a continuation pause a half second or so too long, the other man is likely to grab the silence and run off with the conversation.

Gestures reinforce the speech and the pauses. A person may pause for effect and then add an "uh" or an "um" to signal that he's going to go on again. As he does he may signal the same message with a move of the hand. Gestures are especially important when one speaker does not play the game, jumping a pause, for example, or talking well beyond his turn. At such times, gestures are apt to be touching gestures—a hand on the other's sleeve, for example, as if to say, "I'm not finished yet."

Most touching gestures are friendly; the arm around another's shoulders is one of the more-common ones. But the purpose is often a measure of control. The one who does the touching is dominant—at that particular moment, at least—or seeking to be. When a man who is talking reaches out and touches another's arm, he is giving a command: Don't start talking again now, because I'm not finished yet. A more-open coercion is the grasping of another's arm to stay a departure.

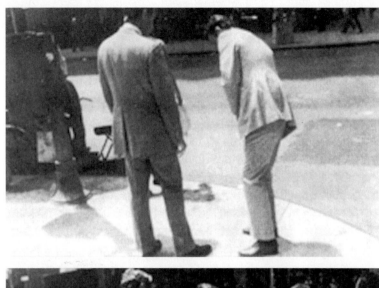

Corner of Wall and
Winter streets: noon.

Who touches whom? Men usually assume that women touch people more than men do. I assumed this and was rather pleased with some excellent examples I filmed of women picking lint from each other's coats and other forms of touching rituals. One of our researchers, a woman, took issue with my assumption, holding that typical male thinking was involved and that some systematic observation might be in order. She was right. In the street encounters we subsequently studied, we found that men did more touching than women. And the kind most frequent was men touching men.

Other studies have arrived at similar findings. Psychologist Nancy Henley found that touching correlates rather strongly with power and status. In the incidents observed, males did the most touching; males touched females more frequently than vice versa; and older people touched younger people more frequently than vice versa. Her analysis of touching in comics and TV movies showed men way in the lead. In fiction, as in life, the boss did the touching.

It is obvious enough that gestures help one person communicate with another. But there is a second function, and it may be the more-important. When one man is saying something to another, he may emphasize his points by gesturing with his hands. But the second man will be looking at his face, not at his hands. The gestures are as much for self as for the other person.

Some of the most interesting gestures are unseen by the other party. The man who's doing the gesturing often does it with his hands behind his back, out of sight of the person for whom they're presumably intended. If you follow a traveling conversation, you will note that very often one of the group will have his hands joined behind his back and will show all sorts of finger and thumb movement, sometimes at variance with the placid mien he's showing his companion. (Occupationally I see a lot of these hidden gestures; when filming traveling conversations on the street, I find it much easier to film them from behind than from the front, and as a result, I've had to pay much more attention to these kinds of gestures than I otherwise might.)

Whatever the function of the gestures and movements, the street is a congenial place for the expression of them. They tend to be more expansive there than in internal spaces. You may see orbiting conversations in a building lobby, but out on the street they may cover far more space. Is there more room on the street? Not really; the highest incidence of encounters is in the most-crowded locations.

The street is a stage, and the sense that an audience is watching pervades the gestures and movements of the players on it. For example, are "girl-watchers" really looking at girls? They are putting on a show of girl-watchers looking at girls. The hard hats appear first and sit on the sidewalk with their backs propped up against the building wall. They are quite demonstrative, much given to whistles and direct salutation to the "girls." If there are several older men among them, the others may josh them, as though they were out of contention. They are a bit cruel: if a bag lady passes, they will hoot at her. White-collar girl-watchers stand or sit on ledges and are quieter. These are connoisseurs, amused and somewhat disdainful. They exchange comments on passersby and snicker and smirk. But it is machismo. I have never seen a girl-watcher make a direct pass at a woman. As our

cameras have recorded, when a *really* good-looking woman goes by, they will be confounded, and they betray it with involuntary tugs on the earlobe and nervous stroking of their hair.

Attractive women can scare them. In an experiment to see how much room strangers would give each other as they passed, James Dabbs and Neil Stokes of Georgia State University recorded passing encounters. Among other things, they found that individual pedestrians would get farther out of the way for an oncoming pair than for a single and would give more room to an oncoming male than a female. But most interesting was the effect of beauty. Would people pass nearer to an attractive woman than to a plain one? Both roles, by the way, were played by the same woman. For one, she was wearing tight-fitting clothes and attractive makeup. For the other, she used no makeup, pulled her hair back, and wore sloppy clothes. Pedestrians gave her a wider berth when she was attractive. It didn't make any difference whether the pedestrians were male or female. They walked notice-ably closer to the unattractive girl, and in several cases, male pedestrians made overtures to her. None did when she was attractive. Dabbs and Stokes believe this behavior is best understood in terms of social power, with a deference given to those further up the scale.

There are many other performers. The Three Jolly Fellows recur so frequently that you would almost think they were an act put on by street entertainers. Lovers are another example, fervently embracing in the most heavily trafficked spots, oblivious of the crowd. But are they so oblivious? I doubt it. Their display of affec-tion may be quite genuine, but it is a display. And they enjoy it very much.

Because I live in New York City, most of my initial research was done there. I have been scolded about this, the city being deemed too unique, too skewed, too

It doesn't take much to draw a crowd in New York.

much of a distorting mirror. There is some truth to this. New York is a place that exaggerates things, no mistake. But it is not necessarily any less informative for that. There one sees in bolder relief patterns of behavior more muted in other places.

Our working assumption was that behavior in other cities would be basically the same, and subsequent comparisons have proved our assumption correct. The important variable is city size. As I will discuss in more detail, in smaller cities densities tend to be lower, pedestrians move at a slower pace, and there is less of the social activity in high-traffic areas. But the basic patterns are there. People are not all that different. Given the elements of a center—high pedestrian volumes, concentration, and mixture of activities—people in one city tend to respond like people in another.

One of the hardest tasks in observing a place is to find out what normal is. We spent a lot of time doing this in several small universes, among them a sleazy stretch of Lexington Avenue. As time went on and we got a better understanding of recurrent patterns, we broadened our field. We did comparative studies in other U.S. cities—in recent years, smaller cities in particular. We also did some observing in a number of major cities abroad. We were glad we did, for they provided more confirmation of basic patterns than did many in the United States.

Pedestrians in the great metropolitan centers act more like one another than pedestrians in smaller cities in their respective countries. Tokyo and New York are examples. The linear development characteristic of Japanese cities is quite unlike the grid pattern of American cities, and the cultural differences are enormous. But when you get people out on the street, the pedestrians of the two cities behave very much the same. They walk fast and aggressively, and cluster in the middle of the way. At Shinjuku Station, the busiest in the world, you will be struck by how much of the congestion is self-congestion. I prize a film record I have of two junior executives solemnly practicing golf swings at a Wall Street corner. But a better one is of three Japanese junior executives going through the same motions in Shinjuku Station in the very middle of the crowd.

In London you see the same recurrent patterns. In the City the financial people use their narrow sidewalks in the same ways New Yorkers do theirs. They block them. Alongside the Bank of England the sidewalk narrows at one point to about four feet, and that spot is favored for conversations. In other respects, people in the City behave very much like those in Wall Street, including the Three Jolly Fellows.

Schmoozers in Milan's Galleria tend to cluster in late afternoon rather than at midday, as in New York. But the basic rhythms are the same, with the schmoozing groups being constantly replenished as new people join and others drop out. Foot motions are as complex and indecipherable as in New York.

That the people of great cities should act alike is not surprising. They are responding to high-density situations and to a range of stimuli not found in smaller cities. It is at once the boon and the bane of smaller cities that they are not crowded. People in smaller cities do walk more slowly; they are not as aggressive and pushy because there is not much to be pushy about. Sidewalks are uncrowded, and there are fewer people blocking the flow.

But similarities of behavior between cities, large or small, are more significant than the differences. And this probably goes back in time. In the streets of the souk in the Old City of Jerusalem you see pedestrian behavior that probably differs very little from what it was centuries before. There are lessons in these old places. In considering plans for new civic spaces people often fret themselves into inaction over the thought of obsolescence. If we design for today's people, they ask, how do we know it will work a generation or so hence? You can't know, of course. But the fact is that spaces designed to work very well for their initial constituency usually work very well for later ones and, indeed, help define them.

BIBLIOGRAPHY

Ashcroft, Norman, and Albert E. Scheflen. *People Space: The Making and Breaking of Human Boundaries.* Garden City, N.Y.: Anchor, 1976.

Bakeman, R., and S. Beck. "The Size of Informal Groups in Public," *Environment and Behavior*, September, 1974.

Barker, Roger. *The Stream of Behavior.* New York: Appleton-Century Crofts, 1963.

Birdwhistle, Ray L. *Kinesics and Context.* Philadelphia: University of Pennsylvania Press, 1970.

Brower, Sidney. "Streetfronts and Sidewalks," *Landscape Architecture*, July 1973.

Ciolek, Matthew T. "Location of Static Gatherings in Pedestrian Areas: an Exploratory Study." Canberra: Australian National University, 1976.

Dabbs, James M., Jr. "Indexing the Cognitive Lead of a Conversation." Paper: Georgia State University, 1980.

————, and Neil A. Stokes III. "Beauty Is Power: The Use of Space on a Sidewalk," *Sociometry*, 1975, Vol. 38, No 4.

Efron, David. *Gesture, Race, and Culture*. The Hague: Mastor, 1972; excerpted in *The Body Reader*, Ted Pelhemus, ed. New York: Pantheon Books, 1978.
A tentative study of some of the spatio-temporal and "linguistic" aspects of the gestural behavior of Eastern Jews and Southern Italians in New York City.

Gehl, Jan. *Pedestrians*. Copenhagen: Arkitekten, 1968.

————. *Life Between Buildings*. New York: Van Nostrand Reinhold, 1987. This book, first published in Copenhagen, is one of a series of studies by architect Gehl that have had a major influence on design and planning in Scandinavia. The patterns of pedestrian life he has observed and the recommendations he has made are highly applicable to American cities. So too are his techniques for studying people—quite objective, but strong on imagination and humor. They are also a primer on the use of photography as a research tool. A splendid piece of work.

Goffman, Erving. *Behavior in Public Places*. New York: Free Press, 1963.

————. *Relations in Public*. New York: Harper & Row, 1971.

Goldberger, Paul. *The City Observed: A Guide to the Architecture of Manhattan*. New York: Vintage Books, 1979.

Hall, Edward T. *The Hidden Dimension*. Garden City, N.Y.: Doubleday & Co., 1966.

————. *The Silent Language*. Garden City, N.Y.: Doubleday & Co., 1969.

Heckscher, August, with Phyllis Robinson. *Open Spaces: The Life of American Cities*. New York: Harper & Row, 1977.

Henley, Nancy M. *Body Politics*. Englewood Cliffs, N.J.: Prentice-Hall, 1977.

Jaffe, Joseph, and Stanley Feldstein. *Rhythms of Dialogue*. Academic Press, 1970.

Lofland, Lyn H. *A World of Strangers: Order and Action in Urban Public Space*. New York: Basic Books, 1973.

Lynch, Kevin. *The Image of the City*. Cambridge, Mass.: M.I.T. Press, 1960.

McPhail, Clark, and Ronald T. Wohlstein. "Using Film to Analyze Pedestrian Behavior," *Sociological Methods and Research*, Vol. 10, No. 3, 1982.

Moudon, Anne Vern, ed. *Public Streets for Public Use*. New York: Van Nostrand Reinhold, 1987.

Proshansky, Harold M., William H. Ittelson, and Leanne G. Rivlin, eds. *Environmental Psychology: Man and His Physical Setting*. New York: Holt, Rinehart & Winston, 1970.

Sennett, Richard. *The Fall of Public Man*. New York: Alfred A. Knopf, 1977.

Sommer, Robert. *Personal Space*. Englewood Cliffs, N.J.: Prentice-Hall, 1969. In this country, psychologist Sommer has been the outstanding exponent of direct observation of the impact of design on behavior, himself a fine observer and walker.

Webb, Eugene J., Donald T. Campbell, Richard D. Schwartz, and Lee Sechrist. *Unobtrusive Measures: Non-reactive Research in the Social Sciences*. Chicago: Rand McNally, 1966.

The Need for Concentration

Jane Jacobs

Jacobs's writings challenge the antiurban, American preference for low density development and extol the economic, social, and cultural virtues of crowded, dense, and diverse cities. In *The Death and Life of Great American Cities*, she describes her own work as no less than an "attack" on conventional planning and building practices (p. 3): "My attack is not based on quibbles about rebuilding methods or hair-splitting about fashions in design. It is an attack, rather, on the principles and aims that have shaped modern, orthodox city planning and rebuilding." In this section of her chapter, "The Need for Concentration," she disputes the belief that high density correlates with "trouble" and overcrowding and distinguishes between dense concentrations of dwellings and dwellings that are overcrowded.

CONDITION 4: *The district must have a sufficiently dense concentration of people, for whatever purpose they may be there. This includes people there because of residence.*

For centuries, probably everyone who has thought about cities at all has noticed that there seems to be some connection between the concentration of people and the specialties they can support. Samuel Johnson, for one, remarked on this relationship back in 1785. "Men, thinly scattered," he said to Boswell, "make a shift, but a bad shift, without many things . . . It is being concentrated which produces convenience."

Observers are forever rediscovering this relationship in new times and places. Thus in 1959, John H. Denton, a professor of business at the University of Arizona, after studying American suburbs and British "new towns" came to the conclusion that such places must rely on ready access to a city for protection of their cultural opportunities. "He based his findings," reported the *New York Times*, "on the lack of a sufficient density of population to support cultural facilities. Mr. Denton . . . said that decentralization produced such a thin population spread that the only effective economic demand that could exist in suburbs was that of the majority. The only goods and cultural activities available will be those that the majority requires, he observed," and so on.

Both Johnson and Professor Denton were speaking about the economic effects of large numbers of people, but not numbers loosely added up indefinitely from thinly spread populations. They were making the point that it seems to matter greatly how thinly or how thickly people are concentrated. They were comparing the effects of what we call high and low densities.

This relationship of concentration—or high density—to conveniences and to other kinds of diversity is generally well understood as it applies to downtowns. Everyone is aware that tremendous numbers of people concentrate in city downtowns and that, if they did not, there would be no downtown to amount to anything—certainly not one with much downtown diversity.

But this relationship between concentration and diversity is very little considered when it comes to city districts where residence is a chief use. Yet dwellings form a large part of most city districts. The people who live in a district also form a large share, usually, of the people who use the streets, the parks and the enterprises of the place. Without help from the concentration of the people who live there, there can be little convenience or diversity where people live, and where they require it.

To be sure, the dwellings of a district (like any other use of the land) need to be supplemented by other primary uses so people on the streets will be well spread through the hours of the day, for economic reasons. These other uses (work, entertainment, or whatever) must make intensive use of city land if they are to contribute effectively to concentration. If they simply take up physical room and involve few people, they will do little or nothing for diversity or liveliness. I think it is hardly necessary to belabor that point.

This same point is just as important, however, about dwellings. City dwellings have to be intensive in their use of the land too, for reasons that go much deeper than cost of land. On the other hand, this does not mean that everyone can or should be put into elevator apartment houses to live—or into any other one or two types of dwellings. That kind of solution kills diversity by obstructing it from another direction.

Dwelling densities are so important for most city districts, and for their future development, and are so little considered as factors in vitality, that I shall devote this chapter to that aspect of city concentration.

High dwelling densities have a bad name in orthodox planning and housing theory. They are supposed to lead to every kind of difficulty and failure.

But in our cities, at least, this supposed correlation between high densities and trouble, or high densities and slums, is simply incorrect, as anyone who troubles to look at real cities can see. Here are a few illustrations:

In San Francisco, the district of highest dwelling densities—and highest coverage of residential land with buildings too—is North Beach-Telegraph Hill. This is a popular district that has spontaneously and steadily unslummed itself in the years following the Depression and the Second World War. San Francisco's chief slum problem, on the other hand, is a district called the Western Addition, a place that has steadily declined and is now being extensively cleared. The Western Addition (which at one time, when it was new, was a good address) has a dwelling-unit density considerably lower than North Beach-Telegraph Hill's, and, for that matter, lower than the still fashionable Russian Hill's and Nob Hill's.

In Philadelphia, Rittenhouse Square is the only district that has been spontaneously upgrading and extending its edges, and is the only inner city area that has not been designated for either renewal or clearance. It has the highest dwelling density in Philadelphia. The North Philadelphia slums currently display some of the city's most severe social problems. They have dwelling densities averaging at most half those of Rittenhouse Square. Vast territories of additional decay and social disorder in Philadelphia have dwelling densities less than half those of Rittenhouse Square.

In Brooklyn, New York, the most generally admired, popular and upgrading neighborhood is Brooklyn Heights; it has much the highest density of dwellings in Brooklyn. Tremendous expanses of failed or decaying Brooklyn gray area have densities half those of Brooklyn Heights or less.

In Manhattan, the most fashionable pocket of the midtown East Side, and the most fashionable pocket of Greenwich Village have dwelling densities in the same high range as the heart of Brooklyn Heights. But an interesting difference can be observed. In Manhattan, very popular areas, characterized by high degrees of vitality and diversity, surround these most fashionable pockets. In these surrounding popular areas, dwelling densities go still higher. In Brooklyn Heights, on the other hand, the fashionable pocket is surrounded by neighborhoods where dwelling unit densities drop off; vitality and popularity drop off too.

In Boston, the North End has unslummed itself and is one of the city's healthiest areas. It has much the highest dwelling densities in Boston. The Roxbury district, which has been steadily declining for a generation, has a dwelling density about a ninth that of the North End's.*

The overcrowded slums of planning literature are teeming areas with a high density of dwellings. The overcrowded slums of American real life are, more and

*Here are the density figures for these examples. They are given in numbers of dwelling units per net acre of residential land. When two figures are given, they represent a range into which the average or averages for the place concerned fall (which is the way this data is often tabulated or mapped). In San Francisco: North Beach-Telegraph Hill, 80–140, about the same as Russian Hill and Nob Hill, but the buildings cover more of the residential ground in North Beach-Telegraph Hill; the Western Addition, 55–60. In Philadelphia: Rittenhouse Square, 80–100; North Philadelphia slums, about 40; row-house neighborhoods in trouble, typically 30–45. In Brooklyn: Brooklyn Heights, 125–174 at heart and 75–124 in most of the remainder; drop-offs to 45–74 beyond; as examples of Brooklyn areas in decline or trouble, Bedford-Stuyvesant, about half at 75–124 and half at 45–74; Red Hook, mostly 45–74; some Brooklyn spots in decay as low as 15–24. In Manhattan: most fashionable pocket of midtown East Side, 125–174, rising in Yorkville to 175–254; Greenwich Village, most fashionable pocket, 124–174, rising to 175–254 for most of remainder with pocket containing stable, old, unslummed Italian community rising above 255. In Boston, North End, 275; Roxbury, 21–40.

For Boston and New York, these figures are from planning commission measurements and tabulations; for San Francisco and Philadelphia they are estimates by planning or redevelopment staff members.

Although all cities make a fetish of minute density analysis in project planning, surprisingly few have much accurate data on nonproject densities. (One planning director told me he could see no reason for studying them except as light on how big the relocation problem would be if they were knocked down!) No city that I know of has studied just what localized, building-by-building variations in density go into the makeup of density averages in successful and popular neighborhoods. "It's too hard to generalize about districts like that," complained a planning director when I asked him about specific density variations, at small scale, in one of his city's most successful districts. It is hard, or impossible, to generalize about such districts precisely because they are, themselves, so little "generalized" or standardized in their groupings. This very capriciousness and diversity of the components is one of the most important, and most ignored, facts about density averages in successful districts.

more typically, dull areas with a low density of dwellings. In Oakland, California, the worst and most extensive slum problem is an area of some two hundred blocks of detached, one- and two-family houses which can hardly be called dense enough to qualify as real city densities at all. Cleveland's worst slum problem is a square mile of much the same thing. Detroit is largely composed, today, of seemingly endless square miles of low-density failure. The East Bronx of New York, which might almost stand as a symbol of the gray belts that have become the despair of cities, has low densities for New York; in most parts of the East Bronx, densities are well below the whole city averages. (New York's average dwelling density is 55 units per net residential acre.)

However, it will not do to jump to the conclusion that all areas of high dwelling density in cities do well. They do not, and to assume that this is "the" answer would be to oversimplify outrageously. For instance, Chelsea, much of the badly failed uptown West Side, and much of Harlem, all in Manhattan, have dwelling densities in the same high ranges as those of Greenwich Village, Yorkville and the midtown East Side. Once-ultrafashionable Riverside Drive, plagued by trouble today, has still higher dwelling densities.

We cannot understand the effects of high and low densities if we assume that the relationship between concentrations of people and production of diversity is a simple, straight mathematical affair. The results of this relationship (which Dr. Johnson and Professor Denton both spoke of in its simple, crude form), are drastically influenced by other factors too.

No concentration of residents, however high it may be, is "sufficient" if diversity is suppressed or thwarted by other insufficiencies. As an extreme example, no concentration of residence, however high, is "sufficient" to generate diversity in regimented projects, because diversity has been regimented out in any case. And much the same effects, for different reasons, can occur in unplanned city neighborhoods, where the buildings are too standardized or the blocks are too long, or there is no mixture of other primary uses besides dwellings.

However, it still remains that dense concentrations of people are *one* of the necessary conditions for flourishing city diversity. And it still follows that in districts where people live, this means there must be a dense concentration of their dwellings on the land preempted for dwellings. The other factors that influence how much diversity is generated, and where, will have nothing much to influence if enough people are not there.

One reason why low city densities conventionally have a good name, unjustified by the facts, and why high city densities have a bad name, equally unjustified, is that high densities of dwellings and overcrowding of dwellings are often confused. High densities mean large numbers of dwellings per acre of land. Overcrowding means too many people in a dwelling for the number of rooms it contains. The census definition of overcrowding is 1.5 persons per room or more. It has nothing to do with the number of dwellings on the land, just as in real life high densities have nothing to do with overcrowding.

This confusion between high densities and overcrowding, which I will go into briefly because it so much interferes with understanding the role of densities, is another of the obfuscations we have inherited from Garden City planning.

Defensible Space

Oscar Newman

Oscar Newman has pioneered in focusing attention on the importance of physical design in controlling human behavior. This chapter discusses how different elements in residential environments can be combined to make a defensible space that discourages crime. Newman proposes a range of mechanisms that can be used to enhance an area's sense of community and to create a physical fabric that inhibits crime. The author defines *defensible space* as "a living residential environment which can be employed by inhabitants for the enhancement of their lives, while providing security for their families, neighbors, and friends" (p. 210).

The crime problems facing urban America will not be answered through increased police force or firepower. We are witnessing a breakdown of the social mechanisms that once kept crime in check and gave direction and support to police activity. The small-town environments, rural or urban, which once framed and enforced their own moral codes, have virtually disappeared. We have become strangers sharing the largest collective habitats in human history. Because of the size and density of our newly evolving urban megalopoli, we have become more dependent on each other and more vulnerable to aberrant behavior than we have ever been before.

In our society there are few instances of shared beliefs or values among physical neighbors. Although this heterogeneity may be intellectually desirable, it has crippled our ability to agree on the action required to maintain the social framework necessary to our continued survival. The very winds of liberation that have brought us this far may also have carried with them the seeds of our demise. It is clear to almost all researchers in crime prevention that the issue hinges on the inability of communities to come together in joint action. The physical environments we have been building in our cities for the past twenty-five years actually prevent such amity and discourage the natural pursuit of a collective action.

The anonymous cities we have built, for maximum freedom and multiple choice, may have inadvertently succeeded in severely curtailing many of our previous options. Collective community action, once easy, is now cumbersome. But even in the absence of a community of minds, joint action has become essential to the survival of urban life in America. Police forces operating without community consent, direction, and control are a wasted effort—more irritant than deterrent. Means must be found for bringing neighbors together, if only for the limited purpose of ensuring survival of their collective milieu. Where the physical design of the living environment can be used for this purpose, it must be so exploited.

Over the past fifteen years, the crime problem in our urban metropolitan areas has become severe enough to prompt a major exodus of middle-income families to the suburbs. However, the results of 1971 crime survey statistics indicate that the crime problem is shifting to the outer reaches of the city.[1] The horizons of escape promised by suburbia and the barricaded inner city towers seem to be narrowing. The only recourse now appears to be total lockup and self-restriction of movement: a self-imposed curfew and police state.

This book is about an alternative, about a means for restructuring the residential environments of our cities so they can again become livable and controlled, controlled not by police but by a community of people sharing a common terrain.

Over the past three years, the New York University Project for Security Design in Urban Residential Areas has been studying the nature, pattern, and location of crime in urban residential areas across the country. Our conclusion is that the new physical form of the urban environment is possibly the most cogent ally the criminal has in his victimization of society. The concentration of population in large metropolitan areas has produced an urban form that makes hapless victims of its occupants.

The time has come to go back to first principles, to reexamine human habitat as it has evolved, to become attuned again to all the subtle devices invented over time and forgotten in our need and haste to house the many. For even within the widespread chaos of our cities, it is still possible to find isolated examples of working living environments which are crime-free, although at times located in the highest crime precincts of cities. Architectural design can make evident by the physical layout that an area is the shared extension of the private realms of a group of individuals. For one group to be able to set the norms of behavior and the nature of activity possible within a particular place, it is necessary that it have clear, unquestionable control over what can occur there. Design can make it possible for both inhabitant and stranger to perceive that an area is under the undisputed influence of a particular group, that they dictate the activity taking place within it, and who its users are to be. This can be made so clearly evident that residents will not only feel confident, but that it is incumbent upon them to question the comings and goings of people to ensure the continued safety of the defined areas. Any intruder will be made to anticipate that his presence will be under question and open to challenge; so much so that a criminal can be deterred from even contemplating entry.

Defensible space is a model for residential environments which inhibits crime by creating the physical expression of a social fabric that defends itself. All the different elements which combine to make a defensible space have a common goal—an environment in which latent territoriality and sense of community in the inhabitants can be translated into responsibility for ensuring a safe, productive, and well-maintained living space. The potential criminal perceives such a space as controlled by its residents, leaving him an intruder easily recognized and dealt with. On the one hand this is target hardening—the traditional aim of security design as provided by locksmiths. But it must also be seen in another light. In middle-class neighborhoods, the responsibility for maintaining security has largely been relegated to the police. Upper-income neighborhoods—particularly those including high-rise apartment buildings—have supplemented police with doormen, a luxury not possible in other neighborhoods. There is serious self-deception in this posture. When people begin to protect themselves as individuals and not as a community, the battle against crime is effectively lost. The indifferent crowd witnessing a violent crime is by now an American cliché. The move of middle- and upper-class population into protective high-rises and other structures of isolation—as well guarded and as carefully differentiated from the surrounding human landscape as a military post—is just as clearly a retreat into indifference. The form of buildings and their arrangement can either discourage or encourage people to take an active part in policing while they go about their daily business. "Policing" is not intended to evoke a paranoid vision but refers to the oldest concept in the Western political tradition: the responsibility of each citizen to ensure the functioning of the *polis.*

"Defensible space" is a surrogate term for the range of mechanisms—real and symbolic barriers, strongly defined areas of influence, and improved opportunities for surveillance—that combine to bring an environment under the control of its residents. A *defensible space* is a living residential environment which can be employed by inhabitants for the enhancement of their lives, while providing security for their families, neighbors, and friends. The public areas of a multi-family residential environment devoid of defensible space can make the act of going from street to apartment equivalent to running the gauntlet. The fear and uncertainty generated by living in such an environment can slowly eat away and eventually destroy the security and sanctity of the apartment unit itself. On the other hand, by grouping dwelling units to reinforce associations of mutual benefit; by delineating paths of movement; by defining areas of activity for particular users through their juxtaposition with internal living areas; and by providing for natural opportunities for visual surveillance, architects can create a clear understanding of the function of a space, and who its users are and ought to be. This, in turn, can lead residents of all income levels to adopt extremely potent territorial attitudes and policing measures, which act as strong deterrents to potential criminals.

The spatial layout of the multi-family dwelling, from the arrangement of the building grounds to the interior grouping of apartments, achieves defensible space when residents can easily perceive and control all activity taking place within it. It is not of course intended that residents take matters into their own hands and personally restrict intrusion. Rather, it is suggested that they employ a full range of encounter mechanisms to indicate their concerned observation of questionable activity and their control of the situation: offers of assistance to strangers in finding their way, as a means for determining their intent and the legitimacy of their presence; continued in-person surveillance and the threat of possible interference; questioning glances from windows; and finally, to be able to set up a situation which will stimulate residents to call the police and insist on their intervention. As we have seen too often lately, the ability of even secure middle-class Americans to intervene, if only by calling the police, is not something that can be depended on any longer. Similarly, self-initiated police intervention in ghetto areas meets at times with community disapproval, even when the community feels intervention is required. The defensible space environment extends the areas of the residential unit into the street and within the area of felt responsibility of the dweller—of both low- and middle-income. By contrast, the resident living within large, apartment tower developments feels his responsibilities begin and end within the boundaries of his own apartment. He has learned to be detached even from what he sees outside his own window.

In our newly-created dense and anonymous residential environments, we may be raising generations of young people who are totally lacking in any experience of collective space, and by extension, of community rights and the shared values of society. In many ways, therefore, defensible space design also attempts to attack the root causes of crime. In the area of crime prevention, physical design has been traditionally relegated the role of *mechanical prevention*, leaving intact the structure of motivation and attitudes which eventually lead to the criminal event. Defensible space design, while it uses mechanical prevention, aims at formulating an architectural model of *corrective prevention*. Our present urban environments, created with such speed and determination, may be little more than the spawning grounds of criminal behavior.

In the evolution of human habitat over the past thousands of years, men in every culture have developed cogent devices to define the territorial realm of their dwellings. The nature and function of these mechanisms evolved slowly through change and adaptation during use. So long as human environment was built within a tradition, simply repeating previous forms ensured the preservation of past learned experience. With the breakdown of building tradition, through the rapid evolution of new techniques and the need to answer the pressing problem of accommodating higher densities, the simple repetition of past practice has become difficult, if not impossible. Unfortunately, the accumulated traditions inherent in the residential forms of the past were not held within the conscious verbal bank of human knowledge. In architectural history there is ample evidence of territorial definition and symbolization in the forms of previous residential environments. There is unfortunately no parallel evidence of their overt discussion. The tradition, grown over thousands of years in man's piecemeal search for a form of residence in an urban setting, has been lost.

In building the residential environments of twentieth-century cities, there was no reference to tradition, simply because the needs seemed so totally new and unlike any experience in the past. In our rush to provide housing for the urban immigrants and to accommodate our high population growth rates, we have been

FIGURE 1 Mud House in the African Sudan. The stoop symbolically defines the entry to the dwelling. It declares simply, but emphatically that this is where the territorial prerogatives of the tribe, defined by the compound, are overridden by the dictates of the members of the family unit. (Reprinted, by permission, from Joop Hardy, "Door and Window," in *Forum*, No. 8, 1960. Photo by Aldo Van Eyck.)

FIGURE 2 Neolithic Settlement, Hacilar, Turkey. Excavation and reconstruction of extended family compound and individual house. There are two entries to the enclave, both of which lead to a central communal area shared by all dwellings. The entry to each family unit is then further defined by a smaller transitional court off the communal area. (Courtesy of The Hamlyn Group)

Excavation of extended family compound

House within family compound

FIGURE 3   Street in Herculaneum. Note stoop at entry to each house and positioning of windows to survey street entry. (Reprinted by permission from M. Grant, *Cities of Vesuvious*, p. 64. Photo by Werner Forman © 1971 by The Macmillan Company.)

building *more* without really asking *what*? The high-rise prototype, with its myriad of resident janitorial and security staff, worked well for upper-middle-income families with few children but cannot be simplistically transplanted, minus the accompanying staff and accouterments, for the use of large, low-income families. It is clear that we built without much thought and without much concern and are now stuck with the results. Poorly designed buildings and projects have crime rates as much as three times higher than those of adjacent projects housing socially identical residents at similar densities.

Considering the needs of low-income families, there is no rationalism to the design of most high-rise residential developments, other than the narrow dictates of investment economics. Once built, they prove dangerous to live in and costly to maintain. The economic argument which led to their initial construction is reversed exactly. Their cost of operation is surpassed only by the social costs borne by the inhabitants. High-rise apartment developments are a new genre, with us little more than a hundred years. As a means for housing low- and middle-income American families, most date back to the early fifties. They are not the result of a careful application of the knowledge employed in housing the few, transferred to the problems of housing the many. Their form evolved in response to pressures for higher densities, with no reference to previous traditions and no attempt at understanding the range of need to be answered in human habitat. Beyond an occasionally suc-

FIGURE 4   Street in Eighteenth-Century Dutch Town. Note how the realm of each dwelling unit is defined by the raised platform at the point where the entry meets the street. Windows further reinforce territorial claim by providing unmistakable surveillance from within the dwelling. (Photo by author)

FIGURE 5   Row-House Street typical of Nineteenth-Century American Cities. It contains the identical ingredients which define the dwellings' relationship to the street found in the Dutch town (fig. 4). (Photo by author)

cessful composition, there is little evidence of any genius and now, in this period of high crime rates, they have become containers for the victimization of their inhabitants. This book presents an alternative—housing of medium density which through its physical design enables residents to control their living environment rather than become its victims.

Defensible space design returns to the productive use of residents the public areas beyond the doors of individual apartments: the hallways, lobbies, grounds,

FIGURE 6   Pruitt-Igoe, St. Louis, Missouri. View of vandalism to windows of public access galleries serving upper levels of the buildings. (Photo by Bob Williams)

and surrounding streets—areas which are now beyond the control of inhabitants. Four elements of physical design, acting both individually and in concert, contribute to the creation of secure environments.

1 The territorial definition of space in developments reflecting the areas of influence of the inhabitants. This works by subdividing the residential environment into zones toward which adjacent residents easily adopt proprietary attitudes.

2 The positioning of apartment windows to allow residents to naturally survey the exterior and interior public areas of their living environment.

3 The adoption of building forms and idioms which avoid the stigma of peculiarity that allows others to perceive the vulnerability and isolation of the inhabitants.

4 The enhancement of safety by locating residential developments in functionally sympathetic urban areas immediately adjacent to activities that do not provide continued threat.

Defensible space can be made to operate in an evolving hierarchy from level to level in the collective human habitat—to extend from apartment to street. It is a technique applicable to low-density row-house groupings as well as to developments composed of high-rise apartment buildings. The small cluster of apartments at each floor of a multi-story building is the first level beyond the apartment unit

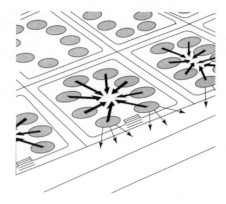

FIGURE 7 Defensible Space. Schematic sketch illustrating territorial definition reinforced with surveillance opportunities (arrows).

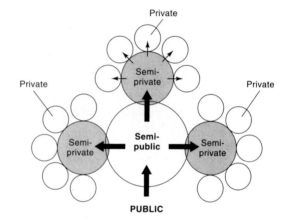

FIGURE 8 Hierarchy of Defensible Space. Schematic diagram illustrating evolving hierarchy of defensible space from public to private. Arrows indicate entries at different levels of the hierarchy.

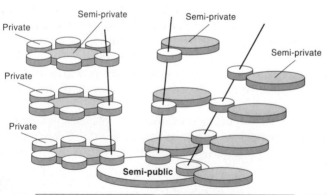

FIGURE 9 Defensible space hierarchy in multi-level dwelling.

where occupants can be made to extend the realm of their homes and responsibilities. The second level is the common entry and circulation paths within their buildings. The third level is the clustering of buildings which define a project's grounds and its entry. The final level in the hierarchy occurs when the housing development stakes its claim on surrounding urban streets.

In our examination of developments in every major city in the country, an effort was made to study the housing of all income groups for the purpose of comparison. A variety of study techniques were employed, including interviews with inhabitants, project managers, and police who serve these developments. Where recorded data on crime, vandalism, and maintenance costs was available, it was incorporated into the analysis. In New York City the analysis has been most extensive and detailed. The New York City Housing Authority is responsible for 150,000 units of public housing located in its five boroughs. This represents approximately 19 percent of all public housing in the country. The Housing Authority keeps computerized files on all its tenants, their incomes, the ages of each of the members of a family, their backgrounds, etc. In addition, the Housing Authority has its own sixteen-hundred-man police force who in turn keeps data on the occurrence and reporting of crime. The unique aspect of the Housing Authority Police data is that it also pinpoints the place of the crime. Specific buildings and interior locations are recorded along with the nature of the crime, victim, and offender. This resource allows us to consider the function of every physical variable and its effect on crime.

The results of our findings from three years of study apply to residential design for most income groups. In all instances, the physical mechanisms suggested to create safety and improve upkeep are tools of "self-help." The designs catalyze the natural impulses of residents, rather than forcing them to surrender their shared social responsibilities to any formal authority, whether police, management, security guards, or doormen. In a sense, this study takes its place as a partner in the political movements calling for the return of participation and control to the local level. However, it must be said that the ideas in this book, when initially presented to police, housing officials, and tenants often met with disbelief. Residents who live in hourly terror pointed at their scarred steel-plated doors and suggested that the author was wonderfully naive. Police officers—turning their attention from bands of teen-agers and addicts who do not appear to seriously weigh the consequences of being caught—pointed out the high costs of physical modification compared to increased police manpower. Ghetto leaders and social scientists have challenged us in our belief that crime, born of a poverty of means, opportunity, education, and representation, could be prevented architecturally.

Some of this skepticism is well-founded—particularly that of a low-income resident who does not believe physical change is likely to occur, regardless of the new-found knowledge. However, the skepticism is based on the assumption that a particular building prototype and project design represents the only available solution to a particular set of density and cost restraints. Most people do not know that different residential building prototypes are available to do the same job. The 150 New York families trapped in apartments that open onto the double-loaded corri-

FIGURE 10 Aerial photo of two adjacent projects of equal density. The one in the foreground consists mostly of walk-ups; the other mostly of high-rises. (Courtesy of New York City Housing Authority)

dors of a seventeen-story high-rise building—whose elevators, fire stairs, hallways, and roofs are freely roamed and ruled by criminals—find it hard to believe that the project across the street, composed of three- to six-story buildings in which two to three families share a hallway and six to twelve an entrance, actually accommodate people at the same densities and could be built at the same cost. The families in the seventeen-story building are continually aware of the fact that they are the constant prey of criminals and are equally aware that things are a lot better across the street. They find it incomprehensible that both projects house families at equal densities, and that the design differences between the two projects are predominantly the result of the whims of each designer. It seems unforgivable that high-rise projects would have been designed to make their inhabitants so vulnerable, when projects across the street were able to avoid these problems simply by not creating them in the first place.

Society may have contributed to the victimization of project residents by setting off their dwellings, stigmatizing them with ugliness; saying with every status symbol available in the architectural language of our culture, that living *here* is falling short of the human state. However, architecture is not just a matter of style, image, and comfort. Architecture can create encounter and prevent it. Certain kinds of space and spatial layout favor the clandestine activities of criminals. An architect, armed with some understanding of the structure of criminal encounter, can simply avoid providing the space which supports it. In discussing our tenant surveys with police, they were surprised to discover that residents of alternate building prototypes have radically different attitudes toward representatives of formal authority, and policemen in particular. These varying attitudes are strongly reflected in the varying rates of reported crime. In the two adjacent projects already mentioned, residents with identical social characteristics hold quite different views of the police. In one high-rise project—a labyrinthine profusion of corridors, fire stairs, and exits—police report great difficulty in locating apartments, to say nothing of pursuing criminals. Officers responding to calls meet tenant indifference if not open hostility. It is not uncommon for tenants to angrily attempt to drive off police responding with well-intentioned assistance. Tenants are skeptical of police effectiveness and fearful of police officers and of police intentions. Records show that only very serious crimes are brought to police attention. A comparison of tenant interviews with police reports shows that only one crime in four is ever reported. The obverse is true as well. In anonymous, crime-ridden high-rises, police officers—whether out of fear or because they respond negatively to the apparent anonymity of the environment—are often dictatorial, arbitrary, and unrespecting of the tenants' rights and needs.

Yet across the street in a development mixing walk-ups and low, elevator buildings, the same policemen behave like polite, conscientious civil servants. Tenants respond positively. Police move easily and familiarly through the project, and tenant-police relations are much better. Tenants in these buildings not only report more of the crimes they are involved in or witness, they make a practice of reporting loitering strangers and potentially threatening situations. In interviews, their trust in the efficacy of police intervention was found to be stronger, possibly not unrelated to their ability to keep police in hand in their own buildings.

The adoption of defensible space design in new building or the modification of existing buildings may well pay for itself in terms of the increased level of police efficiency. Although police expenditures are unlikely to go down in the near future, new projects constructed along defensible space guidelines can help curb an otherwise necessary expansion of police control and budget. If we are ever to lower the expenditures and profile of police in our cities, it will be through measures such as these. In federally supported housing, security personnel—always considered a luxury by the Federal Housing Administration—are increasingly expensive and difficult to support from overextended city and housing authority budgets. In New York it has been demonstrated that because of fringe benefits and time off, making one additional patrolman evident costs the equivalent of the annual salary of ten policemen.[2] The cost of security personnel is beginning to compete with the cost of building maintenance, while the effectiveness of increased manpower is in serious question.

The root causes of inner city and ghetto crime lie deep in the social structure of our nation. Criminal and victim alike come from that strata of the population without the power of choice. In the United States, the correlation of criminal and victim with poverty is unmistakable.[3] To both, access to institutions which lead out of their condition has been denied. Our social and educational systems have not adapted to admit the minority groups who largely make up this population. In a disturbing percentage of the inner city and ghetto population, the one institution normally most resistant to social disruption, the family, is crumbling. Lee Rainwater, in his article "Fear and the House-as-Haven," about his study of Pruitt-Igoe, defines security as the most important need to be satisfied in a residence for low-income groups.[4] Feelings of insecurity about one's residential environment often lead to the adoption of a negative and defeatist view of oneself, to ambivalence about job finding, and to expressions of general impotence in the capacity to cope with the outside world. The secure residential environment—understood by a resident as a haven and interpreted by outsiders as the expression of the inhabitants' egos—may be one of the most meaningful forms of social rehabilitation available to the family and to society. The way in which community attitudes toward security and insecurity act as social causes is still to be studied. Children who live in high-rise buildings seem to have a poorly developed perception of individual privacy and little understanding of territory. There may be evidence that the physical form of a residential environment plays a significant role in shaping the perception of children and in making them cognizant of the existence of zones of influence and, therefore, the rights of others.

It is difficult to isolate the various mechanisms which have been producing the high crime rates we are presently experiencing in our urban core areas. Some contributory causes can be assumed: the concentration of the disadvantaged in these areas; the attraction of criminals to an urban environment which is at the same time increasingly anonymous and decreasingly self-protective; and the evolution of an urban physical form and residential environment which encourages and fosters criminal behavior. The poor are most vulnerable to crime in any setting. But in anonymous buildings which facilitate their victimization, we have the makings of a situation of crisis proportions.

No one has met these problems with conscious solutions. The poor are unable to choose alternatives. Low-middle-income populations that have not succumbed to apathy have fled. The exercise of choice in the housing market has glutted the suburbs with newly transplanted families, who at times feel cut off from the social life of their original neighborhoods, from the convenience of place of work, shopping, entertainment, and friends—but are safe. How quickly suburbs will slide into the same insecurity that plagues the city is open to speculation. For the time, suburban families have avoided the problem for themselves. The problem remains, however, and evasion has its social costs.

Some middle-class families have not fled to the outskirts, but have withdrawn into high-rise security-guarded fortresses of semiluxury. This introversion and intentional isolation inevitably occurs at the expense of adjacent surroundings. But mental and physical withdrawal from the social order and its problems has at least three dangerous attending characteristics. First is the indifference to the problem once it has been evaded. Second—and this follows on the first—is the relegation of the problem of security, the traditional responsibility of the citizenry, to formally designated authority. It is no doubt impossible to imagine a modern city without a functioning police force, although their advent is as little distant as the introduction of the "Bobbys" of London in 1840. But the function of police has traditionally been to apprehend criminals. Fear of apprehension and ensuing speedy prosecution is, of course, a deterrent to criminal behavior. But police alone can in no major way create or foster security. Society, in the persons of citizens, must adopt this function. An apathetic, detached citizenry far too often limits its participation to bitter criticism of police for not accomplishing work which rightly must be undertaken by the citizenry itself. The well-off citizen, by isolating himself in a secure fortress, by restricting his own ventures into the streets, and by demanding that authority assume all responsibility for ensuring the safety of streets, has effectively set the stage for the defeat of his own demands. The street, without the continued presence of the citizen, will never be made to function safely for him. Without the continued presence, focused demand, and responsible overview of the citizen, the police become lackadaisical, their commitments distorted, and they fall easy prey to corruption.

The third characteristic of withdrawal from urban life is the resultant physical design of the buildings of our cities. To provide security by means of a guard or doorman requires that entry to a building complex be restricted to one location. This usually means walling off a two- to ten-acre housing complex from the surrounding neighborhood. By this action, thousands of feet of street are removed from all forms of social and visual contact. A natural mechanism providing safety to our streets has been sacrificed to insure the security of the residents of the walled-off complex.

On the other hand, it is possible to design a multi-family housing complex in which as low a number of units as possible share a common entry off the street. Designers can position units, windows, and entries, and prescribe paths of movement and areas of activity so as to provide inhabitants with continuous natural surveillance of the street and project grounds. The street comes under surveillance from the building, the building entries and lobbys under the surveillance of the street. As with the fortress, this design also provides security. But instead of relegating the responsibility to others, it is assumed by the residents in the natural flow of their everyday activities. Moreover, the building complex and the residents are integrated into the community. The complex protects the street as well as itself. The street life helps, in turn, to protect the complex. Instead of being an act of withdrawal, this design reinforces residents in their expression of concern for their own domain and for the streets and activity areas to which it is tied. In this way, residents do not achieve internal security at the expense of the surrounding area, but by insuring that the surrounding area is equally secure. Their concerns are in harmony with those of the community. This is defensible space design.

For urban residential settings, for low- and moderate-income populations in particular, defensible space design is imperative. In many cases, withdrawal is not an option open to them. Four million people live in federally subsidized low-middle-income housing. For them there is effectively no choice to exercise on the housing market. The same factionalizing of our society which is expressed in middle- and upper-class withdrawal has, moreover, infected the design and structure of their environment. The stigma of poverty and minority group membership has been stamped onto public housing. It has been made to appear as different as possible

FIGURE 11   Aerial view of Co-op City. (Courtesy of Skyviews Survey Inc.)

from its surroundings; it has been marked off as clearly as if by quarantine. It is not our concern here to unravel the social forces which have influenced the architectural form and symbolism of contemporary low-income America, but to offer an alternate model of design. Because of the location of their residences, because of their social position, and because of the design of their housing, the poor are the most consistently victimized of our urban population.[5]

Even those who have fled the old neighborhoods often find they have purchased a transitory security. Thinking they left the victims behind, they have often designed themselves into a victimization which, if it has not yet arrived, is nonetheless on the way. In September 1970, a fifty-thousand-unit housing development, built privately for cooperative ownership, was completed in an outlying area of the Bronx, New York. It was occupied almost overnight, predominantly by an older middle-class population fleeing an adjacent area of the Bronx only a few miles away. Many see that their new homes and environment are inferior to the area they have abandoned. Their apartments are smaller, shopping is inconvenient and

FIGURE 12   Map of Upper Manhattan and The Bronx, locating Co-op City, Grand Concourse, Fordham Road, and Pelham Parkway.

expensive, television provides most of the available entertainment. They have left behind them friends and institutions—a way of life.

Many of these deficiencies will be remedied as the project is completed and the area becomes more heavily populated. Yet the new residents spend little time complaining. In a sense they are pleased with the costs and faults. These are, after all, a small and necessary price to pay for what they most crave—security. They have escaped from a once-friendly environment, which had come to terrify them. Muggings, burglaries, and assaults had made life in their "old neighborhood" impossible for a generation of elders. In a random interview, almost all those questioned admitted that in their abandoned neighborhood they had long ago stopped going out in the evening. All had either experienced robberies or had close friends who had. This is no new story. What is fascinating and fearful is the way this population chose to solve its problems. They fled *en masse* and segregated themselves within a new middle-class ghetto—an isolation of their own making, one which fits their image of the social order. In Co-op City they live among their own kind—45 percent of the adult population is over 50, 65 percent is Jewish, and the average wage earner makes between seven and ten thousand dollars a year.[6] Once a heterogenous, gregarious, active, and culturally involved community, the new residents of Co-op City now are segregated by income and ethnicity and only desire to breathe more easily. Those who fled to this haven would be shocked to know that the buildings and residential settings they now occupy are much less defensible than those they abandoned. The onslaught of only a small percentage of the criminals they fled is all that would be required to make their dream world evaporate.

Co-op City works now because it is far from the site of crime. But, how long before the project is recognized as vulnerable—before the criminal extends his range and mobility? The developers of Co-op City recognized that by ensuring a uniform middle-class population they could ensure a low crime rate. So long as all the families in Co-op City are exclusively white, middle-class, and elderly, the crime rate will stay down. The appearance of anyone else sends out a danger signal as obviously as an alarm bell. But already there are young families moving into Co-op City—black families, Puerto Rican families—seeking the same security and using the same means to achieve it. As the population becomes mixed, the success of this strategy will diminish.

An important principle of defensible space design is that subdivision allows residents to distinguish neighbor from intruder. In Co-op City this is accomplished not through design but by isolating a large, uniform population. Unfortunately, this is only a temporary respite for a small, privileged segment of the population. It employs statistics and segregation as weapons for keeping out those who are already the chief victims of crime—the poor. It will not work for very long, and it is repellent by virtue of the racism and prejudice it practices. It will not, in any way, contribute to the redemption of our cities.

The lesson to be learned from Co-op City is that crime control can be achieved by creating a situation in which it is possible for the potential victim to recognize in advance the potential criminal. A criminal will rarely commit a crime in a building in which he knows he will be easily recognized. Design can facilitate the process of recognition. Rather than the device of uniformity of population, such a design enables a varied and mixed population to know and control its own territory, to distinguish who (in an apparently complex and anonymous urban space) is neighbor and who intruder, and to do this at the level of the building as well as at the individual and communal level.

Subtle difficulties arise in attempting to improve the security of low-income, as compared with middle-income housing; these are mainly a function of the social characteristics of the resident populations. The social characteristics of the middle class greatly facilitate the task of providing them with a secure environment. Middle-class people have developed a refined sense of property and ownership; they have a measure of self-confidence and pride in their personal capabilities. Their everyday experiences reinforce their social competence; they can retain some control over the forces that shape their lives; and they recognize alternatives among which they can choose. These positive social controls give them a feeling of potency in protecting and enforcing their rights within a defined sphere of influence; for

FIGURE 13 Aerial Perspective of Tilden Houses in Brooklyn, New York. (Courtesy of New York City Housing Authority)

instance, they are well-practiced in their demand for and use of police protection.

Security design for a low-income population is very difficult. This is not only because of the economic restraints on cost and the higher concentration of criminal and victim. Daily social experience reinforces among the poor the sense of their own impotence and removes to a level of fantasy the thought of altering or improving the conditions of their lives. Closed out of the game financially, politically, educationally, and in virtually every other way, those among the poor who have not accepted the image of their own impotence are rare. In this light it may be unrealistic to expect an individual to assume positive social attitudes and influence in one sphere of his life—his family and residential environment—when he has learned clearly and consistently in the other facets of his existence that he has no such power.

Defensible space, it may be charged, is middle-class thinking. The poor have their own culture. They don't want the peaceful, secure, dull life of the middle class. They don't want property. They don't want the values middle-class society wishes to foist upon them. Violence, it is contended, is part of their culture. So, apparently, is communality. They don't want walls, whether real ones, or the ones you place in their minds by the design of space.

This romantic view of the poor is without foundation. Interviews with hundreds of low-income housing residents reveal that most hold the goals and aspirations of the middle class. The desire for security is not limited to the middle class. The desire for a living environment over which one has personal control is part and parcel of the desire for a life which one controls. The creation of communities able to keep themselves free of crime—and to keep their members from becoming criminals—is the task of every society. Anonymous, stigmatized high-rise projects are neither the work of nature, nor the free choice of their inhabitants. They do, however, prove to be important contributors to crime. If it is "middle class" to wish to escape this fate, then the overwhelming majority of lower-class people hold middle-class goals and aspirations which are very dear to them.

NOTES

1 The total number of crimes reported in the first nine months of 1971, as compared with the same period in 1970, indicates that crime rose nearly three times as fast in suburban areas as in cities with populations over one million—11 percent as compared with 4 percent. Overall, crime in the suburbs rose nearly twice as fast as in the nation as a whole (*Uniform Crime Report*, Federal Bureau of Investigation, as reported in the *New York Times*, 30 January, 1972, p. 1).

2 *New York City Criminal Justice Coordinating Council Report* (New York, 1971), p. 34.

3 *To Establish Justice, to Insure Domestic Tranquility: Final Report of the National Commission on the Causes & Prevention of Violence* (New York: Bantam Books, 1970), pp. 20–21.

4 Lee Rainwater, "Fear and the House-as-Haven in the Lower Class," *AIP Journal* 32 (January 1966):23.

5 *To Establish Justice*, p. 24.

6 Jane Krause, "Co-op City: Beauty or the Beast?" (Paper, New York University Graduate School of Public Administration, January 1972 [from an interview with Don Phillips, quoting in-house publication, "Projection Completion," of the Office of Cooperative Education, Co-op City, Bronx, N.Y., December 16, 1971]).

FIVE. DESIGN AND URBAN FORM—SUGGESTED READINGS

Alexander, Christopher. 1987. *A New Theory of Urban Design*. New York: Oxford University Press.

Bacon, Edmund N. 1976. *Design of Cities*. New York: Penguin.

Barnett, Jonathon. 1982. *An Introduction to Urban Design*. New York: Harper & Row.

Cullen, Gordon. 1961. *Townscape*. New York: Reinhold.

Howard, Ebenezer. 1946. *Garden Cities of Tomorrow*. London: Faber.

Le Corbusier. 1987. *The City of Tomorrow and Its Planning*. New York: Dover.

Lynch, Kevin. 1960. *Image of the City*. Cambridge, MA: M.I.T.

Lynch, Kevin. 1984. *Site Planning*, 3d ed. Cambridge, MA: M.I.T.

Scully, Vincent. 1969. *American Architecture and Urbanism*. New York: Praeger.

Venturi, Robert. 1977. *Complexity and Contradiction in Architecture*, 2d ed. New York: Museum of Modern Art.

Whyte, William H. 1968. *The Last Landscape*. Garden City, NY: Doubleday.

Whyte, William H. 1988. *City: Rediscovering the Center*. New York: Doubleday.

6

ECONOMIC DEVELOPMENT

Economic Growth and Development: Processes, Stages, and Determinants

Wilbur R. Thompson
Professor Emeritus of Economics, Wayne State University

Wilbur R. Thompson was among the first to recognize that urban economies were an important and unique entity for study. When he wrote *A Preface to Urban Economics*, most of the "serious" economists were studying either the firm or the national economy. In his book, however, Thompson stated that "as the United States tends more and more to be a country of very large cities, the critical national problems of growth and development, stability, greater and more equal opportunity and, ultimately, the pursuit of the 'good life' become urban problems" (p. 1). In this chapter, Thompson sketches the urban growth process. Almost thirty years after the chapter was written, it still stands as a useful and accurate analysis of urban growth.

The principal cause of the dramatic urban growth experienced by the United States since the turn of the century is the great rural to urban migration. By now, however, the significance of the continuing shift from farm to city is well appreciated; we need pause only briefly to recall its main characteristics as background for the principal concern of this chapter.

In brief, a steady advance in agricultural technology has greatly enlarged farm output per man-hour. The rate of annual increase has risen from a little over 1 per cent in the twenties to more than 5 per cent in the years since the Second World War. Our rapidly growing per capita income—the reflection of a generally advancing technology—has not, however, increased the demand for foods and fibers at anywhere near the same rate; food consumption is increasing only about half as fast as over-all productivity and per capita income, and not much more than half as fast as the productivity growth rate in agriculture itself. Thus, national economic development has required that the agricultural sector decline sharply in relative share. The percentage of the labor force engaged in agriculture plummeted from 12 to 6 per cent between 1950 and 1960—while manufacturing and services absorbed expanding shares.

Farm to city migration was, then, dictated by national demand and supply forces and would have occurred even if demographic patterns had been neutral. But a farm birth rate considerably above the urban one resulted in more than proportionate manpower additions in agriculture, during a period when few additions were needed. In sum, the great shift from farm to factory and office is the most basic explanation of urban growth up to now.

But the nation's rural areas are rapidly emptying out; the great farm to city migration has about run its course and will soon belong to economic history. Today, the most challenging urban growth theory and the most compelling urban growth problems arise out of interurban competition for growth and the development of the national system of cities. It is in the size distribution and the spatial pattern of cities that the new vitality of urban economics lies. This chapter emphasizes, then, not the rural to urban migration of the past but the interurban interactions of the present and near future.

THE MANY LINES OF LINKAGE

Some appreciation of the fine web of urban growth forces can be gained by working through a much oversimplified presentation of the lines of linkage between a hypothetical urban area and the outside world, as outlined in Figure 1. We arbitrarily break into the pattern of urban economic development by beginning with three local meat-packing plants (1) which sell outside the locality. These have been drawn together by the mutual advantages they enjoy in tapping a large local pool of specialized and skilled labor (2), created by their own *combined* demand. Because they have clustered together, these three plants have attracted a common supplier, a plant manufacturing meat cutting tools (3), and this integration of sequential operations has added to local exports, indirectly, by increasing the proportion of the meat products sales dollar that remains within the area. In other words, as vertical integration in the local export industries progresses, local value-added and income generated become a higher proportion of sales.

Local slaughtering produces hides as a by-product and this encourages shoe firms (4) to locate nearby to save transportation costs on their chief raw material. The horizontal agglomeration of shoe plants may be reinforced by the fact that shoes are subject to comparative shopping by wholesalers and retailers and an out-of-the-way shoe plant is at a severe disadvantage. All of this greatly increases the demand for local business services (5), such as transportation, financial, and marketing services, and thereby improves their quality and variety and lowers their cost.

As local business services become more varied and improve in quality, they steadily replace similar services (6) previously imported from larger, more highly developed neighboring cities. While the net effect is for the local economy to become ever more self-sufficient in business services, the growing complexity of the local economy will bring a need to import at least a modest amount of new, more esoteric business services (e.g., specialized financial and commercial services related to importing foreign steels for the meat cutting tool firm). Simultaneously, the addition of successive firms augments local payrolls and personal income of local households (7) which, in turn, enriches the consumer service sector (8). As successive consumer spending mounts, the variety store gives way to the department store, and then the "custom shop" and the "salon" are added.

Consumer expenditures rise faster than export industry payrolls as the "multiplier effect" takes hold and employees of the local service facilities (9) take

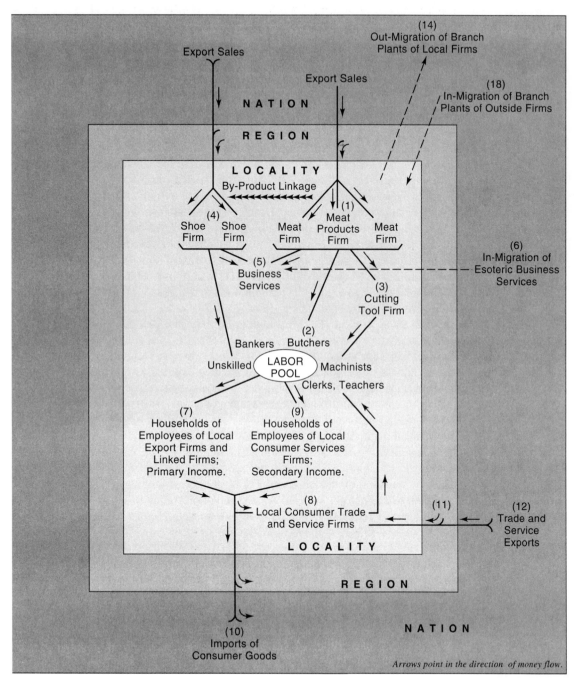

FIGURE 1   The urban growth complex.

incomes earned by servicing the households of employees of the export industries and the linked business service and cutting tool firms, and spend them for more locally produced goods and services. Parallel to the pattern developing in the local business service sector, as the local consumer service sector matures imports of consumer goods and services (10) will decrease, in relative terms, although the absolute amount of consumer imports will probably increase as the local economy grows in size and complexity.

Our hypothetical urban area is now moving up in rank in the hierarchy of cities. As it becomes first a provincial and then a regional capital, its rising status is explicitly recognized by an industrial structure which changes to reflect its new role: an exporter of services. A true metropolis as a "mother city" reaches out and renders the more specialized and skill-demanding administrative, financial, legal, educational, recreational, medical, and governmental services to its satellites. The first step, usually, is to export a growing range of services to nearby cities of the next smaller size (11), which in turn merchandise a somewhat abridged line of services to the next lower level of cities. With growth, however, the metropolis may extend its reach to embrace the whole nation or a very large portion of it (12) for a much narrower group of services: New York with finance, corporate administration, entertainment, and others; Chicago with nearly as broad a group; Miami, recreation and amusement; Washington, government and tourist services; Boston, education and research.

Even local manufacturing tends to become more diversified and self-sufficient, as the growing local market attracts the branch plants of outside firms (13), while the branch plants of the growing local firms are spun off in complementary fashion to the large and growing metropolitan areas elsewhere (14). Piece by piece, additional business and consumer services and manufacturing operations are added to the local economy, as the growing local market affords ever more economies of scale and cuts the cost of local production to the point at which the remaining cost disadvantage vis-à-vis the bigger and/or most efficient operations elsewhere is less than the transportation costs from each of them.

Finally, the metropolis, with its universities, museums, libraries, and research laboratories, becomes one big spatially integrated "coffee house," where bright minds out of diverse cultures clash and strike sparks that ignite the fires of new products and processes—new export industries. We have now come full circle to where we began, or better, we have entered upon an endless and self-regenerative growth cycle.[1]

THE STAGES OF URBAN GROWTH

Can the many aspects of urban-regional growth be grouped and arranged in a time sequence of distinct stages?

We might identify, first, the *Stage of Export Specialization* in which the local economy is the lengthened shadow of a single dominant industry or even a single firm. This initial stage gives way with growth and size to the *Stage of the Export Complex* in which local production broadens to other products and/or deepens by extending forward or backward in the stages of production, by adding local suppliers and/or consumers of intermediate products. Next, the *Stage of Economic Maturation* (Local Service Sector Puberty) follows, in which the principal expansion of local activity is in the direction of replacing imports with new "own use" production; the local economy fills out in range and quality of both business and consumer services. Fourth, the *Stage of Regional Metropolis* is reached, when the local economy becomes a node connecting and controlling neighboring cities, once rivals and now satellites, and the export of services becomes a major economic function.

One more common phase is the *Stage of Technical-Professional Virtuosity*; national eminence in some specialized skill or economic function is achieved. This stage may succeed or precede the status of regional metropolis: Detroit was a national center of automotive design and engineering long before it became a regional metropolis, if indeed it is one now. Boston's acknowledged eminence in education and, more recently, research and development, followed its role as the capital of New England. San Francisco is a national cultural center, perhaps second only to New York, quite apart from its co-captaincy with Los Angeles of the West Coast region.

These purported stages of urban growth are, of course, highly impressionistic generalizations and deserve a hearing only as the most tentative hypotheses from which careful empirical work might be begun. Moreover, these growth sketches leave much too strong a feeling of the inevitability of growth and development—onward and upward forever. And yet we see many examples of local economic stagnation and decay and even demise. What are some of the dampening and restraining forces that surely must exist?

FAILURE OF MOMENTUM BETWEEN STAGES IN GROWTH

Suppose the original growth stimulus—the economic environment at genesis—did not generate a sufficiently strong impulse to lift the economy to a level at which derivative growth forces could take over. For example: the local harbor and connecting waterways may not have been so superior or the local ore deposit so rich, given the current ore prices and the remoteness of the mine and so forth, to create a town large enough or a technology advanced enough to build an attractive labor force. Without this latter attraction, the local economy never drew the manufacturing plants which would have moved the local economy into the second stage of export diversification and into a state of general industrial enrichment, before the preferred mode of transportation changed or the vein of ore gave out. Or, if the small port or mining economy did manage to add a few manufacturing firms and limp through the second stage of growth, not enough of an industrial complex was created to develop the local market to a point where a strong surge of local service industry formation developed, replacing imports with local production. Thus the growth of a local economy may hesitate and stagnate between any of these stages if the momentum at the end of a phase is not strong enough to carry the economy to the point at which the mechanism of the next stage is activated.

An insufficiency of momentum may be relative rather than absolute, especially with reference to the fourth stage, metropolis formation. Typically, one city will rise from a group of rivals to become the "mother city" of the group. Whichever city gets the jump on the others and achieves early economic dominance usually finds that success breeds success as external economies of service industry agglomeration pave the way for progressive, cumulative coups.[2] The wholesale trade center for the group may stand in good way to become the financial center and the latter gain may commonly lead to administrative dominance and subsequent legal eminence and so forth. The sequence as sketched is purely illustrative because historical and/or statistical-empirical work on this facet of urban growth dynamics is scarce.[3]

Promotion up through the hierarchy of cities is, then, partly a matter of the right timing, usually an early lead amply fortified with local leadership. And we count, of course, more losers than winners in this interurban competition; too little and too late, relative to neighboring cities, is a powerful constraint on urban growth and development.

To be sure, a lagging city can forge ahead to dominance through some exceptionally fortunate circumstance, such as being the chance host to a firm which is destined to become the individual "success story" of *the* growth industry of the era (e.g., Ford Motor Company and Detroit) or through the discovery of great natural wealth (e.g., Houston). Ordinarily, however, success breeds success and the rich get richer, at least in the urban growth process.

"CHALLENGE AND RESPONSE": A TALE OF THREE CITIES

If the rich always did get richer (and the poor poorer) in interregional competition, long-range urban forecasting would be much easier than it actually is. But victories can bring complacency and defeats can be challenges. We might postulate a crisis theory of human behavior in regional economic development: a community rises to the occasion in a variation on the Toynbee theme of "challenge and response."

When urban growth slackens or stalls—when the rate of growth of new jobs falls below the rate of natural increase in the local labor force—heavy, chronic unemployment creates local crises: personal, social and governmental. Out-migration, the economist's solution, is often sluggish, especially in a time of ever more pervasive home ownership, tighter job seniority, and broadening unemployment compensation. (Millions for unemployment compensation, but not one cent for relocation expenses!) In depressed areas, sagging tax collections and soaring welfare costs upset municipal budgets and force politicians and public administrators to strain for more imaginative and incisive programs of area industrial development.

Agonizing reappraisals are made of local business taxes relative to competing urban areas, and the efficacy of tax concessions, subsidies in the form of rent-free use of vacant buildings, and other industrial lures are reviewed. One can almost predict the likelihood of "another" state-local tax study from the current rate of local unemployment relative to the current national rate. Comparative transportation facilities, wage rates, utility rates, and other leading plant location factors will also come in for close scrutiny during these trying times. If necessity is the mother of social, as well as technical, invention, the probability of imaginative and effective local action, both public and private, designed to improve the local business climate and nurture new industrial growth will be significantly increased in time of local stagnation.[4]

Perhaps, on close inspection, the recent economic histories of Boston, Pittsburgh, and Detroit would exhibit evidence of a challenge-and-response developmental syndrome. Boston was the first of the three to experience economic stagnation and was a declining economy prior to the outbreak of the Second World War. But shortly after its end, building on a base of superior higher educational facilities that area spawned a complex of research and development work and manufacturing activity in R & D-oriented industries (e.g., electronics, instruments) almost overnight, greatly softening the blow of losing the textile and shoe industries to the South. How much of this new work was generated by increased organized efforts at industrial development and how much was due to the presence of Harvard University and Massachusetts Institute of Technology in the area is impossible to tell. But there is at least evidence of local awareness of a need to rebuild a faltering economy on a new industrial base in the mass of economic studies and reports on the area that poured forth in the prewar and early postwar period.[5]

Contrast the case of Boston with that of Pittsburgh, an economy which boomed during the war and briefly in its aftermath as it worked to supply the backlog demand for steel. Hard hit by the first postwar recession in 1949, for the next half-dozen years Pittsburgh stagnated as local leadership went through a period of intellectual and emotional readjustment, apparently culminating in a clear understanding that this urban area could either stagnate as a steel city or hunt for some broader industrial base for a resurgence. The striking rebirth of Pittsburgh—through smoke abatement programs; physical renewal in the Golden Triangle; the sponsorship of a highly sophisticated economic development study in co-operation with the local universities;[6] and, most recently, the $250 million research center sponsored by the universities of the area—gives every evidence of being just as spectacular as the Boston rebirth, at least if it is conceded that in an age of education and affluence the image and long-run prospects of a steel city are decidedly inferior to those of a center of culture.

Consider now the third city, Detroit, an area which rode through the first two postwar recessions (1949, 1954) relatively unscathed on a huge backlog demand for automobiles. Not until 1955, much later than the other two cities, did automobile manufacturing employment in Detroit reach its peak. For almost five years thereafter, as manufacturing employment sagged lower and lower, the local industrial pundits misread warning signs of structural transformation in the local economy as signaling only a temporary cycle trough. About 1960, the chronic nature of the crushing unemployment left in the wake of an automobile industry which had matured, decentralized, automated and demilitarized—all in an indigestibly short period of time—began to percolate through to the opinion molders in the local economy. True, the first serious stirrings had begun about two years before, with an epic state tax study[7] and a few small-budget industrial development analyses,[8] but serious efforts at organizing industrial development investment funds, industrial parks and the like were five or six years behind the turning point of a trend in local manufacturing employment. The concept of a research park tied in with two large universities of the area was independently "discovered" in 1961 about six years after the first signs of crisis and perhaps a dozen years after Boston's successful venture in hothouse research and development.

An interesting and supporting sidelight here is that Detroit could have carried on its World War II work in aircraft, at least in aircraft engines, granting Southern California's advantage in climate for final assembly and testing. But impatience to get back to the more lucrative automobile business was so great that airplane production was not even accorded a secondary place on Detroit's postwar industrial agenda. Conversely, Los Angeles, with nothing as profitable as making automobiles to reconvert to, fought for and won the postwar airplane business. Accordingly, Michigan's share of total military procurement fell from 10.5 per cent in 1940–45 to 2.7 per cent in 1962, while California's was rising from 9.1 to 23.9 per cent.

On careful quantification, we might find that the challenge of an employment crisis elicits its response in a resurgence of local economic leadership with various lags of roughly predictable length, under various sets of circumstances. For example, in these three industrially mature cities, about a half-dozen years elapsed between the beginning of steady deterioration and widespread appreciation of the structural character of the local malady. Public and private counteraction, in magnitude commensurate with the gravity of the challenge, lagged by another half-dozen years. And industrial reconversion may take a decade or so. Thus, over all, as much as two decades may elapse between shifts from one economic base to a substantially new one. Of course, this is the very kind of knowledge which, once revealed, might effect changes in the developmental pattern and might even shorten the period of response.

THE URBAN SIZE RATCHET

If the challenge of economic adversity does indeed beget the response of renewed community leadership and individual creativity, how can we explain abandoned towns and depressed areas?[9] The coal towns of Pennsylvania, West Virginia, and Kentucky have been challenged by chronic unemployment for decades now with little evidence or prospect of significant response; the smaller urban places in Nebraska, the Dakotas and Montana—the wheat belt—have been declining for decades and give every indication of continuing to do so.

But these illustrations are all of the smaller urban areas. Clearly a scale factor is at work: witness the difficulty of finding a similar illustration of an urban area of over half a million population, one which has suffered an absolute decline in population. How far down in population size must we go to name an urban area that has lost population? Perhaps some critical size exists, short of which growth is not inevitable and even the very existence of the place is not assured, but beyond which absolute contraction is highly unlikely, even though the growth rate may slacken, at times even to zero. In sum, at a certain range of urban scale, set by the degree of isolation of the urban place, the nature of its hinterland, the level of industrial development in the country, and various cultural factors, some growth mechanism, similar to a ratchet, comes into being, locking in past growth and preventing contraction.

A number of possible rationalizations of a hypothetical urban-size ratchet could be adduced. One argument would be that with growth and size comes industrial diversification, and even a random blending of young, mature, and decadent industries tends to produce local growth rates which deviate only slightly from the national average rate, or the rate applicable to the surrounding region. Freedom from rapid rates of decline, moreover, provides the large urban area a grace period in which to react to adversity. Finally, the rich industrial diversification of the large urban area is fashioned in part out of many small firms with extensive and complex linkages to other local businesses. Clearly, it is much harder for these firms to relocate than it is for the large self-sufficient plant characteristic of a small urban area.

A second possible basis for irreversible urban growth after achievement of some threshold size is simply power politics. With a larger population comes greater electoral strength at both the state and national levels and with reference to both executive and legislative bodies. True, political power may increase less than proportionately with population increase, as in malapportioned state legislatures and in the United States Senate; nevertheless, it does increase significantly. Thus, to the extent that federal and state financial aids and public works projects can revive faltering urban economies, the bigger urban areas are the gainers, for they can press harder for government support.

Third, and somewhat related, is the fact that tremendous amounts of fixed capital have been sunk in social and private overhead in the very large urban area—streets, sewers, schools, water mains, electric power lines, stores and housing—so that even if the area's productive facilities for export are worn out or technically obsolete, public service and utility costs are low enough to make it uneconomic to abandon so much immobile capital. No nation is so affluent that it can afford to throw away a major city.

Fourth, a greater and greater proportion of industrial activity is oriented to customers rather than to sources of supply, and the larger urban areas amass potential customers. A large local economy becomes almost self-justifying as a rich product market. New industries, born elsewhere, eventually reach a stage of development at which they are likely to establish branch plants in this large local market, sustaining local growth. Also, the current shift from manufacturing to service activity favors local market-oriented production. With growing size comes a steady improvement in an area's transportation position; every large urban area becomes a transportation hub regardless of its geographical position. In a day when the giant corporation engaged in nationwide operations is growing ever more dominant, the frequency of jet air service may be the critical factor in choosing an area for a headquarters or even a branch operation.

Finally, a large urban area is more likely to give birth to new industries at critical points in its life cycle than is a small urban area—an industrial birth which rescues it from the brink of stagnation or decline. While a large place may not produce more new ideas per thousand population per year than a small place—and some evidence will be cited below to suggest greater industrial creativity in larger places—a surer and steadier supply of invention, innovation, and promotion is to be expected in larger places. To illustrate, suppose that an entrepreneurial genius occurs only once in every 10,000 births, then a 50,000-population urban area with, say, 1,000 births per year will produce this key person only once every ten years, on the average. This area may not have a new industrial savior ready at the time of critical need, whereas the 500,000-population urban area, spawning a genius a year, almost certainly will. Gifted persons, moreover, born in smaller places tend to migrate to bigger cities. Sheer size may stabilize the supply of the key human resources necessary to economic growth and development.

In sum, if the growth of an urban area persists long enough to raise the area to some critical size (a quarter of a million population?),[10] structural characteristics, such as industrial diversification, political power, huge fixed investments, a rich local market, and a steady supply of industrial leadership may almost ensure its continued growth and fully ensure against absolute decline—may, in fact, effect irreversible aggregate growth.

MANAGEMENT AS THE SCARCE FACTOR IN URBAN GROWTH

Absolute size may also be a brake on rate of growth as cities experience, after a certain critical level, increasing cost of public services due to density, congestion, bureaucracy, and so forth. Few statistical studies of public service production functions are available and even with a full portfolio of them one would have to exercise great care in generalizing across diverse urban areas. The principal diseconomy of scale may well turn out to be managerial efficiency, with a high variability between areas. The impression that management may be the limiting factor in urban scale is partly inferential by analogy from orthodox economic thought and partly intuitive.

In search of a theoretical constraint on size of firms, without which neither competition nor the self-regulating price system itself could be preserved, economists long ago found that they were forced to rely primarily on the limited expansibility of the managerial factor. The supply of land, labor, and capital does not seem to pose serious constraints on firm size. Apart from the managerial limitation, economists could rationalize firm-size limits only by turning to imperfect competition or the inability of a firm to sell an endless amount of a given product at a constant price (i.e., a "downward sloping demand curve").[11] If price cuts are necessary to sell additional product, the firm realizes steadily diminishing net additions to revenue and profit with each additional sale, even if its unit costs do not begin to rise. While the firm might continue to grow even here by adding new product lines, multiproduct operations pose even greater managerial demands. Sooner or later, management would come to be the principal limitation or scarce factor, albeit later with multiproduct expansion.

The managerial factor may also be the critical limitation on city size. As the city grows in total population, density of population, and physical extent, a point may be reached at which the unit cost of public services begins to rise or the quality of the service begins to fall appreciably. If so, a force which tends to dampen urban growth will have come into being. Local export firms, with their costs of production rising, find themselves disadvantaged in interregional competition for shares of the national market; manufacturing firms must move their trucks through congested streets to cramped loading docks, while paying higher property taxes for the less efficient urban public services. The city size at which increasing public service costs first turn sharply upward is probably, in large measure, a matter of the current level of urban technology. While the state of the arts in such diverse fields as urban transportation, communication, governmental decision making, and personnel administration is common to all urban areas—for knowledge is freely available—the competency and creativeness of various sets of local public officials are not nearly so uniform. And it is the local public officials, elective and appointive, who are the principal instruments of urban efficiency, together with the private managers of a few key local service industries, such as the utilities, banks, and local transportation and communication systems.

The parallel to the multiproduct firm is the highly interrelated set of local public services that must be integrated or co-ordinated to preserve the efficiency of the city, seen now as a huge factory with its streets, power lines, and pipes as the assembly lines, and its complex of legal, financial, and technical services as a magnified version of the "front office." If we believe that success in business is closely tied to the efficiency and creativity of the firm's management, is it not equally likely that the efficiency of the local public economy will vary widely from place to place according to the quality of urban management? Just as efficient management of the General Motors Corporation can push back the point at which net diseconomies of scale take effect, so public service inefficiency and rising unit costs can be postponed considerably, even if not indefinitely, by able and experienced local public legislators and administrators.

But recruiting able public administrators at the local level is no easy matter. The Municipal Manpower Commission found:

> *Low prestige of government employment adversely affects the quality of local government personnel.* . . . Nearly half of the responses to a survey of local officials conducted by the Public Personnel Association said that low prestige was a major obstacle to recruiting persons to fill key positions in local governments. A still more striking manifestation of the effect of this low prestige of employment in local governments is found in the attitudes of municipal executives themselves. The Commission's study of 1,700 local executives revealed that only 17 per cent would recommend a career in local government.[12]

It is not enough to recruit talented people to serve as public officials, develop a science of local public administration, and professionalize urban management. The organizational and institutional framework within which all this functions is paramount. Even the most able urban managers may not be able to provide efficient government in a politically fragmented, unco-ordinated urban area. The problems of recruitment and political fragmentation, moreover, interact, worsening the situation. The Municipal Manpower Commission also reported that:

> A lack of clear-cut community-wide objectives and of permanent machinery for area-wide planning and policy formulation. . . . The fragmentation of the geographical area among numerous local governments and many leadership groups is a serious barrier to the solution of metropolitan problems which are beyond the capacity of any single jurisdiction or civic organization; it is a cause of frustration for municipal manpower. . . . Furthermore, the small-scale problems faced by such units do not offer much attraction to experienced and able personnel.[13]

Ultimately, then, diseconomies of scale in public services and quasi-public services, such as water supply, sewage disposal, electricity, gas and transportation, may constrain the size of the city; but only if technology progress, political innovation, and administrative ingenuity do not keep pace. Despite the built-in frailties that have been mentioned, they have up to now.

NOTES

1 This summary and loose synthesis of the complex of forces underlying urban-regional economic growth and development draws liberally, of course, from innumerable sources, and only an unabridged history of doctrine in this field of thought would suffice to assign credits of authorship. The most comprehensive review of this literature and the most exhaustive bibliography published to date (or likely to be published for some time to come) is in Walter Isard, *et al., Methods of Regional Analysis: an Introduction to Regional Science* (New York: John Wiley and Sons, Inc., 1960).

2 For example, in the historic rivalry between Chicago and St. Louis for supremacy in the Middle West and as a gateway to the West, natural factors, such as the Mississippi River, as a north-south transportation facility and as an east-west barrier, and social factors, such as a river-minded leadership group in St. Louis and the disruptive effect of the Civil War on the border-state hinterland of St. Louis, all combined to edge Chicago past St. Louis. Cumulative forces in growth then widened the gap. See Lewis F. Thomas, "Decline of St. Louis as Midwest Metropolis," *Economic Geography* (April 1949), pp. 118–27, for a brief account, or Wyatt Winton Belcher, *The Economic Rivalry between St. Louis and Chicago, 1850–1880* (New York: Columbia University Press, 1947), for a more extended treatment.

3 A number of static, cross-section studies have been made which classify cities according to their principal economic function—manufacturing, wholesale trade center, transportation center, seat of government and so forth. But dynamic analyses which take a city through a sequence of functions with sufficient analytical rigor to permit generalization are still to be done or lie hidden in fugitive materials. On the classification of U.S. cities according to economic function see Chauncy D. Harris, "A Functional Classification of Cities in the United States," *Geographical Review* (January 1943), pp. 86–99, and Howard J. Nelson, "A Service Classification of American Cities,"

Economic Geography (July 1955), pp. 189–210, both reprinted in Harold Mayer and Clyde F. Kohn (editor), *Readings in Urban Geography* (Chicago: University of Chicago Press, 1959), Gunnar Alexandersson, *The Industrial Structure of American Cities* (Stockholm: Almquist and Wiksell, 1956), and Otis Dudley Duncan, W. Richard Scott, Stanley Lieberson, Beverly Duncan, and Hal H. Winsborough, *Metropolis and Region* (Baltimore: The Johns Hopkins Press for Resources for the Future, 1960).

4 Perloff and associates found a low *negative* correlation between the location of growth industries and the local growth rate. Harvey S. Perloff, Edgar S. Dunn, Eric E. Lampard, and Richard F. Muth, *Regions, Resources, and Economic Growth* (Baltimore: The Johns Hopkins Press for Resources for the Future, 1960), p. 68. Perhaps this is due to the tendency of invention, innovation, and promotion to come more than proportionately out of the industrially mature regions, a point they themselves make later in their work. This more than proportionate incubation of new industries in the older industrial areas may originate in their greater technological sophistication, and then again it may originate in purposeful desperation as local entrepreneurs rise to the challenge of heavy local unemployment and business losses.

5 Culminating in *The New England Economy*, a Report to the President by the Committee on New England Economy of the Council of Economic Advisers (Washington: U.S. Government Printing Office, 1951).

6 The Economic Study of the Pittsburgh Region was jointly financed by the Commonwealth of Pennsylvania and The Ford Foundation as a successor to the New York Metropolitan Area Regional Study and was sponsored by The Pittsburgh Regional Planning Association and directed by Edgar M. Hoover. The last of the four volumes was published by the University of Pittsburgh Press in late 1964; this study will probably be judged the best piece of empirical work on urban economics to date.

7 *Michigan Tax Study, Staff Papers*, Legislative Committee, House of Representatives, Lansing, Michigan, 1958. This is one of the two best analyses of state and local finance extant, including academic efforts, the other is the earlier *Report of the Governor's Minnesota Tax Study, 1956*. The latter, which goes beyond the usual coverage of such studies to include an excellent analysis of regional economic growth factors was also initiated in response to a local "crisis" of slower-than-average economic growth.

8 For example, William Haber, Eugene C. McKean and Harold C. Taylor, *The Michigan Economy: Its Potentials and Its Problems* (Kalamazoo, Mich.: The W. E. Upjohn Institute for Employment Research, 1959) and Paul W. McCracken (editor), *Taxes and Economic Growth in Michigan* (Kalamazoo: Upjohn, 1960).

9 See *Distressed Areas in a Growing Economy*, A Statement of National Policy by the Research and Policy Committee of the Committee for Economic Development (New York, June 1961), and current unpublished memoranda on area redevelopment circulated by the Manpower and Social Affairs Committee of the Organisation for Economic Cooperation and Development (Paris). The former is directed to U.S. depressed area problems and the latter to the European counterparts.

10 Of the 212 Census-defined standard metropolitan areas, only seven experienced population losses between 1950 and 1960: Texarkana (92,000 population), Altoona (137,000), Wheeling (190,000), Scranton (235,000), Johnstown (280,000), Wilkes-Barre-Hazleton (347,000) and Jersey City (611,000). If Jersey City, N.J., is regarded as one of the central cities of the consolidated New York-Northeastern New Jersey metropolitan area, and it is alternatively classified that way by the Census, then we find no absolute declines in the one-half-million-and-over class and only two cases in the one

quarter to one-half million population class. U.S. Bureau of the Census, *Statistical Abstract of the United States: 1961*, Washington, 1961, Table 10.

11 See the chapter on "monopolistic competition" in any standard Principles of Economics textbook. This idea dates back to the brilliant article by Piero Sraffa, "The Laws of Returns under Competitive Conditions," *The Economic Journal*, Vol. 36 (1926), reprinted in George J. Stigler and Kenneth E. Boulding (editors), *Readings in Price Theory* (Chicago: Richard D. Irwin, 1952), especially pp. 189 ff.

12 *Government Manpower for Tomorrow's Cities,* A Report of the Municipal Manpower Commission (New York: McGraw-Hill Book Co., Inc., 1962), pp. 44–46.

13 *Ibid.*, pp. 30–32.

Development Planning as the Only Game in Town

Lisa Peattie
Massachusetts Institute of Technology

Stephen Cornell
Harvard University

Martin Rein
Massachusetts Institute of Technology

The authors of this article contend that planning for business, or "development planning," is a primary concern of city government. By examining selected development projects in a small city in the Boston metropolitan area, Peattie, Cornell, and Rein show how the interests of different constituencies converge to support development planning. A focus on development planning may have the opportunity cost of "crowding-out" other vital social and political agendas. The authors discuss the risks to the community and express concern about the role of planners in the process.

INTRODUCTION

This paper sets out to explain something which may appear so self-evident as to hardly require explanation. Why is development planning so central in the agenda of American city government? Or, to put it another way, why do alternative agendas for planning fail to thrive in the way development planning does?

Development planning is planning for business. It tries to produce a city environment in which private, profit-making enterprises can successfully function, and to induce such enterprises to locate in the community. However, in a case study of a small northeastern city, we found the development process is a problematic one. Development is difficult to do, for it involves the collaboration of Federal and State governments, City Hall, the local business elite, outside investors, aldermen, and ordinary residents. Specific projects are locally disruptive, while the whole development enterprise threatens the stability of this predominantly working-class community.

Furthermore, there are people in the city who would like to see other sorts of planning going on. While development planning served business interests—and often other interests as well—there are alternative agendas. Among the mass of voters, for example, human services appear to be of more concern than development. Politicians clearly understand this, yet development remains the centerpiece of city planning. Why? Most strikingly, we found that three sharply different mayoral administrations, committed to quite different philosophies, have treated services, not development, as the basis for popularity with the voters, the way to win elections. Yet, each of these very different mayors, once in office, made development planning the central activity of city government.

How are we to explain this? Is it pressure from outside investors—i.e., the imposed interests of capital—which accounts for the salience of development planning? Is it, perhaps, professional planners themselves, simply doing what they have been trained to do, and trying to enhance their professional prestige? Is it the fact that the city needs funds, and the available funds—those from state and federal governments—are development-specific? Or is it, after all, simply in the best interests of the voters, who see that development is a precondition for services and grudgingly respond to that view?

The relevant literature is not particularly helpful. On the one hand, there are Marxist-oriented scholars interested in developing a theory of the State, of which planning is certainly a part; there is also a Marxist literature on the structure of cities. But with a few notable exceptions, such as Cockburn's (1977) study of local government in the London borough of Lambeth and Fainstein et al.'s (1983) recent collection on urban development, the literature on the state tends to be focused on the national as opposed to the local level, while the literature on city structure has paid only sketchy attention to the actual institutional machinery of urban planning and management.

We looked also for guidance within sociology, in community power studies and accounts of community-based social movements, particularly as these confronted local governments (for example, Susser 1982; Katznelson 1981). But such studies have not examined the activities of planners or the constraints and opportunities of planning.

Finally, there is a substantial literature which takes the planner's perspective, focusing on the "how to" issues of professional practice and, in particular, on issues of implementation. Here we found useful the growing literature on public-private partnership and have followed with particular interest the still unpublished study by Frieden and Sagalyn on the development of central city malls. But most such studies are asking, "How should planning and development be done? What is the state-of-the-art professional practice, and how did it evolve?" Even those studies which engage the issue of who benefits—and not many do (Hollister and Lee 1979)—have a prescriptive orientation which separates them from our study.

We are not asking "how to" questions here, and the professional will not find advice on how to plan. The object instead is to explain the dominance of particular policy agenda—development—by showing how particular government and private interests get worked out through specific actors and institutions. Our argument is that the centrality of development planning is not adequately explained as the result of scheming special interests or funding availability or professional imperatives. All these explanations are correct, but each is insufficient. One could say that the entire "system" generates development planning, that is, the urban system is constituted by linkages between diverse interests which are so joined as to consistently produce development planning. But we will try to avoid abstractions such as "politics," "markets," "the system," and "the institution." Our task is to find the concrete form in which these abstractions are embodied, and to show how, for nearly everyone, development becomes the obvious thing to do.

This paper, then, is about how something which is not particularly popular comes to be perceived as not only appropriate, but the only game in town. In what follows, we will describe how the system operates as we came to understand it. One might begin at various points. We began at City Hall with the planners themselves and the mayor, and our investigation radiated outward from there.

The project was organized as a research course offered jointly at MIT and Harvard. Faculty and—much more commonly—students enrolled in the course spent hours roaming the offices, commercial districts, and neighborhoods of the city we were studying. The bulk of our information and most of our ideas emerged from extended interviews with city officials, community organizers, business people, and neighborhood residents. We supplemented interview and observational material with an examination of city budget figures and data on housing, demographics, and economic development.

THE CITY AND DEVELOPMENT PLANNING

The city itself is old, working class, residential. While administratively distinct, it is physically contiguous with and economically part of greater Boston. Craftsmen and operatives were long the largest occupational group, but have been passed in the 1980 census by the technical, sales, and administrative support category. It is in some ways a working class bedroom community; large numbers of residents, now and in the past, work outside the city.

The housing stock is dominated by wooden three-deckers, set close together on small lots close to the road, with few gardens. There is a university whose land holdings constitute the largest open space around; the one district of substantial dwellings is nearby. The university land is tax exempt, and the university pays no service fee to the city. The Irish, the Italians, and the Portuguese are the largest ethnic groups; there are a few blacks and Hispanics and a tiny Asiatic and Haitian minority group. In the 1940s the city was one of the most densely populated in the United States, but since 1945 the population has been declining, especially in the 35–60 age group. The 94,000 inhabitants of the 1960 census had dropped to 88,000 in 1970, and to 77,000 by 1980.

Median income hovers just over the national average, but has been falling relative to the surrounding metropolis. In 1950, it was just above the median of the Boston metropolitan area; by 1980 it had fallen to 77% of that of the SMSA as a whole. The city has few high-income families.

The big economic blow to this working-class community came in 1958 when the Ford assembly plant closed, taking 1,800 jobs with it. A grocery chain located on the vacant plant site. It lasted nearly 20 years but in 1977 also left, costing the city nearly 1,000 jobs and close to $1 million a year in property taxes.

The substrate of city politics is a set of interlinked family groups with connections into state government, but the present mayorality is the third consecutive one in which the chief executive had no strong family-political connections in town. The three mayoralities of the last 15 years have differed sharply in style, moving from progressive reform to conservative reaction to established "clean government." In the late 1960s, after many decades of in-group politics, the city got a dramatically novel reform administration. The new mayor was a minister with a background in civil rights and educational organizing; his platform emphasized political reform and human services. He brought in a small group of like-minded persons who tended to be young, zealous, and relatively inexperienced in government, and who arrived with a feeling of revolutionary triumph. According to one of them, they were "trying to learn how to run a government,"—the city auditor refused them money for postage stamps—but there was a great deal of energy. "The planning organization looked stuck together with chewing gum, but nothing had been done for so long it looked good." The federal tap was flowing. "I was good at getting funds," one planner said, "not because *I* was so good at it but because there were a lot of people who wanted to help us." The new government made it easier for people to find the services they needed, brought in new federally-funded service programs, and brought an existing youth program into City Hall for better control. The City Hall basement became a service center. The reform planners also tried to get federal money to develop open spaces for recreation. The public library was magnificently rehabilitated. Less successfully, they pursued economic development, trying, for example, to get control of some unused railroad yards for development purposes. There was much discussion of what to do with the land vacated by Ford when it gave up assembling Edsels there.

This administration was followed by a much more conservative one. It claimed to have come to "save the city," and described itself as staffed by businessmen as compared to the prior administration which was staffed by school teachers and a priest." It saw itself as redressing the excesses of the reformers—all this has gone too far, running a tight ship, being fiscally cautious. It felt there had been entirely too much emphasis in City Hall on social services. The new mayor pretty much dismantled human services and hired a new federal funds coordinator, saying, "we're going to bring in as much federal dollars as we can." At the same time, Washington's annual Community Development Block Grant (CDBG) program transferring federal funds to localities changed its formula, and the city found itself with a 10-fold increase in CDBG funds.

This administration's major development project was a mall on the land vacated by the old Edsel plant. The initiative came from a private developer who approached the city with a proposal. The planners got the federal funding: a $3.9 million Urban Development Action Grant (UDAG). "The big problem was that there was no access to the site. It was both too much for the developer and too much for the city to make (the development) fly without the UDAG." The planners also helped make the local connections; for example, they found a local restaurant owner who would open a prestigious restaurant in the mall.

But to the great astonishment of the federal funds coordinator, when election time came around, the mayor did not run on his record as a developer, but on the human services theme he originally had disdained: "He cares." As his urban planner told us, "The only thing on development was a leaflet I wrote. We brought in 18 million dollars in a year and a half, a great achievement which was completely ignored in the campaign. I absolutely can't understand why." The conservatives lasted only two years; the third administration chose a middle road between the first two, entering in the spirit of good government and mild reform.

"This mayor understands that it is important not only to do right, but also to stay in power," said his planning director. This planning director, a graduate of the Harvard School of Design, first appeared on our stage as a long-haired negotiator for the reform administration vis-a-vis state transportation planners. Now, with hair cut, energetic and close to the mayor, he presided over the completion of the mall. He and his staff are quite proprietary about this project. They re-wrote the specs for the development contract to "cut out the fat," and modernized the design. The planners see these changes as "important for the reputation and image of the city. Also, developers will know they won't be ripped off; it will be open. Previous development was all by insiders." Despite the emphasis on development planning, this mayor, like his predecessors, feels that what will re-elect him is integrity and personal caring. "The elderly will vote for me because they know I'm a champion of the elderly. The people around the social agencies will vote for me because they know I'm for human services. Ordinary residents will vote for me because they know I'm honest and get things done." In his 1983 State of the City address, he cited development projects but ended by boasting: "People in crisis call me at home at all hours of the night . . . No one is denied my ear." His chief planner told us that in election years they use the CDBG money to fix potholes; in off-years they can put it into development.

While all three mayors, then, have thought of services and personal responsiveness as the way to win elections—and the voters have seemed to agree—development planning has been a central focus in all three administrations.

Of course, the overall rationale usually given for development planning is jobs and the tax base. The city is losing jobs, and until the last couple of years, taxes were rising. A few years ago the property tax rate was the third highest in the state of Massachusetts. A recent state law, however, requires all municipalities, including this one, to lower the property tax rate to 2 and 1/2 percent of assessed value.

THE PLANNING PROCESS

Another route to understanding the logic of development planning is via the process itself. At the center is the development package. A typical package has four components: land, political support, public (federal and state) funds, and private investment. The city planner's job is entrepreneurial: to bring these components together around a particular physical outcome, a program for building. The task involves locating physical opportunities for development, obtaining state or federal funds for site improvement or other aspects of the project, finding private investors and, as part of any or all of these, drumming up political support. This last may involve aldermen, state representatives, and citizens and business groups. The mayor himself is often a critical actor in assembling the package. "I let the experts take care of getting the money," he says, adding proudly, "but when it needs a push, I make the phone calls." The Board of Aldermen must approve all sales of city land and all permits for development projects. Aldermanic attitudes towards development vary. There is the alderman who describes himself as very active in helping neighborhoods resist unwanted development; there is another who, when interviewed, asked rhetorically, "Is an eyesore (in this case, an abandoned lot) better than a high rise?" The general practice, however, is for aldermen to vote according to the wishes of the alderman in whose ward a problem or development project is taking place. While this maximizes the aldermanic system's responsiveness to local interests, it tends to prevent the Board from developing general policy on development issues, and leaves the initiative in development with City Hall.

The various forms which the developing planning process can take may be illustrated by three of the major recent development programs in the city: school re-use, redevelopment of commercial centers, and the new mall.

The school re-use process began with a problem which, oddly, was itself an outcome of previous development efforts. The reform administration, unable to gain much control over educational processes dominated by a largely hostile school committee, chose instead to build new neighborhood schools. Subsequently, as declining enrollments confronted a cut in state funds to the city, the mayor decided to close schools, seven in all.

A school closing is unpopular in any neighborhood. In this case, however, the planning process was able, in effect, to transform growing local concern into political support which, at the same time, would protect the planners' sphere of action. Public meetings were held in each neighborhood where the need for school closings was explained and community participation in planning the re-use or replacement of the buildings was invited. Neighborhood committees served to keep the process open to outside developers and prevent a takeover by local political insiders. (The planners see this as leading to better design.) The planners made available outside the city "developers' kits" describing each site.

Most of the school lands were converted to residential use—apartments and condominiums. One school was leased to the University. One became a boys' club.

Only this last was politically contentious. The school was on the border between two wards: on one side there was substantial neighborhood opposition based on fears of rowdy youth, perhaps including blacks; on the other, the alderman and much of the neighborhood supported the club. The planners and the mayor also favored the club, and the alderman who favored it was faithful at meetings, but in the end it was no contest. A local developer with a competing condominium proposal made a low bid at the outset, eventually decided the project was unprofitable, and withdrew.

A law student who works with one of the reform organizations in the city found it disappointing that a majority of the schools ended up as condominiums. Weren't there alternatives to selling to developers? What about cooperatively-owned options or low-to-moderate income housing, or something to add to community resources, like the Boys' Club? But it appears that there was little support from the citizenry for such a position. The Boys' Club was not popular. At the school re-use hearings, local residents insisted on the importance of increasing the tax base. The planners, however, saw the school developments as constituting an indirect way of adding to the community's resources, by improving the city's image for potential investors. "Investors are keeping an eye out to see what will happen with the schools." A second kind of development packaging occurred with the "squares"— as people of the city call commercial nodes. These, in contrast to the schools, seem to revolve around the flow of federal funds. They involve the planners who, with the help of the mayor and his contacts at the state level, organize a flow of funds which can physically upgrade the squares to make them more appropriate settings for new business.

One of the "squares" projects is the outgrowth of political pressure mounted in the 1960s to extend the metro area subway through the city with a station at this particular point. Both the planner for the reform mayor and the current head of the city's Office of Planning and Community Development were active in organizing the pressure which put the subway stop in the new transportation plan. At the time, there was some criticism of this effort by radicals who expected it to result in rising real estate prices and the displacement of working-class residents and local businesses. Nor was business conspicuous in its support: the Civic Association voted against the subway. Local business people kept their distance also from the attempts which followed to upgrade the square through federally-funded city planning and design.

Here the political base of the planning process seems to have been a combination of contacts reaching up from the mayor and some aldermen to the state and federal governments, along with an active Citizen's Task Force. This latter group legitimized the project by incorporating such citizen concerns as siting of construction so as to reduce the taking of private homes and compensation to property owners for attendant blasting damage. Thanks to this coalition, plans now call for a new food store to encourage a retail mix catering to community needs; an office/parking complex to draw new workers/customers to the area; major store-front renovations and landscaping; and a new elderly housing project. The funding comes largely from a federal UDAG.

While some local enterprises may benefit from all of this—at the very least, the construction firm, part of the empire of a politically potent local developer—in general the program is more geared to bringing in new business than stabilizing old ones. Now that the subway stop has opened, it looks very much as if the early predictions of subsequent gentrification and displacement will be confirmed. The planners' success in converting the local movie theater into an art theater with a grant from the National Endowment for the Arts seems symbolic of a successful development project attracting into the area a younger, more professional and more affluent population. Rents are beginning to rise; the old neighborhood will be to some degree transformed; some current residents and businesses will be replaced. Meanwhile, it will be easier for residents to get downtown; the city's tax base will increase, as will overall use of the area; and an aging city square will have been turned into a showcase.

The other square project centers simply on improving an existing physical setting. Police and fire stations now in this square are to be relocated to a vacant mass transit lot. The vacated fire station is to house studios for a cable television company. Traffic will be re-routed; there will be some store-front renovation; and one of the streets will be closed to create a pedestrian mall.

This project has a political structure very different from the other. The mayor is deeply involved in this project at the level of design. Since the square is also turf of several persons who are powers in traditional city politics, the planners here are serving a small group of powerful decision makers. Local businessmen originally doubted anything would come of the project, but City Hall put a good deal of effort into winning their support. When the mayor went to Washington to meet with the Secretary of Transportation and the Speaker of the House about federal funds, he took the head of the square's businessmen's association along. "Even if nothing happened," says the mayor, "they knew we were trying." Now that the project is under way, not all the business people like it. "I don't know why they want to put this (pedestrian) mall in anyway," said one, "All the businesses in the block are basically convenience-type stores and rely heavily on walk-in business, and by putting a mall in front of us, it's just going to discourage people from going through the hassle of getting here." The residents of the area, meanwhile, are correspondingly less involved.

The largest development project in the city has been the suburban-style shopping mall. It was also the least constrained politically. Its execution spanned two mayoralities. The aldermen and City Council supported the UDAG submission from the start as "there was an agreement that this was good for the city." There was "no organized opposition," in part because the site is physically isolated from the neighborhoods. There was a requirement set for local hiring.

Thus the mall is a project within which the planners see themselves as free to use their professional skills and competence, to perform according to their own criteria, not those imposed by political exigency. They are proud to display to a professional visitor the way they made use of the old industrial architecture and incorporated associations with the old Edsel plant into the mall's logo. Today the mall, which still has some vacancies, consists of two major department stores and a host of smaller shops, restaurants, and services. Adjacent to it are a multi-screen movie theater and an office complex. The theater is doing well and is presently expanding, while some of the offices remain empty and others are being rented at under market value. The floor space in the mall, because of higher prices, also went fairly slowly but is filling up. The president of the development corporation and the mall manager are optimistic. Plans to open a hotel complex there are presently on hold; and in the meantime, the city planners have turned their interests elsewhere.

In 1980, when the mayor issued a progress statement on the mall, he called the developer "the largest employer and taxpayer in (the city) even though they're still in the demolition state. (The city) has continued to have high unemployment, and we certainly need the jobs this project will create." Not only would the project create jobs, he went on, but "much-needed revenue." The facts can be interpreted variously. The city's application to a UDAG projected more than 2,000 mall jobs. As of 1983, the mall employed between 750 and 800 people, less than half local residents. This was less than half the Ford plant's labor force, but as many as the grocery chain. A related new office building, despite renting-up problems, houses another 700 jobs, a quarter of them filled by local residents. The mall pays more taxes than the essentially vacant land it replaced, but is clearly undervalued, and in 1984 represented 1.2 percent of the city's tax base, less than either the Ford plant or the grocery chain in previous years.

In sum, the mall has certainly made a contribution to both jobs and tax base without constituting a major solution to either problem. Even so, it is not altogether popular. Local retailers elsewhere in the city worry about the competition. One alderman considers the mall "just a tax shelter for the developers." One community activist told an interviewer:

I think the new development strategies have a bad effect on the people (of the city). As I explain it, we're being malled to death. They're doing all this work on the new mall when another mall . . . just 10 minutes down the road (in another city) is also growing. A mall is *not* the best use of land . . . Everyone is land poor these days. (The city) had some real valuable property. It could have been used to help out residents . . . The (prior) administration gave the developers a 121A tax agreement. These are big tax breaks they offer as an incentive for them to develop. It was an act of sheer desperation by the major to get people interested in (the city). This was valuable property but they threw it away. And now they've got all those empty stores so they can keep the 121A status for tax breaks . . . The management and good jobs are held by people from outside of the city. They don't provide any good job opportunities for (the city's) people . . . (The city) needs light industry which pays better and employs better . . . Development is a problem.

HUMAN SERVICES PLANNING

What alternative agendas might city government have? Human services is one, and in fact it has an institutional base: the Mayor's Office of Human Services, located in the basement of City Hall. This office links the mayor, via his Human Services Director, with federally- and state-funded social service agencies on the one hand and citizens seeking help on the other. Its major piece of equipment is a telephone.

The office was first established by the 1960s reform mayor, but "the whole thing was dismantled" by the conservative administration which followed. The third and current mayor came into office on a platform including the restoration of City Hall's commitment to people—"a recreation of human services." The restoration doubtless has a political payoff. Now when residents—especially the elderly—need a service, they can call *City* Hall and get connected to the *Mayor's* Office of Human Services. As human services clients are told, "whenever you have a problem, you know who to call." The office then refers citizens to appropriate resources in the outside service network, much of it pocketbook oriented: fuel assistance, health care, meals programs. Thus it maintains connections to outside agencies, but from a distance. It is a cheap way of identifying the mayor with caring for people.

Recently, however, this political payoff has been undermined by declining funds. The office is down to a skeleton referral service with direct project administration "only when required." When the director recently left for another job, he was not replaced; and current staff are uncertain about the future of the office.

When we first began to explore City Hall, the human services staff told us "we're planners, too." We soon came to speak of two kinds of planners: the Third Floor Planners and the Basement Planners. The contrast between the two is striking. On the third floor in the Office of Planning and Community Development is the large group of professionals concerned with the physical reorganization of the city: development planning. Some 30 people work here. All salaries are paid with monies brought in by the office itself through grants and reimbursements, and these support not only planners but certain amenities as well—hanging plants and decorative shades. There is none of this in the tiny basement office of Human Services. Moreover, while Human Services, and its contact with individual voters, is an office with some political impact, the Third Floor Planners, dependent on civil service but working directly with the mayor, are politically critical. In addition to their work on development projects, these planners have been active in the mayor's electoral campaigns. The head of the office, in fact, was the mayor's campaign manager; other staffers contributed money and time. Federal funding, then, also contributes to the dominance of the development agenda.

LAND USE AND HOUSING: A CONTENTIOUS TERRAIN

Development planning not only represents a choice among competing agendas, it has the inherent potential for deep social conflict beyond the issues raised by particular projects. The city is densely settled and close to Boston where real estate prices are soaring. As one informant pointed out, with the decline of industry, real estate has become the biggest business in town. It is also an important area for conflict.

Data on what is happening in the city's housing market lends itself to different interpretations. One is that rents are rising in the private sector; that, owing to changing federal policies, there will be no further increase in subsidized housing and that, as a consequence, gentrification and displacement will become increasingly serious problems for the working class families who dominate the city's population. An opposed interpretation is that those who perceive the threat of gentrification and displacement are barking at shadows. It may well be true gentrification is occurring, but so many families have already left the city, in response to shifts in job markets and other factors, that the new residents pose no threat to remaining inhabitants.

Regardless of which interpretation better conforms to the facts, the concern with gentrification is widespread. Says one resident, "The neighborhoods around the squares will disintegrate through gentrification . . . The sense of neighborhood is gone, 'attractiveness' has driven the people out." Another citizen speaks bitterly of "these landlords who buy up the place and develop it and put the poor people on the street . . . I can take you around and show you where half the block has been bought up and 'developed'—the nicest of the old brick houses where blacks used to live." There is also concern with the capacity of students, banding together in group living arrangements, to bid up rents beyond what the city's working-class tenantry can afford. Indeed, land use and housing have become major political issues.

ISSUE POLITICS

Comments like the attack on the mall by the activist who felt that "development is a problem" represent more than criticisms of specific development projects. They represent a sharply different way of looking at planning: not in terms of programs or institutional arenas, but in terms of issue-based politics. Such politics begin with interests and organization; that is, with the development of collective consciousness around group interests and with organizing to pursue those interests. Because the collective sense and the organizational participation which embodies it are most easily developed through confrontation with the established institutions, issue politics tends to be confrontational.

There are a number of groups in the city working in this mode. One is a Tenants' Union which emerged as an organization in 1969 when university students and local leaders organized the "working class brawl" over a freeway extension which threatened a number of working-class houses. Soon afterwards the rent and eviction control issues appeared, and the Tenants' Union transferred its major effort to this. Another conspicuous organization is a United Neighborhood Committee which was started in 1974–75 by a group of clergy and neighborhood leaders to try to force City Hall to be more responsive to neighborhood needs. In addition, organizers of a state-wide consumer advocacy group are now working in the city. Issue politics is prominent in the media world. Here, a middle-of-the-road commercial newspaper is straddled by another paper seen by many as representing real estate interests, and a socialist paper, run on a collective basis, which prints and distributes 10,000 mostly free copies a month.

Issue politics is in deliberate contrast to the prevailing local style. As a publisher of the community newspaper on the conservative end of the media spectrum put it, with distaste: "They practice confrontation politics instead of working quietly behind the scenes to get things done." Nevertheless, the organizers of issue politics are inter-linked with the regular institutional world of service-providing social agencies. The United Neighborhood committee was first funded by the Catholic Church, and then, in 1978, got five organizers funded by VISTA. The planner of the state-funded community action agency is on the United Neighborhood board. The Tenants' Union is funded by the state, through the community action agency; that agency's housing advocate has worked with the Tenants' Union since 1978. The one paid staff person of the socialist newspaper had previously worked for the city's youth agency for nine years. Such links illustrate how certain groups which intend to confront the establishment on issues such as rent control are also dependent to some degree on the flow of federal and state funds and are inherently in competition with each other for resources.

The main substantive interest around which issue politics has mobilized has been the obverse of City Hall's focus on development: tenant interest in affordable housing. The programmatic issue which has focused this has been rent control. When the United Neighborhood group began their door-to-door canvassing, people's concerns centered on city responsibilities: stop signs and street repairs, crime prevention. More recently, the group has worked on tax reform and the redirection of funding to the neighborhoods. But the organization's spokesman feels—as does the Tenants' Union—that the most important issue in the last few years has been the housing problem and the fight for rent control.

The struggles for rent control at the local level had depended on state action— in turn shaped by national politics. In 1970, the state passed an enabling act permitting certain cities and towns to control rents and evictions. There had been a good deal of active advocacy for such a bill at the local level; and only four days after the state act was approved, the city's major local newspaper ran the headline: "Aldermen to Vote on Rent Control Tonight—Passage is Expected." Actually, local real estate brokers, the Property Owners' Association, and the Chamber of Commerce mustered substantial opposition; and it was only three months later, on a surprise vote with two opponents absent, that the local rent control bill passed the Board of Aldermen. Over time the bill's provisions were weakened. In 1978, under the leadership of a conservative mayorality, rent control in the city was abolished altogether. The reformers did not give up, however, and by March of 1982, "political pressure" about rents had persuaded two aldermen to draw up a new rent control ordinance.

Sentiments pro and con ran high. A new hearing on the issue was crowded, with Tenants' Union members pleading that they needed "affordable" houses to live in and members of the Property Owners' Association maintaining their right to make "reasonable" profits from their property. The emotional climax of the evening was reached with a speech by an alderman representing the property owners' views. It was related that, "He started by talking about his mother, who owned a small house, part of which she rented out, and was dying of cancer. Any law that would deprive her of a living is un-American. (Note, however, that the law did not apply to buildings with fewer than three living units.) He started singing 'God Bless America' at the top of his lungs. All the anti-rent control people joined him. Of course, then the pro-rent control group joined as well, each group trying to sing louder than the other." Rent control lost. "There was a feeling that if the vote were close, or if we were going to win, these people would have beaten up the rent control supporters." The organizers of issue politics are currently in some disarray. There have been attempts to organize around restricting condominium conversion, but the defeat of rent control has been demoralizing; and finding an equally clear target has been difficult. Meanwhile, funding via the state community action agency appears to be dwindling.

The organizers of issue politics differ sharply from the mainstream planners and politicians in seeing specific programmatic objectives as means rather than ends. The goal of the Tenants' Union, according to its organizer, is "to build some sort of working-class-based political movement." The rent control effort was an attempt at movement-building; the focus on evictions and rents is "an organizing tool." It makes it easier to go into buildings, organize, and get people to form building unions, "which is our goal as opposed to rent control." Around what other issues might organization take place? Even more basic than the issue of rents and real estate is the issue of jobs. The metropolitan area of which the city is a part has been changing its economic structure. The departure of the Ford plant was not a unique event; the local economy, like that of the Northeast in general, has been shifting out of manufacturing into services. The voters would like to see the industrial jobs replaced, and city officials responded by including a proposal for an industrial park in the 1978 mall UDAG. Unfortunately, the proposal attracted no firm commitments from industry and was not funded by HUD. Subsequently, there have been efforts by City Hall to attract industrial investment, so far unsuccessful. In any event, it seems clear to everyone that, on the issue of jobs, the city has to adjust to very much bigger trends.

Furthermore, since much of the city's labor force has long worked elsewhere, the jobs issue does not seem to the citizenry to be a local one. Instead, the forces affecting the local economic base tend to be viewed in regional or national terms. For example, how many jobs the mall produces and whether these are "good jobs" or "bad jobs" do get some attention, but do not seem to be central issues in the politics of development. One simply is unlikely to blame City Hall for being unemployed.

But while jobs are not viewed as city business, services are. So far, however, the only service issue which seems to have mobilized a substantial constituency has been education. Indeed, the schools were a central part of the issue politics which brought in the reformers to clean up City Hall. But once the reformers were in power, issue politics ceased to be movement-building and became, again, "getting things done." As the reform mayor's planner said, "The terms were dictated by the political reality of delivering to the citizenry." Like the planners of the present, the reformers were "dependent on federal funds—jerked around by what there was money for." In theory, economic recession might dictate a surge of interest in the basic issues of jobs and income. But in practice, the effect has been the reverse. Federal funds get less; private investment dries up; and development planning looks more important than ever, simply as a way to keep the city going.

DISCUSSION

The mall is a development package in which there was very little need to build political support; support was given by the general belief that new investment is needed for jobs and the tax base. On the other hand, where residences are cleared or construction bothers the neighborhood, or where local businesses are affected, some political work is required to build support and tailor details to take account of criticism. But this usually involves marginal criticism and marginal modification. It is possible to question development—an example is the activist, already quoted, who says, "Development is a problem"—but such a position is heretical vis-a-vis the prevailing orthodoxy.

Nevertheless, we have seen that even in projects where there is a substantial local political base, the impetus for development does not come out of the neighborhoods. It comes, rather, from City Hall and private investors. The Third Floor Planners, working directly for the city administration, see the need for an expanded tax base and new jobs. But they do not merely share a belief in the general benefits of development. It also supports their salaries and comprises the modernization which is the focus of their professional culture. In the world of planners, the logic of the tax base, the interests of investors, the needs of local government for contract patronage and federal funds, and the professional pride in design of the built environment all support and feed on each other.

The planner's role in development is essentially entrepreneurial, capturing resources from the federal (or in some cases the state) government and making them available to private investors. The logic of the projects, however, usually depends on the initiative of those investors. The larger the project, the more dependent are the planners on the private sector, not only for risk capital, but even for planning and design functions. At the center of it all is the concept of the project itself. Here the role of the planner is, in part, to interpret the private project as serving a public use, thus justifying the flow of federal resources for infrastructural development which is an essential prerequisite for any private venture, and underwriting ideologically the particular negotiations producing the requisite political support.

City Hall is involved in other ways as well. While the current mayor thinks largely in terms of symbols and aesthetics—he likes flagpoles, new signs marking the city limits, landscaping—development projects also play an indispensable role in bringing in the funds which give him budgetary leeway and a staff that is *his*, not the civil service's. It is not simply chance that the Third Floor Planners are important in the mayor's campaign.

The crucial resources here are money and land. One is in the hands of private business, one in the hands of the city. Both are essential for development; consequently city and business need each other.

Land is the major resource which the city controls. The Mayor and the Basement Planners deal with services. But funds are diminishing, and the ability of the city to control services is weak. As for jobs, except for a limited amount of contracting—much of which, in turn, depends on physical development projects—the city can do little. Land is the only productive factor that the city can really manipulate; it is the primary thing that the city can bargain with. Control of land use, therefore, whether through zoning or building regulations or ownership of particular sites, becomes the city's central resource, its primary means of attracting investment.

Business, on the other hand, provides the capital which can be used to transform the environment, create jobs, and expand the tax base. Only in certain exceptional instances can city government realize income from land directly. The school sites which are being "packaged" for redevelopment are important as such exceptional opportunities. In general, however, City Hall must draw from land indirectly, via real estate taxation. Thus here, too, government is dependent on private enterprise, the real estate investors—large and small—who maintain or, the city hopes, increase the value of land by building on it. There is no need for "businessmen's development committees" to "actively influence local politics" (Barnekov and Rich, ND). Business interests will dominate the planning agenda anyway. As Elkin (1982), paraphrasing Lindblom, says:

> Government is dependent on business because business enterprises are the custodians of a range of decisions crucial to the public . . . Businessmen appear to government officials not merely as representatives of special interests but as those performing functions that these officials need performed. Business will thus be granted a special place, one defined by the need to induce enterprises to perform their function (pp. 722–23).

Elkin goes on to point out, "Neither businessmen nor government officials wish to undermine the other because each is required for running the system." The recent state law requiring property tax rate reduction to 2 and 1/2 percent of assessed value has thrown the city's assessment and taxation system into disarray, at the very point when federal funds which could cushion tax shrinkage and support needed services are themselves in steep decline. Consequently, government becomes even more anxious to induce business to perform. Not only is government willing to invest growing amounts of energy in attracting outside investment, but it will even give up some of its own control over land and other resources in order to do so. Given all the forces which lead City Hall to focus on development planning, even in a world in which services are what voters want and rent control is the centerpiece of issue politics, we found ourselves thinking of the mayor's appeal to the city's need for a more adequate tax base as more than mere rationalization for development. The property tax arrangement is one part of a complex system which so functions that a variety of actors and interests converge to make development planning seem eminently reasonable and appropriate, and to make the organizers of issue politics appear impractical, even unreasonable.

Yet planning remains a potentially disputatious terrain. In the planners' view, economic development is a prerequisite for service provision. The tax base rationalizes the entry of outside capital into the community as a service to local people. But in the meantime this strategy—the only game in town, it would appear—must, if successful, transform the community into one dominated by outside investing bodies and attractive to outsiders as residents. Instead of reinforcing the working-class community which the services approach embodied, it tends to undermine it.

The kind of inquiry into agenda-setting presented here does not readily lend itself to recommendations for professional practice. Nevertheless, in planning, purpose and possibility are intertwined. While planning is made legitimate in terms of rational decision making, if it is to be planning for action, it cannot be divorced from the sociopolitical reality in which it is grounded. Community-based studies of the planning process, such as this one, may yet provide a bridge between the emerging literature on agenda setting in the policy process and the prescriptive literature on planning practice.

REFERENCES

Barnekov, T. K., and Rich, D. ND. Privatism and Urban Development: An Analysis of the Organized Influence of Local Business 431–460.

Cockburn, C. 1977. *The Local State: Management of Cities and People.* London: Pluto Press.

Elkin, S. L. 1982. Market and Politics in Liberal Democracy. *Ethics.* 92:720–732.

Fainstein, S.; Fainstein, N.; Hill, R.C.; Judd, D.; and Smith, M.P. 1983. *Restructuring the City: The Political Economy of Urban Redevelopment.* New York: Longman.

Hollister, R. and Lee, T. 1979. *Development Politics: Private Development and the Public Interest.* Washington, D.C.: Council of State Planning Agencies.

Katznelson, I. 1981. *City Trenches: Urban Politics and the Patterning of Class in the United States.* New York: Pantheon.

Susser, I. 1982. *Norman Street: Poverty and Politics in an Urban Neighborhood.* New York: Oxford University Press.

Converting the Military Industrial Economy: The Experience at Six Facilities

Catherine Hill
Ph.D candidate, Rutgers University

Sabina Deitrick
Professor of Public and International Affairs, University of Pittsburgh

Ann Markusen
Professor of Urban Planning, Rutgers University

This article focuses on the enormous challenge of converting military facilities to civilian uses. The authors examine four alternative models of conversion from military to civilian use and present six geographically dispersed and industrially diverse case studies of conversion efforts. Given the accelerated pace of defense cutbacks in the Clinton Administration, the findings in this article are of considerable importance to all those communities concerned with their long-term economic stability. Moreover, although its focus is on military conversion, the article has important implications for deindustrialization issues in general. This article received the Association of Collegiate Schools of Planning's 1992 Chester Rapkin Award for the Best Article in Volume 11 of the *Journal of Planning Education and Research.*

The fate of the military budget hangs in the balance and will continue to do so for years to come. The end of the cold war could mean the dismantling of a huge and very expensive arsenal of highly automated, high-tech weaponry which is regarded by many as having sapped the productive vigor of the economy and deflected resources from pressing social and infrastructural needs. In forty-odd years of equipping the nation for cold war many workers, plants, and communities have become dependent, even prosperous, on military contracts. In this paper we address the task of converting this special segment of the economy to other uses, differentiating demand side from supply side approaches. We distinguish four alternative models of conversion from military to civilian use, each organized around a different target: converting the company, converting the community economic base, converting the worker, and converting the facility.

After some discussion of each approach we scrutinize the last of these, which is in many ways the most difficult and yet the most attractive in terms of retaining jobs and stabilizing communities. No comparative research efforts have been done to evaluate the successes and failures of community-, worker-, or local government-initiated efforts at conversion. After stating both strict and broader criteria for judging "success," we present the results of six geographically-dispersed and

Reprinted by permission of the *Journal of Planning Education and Research* 11 (1991), copyright owned and published by the Association of Collegiate Schools of Planning.

industrially-diverse case studies of conversion efforts in the 1980s. While to date none has succeeded in the narrow sense of retaining jobs, these experiments have had an impact on public thinking about the formidable task of conversion. Partially as a result of these efforts, several states have passed legislation to assist conversion. In other cases, ongoing organizations continue to pursue economic development. As a group, the cases demonstrate the ability and willingness of defense workers to plan for civilian work. In some, local conversion planning has led to an alliance between labor and peace organizations which has strengthened the political clout and institutional capabilities of both.

Finally, we address the conditions which have facilitated or impeded success across the case studies. The conversion efforts share several common obstacles: the unsuitability of current business practices for competing in commercial markets, the opposition of key management people to joint planning, and disarray or antagonism among potential members of alternative use planning coalitions. We conclude that worker participation and unity enhance prospects for success, that success requires early warning and financial disclosure on the part of the company, that state or federal government intervention and funding will be necessary for the conversion of many facilities, and that employees and peace activists can overcome differences and work in coalition. We compare facility conversion to the more general case of plant closings and conclude that conversion, because it involves product and market shifts, will require technical assistance from outside parties, particularly in marketing, financial analysis, and social cost accounting. In conclusion, we recommend policies which link conversion planning with a national agenda to redirect military spending toward social and infrastructural needs, like housing, education, mass transit, and infrastructure repair.

THE CONTEXT: MILITARY BUILDDOWN

Political developments in the Soviet Union and Eastern Europe mean some parts of the military budget will be cut. Hostilities in the Middle East have not restored Congress's will to continue high levels of military spending. Currently close to $300 billion a year, military spending accounts for 44% of the nation's discretionary budget, the largest single component of federal spending. Although the administration's budget proposals call for cuts amounting to only 2% in real terms per year, the pressure for deeper cuts is mounting. The Defense Budget Project notes that the budget requests for FY 1991 through FY 1997 are $410 billion below the amount needed to keep pace with inflation; between FY 1991 and FY 1996 they estimate that there will be a 13% reduction in real terms (Cain 1991, 1–2). William Kaufman (1990), of the Brookings Institution, believes that military spending can be cut in half, to about $160 billion within five to ten years, although current debate in Congress does not envision reductions of that scale.

This prospect presents the nation with exciting though difficult choices. On the one hand, it could free up billions of dollars for dedication to other pressing problems. On the other, it could impose serious adjustment difficulties, as resources shift out of one set of industries and product lines and into others. The National

Commission on Economic Conversion and Disarmament (1991, 1) estimates that in 1990, military contract cutbacks led directly to the loss of 81,000 jobs and indirectly to another 73,000 jobs lost. If organizing for the peace dividend is revived after the U.S.-Iraq war, these numbers will be much greater. In 1988, 6,572,000 people worked for the military or for military contractors, and it is estimated that each $1 billion of defense spending generated about 50,000 jobs (Files and Melman 1989). With cuts looming, at least 1 million defense related jobs could vanish between 1989 and 1995, including 830,000 to 1,066,000 in the private sector (Adams 1990, 7). Since military spending is heavily concentrated in certain industries, occupations, regions, and cities, a reduction in military spending may precipitate considerable displacement and community distress unless a concerted effort takes place to help plan and smooth the transition.

The resource issue is not simply one of manpower, however. The stock of physical capital involved in military-dedicated plants, many of which are government-owned, is valued conservatively at more than $500 billion. A considerable share of new industrial investment in the 1980s took place in plants built or equipped for military projects. For example, net investment in plant equipment by all U.S. manufacturing concerns over the three-year period from 1980 to 1982 was $8.8 billion, while in 1982 alone, the Department of Defense invested $3.3 billion in the same (Melman 1983, 150; Dumas 1986, 219, 223; Choate and Walter 1981, 1). This suggests that the nation could suffer from significant capacity underutilization during a transitional period. Direct industrial capacity is supplemented by considerable public infrastructure, including housing, highways, and schools built in communities which are predominantly military-oriented. These, too, could be idled during a major builddown, despite demonstrable national need.

For these reasons, the task of economic conversion attracted considerable interest and debate by the late 1980s.[1] Conferences on conversion were held all over the country—in Orange County, California; in Boston, Massachusetts; in Columbus, Ohio; in Seattle, Washington; in Harrisburg, Pennsylvania. Technical assistance groups, like the Washington, D.C.-based National Commission on Economic Conversion and Disarmament and the California-based Center for Economic Conversion, who had been laboring on the issue for the last decade, found themselves overwhelmed with inquiries. In the summer of 1990, a major Congressional effort resulted in an appropriation of $200 million to help workers and communities adjust to military plant closings. At least two major constituencies, sometimes at odds, are involved in current conversion efforts: 1) the peace movement, with its fears that economic stakes in the military budget will block disarmament; and 2) workers and their unions, community groups, and politicians whose livelihoods are threatened by military cutbacks. The interplay between these groups is a central theme in recent conversion experience.

THE CONVERSION NEXUS: SUPPLY AND DEMAND WHEN GOVERNMENTS ARE THE MARKET

In many ways, the problem of defense plant or base conversion resembles that of any plant closing. Imminent closure threatens a loss of jobs and tax base to the community, while individual workers face an uncertain labor market, and the shock of a move, premature retirement, or sinking to a lower rung of the labor market. Yet conversion of defense facilities is a unique problem because the $300 billion "market" in which such economic units operate is distinctly different from that of sectors like steel, food processing, or insurance where sales are made on an open commercial market. While defense manufacturers can sell abroad, marketing to foreign governments remain tied to the foreign policy directives of politicians (Quigley 1989, 84).

The biggest difference lies on the demand side of this market. Instead of a host of individual consumers or a modest number of big business buyers, firms and plants in the military market sell to a government bureaucracy, the Pentagon, and, through its foreign military sales program, to foreign governments. Generally, weapons systems for the United States military account for the bulk of military contractors' orders, with foreign sales accounting for a significant portion of some military equipment such as fighter aircraft (Quigley 1989, 84). The way the American military decides to buy a particular weapons system (or aircraft part or uniform) is a complex process in which need is articulated by one or more military services (Army, Navy, Air Force), shaped into a budget request by the Department of Defense (DoD) and the President's Office of Management and Budget, and then reshaped by Congress in the appropriations process. To sell a product to this many-faceted customer requires a marketing system wholly unlike that familiar to companies operating in commercial markets, one requiring institutional knowledge of the customer and skill at lobbying Congress and military leaders. Furthermore, such sales are apt to be the culmination of a design, development, and planning process which can take as long as a decade, particularly for the higher technology portion of procurement. By the time money is appropriated for a program like the B-2 bomber, the relationship between buyer and supplier has been cemented through prior contracts for research and development and construction of prototypes.

On the supply side, the military economy consists of a set of very large corporations, many of them born and bred on cold war military budgets (Table 1). Twenty corporations received 47% of the $145 billion in procurement prime contracts in 1988; more than $1 billion was awarded to each contractor. Some, such as General Dynamics, Grumman, and Martin Marietta, sell more than two-thirds of their output to DoD and NASA. Others, for whom prime contracts form a minority of sales—Ford, GM (Hughes), and Unisys, for example—have separate divisions devoted to military markets. Grouped around these prime contractors are thousands of subcontractors, many of whom are also heavily defense-dependent.

In contrast to commercially-oriented production, these companies have relatively small runs or "batch" production systems, eschewing the economies of scale of mass production. They employ large numbers of specialized scientists and engineers and highly skilled blue collar workers, compared to the preponderance of semiskilled assemblers found in commercial operations. Business planning is preoccupied with design and performance requirements rather than with keeping costs down (Markusen and Yudken in press, chs. 3–4).

The fact that a great deal of military equipment is produced by very large corporations often means that segments of management and labor within the industry

TABLE 1 TOP DOD/NASA CONTRACTORS, 1985–1988.

Rank*	Company	Headquarters	Contract awards (DOD+NASA, million $)				Sales (million $)				Ratio (contract awards/sales)			
			1985	1986	1987	1988	1985	1986	1987	1988	1985	1986	1987	1988
1	McDonnel-Douglas Corp.	St. Louis, MO	9,051	6,852	8,000	8,302	11,478	12,661	13,146	15,072	0.79	0.54	0.61	0.55
2	General Dynamics Corp.	St. Louis, MO	7,439	8,013	7,041	6,522	8,164	8,892	9,344	9,551	0.91	0.90	0.75	0.68
3	General Electric Co.	Fairfield, CT	6,036	7,054	6,027	5,912	28,285	35,210	39,315	49,414	0.21	0.20	0.15	0.12
4	Tenneco Inc.	Houston, TX	1,250	477	2,053	5,058	15,270	14,500	14,790	13,234	0.08	0.03	0.14	0.38
5	Lockheed Aircraft Corp.	Calabasas, CA	5,895	5,700	6,168	4,331	9,535	10,273	11,321	10,590	0.62	0.55	0.54	0.41
6	Raytheon Co.	Lexington, MA	3,024	4,332	3,852	4,093	6,406	7,308	7,660	8,192	0.47	0.59	0.50	0.50
7	Martin Marietta Corp.	Bethesda, MD	3,200	3,362	4,052	4,056	4,410	4,753	5,165	5,727	0.73	0.71	0.78	0.71
8	Rockwell International Corp.	El Segundo, CA	7,609	6,746	3,848	3,898	11,741	12,397	11,937	12,134	0.65	0.54	0.32	0.32
9	United Technologies Corp.	Hartford, CT	4,016	3,624	3,753	3,599	14,992	15,669	17,170	18,000	0.27	0.23	0.22	0.20
10	General Motors Corp.	Detroit, MI	5,165	5,069	4,082	3,550	96,372	102,814	101,782	120,388	0.05	0.05	0.04	0.03
11	Boeing Co.	Seattle, WA	5,527	3,669	3,722	3,278	13,636	16,341	15,355	16,962	0.41	0.22	0.24	0.19
12	Grumman Corp.	Bethpage, NY	2,743	2,976	3,416	2,922	3,099	3,502	3,375	3,649	0.89	0.85	1.01	0.80
13	Litton Industries Inc.	Beverly Hills, CA	1,528	1,663	2,035	2,561	4,568	4,291	4,736	4,943	0.33	0.39	0.43	0.52
14	Westinghouse Electric Corp.	Pittsburgh, PA	1,941	1,713	1,684	2,185	10,700	10,731	10,679	12,500	0.18	0.16	0.16	0.17
15	TRW Inc.	Cleveland, OH	1,182	1,138	1,259	1,393	5,917	6,036	6,821	6,982	0.20	0.19	0.18	0.20
16	Unisys Corp.	Blue Bell, PA	1,909	1,897	2,268	1,380	10,774	7,432	9,713	9,902	0.18	0.26	0.23	0.14
17	Honeywell Inc.	Minneapolis, MN	1,908	1,846	2,008	1,366	6,625	5,378	6,679	7,148	0.29	0.34	0.30	0.19
18	Textron Inc.	Providence, RI	1,920	1,671	1,546	1,276	5,721	5,023	5,388	7,286	0.34	0.33	0.29	0.18
19	Texas Instrument Inc.	Dallas, TX	1,426	1,435	1,109	1,232	4,925	4,974	5,595	6,295	0.29	0.29	0.20	0.20
20	Int'l. Business Machines Corp.	Armonk, NY	1,907	1,453	1,894	1,152	50,056	51,250	54,217	59,681	0.04	0.03	0.03	0.02
	TOTAL TOP 20		74,676	70,690	69,817	68,066	322,674	339,435	354,188	397,650				
	TOTAL CONTRACT AWARDS		157,327	152,098	149,024	144,320								
	SHARE OF TOP 20 IN TOTAL AWARDS		47.47%	46.48%	46.85%	47.16%								

* Rank of the top 20 companies by descending order for 1988.
Sources: Aerospace Facts and Figures, 89/90.
Business Week, 1986–1989.

have different stakes in periods of defense builddown. Top corporate managers may prefer diversification—they may have milked profits from a recent buildup period to diversify into other nondefense fields through buyouts and mergers. Workers, including some engineers and managers, may see their futures tied up with the survival of the facility and support conversion planning. In small, one-plant businesses this tension may be absent.[2] In the cases we studied management was steadfastly opposed to conversion for defense facilities while many workers supported conversion planning.

Much of the current debate in the peace movement on the appropriate target for activism centers on this demand/supply dichotomy (Closson 1990, 4). Some would prefer to strike squarely at the demand side through pressure on Congress to lower the defense budget. Others argue that the massiveness and interdependency of the military industrial complex and the vulnerability of the work force and communities dependent upon military spending deter Congressional action and, on moral grounds, argue for direct attention to the supply side. They stress the necessity to engage in direct plant-by-plant alternative use planning along with worker adjustment programs.[3] The labor movement is increasingly interested in the latter approach, as are communities threatened with destruction of a portion of their economic base. However, some peace activists are pessimistic about the prospects for conversion, preferring instead to align themselves with groups like educators, social workers, housing activists, and other constituencies who would presumably benefit from a change in national spending priorities.

Some question whether this kind of conceptual separation between the demand (state) and supply (private sector) sides is meaningful at all. The relationship between the military industrial sectors and the state is addressed by a considerable and lively literature (Lovering 1987, 283–302). Some scholars argue that the level and nature of military demand is predominantly shaped by foreign policy concerns to protect "the national interest." Others stress the systemic need of capitalism for a state which will police the world for the benefit of multinational corporations, while others argue that a recession-prone capitalist economy must dispose of its economic surplus in "nonproductive" activities like defense. Yet others argue that neither foreign policy nor systemic economic imperatives drive the defense budget. Instead, a segment of American industry in partnership with the Pentagon—the Military Industrial Complex—acts as a special interest group to bloat the defense budget at the expense of other public priorities and other segments of capital. In this latter view, supply drives demand.

These positions differ in their prognosis of the potential for defense builddown and the likely effects it will have on the economy. If foreign policy concerns really do drive the budget, then there is little need for a Congressional initiative because the present thaw will by itself drive down military spending. In this case, we need only worry about adjustment assistance. If the builddown is going to precipitate a serious recession, then linking conversion to a macroeconomic spending initiative is essential.[4] If the budget is determined by the power of the military industrial complex rather than by foreign policy or economic rationales, then an attack on Congress is essential. In this case, the economy could be expected to boom given the change to reordered priorities without much supply side intervention. Our analyses of the conversion efforts in the 1980s suggest that management opposition to conversion poses a formidable obstacle for a demand-driven restructuring of the economy, and that failure to offer workers and communities a concrete alternative will result in their support of continued military spending at the federal level. We return to these more general issues about demand formation and its implications for conversion strategies in the final section of our paper.

FOUR ADJUSTMENT MODELS

Several kinds of phenomenon have been described as conversion. We have identified four different approaches to conversion, each with a different target and each with different lead actors. They are the corporate diversification model or converting the company, the economic development model or converting the economic base of a community, the worker adjustment model or converting the individual employee, and the alternative use model or converting the facility. While our case studies involved only this last type of conversion, the first three models are important in that they represent alternative ways to conceptualize and remedy the impact of military plant or base closures.

Converting the Company

In the company-based model conversion is a business adjustment process. When military dollars dry up firms turn to commercial markets and attempt to diversify their facilities and/or investment funds. Firms play the lead role, and the goal is restored profitability for the company as a whole. As the Reagan buildup tapered off, many companies scrambled to diversify through acquisition, merger, or internal development. Some succeeded in bringing down their defense dependency ratios, although existing divisions remained even more military-oriented than before (Markusen and Yudken in press). Raytheon is an example. Over two decades it purchased two appliance manufacturers, an oil exploration firm, an airplane manufacturer, and a publishing house, lowering its defense dependency by the mid-1980s to under 50% (Stevenson 1991). Relying heavily on acquisitions, the Raytheon strategy resulted in few crossovers of workers from military to commercial activities, and thousands of workers were laid off during periods of military cutbacks (Massachusetts State Department of Employment and Training 1989).

A minority of firms tried to market existing military products to commercial users or embarked upon new product development. Only this last strategy promises to stabilize employment in existing plants under a scenario of extensive military spending cuts. The history of such efforts over the whole postwar period is far from encouraging. Murray Weidenbaum (1964) surveyed a host of early conversion efforts and found that military-dependent firms attempted to design and produce a variety of commercial items, ranging from canoes to computers to coffins. "With one major exception [commercial aircraft]," notes Weidenbaum (1964), "these diversification attempts have each been relatively small in comparison with military equipment." Likewise, in a study of conversion and diversification efforts by six companies in the 1960s and 1970s, Robert DeGrasse (1987) found that few were successful at actual conversion of facilities. Rohr and Boeing Vertol failed at their entry into the mass transit market. Raytheon's adaptation of microwave for home use and Kaman's ventures into guitar and bearings production are company success stories, but did not result in reemployment of the defense-related work force (DeGrasse 1987).

One recent success story is the conversion of Frisby Airborne Systems on Long Island, New York, which reduced its reliance on military contracts from 95% in 1985 to 35% in 1990 (McNeilly 1990). Good management-employee relations and a coincidental surge in commercial aircraft sales helped Frisby make the transition. Nevertheless, the number of successful conversion cases is limited. Conversion advocates find themselves citing the same handful of success stories over and over, and executives like Greg Frisby are run ragged with requests to serve on panels and give public speeches. Most analysts have concluded that the big military contractors are still heavily committed to struggling over shares in a dwindling defense market and are most apt to diversify into other military or space lines rather than make the awkward transition to commercial markets (Markusen and Yudken in press, chs. 4, 7). Regrettably, no good comparative research has been done at the aggregate level on firms' strategies, failures, and successes. While we suspect that company-led diversification could work to preserve jobs more often than pessimists or anecdotal accounts suggest, the evidence to date is thin and discouraging.

Converting the Local Economic Base

The economic development model places the local economic base at the center of its agenda, and the lead agents in this process are economic development planners, sometimes with the aid of the Pentagon. In this approach planners attempt to convert the community by replacing the economic stimulus of the lost military dollar with other activities, sometimes reusing the site or space of a closed military base or plant. The existing kit of economic development tools is employed, including tax incentives, training assistance, and marketing help. One important difference between this approach and that of normal economic development activity is that the government is often willing to give away infrastructure at little or no cost.

Community economic adjustment has been the preferred strategy of the Office of Economic Adjustment (OEA), a small unit in DoD whose funding has been maintained by Congress in the face of continual opposition from Republicans in the White House and top DoD management. According to the OEA, some 100 military bases that closed over the past 25 years have been successfully converted into schools, businesses, housing, and other uses, with a net civilian job gain of more than 64,680 (President's Economic Adjustment Committee 1986, 1990). The OEA is explicitly opposed to conversion plans that target particular facilities for conversion, arguing that traditional economic development strategies will suffice to revitalize formerly defense-dependent economies.

Converting communities in this manner from their defense-dependent status employs familiar techniques for planners, but may fall into familiar traps. It is strictly a "professional" development model, banking on improving the business climate and on government incentives to private business to revitalize the community. In some instances the costs of incentives to private business may outweigh the benefits these companies bring to the community. No systematic research has been done to evaluate diversification of military-dependent local economies through economic development approaches. Such research is badly needed, particularly to inform planners about the special opportunities and problems associated with government ownership of facilities.

Converting the Workers

The worker adjustment model of economic conversion approaches the problem in the same vein, but from the point of view of individuals. It counsels scrapping plants and letting companies exit, but helping workers cope through interim support, retraining, and placement services. The notion is that federal income support and adjustment programs, similar to those provided for other special classes of workers, be set up for workers in industries affected by military cutbacks (Kulik and Fairchild 1987, 191). For example, the federal Trade Adjustment Assistance Act provides income support (including extended unemployment insurance, money for training, and relocation expenses) to workers who become unemployed due to import competition. The Title III program of the Job Training Partnership Act, which replaced the Comprehensive Employment and Training Act in 1982, is the other major component of federal worker readjustment programs. The Title III program has been criticized for its focus on short-term retraining and job search rather than on education, and the Trade Adjustment Assistance Act has been criticized for long delays in processing claims and covering too few workers (Wykle et al. 1991). In a program put forward by Oil Chemical and Atomic Workers Union official, Tony Mazzochi, a superfund modeled on the GI bill and environmental cleanup laws would be created for displaced defense workers. Company contributions would enable displaced workers to return to school with income support for enough time to learn new analytical skills. Advocates of the superfund note that in the debate over the original GI Bill, many argued that war-related workers should be included in the program. In the end, however, only veterans were included in the GI Bill (Wykle et al. 1991, 71).

Only small scale programs have been created specifically for displaced war-related workers, and these programs were geared toward technical and professional staff rather than blue collar workers. Defense-related layoffs of engineers and scientists in the early 1970s generated enough concern that the government created a Technology Mobilization and Reemployment Program which involved career counseling, job search grants, on the job training, and relocation assistance. An innovative component of this effort to place former aerospace engineers in professional jobs at state and local government was unsuccessful due to workers' reluctance to relocate, confusion about how skills could be transferred, and lack of funding at the state and local levels (Kulik and Fairchild 1987, 204). A current effort along these same lines is underway in Florida. There, military personnel with scientific or technical backgrounds facing "involuntary separation" from the military are being placed in teaching positions. State education officials hope that these military personnel will fill the shortage of qualified science and math teachers in Florida. They expect the program to be more successful than its predecessors because expected military personnel cutbacks are more substantial (Cooper 1990).

Although proportionally more engineers and scientists may be displaced in military industrial activity than in industries like auto and steel, blue collar workers are still apt to lose jobs in greater numbers. Furthermore, their reemployment prospects are bleaker than those of the college-educated professional. Studies forecasting military workers' displacement experience suggest that blue collar workers will be unemployed for longer stints and will face greater declines in their relative incomes once defense plants close (Howland 1988).

Worker adjustment strategies "convert" the individual from a defense worker to a civilian worker. There are both operational and normative difficulties in pursuing worker conversion. The worker adjustment strategy assumes that jobs for retrained workers will exist in the marketplace. But, if military cutbacks are substantial and add to recessionary tendencies, this may not be the case. Some critics raise normative issues. Do defense workers warrant special treatment? Why shouldn't workers whose industries have been undercut by an industrial policy favoring aerospace also be covered? Should defense workers who, on average, earn more and have had more education invested in them at public expense deserve adjustment assistance not offered to other displaced workers?[5] Defenders of such assistance argue that the public sector has a special responsibility to this group of workers and that achievements for them are a step in the door for other workers.

Converting the Facility

Facility conversion, the final model, envisions alternative use planning as a joint effort of community, labor, and management representatives. It is at once both more narrowly construed—targeted at individual sites—and more ambitious—aimed at maintaining livelihoods for existing workers in existing plants. It calls for more explicit institutional changes, both in the planning and implementation stages, than the previous models. The beneficiary of considerable academic design work and of a number of singular experiments, this strategy is based on a view that management either can't or won't tackle facility conversion on its own. Management requires a blend of "instruction and imposition," involving participation of workers, community groups, and government. In this model, the initiating impulse comes from outside plant management—from the workers, the community, the peace movement, and/or local government staff.

Inspiration for contemporary alternative use planning came originally from the plan by the workers of Lucas Aerospace in Britain to convert their facility in the

1970s. Since then a number of scholars have worked on designs for such planning, chief among them Seymour Melman, long-time scholar of the military industrial complex and a staunch advocate of conversion (see Melman 1988). These designs favor decentralized conversion, eschewing another Washington bureaucracy. They advocate mandatory alternative use planning paid for by companies (and presumably recoverable from government contracts) and conducted by joint local committees of management, labor, and community representatives. Committees researching alternative uses would have access to company data and to outside consultants and marketing help in drafting a new business plan. Government would pitch in with funds for retraining, transitional income support, and coordination via a National Economic Conversion Commission. A version of such alternative use planning is contained in the Weiss Bill currently before Congress, and it was a major bone of contention during the Congressional debates on conversion in the summer of 1990. As of 1991 alternative use planning has not yet been adopted as law.

Despite the interest in this last approach, no evaluative research on cases of community/labor initiated facility conversion has been conducted to date. Because alternative use planning is more directly concerned with job retention than are the other models described above, we decided to further investigate this model and "test" it against experience to date. In the course of our research, we chose to focus on a half dozen controversial and specific cases of facility-based conversion in the past decade, to see how well each matches up to the Melman model and what each reveals about the politics and implementation of such an approach. The results help to illuminate the other models as well, since facility conversion can be an element in a company diversification or community economic development strategy.

FACILITY CONVERSION—AN EVALUATION

The Research Design

Over the first six months of 1990, we investigated six cases of community/union initiated efforts at facility conversion, four at privately-owned plants and two at government-owned, contractor-operated facilities. The cases were chosen on the basis of the relatively well developed campaigns that were conducted on each site, the fact that each involved large numbers of jobs, and the availability of primary and secondary sources.[6] To find them, we canvassed all the groups in the U.S.— from the peace, plant closings, and labor movements—who had been active in and/or interested in conversion. Those sites that we chose were by and large the best known efforts and together constitute a set of "best practice" cases. They are geographically representative and cover a fair spectrum of types of military production: Quincy Shipyards, a division of General Dynamics, making military ships in Massachusetts; Blaw-Knox foundry, a subsidiary of White Consolidated Industries, making tanks in Indiana; the Long Beach plant of McDonnell-Douglas, making military aircraft in California; Lockheed Shipyards, Marine Division, outside Seattle, Washington; Philadelphia Naval Yards, repairing and overhauling military ships in Pennsylvania; and a Unisys Corporation plant in Minneapolis,

Minnesota, producing military computer systems for the Navy. Some of the efforts had been completed as of our inquiries, while others were still in developmental stages.

In each case, we either interviewed the various parties to the effort, including management, labor, and representatives of the community, and/or we relied upon secondary sources where others had already done this investigative work. In each case we asked the following questions. What did the facility make, who owned it, and what was its current predicament? Who initiated the conversion effort? Who were the leaders of the effort? Was there funding and staff for the effort, and who provided it? How broad was the participation in the effort, both on a group-by-group basis and by members within each group? What was the alternative use strategy? Was a social cost calculus applied? What were the attitudes of each of the major players as the process unfolded? What public policy and political issues were generated? How well did the effort "succeed" on the basis of the narrow and broad criteria? How generalizable are the lessons from each?

Criteria for "Success"

In order to evaluate these conversion initiatives, we must first specify the criteria for gauging "success." In this case, because the constituency for conversion is diverse, we developed both narrow and broad criteria. The narrow, and more demanding goal, is the preservation of jobs in the existing plant in the community. Does the alternative use plan provide a similar number of jobs with similar salaries and wages? Is the plan "practical," i.e. can stockholders make an acceptable return on their investment? This narrow criterion is the one of most immediate interest to workers, managers, and local governments directly involved in a military facility closing.

Because the peace movement is also a constituency for conversion planning, and given the magnitude of the changes necessary for successful conversion, a broader criterion is also appropriate. In it, conversion planning can be considered a success if it succeeds in educating management and workers, on the one hand, about their prospects, and educating voters, including peace activists themselves, on the other hand, about how difficult a contraction might prove and how badly conversion is needed. In other words, a conversion effort, even if it fails as a jobs-preservation project, might have salutary effects overall. On the supply side each effort moves us up the learning curve and helps educate and empower the constituencies most affected, while on the demand side it can feed into the sophisticated crafting of a political response to the spending-preserving efforts of the military industrial complex. While this is more difficult to measure, it is important to recognize how these efforts contributed to the conversion debate overall.

Six Conversion Efforts: A Synopsis

Quincy Shipyards   Quincy Shipyards, a 180-acre yard located south of Boston, Massachusetts, belonged to General Dynamics, the biggest purely military conglomerate in the nation. Quincy Yard employed more than 11,000 workers in the 1960s and 5,000 as recently as the mid-1980s, although the number of jobs fluctuated with the rise and fall of big projects. In 1982 its future looked grim as a large commercial effort failed and competition for military contracts heightened. Employment had fallen to 1,100, and the yard seemed destined to be smaller and more military-dependent than ever. At that point a group of activist rank and file workers in the local shipbuilder's union initiated the South Shore Conversion Committee (SSCC), creating a coalition with local peace activists. Without management, outside consultants, or local government involvement, they researched alternative uses and proposed that the yard pioneer in making an ocean thermal energy conversion plantship to produce electricity at sea. Other new products that SSCC believed were feasible and did not require major new investment included oil rigs, rail cars, and bridge spans (Sherman and Meacham 1983). The South Shore Conversion Committee hoped that the Quincy Yard, as well as other shipyards, could stop competing for military work and redirect their industry toward civilian products.

The Quincy effort ran into a number of organizational problems. On the whole, many rank and file members of the union were either indifferent or hostile, as was the "old guard" of the union leadership. At least one of the leaders interpreted this, retrospectively, as a strategic error in organizing. "The peace movement preached morality," he said, "and closed people's minds." There were also practical problems with organizing. Many of the workers were commuters eager to hit the road after work rather than attend lengthy planning meetings. The City of Quincy, reeling from a lawsuit which awarded General Dynamics $28 million for overassessment of property, was in no position to financially support alternative use planning for the yard.

More importantly, General Dynamics adamantly opposed the alternative use effort. The company claimed to have researched alternatives without finding a viable product. Moreover, the company had just completed a financially disastrous commercial venture building liquefied natural gas tankers. General Dynamics focused its energies on getting new Navy contracts, and in 1983 it was successful with a $409 million contract for cargo ships for the Navy's Rapid Deployment Force.

The new contract was a kiss of death for the conversion effort, detracting the attention of all but a few committed activists. However, the Navy contract won in 1983 proved to be the shipyard's last and in 1986 the facility closed. In the final six months of the shipyard's operation, interest in conversion renewed, and the State of Massachusetts commissioned a study of the yard's future. The study concluded that shipbuilding was impractical until 1988 when the commercial shipbuilding market was forecasted to improve. The consultants noted that a new owner could make money on the yard but that the owner "will likely have an entirely different marketing philosophy, cost structure, and pricing policy than the existing owner" (Booz Allen and Hamilton 1986, 5).

General Dynamics sold the site to the Massachusetts Water Resources

Department for $48 million, a bonus for exiting. As of 1990 the government used the site for storing and shipping barge equipment. In 1991 the state hopes to have a secondary sludge treatment facility under construction. Other parts of the yard are used for the storage of vehicles; a 70-acre section was set aside for the shipbuilders union for reuse as a shipyard. In 1990, 1,000 former shipyard workers created a plan to reopen the yard where they would be the new owners. Drexel Burnham Lambert offered financing of $17 million contingent upon a $10 million loan guarantee from the U.S. Economic Development Administration, who thus far has balked at the project. Advocates claim that the yard could take advantage of the strong global demand for shipbuilding and that the land and equipment costs of reopening would be minimal as the site is state owned and former General Dynamics equipment has been maintained (Primack 1990). Critics claim that increased foreign demand may be transitory as foreign governments may increase their shipbuilding capacities despite restrictive international agreements. Ironically, U.S. public and private capital investment is more likely in Poland's Gdansk yard than the Quincy yard.

Overall, on the narrow criterion, the South Shore Conversion project was not successful. The yard was dismantled, and 5,000 jobs disappeared. The possibility of a smaller worker-owned shipyard has run into government opposition, although there may yet be a change of heart in the Economic Development Administration. Nor did the Quincy effort bear much fruit in terms of a larger effort at conversion planning, although one of the major participants did go on to work on the Philadelphia Naval Shipyards conversion effort. If anything, the Quincy case appears to have convinced Boston area peace activists interested in conversion to concentrate on the demand side, working with groups like teachers and housing activists to push for a change in federal spending priorities rather than targeting the point of production. On the other hand, the work done analyzing what could be made at shipyards and publicizing the social costs of closing was a valuable contribution to future conversion efforts.

Blaw-Knox Foundry   Blaw-Knox Foundry of East Chicago, Indiana, was a 70-year-old maker of heavy castings. Up through the late 1960s, it employed about 1,400 mainly semiskilled workers, producing steel mill equipment, although about 15% of its output consisted of tanks, which it first made in World War II. But in the 1970s, a new conglomerate owner, White Consolidated Industries, began switching to production of the M-60 tank for the Army and foreign governments. By the mid- to late 1970s, the plant was making 4-5 tanks a day, working three shifts, and employing approximately 2,500 workers. By then, Pentagon orders accounted for 85 to 95% of its output. Meanwhile, its steel business languished, chiefly because foreign competitors, especially the Japanese, made considerable inroads into the steel mill market.[7]

In 1984 a researcher at the local Calumet Project on Industrial Jobs, a community-based antiplant-closing group, spotted a note in the trade press suggesting that White Consolidated might sell and/or close the plant. Its M-60 was being displaced by the fancier M-1 tank, which did not require Blaw-Knox services. He notified the president of the Steelworker's union local at the plant, who called a meeting, at which the Blaw-Knox Steering Committee was born. The committee consisted of representatives from the union, management, the community, and local and regional economic development agencies. They commissioned a study by A. D. Little which recommended that the plant be retooled, at a cost of $20 to $24 million, to produce smaller sized commercial castings (Moberg 1986, 32). The investment was crucial because, despite twenty years of profitability and lucrative military contracts, White Consolidated had not put in a cent of new equipment. While the government would have to put up between $4 and $7 million, the savings in social costs which would be incurred if the plant, with its 800 workers, was to be shut down would be substantial.

The alternative use plan was never implemented, and the plant closed down in 1986. In the interim, White sold out to another holding company, NESCO, which took control of the planning process and redirected it single-mindedly toward a lobbying effort to keep Pentagon orders coming. Cleavages within the conversion committee paralyzed opposition to NESCO's strategy. The union local refused to play a major leadership role, and the international union was preoccupied with collective bargaining issues. The community groups—the Calumet Project and the United Community Organization—had an alternative vision but little clout. They refused to participate in NESCO's lobbying efforts, trying instead to generate support for a public jobs authority, modeled on the successful Steel Valley Authority in Pittsburgh, with the powers of eminent domain. Meanwhile, the economic development people and the Indiana politicians, including the state's two senators and the local congressman, were co-opted into the company's losing strategy of begging for more tanks.

Although the Blaw-Knox effort did not succeed according to the narrow criterion of job preservation, it has borne fruit in a larger, ongoing effort on the part of the Calumet Project to avert plant closings and facilitate management turnover of endangered plants. In late 1989 the Project published a much-quoted retrospective study of Blaw-Knox and more than a dozen other closings in the area, concluding that many of them, including Blaw-Knox, could have been averted had certain public policies and institutions been in place. Its ongoing efforts include a project to create and fund a public jobs authority which would operate an advanced warning system, provide "one-stop shopping" to plants in trouble, and give technical assistance and support to workers, unions, and business to stabilize jobs and prevent job loss. It would also assist in management turnover, using eminent domain if necessary (Calumet Project on Industrial Jobs 1989).

Philadelphia Naval Yards   The Philadelphia Navy Shipyard is part of a Navy base comprised of two dozen naval commands where engineering research and design is conducted. It is a stable source of employment and income for many Philadelphians. The future of the shipyard and the adjacent Navy hospital has been much less certain; the Pentagon planned to close the yard and the hospital in the mid-1980s, and while the shut down was temporarily averted, both are on the 1991 closure list. The efforts of Jobs With Peace (1986) and union activists in the mid-1980s have become relevant again as plans for closure appear to be moving forward.

In the 1980s, like the Quincy shipyards, the Philadelphia yards faced cuts in naval spending without commercial work to cushion the blow. The yard has several strikes against it in the competition for Navy work. Jobs With Peace activist George Lakey (1986) noted that, "Philadelphia is a non-nuclear yard, which is reassuring for the health of Philadelphians but could be a disadvantage in the scramble for work." Lakey also pointed out that Philadelphia's status as a government-owned yard was not necessarily an asset since privately-owned yards were increasingly undercutting the prices charged by public yards. Because it was futile to demand that the Navy conduct commercial work on government property, conversion advocates suggested that "full use" for the yard be attained by portioning off a section of the yard for sale and then using that site for commercial work. In response to the threatened closure, the League Island Development Corporation (LIDC) was formed with financial support from Jobs With Peace's Philadelphia office. It was a joint effort of neighborhood and peace activists. The LIDC had an explicitly pro-labor conversion strategy:

> We believe that the skills of dislocated workers should not go to waste, but rather, should become a resource for economic development programs benefitting them and their communities. In response to long term decline, the Corporation has focused its initial programs on bringing underutilized sites in and around the Philadelphia Naval Base up to their most productive, job creating capacity (Jobs With Peace 1986).

Despite its pro-labor position the organization had little success with the Metal Trades Council which represented the approximately 10,000 workers of the yard. Jon Brandow (1987), president of the LIDC, believes that there were tactical errors in the way peace activists approached workers in that they appeared to have an agenda. Failure to gain union support became a major stumbling block for the conversion effort and the unions' persistent lack of interest caused the League to cease organizing.

A contributing factor to the effort's demise was the resolution of the immediate crisis. At the end of 1986 the shipyard was informed that it would receive three major ship overhauls which would keep approximately 10,000 skilled blue collar workers busy through 1990. While the League tried to raise the specter of 1991, workers were not interested. In the ensuing two years, the group refocused its work on two other major conversion projects: a shipyard in Chester, Pennsylvania, and the Navy hospital adjacent to the shipyards. While neither plan has yet been adopted, the feasibility studies represent a contribution to conversion efforts nationally.

The Philadelphia conversion-organizing efforts have not been successful yet in terms of job retention or reuse of the site. Continuing efforts in Philadelphia may yet bear fruit of that variety; plans for reuse of the Navy hospital appear to be well underway. Like the Quincy shipyard effort, organizing in Philadelphia publicized alternative uses for shipyards and their plans illustrate the technical feasibility of conversion. Moreover, Jobs With Peace activists have gone on to craft and push state legislation to assist conversion efforts.[8]

McDonnell-Douglas Aircraft By the early 1980s the former Douglas Aircraft Company in Long Beach, California, found itself in longstanding financial difficulty. Once the leader in commercial aviation, the company never recovered from Boeing's entry into the jet airliner market in the late 1950s, nor had it recouped its development costs from the DC-8.[9] In 1967, McDonnell Aircraft of St. Louis, Missouri, had stepped in to attempt to "rescue" the larger Douglas. Unfortunately, the merger did not return Douglas to its former profitability or production levels. In the Long Beach plant that once employed 33,000 workers at its peak in the late 1960s, employment plunged sharply over the intervening years. By the early 1980s the Long Beach plant was operating at about 20% capacity. Between 1980 and 1982 the number of United Auto Workers (UAW) at the plant fell from over 12,000 workers to under 5,000, while the engineering, scientific, and technical workforce was cut in half from its previous level of 7,000. McDonnell chose to do nothing about continued attrition of the Douglas plant business. Instead, it was banking on a C-17 cargo carrier contract, even though it had yet to be approved by Congress.

After the rash of 1982 layoffs, United Auto Workers Local 148 President Bob Berghoff sought alternatives for reemploying his 10,000 members. The Los Angeles Coalition Against Plant Shutdowns (LACAPS), a broad-based coalition of labor, community, and religious activists, met with Berghoff to discuss the idea of conversion planning. The UAW's goals were to reemploy its workers and rebuild its strength in the plant. Working together with the state government and the Mid-Peninsula Conversion Project (MPCP), now known as the Center for Economic Conversion, and an unofficial representative of the engineers' union, the local identified several feasible alternatives for the plant, including light rail transit assembly, a cogeneration project, and commuter aircraft production.

The transit project was particularly attractive since two new light rail systems were underway in California, and Douglas management expressed interest in it. Plant managers and the union, working together with MPCP and the state, began to negotiate informally. While the labor-management committee was never formally established, management's willingness to seriously consider workers' ideas was a significant step. Both labor and management felt they had stakes in the effort. The involvement of the state facilitated both labor's and management's willingness to work together.

What, then, went wrong? First, McDonnell-Douglas did not act quickly enough on the transit project and lost the contract. Secondly, during the course of negotiations, Berghoff led a 113-day strike against a proposed two-tiered wage system and cut in other benefits. It is unclear whether the strike affected the project, although Douglas representatives were willing to continue negotiating with the union concerning new products. Perhaps most significantly, McDonnell management in St.

Louis was ambivalent about the effort. It had earlier rejected Douglas attempts to move into new product lines and continued to stress military work. The rail project was abandoned when Congress approved the C-17 for Douglas Aircraft Company.

The conversion effort was not a success in the narrow sense of preserving jobs. In 1990 the layoffs again numbered in the thousands, due to civilian-related layoffs and no new military prospects. The conversion effort did garner a fair amount of publicity in the Los Angeles area, however. It helped put ideas about alternative high-technology production, and rail projects in particular, on the table, ideas picked up again with enthusiasm in 1990 when a number of local officials in Orange County began to search for projects to counter military cutbacks.

Lockheed Shipyards   On November 17, 1986, the Lockheed Shipbuilding Corporation locked out 685 union workers at its Seattle shipyard with only 48 hours notice after workers had received a 45% wage cut.[10] Lockheed demanded unilateral work rule changes and refused to bargain in good faith. Many observers now believe that by the time of the lockout Lockheed had already made the decision to close its Puget Sound operation, a shipbuilding subsidiary acquired in 1959 from Puget Sound Bridge and Drydock. After the lockout the Seattle Worker Center stepped in to help. The Worker Center, organized in 1986 by representatives of labor, churches, government, industry, academia, and the community, served as an early warning center for plant closures and intervened to help save jobs and to advocate for dislocated workers.

The Seattle Worker Center launched a campaign with two initiatives. First, it worked with people who were locked out and denied their unemployment benefits. Targeting bills to deal with employer-generated lockouts, the Center helped the shipyard workers develop a legislative campaign to take to Olympia, the state capital. The campaign united locked out workers across the state, and the effort succeeded in winning $5 million in unemployment benefits for those locked out. Second, the campaign aimed to convert the Lockheed Shipyards, targeting potential new operations in nonmilitary boat-building, such as fish processing boats.

The campaign ultimately failed in its effort to keep the yard open. The campaign did not receive the support of Lockheed management nor did it generate sufficient political clout to help keep Lockheed in Seattle. Lockheed permanently closed the Seattle yard in December 1987 and sold all its equipment at auction in May 1988. Only 45% of the ex-Lockheed workers found new jobs in the maritime industry. Many of the former Lockheed employees went to work for Boeing, just then enjoying an enormous boom.

However, the shipyard jobs campaign helped save other maritime jobs. The campaign was expanded to target the entire Port of Seattle. The Worker Center helped a worker buyout of a bankrupt tug and barge operation and repair yard. The new worker-owners included many former Lockheed workers. The campaign also helped focus public attention on Puget Sound shipyards and shipyard job loss. It publicized the fact that between 1982 and 1987, shipyard jobs fell from 10,700 to 3,000. In response, the government embarked upon an 18-month research and development effort concerning the state of the industry and its prospects for future growth. The research effort culminated in a report for the governor and legislature, Recapturing Markets for Puget Sound Shipyards (Puget Sound Shipyards Industrial Jobs Commission 1989). Among other provisions, it recommended the creation of an industry-wide labor-management committee, and policy support for shipyard modernization and job retraining programs.

Unisys Defense Computer Systems   In 1986 Sperry and Burroughs corporations merged, combining their military work into one Computer Defense Division heavily concentrated in the St. Paul, Minnesota, area with around 5,000 workers. Shortly thereafter, caught bribing consultants for bid-related information and suspended from bidding on Navy contracts for several months, Unisys lost ground to competitors. When the Navy, which accounted for more than 70% of Unisys' $2.4 million annual military sales, announced a shift to commercial grade from military specifications, Unisys' military sales slumped further. The company began a long series of layoffs with no apparent desire to convert military-oriented facilities to other uses (Duncan 1990, 14; see also Markham and Associates 1989).

In 1985 concerned members of International Brotherhood of Electrical Workers (IBEW) Local 2047 contacted the AFL-CIO and the State Task Force on Economic Conversion to ask for help in challenging these layoffs. A new working group, the Alternative Use Project, was formed with members from the IBEW local, the state AFL-CIO, the Working Group on Economic Dislocation (an antiplant-closing group), and Jobs With Peace. With technical and financial assistance from state and city governments, the group hired an independent consultant to produce an alternative use plan. The result was a careful analysis of over forty new product ideas, including pollution monitoring devices, automobile computers, home security systems, smart irrigation, low power electronic lighting ballasts, adaptive technologies for the physically disabled, light rail transit controls, and monitoring systems. All could be manufactured, the study contended, with little or no change in equipment and with the existing workforce.

However, the company remained adamantly opposed to alternative use planning. It refused to meet with the group, rejected a request for a six-month moratorium on layoffs, and claimed that Unisys was already a "converted company" because it already had divisions producing for the commercial market. The company spokesman belittled the alternative use study, suggesting that management had access to better engineering and new product talent, which, however, it was unwilling to disclose or share. Because the company would not cooperate, additional funding for alternative use planning provided by the state legislature could not kick in, since it required the participation of management. Ironically, the company has recently announced plans to build one of the products suggested in the task force's plan, a satellite-based remote sensing system, but plans to produce it in Salt Lake City rather than in St. Paul (Maki et al. 1991, 15).

To date the Unisys project has not successfully retained jobs. However, Unisys has been attempting to sell its defense division and, if successful, a new management may consider conversion planning more favorably. The alternative use project continues to recruit advocates and amass technical assistance and they may be successful in the future. More importantly, the Unisys project has served as an example of labor, community, and peace activist cooperation. The union's plan received support from many corners. Local academics studied the problem of defense dependency in the region and proved that plans for civilian production made better economic sense for the region (Maki et al. 1989). After a major layoff of 151 workers in January of 1990, the Governor of Minnesota and the Mayor of St. Paul went to the plant gates to welcome fired workers and walk the picket line, the first ever where the issue at stake was conversion. Activists are also trying to channel political support for conversion into state legislation which would mandate alternative use committees for military companies in Minnesota which receive any assistance from the state. As in the other cases, political activism has not yet retained jobs, but does demonstrate the potential, as well as problems, of conversion.

The Cases Compared

From these cases, we can draw some tentative conclusions. We found that peace activists and labor unions were able to work together, and that the deeper the level of consensus among workers in particular, the more powerful the movement. In all cases, management opposed conversion planning, and this crippled the efforts. State intervention, then, is necessary if conversion is to take place. Early warning legislation, particularly legislation which provides a long lead time, would prove useful so that organizers could speak with certainty about when layoffs or closure would occur and plan accordingly. Finally, organizers admitted to us that more technical assistance, particularly in marketing, would be useful. Workers may have good ideas about what products they can produce at a facility, but they don't know what products will sell. These precursors mostly illustrate the obstacles facing conversion; however, these problems are not insurmountable. Nor did we find defense-dependent workers or regions opposed to conversion. By identifying the problems facing conversion in the late 1980s, we can better consider prospects for conversion in the 1990s.

Leadership and Participation The cases differ in the quality of leadership and the degree of broad-based participation in the conversion initiative. Where the initiative came from outside the union or the workforce, as at the Philadelphia Naval Shipyards, developing clout to put pressure on the operator was almost impossible. Narrowly-based efforts, as in the Quincy and Philadelphia shipyards, foundered because of lack of support from the majority of workers and the community, not to mention management. Without such political pressure, response by policymakers was too little, too late.

Labor participation and unity is crucial to mounting a successful case. Unions bring with them an activist tradition. They know how to use strikes and pickets effectively for generating public support and media coverage. Larger trade union offices have resources for funding feasibility studies and research. Where a rank and file dissident group lacked local union support, as at Quincy, management felt no need to take the effort seriously. Support at higher levels of the union hierarchy also helped, but was not crucial. Not having it at Blaw-Knox was a disadvantage, but at McDonnell-Douglas the local effort proceeded quite well without such support. At Unisys, where local union leadership was backed by both the international and the state AFL-CIO, support from politicians and the public sector was easier to generate quickly. On the other hand, an effort mounted strictly within the boundaries of collective bargaining was apt to degenerate into contractual demands for severance pay, job transfer rights, or control over subcontracting—issues which complicated the Blaw-Knox and Quincy cases. Provisions for plant closings can be explicitly bargained into labor contracts. For instance, a machinists union local at Kollmorgen Electro-optical Division in Northampton, Massachusetts, a 75% defense-dependent facility, bargained successfully for the establishment of a joint union-company committee to address issues of mutual concern, among them the prospects for work under future defense cuts (Ruzkowski 1990).

The cases illustrate that potential divisions between peace activists, communities, and trade unionists can and should be bridged.[11] Peace groups often bring with them financial resources, visibility, and manpower to supplement a workplace-based effort. Community groups, too, have helped out by bringing in politicians and local government support. The Unisys effort enjoyed community, peace movement, and public sector support and could enter terrain not generally accessible to workers and their organizations. Peace activists demonstrated their commitment to taking care of those most adversely affected by the demilitarization of the economy, while trade unionists came out strongly in favor of the peace dividend. As Vic Globa (1990), President of IBEW Local 2047 put it, "We have taken the leadership to demonstrate that the cuts to the military budget do not have to cause job loss . . . Our people are extremely talented and can make many useful and profitable products." In the Blaw-Knox case the union local refused the company's demands that they write patriotic letters pushing tank contracts to their congressional representatives.

Management Cooperation   To make conversion work, management must be willing to participate in the effort. In all six cases studied, key managers refused to cooperate in alternative use planning, even when plant-level managers were favorably inclined. This coincides with other research findings and press accounts that generally most military contractors are neither interested in nor capable of refurbishing military-dedicated facilities to alternative production, but prefer strategies of acquisition and merger or, in the rarer cases of successful diversification, undertake new plant construction elsewhere (Yudken 1984, 4–5). In one case, Blaw-Knox, where management initially joined the team, it squelched the effort at its most creative junction and redirected it into political lobbying for more defense spending. At McDonnell-Douglas, where the plant management participated actively, central office management undermined the commercial effort with their preoccupation with military work. The more or less predictable opposition of management to conversion initiatives forms a formidable barrier to the facility conversion strategy.

Management opposition was sometimes tied to evidence of incompetence or dishonesty. In several of the cases, conversion research uncovered failures to maintain and upgrade equipment making commercial competitiveness difficult (Blaw-Knox) or outright corruption damaging the plants' reputation with the Pentagon (Quincy, Unisys). Facilities involved were often subjects of recent mergers (Unisys) or buyouts (Blaw-Knox), which might have contributed to the propensity for closure. Some facilities, like Blaw-Knox, had been "milked" for years on profitable Pentagon contracts with no reinvestment.

Competent and honest managers may also have strong reasons for opposing joint conversion efforts, especially when initiated by workers or community groups. Companies in each case asserted their proprietary rights to plan, opposing the notion that they would have to open their books to joint committee members. Some companies have had historically bad labor relations which are difficult to transcend. Some oppose conversion out of fear of the unknown and unwillingness to invest in dark horses. Then, too, the general economic climate matters as well. Throughout most of the period we studied, defense outlays continued to rise, creating short-term sales for the companies involved and lessening their incentive to consider the alternatives. For the most part, the companies studied here disparaged conversion efforts and politically opposed legislation for mandatory alternative use planning. Their stance is reminiscent of similar stands taken by business organizations against plant-closing legislation and environmental regulations, analogies which suggest that business opposition need not prevail.

The Need for Information: Early Warning and Disclosure The cases taken together suggest that the longer the lead time, the better prepared and positioned the community/union coalitions are to cope with military cutbacks. Knowledge about company and Pentagon plans was essential to each strategy. In some cases the initiating group came upon crucial information only by chance (Blaw-Knox). In others, general information about product and weapons systems gave workers and locals a fairly clear signal about a facility's future. Where lead time was longer, as in Unisys, it was easier to complete coalition building and preliminary studies. Where it was short, or where lags took place in response, facilities ended up being shuttered before planning could produce a reasonable alternative (Quincy, Blaw-Knox).

Access to company books and strategic plans also proved to be essential to the planning process. In general, this is proprietary turf, closely guarded by companies. Especially when a plant is just one of many facilities under a corporate umbrella, the profitability of existing operations is impossible to ascertain without access to the books. Also, while workers often suspected they were the subjects of slash-and-burn or milking tactics on the part of top financial managers, as at Blaw-Knox, this too was hard to prove without such disclosure. The cases suggest that companies will only share such information when required.

Technical Assistance   The case studies all reveal, in varying degrees, deficiencies in technical expertise available to community/union conversion initiators. In order to accomplish social cost accounting, new product assessment, marketing studies, financial feasibility, and business plans, coalitions had to turn to academics or consultants willing to do so for modest amounts of money. In some cases, insiders in plant management or among engineers were supportive and willing to help anonymously. But even friendly managers are often at a loss in thinking about designing or marketing entirely new products. Although it is an appealing and probably correct notion that workers might have good ideas for new products and know the capabilities of their workplaces, in fact they too are not well equipped to tackle the entrepreneurial tasks of business restructuring.

In no case did a coalition come up with a complete business plan or get as far as proposing a worker or community buyout, although over time groups demonstrate more awareness that this kind of design work is necessary. After ten years or more of massive plant closings in their industries, unions like the United Auto Workers and the United Steelworkers have learned that worker buyouts can be successful, although in every case outside professional help has been required, at a price. Financial resources to enable the purchase of these services must be found if such buyouts are to succeed. Alternatively, they could be provided by the state. The McDonnell-Douglas case and the Unisys case both enjoyed capable third party intervention from the state to work with both management and labor, with prospects for state aid if the joint efforts had succeeded.

Technical assistance in a timely fashion is crucial because not all plants and facilities should be saved. Some are simply too old and without redeeming characteristics; too expensive to refurbish; or polluted with chemicals, nuclear contaminants, or metals residues. Workers and communities hosting these plants should be able to get an assessment of their prospects as soon as possible to avoid delays in retraining and other forms of adjustment assistance which will be necessary when employment evaporates.

The Next Steps: Social Cost Calculus and Public Policy   The cases together demonstrate the need for a social cost accounting framework to be applied to the conversion issue. In the case of Quincy shipyards, for example, the state expenditure for the study of the shipyard and latter acquisition of the site could have been combined with the federal worker training funds to convert the yard. More research is needed to calculate the social costs of closing compared with the public investment needed to convert. We also recommend that more research be conducted on technical assistance and early warning programs similar to those already existing in state and local economic development operations, and on structural innovations like the jobs authority concept and the extension of eminent domain powers to the industrial arena. In most cases, the community or union initiative, if well organized, generated a set of legislative proposals which would pioneer new institutions to monitor military-related plant closings and to respond to them.

Some of the cases we studied generated state legislation. Proposals for state conversion legislation have reflected the experience of local organizing efforts

(Hill 1991). The Pennsylvania bill mandates community-led alternative use committees created by residents and/or workers, reminiscent of the composition of the League Island Development Corporation. The proposed Minnesota legislation mandates the creation of alternative use committees at every defense related facility, reflecting the needs articulated by the Unisys workers. While only a few states (Connecticut and Washington) have passed effective conversion legislation, many states have conducted studies on military spending and/or conversion and are considering proposals. The state of Washington combined proposals for alternative use planning with a proposal for state economic diversification. It passed into law on June 7, 1990. Historically, state legislation is important in that it has been a precursor for national legislation. For example, national plant-closing legislation borrowed heavily from state legislation (Kerson and LeRoy 1989, 6). The efforts of states to encourage conversion serve as a model for national legislation. Inclusion of local alternative use planning mechanisms within state legislation may lend authority to the Weiss conversion bill's effort to mandate alternative use committees for all defense firms.

Overall, and despite some hope for future conversion at Unisys and Philadelphia shipyard, we found that none of the cases has been successful on the basis of the stricter criterion of maintaining a plurality of workers on the site. Failure can be ascribed to both organizational difficulties and management resistance. However, the efforts have been successful in other ways. In each case they have helped to instruct peace movement activists about the costs and difficulties of military shutdowns. Groups such as SANE/FREEZE have added conversion to their agenda. Each case has involved the education of at least some workers into the rudiments of plant management and business planning. Efforts in Seattle, for example, led activists and workers to successfully create a worker buyout of a maritime company. Cumulatively, the cases have contributed to a body of knowledge and practice about conversion planning which has proven helpful to new groups starting out.

We are guardedly optimistic because we view these cases as pilot projects. Any innovation goes through a period of frequent failures before it catches hold. Furthermore, these efforts all took place during a period of military buildup, and a majority of them foundered on management preference for short-term defense contracts over long-term and riskier alternative use planning. If the military budget is indeed reduced, management at defense-dependent plants may not be as hostile to conversion.

It is too soon to tell whether or not the lessons of these cases can be applied to other instances of military-related plant closings.[12] However, the progression in sophistication and cooperation among interested parties in the cases examined is heartening. In 1990 a number of new initiatives cropped up around the country, including conversion efforts around Bath, Maine, shipyards; Oak Ridge, Tennessee, nuclear facilities; a Burlington, Vermont, General Electric gatling gun producer; western Massachusetts machine tool makers; Long Island, New York, area aircraft plants; and several Connecticut engine and machining factories. Groups in several cities and regions, including Boston and Cambridge, Massachusetts; St. Louis, Missouri; Seattle, Washington; Baltimore, Maryland;

Orange County, California; and the Naugatuck Valley, Connecticut, have initiated public sector or nonprofit conversion efforts designed to monitor, cajole, and act when military plant closings occur. All stand to benefit from the experience of these six pioneering efforts.

We recommend a number of strategies to encourage conversion. First, conversion activists must work diligently to secure management cooperation. However, planners and activists must expect antagonism, at least initially, from the contractor sector and be ready to consider regulation rather than relying on voluntary action. This is equivalent to the histories of environmental protection, worker health and safety laws, and early warning notification in the case of plant closings.[13] In each case, behavioral norms had to be imposed on companies and monitored by the public sector. All such regulations were opposed by organized business interests, who sometimes succeeded in watering down but not defeating them. Most companies, however, have learned to live with them in the longer run.

Companies should be offered carrots, as well as threatened with sticks, to engage in conversion planning. Existing tax incentives that encourage companies to close facilities should be eliminated and, in their place, cost sharing for planning as well as technical and financial assistance for new ventures should be provided. These should be equally available to old as well as new owners, whether private or public, and should require evidence of ongoing worker and community involvement before being awarded. Getting military contractors to face the new reality of shrinking budgets may not prove any more difficult than bringing auto and steel company managements into the modern era of international competition. A concerted public sector program of education, incentives, and judicious regulation is the only hope, in our view.

Second, conversion efforts should focus on facilities but not necessarily on current management. New institutions should be built to operate as storefronts of "first resort" for military plants in trouble. Operating with the powers that local and regional authorities like urban renewal or the Tennessee Valley Authority have in the past, jobs authorities encompassing both military and civilian plant closings could help a specific constituency survey its options. They could conduct prefeasibility studies; package financial assistance for further product, marketing, and financial studies; exercise the power of eminent domain in the public interest to facilitate management turnover; and participate as an active party in plant restructuring, perhaps as landlord or as an equity partner. The Steel Valley Authority in the Pittsburgh area is an innovative new organization set up to perform these tasks and has been breaking new ground.

Third, site-based conversion planning will only work if the policies needed to support it become codified into law and exercised in the public domain. Legislation mandating alternative use planning and providing financial assistance for it has been introduced in both national and state legislatures. At the national level, the 101st Congress considered proposals by Weiss (H.R. 101), Gejdenson/Mavroules (H.R. 2252), Oaker (H.R. 486) and Pell (S.2097). House Majority leader Gephardt supported conversion legislation and advanced a consolidation measure for amendment to the FY 1991 Defense Authorization Bill which passed in October 1990.

The amendment provides $200 million for assistance to the individuals and communities affected by military cutbacks. The amendment did not include the more controversial aspect of the Weiss bill, namely its requirement that alternative use committees be established by all large military contractors. However, as the number of defense plant closings balloons, pressures to enact such national legislation increases.

We recommend state legislation which sets aside financial resources for conversion planning. This may play an important role in financing feasibility and marketing studies. State and local governments can also act as a catalyst for conversion by acting as a first market for new civilian products. Nevertheless, state legislation may not be sufficient to induce contractors to create alternative use committees nor can it channel enough financial resources to substitute for a national industrial and/or conversion policy. State and local legislation should work in tandem with federal policies.

These recommendations and the rationale for them return us to our theme of supply and demand side approaches to conversion. In general, dramatic shifts in the federal budget away from defense and toward social spending are not apt to happen, especially in an era of recession, without complementary initiatives on the supply side that will insure those with a stake in military production against the devastation of permanent job loss. However, the prospects for a purely supply side approach will be much less effective if not accompanied by new commitments from the federal government for expenditures on infrastructure, housing, the environment, and education. Many of the alternative products proposed at these six facilities—light rail at McDonnell-Douglas, Energy Conversion Plantship at Quincy, pollution monitoring devices at Unisys—require a government induced market either directly or through regulation. Prospects for orders for mass transit vehicles, multifamily housing, pollution control equipment, or new solid waste disposal technologies, for instance, would encourage some firms to make the costly transition from military production to commercial work (Faux and Sawicky in press).

Overall, our conclusions are at odds with those who dismiss facilities-based planning in favor of conventional economic development planning on the supply side and targeting the national budget on the demand side (Adams 1986, 24–28). The latter approach underestimates, in our view, the resistance that defense-dependent companies and communities can and have successfully put up to cuts in their programs without assurance of alternative livelihoods. It underestimates, too, the enthusiasm that workers can bring to a conversion effort, including being pro-peace, and the support that unions at the district and national level are willing to give to such initiatives. During the 1980s, in many other heavy industries, unions learned that their best bet may be something far more activist than adversarial collective bargaining—it may be assuming ownership of plants and running them themselves. Furthermore, the most powerful way of raising consciousness about national budgetary priorities may be the drama of tackling, case-by-case, military base closings and provoking creative thinking about what the local economy could be making instead.

Critics of facility conversion strategies suggest that they put supporters in an inherently marginal political position. We found that on the contrary, participation in such efforts proved to be empowering, broadening the political base for demilitarization and creating experiments and legislative innovations at the state and local level. Slowly, this entrepreneurial attitude is percolating up through political circles, challenging the view that in the United States the arms race originates and is sustained by decisions made in centralized bureaucracies in Washington impervious to public will. Unless attention is focused on displacement on a facility-by-facility basis, workers will be displaced and communities will face hardships. Fear of such a fate may feed into support for extending military spending and, worse, into support for more militaristic forays around the globe. We cannot do better than to echo IBEW local member Claudette Munson of Unisys: "Peace shouldn't be a hardship for anyone!"

NOTES

1 Conversion efforts were building throughout the 1980s, and a number of seminal books and articles have been written examining the case for conversion and suggesting how it might be done. See Greg Bischak (1991), Michael Renner (1990), Lloyd Dumas and Marek Thee (1989), Seymour Melman (1988), John Lynch (1987), Suzanne Gordon and Dave McFadden (1984), and Philip Webre (1979).

2 This is analogous to the case of commercial plant closings, where researchers have found that multiplant absentee-owned firms are more apt to close facilities than are single plant locally-owned firms (See for instance Bluestone and Harrison 1982, Calumet Project 1989).

3 The federal government owns a considerable number of defense plants, some dating from World War II and others more recently built. Some of these, often the most critical nuclear facilities, are GOGOs (government-owned and government-operated) such as the Hanford nuclear weapons facility currently being dismantled. Others, including many aircraft plants, are government-owned, contractor-operated plants.

4 A number of macroeconomists point out that in addition, military spending has been countercyclical. One Congressional Budget Office analyst stated in late 1990 that if a recession were to take place in 1991, military spending would be the most likely candidate in an effort to stimulate the economy (Hale 1990).

5 In Massachusetts, for example, annual earnings in the seven defense-related industries taken together approximately $33,000 in 1987, over 25% above the corresponding figure (roughly $26,000) in nondefense-related manufacturing and almost 60% above the average wage (approximately $21,000) in nonmanufacturing industries (Massachusetts State Department of Employment and Training 1989).

6 Other communities where organizing for conversion has taken place include Savannah, South Carolina; St. Louis, Missouri; Baltimore, Maryland; Chicago, Illinois; and San Diego, California. Generally these efforts have been community oriented rather than plant specific.

7 The Blaw-Knox case has been written up by the Calumet Project on Industrial Jobs (1989), Moberg (1986), and LeRoy and Feekin (1985). The following summary draws from all of these.

8 The bill, HB 697, would create an economic adjustment board within the State Department of Labor and Industry, consisting of representatives from business, labor, executive agencies, and the legislature. The board would be responsible for developing and monitoring an economic adjustment strategy and would fund local adjustment committees which would identify alternative business activities which could maximize employment and minimize dislocation in the event of crisis. The bill proposes $2 million appropriation for the economic adjustment board for its first year.

9 This section is based on personal interviews with Joel Yudken, Menlo Park, California, and Kate Squire, Berkeley, California. See also Yudken (1984).

10 This section is based on an interview with Tom Croft, Steel Valley Authority, former director of the Seattle Worker Center and documents from the Puget Sound Shipyards Industrial Jobs Commission (1989).

11 See the analysis of obstacles to organizing across such groups in Bean (1988).

12 See Bischak (1989) for an analysis of conversion of government-owned facilities.

13 See the analysis and proposals in Tri-State Conference on Steel (1989).

REFERENCES

Adams, G. 1986. Economic conversion misses the point. *Bulletin of Atomic Scientists* February:24–28.

Adams, G. 1990. *Potential Impact of Defense Spending Reductions on the United States Economy and State Employment*. Washington, D.C.: Defense Budget Project.

Bean, K. 1988. Reconversion in Connecticut. *Social Policy* Winter:46–49.

Bischak, G. 1989. Facing the second generation of the nuclear weapons complex: Renewal of the nuclear production base or economic conversion. In *Making Peace Possible: The Promise of Economic Conversion*, eds. L. Dumas and M. Thee. Oxford: Pergamon Press.

Bischak, G., ed. 1991. *Toward a Peace Economy in the United States*. New York: St. Martins Press.

Bluestone, B., and B. Harrison. 1982. *The Deindustrialization of America*. New York: Basic Books.

Booz Allen & Hamilton, Inc. 1986. *Potential Reuse Study of the Quincy Shipyard*. Bethesda, Maryland.

Brandow, J. 1987. *The Philadelphia Story*. Mountain View, California: Plowshare Press.

Cain, S. 1991. *Analysis of the FY 1992–93 Defense Budget Request*. Washington, D.C.: Defense Budget Project.

The Calumet Project on Industrial Jobs. 1989. *Preventing Plant Closings in Northwest Indiana: A Public Policy Program for Action*. East Chicago, Indiana.

Choate P., and S. Walter. 1981. *America in Ruins: Beyond the Public Pork Barrel*. Washington, D.C.: Council of State Planning Agencies.

Closson, M. 1990. *Economic Diversification: Opportunities and Problems*. Speech for Roundtable Conference on Economic Diversification 26 February. City Hall, Irvine, California.

Cooper, K. 1990. Recruiting among the ex-military. *The Washington Post* August 6:A9.

DeGrasse, R. 1987. Corporate diversification and conversion experience. In *Economic Adjustment and Conversion of Defense Industries*, ed. J. Lynch. Boulder and London: Westview Press.

Dumas, L. 1986. *The Overburdened Economy*. Berkeley and Los Angeles: University of California Press.

Dumas, L., and M. Thee 1989. *Making Peace Possible: The Promise of Economic Conversion*. Oxford: Pergamon Press.

Duncan, M. 1990. Local planning in Minnesota. *Nuclear Times* Summer:14.

Faux, J., and M. Sawicky. In press. *Investing the Peace Dividend: How to Break the Gramm-Rudman-Hollings Stalemate*. Washington, D.C.: Economic Policy Institute.

Files, C., and S. Melman. 1989. *Are the Defense Cuts Real?* mimeo, Washington, D.C.: National Commission for Economic Conversion and Disarmament.

Globa, V. 1990. Perpick, workers demand Unisys act to stop layoffs. *The Union Advocate* 93(18):1.

Gordon, S., and D. McFadden, eds. 1984. *Economic Conversion: Revitalizing America's Economy*. Cambridge, Massachusetts: Ballinger.

Hale, R. 1990. *The Outlook on Peace Dividend*. Paper presented at the Conference on Economic Issues of Disarmament, 30 November. South Bend, Indiana: University of Notre Dame.

Hill, C. 1991. *State and Local Legislation on Conversion of a Military to a Civilian Economy*. Washington, D.C.: National Commission on Economic Conversion and Disarmament.

Howland, M. 1988. *Plant Closings and Worker Displacement: The Regional Issues*. Kalamazoo, Michigan: W. E. Upjohn Institute for Employment Research.

Jobs With Peace. 1986. *League Island Development Corporation Mission Statement*. Philadelphia, Pennsylvania.

Kaufman, W. 1990. *Glasnost, Perestroika, and U.S. Defense Spending*. Washington, D.C.: Brookings Institution.

Kerson, R., and G. LeRoy. 1989. *State and Local Initiatives on Development Subsidies and Plant Closings*. Chicago: Federation for Industrial Retention and Renewal.

Kulik, J., and C. Fairchild. 1987. Worker assistance and placement experience. In *Economic Adjustment and Conversion of Defense Industries*, ed. J. Lynch. Boulder and London: Westview Press.

Lakey, G. 1986. *In the Liberty Bell's Shadow: Converting the Philadelphia Navy Yard*. Mountain View, California: Plowshare Press.

LeRoy, G., and L. Feekin. 1985. Converting tanks in Indiana. *Labor Research Review* 7:59–68.

Lovering, J. 1987. Militarism, capitalism, and the nation-state: Toward a realist synthesis. *Environment and Planning D* 5:283–302.

Lynch, J., ed. 1987. *Economic Adjustment and Conversion of Defense Industries*. Boulder and London: Westview Press.

Maki, W., D. Bogenschultz, C. Evans, and M. Senese. 1989. *Military Production and the Minnesota Economy: A Report for the Minnesota Task Force on Economic Conversion*. St. Paul: Department of Jobs and Training.

Maki, W., R. Bolan, and H. Akhavi-Pour. 1991. *Forging a Peace Economy in Minnesota:*

A Report for the Minnesota Task Force on Economic Conversion. St. Paul, Minnesota: Department of Jobs and Training.

Markham, J., and Associates. 1989. *The Unisys Alternative Use Project, Parts I and II.* St. Paul, Minnesota: Alternative Product Development Committee.

Markusen, A., and H. Yudken. In press. *Dismantling the Cold War Economy.* New York: Basic Books.

Massachusetts State Department of Employment and Training. 1989. *Defense Industry Profile.* Boston: Field Research Services.

McNeilly, M. 1990. *Braving the New World.* Mountain View, California: Plowshare Press.

Melman, S. 1983. *Profits Without Production.* New York: Alfred Knopf.

Melman, S. 1988. *The Demilitarized Society: Disarmament and Conversion.* Montreal: Harvest House.

Moberg, D. 1986. Hooked on tanks. *The Progressive* September:30–32.

National Commission for Economic Conversion and Disarmament. 1991. *Estimate of National Defense Industry Job Layoffs in 1990.* Washington, D.C.

President's Economic Adjustment Committee, Office of Economic Adjustment. 1986. *25 Years of Civilian Reuse: Summary of Completed Military Base Economic Adjustment Projects.* Washington, D.C.: Government Printing Office.

President's Economic Adjustment Committee, Office of Economic Adjustment. 1990. *Civilian Reuse of Former Military Bases.* Washington, D.C.: Government Printing Office.

Primack, P. 1990. Quincy Shipyard's Second Chance. *Boston Herald* Massachusetts: January 1.

Puget Sound Shipyards Industrial Jobs Commission. 1989. *Recapturing Markets for Puget Sound Shipyards: Survey, Analysis, Recommendations.* Seattle, Washington.

Quigley, P. 1989. Arms exports: The stop-gap alternative to Pentagon contracts. In *Making Peace Possible: The Promise of Economic Conversion*, eds. L. Dumas and M. Thee. Oxford: Pergamon Press.

Renner, M. 1990. *Swords into Plowshares: Converting to a Peace Economy.* Washington, D.C.: Worldwatch Institute.

Ruzkowski, J. 1990. *Early Warning Network Model.* Speech presented to the Labor and Business Working Group, Pennsylvania Economic Conversion Conference, 4 October. Harrisburg.

Sherman, E., and S. Meacham. 1983. *Conversion: New Hope for Shipbuilding?* (pamphlet) Weymouth, Massachusetts: South Shore Conversion Committee.

Stevenson, R. 1991. Contractor plans cutback of 27,000 jobs. *New York Times* May 2.

Tri-State Conference on Steel. 1989. *Industrial Renaissance: Building Support for National, Regional and Sectoral Reindustrialization.* Pittsburgh, Pennsylvania.

Webre, P. 1979. *Jobs to People—Planning for Conversion to New Industries.* Washington, D.C.: Exploratory Project on Economic Alternatives.

Weidenbaum, M. 1964. The transferability of defense industry resources to civilian uses. In *Convertability of Space and Defense Resources to Civilian Needs: A Search for New Employment Potentials.* Washington, D.C.: Subcommittee on Employment and Manpower. (Reprinted in J. Clayton, ed. 1970. *The Economic Impact of the Cold War.* New York: Harcourt, Brace & World.)

Wykle, L., W. Morehouse, and D. Dembo. 1991. *Worker Empowerment in a Changing Economy: Jobs, Military Production and the Environment*. New York: Apex Press.

Yudken, J. 1984. Conversion in the aerospace industry: The McDonnell-Douglas Project. In *Economic Conversion: Revitalizing America's Economy*, eds. S. Gordon and D. McFadden. Cambridge, Massachusetts: Ballinger.

The Los Angeles Rebellion: A Retrospective View

James H. Johnson, Jr.
Professor of Geography, University of California

Cloyzelle K. Jones
Professor of Education, University of Michigan

Walter C. Farrell, Jr.
Professor of Educational Policy and Community Studies, University of Wisconsin

Melvin L. Oliver
Associate Professor of Sociology, University of California

Although American cities have been rocked many times in recent decades by episodes of violent civil unrest, the 1992 Los Angeles riots—in terms of losses to life and property—were the worst in recent United States history. This article analyzes the causes of the Los Angeles "rebellion" and offers a critical review of existing public policies. The authors note that "the fires have been extinguished in south central Los Angeles and other cities, but the anger and rage continue to escalate, and they are likely to reemerge during another long, hot summer in our large urban centers" (p. 300). The authors conclude with a strategy for addressing the "seeds" of the rebellion.

This article was written nearly six weeks after widespread civil unrest erupted in Los Angeles on April 29, 1992, following the not-guilty verdict in the trial of the four white police officers accused of using excessive force in the arrest of Rodney King, a black motorist, approximately 15 months earlier. The looting and fire bombings have stopped, the fires have been extinguished, the National Guardsmen and the federal troops have been withdrawn, the loss of life and property has been assessed, and efforts to clean up and rebuild Los Angeles are under way. For the most part, a sense of calm—albeit ever so tenuous—has returned to the city, affording academics, government officials, the media, and the general public the opportunity to reflect on the causes and consequences of civil unrest.

In this article, we reflect on the Los Angeles civil disorder of 1992 from an urban political economy perspective. We begin by discussing the anatomy of the civil unrest and comparing it with other civil disorders in recent history. We then make a few retrospective comments about the police brutality trial and the events that occurred in its immediate aftermath. Next, we situate the civil unrest within the broader context of the recent demographic, social, and economic changes occurring in the Los Angeles society. We follow this with a brief but critical review of the existing policies and proposals that have been advanced to "rebuild" Los

Reprinted by permission of *Economic Development Quarterly* 6, 4, November 1992, Sage Publications.

Angeles. Finally, we outline our own strategy for redeveloping south central Los Angeles, one which is designed to address the real "seeds" of the civil unrest.

ANATOMY OF THE REBELLION

The recent civil unrest in Los Angeles was the worst such event in recent U.S. history. None of the major civil disorders of the 1960s, including the Watts rebellion of 1965, required a level of emergency response or exacted a toll—in terms of loss of life, injuries, and property damage and loss—comparable to the Los Angeles rebellion of 1992 (Table 1). The burning, looting, and violence that ensued following the rendering of a not-guilty verdict in the police brutality trial required the deployment of not only the full forces of the LAPD and the Los Angeles County Sheriff's Department, but also 10,000 National Guardsmen and 3,500 military personnel (Table 2). The Fire Department received 5,537 structure fire calls and responded to an estimated 500 fires. An estimated 4,000 businesses were destroyed. Forty-three people died and 2,383 people were injured, including 20 law enforcement and fire personnel. Property damage and loss has been estimated at between $785 million and $1 billion (Table 1).

TABLE 1   TOLL FROM SELECTED REBELLIONS

City/State	Date	Number arrested	Number injured	Number dead	Property damage	Other characteristics
Newark, NJ	July 12–17, 1967	n.a.	1,500	26	$58,796,605	300 fires set
Detroit, MI	July 23–28, 1967	7,000	2,000	43	$162,396,707	—
Los Angeles, CA	August 11–17, 1965	n.a.	1,032	34	$182,565,079	—
Washington, DC	April 4–9, 1968	6,036	1,202	9	$45,292,079	—
Los Angeles, CA	April 29–30, 1992	16,291	2,383	43	$785 million–$1 billion	500 fires set

Source: Data from "Toll from Other Riots," *USA Today,* May 5, 1992, p. 4A; Timothy Noah and David Wessel, "Urban Solutions: Inner City Remedies Offer Novel Plans—and Hope, Experts Say," *Wall Street Journal,* May 4, 1992, pp. A1, A16.
NOTE: n.a. = not available.

TABLE 2   LAW ENFORCEMENT PERSONNEL ON DUTY

Los Angeles Police and County Sheriff's Deputies	3,720
California Highway Patrol	2,300
Fire	2,700
National Guard	10,000
Army	2,500
Marines	1,500

Source: Data from "L.A. Aftermath at a Glance," *USA Today,* May 6, 1992, p. 3A.

TABLE 3 LOS ANGELES REBELLION, 1992: ARREST BY RACE/ETHNICITY
(APRIL 30 THROUGH MAY 4, 1992)

	LAPD	Sheriff's Department
Latino	2,764	728
Black	2,022	810
White	568	72
Other/unknown	84	2,408
Total	5,438	4,018

Source: Data from Virginia I. Postrel, "The Real Story Goes Beyond Black and White," *Los Angeles Times*, May 8, 1992, p. A11.

TABLE 4 LOS ANGELES REBELLION, 1992: ILLEGAL
ALIENS ARRESTED AND DEPORTED BY
COUNTRY OF ORIGIN

Mexico	360
El Salvador	62
Guatemala	35
Honduras	14
Jamaica	2
Other countries	4
Total (*N*)	477

Source: Data from George Ramos and Tracy Wilkinson, "Unrest Widens Rifts in Latino Population," *Los Angeles Times*, Washington edition, May 8, 1992, p. 1.

In contrast to the civil disorders of the 1960s, this was a multiethnic rebellion. The diversity is reflected in Table 3, which depicts, for the period April 30 through May 4, arrests by race/ethnicity. It has been estimated that 1,200 of the 16,000-plus arrested were illegal aliens, roughly 40% of whom were handed over to INS officials for immediate deportation (Table 4). Also in contrast to the civil disorders of the 1960s, the burning and looting were neither random nor limited to a single neighborhood; rather the response was targeted, systematic, and widespread, encompassing much of the legal city. This fact has led us to purposefully and consistently refer to the civil unrest as a *rebellion* as opposed to a *riot*.

THE VERDICT AND THE REBELLION IN RETROSPECT

We think it is safe to say that both the verdict rendered in the police brutality trial, and the widespread burning, looting, and violence that ensued after the jury issued its decision, *shocked* most Americans. In retrospect, however, we would like to suggest that both the verdict and the subsequent rebellion were quite predictable.

The outcome of the trial, in our view, was predictable for two reasons. The first pertains to the defense attorney's successful bid for a change of venue for the trial.

Simi Valley, the site of the trial, as well as Ventura County more generally, is a predominantly white community known for its strong stance on law and order, as evidenced by the fact that a significant number of LAPD officers live there.[1] Thus the four white police officers were truly judged by a jury of their peers.[2] Viewed in this context, the verdict should not have been unanticipated.

The second development that made the outcome of the trial predictable, in retrospect, was the defense attorneys' ability to put King, instead of the four white police officers, on trial. (We should note here, parenthetically, that the media are also guilty in this regard, as evidenced by their consistent characterization of the case as "The Rodney King Trial.") The defense attorneys, in effect, played the so-called race card; they painted King as unpredictable, dangerous, and uncontrollable, much as George Bush, in the 1988 presidential campaign, used Willie Horton, the convicted rapist released on a temporary work furlough only to commit another heinous crime, to paint Michael Dukakis as being soft on crime.[3]

In today's society, the Willie Horton stereotype, recent surveys tell us, is often applied categorically to black males, irrespective of their social and economic status, but especially if they reside in the inner city.[4] It is our contention that the jury agreed with the defense attorneys' portrayal of King as dangerous and uncontrollable, and thus rendered a verdict in favor of the four white police officers, notwithstanding the seemingly irrefutable videotaped evidence.

Why do we think, in hindsight, that the civil unrest following the verdict in the police brutality trial was predictable? We believe that the response was not about the verdict in the police brutality trial per se; rather, the civil unrest reflected the high degree of frustration and alienation that had built up among the citizens of south central Los Angeles over the past 20 years. The rebellion, as we view it in retrospect, was a response not to a *single* but rather *repeated* acts of what is widely perceived in the community to be blatant abuse of power by the police and the criminal justice system more generally.[5]

The civil unrest, as we view it in retrospect, was also a response to a number of broader, external forces that have increasingly isolated the south central Los Angeles community, geographically and economically, from the mainstream of the Los Angeles society.[6] These forces include recent structural changes in the local (and national) economy; wholesale disinvestment in the south central Los Angeles community by banks and other institutions, including the local city government; and nearly 2 decades of conservative federal policies that have simultaneously adversely affected the quality of life of the residents of south central Los Angeles and accelerated the decline and deterioration of their neighborhoods.

Moreover, these developments were occurring at a time when the community was experiencing a radical demographic transformation, an unprecedented change in population accompanied by considerable tensions and conflict between long-term residents and the more recent arrivals.[7] Viewed from this perspective, the verdict in the police brutality trial was merely the straw that "broke the proverbial camel's back."[8]

SEEDS OF THE REBELLION

The videotaped beating of Rodney King was only the most recent case in which there were serious questions about whether LAPD officers used excessive force to subdue or arrest a black citizen. For several years the LAPD has spent millions of taxpayers' dollars in compensation to local citizens who were victims of abuse, illegal search and seizures, and property damage. Moreover, the black citizens of the city of Los Angeles have been disproportionately victimized by the LAPD's use of the choke hold, a tactic employed to subdue individuals who are perceived to be uncooperative. During the 1980s, 18 citizens of Los Angeles died as a result of LAPD officers' use of the choke hold, and 16 of them reportedly were black.[9]

Accordingly, the not-guilty verdict rendered in the police brutality trial was also only the most recent in a series of cases in which the decisions emanating from the criminal justice system were widely perceived in the black community to be grossly unjust. This decision came closely on the heels of another controversial verdict in the Latisha Harlins case. A videotape revealed that Harlins—an honor student at a local high school—was fatally shot in the back of the head by a Korean shopkeeper following an altercation over a carton of orange juice. The shopkeeper was sentenced to 6 months of probation.[10]

These and related events have occurred in the midst of drastic demographic change in south central Los Angeles. Over the past 2 decades, the community has been transformed from a predominantly black to a mixed black and Latino area (Figure 1). Today, nearly one-half of the south central Los Angeles population is Latino. In addition, there also has been an ethnic succession in the local business environment, characterized by the exodus of many of the Jewish shopkeepers and a substantial influx of small, family-run Korean businesses. This ethnic succession in both the residential environment and the business community has not been particularly smooth. The three ethnic groups—blacks, Latinos, and Koreans—have found themselves in conflict and competition with one another over jobs, housing, and scarce public resources.[11]

Part of this conflict stems from the fact that the Los Angeles economy has undergone a fairly drastic restructuring over the past 2 decades.[12] This restructuring includes, on one hand, the decline of traditional, highly unionized, high-wage manufacturing employment; and on the other, the growth of employment in the high-technology manufacturing, the craft specialty, and the advanced services sectors of the economy. As Figure 2 shows, south central Los Angeles—the traditional industrial core of the city—bore the brunt of the decline in manufacturing employment, losing 70,000 high-wage, stable jobs between 1978 and 1982.[13]

At the same time that these well-paying and stable jobs were disappearing from south central Los Angeles, local employers were seeking alternative sites for their manufacturing activities. As a consequence of these seemingly routine decisions, new employment growth nodes or "technopoles" emerged in the San Fernando Valley, in the San Gabriel Valley, and in El Segundo near the airport in Los Angeles County, as well as in nearby Orange County (Figure 3).[14] In addition, a number of

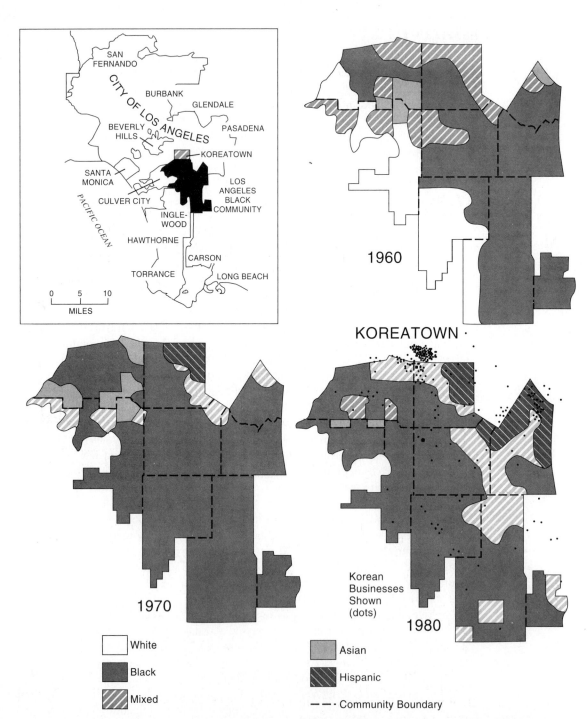

FIGURE 1 Ethnic Change in South Central Los Angeles, 1960–80, and Locations of Korean Businesses, 1987. *Source*: Los Angeles Community Development Department, *Ethnic Clusters of Los Angeles* (Los Angeles: Community Development Department, 1977, 1982); and Korean Chamber of Commerce of Los Angeles, *Directory of Korean Businesses* (Los Angeles: Korean Chamber of Commerce of Los Angeles, 1987).

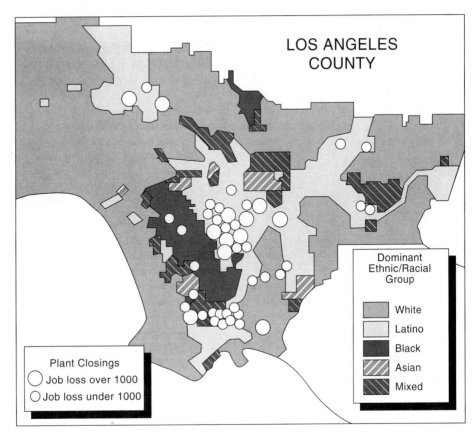

FIGURE 2   Plant Closings in L.A. County, 1978–82. *Source*: Data from U.S. Bureau of the Census, *1990 Census of Population* (Washington, DC: U.S. Department of Commerce, 1991); and The Data Center, *Plant Shutdown Directory* (Oakland, CA: The Data Center, 1978–1982).

Los Angeles-based employers established production facilities in the Mexican border towns of Tijuana, Ensenada, and Tecate. Between 1978 and 1982, over 200 Los Angeles-based firms, including Hughes Aircraft, Northrop, and Rockwell, as well as a host of smaller firms, participated in this deconcentration process.[15] Such capital flight, in conjunction with the plant closings, has essentially closed off to the residents of south central Los Angeles access to what were formerly well-paying, unionized jobs.[16]

It is important to note that, although new industrial spaces were being established elsewhere in Los Angeles County (and in nearby Orange County as well as along the U.S.-Mexico border), new employment opportunities were emerging within or near the traditional industrial core in south central Los Angeles (Figure 3). But, unlike the manufacturing jobs that disappeared from this area, the new jobs are in competitive sector industries, which rely primarily on undocumented labor and pay, at best, minimum wage.

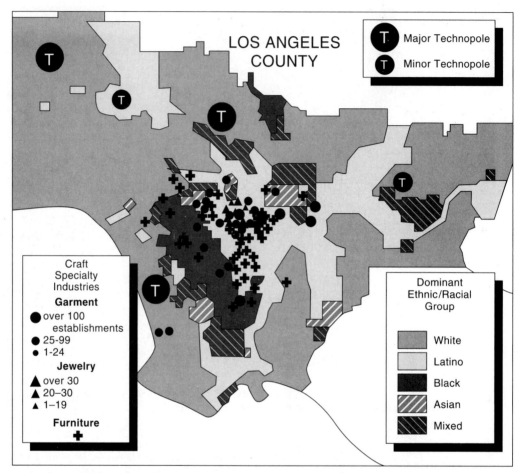

FIGURE 3 Locations of Craft Specialty Industries and Job Growth Technopoles in L.A. County, 1990. *Source*: Data from Maya Blum, Kathryn Carlson, Estela J. Morales, Ross Nussbaum, and Patricia J. Wilson, "Black Male Joblessness, Spatial Mismatch, and Employer Preferences: A Case Study of Los Angeles," unpublished paper, Center for the Study of Urban Poverty, University of California, Los Angeles, May 1992.

In part as a consequence of these developments, and in part as a function of employers' openly negative attitudes toward black workers, the black male jobless rate in some residential areas of south central Los Angeles hovers around 50%. Whereas joblessness is the central problem for black males in south central Los Angeles, concentration in low-paying, bad jobs in competitive sector industries is the main problem for the Latino residents of the area. Both groups share a common fate: incomes below the poverty level (Figure 4). One group is the working poor (Latinos) and the other is the jobless poor (blacks).[17]

In addition to the adverse impact of structural changes in the local economy,

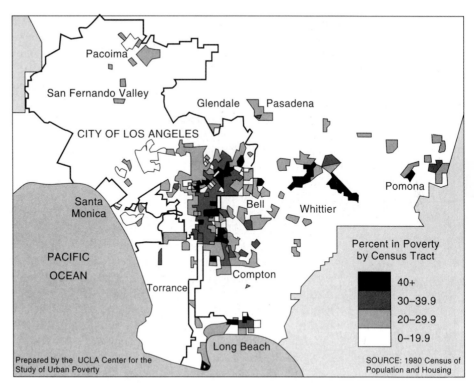

FIGURE 4   Poverty Areas in the Los Angeles Area. *Source*: Data from U.S. Bureau of the Census, *1980 Census of Population and Housing, Census Tracts* (Washington, DC: U.S. Department of Commerce, 1981).

south central Los Angeles also has suffered as a result of the failure of local institutions to devise and implement a plan to redevelop and revitalize the community. In fact, over the past 2 decades, the local city government has pursued consciously a policy of downtown and westside redevelopment at the expense of south central Los Angeles. One only needs to look at the skyline of downtown and the so-called Wilshire corridor—that 20-mile stretch extending along Wilshire Boulevard from downtown to the Pacific Ocean—to see the impact of this policy.[18]

Finally, the seeds of the rebellion are rooted in nearly 2 decades of conservative policy making and implementation at the federal level. Many policy analysts talk about the adverse impact on minorities and their communities of Democratic President Lyndon Johnson's "War on Poverty" programs of the 1960s, but we must not lose sight of the fact that the Republicans have been in control of the White House for all but 4 (the Carter years) of the past 20 years.[19] A number of public policies implemented during this period, and especially during the years when Ronald Reagan was president, we contend, served as sparks for the recent civil unrest. Three of these policy domains are worthy of note here.

The first pertains to the federal government's establishment of a laissez faire business climate in order to facilitate the competitiveness of U.S. firms. Such a policy, in retrospect, appears to have facilitated the large number of plant closings in south central Los Angeles and capital flight to the U.S.-Mexico border and other Third World countries. Between 1982 and 1989, there were 131 plant closings in Los Angeles, idling 124,000 workers. Fifteen of those plants moved to Mexico or overseas.[20]

The second involved the federal government's dismantling of the social safety net in minority communities. Perhaps most devastating for the south central Los Angeles area has been the defunding of community-based organizations (CBOs). Historically, CBOs were part of that collectivity of social resources in the urban environment that encouraged the inner-city disadvantaged, especially disadvantaged youth, to pursue mainstream avenues of social and economic mobility and discouraged dysfunctional or antisocial behavior. In academic lingo, CBOs were effective "mediating" institutions in the inner city.[21]

During the past decade or so, however, CBOs have become less effective as mediating institutions. The reason for this is that the federal support they received was substantially reduced. In 1980, when Reagan took office, CBOs received an estimated 48% of their funding from the federal government.[22] As part of the Reagan Administration's dismantling of the social safety net, many CBOs were forced to substantially reduce programs that benefited the most disadvantaged in the community. Inner-city youth have been most adversely affected by this defunding of community-based initiatives and other safety-net programs.

It should be noted, moreover, that the dismantling of the social safety net has been replaced with a criminal dragnet. That is, rather than allocate support for social programs that discourage or prevent disadvantaged youth from engaging in dysfunctional behavior, over the past decade or so, the federal government has pursued a policy of resolving the problems of the inner city through the criminal justice system.

Given this shift in policy orientation, it should not be surprising that, nationally, 25% of prime working-age young black males are either in prison, in jail, on probation, or otherwise connected to the criminal justice system.[23] Although reliable statistics are hard to come by, the anecdotal evidence suggests that at least 25% of the young black males in south central Los Angeles have had a brush with the law. What are the prospects of landing a job if you have a criminal record? Incarceration breeds despair and in the employment arena, it is the scarlet letter of unemployability.[24]

Educational initiatives enacted during the late 1970s and early 1980s, which were designed to address the so-called crisis in American education, constitute the third policy domain. There is actually a very large body of social science evidence that shows that such policies as tracking by ability group, grade retention, and the increasing reliance on standardized tests as the ultimate arbiter of educational success, have, in fact, disenfranchised large numbers of black and brown youth. In urban school systems they are disproportionately placed in special education classes and are more likely than their white counterparts to be subjected to extreme disciplinary sanctions.[25]

The effects of these policies in the Los Angeles Unified School District (LAUSD) are evident in the data on school-leaving behavior. For the Los Angeles Unified School District as a whole, 39.2% of all of the students in the class of 1988 dropped out at some point during their high school years. However, for high schools in south central Los Angeles, the drop-out rates were substantially higher, between 63% and 79% (Figure 5). It is important to note that the drop-out problem is not limited to the high school population. According to data compiled by LAUSD, approximately 25% of the students in the junior high schools in south central Los Angeles dropped out during the 1987–88 academic year (Figure 6).

Twenty years ago it was possible to drop out of school before graduation and

FIGURE 5   Dropout Rates in Los Angeles Unified School District Senior High Schools, Class of 1988. *Source*: California Basic Educational Data System, *Three Year Summary: Number of Dropouts in California Public High School Instruction* (Sacramento, CA: CBEDS, 1989).

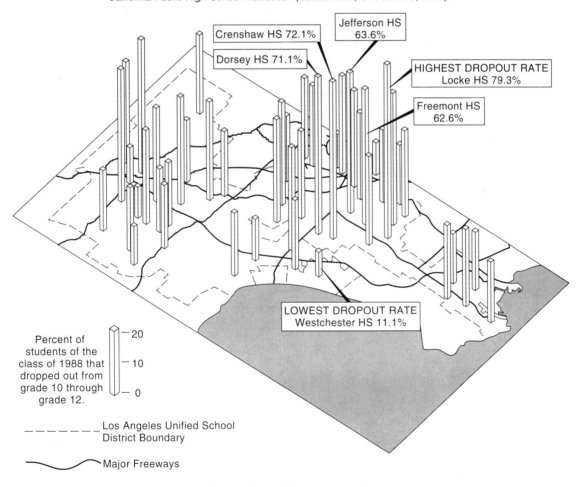

Jefferson HS
63.6%

Crenshaw HS 72.1%

Dorsey HS 71.1%

HIGHEST DROPOUT RATE
Locke HS 79.3%

Freemont HS
62.6%

LOWEST DROPOUT RATE
Westchester HS 11.1%

Percent of students of the class of 1988 that dropped out from grade 10 through grade 12.
— 20
— 10
— 0

_ _ _ _ _ _ _ Los Angeles Unified School District Boundary

⌒⌒⌒ Major Freeways

Prepared by the UCLA Center for the Study of Urban Poverty
Chase Langford, Cartographer

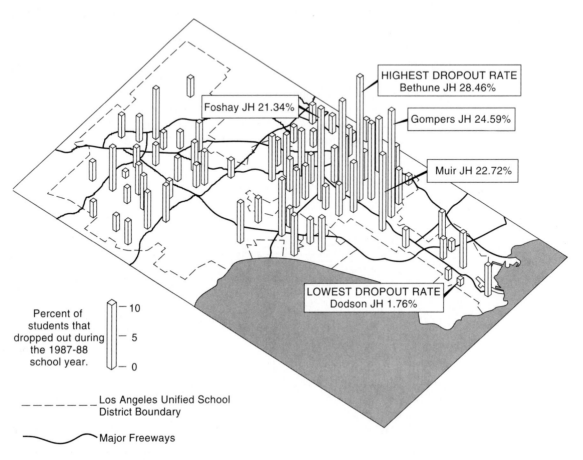

Percent of students that dropped out during the 1987-88 school year.

– – – – – – Los Angeles Unified School District Boundary

⌒⌒⌒⌒ Major Freeways

Prepared by the UCLA Center for the Study of Urban Poverty
Chase Langford, Cartographer

FIGURE 6   Dropout Rates in Los Angeles Unified School District Junior High Schools, 1987–88. *Source*: LAUSD, *Dropout Rates in LAUSD Junior High Schools, 1978–88*. Research Development Department (Los Angeles: Los Angeles Unified School District, 1989).

find a well-paying job in heavy manufacturing in south central Los Angeles. Today, however, those types of jobs are no longer available in the community, as we noted previously. Juxtaposing the adverse effects of a restructured economy and the discriminatory aspects of education reforms, what emerges is a rather substantial pool of inner-city males of color who are neither at work nor in school. These individuals are, in effect, idle; and previous research shows us that it is this population that is most likely to be in gangs, to engage in drug trafficking, and to participate in a range of other criminal behavior.[26] Moreover, we know that it is this population of idle minority males who experience the most difficulty forming and maintaining stable families, which accounts, at least in part, for the high percentage of female-headed families with incomes below the poverty level in south central Los Angeles.

THE FEDERAL BLUEPRINT

How do we simultaneously deal with the seeds of the rebellion, as we have characterized them above, and rebuild the physical infrastructure of south central Los Angeles? In attempting to answer this question, we shall limit the discussion here to the federal government's blueprint, as the local "Rebuild LA" initiative remains somewhat vague in both scope and content.[27]

Table 5 highlights the Bush Administration's plan to revitalize the south central Los Angeles community. In actuality, the main elements of the plan constitute what Secretary of Housing and Urban Development, Jack Kemp, termed, prior to the Los Angeles rebellion, as his blueprint for a "Conservative War on Poverty."[28]

Kemp promotes enterprise zones, as Table 5 shows, as being the key to job creation and retention in the inner cities. He proposes to eliminate capital gains taxes and reduce levies for business that will locate in specified inner-city areas. However, there is no history of success of such strategies in poor communities like south central Los Angeles.

Moreover, recent research has indicated, as we noted earlier, that those white businesses in the inner city are especially reluctant to hire black males. Employer responses to a field survey in Chicago showed that they generally embrace the prevailing racial stereotypes about this group—that they are lazy, lack a good work ethic, are ineducable, and, perhaps most important, dangerous.[29]

TABLE 5   THE FEDERAL BLUEPRINT

Program	Description	$ Allocation
Emergency aid	To address immediate needs of citizens impacted by the crisis.	$600 million
"Weed and Seed"	Beef up law enforcement and social services (Headstart, Job Corps, WIC, Safe Haven Program) in the inner city.	$500 million
"Project HOPE"	Encourage homeownership among residents of public housing projects	$1 billion
"Move to Opportunity"	Five-city plan to subsidize welfare families that move from depressed inner-city areas, using housing vouchers and providing advice.	$20 million
Welfare reform	Raise to $10,000 from $1,000 the amount of assets that welfare recipients may accumulate without losing benefits. Builds on a Wisconsin Plan to discourage welfare mothers from having more babies.	
Urban enterprise zones	Establishment of specifically designated areas where investment and job creation would be encouraged through incentives such as tax breaks and regulating relief.	

Source: Data from Jessica Lee, "Bush Presents His Urban Policy," *USA Today,* May 6, 1992, p. 8A.

Couple this social reality with the fact that the major priorities for businesses when making locational decisions are access to markets, access to a quality labor force (code words for no blacks), infrastructure, and crime rates. These business factors are considered to be much more important in site selection than tax rates. And where enterprise zones have been successful, employers have brought their work force with them rather than employing community residents, or they used these enterprise locations as warehouse points where there is a need for few workers.[30]

Secretary Kemp has had a long-term commitment to empower the poor by making them homeowners—the theory being that individuals will have a stronger commitment to maintaining that which they own and to joining in other efforts to enhance their general neighborhood environment. Project HOPE, as it is called, would make homeownership affordable (Table 5). This idea had languished in the Bush Administration for the past 4 years, until the Los Angeles rebellion pushed it to center stage.[31]

However, this program would lock poor people into communities that are isolated, socially and economically, from the mainstream employment and educational opportunities. And it would do nothing to expand the housing stock. Project HOPE is analogous to the reservation status provided to Native Americans in the government's effort to empower them. As a result, in part, of their isolation over time, Native Americans currently have some of the highest rates of unemployment, alcoholism, and domestic abuse of any American ethnic and racial group.

The federal blueprint, as Table 5 shows, also includes monies to give the poor inner-city residents of south central Los Angeles greater choice in deciding what school their children will attend. The encouragement of educational choice among public and private schools—using public dollars—needs to be carefully monitored. Although promoted as the solution to the crisis in public education, poor parents are at risk of being losers in a system where choice is "unchecked." The much heralded Wisconsin Parental Choice Plan has achieved a modicum of success because this public/private initiative was carefully designed to meet the educational needs of poor children. The legislature structured it to mandate that private educational providers would develop their recruitment strategies and curricular offerings to specifically accommodate poor students. Because nonpoor youngsters already had a wide range of educational choice, it was appropriate that poor children—who are the least well served in our educational system—have their interests served. Educational choice should be driven by the needs of the poor if we are to revitalize education in inner cities.[32]

Finally, the Bush Administration proposes to spend $500 million on a "Weed and Seed Program," which is designed to rid the community of the violent criminal element and to provide support for programs like Headstart and Job Corps, which are known to benefit the urban disadvantaged and their communities (Table 5). As it is currently envisioned, however, the program places too much emphasis on the "weed" component and not enough on the "seed" component. Of the $500 million proposed for the program, only $109 million is targeted for "seed" programs like Headstart. With nearly 80% of the proposed funding targeted for the "weed" component, the primary goal of the program is, clearly, to continue the warehousing of large numbers of poor, inner-city youth in the penal system.[33]

This, in our view, is a misplaced programmatic focus, as it is ever so clear that harsher jail and prison terms are not deterrents to crime in inner-city areas like south central Los Angeles. What is needed in south central Los Angeles, instead, is more "seed" money; and to the extent that increased police power is deployed in south central Los Angeles, it should be via a community policing construct where officers are on the street interfacing with community residents prior to the commission of a crime.

We are, quite frankly, dubious of the so-called conservative war on poverty and, in particular, of its likely impact in south central Los Angeles. The federal blueprint, and apparently the local "Rebuild LA" initiative headed by Peter Ueberroth as well, are built on the central premise that, if the proper incentives are offered, the private sector will, in fact, play the leading role in the revitalization and redevelopment of south central Los Angeles. We do not think this is going to happen for the reasons stated earlier: The types of governmental incentives currently under consideration in Washington are not high on private businesses' locational priority list.

In view of these facts—and the social science evidence is clear on the ineffectiveness of enterprise zone legislation both in Britain and in 36 states in this country[34]—we firmly believe that what is needed to rebuild south central Los Angeles is a *comprehensive public works employment program*, modeled on President Roosevelt's Works Progress Administration (WPA) program of the 1930s. Jobs to rebuild the infrastructure of south central Los Angeles can provide meaningful employment for the jobless in the community, including the hard-core disadvantaged, and can be linked to the skilled trades' apprenticeship training programs.

To incorporate the hard-core disadvantaged in such a program, however, would require a restructuring of the current Private Industry Council, Job Training Partnership Act Program (JTPA). The program must dispense with its performance-based approach in training where funding is tied to job placement. This approach does not work for the hard-core disadvantaged because training agencies, under the current structure, have consistently engaged in creaming—recruiting the most "job ready" segment of the inner-city population—to ensure their continued success and funding. Meanwhile, the hard-core unemployed have received scant attention and educational upgrading.[35]

We are convinced that a WPA-type initiative combined with a restructured JTPA program will go a long way toward resolving the chronic jobless problem, especially among young males of color in the community, and toward rebuilding the infrastructure of south central Los Angeles. Such a program would have several goals that would enhance the social and economic viability of south central Los Angeles. First, it would create meaningful jobs that could provide the jobless with skills transferable to the private sector. Second, it would rebuild a neglected infrastructure making south central Los Angeles an attractive place to locate for business and commerce. Third, and most important, by reconnecting this isolated part of the city to the major arteries of transportation, by building a physical infrastructure that could support the social and cultural life of this rich multicultural area (e.g., museums, public buildings, housing), and by enhancing the ability of community and educational institutions to educate and socialize the young, this plan would go far in providing a sustainable "public space" in the community. For it is our contention that only when south central Los Angeles is perceived as an economically vibrant and socially attractive public space will the promise of this multicultural community be fulfilled. Thus far, private sector actions and federal government programs and proposals have done nothing to facilitate this goal.

CONCLUSIONS

The fires have been extinguished in south central Los Angeles and other cities, but the anger and rage continue to escalate, and they are likely to reemerge during another long, hot summer in our large urban centers. Political, business, and civic leaders have rushed to advance old and new strategies and solutions to this latest urban explosion. But much of what is being proposed is simply disjointed and/or deja vu.

Clearly there is a need for additional money to resolve the underlying causes of this urban despair and devastation, but money alone is not enough. Government is constitutionally mandated to ensure "domestic tranquility," but government alone cannot empower poor communities. And although blacks and other people of color have a special role and obligation to rebuild their neighborhoods because they are the majority of the victims and the vandals, they cannot solely assume this burden of responsibility.

What is needed, in our view, is a reconceptualization of problem solving where we meld together, and invest with full potential, those strategies offered from liberals and conservatives, from Democrats and Republicans, and from whites and people of color. Three cities (Milwaukee, Los Angeles, and Detroit, respectively) have served, individually and collectively, as urban laboratories where we have engaged in action research and proffered solutions to urban problems, which have generated violent outbursts.

The contentious state of police/minority community relations has served as the linchpin of urban unrest in each instance. While relations have improved in several large cities in recent years, the Los Angeles Police Department (LAPD) has been frozen in time. Black and Hispanic males have been particularly brutalized in their encounters with police, the majority of whom are white males. But more disconcerting is the fact that poor, central-city minority communities have become more crime ridden of late. Thus minorities find themselves in the ambiguous situation of needing greater police services on the one hand and protection from the excesses of those same services on the other. This contradictory situation had kept relations between these groups at a race/class boiling point.

More police officers are desperately needed in high-crime communities disproportionately populated by the poor. Local, state, and federal dollars (federal funds for this initiative are in the crime bill before Congress) need to be quickly allocated toward this end. At present, violent felons are beginning to outnumber police officers in many of our urban centers.[36] As we noted previously, this increase in police power should be deployed via a community policing program. Such an effort can serve to control minor offenses and to build trust between police and community residents. Community policing has evidenced positive results in Detroit and Philadelphia, and is showing encouraging signs in Milwaukee and numerous other large and small cities. In addition, the intensive recruitment of minority officers and specific, ongoing (and evaluated) diversity training will further reduce police/minority community tensions. But most important in this effort is enlightened, decisive leadership from the office of the chief, a position of abysmal failure in Los Angeles.

If the central-city poor are provided comprehensive assistance, there is a high probability that we can bring them into mainstream society, enhance their acceptance of personal responsibility, and improve their personal values. But a change in personal values alone, as suggested by some public experts, will not substitute for job training, job creation, and the removal of racial stereotypes and discrimination.[37] The spatial concentration of contemporary poverty presents significant challenges to policymakers and human service providers alike. Although numerous programs and initiatives have been instituted to combat these problems, they suffer from three important weaknesses.

First, there is a lack of coordination among programs aimed at improving the life chances of citizens in poor communities. Second, no systematic steps have been taken to evaluate existing efforts, to insure that the programs are effectively targeting the "hardest to serve" adults with low skills and limited work history and youth who are teen parents or school dropouts. Third, there is no comprehensive strategy for planning future resource allocations as needs change and as these communities expand in size.

A recent national study of training and employment programs under the Job Training and Partnership Act revealed that little has been done to address the remedial educational needs of high school drop-outs, and that those with the greatest need for training and employment services are not targeted. However, overcoming these and other program weaknesses is not sufficient to solve these complex problems. A strategic plan is needed to alleviate the social ills associated with concentrated poverty.

There is a need to conduct a comprehensive inventory of agencies and institutions that provide services to populations in poverty areas. We also need to assess and evaluate the service providers' performance in an attempt to identify strengths, weaknesses, and missing links in their service delivery systems. Based on these findings, a strategy should be devised for a more effective and coordinated use of existing resources and for generating new resources to address unmet needs. Finally, we need to propose a plan of action that would encourage development in the 1990s—those that link together the various program initiatives.

And most important, representatives of the affected ethnic and racial groups must be in key decision-making roles if these efforts are to achieve success.[38] Citizens of color, individually and through their community, civic, and religious institutions, bear a responsibility to promote positive values and lifestyles in their communities and to socialize their youth into the mainstream. But they cannot do this alone.

They cannot be held accountable for the massive plant closings, disinvestments, and exportation of jobs from our urban centers to Third World countries. There must be an equality in status in responsibility and authority across race and class lines if we are to resolve our urban crises. Government, in a bipartisan fashion, must direct its resources to those programs determined to be successful with the poor, the poor must be permitted to participate in the design of programs for their benefit, and society at all levels must embrace personal responsibility and a commitment to race and gender equity.

Let us conclude, simply, by saying that if we do not take vigilant and positive action quickly to become more actively involved in south central Los Angeles and in poor communities in other U.S. cities, there will be a fire next time, only the next time will be much sooner than it was the last time.

NOTES

1 Jane Gross, "In Simi Valley, Defense of a Shared Way of Life," *The New York Times*, May 4, 1992, p. A9.

2 David Margolick, "As Venues Are Changed, Many Ask How Important a Role Race Should Play," *The New York Times*, May 23, 1992, p. A1.

3 Walter C. Farrell, Jr., James H. Johnson, Jr., and Cloyzelle K. Jones, "Field Notes from the Rodney King Trial and the Los Angeles Rebellion," April 28, 29, May 2, 3, and 4.

4 See, for example, Joleen Kirschenman and Kathryn Neckerman, "We'd Love to Hire Them But . . . : The Meaning of Race for Employers," in *The Urban Underclass*, eds. Christopher Jencks and Paul Peterson (Washington, DC: Brookings, 1990), pp. 203–24; Margaret Austin Turner, Michael Fix, and Raymond Struyk, *Opportunities Denied, Opportunities Diminished: Discrimination in Hiring*, unpublished project report (Washington, DC: Urban Institute Press, 1991).

5 Jason De Parle, "Year-Old Study on Police Abuse Is Issued by U.S.," *The New York Times*, May 20, 1992, pp. A1, A10; Joseph D. MacNamara, "When the Police Create Disorder," *Los Angeles Times*, May 1992, pp. M1, M6; Melvin L. Oliver, Walter C. Farrell, Jr., and James H. Johnson, Jr., "A Quarter-Century of Slipping Backward," *Los Angeles Times*, August 10, 1990, p. B7; Dennis Schatzman, "50–60 Percent of Riot Arrestees Had No Prior Contact with the Law," *Los Angeles Times*, May 28, 1992, pp. A1, A16; David K. Shipler, "Khaki, Blue, and Blacks," *The New York Times*, May 26, 1992, p. A15.

6 Ed Soja, Rebecca Morales, and Goetz Wolff, "Urban Restructuring: An Analysis of Social and Spatial Change in Los Angeles," *Economic Geography* 58 (1983): 221–35; Melvin L. Oliver and James H. Johnson, Jr., "Interethnic Conflict in an Urban Ghetto: The Case of Blacks and Latinos in Los Angeles," *Research in Social Movements, Conflicts, and Change* 6 (1984): 57–94; James H. Johnson, Jr. and Melvin L. Oliver, "Interethnic Minority Conflict in Urban America: The Effects of Economic and Social Dislocations," *Urban Geography* 10 (1989): 449–63; James H. Johnson, Jr. and Melvin L. Oliver, "Economic Restructuring and Black Male Joblessness: A Reassessment," in *Urban Labor Market and Job Opportunity*, ed. George Paterson and Wayne Vrohman (Washington, DC: Urban Institute, 1992), pp. 113–47.

7 Oliver and Johnson, "Interethnic Conflict in Urban Ghetto"; Johnson and Oliver, "Interethnic Minority Conflict in Urban America."

8 Melvin L. Oliver, "Its the Fire Everytime, And We Do Nothing," *Los Angeles Times*, May 1, 1992, p. A10.

9 Farrell, Johnson, and Jones, "Field Notes."

10 Elaine Kim, "They Armed in Self-Defense." *Newsweek*, May 18, 1992, p. 10; Seth Mydans, "Jury Acquits Los Angeles Policemen in Taped Beating," *The New York Times*, April 29, 1992, pp. A1, A8.

11 Oliver and Johnson, "Interethnic Conflict in an Urban Ghetto"; Johnson and Oliver, "Interethnic Minority Conflict in Urban America"; and James H. Johnson, Jr. and Curtis C. Roseman, "Increasing Black Outmigration from Los Angeles: The Role of Household Dynamics and Kinship Systems," *Annals of the Association of American Geographers* 80 (1990): 205–22.

12 Soja, Morales, and Wolff, "Urban Restructuring"; Johnson and Oliver, "Economic Restructuring and Black Male Joblessness in U.S. Metropolitan Areas"; Johnson and Oliver, "Economic Restructuring and Black Male Joblessness in U.S. Metropolitan Areas: A Reassessment."

13 Soja, Morales, and Wolff, "Urban Restructuring."

14 A. J. Scott, "Flexible Production Systems and Regional Development: The Rise of New Industrial Spaces in North America and Western Europe." *International Journal of Urban and Regional Research* 12 (1988): 61–113; A. J. Scott, *Metropolis: From Division of Labor to Urban Form* (Berkeley: University of California Press, 1986).

15 Soja, Morales, and Wolff, "Urban Restructuring."

16 Johnson and Oliver, "Economic Restructuring and Black Male Joblessness."

17 Johnson and Oliver, "Economic Restructuring and Black Male Joblessness"; Soja, Morales, and Wolff, "Urban Restructuring"; Ed Luttwak, "The Riots: Underclass vs. Immigrants," *The New York Times*, May 15, 1992, p. A15.

18 Robert Beauregard and H. Braviel Holcomb, *Revitalizing Cities*, Resource Publication in Geography (Washington, DC: Association of American Geographers, 1981).

19 See Gary Orfield and Carole Ashkinaze, *The Closing Door: Conservative Policy and Black Opportunity* (Chicago: University of Chicago Press, 1991).

20 These statistics were extracted from The Data Center's *Plant Shutdowns Monitor Directory* for the years 1982 through 1989.

21 See P. L. Berger and R. J. Newhaus, "To Empower People: The Role of Mediating Structures in Public Policy" (Washington, DC: American Enterprise Institute, 1977); Melvin L. Oliver, "The Urban Black Community as Network: Toward a Social Network Perspective," *Sociological Quarterly* 29 (1988): 623–45.

22 L. M. Salamon, "Non-Profit Organizations: The Lost Opportunity," in *The Reagan Record*, eds. John L. Palmer and Isabel V. Sawhill (Cambridge, MA: Ballinger, 1984), pp. 261–85.

23 Marc Mauer, "Americans Behind Bars," *Criminal Justice*, Winter 1992, pp. 12–18, 38.

24 Johnson and Oliver, "Economic Restructuring and Black Male Joblessness."

25 Gary Orfield, "Exclusion of the Majority: Shrinking College Access and Public Policy in Metropolitan Los Angeles," *The Urban Review* 20 (1988): 147–63.

26 W. K. Viscusi, "Market Incentives for Criminal Behavior," in *The Black Youth Employment Crisis*, eds. R. B. Freeman and H. J. Holzer (Chicago: University of Chicago Press, 1986).

27 Richard Stevenson, "With Few Tools, Ueberroth Begins Mission in Riot Areas," *The New York Times*, May 5, 1991, p. A23.

28 Marshall Ingwerson, "Radical Intent: HUD Chief Wants Poverty to Top Conservative Agenda," *The Christian Science Monitor*, October 11, 1991, p. 9.

29 Kirschenman and Neckerman, "We'd Love to Hire Them But."

30 David Osborne, "The Kemp Cure-All," *The New Republic*, April 3, 1989, pp. 21–25; and Neal R. Pierce, "Kemp's Enterprise Zones: Breakthrough or Chimera?" *Nation's Cities Weekly*, June 5, 1989, p. 4.

31 Kathleen Decker, "Kemp Champions Blacks and Poor: Secretary Preaches Theme of Hope in Squalor of Ghettos," *Los Angeles Times*, April 19, 1989, p. A1.

32 Walter C. Farrell, Jr. and Jackolyn E. Mathews, "School Choice and the Educational Opportunities of African American Children," *Journal of Negro Education* 59 (1990): 526–37; Gary George and Walter C. Farrell, Jr., "School Choice and African American Students: A Legislative View," *Journal of Negro Education* 59 (1990): 521–25.

33 Terry Eastland, "Weed and Seed: Root Out Crime, Nurture Poor," *Wall Street Journal*, May 14, 1992, p. A1.

34 Osborne, "Kemp Cure-All."

35 "90 Days to Learn to Scrub? Sure, If Uncle Sam's Paying," *Business Week*, January 20, 1992, p. 70.

36 "Put Police Before Prisons" (The New York Times Editorial), *The New York Times*, May 23, 1992, p. A10.

37 John D. Kasarda, "Why Asians Can Prosper Where Blacks Fail," *Wall Street Journal*, May 28, 1992, p. A20; Lawrence M. Meade, "Job Programs and Other Bromides," *The New York Times*, May 19, 1992, p. A15; James Q. Wilson, "How to Teach Better Values in Inner Cities," *Wall Street Journal*, May 18, 1992, p. A14.

38 Robert Woodson, "Transform Inner Cities from the Grassroots Up," *Wall Street Journal*, June 1, 1992, p. A12.

SIX. ECONOMIC DEVELOPMENT—SUGGESTED READING

Beauregard, Robert. 1989. *Economic Restructuring and Political Response.* Newbury Park, CA: Sage Publications.

Becker, Gary. 1975. *Human Capital*, 2d ed. New York: Columbia.

Blakely, Edward J. 1989. *Planning Local Economic Development: Theory and Practice.* Newbury Park, CA: Sage Publications.

Bluestone, Barry, and Bennett Harrison. 1982. *The Deindustrialization of America.* New York: Basic Books.

Goldsmith, William W., and Edward J. Blakely. 1992. *Separate Societies: Poverty and Inequality in U.S. Cities.* Philadelphia: Temple University Press.

Hughes, Mark Alan. 1991. "Employment Decentralization and Accessibility: A Strategy for Stimulating Regional Mobility." *Journal of the American Planning Association* 57, 3.

Jacobs, Jane. 1969. *The Economy of Cities.* New York: Random House.

Mills, Edward. 1979. "Economic Analysis of Urban Land Use Controls." In *Current Issues in Urban Economics* edited by Peter Mieszkowski and Mahlon Straszheim. Baltimore: Johns Hopkins.

Myrdal, Gunnar. 1957. *Rich Lands and Poor.* New York: Harper.

Reich, Robert. 1992. *The Wealth of Nations.* New York: Vantage Books.

Rubin, Barry M., and Margaret G. Wilder. 1989. "Urban Enterprise Zones: Employment Impacts and Fiscal Incentives." *Journal of the American Planning Association* 55, 4.

Sagalyn, Lynne B. 1990. "Explaining the Improbable: Local Redevelopment in the Wake of Federal Cutbacks." *Journal of the American Planning Association* 56, 4.

Tabb, William K., and Lang Sawyer. 1984. *Marxism and the Metropolis: New Perspectives in Urban Political Economy.* New York: Oxford University Press.

7

TRANSPORTATION

Autos, Transit, and the Sprawl of Los Angeles: The 1920s

Martin Wachs
Professor of Urban Planning, University of California

Martin Wachs presents a historical analysis of Los Angeles to show how critical decisions made sixty and seventy years ago about land-use and transportation systems have shaped the city's current fabric. Well before the construction of its freeways, Los Angeles showed a preference for the low density development that has become the sprawl of today. The article offers important insights into the relationships among land use, politics, cultural values, and transportation planning.

Throughout the world, Los Angeles is known for its unique urban form and distinctive lifestyle. Some consider it glamorous and others find it sterile, but the name generally evokes images of freeways, sprawling low-density communities of single-family homes, and dependence on the automobile. Although many share these images, it proves difficult to explain how or why Los Angeles got to be the way it is. In the popular press, its decentralization is often attributed to the freeway building program and the suburban housing boom that followed the Second World War; yet historical evidence shows that the familiar Los Angeles pattern existed well before 1930 and that freeways were as much a response to decentralization as its cause.

The characteristic low density of Los Angeles was recognizable before 1900 and well established by 1930. It was the product of many interacting influences. The automobile was a critical ingredient, but so were street railways, attitudes of real estate speculators, the nature of the city's economy, and the timing of the region's most rapid growth. The decade between the end of World War I and the start of the Great Depression was probably the single most important period in the determination of Los Angeles' lifestyle and its accommodation to the automobile. Today's most complex decisions about land use, highways, and transit all have their roots in the twenties.

The automobile was being adopted widely during the 1920s, precisely when Los Angeles was experiencing its most explosive growth. At the same time, the city planning movement was attempting to establish its influence over the growth and form of the city. By studying the ideas, plans, and politics of that period, we learn that the decentralization of Los Angeles and the growth of the planning profession there had common roots.

Los Angeles in the 1920s provides another lesson to students of urban form and planning. Many portray public transit investments as ways to create urban areas of

Reprinted by permission of the *Journal of the American Planning Association* 50, 3, Summer 1984.

greater concentration and higher densities, while automobiles and highways are seen as countervailing influences leading inevitably to lower densities and sprawl (Taebel and Cornehls 1977). Historical analysis of Los Angeles, however, shows that during the formative decade of the twenties, highways and rail lines were not seen as competing influences on urban form. They were portrayed as complementary elements of regional plans, contributing in concert to the decentralization of the metropolis at a time when low-density development was being vigorously pursued by businessmen, political leaders, and planners.

THE FIRST GREAT BOOM

Los Angeles was first settled in 1781, and it remained a sleepy and relatively unimportant town for nearly its first hundred years; its population was about six thousand in 1870. The town was first linked to the growing national railroad network in 1876, when the Southern Pacific completed a line between Los Angeles and San Francisco. In 1881 the SP completed a more direct rail link between Los Angeles and the east, and in 1885 the Santa Fe opened its competing railroad. By 1890, the city's population had grown to more than fifty thousand, and the county's reached 100,000. While the European migrants to New York, Boston, and Philadelphia filled those cities with relatively poor and unskilled newcomers, the people arriving in Los Angeles were of a very different background (Brodsly 1981, 63; Fogelson 1967, 54–55).

Most of the new arrivals to Los Angeles were American-born, many came from the Middle West, and a large proportion were people of some means. Prosperous middle-western farmers turned their holdings over to their children and moved west to try their hands at citrus growing. Wealthy invalids sought a warmer climate in which to retire. Merchants and businessmen sought new markets and profits in speculation. Thus one observer described the new residents of Los Angeles as ". . . the best American stock; the bone and sinew of the nation; the flower of the American people," and a San Francisco newspaper noted that "the outstanding quality of the newcomers was their prosperity" (Brodsly 1981, 64). Another observer described the new settlers as "immigrants coming in palace-cars instead of 'prairie schooners,' and building fine houses instead of log shanties, and planting flowers and grass lawns before they planted potatoes or corn" (Fogelson 1967).

With rural American backgrounds and the means to implement their ideals, the immigrants to Los Angeles pursued, even in those early years, an ideal of low-density, single-family living, well before the automobile placed that lifestyle within reach of millions. Fogelson (1967, 144–45) has described their pursuit of this vision as follows:

> Americans came to Los Angeles with a conception of the good community which was embodied in single-family houses, located on large lots, surrounded by landscaped lawns, and isolated from business activities. Not for them multi-family dwellings, confined to narrow plots, separated by cluttered streets, and interspersed with commerce and industry. Their vision was epitomized by the residential suburb—spacious, affluent, clean, decent, permanent, predictable, and homogeneous—and violated by the great

PHOTO 1A In eastern cities like New York, new transit technology was added to densely developed communities. ("The S-curve of the Third Avenue El," from *32 Picture Postcards of Old New York* by Hayward Cirker, 1976, Dover Publications, Inc., New York. From the collection of E. B. Watson. Used by permission.)

PHOTO 1B In Los Angeles, the Pacific Electric was used to develop low-density, outlying areas. (From *Los Angeles: An Illustrated History*, by Bruce Henstell, New York, Alfred A. Knopf, 1980. Used by permission.)

city—congested, impoverished, filthy, immoral, transient, uncertain, and heterogeneous. The late nineteenth- and early twentieth-century metropolis, as the newcomers in Los Angeles perceived it, was the receptacle for all European evils and the source of all American sins. It contradicted their long-cherished notions about the proper environment and compelled them to retreat to outskirts uncontaminated by urban vices and conducive to rural virtues. And though native [-born] Americans everywhere shared these sentiments, they formed a larger portion of the populace in Los Angeles than in other great metropolises. Here then was the basis for the extraordinary dispersal of Los Angeles.

THE ROLE OF EARLY TRANSIT SYSTEMS

Between 1870 and 1910, the technology of urban transportation was advancing substantially. Entrepreneurs were replacing horse car lines with cable, steam, and electric traction street railways in Boston, Chicago, New York, and Philadelphia. Similar technology was introduced in Los Angeles, but there it had different effects on the city. The eastern and midwest metropolises already had become mature cities before extensive street railway networks were developed, and they were characterized by high residential densities, with living quarters in proximity to industrial and commercial districts. The street railways enabled those cities to add new residential districts beyond their older cores, through processes described by Sam Bass Warner in his classic book, *Streetcar Suburbs* (1962). Los Angeles, however, was just growing to maturity as a city when street railways were introduced, and it had never developed a significant commercial and industrial core. Its first period of rapid growth, from a population of five thousand in 1870 to nearly 320,000 in 1910, coincided with the introduction of street railways and interurban electric lines. These made residential growth possible at relatively long distances from the industrial and commercial center, even when the region's population was quite small. While new industries and businesses concentrated near the downtown railhead in the days before motor trucks and telephones, the street railways made it possible for real estate speculators to develop low-density residential estates in outlying sections catering to the obvious preferences of the newcomers. Since the denser, congested, eastern cities were regarded as sources of illness and vice, the low-density, outlying suburban growth of newer cities was regarded as an advance that contributed to substantial improvement in the quality of life. Charles Horton Cooley, who was one of the early leaders of the emerging discipline of sociology and whose doctoral dissertation was titled *A Theory of Transportation* (1894), illustrated the common view of the benefits of decentralization made by the street railways when he wrote this in 1891:

> Humanity demands that man should have sunlight, fresh air, the sight of grass and trees. It demands these things for the man himself, and it demands them still more urgently for his wife and children. No child has a fair chance in the world who is condemned to grow up in the dirt and confinement, the dreariness, ugliness, and vice of the poorer quarter of a great city. . . . There is, then, a permanent conflict between the needs of industry and the needs of humanity. Industry says men must aggregate. Humanity says they must not,

PHOTO 2   Advertisements for land subdivisions in Los Angeles, illustrating the prominence of railway access in the promotion of real estate. (From *Los Angeles: An Illustrated History*, by Bruce Henstell, New York, Alfred A. Knopf, 1980. Used by permission.)

or if they must, let it be only during working hours and let the necessity not extend to their wives and children. It is the office of the city railways to reconcile these conflicting requirements. (Cooley 1891)

With preferences for single-family, low-density living so prevalent, and a population of relatively greater economic means, it was inevitable that technological advances in transit would be coupled with ventures in real estate speculation. Between 1880 and 1910, cable car and electric trolley lines were built by holders of large tracts of vacant land with the specific intention of subdividing that land and profiting from the sale of homesites made accessible to downtown by transit (Foster 1971). Often mechanically unreliable, and even more often on unsound financial footings, the street railways rarely turned profits as transportation businesses, though they often contributed to huge speculative profits in real estate. Despite many failures and bankruptcies of smaller transit companies, the period from 1901 to 1911 saw the development in Los Angeles of the largest system of interurban electric lines in the country. The Pacific Electric System, assembled and extended by Henry Huntington from seventy-two separate companies, by 1923 offered service over 1,164 miles of single track and a network that extended more than 100 miles from one end to the other. The Pacific Electric offered interurban service from Los Angeles to outlying towns and villages, while the Los Angeles Railway operated local service on an additional 316 miles of single track within the

PHOTO 3 The opening of a suburban subdivision in Monrovia in 1887. Despite the sign's implication, the ocean was many miles away. (From *Los Angeles: An Illustrated History*, by Bruce Henstell, New York, Alfred A. Knopf, 1980. Used by permission.)

city. Many think of the sprawling Los Angeles metropolis in terms of the automobile and freeways, but Spencer Crump (1962, 96) is more accurate when he observes that "unquestionably it was the electric interurbans which distributed the population over the countryside during the century's first decade and patterned Southern California as a horizontal city rather than one of skyscrapers and slums." By 1910, largely because of the Pacific Electric System, Los Angeles was functionally integrated with Long Beach, Santa Monica, and San Bernardino. The extent of the metropolitan region has not grown substantially since then, and most of the more recent growth has consisted instead of filling in the spaces between outlying centers associated with important stations on the Pacific Electric.

THE ARRIVAL OF THE AUTOMOBILE

During the very years of consolidation and expansion of the public transportation system, which made dispersed residential development possible in Southern California, the automobile was being introduced and perfected. At first it was available only to the wealthy. In addition, before 1920, almost all automobiles were open to the elements, and therefore extremely unattractive in the cold, rain, or snow. Early cars were difficult to operate where there were few paved roads, especially when winter weather turned dirt roads into quagmires. No wonder, then, that the auto was adopted early in Southern California. The mild and dry climate made driving in open cars relatively comfortable and kept early roads reasonably passable. A greater proportion of Los Angeles' relatively affluent citizenry had the economic means to buy automobiles than was the case in eastern cities, and lower-density, single-family neighborhoods provided ample space to store and maintain cars, in comparison with eastern tenement communities. Thus by the end of 1919, an article in *Scientific American* describing automobile ownership patterns in the United States expressed amazement that California led the nation in per capita automobile ownership:

> [I]f we had any idea that states would follow along in the approximate order of their population we would be speedily disillusioned to learn that California has 2,000 more vehicles than Pennsylvania, and leads seven other states which are credited with greater population. We find, then, that the banner is to be awarded to California, with her perpetual summer, her tourist industry, and her wonderful roads.

When that article was written, Los Angeles already had the highest ratio of automobiles per capita of any large city in the United States—about one auto per nine people. Yet Los Angeles was poised on the edge of its second and greatest boom. Between 1910 and 1920, the great aqueduct was completed from the Owens Valley, providing the city with a reliable supply of water and relief from the problem of periodic drought. Before 1910, voters in Los Angeles approved the development of a harbor at San Pedro and Wilmington, and a series of improvements to that harbor continued into the twenties, allowing Los Angeles to compete successfully to

PHOTO 4 The opening of the cable car to the suburban community of Boyle Heights, across the Los Angeles River from downtown, in 1889. (From *Los Angeles: An Illustrated History*, by Bruce Henstell, New York, Alfred A. Knopf, 1980. Used by permission.)

become the largest west coast port by 1930. The decade after the First World War was the city's period of most rapid growth, decentralization, and automobile acquisition, and the low-density, single-family lifestyle that has come to be identified with this city was solidified during that period of dramatic growth.

THE GREAT BOOM OF THE TWENTIES AND THE DISPERSION OF ECONOMIC ACTIVITY

Between 1920 and 1930, the population of the City of Los Angeles grew from 577,000 to 1,240,000, while the population of the county increased from 1,238,000 to 2,200,000. This phenomenal rate of increase was described by one scholar of the period as "the largest internal migration in the history of the American people" (Thornthwaite 1934, 18). By 1930, only 20 percent of the residents of Los Angeles had been born in California, while by contrast more than two-thirds of all Americans resided in the states where they were born (Findley 1958, 24). The population distribution for Los Angeles showed that it had a larger proportion of middle-aged and older residents than did the country as a whole. And median income was relatively high, at least partly because the growth rate in employed workers exceeded the growth rate in population. While manufacturing industries grew, the proportion of employed workers engaged in manufacturing declined from 28 percent in 1920 to 22 percent in 1930, and Los Angeles was increasingly described as a "white collar" town; real estate, finance, and tourism expanded most prominently (Findley 1958).

The rapid growth of Los Angeles was, of course, not accidental. Like earlier booms, it was fostered by speculators, bankers, and businessmen who derived profits from the great boom of the twenties. In 1921, the "All Weather Club" was formed to advertise the wonders of Southern California in the East and especially to promote tourism, in the belief that a substantial proportion of those who vacationed in Southern California would be "sold" on the idea of staying permanently (Foster 1971, 26).

During the first wave of Los Angeles' dispersal, between 1880 and 1910, residential subcenters grew up in outlying areas in response to accessibility provided by street railways. Most businesses, with the exception of local services, remained downtown. The boom of the twenties, however, was accompanied by decentralization of much business and commercial activity as well as the continuation of residential dispersal. By the end of the First World War, the motor truck was available to free some businesses of their dependence on proximity to rail lines, and the availability of the telephone made it possible for businesses to communicate with one another without face-to-face contact. In addition, three factors unique to Los Angeles contributed directly to the dispersion of growth during the boom of the twenties: the central role of the petroleum industry in the local economy, the development of a port located far from the downtown area, and the adoption of a height limitation on buildings because of the danger of earthquakes.

With little coal except what was imported from great distances, local oil production fueled industrial growth and provided gasoline to operate the region's growing auto and truck fleet. As the twenties began, low petroleum prices and stable production gave way to tremendous fluctuations in prices and in the flow of capital into this industry. In 1920 there was a shortage of gasoline and a public outcry over rising gasoline pump prices. That, in turn, spurred increased investments in oil exploration, and several large, new fields were discovered in the early twenties. Later their collective production glutted the market and caused prices to plummet. Because some of the oil fields were located more than twenty miles from the central city, in places like Seal Beach, Signal Hill, and Fullerton, capital investments made in those outlying areas were another force for the spatial decentralization of Los Angeles during the twenties. Coupled with that investment was the development of refining and storage facilities near the port. The petroleum industry, one of the most important in the boom of Los Angeles in the twenties, is inherently dispersed, and that certainly contributed to the sprawl of the metropolis during the decade. To a lesser extent, the arrival of the movie industry in the twenties had a similar effect. Seeking large lots and a variety of settings for movie production, the film industry also developed a dispersed pattern of investments as it took an important place in local economic growth.

The harbors of many eastern cities were the sources of their early commercial growth and determined the locations of their central business districts, but the Los Angeles Harbor played a small role in the early development of the town. When the seaport did begin to develop as a significant part of the local economy, between 1890 and 1920, its growth took place about twenty miles from the business center of the city. The harbor was an important element in the economic boom of the twenties, in part because of the growth in exports of the region's petroleum. The distance of the harbor from downtown meant that its growth fostered the decentralization of economic activity. In fiscal year 1920, 2,886 ships entered Los Angeles Harbor, carrying 3.5 million tons of cargo valued at $154 million. In the fiscal year ending in June 1930, the number of vessels entering the port had grown to 8,633, carrying 26 million tons of cargo valued at more than a billion dollars (Findley 1958, 110). By that time, the port of Los Angeles ranked third nationally in total commerce and second in export tonnage (Findley 1958, 111), and the associated growth in warehousing and commercial activity took place along forty miles of waterfront in the Long Beach, San Pedro, and Wilmington areas, quite distant from the traditional commercial core of the city. In response, new residential communities sprang up on previously undeveloped land between the downtown and port areas.

In 1906, after the disastrous San Francisco earthquake, the Los Angeles City Council passed an ordinance limiting the height of buildings in the city to 150 feet. The ordinance remained in effect until the mid-1950s; the only exception was the construction of the 28-story Los Angeles City Hall, completed in 1928. The limit on building height reduced the attractiveness of the central business district to office developers, thus contributing to the decentralization of economic activity. Certainly, after the elimination of the height limitation at about the same time that freeway construction was at its peak, there was a surge of high-rise development in the downtown area (Scott 1971, 189–190).

AUTOS AND TRAFFIC IN THE BOOM OF THE TWENTIES

The extensive network of interurban and local street railways at first benefited from the dispersed growth of the twenties. Because the system had been "overbuilt" in pursuit of earlier real estate profits, it had the capacity to carry more and more passengers as suburban growth accelerated after the First World War. While the Pacific Electric System had carried about 74 million passengers in 1919, in 1924 it carried its highest annual passenger total of more than 109 million, an increase of 47 percent in only six years (Crump 1962, 251). This growth, however, was much smaller than the growth in automobile ownership during the same period, and interurban patronage fell off after 1924 as reliance on the automobile increased.

The growth of Los Angeles, which peaked in the early twenties, was accompanied by the public's greater financial access to automobiles, which followed the introduction of assembly line techniques and installment buying. Expansion of the automobile industry was simultaneously the cause and the result of a decline in the price of cars. Whereas the Ford Model T sold for $950 in 1909 and a Ford runabout sold for $390 in 1916, by 1926 a Ford runabout cost $260 and a Model T carried a price tag of $290. In 1926, moreover, the price tag was attached to a car that protected its occupants better from rain, dust, and direct sun (Berger 1979, 44).

PHOTO 5 Map shows the major streetcar and interurban transit routes serving Los Angeles in 1925. (From *The Fragmented Metropolis: Los Angeles 1850–1930*, by Robert M. Fogelson, Cambridge, Harvard University Press, 1967. Used by permission.)

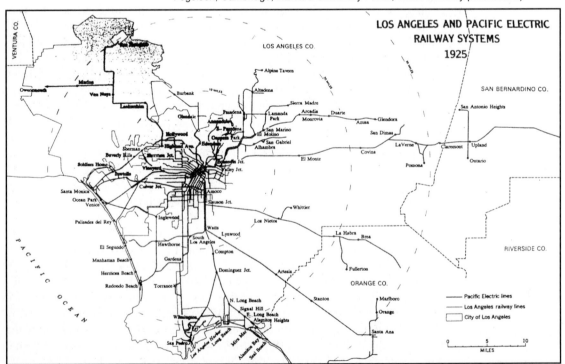

Los Angeles had an unusually high rate of automobile ownership before 1920, but during the twenties its familiar pattern of reliance on automobile travel was solidified. Between 1919 and 1929 the number of autos registered in the county increased from 141,000 to 777,000 (Foster 1971, 143). This rate of increase (about 550 percent) was many times the rate of increase in population, and the ratio of people per car dropped in ten years from nine to one to roughly three to one. Nearly fifty years passed before the city reached the present ratio of people to cars—about 1.7 to one (California Department of Transportation 1979)—indicating that 1920–1930 was the watershed decade for Los Angeles' adoption of the automobile.

It is difficult and probably fruitless to determine whether the decentralization of Los Angeles caused or resulted from this explosive growth in the use of the automobile; but the combination clearly gave the city its familiar character during the twenties. Foster (1971, 144), for example, reports that despite the dispersal of economic activity,

> . . . a 1933 study of traffic in ten major United States cities revealed that over twice as many vehicles invaded downtown Los Angeles in a twelve-hour period as any other city studied. Roughly 277,000 automobiles entered downtown Los Angeles' central business district. Of cities with roughly equal-sized central districts, Chicago was visited by 113,000 automobiles in the same time period, Boston by 66,000, and St. Louis by only 49,000.

A cordon count revealed that in 1924, 48 percent of all those entering the central business district of Los Angeles came by car; by 1931 another cordon count showed that the proportion had risen to 62 percent (Foster 1971, 144). Amazingly, the passage of fifty years and the construction of hundreds of miles of freeways have not really changed the basic pattern, for a 1980 cordon count showed that about two-thirds of those entering the Los Angeles CBD on a typical workday arrived in autos, vans, and trucks (Los Angeles Department of Transportation 1980).

The rapid growth in automobile ownership and use during the early twenties had two important effects on Los Angeles. First, it increased congestion on the streets at a much faster rate than street widenings, straightenings, and new street openings could cope with. Second, the growth in automobile traffic had a devastating effect on street railway operations, which already had been in financial difficulty before the widespread adoption of the automobile. The automobile first deprived the street railways of their weekend excursion traffic to beaches and mountain resorts, as people began to substitute Sunday drives for trolley car outings. For the financially strapped public transit systems, the withdrawal of that traffic was quite damaging. Their rush-hour commuting patronage remained stable at first, but profit margins disappeared because of lost revenue from recreational traffic. The loss forced a reduction in maintenance and a decrease in the frequency with which old vehicles were replaced. Some marginal routes were abandoned in the early twenties, and frequencies of service were decreased. Repeated requests for fare increases were denied by the city council, leading to further reductions in levels of service.

As transit service declined, more and more people took to automobiles for work trips, further crowding the streets that autos shared with transit cars. That, in turn, slowed transit service, increased operating costs, and caused even larger numbers of commuters to abandon the trolleys in favor of auto commuting. In spite of continued population growth, the number of revenue passengers on the Pacific Electric declined from 109 million in 1923 to 100 million in 1931 (Crump 1962, 251). The slow speeds and declining quality of transit service caused citizens to be outraged whenever proposals for fare increases were made, and the deterioration of service accelerated as traffic congestion grew. Even before 1920, the Automobile Club, the Business Men's Cooperative Association, officers of the Pacific Electric Railway, and members of the city council all had addressed the problem with a variety of proposals for potential solutions. They all widely publicized the idea that Los Angeles had a severe congestion problem primarily because it had an inadequate street system. They pointed out that Washington, D.C., at the time devoted 44 percent of its central city area to streets, and San Diego's CBD had 41 percent of its area devoted to streets, while Los Angeles' central area had narrow and discontinuous streets amounting to a mere 21.5 percent of its total downtown area. Street widenings and extensions would help automobile and transit commuters, since both modes shared the streets. In addition, proposals were made to initiate a system of traffic controls, including stop signs and traffic signals, and limitations on parking on the streets (Los Angeles Traffic Commission 1922).

From January through April 1920, the city council considered instituting a ban on curb parking in the central business district, an action that proved controversial. Some business groups supported the ban, while others opposed it vehemently, fearing that it would lead to a decline in central city sales, and an abandonment of the central district by many smaller businesses (Bottles 1983). The Board of Railway Commissioners argued that the ban was needed to reduce interference of auto traffic with the operations of the street railways and to avoid fare increases. The ban on parking was finally approved, but within days of its implementation it spurred protest meetings where hundreds of businessmen reported dramatic losses of trade. The newspapers joined in criticizing the parking ban, and the city council was finally forced to amend the ordinance, allowing 45-minute parking on the streets between the hours of 10 a.m. and 4 p.m. and keeping the no-parking rule in effect from 4 p.m. until 6:45 p.m. In the same year, the Automobile Club installed the first traffic signal as an "experiment." Despite confusion and early violations, this innovation in traffic control took hold, and in time it was widely accepted and obeyed.

THE ROLE OF CITY AND REGIONAL PLANNING

The twin explosions of population growth and automobile use occurred in the early 1920s in Los Angeles, just as the city planning movement was gaining momentum. Foster (1979) has argued that city planners were so busy establishing the legitimacy of their undertakings that they were forced to accept and adapt to the automobile rather than control it. If that occurred in eastern cities, where population

PHOTO 6   Traffic in downtown Los Angeles in the mid-twenties. (From *Los Angeles: An Illustrated History*, by Bruce Henstell, New York, Alfred A. Knopf, 1980. Used by permission.)

growth had peaked decades earlier and urban cores of higher density were long established, it was even more obviously true in southern California, where a commitment to decentralization was stronger.

The nascent "city planning" movement of the first decade of the century had resulted in the creation of several "city beautiful" organizations, whose members feared that growth would lead to congestion and a decline in the quality of life; but the potential for profit was so great that opposition to growth was ineffectual. An accommodation was reached, over time, between boosters of growth and promoters of the "city beautiful." Both groups regarded East Coast and European cities to be models of what should be avoided in Los Angeles, and both identified high densities and congestion as the greatest dangers facing their city. Promotion of low-density and dispersed growth, they finally agreed, could serve the interests of both boosters and reformers. The city of Los Angeles established a planning commission in 1920, and the commissioners spoke out for a dispersed city, avoiding eastern-style skyscrapers. The most tangible manifestation of their commitment to decentralization was their leadership in the creation in 1923 of the nation's first regional planning commission, joining together planning proponents from thirty-nine cities in the County of Los Angeles. In the words of Fogelson (1967, 250), "From their conception of congested eastern and midwestern metropolises, the planners assumed that the great city was no longer the most pleasant place for living or the most efficient location for working. They proposed, as an alternative, residential dispersal and business decentralization. . . ." This view was reinforced by the appointment of real estate agents, bankers, and land developers to the two new planning commissions. While advocating orderly decentralized growth, the commissions, for all practical purposes, focused their everyday staff activities on two principal tasks: the rationalization of land subdivision activity in the county, and the provision of adequate streets and highways, primarily through negotiated agreements with the land developers.

Against the backdrop of growing traffic congestion and increasing political salience of the traffic issue, Los Angeles in the early twenties considered two different regional transportation plans that would determine the directions of transportation policy in that city for decades to come. The first dealt primarily with highways and the second primarily with transit.

THE MAJOR TRAFFIC STREET PLAN

The Automobile Club and a voluntary association of civic leaders calling itself the Los Angeles Traffic Commission both surveyed traffic conditions and called on the city council in the early twenties to develop a single comprehensive highway and street plan for Los Angeles, to include street widenings, straightenings, and extensions in accordance with a set of principles for improved traffic flow throughout the city. At the time, individual subdivisions were platted with little reference to the pattern or capacity of the overall street network, and street widenings were considered only when petitions were received from property owners along the streets. Petitions were reviewed, on a case-by-case basis, by the city engineer. If the proposals were approved, property owners would be assessed the cost of improvements and a contractor retained to do the work. There was no master plan for such actions, and the individual projects were uncoordinated. After several independent proposals and plans for the improvement of traffic in Los Angeles, twenty-three members of the Traffic Commission were appointed and constituted as a "Major Highways Committee," and each donated $1,000 toward financing and drafting a comprehensive traffic plan. They retained Frederick Law Olmsted, Jr., Harland Bartholomew, and Charles H. Cheney; the three considered the many independent proposals and distilled from them the influential *Major Traffic Street Plan for Los Angeles* of 1924. The plan argued for the widening, extension, and straightening of many streets and the provision of a network of major streets. It proposed the first continuous grade-separated parkway, similar to those under development at the time in the New York area. The proposed Arroyo Seco Parkway would connect Pasadena to the central business district and later would be incorporated into the freeway system as the Pasadena Freeway. Several principles were proposed that in retrospect can be seen as the rudiments of the huge regional freeway network.

A strong case was made, for example, for the separation of different classes of traffic. Through traffic should not mix with local traffic, and streetcars should be separated, to the extent feasible, from automobiles. Underpasses and viaducts were proposed at the busiest intersections to separate traffic moving in different directions, and the concept of an elevated highway was introduced to separate automobiles from streetcars. While some of these more exotic concepts were adopted in

PHOTO 7 Traffic congestion in downtown Los Angeles, circa 1920. (Courtesy of the California Historical Society/Los Angeles History Center Title Trust and Insurance Collection)

later years, the immediate effect of the plan was a general consensus for its two hundred specific proposed widenings, extensions, and straightenings of streets, and for the concept of an integrated regional road network. The plan was quickly supported by the major newspapers, business associations, the Automobile Club, and the planning commission. Foster (1971, 209) reports that even before its adoption, employees of the planning commission were referring to the plan as a comprehensive guide to the street system as they negotiated with real estate developers over individual subdivisions.

Transit executives also joined in support of the plan, believing that street improvements were an important step toward more efficient transit operations. The plan was presented to the city council in July 1924, and the Major Highways Committee of the Traffic Commission urged that a measure approving the plan be placed on the ballot at the next election to enable the citizenry to voice its support of the plan. The council voted unanimously to put the street plan on the ballot, and also to put on the ballot a $5 million bond issue to begin implementation of the plan. A combination of general revenues, bond issues, and local assessments of affected property owners was advocated as a fair and balanced way of implementing the plan over the coming years.

Support for the two ballot measures was widespread, though there was some opposition, primarily related to the high cost of the project and its financing mechanisms (Foster 1971, 158–160). Some homeowner groups thought special assessments were unfair, in that property owners abutting the improved roads would bear much of the cost, while many nonresident users would benefit. The bond issue also was opposed by some who argued that the growing population had greater need for schools and health care facilities than for roads. In fact, the proposed bond issue would raise an amount of money that could only provide a modest start toward implementing a street program expected to cost hundreds of millions. Yet a modest start was advocated precisely because the city council feared public opposition to larger spending programs. Both propositions were approved by wide margins, and the Major Traffic Street Plan had been adopted.

By the end of the twenties, only a small proportion of the projects included in the street plan had been implemented, but progress was under way. Significantly, the consensus that these projects were important remained strong throughout the Depression years, and nearly every subsequent plan for highway or freeway improvements resembled the initial one in many ways. As new subdivisions were opened in later years, streets were extended and patterned after the 1924 plan, and its influence can be seen today throughout Los Angeles.

A COMPREHENSIVE RAPID TRANSIT PLAN

Everyone agreed the automobile was critical to the future prosperity of Los Angeles, yet few in the early twenties believed that rapid transit would not also be a critical element in the city's transportation system. Support for the highway plan and parking controls were both predicated, in part, on the improvements they would engender in transit service as well as their benefits to auto commuters. Yet the public and the press were extremely critical of the Los Angeles Railway and the Pacific Electric, complaining about the quality of service and opposing every effort to raise fares. After a series of critical articles in the local press, and outraged testimony before the city council, in 1923 the council and the Board of Public Utilities agreed to work with the railways to improve service (Bottles 1983). Although there had been many proposals for rail rapid transit projects dating back to 1906, local planners urged that transit improvements should be undertaken only in accordance with a metropolitan comprehensive plan for transit improvements. Although construction was under way on a subway project, which would permit streetcars to travel underground through one of the most congested central city areas to a downtown terminal building of the Pacific Electric, the city charter revisions of 1924 included a provision that no rapid transit construction could be undertaken until a citywide plan was completed and approved (Foster 1971, 112). In 1924 the city council and the county board of supervisors agreed to share the cost of hiring a firm of transit experts to prepare a comprehensive transit plan for Los Angeles. The Chicago firm of Kelker, DeLeuw, and Company was chosen, and in 1925 they submitted the *Report and Recommendations on a Comprehensive Rapid Transit Plan for the City of Los Angeles.*

The plan called for the construction of 26.1 miles of subways and 85.3 miles of elevated railways during the next ten years and proposed many miles of feeder bus lines and bus routes in outlying areas. The report estimated the total capital cost of the transit system to be $133.4 million. The authors acknowledged that Los

Angeles would continue to be a low-density metropolis of single-family homes and that rapid transit could not be financed solely from operating revenues in such an environment. It recommended that the city make special assessments in the vicinity of the stations and participate in the real estate gains that would flow from the investment by acquiring vacant property along the route; rental income in later years would go to pay off bonded indebtedness that would be used to cover construction costs. Finally, it acknowledged that an increase in transit fares would be required, probably from the 1925 level of five cents to a new level of eight cents, to make the project a reality (Kelker, DeLeuw, and Co. 1925, 163–181).

While many central city business groups supported the transit plan, and eventually some suburban chambers of commerce also endorsed it, the transit plan met from the start with much greater opposition than did the highway plan. Many questioned the wisdom of spending so much public money to benefit the privately owned Pacific Electric and Los Angeles Railway, especially considering their poor record of service. Others decried the fare increase that likely would be required. While an eight-cent fare may seem tolerable looking back on these events from the perspective of the eighties, it actually constituted a 60 percent increase in fares and was greeted by the public as would any current proposal to raise transit fares by an equivalent percentage. There was also damaging opposition to the proposal that the majority of the proposed transit routes be elevated, and many homeowner groups decried elevated transit lines as dirty, rickety, noisy, and blighting. Reports appeared in the local press of depressed property values in New York, Chicago, and Philadelphia where elevated railways already had been built. The consultants pointed out, however, that four miles of elevated line could be built for a cost equivalent to that of one mile of subway.

At the time the Kelker-DeLeuw recommendations were made, the City of Los Angeles for years had been attempting to force the major railways serving Los Angeles to abandon their separate downtown terminals and to jointly finance a "union station," located west of the plaza marking the point where the city was supposedly founded. The railroads preferred to maintain their independent terminals for a number of reasons, not the least of which was fear that they would be forced to permit intercity service by new competing carriers from the union station. At the time they could effectively exclude new rail carriers from serving Los Angeles because the Santa Fe, Union Pacific, and Southern Pacific controlled the downtown terminals and the most economic rights-of-way providing access to downtown. The *Los Angeles Times* favored a union station at the plaza site, while several other newspapers favored the railroads' position. The railroads offered to elevate the tracks serving their existing downtown terminals, thus eliminating many grade crossings, reducing safety hazards, and easing the flow of downtown traffic. They also agreed to allow the Pacific Electric to use the proposed elevated rights-of-way, providing convenient access between the intercity railroad terminals and the public transit system. The issue became heated, and the debate lasted for years. Charges were made that crooked real estate deals were really behind the different positions, and several public commissions studied the issue without resolution. Finally, the controversy led in 1926 to two ballot propositions. The first asked voters to approve or disapprove of a union station; and the second asked them to approve or disapprove of the proposed plaza site. The battle peaked as the election neared, and the opposition to the railroads' position, articulated by the Taxpayers Anti-Elevated League, was based in large part upon the environmental damage elevated lines would have done.

Consideration of the Kelker-DeLeuw plan was deferred until the union station issue was resolved, but the implications were clear. A defeat of the railroads' proposal would severely damage prospects for implementation of the transit plan, since the acceptance of elevated railways was central to the debate over the terminal. The voters approved the concept of a union station by a margin of 61 percent to 39 percent and also chose the plaza site, though by a smaller margin. In reaching that decision, the voters had overwhelmingly rejected elevated transit. The city council could no longer consider the Kelker-DeLeuw proposal, and as the Depression arrived it had not adopted that plan or acted to implement a rapid transit system for Los Angeles.

THE LEGACY OF THE TWENTIES

City planners and businessmen agreed that dispersal of Los Angeles was desirable and recognized that pursuit of this objective required large capital investments in the capacity to move people between many activity centers. They agreed that investments in highways *and* transit would be necessary to support decentralization. Yet there were several practical reasons the highway plan was implemented while the rail transit plan was not. It appears, in retrospect, that these circumstances, rather than a clear preference for automobiles, governed decisions in the twenties.

The highway plan consisted of hundreds of individual, functional improvements that could be implemented in piecemeal fashion over many years, while the transit plan would require more "lumpy" capital investments, each quite expensive and concentrated in space and time. The tiny staff of the city planning commission, numbering about fourteen in 1925 and seventeen in 1931 (Foster 1971, 218), could address specific street dedications and widenings as it went about its primary activity of reviewing subdivision applications. The planners could use their subdivision approval authority to gain compliance from the developers, who, in the end, realized that successful marketing of their subdivisions depended on adequate street access. The financial burden of implementing the street and highway improvements was imposed on particular property owners, who recovered their costs from the sale of the subdivided lots.

The transit plan was more difficult to implement for several reasons. Because particular elements of the plan were of much larger scale and greater cost than most of the highway projects, regional tax assessments and fare increases would be required to implement them. Yet the public was already critical of the private transit companies and did not welcome the prospect of paying for improvements to services that would yield private profits. In addition (though today it seems ironic in a city internationally known for its air pollution), the elevated transit lines were

PHOTO 8   Suburban residential communities of Los Angeles in the twenties. (Courtesy of the Los Angeles Public Library/Security-Pacific Photographic Collections)

viewed in the twenties as environmentally damaging. They would bring noise and shadows to a city in which sunlight and views were highly valued. The transit plan also suffered because it was closely associated with the dispute over the union station, which tended to identify the rail plan with crooked politicians, kickbacks, and land grabs. City planners were too busy implementing the highway plan and too vulnerable to political criticism to adopt a high profile in support of the rail transit plan.

As the citizens of Los Angeles debated the highway and transit plans, real estate speculators, building on widespread preferences for single-family living and the availability of autos, continued their practice of opening new subdivisions, often using fraudulent promotional tactics. By July 1925, there were nearly half a million vacant but subdivided residential lots in Los Angeles county, meaning that more than 55 percent of the subdivided lots were as yet undeveloped (Foster 1971, 183). Although the real estate speculators experienced a substantial decline in volume of transactions during the late twenties, their earlier activity ensured the continuation of the decentralized pattern that had been established in the days of the street railways.

By 1930, Los Angeles led the nation's cities in the proportion of its dwelling units that were single-family homes, at an astounding 93.7 percent. The same census showed, by comparison, that New York, Boston, and Chicago all had housing stocks of which less than 53 percent of the dwellings were single-family units (U.S. Bureau of the Census 1930, 450–51). In 1930 the Census Bureau reported that Los Angeles had a population density of only 2,812 people per square mile. That figure may be somewhat misleading, since it is based on a land area that includes the large and then-sparsely developed San Fernando Valley, annexed to the city after completion of the Owens Valley aqueduct project. Excluding that portion of the city, the density was about six thousand people per square mile, still dramatically lower than the reported figure of more than 23,000 residents per square mile in New York, nearly 18,000 per square mile in Boston, and nearly 17,000 per square mile for Chicago (U.S. Bureau of the Census 1930, 77).

By 1930 it was also clear that businesses, services, and commercial activities had dispersed to a far greater extent in the twenties than they had in the previous four decades. For example, whereas 55 percent of all the city's banks were located downtown in 1920, only ten years later that proportion had declined to 11 percent, as hundreds of branch banks opened throughout the area. The proportion of dentists' offices outside the central city increased from 16 percent in 1920 to 55 percent in 1930; and the proportion of the city's theaters that were in the central city declined from 73 percent in 1920 to just 20 percent in 1930. Whereas fewer than half of the city's delicatessens were in outlying locations in 1920, 93 percent were located outside the central city by 1930 (Reeves 1932, 19). By all accounts, then, the dispersed pattern typical of Los Angeles was clearly established during the twenties, long before the start of construction on the region's freeways.

The great boom of the twenties ended with a dramatic slowing of economic growth, bankruptcies of many real estate agents and speculators, and a slowing of the pace at which citizens of Los Angeles bought more automobiles. The pattern of the twenties persisted—the street railways slowly declined during the thirties and prospered briefly during the war years in response to gasoline rationing and military production in Los Angeles. Each year, bus routes were expanded and street railway lines abandoned. Buses could serve a large, low-density metropolitan area more economically, and that pattern had been well established before 1930. There were many proposals for transit improvements, but they all failed to capture the imagination of the public and its political leadership.

After the Second World War, when suburban growth again boomed in Los Angeles, the freeway building program began. In the early 1960s the last rail transit line was replaced by buses, and since then at least half a dozen major rapid transit plans have been considered as hundreds of miles of freeways were built. Los Angeles now has the largest all-bus transit fleet in the United States, and it appears that, after sixty years, a start will be made soon on a rail rapid transit system. The arguments for and against the most recent subway proposals for the city have been substantially identical to those offered in the 1920s, and the major stumbling block continues to be failure to secure the necessary funding for a rail transit system in a growing and vital but decentralized metropolitan area.

Author's Note

The author gratefully acknowledges financial support from the Institute of Transportation Studies of the University of California. Deborah H. Redman conducted much of the library research necessary to identify critical sources used in this study. Scott L. Bottles provided several key interpretations of events in the 1920s. I also am indebted to James Clifford Findley and Mark Foster, whose doctoral dissertations were the source of a great deal of material included in this paper. Professors James J. Flink, Donald A. Krueckeberg, and John Pucher offered useful comments on the manuscript.

REFERENCES

Berger, Michael L. 1979. *The devil wagon in God's country: The automobile and social change in rural America, 1893–1929.* Hamden, Conn.: Archon Books.

Bottles, Scott L. 1983. A search for rapid transit. Unpublished manuscript.

Brodsly, David. 1981. *L.A. Freeway: An appreciative essay.* Berkeley: University of California Press.

Brownell, Blaine A. 1980. Urban planning, the planning profession, and the motor vehicle in early twentieth century America. In *Shaping an Urban World,* edited by Gordon E. Cherry. London: Mansell.

California Department of Transportation and Southern California Association of Governments, 1979. *1976 urban and rural travel survey, volume IV: Summary of findings: Travel data.* Los Angeles.

Cooley, Charles Horton. 1891. The social significance of street railways. *Publications of the American Economic Association* VI: 71–73.

———. 1894. A Theory of Transportation. *Publications of the American Economic Association* IX, 3.

Crump, Spencer, 1962. *Ride the big red cars: How trolleys helped build southern California.* Corona del Mar: Trans-Anglo Books.

Findley, James Clifford. 1958. *The economic boom of the twenties in Los Angeles.* Doctoral dissertation. Claremont: Claremont Graduate School.

Fogelson, Robert M. 1967. *The fragmented metropolis: Los Angeles, 1850–1930.* Cambridge: Harvard University Press.

Foster, Mark S. 1971. The decentralization of Los Angeles during the 1920s. Doctoral dissertation. Los Angeles: University of Southern California, Department of History.

———. 1979. City planners and urban transportation: The American response, 1900–1940. *Journal of Urban History* 5, 3 (May): 365–396.

Kelker, DeLeuw, and Company. 1925. *Report and recommendations on a comprehensive rapid transit plan for the City and County of Los Angeles.* Chicago: Kelker, DeLeuw, and Company.

Los Angeles Department of Transportation. 1980. Central business district cordon count. Los Angeles.

Los Angeles Traffic Commission. 1922. The Los Angeles plan: A selected traffic program. December. Los Angeles.

Olmsted, Frederick Law; Harland Bartholomew; and Charles Henry Cheney. 1924. *A major traffic street plan for Los Angeles.* Prepared for the Committee on Los Angeles Plan of Major Highways of the Traffic Commission of the City and County of Los Angeles.

Reeves, Cuthbert D. 1932. *The valuation of business lots in downtown Los Angeles.* Los Angeles: Bureau of Municipal Research.

Scientific American. 1919. Automobiles and People. CXXI, 26 (December 27).

Scott, Mel. 1971. *American city planning since 1890.* Berkeley: University of California Press.

Taebel, Delbert A., and James V. Cornehls. 1977. *The political economy of urban transportation.* Port Washington, N.Y.: Kennikat Press.

Thornthwaite, C. Warren. 1934. *Internal migration in the United States.* Philadelphia: University of Pennsylvania Press.

U.S. Bureau of the Census, Department of Commerce. 1930. *Abstract of the Census, 1930.* Washington: U.S. Government Printing Office.

Warner, Sam Bass. 1962. *Streetcar suburbs: The process of growth in Boston, 1870–1900.* Cambridge: Harvard University Press.

Causes of Recent Increases in Traffic Congestion

Anthony Downs
Senior Fellow, Brookings Institution

Stuck in Traffic examines the causes and possible remedies for the continuing increase in traffic congestion in American communities. Traffic congestion is not only an exasperating condition for citizens, but also causes economic inefficiency in terms of the opportunity cost of lost time. In this chapter, Anthony Downs analyzes several important reasons for the increase in congestion, including the intensified use of the automobile, the desire for low density residential development, and our failure to require drivers to pay the full marginal cost of their behavior.

The goal of reducing traffic congestion has caused several communities to enact growth management legislation. This chapter should help the reader understand the causes of congestion. For remedies, the reader is encouraged to refer to the remainder of Downs's book, which discusses many imaginative strategies for reducing congestion.

The main causes of peak-hour traffic congestion are deeply rooted in American desires and behavior patterns. Some are even built into the basic physical and social structures of U.S. metropolitan areas. Policymakers hoping to reduce congestion therefore must persuade millions of Americans to alter some of their most cherished social goals and comfortable personal conduct.

The causes of rising congestion can be divided into two basic categories: immediate and long term. At least four immediate causes have been identified, each of which tends to reinforce the impact of the others and thereby heighten congestion.

RAPID POPULATION AND JOB GROWTH

Rapid growth in the number of households and jobs in an area inevitably increases the daily flow of traffic through it. Growth can be rapid because it is either absolutely large or occurs at a high rate or both. Absolutely large growth recently occurred concerning jobs, though not always population, in the twenty-one metropolitan areas with 1990 populations exceeding 2 million. All experienced substantial absolute gains in the number and use of vehicles during the 1980s, even if their total populations remained stationary. Absolutely large population growth—defined as a gain of 250,000 persons or more from 1980 to 1990—took place in thirteen of those large metropolitan areas and in eight others with populations less than 2 million. Rapid rates of population growth—defined as percentage gains more than four times greater than the 1980–90 average for all U.S. metropolitan areas—happened in eighteen metropolitan areas with population increases of 45 percent or more.

These changes occurred in thirty-six American metropolitan areas, which were therefore most likely to have experienced rising traffic congestion in the past decade (table 1-1). Their combined population increase in the 1980s was 15.3 percent, in comparison with 9.8 percent for the United States as a whole. If one excludes New York, Pittsburgh, Nassau-Suffolk, Chicago, Detroit, Philadelphia, St. Louis, and Boston—included because of their large size but having low growth rates (or actual contractions)—the remaining twenty-eight grew 27.3 percent in the past decade. Yet all thirty-six combined contained only about 35 percent of the total U.S. population.[1]

Employment growth in the 1980s, which reached 14.4 percent, perhaps had an even greater impact in causing congestion than population growth. For every 1 percent increase in population, there was a 1.53 percent increase in jobs outside the home. This meant that areas with relatively low rates of population growth nevertheless had more workers commuting daily. The Detroit metropolitan area, for instance, experienced an increase in employment between 1980 and 1990 despite a 2.4 percent decrease in population.[2]

Congestion is thus not growing at an alarming rate throughout the nation but primarily in areas experiencing rapid population or job growth. That is probably why the first congestion remedy tried by most local governments is to slow their own growth. Not only is rapid growth the most visible cause, but local officials believe—correctly—that they have more control over local growth than over any other cause. Also, for reasons discussed later, they feel they are less likely to upset voters by adopting growth-slowing policies than by using other congestion remedies.

MORE INTENSIVE USE OF AUTOMOTIVE VEHICLES

During the past fifteen years, the intensity with which Americans have used automotive vehicles has risen sharply. This has compounded the increase in vehicle travel resulting from population growth alone. Thus the number of cars and trucks in use increased nearly 50 percent, and the number of miles driven per vehicle increased 14.2 percent (table 1-2). Hence the total number of miles traveled by all motor vehicles annually soared 61.9 percent. The number of cars and light trucks available for personal driving during peak periods rose twice as fast as the number

TABLE 1–1   GROWTH OF SELECTED METROPOLITAN AREAS, 1980–90[a]

Area[b]	Population (April 1, 1990)	Population change 1980–90	
		Number	**Percent**
Los Angeles-Long Beach	8,863,164	1,385,925	18.54
New York	8,546,846	271,885	3.29
Chicago	6,069,974	9,591	0.16
Philadelphia	4,856,881	140,322	2.98
Detroit	4,382,299	−105,725	−2.36
Washington, D.C.	3,923,574	672,653	20.69
Boston	3,783,817	120,929	3.30
Houston	3,301,937	567,320	20.75
Atlanta	2,833,511	695,375	32.52
Nassau-Suffolk, N.Y.	2,609,212	3,399	0.13
Riverside-San Bernardino	2,588,793	1,030,578	66.14
Dallas	2,553,362	595,932	30.44
San Diego	2,498,016	636,170	34.17
Minneapolis-St. Paul	2,464,124	326,991	15.30
St. Louis	2,444,099	67,131	2.82
Anaheim-Santa Ana	2,410,556	477,635	24.71
Baltimore	2,382,173	182,675	8.31
Phoenix	2,122,101	612,926	40.61
Oakland	2,082,914	321,204	18.23
Tampa-St. Petersburg-Clearwater	2,067,959	454,359	28.16
Pittsburgh	2,056,705	−162,165	−7.31
Seattle	1,972,961	365,343	22.73
Miami	1,937,094	311,585	19.17
Sacramento	1,481,102	381,288	34.67
Fort Worth-Arlington	1,332,053	358,915	36.88
Orlando	1,072,748	372,844	53.27
West Palm Beach-Boca Raton-Delray Beach	863,518	286,760	49.72
Austin	781,572	244,884	45.63
Las Vegas	741,459	278,372	60.11
Melbourne-Titusville-Palm Bay, Fla.	398,978	126,019	46.17
Manchester, N.H.	336,073	59,465	45.99
Fort Myers-Cape Coral	335,113	129,847	63.26
Fort Pierce, Fla.	251,071	99,875	66.06
Ocala, Fla.	194,833	72,345	59.06
Naples, Fla.	152,099	66,128	76.92
Bangor, Me.	146,601	62,682	74.69
Totals	86,839,291	11,521,462	15.30
Average	. . .	. . .	31.00

Sources: Bureau of the Census, *Statistical Abstract of the United States: 1991* (1991), pp. 29–31; and Joe Schwartz, "This World Is Flat," *American Demographics,* vol. 13 (April 1991), pp. 34–39.

[a] Includes metropolitan areas with 1990 populations greater than 2 million, or those with growth of 45 percent or more from 1980 to 1990, or those with growth of 250,000 from 1980 to 1990.

[b] Ranked by 1990 population.

of households in absolute terms and one-third faster in relative terms. It also rose much faster than the number of licensed drivers. Total motor vehicle miles traveled increased faster than any other variable shown in table 1-2.

This intensified use of vehicles has contributed even more than population growth to the worsening congestion, except in very fast-growing areas. Consider a typical metropolitan area containing 100,000 residents in 1975. From 1975 to 1990 the number of vehicles in use would have risen 29.7 percent even if there had been no population growth at all. The number of miles driven per vehicle increased too; so total vehicle miles driven would have shot up 51.9 percent—also without any population rise. However, during the same fifteen years the nation's total population rose 15.2 percent. If this community had grown at that same rate, by 1990 its total population would be generating 75 percent more vehicle miles of driving than in 1975.[3]

The widespread occurrence of this vehicle population explosion is shown by table 1-3. From 1980 to 1990 the absolute number of registered vehicles rose 34.4 million, or 55.2 percent more than the human population, which grew by 22.2 million. Vehicle populations increased more than human populations in thirty-six states and the District of Columbia.

This intensification of vehicle ownership and usage can be traced in part to the sharp increase in households having more than one person working outside the home, as more women entered the job market. The fraction of all households owning two or more vehicles rose from 29 percent in 1969 to 53 percent in 1988.[4] Vehicle usage was also affected by the growth of suburbs not well served by pub-

TABLE 1-2   CHANGES IN KEY TRANSPORTATION VARIABLES, 1975–90
(Millions Unless Otherwise Specified)

	Increase	
Variable	**Number**	**Percent**
Civilian population	34.0	15.9
Number of households	22.2	31.3
Civilian employment	32.1	37.4
Licensed drivers	38.0	29.3
Cars and light trucks in use	45.8	41.9
All cars and trucks in use	59.2	49.3
Total vehicle miles traveled annually		
All motor vehicles	821.8	61.9
All passenger cars	451.5	43.6
Annual miles traveled per vehicle[a]		
All motor vehicles	1,365	14.2
All passenger cars	692	7.1

Sources: Motor Vehicle Manufacturers Association, *Motor Vehicle Facts and Figures '91* (Detroit, 1991), pp. 28–29, 38–39, 43, 53; and Bureau of the Census, *Statistical Abstract of the United States: 1982–83*, pp. 7, 45, 384, 614.
    [a] For 1975–89.

lic transit, the scattering of jobs, and a decline in the use of public transit for commuting trips.

FAILURE TO BUILD NEW ROADS

Between 1981 and 1989, total highway mileage in the United States went from 3.853 million to 3.877 million, an increase of only 0.6 percent in a period when the number of cars and trucks in use rose by 24.0 percent and total vehicle miles driven soared 33.6 percent.[5] Urban road mileage went from 624,000 miles in 1980 to 753,000 in 1989, a gain of 20.7 percent.[6] These data do not take into account the widening of existing roads. But the Texas Transportation Institute compared changes in daily vehicle miles traveled with changes in lane miles of both expressways and major arteries in thirty-nine large urban areas for 1982–88. Total driving increased more than twice as fast as roadway capacity. As a result, the number of urban areas classified by the institute as suffering from congestion rose from ten in 1982 to eighteen in 1988. Thirty-five of the thirty-nine areas had higher congestion indexes in 1988 than in 1982.[7]

FAILURE TO MAKE DRIVERS BEAR FULL COSTS THEY GENERATE

Another immediate cause of traffic congestion long noted by economists but ignored by government officials is that commuters are not required to pay the full marginal costs of driving during peak periods. Drivers are only responsible for vehicle operating costs and the time spent commuting. Since they will probably be caught in heavy congestion during peak periods, they recognize that their commuting time will be higher then than during other periods. But by commuting during peak hours, each employee can work the same hours as most others do. As long as this benefit outweighs the private costs described earlier, many commuters will travel in peak periods.

What these drivers fail to consider, however, are the costs of delay that their entry imposes on all other persons traveling along a congested roadway at the same time. Unless society compels them to do otherwise—say, by charging a toll or parking fee for driving during the most popular periods—commuters will continue to underestimate this collective cost. The main reason they and most public officials think this way is that traditionally most roads have been freely accessible to all motorists. People could certainly recognize that offering unlimited access to hearty free meals at restaurants would cause chronic overcrowding there, as happens at many shelters for the homeless. Similarly, they see that offering public housing units at below cost has generated massive waiting lists among potential occupants. But they fail to connect the congestion they abhor with free access to crowded expressways during peak hours. Clearly, no strategy for remedying peak-hour congestion will be effective unless this relationship is fully recognized and taken into account.

TABLE 1-3 CHANGES IN POPULATION AND NUMBER OF AUTOMOTIVE VEHICLES, BY STATE, 1980–90

State	Change in population		Change in registered automotive vehicles		Ratio of change in vehicle numbers to change in population	Vehicles per 100 persons 1990
	Thousands	Percent	Thousands	Percent		
Alabama	150	3.9	745	25.36	4.97	91.2
Alaska	150	37.5	106	40.46	0.71	66.9
Arizona	947	34.8	934	48.72	0.99	77.8
Arkansas	64	2.8	−126	−8.01	−1.97	61.6
California	6,091	25.7	5,303	31.43	0.87	74.5
Colorado	405	14.0	902	38.51	2.23	98.5
Connecticut	179	5.8	525	24.45	2.93	81.3
Delaware	71	11.9	134	33.75	1.89	79.7
District of Columbia	−32	−5.0	−14	−5.22	0.44	41.9
Florida	3,197	32.8	3,918	51.46	1.23	89.1
Georgia	1,014	18.6	1,560	40.86	1.54	83.0
Hawaii	143	14.8	190	33.33	1.33	68.6
Idaho	62	6.6	200	23.98	3.23	102.7
Illinois	12	0.1	646	8.64	53.83	71.1
Indiana	54	1.0	588	15.37	10.89	79.6
Iowa	−137	−4.7	270	11.59	−1.97	93.6
Kansas	114	4.8	−5	−0.25	−0.04	80.8
Kentucky	24	0.7	297	11.45	12.38	78.4
Louisiana	15	0.4	234	8.42	15.60	71.4
Maine	102	9.1	222	30.66	2.18	77.0
Maryland	565	13.4	777	27.72	1.38	74.9
Massachusetts	279	4.9	38	1.01	0.14	62.9
Michigan	37	0.4	722	11.13	19.51	77.6
Minnesota	298	7.3	250	8.09	0.84	76.4
Mississippi	52	2.1	325	20.61	6.25	73.9
Missouri	200	4.1	619	18.92	3.10	76.0
Montana	12	1.5	78	11.47	6.50	94.9
Nebraska	8	0.5	133	10.61	16.63	87.9
Nevada	402	50.3	192	29.31	0.48	70.5
New Hampshire	188	20.4	251	35.65	1.34	86.1
New Jersey	366	5.0	832	17.48	2.27	72.4
New Mexico	215	16.5	251	23.50	1.17	87.1
New York	432	2.5	2,155	26.93	4.99	56.5
North Carolina	754	12.8	694	15.31	0.92	78.8
North Dakota	−15	−2.3	2	0.32	−0.13	98.5
Ohio	50	0.5	1,620	20.85	32.40	86.6
Oklahoma	120	4.0	9	0.35	0.08	82.4
Oregon	209	7.9	359	17.25	1.72	85.8
Pennsylvania	14	0.1	1,101	15.90	78.64	67.6
Rhode Island	56	5.9	46	7.38	0.82	66.7
South Carolina	367	11.8	559	28.01	1.52	73.3
South Dakota	6	0.9	121	20.13	20.17	103.7
Tennessee	286	6.2	1,138	34.79	3.98	90.4
Texas	2,758	19.4	2,233	21.32	0.81	74.8
Utah	261	17.9	199	20.06	0.76	69.1
Vermont	51	10.0	123	35.45	2.41	83.5
Virginia	841	15.7	1,356	37.40	1.61	80.5
Washington	736	17.8	1,066	33.05	1.45	88.2
West Virginia	−157	−8.1	−98	−7.42	0.62	68.1
Wisconsin	186	4.0	626	21.29	3.37	72.9
Wyoming	−18	−3.8	26	5.57	−1.44	108.7
United States	22,184	9.8	34,432	22.10	1.55	76.5

Sources: Human populations data are from *Numbers News*, vol. 11 (February 1991), p. 2. Vehicle populations data are from Bureau of the Census, *Statistical Abstract of the United States, 1982–83*, p. 614; Motor Vehicle Manufacturers Association, *Motor Vehicle Facts and Figures '91* (Detroit, 1991), p. 22.

LONG-TERM CAUSES

Suburban traffic congestion in growing metropolitan areas is also intensified by a number of long-term, or indirect, causes.

Concentration of Work Trips in Time

Many work trips are concentrated in relatively short periods each day, mainly in the morning (6 to 9 a.m.) and evening (4 to 7 p.m.) rush hours. About 17 percent of all trips occur during the morning peak period, and 23 percent during the evening peak (figure 1-1). The heaviest concentration per hour is from 4 to 7 p.m. for all trips, and from 6 to 9 a.m. for work trips. Since 1983 this concentration has been compounded by a 25.2 percent increase in the total number of vehicle trips made daily and by a 40.6 percent jump in the total vehicle miles driven daily.[8]

Trips cluster in this way because most organizations start and end their work days at the same time so that their employees can interact with workers in other organizations. The resulting efficiency is thought to outweigh the costs of delay that arise because their workers all have to commute at the same time.[9] As long as organizations hold this view, they will continue to have roughly the same working hours.

Currently, the private marginal costs of the work pattern for each firm are smaller than the social marginal costs it causes. Each firm suffers—mainly indirectly—only from the time losses its own employees experience commuting to work; it does not have to pay any of the costs their peak-hour travel imposes on other firms and workers. Firms thus put less effort into adjusting work hours than they would if they had to pay the full costs of the present arrangement. This causes a socially inefficient allocation of resources. It could be corrected by placing a price on travel during peak hours through assessing special tolls.

Many nonwork trips are also concentrated close to the peak commuting periods: people taking children to school or running errands before or after work. In 1983

FIGURE 1-1   Share of Weekday Vehicle Trip Miles, by Type of Trip and Time Period. *Source*: Federal Highway Administration, *Personal Travel in the U.S.*, vol. 1: *1983–1984 Nationwide Personal Transportation Study* (Department of Transportation, 1986).

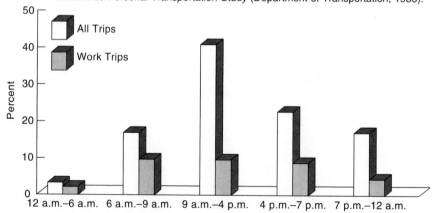

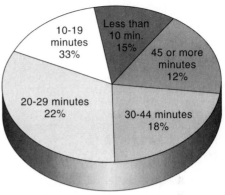

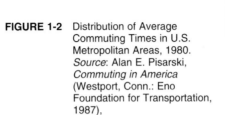

FIGURE 1-2 Distribution of Average Commuting Times in U.S. Metropolitan Areas, 1980. *Source*: Alan E. Pisarski, *Commuting in America* (Westport, Conn.: Eno Foundation for Transportation, 1987),

weekday nonwork trips made up 49.7 percent of all morning peak-hour trips and 68.9 percent of all evening peak-hour trips.[10]

Desire to Choose Where to Live and Work

Many commuters are willing to travel long distances or to tolerate the time wasted in heavy traffic so they can work and live where they choose. If they commute relatively long distances, they add to total peak-period travel. In 1980 the average commuting trip took 21.7 minutes, but 30 percent of all commuters traveled 30 minutes or more, and 12 percent traveled 45 minutes or more (figure 1-2). In large metropolitan areas the average trip time is longer and the percentage of commuters traveling for long periods is higher. In the New York City area, for example, the average commuting time was 32.3 minutes, and nearly 30 percent of all commuters traveled 45 minutes or more.[11]

From 1983 to 1990 the average work trip has increased from 8.6 miles to 10.98 miles (or 27 percent).[12] People's willingness to commute long distances has repeatedly undermined attempts to shorten commuting times by building housing near workplaces and encouraging workers to occupy that housing. Almost invariably, many choose to live in distant communities, while many occupants of the adjacent housing work miles away.

The reasons for this behavior are rooted in fundamental American values. In a 1980 national sample of workers commuting more than five miles to and from work daily, respondents were asked to state the most important reason they lived so far from their jobs. About 38 percent cited good schools; 24 percent said they liked their house; 17 percent said they liked their neighbors; and 10 percent said their own jobs were too far from the jobs of other family members.[13]

Desire for Low-Density Neighborhoods

A goal of most American households is to own single-family detached homes with private open space next to each dwelling. The low-density pattern required to meet

TABLE 1-4 DENSITIES OF LARGE U.S. CITIES, BY REGION, 1986[a]

Region	Number of cities[a]	Total population	Total cities area (square miles)	Average overall density	Average individual city density[b]	Average city population	Average city area (square miles)
Northeast	22	12,846,880	960.8	13,371	9,147	583,949	43.7
Midwest	39	12,880,140	3,172.2	4,060	3,857	330,260	81.3
South	47	11,664,880	5,603.0	2,082	3,203	248,189	119.2
Southwest	27	9,794,860	4,497.4	2,178	2,390	362,773	166.6
West	47	14,079,490	8,116.2	1,735	4,585	299,564	172.7
United States	182	61,266,250	22,349.6	2,741	4,298	336,628	122.8

Source: Author's calculations based on data from Bureau of the Census, *Statistical Abstract of the United States: 1990* (1990).
[a] Population of 100,000 or more.
[b] Average population per square mile.

this goal spreads housing over a much larger area than it would occupy in high-density settlements. Thus it is not surprising that central cities' share of all metropolitan-area workers' homes declined from 53.2 to 45.7 percent in the 1970s.[14]

The nation's average residential densities have also been affected by the relative movement of population from metropolitan areas in the Northeast and Midwest to ones in the South and West built mainly in the automobile era. Of the 182 cities that contained more than 100,000 persons in 1986, the 22 in the Northeast had an average density more than triple that of the 39 in the Midwest and more than six times the average of cities in the other three regions (table 1-4).

Density in the suburbs—computed for seven metropolitan areas in the Northeast and Midwest (total population 30.7 million) and seven in the South and West (total population 27.6 million)—shows a similar trend. Average densities per square mile outside central cities were 1,319 for the Northeast and Midwest and 498 for the South and West. Note, however, that counties in many western metropolitan areas include much larger portions of unsettled territory than do those in eastern areas.

The fastest-growing suburbs are almost always those at the edges of the built-up parts of metropolitan areas. These peripheral suburbs typically have densities much lower than suburbs closer in. Hence most new growth is occurring at low densities that generate more travel per resident than would higher-density settlements.

Preference for Low-Density Workplaces

Many suburbs—exercising their rights of local governance—require offices, retail facilities, and other workplaces to be housed in low-rise structures with low ratios of floor area to ground area. Such regulations cause jobs to become widely dispersed across a metropolitan area. This is what has happened in the greater Los Angeles area. By 1980 the nineteen largest clusters of jobs there—including downtown Los Angeles—accounted for only 17.5 percent of all jobs in the area's five counties.[15] In other words, 82.5 percent of all jobs were widely spread throughout the region.

Both local residents and building tenants like the adjacent free ground-level parking and attractive landscaping possible in such low-density work areas. Therefore, developers of suburban workplaces have typically found it easier to rent or sell space in these parklike settings. An exception is where workplaces are close to an airport, a regional shopping center, or similar amenities. Then more intensive use of the land with high-rise structures becomes a more important consideration than aesthetic effects.

Some jobs have shifted to low-density workplaces because computers, fax machines, and other telecommunications devices have made it possible to separate lower-level activities from executives without much loss of efficiency. Suburban office space generally costs less to rent than downtown space. So more firms have been moving operations to the suburbs, where lower land costs and aesthetic and zoning considerations encourage them to select low-density workplaces.

The density of suburban workplaces affects congestion because more new jobs are being created in suburbs than in central cities. In the fifty metropolitan areas where Coldwell Banker tracked office space in 1989, the suburbs attracted 72 percent of the new office space built and 74 percent of the office space actually absorbed.[16] Between 1970 and 1980 the suburban share of jobs rose from 46.9 to 52.5 percent in the twenty-five largest metropolitan areas and from 41.9 to 44.3 percent in all urban areas.

The combination of low-density settlements and low-density workplaces reduces the feasibility of commuting by mass transit. Such commuting is efficient mainly when many passengers' points of origin or destination are massed in a few large centers, so that routes and vehicles can converge at one end of the journey or the other. But when both ends of their trips are widely scattered, mass transit does not work efficiently. For the same reason, such dispersal also discourages use of car pooling, van pooling, and other ride sharing.

Some have suggested that dispersal of suburban workplaces decreases commuting times and distances by moving jobs closer to where workers live. In that case, low-density workplaces might have a beneficial effect on traffic congestion. Indeed, a 1980 study found that people who both lived and worked in the suburbs had the shortest average commuting time of all workers grouped by job and housing locations (table 1-5). But this does not necessarily mean that dispersed suburban jobs generate shorter average commuting distances. In fact, some suburban areas are so spread out, with structures separated by seas of parking spaces, that workers typically drive even when just moving from one building to another, thereby worsening congestion.

Desire to Travel in Private Vehicles

Most Americans prefer traveling in private vehicles, usually alone, because such travel provides convenience, comfort, privacy, and speed far superior to that of

TABLE 1-5   AVERAGE MINUTES OF ONE-WAY COMMUTING, BY LOCATION OF
RESIDENCE AND WORKPLACE, 1980.

	Workplace		
Residence	Central business district	Elsewhere in city	Suburb
City	24.9	20.0	26.4
Suburb	35.1	27.2	18.8

Source: William P. O'Hare and Milton Morris, *Demographic Change and Worktrip Travel
Trends*, vol. 2: *Statistical Tables* (Washington: Joint Center for Political Studies, 1985), table
I-80.

public transit.[17] This preference immensely increases the number of vehicles on the
roads during peak hours, compared to more widespread use of public transit. It also
explains why public transit usage in peak periods declined between 1977 and 1983.
By 1983 only 5.9 percent of all commuters were using public transit in the morning peak and 5.4 percent in the evening peak, whereas 88.5 percent were using private vehicles in the morning and 86.2 percent in the evening.[18] Any large increase
in the fraction of commuters sharing rides could significantly reduce peak-hour
congestion. Nonetheless, statistics show that close to 70 percent of all commuters
drive cars alone. Clearly the benefits of doing so, net of costs, still exceed the net
benefits of public transit and ride sharing. The commuter who drives alone enjoys
not only greater privacy and comfort, but also shorter travel times, more convenient
timing, and, if parking is free, lower day-to-day cash outlays.

To persuade more commuters to shift modes without changing the locations of
their homes or jobs, it would be necessary to make net benefits of solo driving less
than those of travel by other modes. That would require either increasing the net
benefits of the other modes or decreasing those of driving alone. Unfortunately, it
is extremely difficult to increase the benefits of alternative modes. So the most
effective course of action is likely to be decreasing the net benefits of driving alone,
mainly by raising the costs. A great many of the tactics analyzed later in this book
are designed to do just that.

FUTURE TRENDS

A recent analysis by Charles Lave suggests that traffic congestion in the 1990s will
not continue to increase as it did in the 1970s and 1980s because its primary causes will have abated.[19] There will not soon be another baby-boom generation coming of driving age. The number of women obtaining driver's licenses will have lev-
eled off in comparison with when they were first seeking independence and the
percentage working outside the home began rising sharply. Also, household
incomes will no longer be rising rapidly and allowing more people to own vehi-

cles. In this view traffic congestion will not grow any faster than the population of driving-age persons.

Some of the data to support this view come from California. The ratio of vehicles in California "usable for commuting" (autos plus vans plus 57 percent of light trucks) to the total population of driving age (fifteen to sixty-four years) rose from 0.523 in 1940 to 0.76 in 1960 and 1.0 in 1986. But this rate of increase appears to be slowing as the ratio approaches or surpasses one vehicle for each potential driver. That seems to indicate true saturation of the population with vehicles. After all, every potential driver cannot drive more than one vehicle at a time. Lave also says that because the average number of miles each vehicle travels a year is relatively constant, congestion will stop intensifying.

But these statistics do not necessarily mean that congestion will stop getting worse. Even if vehicle use rises no faster than population, the latter can still soar in fast-growing areas. For example, the Southern California Association of Governments has forecast just such an increase in its six-county area. That region is already plagued by heavy traffic congestion, but its population is expected to rise by 5.8 million persons between 1985 and 2010.[20]

The suggestion that more intensive use of automotive vehicles will be less of a problem in the future is also questionable. According to the Department of Transportation, average miles driven per vehicle increased 22 percent from 1983 to 1990. If this trend continues, it will offset any stabilization in the number of vehicles per person of driving age. Moreover, although women now drive less than men, they might indeed catch up in the future. Since 1983, average annual miles per driver has risen 50 percent among women, compared with 28 percent among all drivers.[21] Further catching up by women would continue to intensify vehicle use. And because household vehicle ownership rises with income, if real incomes of low-income households rise in the 1990s, vehicle ownership will also increase.[22] Finally, since many households with multiple workers now have fewer vehicles than workers, more may buy vehicles to equal their number of workers.

This analysis implies that traffic congestion is almost certain to continue worsening in fast-growing metropolitan areas unless effective remedies can be found and implemented. Congestion may get worse in other areas too in the absence of such remedies. Moreover, the evidence suggests that many key causes of traffic congestion are rooted in long-established beliefs and behavior patterns. Any notable relief will therefore depend on whether these patterns can be changed through deliberate policies.

NOTES

1 This list corresponds to large urban areas classified as congested in a 1990 study of thirty-nine areas by the Texas Transportation Institute. Eighteen of that group were found to be congested overall in 1988; seventeen are on the list in table 1-1 (San Francisco is not, but Oakland is). Of the thirty-six areas discussed in this chapter, seventeen were classified by the study as congested overall, ten were not covered, three were incorporated into larger areas counted as congested, and only six were studied but not classified as congested. See James W. Hanks, Jr., and Timothy J. Lomax, *Roadway Congestion in Major Urbanized Areas, 1982 to 1988* (College Station: Texas Transportation Institute, 1990), p. 24.

2 Data for 1980 employment from Bureau of the Census, *State and Metropolitan Area Data Book: 1986* (Department of Commerce, 1986), p. 14; for 1990, see Salomon Brothers, *Real Estate Market Review: Supplement Edition* (January 1991), pp. 16–17.

3 Motor Vehicle Manufacturers Association, *Automobile Facts and Figures* (Detroit, various years).

4 Automobile Manufacturers' Association, *1970 Automobile Facts and Figures* (Detroit, 1970), p. 47; Motor Vehicle Manufacturers Association, *Motor Vehicle Facts and Figures '90* (Detroit, 1991), p. 44.

5 Bureau of the Census, *Statistical Abstract of the United States: 1991* (1991), p. 605; and Motor Vehicle Manufacturers Association, *Motor Vehicle Facts and Figures '90*, pp. 50, 53. The 1989 figure for total vehicle miles driven was estimated by extrapolating the rate of change from previous years.

6 Bureau of the Census, *Statistical Abstract of the United States: 1991*, p. 599.

7 Hanks and Lomax, *Roadway Congestion*, pp. C-3–C-16.

8 Federal Highway Administration, *1990 Nationwide Personal Transportation Study*, p. 17. Because total travel each day rose so sharply, it was not necessary for the degree of concentration of trips during rush hours to increase in order for such concentration to contribute to greater congestion during those hours.

9 I am indebted to Herbert Mohring of the University of Minnesota for emphasizing this underlying economic rationale for simultaneous working hours and for pointing out the socially inefficient nature of current practices. One tactic for reducing congestion analyzed later is staggering working hours. But even when work starting times are staggered, most work hours overlap with those of other workers so that the interorganizational efficiency of simultaneity can be retained.

10 Federal Highway Administration, *Personal Travel in the U.S.*, vol. 1: *1983–1984 Nationwide Personal Transportation Study* (Department of Transportation, 1986), p. 6-28.

11 Computed from Department of Transportation, *Transportation Planning Data for Urbanized Areas Based on the 1980 Census* (1985), chaps. 1, 2.

12 Federal Highway Administration, *1990 Nationwide Personal Transportation Study*, p. 9.

13 William M. Rohe and others, *Travel to Work Patterns: A Preliminary Analysis of Selected Data from the Annual Housing Survey Travel-to-Work File* (University of North Carolina, Department of City and Regional Planning, 1980), p. 145.

14 William P. O'Hare and Milton Morris, *Demographic Change and Recent Worktrip Travel Trends*, vol. 1: *Final Report* (Washington: Joint Center for Political Studies, 1985), p. 104.

15 See Peter Gordon, Harry Richardson, and Genevieve Giuliano, *Travel Trends in Non-CBD Activity Centers* (University of Southern California, School of Urban and Regional Planning, 1989), p. 16.

16 Coldwell Banker Commercial Toro Wheaton Services, *Coldwell Banker Commercial Office Vacancy Index of the United States, December 31, 1989* (Boston, 1990), p. 1.

This publication does not list (or apparently, track) office space within central cities but outside downtown markets.

17 In some areas and under some circumstances driving alone may take more time and be less convenient than ride sharing or using public transit. But on average this is not the case. In 1983 average commuting times were 19.1 minutes for persons using private passenger cars, 20.1 minutes for those using trucks, vans, and other private vehicles, and 46.1 minutes for those using public transportation. Average speeds were 31.1 miles per hour for the first group, 33.7 for the second, and 19.7 for the third. Federal Highway Administration, *Personal Travel in the U.S.*, vol. 1, p. 7-9.

18 See Federal Highway Administration, *Personal Travel in the U.S.*, vol. 1, p. 7-19. In 1977, 72.0 percent of all morning peak-period commuters were private vehicle drivers and 18.3 percent were passengers, while the average car pool then held 1.52 passengers. By 1983 these figures had changed to 76.7 percent, 11.8 percent, and 1.49 respectively.

19 Charles Lave, *Things Won't Get a Lot Worse: The Future of U.S. Traffic Congestion* (University of California at Irvine, Institute of Transportation Studies and Department of Economics, 1990).

20 Southern California Association of Governments, *Regional Mobility Plan* (February 1989), p. III-1.

21 Federal Highway Administration, *1990 Nationwide Personal Transportation Study*, pp. 19, 37.

22 In 1988, households with 1987 incomes less than $10,000 owned an average of 1.3 vehicles; those with incomes of $25,000 to $34,000 owned 1.8; and those with incomes of $35,000 to $49,999 owned 2.2. Motor Vehicle Manufacturers Association, *Motor Vehicle Facts and Figures '90*, p. 45.

Needed: A Marshall Plan for Ourselves

Richard P. Nathan
University at Albany, State University of New York

Richard P. Nathan reviews several recent studies that document an insufficient United States investment in public infrastructure—roads, bridges, sewer and water systems, and so forth. While demand for the construction and maintenance of infrastructure has increased over the past fifteen years, spending on public works has actually declined. There has been a real, inflation-adjusted decline in federally financed net investment in public physical capital and in total state and local government capital spending. Nathan calls for new priorities—a "Marshall Plan"—for investment in public infrastructure and stimulation of economic growth.

Reprinted by permission of *Economic Development Quarterly* 6, 4 (November 1992), Sage Publications.

Grid•lock *n.* (1980) 1. A traffic jam in which a grid of intersecting streets is so completely congested that no vehicular movement is possible.

2. A situation resembling a gridlock (as in congestion or lack of movement).

Source: Webster's Ninth New Collegiate Dictionary, 1989.

By the time "gridlock" traffic jams got into *Webster's* in 1980, we had become all too familiar with their meaning for America's cities. Visit almost any big city today and you can learn about blocked roads, jammed traffic, closed bridges, flooded streets, and blown sewers. Gridlock also has a second definition in *Webster's*, as quoted above, that can be political: "lack of movement." The two kinds of gridlock—physical and political—go together. Until recently, when Congress passed the Intermodal Surface Transportation Efficiency Act of 1991 (quickly dubbed "iced tea"), the national government, and for that matter many state and local governments, have had a congested policy backlog with little movement on measures to keep up and build up the nation's public physical plant.

The United States has been strong in demanding that other countries adopt policies to stimulate economic growth. We need to take some of our own medicine. The national government cannot keep hiding behind the budget deficit; it must adopt policies to stimulate the investment side of the economic equation.

The time has come for a shift in U.S. economic policy to favor investment, including state and local infrastructure investment. A special fund is needed to rebuild the nation's roads, bridges, water and sewer systems, waste treatment systems, and other public facilities in order to spur the economy. What we need now is a Marshall Plan for ourselves.

The 1992 presidential campaign heightened concern about the sluggishness of the national economy. As the new presidential term begins, we can expect (or at least hope for) attention to the nation's domestic agenda. One would anticipate the focus to be on the economy. The key is likely to be to *investment* to increase economic growth and enhance the nation's competitiveness.

The 1991 Surface Transportation Act authorizes spending of $155 billion over 6 years, gives states added flexibility, and increases the national commitment to urban mass transit. Federal matching grants would be provided on an 80/20 cost sharing basis, including:

$121 billion for highways,
$31.5 billion for mass transit, and
$3 billion for safety and research programs.[1]

There is growing recognition that further action is needed to improve our public capital stock beyond the 1991 Surface Transportation Act. We need investments that will enhance the movement of goods and provide transportation and other public services essential to the efficient working of markets and the smooth flow of goods and the factors of production.

Going back over a decade, there has been a series of studies documenting public infrastructure needs and urging action.

• The *Hard Choices* report prepared for the Joint Economic Committee of the U.S. Congress (1984) proposed a partnership between federal, state, and local governments in the form of a National Infrastructure Fund, with the planning and implementation of aided projects assigned to state and local governments.[2]

• The National Council on Public Works Improvement in *Fragile Foundations* (1988) argued that the quality of America's infrastructure was barely adequate to fulfill current requirements and insufficient to meet the demands of future economic growth and development.[3]

• In *Rebuilding the Foundations* (1990), the Office of Technology Assessment said that it is time for the federal and state governments to create a coherent, supportive, management framework for infrastructure projects that includes adequate financing.[4]

A growing body of public opinion and analysis argues that government spending for infrastructure is deficient and should be increased. Many experts are urging us to take action now:

• Robert Reich in *The Work of Nations* (1988) sees the federal withdrawal from infrastructure spending as precipitous and recommends that savings from the defense budget be applied to public investment in infrastructure, education, and training.[5]

• Felix Rohatyn recently called for "a vast national public investment program" in the New York Review of Books, both to meet the long-term needs of the country and to provide a countercyclical boost to the weak economy.[6]

• Economist Robert M. Solow believes it is essential for the U.S. to get serious now about private and public investment to make our economy competitive. He sees the United States as looking feckless and drifting in the eyes of other industrial countries.[7]

Historically, federal funds have been an indispensable part of the financing for public capital for ports, highways, bridges, transit systems, airports, wastewater treatment, and water supply plants and systems. However, over the past decade, the federal government has withdrawn much of this support for state and local infrastructure. The Congressional Budget Office's latest report on federal capital spending shows a steady decline in infrastructure spending as a percentage of all federal outlays, hitting a low of 2.5% in 1990. It was 4.5% a decade earlier in 1980, and throughout the seventies this ratio was over 4%. The downward trend of infrastructure spending is depicted in Figure 1 which shows that the amount of nondefense public physical capital public investment—on a net basis—has changed dramatically since 1970. Measured in constant dollars, net investment financed by federal grants-in-aid declined by 60% from 1970.

The reduction of federal assistance in the 1980s has been wrenching and painful for state and local governments. Both construction and maintenance expenditures for public infrastructure have been the victim of fiscal stress. Over the last decade, cities and states across the United States have been caught between demands for better services, rising costs, the inability to raise and accumulate revenues, and decreased funding from the federal government. Recent data show a decline in

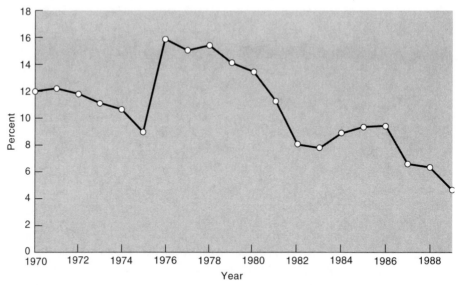

FIGURE 1 Federally Financed Net Investment in Nondefense Public Physical Capital (constant 1982 billion dollars). *Source*: Executive Office of the President. Office of Management and Budget. *Special Analyses: Budget of the U.S. Government, 1989.* Washington, DC: U.S. Government Printing Office.

total state and local government capital spending over the last 15 years (Figure 2). As a percentage of state and local government expenditure, capital spending from all sources declined from 16.6% in 1975 to 10.8% in 1989. Cities and states are unable to raise enough revenue to keep up and fix aging roads, outdated water supply systems, overcrowded airports, and other public facilities.

AMERICA IN RUINS

Ten years ago, Pat Choate and Susan Walter published a report, *America in Ruins, Beyond the Public Works Pork Barrel* that dramatized the case for rebuilding our public capital infrastructures. The message of this report is just as alive today:

> A large and growing number of communities are now hamstrung in their economic revitalization efforts because their basic public facilities—their streets, roads, water systems, and sewerage treatment plants—are either too limited, obsolete, or worn out to sustain a modernized industrial economy.[8]

Choate and Walter reviewed the major past efforts to use infrastructure investment for countercyclical policy purposes. The most recent such effort was the $6 billion Local Public Works (LPW) Impact Program in 1976–77. Choate and Walter's description of this program showed how good intentions can go awry. Like its predecessors, the LPW was unable to meet its objective of stimulating employment in distressed areas during an economic downturn. Choate and Walter said:

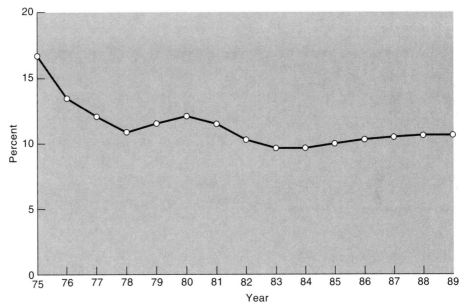

FIGURE 2   Real Capital Expenditure as a Percentage of Total Expenditures (constant 1982 billion dollars). *Source*: U.S. Census Bureau, Government Finances, selected years.

The temporary countercyclical Local Public Works program of 1976–1977 did nothing to relieve the 1974–1977 recession until late 1976. Over 80 percent of the direct employment generated by the LPW projects did not occur until the recovery phase of the cycle had begun.[9]

Choate and Walter found the LPW to be inadequate primarily because of legislative and executive incapacity, rather than failures with the program concept itself. "Lags occurred because of delays in securing passage of legislation, Presidential approval, appropriation of funds, selection of projects, and construction."[10]

Infrastructure and the Economy

The condition of our public infrastructure is intrinsically bound up in our economic renewal. Evidence suggests that infrastructure expenditures have been a key ingredient to the robust performance of the economy in the 1950s and 1960s.[11] Carefully selected public investment in infrastructure can improve national productivity and output. The building of the interstate highway system was a major contributor to the rise in national productivity during the 1960s.[12]

The argument made here that the United States has underinvested in public capital and that public capital has a positive impact on economic activity does not mean that the United States should suddenly and indiscriminately pump up the amount of money it spends on public capital, nor does it mean that careful cost-benefit analyses are no longer needed for individual projects.[13] Wisely planned infrastructure investments, coupled with efficient pricing, can improve federal and state finances and national economic conditions now and over the long run.[14]

HARD CHOICES REPORT

Three years after the Choate-Walter report was published in 1981, the National Infrastructure Study, prepared by the University of Colorado under the direction of the National Infrastructure Advisory Committee, produced the report called *Hard Choices*. This study was done for a subcommittee of the Joint Economic Committee of the U.S. Congress. The study group was chaired by Henry S. Reuss, former chair of the Joint Economic Committee. The two vice chairs were Peter C. Goldmark, Jr., Executive Director of the Port Authority of New York and New Jersey, and Lee White of Smith Barney.

Hard Choices analyzed national infrastructure repair needs and policy options in 23 states and evaluated projected repair needs and financial resources for highways and bridges, transportation facilities, water supply and distribution, and waste-water collection and treatment. The report highlighted the increasing gap between America's infrastructure needs and the ability to pay for them. The authors concluded that infrastructure deterioration had reached the point where it limits the ability of the U.S. to achieve a satisfactory rate of economic growth. Other conclusions of the National Infrastructure Advisory Committee were:

- The problem is national in scope, and it is not limited to a region or to any state.
- The problem is manageable, if the public sector's capacity to define needs and budget scarce resources is increased.
- The problem requires that state and local governments assume basic management and funding responsibilities.

The problem requires a predictable and long-term response by the federal government.[15]

The examination of infrastructure needs and revenues in this report indicated:

For the 23 states studied, total infrastructure needs (highways, other transportation, water sewerage) for the 1983 to 2000 period are projected to be about $750 billion in 1982 dollars. Revenue to meet these needs is to be about $460 billion resulting in a revenue shortfall of $290 billion.

For the country as a whole, infrastructure needs for the four categories addressed in this study are estimated to be $1,160 billion in 1982 dollars. Revenue to meet these needs is projected to be $710 billion leaving a financing gap of $450 billion.[16]

The authors found that the single most dominant need across the country is for additional spending on highways and bridges—an infrastructure category traditionally financed in large measure by the federal government. This study also looked at waste treatment and the needs of the water supply.

This report proposed that a new infrastructure-financing mechanism be established capitalized with long-term federal debt issued over a period of 10 years.

Interest on this debt would be borne by the federal government. The report said that the National Infrastructure Fund would provide state and local governments with a means to increase available capital at reasonable rates. It would avoid the numerous legal, financial, and institutional problems that 50 state governments and more than 10,000 local governments would encounter in trying to raise the same amount of capital through many individual debt issues.

1984 NATIONAL COUNCIL

In 1984 the National Council on Public Works Improvement was established by Congress to analyze the nation's public works improvements, including their age and condition, changes in their condition from preceding years, their maintenance needs and projected expenditures, and their capacity to sustain economic development and to support an expanding economy.[17]

This congressionally established council concluded that the quality of America's infrastructure—highways, mass transit, aviation, water resources, water supply, waste water, solid waste, hazardous waste handling, and so on—is barely adequate to fill current requirements and is insufficient to meet the demands of future economic growth and development.[18] It recommended a national commitment shared by all levels of government to upgrade the infrastructure that could require an annual national capital investment increase of up to 100% in new and existing public works.

THE CASE OF NEW YORK STATE

New York offers a good example of the problems in state and local capital investment. According to the U.S. Census, capital investment by all levels of government in New York State declined in 1982 dollars throughout the 1970s and early 1980s. This was especially true of highway-related expenditures. As a result of this decline, New York State now faces the serious consequences that come from inadequate maintenance and aging facilities. A report by a national group of government organizations described the problems facing New York's public facilities, and concluded:

> Over the next five years, 78 projects must be built to bring New York's municipalities into compliance with water quality standards mandated by the Clean Water Act, at a cost of $1.7 billion. To remain in compliance with these standards, in the next five years 547 additional projects must be funded at a cost of $5.6 billion.
>
> Of New York's 17,313 bridges, 11,808 (63 percent) are either structurally deficient or functionally obsolete.
>
> Three percent, or 798 miles, of paved rural highway miles in the state are rated as deficient under the Federal Highway Administration pavement conditions rating system; that is, the pavement is in "poor" condition and is therefore in need of resurfacing, rehabilitation, or reconstruction.[19]

The numbers are high, and may be overestimated, but the general assessment is on target.

New York is now trying to take up the challenge and reverse the decline in its capital stock. Governor Mario M. Cuomo has proposed an $800 million infrastructure bond act to pump prime the economy and lay a foundation for future economic growth. The money from the Jobs Bond Act would be disbursed among local governments to finance improvements of public facilities and create private-sector jobs.

As noted above, state and local government spending has declined over the past 15 years and cities and states are unable to keep up. No state can entirely fill the vacuum created by the reductions in federal public works support because right now they are under the gun to meet many burdens, for example, of Medicaid, education, and corrections.

Federal support of state and local capital investment should be more than a jobs program. It should go beyond the 1991 Surface Transportation Act and address a range of needs intrinsic to the growing national concern about America's economic future. According to the Office of Technology Assessment, a strong case can be made for a dedicated federal fund to assist states and local governments in the construction and repair of deteriorating public facilities.

A CAPITAL INVESTMENT BLOCK GRANT

The history of federal grant-in-aid programs in the United States suggests a number of lessons for thinking about how the federal government should operate in this field. What is needed now is a Capital Investment Block Grant. Such a fund, administered by the U.S. Treasury, would be used to expand and modernize capital facilities. Aid should be provided on a flexible basis to avoid interference with state and local practices. It should be allocated according to a redistributive formula, favoring communities and regions with the greatest capital deficiencies and economic needs. States should be free to use these grant funds for a wide range of capital investments, including roads, bridges, other transportation facilities, waste treatment, water systems, mass transit, schools, and other public facilities. The Capital Investment Block Grant should be a multiyear program.

1 Grants of $25 billion per year should be made annually to the states in predictable annual installments.

2 States should be required to use 60% of the total funding received for areas that are eligible for aid under a similar program, the Community Development Block Grant, that has withstood the test of time and aids urban development. This requirement could be waived by the Secretary of the Treasury for sparsely settled and smaller states.

3 Funds should not be used as a substitute for planned or existing state and local public works projects.

4 The Secretary of the Treasury should be required to issue an annual inventory statement on infrastructure needs, an evaluation of basic infrastructure conditions in the states, and a report of the uses of the grant funds provided under this program.

5 An automatically triggered 50% countercyclical add-on should be provided when there is a one quarter decline in GNP or the classification of a given period as a recession by the National Bureau of Economic Research, whichever comes sooner.

The Capital Investment Block Grant would be an instrument of both long-term and countercyclical economic policy. Pat Choate and Susan Walter, in *America in Ruins* (1981), analyzed the ways capital investments can be used to stabilize the economy. The basic problem limiting the impact of public works investment in the past, they said, has been the tendency to increase expenditures during expansionary phases and decrease them during contractionary periods.

Under the Capital Investment Block Grant Fund proposed here, states and local governments would be required to maintain a list of projects that would be ready to go as the economy begins to slide into recession. There would be a number of benefits from having the fund have a permanent countercyclical add-on:

• It would reduce the adverse consequences caused by procyclical investment patterns of these investments;

• A permanent, more systematic countercyclical public works policy would reduce the "crisis" management atmosphere which surrounds temporary public works programs;

• It would reduce the lag between the beginning of a recession and the time when benefits flow;

• It would facilitate better targeted investments in order to address regional and sectoral variations in the economic cycle; and

• It would improve fiscal stability to state and local finance.[20]

At the state level, I favor a requirement under this block grant for the establishment by the states of panels like the U.S. military base-closing commissions. The panels would be charged to recommend a program of priority projects for development that the governor and legislature would have to consider en bloc. They could send it back, but not modify the list.

A critical operational question for such a program is what is its *impact*? One needs to think through the substitution issue carefully. Our earlier evaluation research on revenue sharing and block grants suggests that for capital projects this is a harder issue to deal with than in the case of operating programs. For the latter, recipient jurisdictions of revenue sharing and block grant funds tend to avoid substitution, not wanting to lock in new operational commitments that would be hard to cut off if and when the federal government—often unpredictable and fickle—cuts their money or changes the rules.[21]

Substitution is not always bad. The issue is complicated. One good way to handle it would be to empower the Secretary of the Treasury to establish oversight committees in each state to report on the use of Capital Investment Block Grant funds and on the substitution issue, assuming the law requires "maintenance of effort," which I believe it should. In any event, Congress is likely to want to do this. These state committees in turn would be charged to report publicly on an annual basis, would have access to state and local records, and would use a common analytical framework and structure for their reports. The Secretary of the Treasury on a longer-term, follow-up basis would be required to compile these reports and submit an overall report to the Congress on the use of these block grant funds and compliance with maintenance of effort.

In long run, my Rockefeller Institute colleague Steven D. Gold and I favor special borrowing through a federal capital budget for these types of investment purposes. In the near term, an increase in the gasoline tax is also a possible and logical funding source for the Capital Investment Block Grant. Another funding option for such a program is to adopt the approach of the "National Infrastructure Fund" proposed in the 1984 *Hard Choices* report (cited above), though on balance I think the block grant approach suggested above is a better way to proceed.

The start of a new presidential term in 1993 should serve as the impetus for adopting new economic and domestic policies, including a public capital program—on a substantial scale—what I called earlier, "a Marshall Plan for ourselves." The program described here could generate upwards of half a trillion dollars in investments in public facilities (planned, committed, or under way) between now and the millennial year, 2000.

The economy of the United States has been a beacon for industrial development throughout the world. Its hallmark is a high standard of personal consumption for all of its citizens. But we got lost in the 1980s. We overdid it. We ate our seed corn. Now we need to adopt such a Marshall Plan for ourselves to stimulate the investment side of the American economic equation. This would be sound economics, good for growth, and good for the American future.

Author's note: I gratefully acknowledge help from Robert M. Solow, Steven D. Gold, Paul Page, and our competent editor, Laurie Norris, in writing this article. The ideas here, however, are in the usual way my responsibility.

NOTES

1 U.S. Congress, House of Representatives, *Intermodal Surface Transportation Efficiency Act of 1991* (Washington, DC: U.S. Government Printing Office, 1991), pp. 4–8.

2 U.S. Congress, Joint Economic Committee, *Hard Choices* (Washington, DC: U.S. Government Printing Office, 1984).

3 National Council on Public Works Improvement, *Fragile Foundations: A Report on America's Public Works* (Washington, DC: U.S. Government Printing Office, 1988).

4 U.S. Congress, Office of Technology Assessment, *Rebuilding the Foundations: Public Works Technologies, Management and Financing* (Washington, DC: U.S. Government Printing Office, 1990).

5 Robert Reich, *The Work of Nations* (New York: Vintage Books, 1992), pp. 254–60.

6 Felix Rohatyn, "The New Domestic Order?" *The New York Review of Books* (New York, November 21, 1991), p. 8.

7 Robert M. Solow, Address on the occasion of his receiving an honorary degree from the University at Albany, State University of New York, May 26, 1991.

8 Pat Choate and Susan Walter, *America in Ruins, Beyond the Public Works Pork Barrel,* Council of State Planning Agencies (Washington, DC, 1981), p. 15.

9 Ibid., p. 24.

10 Ibid.

11 David A. Aschauer, "Why Is Infrastructure Important?" in *Is There a Shortfall in Public Infrastructure?* Conference proceedings, ed. A. H. Munnell (Harwich Port, MA: Federal Reserve Bank of Boston, June 1990), p. 48.

12 Charles L. Schultze, "The Federal Budget and the Nation's Economic Health," in *Setting National Priorities: Policy for the Nineties,* ed. Henry J. Aaron (Washington, DC: Brookings, 1990).

13 Alicia H. Munnell, *Is There a Shortfall in Public Capital Investment?* Conference proceedings, ed. A. H. Munnell (Harwich Port, MA: Federal Reserve Bank of Boston, June 1990), pp. 94–95.

14 Clifford M. Winston, "How Efficient Is Current Infrastructure Spending and Pricing?" in Munnell, *Is There a Shortfall in Public Capital Investment?*, p. 199.

15 U.S. Congress, Joint Economic Committee, *Hard Choices,* p. 113.

16 Ibid., p. 8.

17 The chairman of this National Council was Joseph M. Giglio, Managing Director, Bear, Stearns and Company.

18 National Council on Public Works Improvement, *Fragile Foundations,* p. 10.

19 Rebuild America Coalition, "America's Infrastructure: Preserving Our Quality of Life," in *U.S. Congress, Committee on Public Works and Transportation, To Examine the Future of Our Nation's Infrastructure Needs* (Washington, DC: U.S. Government Printing Office, 1991), p. 163.

20 Choate and Walter, *America in Ruins*, pp. 25–26.

21 Earlier research is discussed in Richard P. Nathan, Allen D. Manvel, Susannah E. Calkins, and Associates, *Monitoring Revenue Sharing* (Washington, DC: Brookings, 1975): Richard P. Nathan, Charles F. Adams, Jr., and Associates, *Revenue Sharing: The Second Round* (Washington, DC: Brookings, 1977); Richard P. Nathan, Paul R. Dommel, Sarah F. Liebschutz, Milton D. Morris, and Associates, *Block Grants for Community Development* (Washington, DC: U.S. Department of Housing and Urban Development, January, 1977); and Richard P. Nathan, Robert F. Cook, V. Lane Rawlins, and Associates, *Public Service Employment: A Field Evaluation* (Washington, DC: Brookings, 1981).

SEVEN. TRANSPORTATION—SUGGESTED READINGS

Cervero, Robert. 1986. *Suburban Gridlock*. New Brunswick, NJ: Center for Urban Policy Research, Rutgers University.

Cervero, Robert. 1989. "Jobs-Housing Balancing and Regional Mobility." *Journal of the American Planning Association* 55, 2.

Choate, Pat, and Susan Walter. 1981. *America in Ruins, Beyond the Public Works Pork Barrel*. Washington, DC: Council of State Planning Agencies.

Dickey, J. 1990. *Metropolitan Transportation Planning*. Washington, DC: Scripta Book.

Hanson, Susan, ed. 1986. *The Geography of Urban Transportation*. New York: Guilford Press.

Hanson, Susan, ed. 1986. *The Car and The City*. New York: Guilford Press.

Meyer, John R., and Jose A. Gomez-Ibanez. 1981. *Autos, Transit and Cities*. Cambridge, MA: Harvard.

Stein, Jay M. 1988. *Public Infrastructure Planning and Management*. Newbury Park, CA: Sage Publications.

Wachs, Martin, and Margaret Crawford. 1992. *The Geography of Urban Transportation*. Ann Arbor: The University of Michigan Press.

8

HOUSING, SOCIAL AND COMMUNITY PLANNING

A Ladder of Citizen Participation

Sherry R. Arnstein

Sherry R. Arnstein's article offers a typology of eight levels of citizen participation arranged in a ladder pattern. The "ladder" contains rungs of power. The first rung is the least powerful position of "manipulation," while the highest rung is for real "citizen control." For Arnstein, meaningful citizen participation means citizen power. She states that it is a strategy by which the have-nots "can induce significant social reform which enables them to share in the benefits of the affluent society" (p. 359).

The idea of citizen participation is a little like eating spinach: no one is against it in principle because it is good for you. Participation of the governed in their government is, in theory, the cornerstone of democracy—a revered idea that is vigorously applauded by virtually everyone. The applause is reduced to polite hand-claps, however, when this principle is advocated by the have-not blacks, Mexican-Americans, Puerto Ricans, Indians, Eskimos, and whites. And when the have-nots define participation as redistribution of power, the American consensus on the fundamental principle explodes into many shades of outright racial, ethnic, ideological, and political opposition.

There have been many recent speeches, articles, and books[1] which explore in detail *who* are the have-nots of our time. There has been much recent documentation of *why* the have-nots have become so offended and embittered by their powerlessness to deal with the profound inequities and injustices pervading their daily lives. But there has been very little analysis of the content of the current controversial slogan: "citizen participation" or "maximum feasible participation." In short: *What* is citizen participation and what is its relationship to the social imperatives of our time?

CITIZEN PARTICIPATION IS CITIZEN POWER

Because the question has been a bone of political contention, most of the answers have been purposely buried in innocuous euphemisms like "self-help" or "citizen involvement." Still others have been embellished with misleading rhetoric like "absolute control" which is something no one—including the President of the United States—has or can have. Between understated euphemisms and exacerbated rhetoric, even scholars have found it difficult to follow the controversy. To the headline reading public, it is simply bewildering.

My answer to the critical *what* question is simply that citizen participation is a categorical term for citizen power. It is the redistribution of power that enables the

Reprinted by permission of the *Journal of the American Institute of Planners* 8, 3, July 1969.

FIGURE 1   French Student Poster. In English, I participate; you participate; he participates; we participate; you participate . . . **They profit.**

have-not citizens, presently excluded from the political and economic processes, to be deliberately included in the future. It is the strategy by which the have-nots join in determining how information is shared, goals and policies are set, tax resources are allocated, programs are operated, and benefits like contracts and patronage are parceled out. In short, it is the means by which they can induce significant social reform which enables them to share in the benefits of the affluent society.

Empty Ritual Versus Benefit

There is a critical difference between going through the empty ritual of participation and having the real power needed to affect the outcome of the process. This difference is brilliantly capsulized in a poster painted last spring by the French students to explain the student-worker rebellion.[2] (See Figure 1.) The poster highlights the fundamental point that participation without redistribution of power is an empty and frustrating process for the powerless. It allows the powerholders to claim that all sides were considered, but makes it possible for only some of those sides to benefit. It maintains the status quo. Essentially, it is what has been happening in most of the 1,000 Community Action Programs, and what promises to be repeated in the vast majority of the 150 Model Cities programs.

TYPES OF PARTICIPATION AND "NONPARTICIPATION"

A typology of eight *levels* of participation may help in analysis of this confused issue. For illustrative purposes the eight types are arranged in a ladder pattern with each rung corresponding to the extent of citizens' power in determining the end product.[3] (See Figure 2.)

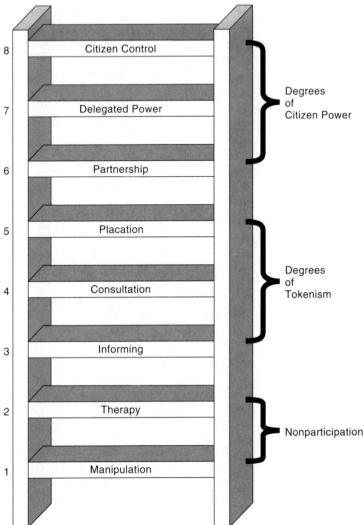

FIGURE 2 Eight Rungs on a Ladder of Citizen Participation.

The bottom rungs of the ladder are (1) *Manipulation* and (2) *Therapy*. These two rungs describe levels of "non-participation" that have been contrived by some to substitute for genuine participation. Their real objective is not to enable people to participate in planning or conducting programs, but to enable powerholders to "educate" or "cure" the participants. Rungs 3 and 4 progress to levels of "tokenism" that allow the have-nots to hear and to have a voice: (3) *Informing* and (4) *Consultation*. When they are proffered by powerholders as the total extent of participation, citizens may indeed hear and be heard. But under these conditions they lack the power to insure that their views will be *heeded* by the powerful. When participation is restricted to these levels, there is no followthrough, no "muscle," hence no assurance of changing the status quo. Rung (5) *Placation*, is simply a higher level tokenism because the groundrules allow have-nots to advise, but retain for the powerholders the continued right to decide.

Further up the ladder are levels of citizen power with increasing degrees of decision-making clout. Citizens can enter into a (6) *Partnership* that enables them to negotiate and engage in trade-offs with traditional powerholders. At the topmost rungs, (7) *Delegated Power* and (8) *Citizen Control*, have-not citizens obtain the majority of decision-making seats, or full managerial power.

Obviously, the eight-rung ladder is a simplification, but it helps to illustrate the point that so many have missed—that there are significant gradations of citizen participation. Knowing these gradations makes it possible to cut through the hyperbole to understand the increasingly strident demands for participation from the have-nots as well as the gamut of confusing responses from the powerholders.

Though the typology uses examples from federal programs such as urban renewal, anti-poverty, and Model Cities; it could just as easily be illustrated in the church, currently facing demands for power from priests and laymen who seek to change its mission; colleges and universities which in some cases have become literal battlegrounds over the issue of student power; or public schools, city halls, and police departments (or big business which is likely to be next on the expanding list of targets). The underlying issues are essentially the same—"nobodies" in several arenas are trying to become "somebodies" with enough power to make the target institutions responsive to their views, aspirations, and needs.

Limitations of the Typology

The ladder juxtaposes powerless citizens with the powerful in order to highlight the fundamental divisions between them. In actuality, neither the have-nots nor the powerholders are homogeneous blocs. Each group encompasses a host of divergent points of view, significant cleavages, competing vested interests, and splintered subgroups. The justification for using such simplistic abstractions is that in most cases the have-nots really do perceive the powerful as a monolithic "system," and powerholders actually do view the have-nots as a sea of "those people," with little comprehension of the class and caste differences among them.

It should be noted that the typology does not include an analysis of the most significant roadblocks to achieving genuine levels of participation. These roadblocks lie on both sides of the simplistic fence. On the powerholders' side, they include racism, paternalism, and resistance to power redistribution. On the have-nots' side, they include inadequacies of the poor community's political socioeconomic infrastructure and knowledge-base, plus difficulties of organizing a representative and accountable citizens' group in the face of futility, alienation, and distrust.

Another caution about the eight separate rungs on the ladder: In the real world of people and programs, there might be 150 rungs with less sharp and "pure" distinctions among them. Furthermore, some of the characteristics used to illustrate each of the eight types might be applicable to other rungs. For example, employment of the have-nots in a program or on a planning staff could occur at any of the eight rungs and could represent either a legitimate or illegitimate characteristic of citizen participation. Depending on their motives, powerholders can hire poor people to coopt them, to placate them, or to utilize the have-nots' special skills and insights.[4] Some mayors, in private, actually boast of their strategy in hiring militant black leaders to muzzle them while destroying their credibility in the black community.

CHARACTERISTICS AND ILLUSTRATIONS

It is in this context of power and powerlessness that the characteristics of the eight rungs are illustrated by examples from current federal social programs.

1. Manipulation

In the name of citizen participation, people are placed on rubberstamp advisory committees or advisory boards for the express purpose of "educating" them or engineering their support. Instead of genuine citizen participation, the bottom rung of the ladder signifies the distortion of participation into a public relations vehicle by powerholders.

This illusory form of "participation" initially came into vogue with urban renewal when the socially elite were invited by city housing officials to serve on Citizen Advisory Committees (CACs). Another target of manipulation was the CAC subcommittees on minority groups, which in theory were to protect the rights of Negroes in the renewal program. In practice, these subcommittees, like their parent CACs, functioned mostly as letterheads, trotted forward at appropriate times to promote urban renewal plans (in recent years known as Negro removal plans).

At meetings of the Citizen *Advisory* Committees, it was the officials who educated, persuaded, and advised the citizens, not the reverse. Federal guidelines for the renewal programs legitimized the manipulative agenda by emphasizing the terms "information-gathering," "public relations," and "support" as the explicit functions of the committees.[5]

This style of nonparticipation has since been applied to other programs encompassing the poor. Examples of this are seen in Community Action Agencies (CAAs) which have created structures called "neighborhood councils" or "neighborhood advisory groups." These bodies frequently have no legitimate function or power.[6] The CAAs use them to "prove" that "grassroots people" are involved in the program. But the program may not have been discussed with "the people." Or it may have been described at a meeting in the most general terms; "We need your signatures on this proposal for a multiservice center which will house, under one roof, doctors from the health department, workers from the welfare department, and specialists from the employment service."

The signators are not informed that the $2 million-per-year center will only refer residents to the same old waiting lines at the same old agencies across town. No one is asked if such a referral center is really needed in his neighborhood. No one realizes that the contractor for the building is the mayor's brother-in-law, or that the new director of the center will be the same old community organization specialist from the urban renewal agency.

After signing their names, the proud grassrooters dutifully spread the word that they have "participated" in bringing a new and wonderful center to the neighborhood to provide people with drastically needed jobs and health and welfare services. Only after the ribboncutting ceremony do the members of the neighborhood council realize that they didn't ask the important questions, and that they had no technical advisors of their own to help them grasp the fine legal print. The new center, which is open 9 to 5 on weekdays only, actually adds to their problems. Now the old agencies across town won't talk with them unless they have a pink paper slip to prove that they have been referred by "their" shiny new neighborhood center.

Unfortunately, this chicanery is not a unique example. Instead it is almost typical of what has been perpetrated in the name of high-sounding rhetoric like "grassroots participation." This sham lies at the heart of the deep-seated exasperation and hostility of the have-nots toward the powerholders.

One hopeful note is that, having been so grossly affronted, some citizens have learned the Mickey Mouse game, and now they too know how to play. As a result of this knowledge, they are demanding genuine levels of participation to assure them that public programs are relevant to their needs and responsive to their priorities.

2. Therapy

In some respects group therapy, masked as citizen participation, should be on the lowest rung of the ladder because it is both dishonest and arrogant. Its administrators—mental health experts from social workers to psychiatrists—assume that powerlessness is synonymous with mental illness. On this assumption, under a masquerade of involving citizens in planning, the experts subject the citizens to clinical group therapy. What makes this form of "participation" so invidious is that citizens are engaged in extensive activity, but the focus of it is on curing them of their "pathology" rather than changing the racism and victimization that create their "pathologies."

Consider an incident that occurred in Pennsylvania less than one year ago. When a father took his seriously ill baby to the emergency clinic of a local hospital, a young resident physician on duty instructed him to take the baby home and feed it sugar water. The baby died that afternoon of pneumonia and dehydration. The overwrought father complained to the board of the local Community Action Agency. Instead of launching an investigation of the hospital to determine what changes would prevent similar deaths or other forms of malpractice, the board invited the father to attend the CAA's (therapy) child-care sessions for parents, and promised him that someone would "telephone the hospital director to see that it never happens again."

Less dramatic, but more common examples of therapy, masquerading as citizen participation, may be seen in public housing programs where tenant groups are used as vehicles for promoting control-your-child or cleanup campaigns. The tenants are brought together to help them "adjust their values and attitudes to those of the larger society." Under these groundrules, they are diverted from dealing with such important matters as: arbitrary evictions; segregation of the housing project; or why is there a three-month time lapse to get a broken window replaced in winter.

The complexity of the concept of mental illness in our time can be seen in the experiences of student/civil rights workers facing guns, whips, and other forms of terror in the South. They needed the help of socially attuned psychiatrists to deal with their fears and to avoid paranoia.[7]

3. Informing

Informing citizens of their rights, responsibilities, and options can be the most important first step toward legitimate citizen participation. However, too frequently the emphasis is placed on a one-way flow of information—from officials to citizens—with no channel provided for feedback and no power for negotiation. Under these conditions, particularly when information is provided at a late stage in planning, people have little opportunity to influence the program designed "for their benefit." The most frequent tools used for such one-way communication are the news media, pamphlets, posters, and responses to inquiries.

Meetings can also be turned into vehicles for one-way communication by the simple device of providing superficial information, discouraging questions, or giving irrelevant answers. At a recent Model Cities citizen planning meeting in Providence, Rhode Island, the topic was "tot-lots." A group of elected citizen representatives, almost all of whom were attending three to five meetings a week, devoted an hour to a discussion of the placement of six tot-lots. The neighborhood is half black, half white. Several of the black representatives noted that four tot-lots were proposed for the white district and only two for the black. The city official responded with a lengthy, highly technical explanation about costs per square foot and available property. It was clear that most of the residents did not understand his explanation. And it was clear to observers from the Office of Economic Opportunity that other options did exist which, considering available funds, would have brought about a more equitable distribution of facilities. Intimidated by futility, legalistic jargon, and prestige of the official, the citizens accepted the "information" and endorsed the agency's proposal to place four lots in the white neighborhood.[8]

4. Consultation

Inviting citizens' opinions, like informing them, can be a legitimate step toward their full participation. But if consulting them is not combined with other modes of participation, this rung of the ladder is still a sham since it offers no assurance that citizen concerns and ideas will be taken into account. The most frequent methods used for consulting people are attitude surveys, neighborhood meetings, and public hearings.

When powerholders restrict the input of citizens' ideas solely to this level, participation remains just a window-dressing ritual. People are primarily perceived as statistical abstractions, and participation is measured by how many come to meetings, take brochures home, or answer a questionnaire. What citizens achieve in all this activity is that they have "participated in participation." And what powerholders achieve is the evidence that they have gone through the required motions of involving "those people."

Attitude surveys have become a particular bone of contention in ghetto neighborhoods. Residents are increasingly unhappy about the number of times per week they are surveyed about their problems and hopes. As one woman put it: "Nothing ever happens with those damned questions, except the surveyor gets $3 an hour, and my washing doesn't get done that day." In some communities, residents are so annoyed that they are demanding a fee for research interviews.

Attitude surveys are not very valid indicators of community opinion when used without other input from citizens. Survey after survey (paid for out of antipoverty funds) has "documented" that poor housewives most want tot-lots in their neighborhood where young children can play safely. But most of the women answered these questionnaires without knowing what their options were. They assumed that if they asked for something small, they might just get something useful in the neighborhood. Had the mothers known that a free prepaid health insurance plan was a possible option, they might not have put tot-lots so high on their wish lists.

A classic misuse of the consultation rung occurred at a New Haven, Connecticut, community meeting held to consult citizens on a proposed Model Cities grant. James V. Cunningham, in an unpublished report to the Ford Foundation, described the crowd as large and "mostly hostile":[9]

> Members of The Hill Parents Association demanded to know why residents had not participated in drawing up the proposal. CAA director Spitz explained that it was merely a proposal for seeking Federal planning funds—that once funds were obtained, residents would be deeply involved in the planning. An outside observer who sat in the audience described the meeting this way:
>
> "Spitz and Mel Adams ran the meeting on their own. No representatives of a Hill group moderated or even sat on the stage. Spitz told the 300 residents that this huge meeting was an example of 'participation in planning.' To prove this, since there was a lot of dissatisfaction in the audience, he called for a 'vote' on each component of the proposal. The vote took this form: 'Can I see the hands of all those in favor of a health clinic? All those opposed?' It was a little like asking who favors motherhood."

It was a combination of the deep suspicion aroused at this meeting and a long history of similar forms of "window-dressing participation" that led New Haven residents to demand control of the program.

By way of contrast, it is useful to look at Denver where technicians learned that even the best intentioned among them are often unfamiliar with, and even insensitive to, the problems and aspirations of the poor. The technical director of the

Model Cities program has described the way professional planners assumed that the residents, victimized by high-priced local storekeepers, "badly needed consumer education."[10] The residents, on the other hand, pointed out that the local storekeepers performed a valuable function. Although they overcharged, they also gave credit, offered advice, and frequently were the only neighborhood place to cash welfare or salary checks. As a result of this consultation, technicians and residents agreed to substitute the creation of needed credit institutions in the neighborhood for a consumer education program.

5. Placation

It is at this level that citizens begin to have some degree of influence though tokenism is still apparent. An example of placation strategy is to place a few hand-picked "worthy" poor on boards of Community Action Agencies or on public bodies like the board of education, police commission, or housing authority. If they are not accountable to a constituency in the community and if the traditional power elite hold the majority of seats, the have-nots can be easily outvoted and outfoxed. Another example is the Model Cities advisory and planning committees. They allow citizens to advise or plan ad infinitum but retain for powerholders the right to judge the legitimacy or feasibility of the advice. The degree to which citizens are actually placated, of course, depends largely on two factors: the quality of technical assistance they have in articulating their priorities; and the extent to which the community has been organized to press for those priorities.

It is not surprising that the level of citizen participation in the vast majority of Model Cities programs is at the placation rung of the ladder or below. Policymakers at the Department of Housing and Urban Development (HUD) were determined to return the genie of citizen power to the bottle from which it had escaped (in a few cities) as a result of the provision stipulating "maximum feasible participation" in poverty programs. Therefore, HUD channeled its physical-social-economic rejuvenation approach for blighted neighborhoods through city hall. It drafted legislation requiring that all Model Cities' money flow to a local City Demonstration Agency (CDA) through the elected city council. As enacted by Congress, this gave local city councils final veto power over planning and programming and ruled about any direct funding relationship between community groups and HUD.

HUD required the CDAs to create coalition, policymaking boards that would include necessary local powerholders to create a comprehensive physical-social plan during the first year. The plan was to be carried out in a subsequent five-year action phase. HUD, unlike OEO, did not require that have-not citizens be included on the CDA decision-making boards. HUD's Performance Standards for Citizen Participation only demanded that "citizens have clear and direct access to the decision-making process."

Accordingly, the CDAs structured their policymaking boards to include some combination of elected officials; school representatives; housing, health, and welfare officials; employment and police department representatives; and various civic, labor, and business leaders. Some CDAs included citizens from the neighborhood. Many mayors correctly interpreted the HUD provision for "access to the decision-making process" as the escape hatch they sought to relegate citizens to the traditional advisory role.

Most CDAs created residents' advisory committees. An alarmingly significant number created citizens' policy boards and citizens' policy committees which are totally misnamed as they have either no policy-making function or only a very limited authority. Almost every CDA created about a dozen planning committees or task forces on functional lines: health, welfare, education, housing, and unemployment. In most cases, have-not citizens were invited to serve on these committees along with technicians from relevant public agencies. Some CDAs, on the other hand, structured planning committees of technicians and parallel committees of citizens.

In most Model Cities programs, endless time has been spent fashioning complicated board, committee, and task force structures for the planning year. But the rights and responsibilities of the various elements of those structures are not defined and are ambiguous. Such ambiguity is likely to cause considerable conflict at the end of the one-year planning process. For at this point, citizens may realize that they have once again extensively "participated" but have not profited beyond the extent the powerholders decide to placate them.

Results of a staff study (conducted in the summer of 1968 before the second round of seventy-five planning grants were awarded) were released in a December 1968 HUD bulletin.[11] Though this public document uses much more delicate and diplomatic language, it attests to the already cited criticisms of non-policymaking policy boards and ambiguous complicated structures, in addition to the following findings:

1 Most CDAs did not negotiate citizen participation requirements with residents.

2 Citizens, drawing on past negative experiences with local powerholders, were extremely suspicious of this new panacea program. They were legitimately distrustful of city hall's motives.

3 Most CDAs were not working with citizens' groups that were genuinely representative of model neighborhoods and accountable to neighborhood constituencies. As in so many of the poverty programs, those who were involved were more representative of the upwardly mobile working-class. Thus their acquiescence to plans prepared by city agencies was not likely to reflect the views of the unemployed, the young, the more militant residents, and the hard-core poor.

4 Residents who were participating in as many as three to five meetings per week were unaware of their minimum rights, responsibilities, and the options available to them under the program. For example, they did not realize that they were not required to accept technical help from city technicians they distrusted.

5 Most of the technical assistance provided by CDAs and city agencies was of third-rate quality, paternalistic, and condescending. Agency technicians did not suggest innovative options. They reacted bureaucratically when the residents pressed for innovative approaches. The vested interests of the old-line city agencies were a major—albeit hidden—agenda.

6 Most CDAs were not engaged in planning that was comprehensive enough to expose and deal with the roots of urban decay. They engaged in "meetingitis" and were supporting strategies that resulted in "projectitis," the outcome of which was a "laundry list" of traditional programs to be conducted by traditional agencies in the traditional manner under which slums emerged in the first place.

7 Residents were not getting enough information from CDAs to enable them to review CDA developed plans or to initiate plans of their own as required by HUD. At best, they were getting superficial information. At worst, they were not even getting copies of official HUD materials.

8 Most residents were unaware of their rights to be reimbursed for expenses incurred because of participation—babysitting, transportation costs, and so on.

9 The training of residents, which would enable them to understand the labyrinth of the federal-state-city systems and networks of subsystems, was an item that most CDAs did not even consider.

These findings led to a new public interpretation of HUD's approach to citizen participation. Though the requirements for the seventy-five "second-round" Model City grantees were not changed, HUD's twenty-seven page technical bulletin on citizen participation repeatedly advocated that cities share power with residents. It also urged CDAs to experiment with subcontracts under which the residents' groups could hire their own trusted technicians.

A more recent evaluation was circulated in February 1969 by OSTI, a private firm that entered into a contract with OEO to provide technical assistance and training to citizens involved in Model Cities programs in the northeast region of the country. OSTI's report to OEO corroborates the earlier study. In addition it states:[12]

> In practically no Model Cities structure does citizen participation mean truly shared decision-making, such that citizens might view themselves as "the partners in this program. . . ."
>
> In general, citizens are finding it impossible to have a significant impact on the comprehensive planning which is going on. In most cases the staff planners of the CDA and the planners of existing agencies are carrying out the actual planning with citizens having a peripheral role of watchdog and, ultimately, the "rubber stamp" of the plan generated. In cases where citizens have the direct responsibility for generating program plans, the time period allowed and the independent technical resources being made available to them are not adequate to allow them to do anything more than generate very traditional approaches to the problems they are attempting to solve.
>
> In general, little or no thought has been given to the means of insuring continued citizen participation during the stage of implementation. In most cases, traditional agencies are envisaged as the implementors of Model Cities programs and few mechanisms have been developed for encouraging organizational change or change in the method of pro-

gram delivery within these agencies or for insuring that citizens will have some influence over these agencies as they implement Model Cities programs. . . .

By and large, people are once again being planned *for*. In most situations the major planning decisions are being made by CDA staff and approved in a formalistic way by policy boards.

6. Partnership

At this rung of the ladder, power is in fact redistributed through negotiation between citizens and powerholders. They agree to share planning and decision-making responsibilities through such structures as joint policy boards, planning committees and mechanisms for resolving impasses. After the groundrules have been established through some form of give-and-take, they are not subject to unilateral change.

Partnership can work most effectively when there is an organized power-base in the community to which the citizen leaders are accountable; when the citizens group has the financial resources to pay its leaders reasonable honoraria for their time-consuming efforts; and when the group has the resources to hire (and fire) its own technicians, lawyers, and community organizers. With these ingredients, citizens have some genuine bargaining influence over the outcome of the plan (as long as both parties find it useful to maintain the partnership). One community leader described it "like coming to city hall with hat on head instead of in hand."

In the Model Cities program only about fifteen of the so-called first generation of seventy-five cities have reached some significant degree of power-sharing with residents. In all but one of those cities, it was angry citizen demands, rather than city initiative, that led to the negotiated sharing of power.[13] The negotiations were triggered by citizens who had been enraged by previous forms of alleged participation. They were both angry and sophisticated enough to refuse to be "conned" again. They threatened to oppose the awarding of a planning grant to the city. They sent delegations to HUD in Washington. They used abrasive language. Negotiation took place under a cloud of suspicion and rancor.

In most cases where power has come to be shared it was *taken by the citizens*, not given by the city. There is nothing new about that process. Since those who have power normally want to hang onto it, historically it has had to be wrested by the powerless rather than proffered by the powerful.

Such a working partnership was negotiated by the residents in the Philadelphia model neighborhood. Like most applicants for a Model Cities grant, Philadelphia wrote its more than 400 page application and waved it at a hastily called meeting of community leaders. When those present were asked for an endorsement, they angrily protested the city's failure to consult them on preparation of the extensive application. A community spokesman threatened to mobilize a neighborhood protest *against* the application unless the city agreed to give the citizens a couple of weeks to review the application and recommend changes. The officials agreed.

At their next meeting, citizens handed the city officials a substitute citizen participation section that changed the groundrules from a weak citizens' advisory role to a strong shared power agreement. Philadelphia's application to HUD included the citizens' substitution word for word. (It also included a new citizen prepared introductory chapter that changed the city's description of the model neighborhood from a paternalistic description of problems to a realistic analysis of its strengths, weaknesses, and potentials.)

Consequently, the proposed policy-making committee of the Philadelphia CDA was revamped to give five out of eleven seats to the residents' organization, which is called the Area Wide Council (AWC). The AWC obtained a subcontract from the CDA for more than $20,000 per month, which is used to maintain the neighborhood organization, to pay citizen leaders $7 per meeting for their planning services, and to pay the salaries of a staff of community organizers, planners, and other technicians. AWC has the power to initiate plans of its own, to engage in joint planning with CDA committees, and to review plans initiated by city agencies. It has a veto power in that no plans may be submitted by the CDA to the city council until they have been reviewed, and any differences of opinion have been successfully negotiated with the AWC. Representatives of the AWC (which is a federation of neighborhood organizations grouped into sixteen neighborhood "hubs") may attend all meetings of CDA task forces, planning committees, or subcommittees.

Though the city council has final veto power over the plan (by federal law), the AWC believes it has a neighborhood constituency that is strong enough to negotiate any eleventh-hour objections the city council might raise when it considers such AWC proposed innovations as an AWC Land Bank, an AWC Economic Development Corporation, and an experimental income maintenance program for 900 poor families.

7. Delegated Power

Negotiations between citizens and public officials can also result in citizens achieving dominant decision-making authority over a particular plan or program. Model City policy boards or CAA delegate agencies on which citizens have a clear majority of seats and genuine specified powers are typical examples. At this level, the ladder has been scaled to the point where citizens hold the significant cards to assure accountability of the program to them. To resolve differences, powerholders need to start the bargaining process rather than respond to pressure from the other end.

Such a dominant decision-making role has been attained by residents in a handful of Model Cities including Cambridge, Massachusetts; Dayton, and Columbus, Ohio; Minneapolis, Minnesota; St. Louis, Missouri; Hartford and New Haven, Connecticut; and Oakland, California.

In New Haven, residents of the Hill neighborhood have created a corporation that has been delegated the power to prepare the entire Model Cities plan. The city, which received a $117,000 planning grant from HUD, has subcontracted $110,000 of it to the neighborhood corporation to hire its own planning staff and consultants. The Hill Neighborhood Corporation has eleven representatives on the twenty-one-member CDA board which assures it a majority voice when its proposed plan is reviewed by the CDA.

Another model of delegated power is separate and parallel groups of citizens and powerholders, with provision for citizen veto if differences of opinion cannot be resolved through negotiation. This is a particularly interesting coexistence model for hostile citizen groups too embittered toward city hall—as a result of past "collaborative efforts"—to engage in joint planning.

Since all Model Cities programs require approval by the city council before HUD will fund them, city councils have final veto powers even when citizens have the majority of seats on the CDA Board. In Richmond, California, the city council agreed to a citizens' counter-veto, but the details of that agreement are ambiguous and have not been tested.

Various delegated power arrangements are also emerging in the Community Action Program as a result of demands from the neighborhoods and OEO's most recent instruction guidelines which urged CAAs "to exceed (the) basic requirements" for resident participation.[14] In some cities, CAAs have issued subcontracts to resident dominated groups to plan and/or operate one or more decentralized neighborhood program components like a multipurpose service center or a Headstart program. These contracts usually include an agreed upon line-by-line budget and program specifications. They also usually include a specific statement of the significant powers that have been delegated, for example: policy-making; hiring and firing; issuing subcontracts for building, buying, or leasing. (Some of the subcontracts are so broad that they verge on models for citizen control.)

8. Citizen Control

Demands for community controlled schools, black control, and neighborhood control are on the increase. Though no one in the nation has absolute control, it is very important that the rhetoric not be confused with intent. People are simply demanding that degree of power (or control) which guarantees that participants or residents can govern a program or an institution, be in full charge of policy and managerial aspects, and be able to negotiate the conditions under which "outsiders" may change them.

A neighborhood corporation with no intermediaries between it and the source of funds is the model most frequently advocated. A small number of such experimental corporations are already producing goods and/or social services. Several others are reportedly in the development stage, and new models for control will undoubtedly emerge as the have-nots continue to press for greater degrees of power over their lives.

Though the bitter struggle for community control of the Ocean Hill-Brownsville schools in New York City has aroused great fears in the headline reading public, less publicized experiments are demonstrating that the have-nots can indeed improve their lot by handling the entire job of planning, policy-making, and managing a program. Some are even demonstrating that they can do all this with just one arm because they are forced to use their other one to deal with a continuing barrage of local opposition triggered by the announcement that a federal grant has been given to a community group or an all black group.

Most of these experimental programs have been capitalized with research and demonstration funds from the Office of Economic Opportunity in cooperation with other federal agencies. Examples include:

1 A $1.8 million grant was awarded to the Hough Area Development Corporation in Cleveland to plan economic development programs in the ghetto and to develop a series of economic enterprises ranging from a novel combination shopping-center-public-housing project to a loan guarantee program for local building contractors. The membership and board of the non-profit corporation is composed of leaders of major community organizations in the black neighborhood.

2 Approximately $1 million ($595,751 for the second year) was awarded to the Southwest Alabama Farmers Cooperative Association (SWAFCA) in Selma, Alabama, for a ten-county marketing cooperative for food and livestock. Despite local attempts to intimidate the coop (which included the use of force to stop trucks on the way to market), first year membership grew to 1,150 farmers who earned $52,000 on the sale of their new crops. The elected coop board is composed of two poor black farmers from each of the ten economically depressed counties.

3 Approximately $600,000 ($300,000 in a supplemental grant) was granted to the Albina Corporation and the Albina Investment Trust to create a black-operated, black-owned manufacturing concern using inexperienced management and unskilled minority group personnel from the Albina district. The profit-making wool and metal fabrication plant will be owned by its employees through a deferred compensation trust plan.

4 Approximately $800,000 ($400,000 for the second year) was awarded to the Harlem Commonwealth Council to demonstrate that a community-based development corporation can catalyze and implement an economic development program with broad community support and participation. After only eighteen months of program development and negotiation, the council will soon launch several large-scale ventures including operation of two supermarkets, an auto service and repair center (with build-in manpower training program), a finance company for families earning less than $4,000 per year, and a data processing company. The all black Harlem-based board is already managing a metal castings foundry.

Though several citizen groups (and their mayors) use the rhetoric of citizen control, no Model City can meet the criteria of citizen control since final approval power and accountability rest with the city council.

Daniel P. Moynihan argues that city councils are representative of the community, but Adam Walinsky illustrates the nonrepresentativeness of this kind of representation:[15]

Who . . . exercises "control" through the representative process? In the Bedford-Stuyvesant ghetto of New York there are 450,000 people—as many as in the entire city of Cincinnati, more than in the entire state of Vermont. Yet the area has only one high school, and 80 per cent of its teen-agers are dropouts; the infant mortality rate is twice the national average; there are over 8000 buildings abandoned by everyone but the rats, yet the area received not one dollar of urban renewal funds during the entire first 15 years of that program's operation; the unemployment rate is known only to God.

Clearly, Bedford-Stuyvesant has some special needs; yet it has always been lost in the midst of the city's eight million. In fact, it took a lawsuit to win for this vast area, in the year 1968, its first Congressman. In what sense can the representative system be said to have "spoken for" this community, during the long years of neglect and decay?

Walinsky's point on Bedford-Stuyvesant has general applicability to the ghettos from coast to coast. It is therefore likely that in those ghettos where residents have achieved a significant degree of power in the Model Cities planning process, the first-year action plans will call for the creation of some new community institutions entirely governed by residents with a specified sum of money contracted to them. If the groundrules for these programs are clear and if citizens understand that achieving a genuine place in the pluralistic scene subjects them to its legitimate forms of give-and-take, then these kinds of programs might begin to demonstrate how to counteract the various corrosive political and socioeconomic forces that plague the poor.

In cities likely to become predominantly black through population growth, it is unlikely that strident citizens' groups like AWC of Philadelphia will eventually demand legal power for neighborhood self-government. Their grand design is more likely to call for a black city hall, achieved by the elective process. In cities destined to remain predominantly white for the foreseeable future, it is quite likely that counterpart groups to AWC will press for separatist forms of neighborhood government that can create and control decentralized public services such as police protection, education systems, and health facilities. Much may depend on the willingness of city governments to entertain demands for resource allocation weighted in favor of the poor, reversing gross imbalances of the past.

Among the arguments against community control are: it supports separatism; it creates balkanization of public services; it is more costly and less efficient; it enables minority group "hustlers" to be just as opportunistic and disdainful of the have-nots as their white predecessors; it is incompatible with merit systems and professionalism; and ironically enough, it can turn out to be a new Mickey Mouse game for the have-nots by allowing them to gain control but not allowing them sufficient dollar resources to succeed.[16] These arguments are not to be taken lightly. But neither can we take lightly the arguments of embittered advocates of community control—that every other means of trying to end their victimization has failed!

NOTES

1 The literature on poverty and discrimination and their effects on people is extensive. As an introduction, the following will be helpful: B. H. Bagdikian, *In the Midst of Plenty: The Poor in America* (New York: Beacon, 1964); Paul Jacobs, "The Brutalizing of America," *Dissent*, XI (Autumn 1964), p. 423–8; Stokely Carmichael and Charles V.

Hamilton, *Black Power: The Politics of Liberation in America* (New York: Random House, 1967); Eldridge Cleaver, *Soul on Ice* (New York: McGraw-Hill, 1968); L. J. Duhl, *The Urban Condition; People and Policy in the Metropolis* (New York: Basic Books, 1963); William H. Grier and P. M. Cobbs, *Black Rage* (New York: Basic Books, 1968); Michael Harrington, *The Other America: Poverty in the United States* (New York: Macmillan, 1962); Peter Marris and Martin Rein, *Dilemmas of Social Reform: Poverty and Community Action in the United States* (New York: Atherton Press, 1967); Mollie Orshansky, "Who's Who Among the Poor: A Demographic View of Poverty," *Social Security Bulletin*, XXVII (July 1965), 3–32; and Richard T. Titmuss, *Essays on the Welfare State* (New Haven: Yale University Press, 1968).

2 The poster is one of about 350 produced in May or June 1968 at Atélier Populaire, a graphics center launched by students from the Sorbonne's École des Beaux Art and École des Arts Decoratifs.

3 This typology is an outgrowth of a more crude typology I circulated in March 1967 in a HUD staff discussion paper titled "Rhetoric and Reality." The earlier typology consisted of eight levels that were less discrete types and did not necessarily suggest a chronological progression: Inform, Consult, Joint Planning, Negotiate, Decide, Delegate, Advocate Planning, and Neighborhood Control.

4 For an article of some possible employment strategies, see, Edmund M. Burke, "Citizen Participation Strategies," *Journal of the American Institute of Planners*, XXXIV, No. 5 (September 1968), 290–1.

5 U.S., Department of Housing and Urban Development, *Workable Program for Community Improvement, Answers on Citizen Participation*, Program Guide 7, February, 1966, pp. 1 and 6.

6 David Austin, "Study of Resident Participants in Twenty Community Action Agencies," CAP Grant 9499.

7 Robert Coles, "Social Struggle and Weariness," *Psychiatry*, XXVII (November 1964), 305–15. I am also indebted to Daniel M. Fox of Harvard University for some of his general insights into therapy being used as a diversion from genuine citizen participation.

8 See, Gordon Fellman, "Neighborhood Protest of an Urban Highway," *Journal of the American Institute of Planners*, XXXV, No. 2 (March 1969), 118–22.

9 James V. Cunningham, "Resident Participation," Unpublished Report prepared for the Ford Foundation, August 1967, p. 54.

10 Interview with Maxine Kurtz, Technical Director, Denver CDA.

11 U.S., Department of Housing and Urban Development,"Citizen Participation in Model Cities," *Technical Assistance Bulletin*, No. 3 (December 1968).

12 Organization for Social and Technical Innovation, *Six-Month Progress Report to Office of Economic Opportunity, Region 1*, February 1, 1969, pp. 27, 28, and 35.

13 In Cambridge, Massachusetts, city hall offered to share power with residents and anticipated the need for a period in which a representative citizens group could be engaged, and the ambiguities of authority, structure, and process would be resolved. At the request of the mayor, HUD allowed the city to spend several months of Model Cities planning funds for community organization activities. During these months, staff from the city manager's office also helped the residents draft a city ordinance that created a CDA composed of sixteen elected residents and eight appointed public and private agency representatives. This resident-dominated body has the power to hire and fire CDA staff, approve all plans, review all model city budgets and contracts, set policy, and so forth. The ordinance, which was unanimously passed by the city council also includes a requirement that all Model City plans must be approved by a majority of residents in the neighborhood through a referendum. Final approval power rests with the city council by federal statute.

14 U.S., Office of Economic Opportunity, *OEO Instruction, Participation of the Poor in the Planning, Conduct and Evaluation of Community Action Programs* (Washington, D.C.: December 1, 1968), pp. 1–2.

15 Adam Walinsky, "Review of *Maximum Feasible Misunderstanding*" by Daniel P. Moynihan, New York Times *Book Review*, February 2, 1969.

16 For thoughtful academic analyses of some of the potentials and pitfalls of emerging neighborhood control models, see, Alan Altshuler, "The Demand For Participation in Large American Cities," An Unpublished Paper prepared for the Urban Institute, December 1968; and Hans B. C. Spiegel and Stephen D. Mittenthal, "Neighborhood Power and Control, Implications for Urban Planning," A Report prepared for the Department of Housing and Urban Development, November 1968.

The Ghetto as a Resource for Black America

William W. Goldsmith

Professor of City and Regional Planning, Cornell University

In this article, William W. Goldsmith brings a new perspective to our view of the ghetto. Rather than subscribing to the prevalent negative view of an unsafe, crime-infested environment, Goldsmith argues that the American black ghetto has considerable economic and political strengths that can be used to further black development.

At Harlem's density, one of every five people in the United States could be squeezed into apartments in the five boroughs of New York City. More than fifteen million black Americans are already jammed in the biggest cities, most of them in areas like Harlem that we have all heard of: Hunters Point, Watts, the Fillmore, Hough, Bedford-Stuyvesant, Roxbury, and so on. We all know where black people are supposed to live, where they do live, and where they will continue to live. They live where housing conditions are appalling, where jobs are so hard to get that sometimes half the potential work force is underemployed, where schools are inferior, and where the police form an occupation army.

There has been a vast writing of anger and grief over the ghetto for about five years, much of it proposing to plan or develop the political economy of the future of black America. We have heard most about the ideas of liberal Democrats, who have proposed either programs for "improvement" of individuals, such as job train-

Reprinted by permission of the *Journal of the American Institute of Planners* 40, 1, January 1979.

ing, or unlikely industrial relocations, such as the Bedford Stuyvesant IBM plant, or practical impossibilities, such as rapid suburbanization. Alternative proposals from the black community and a few whites see the ghetto as a colony and call for relative political autonomy and economic autarchy. Still, except for an occasional lapse into emotional polemic, most who write about the American black ghetto mask the real dilemma: although political power and economic strength are mutually reinforcing, it is very difficult to establish either one without the existence of the other.

There is a wide array of forces keeping blacks concentrated and their conditions degraded. Ghetto walls are buttressed most firmly by housing and job discrimination, but such things as slum-lord profits, low-wage benefits to employers, and the need for household domestic workers all reinforce the concentration.

White racism accounts directly for as much as half the housing segregation, the remainder caused by low incomes, social class, job location, and voluntary isolation.[1] Job discrimination is so strong that even education makes no appreciable difference for a black job applicant.[2] Poor training, relocation of manufacturing plants to suburbs, and reduced need for unskilled labor in the economy further reduce opportunities for work.[3] Industrialists and managers benefit from such conditions, of course, because they can play black employees off against whites. Landlords can increase profits by crowding ghetto real estate. And, in the short-run, marginal businesses and workers can benefit by reduction in black competition for their markets and jobs (Baran and Sweezy, 1966: 263–264).[4]

The political weakness of the ghetto is accentuated by the decline in local control and patronage that used to fall to other groups near the bottom of the city heap. And as the ghetto begins to threaten the citywide electorate, metropolitan government may move in.[5]

The result is that most black people live in areas with very high unemployment; have incomes about half their white co-workers'; suffer from poorer public services, chaotic market conditions, and negligible control over local business; rarely own their homes; rent substandard apartments; hold almost no power over political institutions; and suffer constant physical and psychological danger from crime, drugs and alienation.[6] Living elsewhere would hardly be better for most of them, however, since the ghetto at least provides company for misery and safety from the crush of the nonblack world. There can be little doubt that the ghettos will be here in the near future, for even in the unlikely event of active national employment and urbanization policies, the ghetto's existence is guaranteed by continued migration, residual antagonisms, and just plain inertia.

Nevertheless, most responses to the black man's condition ignore the fact that the ghetto is here to stay for awhile. Some forget that it is here at all. The weakest approaches to black development in America, which tend to view the ghetto entirely negatively, emphasize either neglect or repression, suburbanization, or public employment and general increase in national employment. The following analysis begins with proposals of this sort, which usually fail to recognize that the problems are immense and that the government so far has consistently either treated symptoms or avoided action. The discussion then moves to stronger proposals which would make use of potential ghetto markets and resources, however limited they may be, to promote black commercial and industrial activity. Here the ghetto is seen primarily as an obstacle to be overcome while black owners, managers, and workers integrate into the white economy. Only a third set of proposals really responds to the fact of the ghetto, seeing it at least temporarily as a force for positive change, as a means for gathering both economic and political power. As background for these "separatist" proposals, a number of colonial analogies are then examined. Throughout the article, as alternative approaches are explored, the case for relative and temporary separation is examined. Finally, the potential of the ghetto as a resource for black development is evaluated.

SUBURBANIZATION AND EMPLOYMENT

As Anthony Downs has argued, a continuation of the current policy of neglect is almost certainly impossible, for it will lead to eventual confrontation. Indeed, much of the black radical rhetoric and a good deal of the rational argument warns of a conscious policy of repression (Cleaver, 1969). Of course, violent repression may not come; cooptation, careful police control, and other tactics that have succeeded for many years in third-world colonies may also work in American ghettos. In any case, most planners would not admit to being part of such policies, and the examination of the obvious negative consequences seems pointless.

The first positive proposal, suburbanization, has been urged most vociferously by economist John Kain, who writes, "the only efficient and satisfactory long run solution to ghetto problems [is] suburbanization of the Negro population," and current policies should at least be compatible with such a solution (Kain, 1969: 20). The essence of this argument, to which most public rhetoric subscribes, is that—in addition to limitations on jobs due to low skills, poor working habits, and overt discrimination—residential segregation at large distances from appropriate suburban workplaces combined with inadequate information and high transportation costs make jobs essentially unavailable to blacks.

Policies should be designed to "weaken the ties of the ghetto," and suburban integration, formal schooling, school busing, etc., should all be employed to "weaken the geographic dominance of the ghetto." These arguments are supplemented with proposals to meet "immediate needs of ghetto residents" by income transfers, but with an emphasis on "providing resources to individuals and not freezing them into geographic areas" (Kain and Persky, 1969: 23).

Finally, write the same analysts, others "would have us view the ghetto as something of a community unto itself, a community that could substantially benefit from economic development and especially heavy investments of social capital." The problem, they continue, is that this position ignores "the serious implications of the growing ghetto for the metropolis as a whole" and fails to notice that "many of the most visible problems which affect urban Negroes directly are dependent for much of their adverse impact on the very existence of the ghetto" (Kain and Persky, 1969: 3). Indeed Downs claims that suburbanization of blacks will integrate social classes as well as races, provide housing space, and prevent violence. Although he is concerned that there might appear black "ghetto-lets" or "mini ghettos" in all white suburbs, he believes that ghetto "pathologies" will be much less pronounced in such suburban concentrations (Downs, 1968). Attorney Herbert Hill, NAACP Labor Secretary, agrees that the ghettos contribute to the alienation of an American underclass and vociferously advocates black dispersal (Hill, 1966).

In a realistic appraisal of tendencies toward suburbanization, Downs (1968) worries that there is only a small minority of interests who favor suburbanization: suburban industrialists who need low-skill labor; downtown retailers, bankers, and entertainment people who need calm; home builders who want business; white central city politicians who would like to keep out some of the future black voters; businessmen with offices or plants "locked in" the central city; and good liberals. The key, he argues, along with political scientist Theodore Lowi (1968), is for the government to recognize its responsibility and heavily subsidize programs of enrichment and dispersal, whether integrated or segregated.

Daniel Patrick Moynihan (1970) has been the most outspoken to argue that the creation of general employment opportunity is the most critical factor. "The Negro lower class must be dissolved by transforming it into a stable working class population." Consequently, we must transform these slum dwellers into "truck drivers, mail carriers, assembly line workers—people with dignity, purpose, and in the United States, a very good standard of living indeed" (quoted in Tabb, 1970: 5). For perhaps other reasons, others agree. Labrie (1970:I, 24–25) writes that "black central city employment problems . . . stem not so much from suburban shifts in metropolitan employment as from job shortages and imbalances in the national economy."

Proposals for increases in general employment take two forms. The first one demands vast increases in public service employment. Bennett Harrison, for example, notes the "bluntly political" reason for public service jobs:

> There is not the slightest indication that the private sector is going to be any more willing in the future than it has been in the past to actively seek black Americans as co-workers, neighbors, or employees.

Then, from his studies of training programs, Harrison (1969: 20) concludes that there are also national economic reasons for public service jobs: direct benefits from increases in GNP (a multiplier between four and ten) and indirect training benefits.

Unfortunately, there is no way to guarantee that such jobs are forthcoming. Moynihan had access to the White House, but unemployment in the ghetto did not drop. Perhaps in frustration over such failures of public policy, other writers have developed what Kenneth Clark calls the "ethnic lock" argument:

> Probably the most significant factor in restricting employment opportunities for Negroes in certain skilled crafts and certain other high paying occupations is due to the phenomenon of the "ethnic lock" on jobs.
>
> Through historical processes certain ethnic or religious minority groups come to predominate in certain kinds of jobs: the waterfront for the Italian, the police force for the Irish, the school system for the Jews, and the personal services for Negroes. In addition,

most skilled garment workers in New York are Jewish of eastern European origin, or Italian. Many tool and die makers are of British and German extraction. The "ethnic lock" that is held by these groups over certain jobs means that employment opportunities in these fields, and the saliency of these fields as future occupations, are known and restricted primarily to members of these ethnic groups. (1964: 270)[7]

This essentially negative position has been elaborated and transformed to provide a test of the hypothesis that blacks can use the "ethnic lock" to their advantage in moving into new employment areas. Stephen Rattien (1970: 249–250) suggests four stages in the economic development of minority groups in the United States.

• The first stage provides low paying jobs in few industries, with clear inferiority and lack of power, resulting in both industrial and occupational concentrations. There are no minority institutions, no residential isolation, and a small population. This period in U.S. cities was of great duration for other ethnic groups, and is certainly reason for dismal forecasts.

• In the second period, there is high migration to cities, with growth in ethnic community solidarity, leading to improvement for some at the expense of others. Wages stay depressed because of competition for similar positions, all still at the bottom. Forces of discrimination become clear, but the larger minority population leads to a broadening of the distribution of employment opportunities to include more industries.

• In the third stage, migration to the cities diminishes. Positive effects of group solidarity emerge. "Minority group employment begins to concentrate in those industrial categories in which minority group specialization and dominance can develop . . . [usually] categories of national or regional industrial employment expansion." A sheltered industrial environment allows members to move to higher occupational positions. Unionization is aided by ethnic cohesion, and so forth.

• In the final state, transfer takes place from high occupational categories in ethnically controlled industries to other industrial sectors. This is a slow process.

Rattien looks at shifts in black occupation and industry for nine northeastern U.S. metropolitan areas from 1950 to 1960 and finds some evidence of occupational and industrial shift patterns similar to those hypothesized. Quite clearly, though, the shifts are insufficient to alleviate employment and income problems for blacks. More important, Rattien finds that there is significant covariation between amount of shift and the size of the metropolitan area. Two things seem to be critical. First, a "critical minority group population mass is necessary before certain industrial specializations can be generated." Second, the urban area must grow rapidly to allow minority specialization with less resistance.

Indeed, there seems to be no argument in the literature to counter the position that aggregate demand for black employment must be increased dramatically and that such an increase is most likely to take place within relatively restricted industrial sectors, whether public or private, integrated or separated, individually or community controlled, in the ghetto or outside.[8] The only arguments are whether and how this is done.

GHETTO CAPITALISM

The first proposals that face the real issues call for ghetto capitalism. There are two lines of thought. One argues for the development of more or less separate but parallel capitalist organizations in the ghetto. The other pleads for more involvement of white business with ghetto entrepreneurs and ghetto enterprises in general. Perhaps the essence of the latter position was stated by A. W. Elliott of the National Association of Manufacturers (Haddad and Pugh, 1969),

> Black leadership must [recognize] the gap—financial, technological, and experiential—that currently exists between white and black America. . . . it must perceive and acknowledge the need to close the gap, hence the need for white "things," white experience, white personnel.

The Bankers Committee on Urban Affairs agrees:

> Bankers are proud that they helped build the cities of America. They have begun to recognize a responsibility to contribute positively to the revitalization of these same cities . . . to stimulate bank participation in the economic development of these cities, and their economically depressed communities in particular. The banking industry is moving toward positive, responsible action seeking sustained results. (McNeish, in Haddad and Pugh, 1969)

The evidence is less persuasive. Part of this "black-white" capitalism effort has concentrated on the location of branch plants of major national manufacturing firms, such as the IBM plant in New York's Bedford Stuyvesant ghetto, the Watts Manufacturing Company in Los Angeles, and the Xerox-FIGHTON plant in Rochester (Levitan et al., 1970). Until recently, at least, the two dozen or so new efforts were all modest in size, from one to two million dollars, and turned out unsophisticated products. The effort has been hardly more than an experiment, and nearly all agree that without really dramatic government subsidy, serious efforts of plant location in ghettos will not be made by major white corporations.[9]

Most of the effort in black capitalism by white corporations has been in programs of training and job placement. There have, of course, been many efforts, widely advertised in the business press. But even the most enthusiastic and sympathetic observers agree that so far the programs are insignificant. Even were they to be dramatically successful, these employment programs would not make a dent in black ghetto underemployment.

> The Administration's three-year target of 500,000 jobs is the official estimate of hard-core unemployment in the 50 cities. . . . But many experts believe that the real number is two to six times the 500,000.
>
> As fast as some hard-core unemployed find jobs, the other low-skilled workers are losing theirs to automation and other factors. . . . Even if the 500,000 goal is fully achieved, says manpower specialist Garth Mangum of George Washington University, "we will never notice the difference." (Henderson, 1968)

As soon as one moves to programs for relatively independent development of capitalism in the ghetto, support from corporate and government representatives wanes and gives way to more enthusiasm from black elites. A *New York Times* editorial November 19, 1969 asked, "What Do the Negroes Want?" and claimed that blacks are asking for "hopelessly utopian claims that the United States has never honored for any other group." Perhaps the most dramatic approach to black capitalism is Richard America's response: "a working mechanism is required for the transfer of some major national corporations to black control" (America, 1970: 47). Professor America envisions a process involving transfer of eight major corporations in fifteen years, a shift of about two billion dollars a year, with control essentially in the hands of black stockholders. He cites precedent for such transfers in the railroad land appropriations of the nineteenth century, private rights to inventions sponsored with federal funds, and the Urban Renewal Program.

The most well-developed program for black capitalism came from Roy Innis and CORE, which has made a number of proposals, including the Congressional Community Self-Determination and Rural Development Incentives Bills (HR 18709 and HR 14600) both in 1968, which propose federal funding of from 50 million to 125 million dollars per year for financing the development of business whose shares (five dollars) would be sold to members of the community (Innis, 1969; Henderson and Ledbur, 1970: 92–93). Although Innis claims the form of economic activity is irrelevant, he argues that there is a striking similarity between the exploitation of the ghetto and of most undeveloped countries, and calls for community corporations to control investment, the essence of the program is close to white capitalism for blacks. The economic benefits from control over capital would be control over budgets for urban services, guaranteed markets, and internal circulation of jobs, contracts, and money. Although there was widespread public, bipartisan support in the Congress for the community development corporation bill, it never got out of committee. There was concern by liberals about encouraging "apartheid," by others about using democratic participation rather than competence as a business norm, by still others about conflicts that might arise between the CDC's and private entrepreneurs, and by the AFL-CIO in general. In any case, neither bill passed in 1968 and neither has been seriously advocated since, although some elements have been embodied in various federal programs.[10]

A number of other proposals for encouragement of black capitalism have been made, and several have been at least partially implemented. One of the best known is Dunbar McLaurin's Ghetto Economic Development and Industrialization Plan submitted in 1968 to the New York City Human Resources Administration (McLaurin, 1968). The plan proposes black ghetto resident stock ownership in small and (preferably) big businesses, with funding by city deposits in ghetto controlled banks and with sales guaranteed by city purchasing. Many have argued for the efficacy of such financing and purchasing programs to guarantee ghetto export sales. Neidercorn and Browne, in complementary papers in 1971, have argued that multipliers of ghetto programs are greatest, in declining order, for the expansion of export industries owned and operated by blacks, black jobs outside the ghetto, and expansion of basic industries owned and operated by whites in the ghetto. Eugene Foley has made parallel arguments for ghetto capitalism, both in and out of government, for many years (Foley, 1969). But whatever the program, ghetto multipliers are small indeed—much smaller even than in comparably sized suburban areas.[11]

Undoubtedly the most successful program, primarily for "import substitution," is the Reverend Leon Sullivan's Opportunities Industrialization Center, begun in Philadelphia in 1964, the prototype for dozens of other centers in all parts of the country. Locally owned and black managed with funds raised from white business contributions, the OIC programs combine training, securing of jobs, and encouragement and establishment of black enterprises, such as Progress Plaza in Philadelphia (Sullivan, 1969). By mid-1969, more than 80,000 people were participating in various OIC programs (Henderson and Ledbur, 1970: 127), and it has subsequently expanded further.

Several lesser proposals for encouragement of black capitalism have also been put forward, arguing the need for leverage or borrowing ability, for risk capital, and for entrepreneurial skills in production and marketing (Cross, 1969). Two men associated with the Columbia University OEO Harlem Development Project saw the obstacle in funding, so they proposed a domestic "World Bank," with money for clearly bankable projects, for equity on development projects, and for long-term projects that would not normally qualify (Heilbrun and Wellisz, 1968). The new journal *Black Enterprise* continually advocates and points to successes of funding small businesses and advertises the prerequisites that go with dramatic financial success (Venable, 1971). At its extreme, the position is clear:

> Why stay middle class? There's nothing wrong with our getting wealthy. If we have 10% of the population, let's have 10% of the multi-millionaires.[12]

Both the black-white and the black capitalism programs and proposals fit into two basic approaches: skills training and job placement, on the one hand, and investment expansion, on the other. Whether these are controlled individually by blacks or not, whether they take place within the ghetto or not, are, of course, very important considerations, but one should not neglect the essential similarity of the proposals. They all propose working within the existing American capitalist and welfare-state system, and they are all grossly inadequately funded. Indeed, in all the discussion reviewed above there has been little serious recognition of the magnitude of the problem and the incredible failure of the government to act.

The proposals provide little more than a Hobson's choice among equally paltry alternatives. They talk only of marginal changes and ignore the social and political conditions that might give rise to even these changes, when in fact almost all analysts agree from both moral and practical positions that radical and drastic changes are needed. Indeed, with the exception of the calls for Community Development Corporations, the superficiality of the proposals is underscored by their failure in implementation.[13] The reason is abundantly clear: there are few opportunities for legitimate and profitable business in the ghetto. Hence we turn to a final set of proposals that despair of solution within today's American institutions and argue for really dramatic political change.

INTERNAL COLONIALISM

A view of the ghetto as a colony, or even the entire U.S. black population as a colony, provides a basis for discussion of more substantial change. A little less than ten years ago proponents of American programs for social change and theorists of economic development in the emerging nations began to get together.[14] Out of their discussions came a view of ghetto as an entirely interdependent but subjugated part of the American economy and society. Robert Allen's *Black Awakening in Capitalist America* puts the discussion in the content of general black solidarity and black separatist movements.

> The fact of black America as a semicolony, or what has been termed *domestic colonialism*, . . . is at one and the same time the most profound conclusion to be drawn from a survey of the black experience in America, and also the basic premise upon which an interpretation of black history can be constructed. (Allen, 1970: 2)[15]

As William Tabb points out,[16] the typical former colony in the third world today can be characterized by (1) poverty of material goods, (2) high population growth rates, (3) a few wealthy and many poor people, (4) a small basic industrial sector, (5) low labor productivity, low savings, and little investment, (6) dependence on an export whose supply is not fully utilized no matter how low the price, (7) dependence on imports for consumption, often encouraged by advertising from the exterior, and finally (8) outside ownership of much of the local economy. In addition, of course, the neocolonialist citizens are restrained from movement to other places by citizenship, language, and skills, as well as race, religion, and social affinity. Does this sound like a ghetto, which, after all, is usually within walking distance of the main offices of the wealthiest economy in the world? One by one: (1) ghetto residents are poor; (2) they have high birth rates; (3) their incomes are highly skewed, a few high and many low; (4) there is almost no basic industry in the ghetto; (5) labor productivity is low,[17] and savings and investment are low, too; (6) the major ghetto export is labor, which is tremendously underemployed, even at low wages; (7) almost all ghetto consumption is supplied from the outside, most of it conforming to outside (advertised) consumption standards; and, finally, (8) practically the entire ghetto economy is owned externally. Like the former colonials, and partly as a result of many of these conditions, people usually are unable to leave the ghetto.[18]

How have liberated colonies responded to such conditions? Basically in two ways: they have either become neocolonies and maintained most of their social, political, and economic relations with the mother country, concomitantly maintaining most of their colonial conditions; or they have broken with the colonial master, turned inward, and attempted to attack the root problems directly.

The central process of economic development is the same everywhere. A surplus of income beyond subsistence must be generated and used to establish and support social institutions and physical capital that will lead to further development. Development theorists have usually focused on one of these problems to the exclusion of the others. Some have concentrated on the *generation* of surplus, arguing for the most efficient kinds of production. Many of the horrors of the English industrial revolution and the Soviet industrialization can be traced to the presumed importance of generating a surplus through efficient work practices: getting to work on time, working long hours, adapting to production line techniques, or, as many would put it, changing values from traditional to modern behavior. Here the argument is, generally, that *discipline of work* is essential to the generation of a surplus, and that in most cases it must be imposed from above. Such language, of course, smacks of totalitarian ways and personality manipulation. Nevertheless, if development is the goal, there must be a way to generate a surplus, and sweat is the usual prescription, whether off the back of a Chinese laborer for the Union Pacific, a small American freeholder for his own farmhouse, or a Cuban worker for the Revolution. The trouble is, usually when this argument is invoked it is ethnocentric and racist: "If they had more drive, they could help themselves." In economics there is the well-known "backward-bending labor supply curve," describing the situation where presumedly lazy African mine workers choose less income for more leisure, at a point where an energetic European counterpart would still be hard at work. The term now is "welfare chiseler."

Marxists have emphasized the other aspect of economic surplus: the use to which it is put, or, more directly, *who gets it*. Contemporary writers have emphasized that underdeveloped areas (ghettos, third-world nations, depressed regions) are not primitive and in an "original" state, that is, not undeveloped, but instead are transformed, or *under*developed, through contact with more powerful and richer states or regions. "Underdevelop" is a transitive verb. At its best, the analysis of underdevelopment suggests that even the poorest communities do generate a surplus. According to Keith Griffin, even the highland Indians of Peru have generated a surplus that could have sustained economic and institutional growth, had the surplus not been appropriated by landlords for use in Lima and elsewhere. Ralph Nader reports that neighborhood banks in New York City transfer the surplus of their depositers from working class neighborhoods to central banks for investment elsewhere. Milton Kotler has calculated that the poorest urban neighborhoods get back only about 75 percent of their tax contributions in tangible services and benefits. For richer neighborhoods the figure is probably 60 percent. In all these cases, there is a surplus being generated.[19]

The English gathered their surplus by pauperizing farmers and making children work, allowing a capitalist class to own the funds and invest them in physical capital for production. The Soviet Union used forced collectivization and rigidly enforced consumption limits. Many new world countries used slaves. Today's Chinese farmers seem to be keeping more of their surplus, according to reports that rural incomes are increasing more rapidly than city incomes. So far, ghetto blacks have no way to keep their surplus at home. The annual *per capita* income in Harlem, over $1000, is roughly equal to that of several western European countries, a striking argument for the potential availability of an investible resource, should there be some way to keep it from being taken by the capitalists and tax collectors (Vietorisz and Harrison, 1971).[20]

Most studies that look at the distribution of surplus conclude that real improvement for colonial subjects will come only when their colonial (or neocolonial) status is abolished. Therefore, such things as wars of independence and wars of liberation seem to be the rule rather than the exception for countries that try to escape from colonial bonds. What matters to the colonial subjects is control over their own affairs, collection of the benefits of their own activities. With these conditions material well-being for the masses finally becomes a possibility.

The same arguments are now made about American black ghettos. That is, control over affairs, collection and distribution of benefits, should be in the hands of the colonial subjects, the ghetto residents. Colonial arguments and proposals came as early as 1900, from no less a figure than W.E.B. DuBois:

> Under economic cooperation we must strive to spread the idea among colored people that the accumulation of wealth is for social rather than individual ends. We must avoid, in the advancement of the Negro race, the mistakes of ruthless exploitation which have marked modern economic history. To this end we must seek not simple home ownership, small landholdings and savings accounts, but also all forms of cooperation, both in production and distribution, profit-sharing, building and loan association, systematic charity for definite, practical ends. (Broderick, 1959: 102)

Although DuBois continually resisted long-run separatist arguments and proposals for complete socialization of the economy, his advocacy of at least temporary cultural separatism and nationalism provided the basis for other writers. Marcus Garvey, antagonistic to DuBois' socialism and generally procapitalist, nevertheless stated:

> The Negro will have to build its own government, industry, art, science, literature and culture, before the world will stop to consider him. Until then we are but wards of a superior race and civilization, and outcasts of a standard social system. (Garvey, 1967: 21)

Malcolm X identified the essence of the black situation in this country as internal colonialism, and Stokely Carmichael said, "The struggle for black power . . . is the struggle to free these colonies from external domination" (quoted in Allen, 1970: 248). Even proposals for black capitalism have called forth a similar response, claiming that each effort is merely an attempt at a shift from colonialism, with white landlords, employers and politicians being replaced by their black lackeys:

> The creation of a new, invigorated black bourgeoisie . . . is high on corporate America's agenda for the black colony. From the corporate standpoint, such a class would help to stabilize the ghettos and provide a subtle means of social control. (Allen, 1970: 178)

Indeed, points out Martin Rein, worry about social peace and lower class behavior leads to interest in an intermediary between white power and poor, unruly blacks, which gives rise to "a powerfully 'conservative' network for black power" that urges "the development of a Negro middle class" (Rein, 1969: 46). Tom Hayden puts this idea succinctly:

> During times of relative social peace, the issue of race goes unresolved. When the issue

is forced by black people for reasons of dignity and survival, the answer is to suspend politics and restore order. When the streets are occupied by troops the ultimate colonial substance of the system is revealed. (Hayden, 1969: 177)[21]

The trouble with the colonial or neocolonial analogy is that, appropriate as it may be for illuminating conditions, it ignores some important changes in context from most third world nations to the American ghetto.

> The exploiters are not a minority and in [a] strange land far from their own shores. They are not the British in India, the Dutch in Southeast Asia, the French in Africa. White Americans are an overwhelming and powerful majority in their own land. In the face of Black Rebellion and revolution white Americans will not retreat to a distant homeland from which they once set sail to build a far-flung empire. Long before the point where retreat is indicated the reaction will set in. (Binstock, 1969: 195)

Analogies to "official" colonies and their neocolonial successors and especially to the process of colonization are strong, but the solutions for breaking colonial and neocolonialism bonds—harrassment, terrorism, war—are either insufficient or too dangerous for blacks in America. The usual colonial prescription—make a strong political, even physical, break and then organize the society and economy on local terms and in local ways—is inappropriate in the ghetto because the break cannot be made without the organization first completed. Harlem cannot withdraw from New York and the United States. A small cadre, even with widespread support by the people, cannot throw off the oppressors. There will never be the geographic isolation to enable blacks to settle down and make independent decisions. Black activity will have to be in the context of a dominant white society.

THE GHETTO AS A RESOURCE

The colonial analogy aside for the moment, the brunt of the argument made so far by most writers suggests that a number of common proposals ought to be adopted, including ghetto dispersal, suburban housing desegregation through legal action, school integration, job training, action against employment discrimination, provision of better information and transportation for suburban jobs, subsidy for ghetto branch plants, and encouragement of technical assistance for entrepreneurs. Really what we need, these people say, is simply to enforce liberalism, to make political pluralism work. One can be of two minds about this. Of course it is necessary to sue for the right to housing occupancy, of course black children must have as much choice of schools as whites, of course discrimination in employment must be sought out and fought. There is no material here for debate. The other argument tends to be neglected, and needs to be aired. *Even* in a liberal, pluralist community or society, interest groups are supposed to have power. And the issue for black people, even if we adopt the pluralist view of the world,[22] is to create their own power. This issue is left unresolved, almost untouched, by nearly all the proposals for suburbanization, employment, or black and black-white capitalism.

Hence, we return to pick up elements of the colonialism argument. It is clear that political autonomy is not an option. It seems that, rather than to see political autonomy as a precondition for the establishment of economic isolation, proponents of ghetto development must see it the other way around, or at least as a circular process. The economy must be organized to facilitate the emergence of political solidarity which will then enable black people to dispute internal colonial rule. This is not to argue that adequate economic improvement of individuals must precede integration: it is to argue that adequate economic improvement for most black people of the United States is dependent on their political and social organization, which in turn is largely dependent on economic control over their own resources. Really to come to grips with problems of control, it is necessary to change completely the perspective and see ghetto "problems" as potential solutions, to focus in the first place on the community, and to examine how the ghetto stimulates social solidarity and local organization.

There are a number of arguments in the literature which, if explored further, would lead one to such a conclusion. Those ideas for ghetto development that fit most closely with the need for wresting control of the "colony" from the hands of the larger society all emphasize the importance of widespread participation, communal activity, community control, and the integration of economic and political activity: DuBois proposed a "planned, communal social system in black America"; Harold Cruse later made a similar proposal for Harlem; Innis' CORE proposal began with demands for real community control; and some recent black political activity has been similarly oriented. Vietorisz and Harrison, in their plan for the economic development of Harlem, repeatedly argue that control over activity is much more important than economic efficiency, that community organization, political power, training, and participation should be seen as the *primary objectives* of ghetto development, with minimum economic viability simply a constraint. They emphasize that the specific economic techniques proposed for ghetto development are not new to the American scene. Consumers' and producers' cooperatives, nonprofit development corporations that consider community values, backward economic integration from market-shelf space to producers, infant industry subsidies, and merchandising cooperatives have all been successfully tried by white communities already politically organized. What is new "is the articulation of these techniques into a system," their use for community organization. The use of these conventional activities in combination could provide "a formidable economic planning instrument" (Vietorisz and Harrison, 1971: 27). There would seem to be few other ways ever to gain real control over ghetto economic activity and to use it for long-run political and social improvement. These economic techniques provide a basis for community organization, the only means through which economic success will lead to political power.

This idea finds support in the work on ethnic locks discussed above, in which it was found that one of the strongest "causes" of black movement into a concentrated industrial activity was the absolute size of the black population in the city, presumably because of combined political-economic power such numbers tend to bring. It is quite possible, though far from proved, that this size factor is reinforced by concentration in ghettos.

Further support comes from social theorists. It has been pointed out that even if there exists competition among interest groups, the poor (and therefore many blacks) are usually unable to form the coalitions that are necessary to win their political battles. This is true largely because they must fight several adversaries at once: the group from which they are trying to win a concession, say the school system; agencies of publicity or propaganda, such as newspapers; third parties, such as reform political clubs; and, finally, diversity within the protesting group itself. The only one of these four difficulties directly within reach is the last, group solidarity, and this points in the direction of organization building, with resources used for the development and maintenance of community institutions (Lipsky, 1968).[23]

Other writers have pointed out that in many cases isolation may be beneficial to struggling groups. Lowi has criticized federal poverty programs for arriving too soon, before local communities had put their programs in order, so that money was wasted and local energies dissipated (Lowi, 1971: 59).[24] Others have studied group movements such as boycotts, protests, riots, and demonstrations in a variety of circumstances. Social movements as disparate as the Cargo Cults on South Pacific Islands and Calvinism in Western Europe seem to indicate that cohesion emerges in a group as a result of its internal complexity or "competence" outweighing the strength of its connections with the rest of the world (Young, 1970, 1971). Similar interpretations of black movements in the United States are credible and popularly discussed, although they have not been formally tested.

The ghettos of most big cities for the last ten years or so have exhibited such strains; so has the entire national black "community." Levels of capability and competence have been rising in ghettos but interaction with the outside has not kept pace. Both the ghettos and the black community in general have in many ways been increasingly isolated. Group solidarity, with all the attendant imagery and ideology, has appeared, and it has sought various expressions, from urban riots and rebellions to the formation of community corporations.[25]

The evidence for American black ghettos points toward a combination of growing community development, education, skills, and awareness and insufficiently growing external connections, a combination likely to sustain the solidarity movement we have been watching, joining, or resisting in the last several years. Even psychological studies seem to point in the same directions: black social movements are contributing to "the internal cohesion and authority required for internal group discipline," and they help "to develop and organize resources and power" (Pinderhughes, 1968).

Where does this leave the various proposals for ghetto development? To answer, let us distinguish them by the way they treat the economic isolation of the ghetto (autarchy), its political isolation (autonomy), and its centralization of control over production, distribution, and services (community).

The essence of the suburbanization argument, it turns out, is not that employment is inaccessible to central city blacks, but either that segregation is morally wrong or that the ghettos present a threat to continued operation of the American economy and society on its usual terms. Peter Labrie correctly argues that where there is heavy demand for unskilled workers, information flow about the jobs would be no problem and transport time and cost could be overcome without great difficulty (Labrie, 1970: I). Piven and Cloward (1967) go further and argue that attempted integration has been detrimental to blacks because programs tied to integration, such as housing and schools, have often failed precisely because of resistance to integration. In addition, they argue, "class power in the U.S. is intimately connected with the strength of ethnic institutions. . . . Integration must be understood, not as the mingling of bodies in school and neighborhood, but as participation in and shared control over the major institutional spheres of American life."

Programs for suburbanization might eliminate much of the potential for planned, coordinated development of ghetto areas and would encourage (rather than allow) draining off of organizational and financial surpluses. Suburbanization would decrease economic and political isolation and would reduce internal centralization of control. There is little doubt, in fact, that some proponents see these proposals in precisely this light: they want to prevent black takeovers of whatever is left of city governments, and they want to diffuse potential for organized challenge to the usual way of doing things.

Similarly, the proposals for massive increases in employment to be generated by federal economic policy ignore that fact that there is simply no national lobby to make black unemployment and subemployment felt, and they neglect the potential of well-organized and cohesive ghettos for raising national issues and forcefully fighting for them.

So, we proceed to the other proposals. The black-white capitalism proposals can be rejected as blunt attempts at extension of neocolonial control and cheap liberal advertising. If the proposals were to succeed at anything other than creation of a black elite of managers, they would simply pay a few black workers more money and split them from the bulk of the black community. Their effects would be particularly disruptive. They directly reduce economic and political isolation and make community control almost impossible.[26]

The black capitalism proposals are a little harder to reject. They do to some extent encourage economic exchange within the ghetto and provide potential for organization of ghetto politics. But again, they split the ghetto community into capitalist and worker, and they necessitate strong alliances between the ghetto capitalist and the external, white capitalists. They depend not upon the support of serious black movements, but only upon periodic rebellion to raise worries and provide private and public funds. "Ten percent of the multi-millionaires" won't help many blacks, either directly or indirectly. The accepted theory of capitalist development is that the rich will accumulate funds to invest to make the economy grow most rapidly, to thereby trickle down and benefit all. One need not be a Maoist to reject such an argument in the late twentieth century, particularly for a ghetto. But if one does believe in community control, participation, and all that the national liberal rhetoric proclaims, then the capitalist route to ghetto development is impossible.

The alternative route—through community controlled, probably worker managed, low-profit corporations—to a set of coordinated and cohesive training, employment, production, and marketing operations, seems the most desirable possibility. So far, realistic proposals of this kind have fallen on deaf ears among ghetto leadership. *The Economic Development of Harlem* grew out of such a proposal that was rejected by business interests. And the thirty-odd Community Development Corporations that now operate in most of the biggest ghettos fail either to integrate with other activities or to plow potential profits back into training and community organization.[27] Many of them also depend almost entirely on ghetto leadership for support. If there is to be success, one element will certainly be, as James Boggs (1968) points out, dependence on the neglected "black street force" that started the urban rebellion and that is only temporarily pacified by the programs in response.[28] The weakness of all the proposals is that they stop short of serious analysis of the ways groups do organize for political activity. Even the best proposals that clearly recognize the need for organized strength from the ghettos themselves fail to speculate, much less study, how this might come about. The dilemma of the ghetto is resolved only if the two streams of thought are brought together. When they are, it is clear that the ghetto is today probably the black community's best hope for power and wealth in the future.

WHAT ARE THE CHANCES?

The most dismal forecast for the ghetto is that it will be torn with strife, will violently confront white society, and will be repressed. From this point of view, the colonial analogy is inapt because the exploitation of blacks is no longer necessary for the mainstream of the American economy. Hence poor blacks *can* be written off. They could be more trouble than they are worth to corporate America. The Indians apparently are.

The second possibility is that neocolonial cooptation will be widespread and successful, leadership will be continually removed from its community, and conditions for the masses will improve very slowly at best. Such a situation could continue for some time, but it would require careful planning. Hence it would be likely to devolve to the first.

The third and only desirable possibility, and for almost everyone in the next generation the most practical, is that blacks and their white allies focus on mobilization of concentrated economic and political power and pool and organize resources to develop some independence from the dominant society. How can this be done? One part of the effort will have to be ghetto mobilization. Another will be, as Malcolm X, Cleaver and others have pointed out, some weakening of the white corporate structure, as active critics and reformers take corporate jobs. A supporting trend, as Victor Thompson has for some time predicted (1964), is that corporations will be forced to loosen their hierarchies as they employ larger proportions of technically competent people with support from professions and with the strength to heed their own values.[28] A third element, more speculative yet, is the possibility that black students trained in all kinds of skills will return to work with their communities because they have been at schools with an atmosphere of sympathy, interest, and enthusiasm for real community development. There is some evidence of such shifts among students in the social sciences in general (Gouldner, 1970). Finally, perhaps the mounting third world opposition to American corporate policies will cause the country to reexamine its opposition to social change around the globe. But this is speculation, and the likelihood of all these things happening does not seem great.

NOTES

1 Pascal (1970: 402) shows, for example, that in 1960 although black people constituted 17 percent of the population of the largest U.S. central cities, they made up only 5 percent of the suburban population; in fact a higher percentage of poor whites than well-off blacks lived in the suburbs. In 1970 such analysis is not yet possible, but statistics in *The Social and Economic Status of Negroes* (1970) do nothing to suggest any change. Although it is difficult to be certain because of circularity, family income difference seems to account for no more than half the residential segregation. See Pascal (1967, 1970: 407–409). For documentation of increase in segregation in recent decades at least to 1960 see Lee (1965) and Taeuber and Taeuber (1965). Mechanisms of enforcement work through legislation or administrative rules such as the old FHA "homogeneous neighborhood" strictures, threat of violence, premium payments either by whites voluntarily or blacks involuntarily, reduced flow of information, and simple refusal to rent or sell to blacks. Peter Labrie adds that in the face of widespread hostility to blacks outside the ghetto, blacks simply want to live with friends, so that what is measured as "voluntary" segregation is increased (1971, Part II).

2 Metropolitan area data for 1966 and 1967 indicate also that even migration from ghetto to suburb makes little difference for the income of black workers, while the same educational or residential changes for whites are associated with marked increases in income. See Harrison (1970).

3 This is elaborated on by Meyer, Kain and Wohl (1965: ch. 7), Kain (1968), and the National Advisory Commission (1968), quoted in Mermelstein (1970: 315).

4 Reich's data (1971) suggests that job and income discrimination against blacks lead to larger income and educational distance between working class and upper class whites, and he claims that this is because it is in the interests of business managers and owners to play off black and white workers against one another.

5 On decline in patronage, see National Advisory Commission, ibid. On metropolitan "reform" see Cloward and Piven (1968: 167) and Canty (1969: 153), who gives a preview when he writes that Atlanta "has had an interesting history of annexing new (white) territory with each increase in the city's black electorate."

6 On employment and incomes see Harrison (1970) who, using U.S. Department of Labor data, shows that in ten major ghettos in 1966 the *best* rate was one in four sub-employed, the worst, half the labor force sub-employed, and median income for black workers was about half that for whites. Sub-employment is a much better index than unemployment. It is equal to the sum of unemployed + part-time seeking full-time work + head of HH under 65 earning less than $60/week full-time + non-head of household under 65 earning less than $56/week full-time + 1/2 male non-participants 20–64 + 1/2 "unfound males" not identified in the survey. On market conditions see Sturdivant (1969: x) and Caplovitz (1969). On lack of control over local business see Samuels (1969), DeLorean (1969), Fusfeld (1970: 378), and Reiss and Aldrich (1971). On home ownership see Kain and Quigley (1970). On lack of political control see Broder (n.d.), Baron (1965), and Browne (1970). The best analyses see these conditions not as a result of a culture of poverty, but as a response to external conditions. See Leibow (1967),

Valentine (1968), and Wilson (1968). For a lengthy review of the general condition of black powerlessness in America, see Schuchter (1968).

7 It is interesting to note that even some of these "ethnic-locks" have shifted.

8 Pascal (1970) proposes that the government aid blacks to take over a large number of the quarter-million gasoline service stations in the U.S., in order to establish an "industrial foothold," and "sectoral dominance," but outside the ghetto, in the essentially white market. Schuchter (1968) calculates that the total bill for any adequate restructuring and transfer of ownership, management, and consumption will take a government budget of about 50 billions of dollars *per year* (chs. 2–3, and p. 40).

9 See Martin Skala, "Inner City Enterprises: Current Experience," in Haddad and Pugh (1969), David B. Hertz, "Is Partnership Possible?" in Haddad and Pugh (1969), Levitan *et al.* (1970), Aldrich and Reiss (1970), Reiss and Aldrich (1971), and Henderson and Ledbur (1970: chs. 6 and 7).

10 See McClaughry (1969), Innis (1969), and Sturdivant (1969). The latter strongly opposed the separatist features of the bill and even argued the Horatio Alger story for blacks in white businesses (263). Some elements of the CDC proposals have been embodied in Small Business Administration, EDA, and other federal programs.

11 Other things being equal, one would expect larger areas to have higher internal spending propensities. Table 5 of Oakland, Sparrow and Stettler (1971) reports the following populations and propensities to spend locally:

12 F. Naylor Fitzhugh, former professor at Howard University, Vice President of Pepsi

Ghettos			Other areas		
Hough	59,000	.38	Winnetka	15,000	.30
South Central LA	168,000	.38	Redondo Beach	50,000	.40
East LA	178,000	.48	Evanston	72,000	.50
Bedford-Stuyvesant	378,000	.55			

Cola, and head of an advisory group to the Washington, D.C. Small Business Development and Guidance Center. Personal interview quoted in Henderson and Ledbur (1970: 129).

13 Tabb wrote in 1970 that even the capitalism proposals, "which promise to 'give them a piece of the action,' as President Nixon often phrased it during the last presidential campaign, are little heard of these days. The reason is evident in government statistics. There are not many profitable honest business opportunities available in the ghetto. As the minority group program of the Small Business Administration expanded in recent years, the default rate also climbed to unacceptable rates and the program has been downgraded. Similarly job creation in the private sector has been quietly shelved as the economy has moved downward" (1970: 30).

14 I was first introduced to this convergence of interest and theory by Chandler Morse at Cornell University in 1965.

15 For earlier statements see Clark (1964, 1965), Carmichael and Hamilton (1967), and Cruse (1968).

16 The arguments have been made most directly, and in economic terms, by Allen (1970), Harrison (1968), Tabb (1970: ch. 2). Williams (1944) viewed black slavery in an essentially colonial context.

17 Perhaps the most crushing statement in Leibow's masterful ethnology is his conversation with Tally, who explains his own productive inadequacy: "That's different. Look, can anybody do what you're doing? Can anybody just come up and do your job? Well,

in one week I can teach you cement finishing. You won't be as good as me 'cause you won't have the experience but you'll be a cement finisher. That's what I mean. Anybody can do what I'm doing and that's what gives me this feeling." (1967, p. 62).

18 Colonialism and neo-colonialism—the transfer of colonial control to a local elite that behaves with the mother country's interests at heart—is of course only one of many variables influencing underdevelopment and development. Natural resource endowment, location, size, and initial conditions are among the other most significant variables. When one looks to popular undergraduate texts for a list of traditionally accepted colony conditions, although other characteristics of underdevelopment are discussed, colonial heritage is seldom more than noted in passing, hence the enthusiasm with which recent anti-imperialist works by Frank, Baran, and Griffen are received by university students, and also the excitement over the revisionist historians who see American capitalist power as a pervasive negative influence in world politics. See Williams (1971a, 1971b). Semi-popular writers on economic development omit all serious discussion of colonialism or imperialism from their works. The following list from a quick survey of the Cornell library shelves indicates for several well-known books the total number of index page references to the headings "colony," "colonialism," "neo-colonialism," "empire," "imperialism," etc.: Bauer (1957) 6 references; Galbraith (1962) 0; Gill (1963) 1; Myint (1964) 6; Heilbroner (1963) 6. That is 13 pages out of a total of nearly 700 pages; it is apparently not a very public topic.

It appears that it is only within the last five years that a large number of students have widely read radical criticism. Previously there was such a deep division between acceptable "scientific" social science—including planning—and serious social criticism, that only the most exceptional students had the time or energy to study both. With the explosion of the "underground" journals—*The Review of Radical Political Economy, The Health Pac Newsletter, The NACLA Newsletter*, to name but a few, an integration has begun.

19 See Frank (1969), Griffin (1970), and Kotler (1969; and lecture in Ithaca, N.Y., 1971).

20 Also see Schuchter (1971), who discusses the need for resource transfers from the white economy.

21 Although, as the following section argues, there are problems with the *colonial* analogy, there is no such difficulty with colonization. In fact, the "colonization" of black Americans is probably the most disastrous act of international exploitation in memory. Blauner (1969) makes several important points. (1) "Recall that American slavery lasted 250 years and its racist aftermath another 100. Colonial dependency in the case of British Kenya and French Algeria lasted only 77 and 125 years respectively." (2) Even compared to slave states in the Caribbean and Brazil, American slavery more systematically destroyed African cultures—language, religion, national loyalties, even families were broken up. (3) Other ethnic minorities came to America voluntarily, with their cultures intact, and with at least segments of the society and economy open to them, transforming "their culture at their own pace—giving up ethnic values and institutions when it was seen as a desirable exchange for improvements in social position."

22 Most people today, from writers in the *Wall Street Journal* to full-time social critics, reject the notion that a pluralist system *exists* in the U.S. Instead, it is fairly widely agreed that political and economic power are concentrated in the hands of very few men and institutions. See, for example, Mills (1959) and Domhoff (1967, 1970). In this case, of course, the need for power for a group to be effectively heard is even more clear.

23 Alinsky's programs recognize this point (Lipsk, 1968: 234).

24 I don't want to carry this point too far, though. Without the support from poverty programs it is quite possible that things would have been even worse in the 1960's.

25 Studies of various communities in the United States other than ghettos report various responses which appear to depend partly on the nature and degree of the initial imbalance and partly on conditions of general opportunity. The more complex the community, it seems, the more likely will it organize and succeed (Cottrell, 1951). Many urban renewal programs, foisted on ghettos unlettered in planning and land use law, have large building programs, big political deals, and million dollar transactions, with the well-known result of reduced community cohesiveness. Other city and federal program intrusions into the ghetto can sometimes be seen in the same light. They are often designed for co-optation, that is, the reduction of group solidarity. Also see Clavel et al. (1969).

26 Profiles for about thirty CDC's in New York, Chicago, Los Angeles, Detroit, Philadelphia, Boston, Washington, St. Louis, Cleveland and thirteen other cities were available as of early 1971. See Tobier (1971).

27 Also see Mueller (1971).

28 Cary Hershey's research in this area (1971) suggests that protest movements are usually *not* successful in bureaucracies. But I think his findings are too early to pick up more promising and recent trends.

BIBLIOGRAPHY

Aldrich, Howard, and Albert J. Reiss, Jr. (1970) "The Effect of Civil Disorders on Small Business in the Inner City," *Journal of Social Issues* 26: 187–206.

Allen, Robert I. (1970) *Black Awakening in Capitalist America.* Garden City, N.Y.: Anchor.

America, Richard F., Jr. (1970) "What Do You People Want?" *Review of Black Political Economy* 6 (Spring-Summer): 45–57.

Baran, Paul, and Paul Sweezy (1966) *Monopoly Capital.* New York: Monthly Review, 1966.

Baron, Harold M. (1965) "Black Powerlessness in Chicago," *Transaction* (Nov.).

Binstock, Robert H. (1969) "The Ghetto and the New Left," in Warren (1969): 191–196.

Boggs, James (1968) *Manifesto for a Black Revolutionary Party.* Philadelphia: Pacesetters.

Broderick, Francis L. (1959) *W.E.B. DuBois: Negro Leader in a Time of Crisis.* Stanford: Stanford University Press.

Browne, Robert S. (1970) "Barriers to Black Participation in the American Economy," *Review of Black Political Economy* 1 (Autumn).

Canty, Donald (1969) *A Single Society: Alternatives to Urban Apartheid.* New York: Praeger.

Caplovitz, David (1969) "The Merchant and the Low-Income Consumer," in Sturdivant (1969): 61–75.

Carmichael, Stokely, and Charles Hamilton (1967) *Black Power.* New York: Random House.

Clavel, Pierre, H. C. Capener, and B. G. Jones (1969) *Alternative Organizational Models for District Development*, Cornell University, Department of Rural Sociology.

Clark, Kenneth (1964) *Youth in the Ghetto: A Study of the Consequences of Powerlessness and a Blueprint for Change.* New York: Haryou Association, Harlem Youth Opportunities Association.

Clark, Kenneth (1965) *Dark Ghetto.* New York: Harper & Row.

Cleaver, Eldridge (1969) "Affidavit #2" *Post-Prison Writings and Speeches.* New York: Vintage.

Cloward, Richard A., and Francis Fox Piven (1967) "Ghetto Redevelopment: Corporate Imperialism for the Poor," *The Nation* (Oct. 16).

Cloward, Richard A., and Francis Fox Piven (1968) "Urban Crisis and the Consolidation of National Power" in Connery (1968).

Connery, Robert H., ed. (1968) "Urban Riots: Violence and Social Change," *Proceedings of the Academy of Political Science* 29: 190 + x.

Cottrell, W. F. (1951) "Death by Dieselization: A Case Study of the Reaction to Technological Change," *American Sociological Review* 16: 358–365.

Crecine, John P. (1970) *Financing the Metropolis.* Los Angeles: Sage.

Cross, Theodore (1969) *Black Capitalism: Strategy for Business in the Ghetto.* New York: Atheneum.

Cruse, Harold (1968) *Rebellion or Revolution.* New York: Morrow.

DeLorean, John Z. (1969) "The Problem," in Haddad and Pugh (1969).

Domhoff, G. William (1970) *The Higher Circles: The Governing Class in America.* New York: Random House.

———— (1967) *Who Rules America?* Englewood Cliffs, New Jersey: Prentice Hall.

Downs, Anthony (1968) "Alternative Futures of the American Ghetto," *Daedalus* 97 (Fall): 1331–1378.

Foley, Eugene P. (1969) *The Achieving Ghetto.* Washington, D.C.: The National Press.

Frank, Andre G. (1969) *Latin America: Underdevelopment or Revolution.* New York: Monthly Review.

Fusfeld, Daniel R. (1970) "The Basic Economics of the Urban and Racial Crisis," *Review of Black Political Economy* 1 (Spring-Summer): 58–83.

Fusfeld, Daniel (1970) "The Economy of the Urban Ghetto" in Crecine (1970): 369.

Gouldner, Alvin W. (1970) *The Coming Crisis of Western Sociology.* New York: Basic Books.

Griffin, Keith (1970) "Reflections on Latin American Development," in *Latin America: Problems in Economic Development.* New York: Oxford University Press.

Haddad, William and G. Douglass Pugh, ed. (1969) *Black Economic Development.* Englewood Cliffs, New Jersey: Prentice Hall.

Harrison, Bennett (1968) "A Pilot Project in Economic Development Planning for American Urban Slums," *International Development Review* (March).

———— (1969) "Public Service Jobs for Urban Ghetto Residents," *Good Government* (Fall): 1–20.

———— (1970) "Education, Training, and The Urban Ghetto." Unpublished Ph.D. dissertation, Department of Economics, University of Pennsylvania.

Hayden, Tom (1969) "Colonialism and Liberation as American Problems," in Warren (1969): 170–190.

Heilbroner, Robert L. (1963) *The Great Ascent: The Struggle for Economic Development in Our Time.* New York: Harper and Row.

Heilbrun, James, and Stanislaw Wellisz (1968) "An Economic Program for the Ghetto," in Connery (1968): 73–86.

Henderson, William L., and Larry C. Ledbur (1970) *Economic Disparity: Problems and Strategies for Black America.* New York: The Free Press.

Hershey, Cary (1971) "Protest in the Public Service." Unpublished Ph.D. dissertation, New York University.

Hill, Herbert (1966) "Demographic Change and Racial Ghettos: The Crisis of American Cities," *Journal of Urban Law* 44 (Winter): 231–285.

Innis, Roy (1969) "Separatist Economics: A New Social Contract," in Haddad and Pugh (1969): 50–59.

Kain, John F. (1968) "Housing Segregation, Negro Employment, and Metropolitan Decentralization," *Quarterly Journal of Economics* (May).

——— (1969) "Coping with Ghetto Unemployment," *The Research Review* (August), U.S. Dept. of Commerce, Economic Development Administration.

——— (1970) "National Priorities for Regional Development," Harvard Program in Regional and Urban Economics, Discussion Paper No. 61, May.

———, and Joseph Persky (1969) "Alternatives to the Guilded Ghetto," *Public Interest* 14 (Winter).

———, and John M. Quigley (1970) "Housing Market Discrimination, Homeownership, and Savings Behavior," Harvard Program on Regional and Urban Economics, No. 58 (Jan.).

Kilby, Peter (1971) *Entrepreneurship and Economic Development.* New York: Free Press.

Kotler, Milton (1969) *Neighborhood Government: The Local Foundations of Political Life.* Indianapolis: Bobbs Merrill Co.

Labrie, Peter (1970–1971) "Black Central Cities: Dispersal or Rebuilding." Parts I and II. *The Review of Black Political Economy* 1 (Autumn): 1–20; and (Winter-Spring 1971): 78–99.

Levitan, Sar, Garth Mangum, and Robert Taggart III (1970) *Economic Opportunity in the Ghetto: The Partnership of Government and Business.* Baltimore: Johns Hopkins.

Lowi, Theodore J. (1968) "American Cities: Old Shame and New" *Midway* 9 (Autumn): 27–47.

——— (1971) *The Politics of Disorder.* New York: Basic Books.

McClaughry, John (1969) "Black Ownership and National Politics," in Haddad and Pugh (1969).

McLaurin, Dunbar (1968) *The Ghediplan. An Economic Development Plan.* New York: Human Resources Administration.

Mermelstein, David, ed. (1970) *Economics: Mainstream Readings and Radical Critiques.* New York: Random House.

Meyer, John, John Kain, and Martin Wohl (1965) *The Urban Transportation Problem.* Cambridge, Mass.: Harvard University Press.

Mills, C. Wright (1959) *The Power Elite.* New York: Oxford University Press.

Moynihan, Daniel P. (1970) "Memorandum for the President on the Position of Negroes," text reprinted in *The New York Times*, March 1.

Mueller, Carol E. (1971) Unpublished Ph.D. dissertation, Department of Sociology, Cornell University.

Pascal, Anthony H. (1967) *The Economics of Housing Segregation.* Santa Monica, Calif.: RAND.

——— (1970) "Black Gold and Black Capitalism," *The Public Interest* 19 (Spring): 111–119.

Pinderhughes, Charles A. (1968) "The Psychodynamics of Dissent" in *The Dynamics of Dissent*. New York: Grune and Stratton.

Piven, Frances Fox, and Richard A. Cloward (1967) "The Case Against Urban Desegregation," *Social Work* 12 (Jan.): 12–21.

Rattien, Stephen (1970) "Industrial Specialization and Minority Group Upward Mobility: A Study of Negro Employment Patterns in Selected S.M.S.A.'s, 1950 and 1960." Unpublished Ph.D. dissertation, Department of City and Regional Planning, Cornell University.

Reich, Michael (1971) "The Economics of Racism," *Upstart* 1 (Jan.): 55–65.

Rein, Martin (1969) "Social Responsibility and Black Ghettos," in Warren (1969): 44–58.

Reiss, Albert J., and Howard Aldrich (1971) "Absentee Ownership Management in the Black Ghetto: Social and Economic Consequences," *Social Problems* (Winter).

Samuels, Howard J. (1969) "Compensatory Capitalism," in Haddad and Pugh (1969): 60–73.

Schuchter, Arnold (1968) *White Power, Black Freedom*. Boston: Beacon.

Sturdivant, Frank D., ed. (1969) *The Ghetto as Marketplace*. New York: The Free Press.

Sullivan, Leon H. (1969) *Build, Brother, Build*. Philadelphia: Macrae Smith.

Tabb, William K. (1970) *The Political Economy of the Black Ghetto*. New York: W. W. Norton.

Taeuber, Karl E. and Alma F. (1965) *Negroes in Cities: Residential Segregation and Neighborhood Change*. Chicago: Aldine.

Thompson, Victor A. (1964) *Modern Organization*. New York: Knopf.

Tobier, Arthur (1971) "Profiles in Community Based Economic Development," Cambridge, Mass.: Center for Community Economic Development and the Cambridge Institute.

Valentine, Charles A. (1968) *Culture and Poverty*. Chicago: University of Chicago Press.

Venable, Abraham S. (1971) "Black Business Development: Chaos in Transition?" *Black Enterprise* 2 (Sept.): 20–23.

Vietorisz, Thomas, and Bennett Harrison (1970) *The Economic Development of Harlem*. New York: Praeger.

——— (1971) "The Uncertain Prospects for Ghetto Development," *Challenge* (March).

Warren, Roland L., ed. (1969) *Politics and the Ghettos*. New York: Atherton.

Williams, Eric (1944) *Capitalism and Slavery*. Chapel Hill: University of North Carolina Press. Capricorn Books, 1966.

Williams, William A. Reviews in the *New York Review Books*, (a) Nov. 5, 1971 and (b) Dec. 2, 1971.

Young, Frank W. (1970) "Reactive Subsystems," *American Sociological Review* (Apr.).

——— (1971) "Macrosociological Interpretation of Entrepreneurship," in Kilby (1971).

The First Twenty Years of HUD

Robert C. Weaver

Distinguished Professor Emeritus of Urban Affairs, Hunter College

This article was part of the *Journal of the American Planning Association*'s special symposium issue on housing to celebrate the twentieth anniversary of President Johnson's signing into law the Department of Housing and Urban Development (HUD) Act in September 1965. This act gave cabinet-level status to HUD. In September 1966, Robert C. Weaver was appointed secretary of the new department. He is thus in a unique position to review HUD's performance. HUD began with great expectations for solving urban problems, but twenty years later it was surrounded with dashed hopes and considerable disappointments. As Weaver notes, "Twenty years later, those hopes and expectations have not been realized" (p. 400). On an optimistic note, however, he also states that the experiences gained and the political power delivered by Model Cities to low-income neighborhoods will endure beyond cutbacks in federal programs.

When the U.S. Department of Housing and Urban Development was formed, the urban crisis seemed to be at its height. Civil unrest in the nation's largest cities had greeted a new president's commitment to eradicate poverty. Less dramatic but equally significant were the economic ills that beset the central cities as they lost population, industrial and commercial activity, and tax revenue in the wake of the rapid expansion of suburbia. Urban renewal often had been insensitive to human problems, and housing production seemed destined to lag behind the anticipated demographic trends of urban America. These longstanding problems also were part of the urban crisis. Given the severity of that crisis, it was believed that only a new department focusing on urban and housing problems would be able to muster and coordinate the variety of federal resources needed to aid the cities and provide adequate shelter for our people. Consequently, President Johnson's view of the proposed department suggested that it would become the focal point of thought, innovation, and imagination about the problems of our cities.

At the time President Johnson proposed to establish HUD, I had served four years as administrator of HUD's predecessor, the Housing and Home Finance Agency. As such I became involved in executive branch discussions of what the proposed new department's mission and structure would be. I found myself in a dilemma: should I join the clamor for a superdepartment that would consolidate all or most major activities related to urban development and housing, or should I advocate more modest goals of coordination that seemed achievable based on my experience at HHFA?

Coordination, rather than consolidation, seemed to be the only way HUD could

Reprinted by permission of the *Journal of the American Planning Association* 51, 4, Autumn 1985.

assist in shaping national urban policy effectively. I had little hope that all, or even most, federal activities related to urban affairs could be consolidated into a single department. Even in housing, where HHFA had a large share of the federal programs already, that seemed impossible. Essential programs, such as Veterans Administration guaranteed mortgages, were housed in agencies whose strong lobbies would fight hard to keep them independent. As subsequent events should show, it would have been very difficult to move such activities to HUD.[1] Transfer of budget and many credit-related departments, agencies, or semi-autonomous boards that had principal missions other than housing would have been equally difficult. Moreover, in turf-conscious Washington, the idea that HUD would become the new central authority in urban policy evoked images of widespread transfer of functions and altering of congressional committee jurisdictions. I realized that proposals for such action would imperil legislation to establish the new department.

Although the White House had hesitated to assume the role of coordinator of governmental efforts in urban affairs, I was convinced that only the President could perform that function. One solution to the coordination problem was proposed by the same 1964 Presidential Task Force on Metropolitan and Urban Problems that recommended creation of HUD—to set up an urban affairs council in the White House. I strongly opposed setting up such a council at that time, however, since I believed that, too, could kill legislation to establish HUD. The Republicans already had recommended a similar office in the White House as an alternative to a new department (Weaver 1964). I expected that once HUD began to function effectively, the political climate would permit establishment of an urban affairs council (or some other presidential instrument for coordination) in the White House without its becoming a substitute for HUD.

In January 1966 I was appointed secretary of the new department which was authorized by the Department of Housing and Urban Development Act of 9 September 1965. At that time many and diverse expectations for the department were articulated. They ranged from a concept of almost or complete concentration of all federal housing and urban development activities in HUD to prophecies that the department would become a meaningless symbol. My position was at neither extreme. I started in full agreement with the words of the declaration of purpose contained in the law that authorized formation of HUD: one of the duties of the new department, it said, was "to assist the President in achieving maximum coordination of the various Federal activities which have a major effect upon urban community, suburban, or metropolitan development."

MY ORIGINAL HOPES FOR HUD

My top priority for HUD was to coordinate the existing constituent units of HHFA—the Federal Housing Administration, the Public Housing Administration, the Urban Renewal Administration, the Community Facilities Administration, and the Office of the Administrator—and to structure the new department to promote such coordination. I also sought significant expansion of existing HHFA programs; enactment of legislation authorizing an experimental effort to demonstrate how the quality of life in low-income neighborhoods could be raised by integrating physi-cal and social planning and rehabilitation activities; enactment of an effective fair housing law; and enactment of a comprehensive housing and urban development act that would, among other things, significantly increase production of housing for all income groups and provide access to that housing through adequate mort-gage credit. Another high-priority goal was development of a policy for optioning or buying land for future urban development.

It was my hope that achievement of those and related goals would focus more public attention on urban development and housing issues, persuade the federal government to provide more funds to address those issues, and develop a pool of experts capable of dealing with them. I hoped those results, combined with presi-dential intervention to coordinate urban efforts among numerous agencies, would appreciably increase the effectiveness and clout of HUD.

Twenty years later, those hopes and expectations have not been realized. Nevertheless, I think HUD got off to a fairly good start. Even though pursuit of the Vietnam War distracted him from domestic issues and led him to divert more and more resources to the war, Lyndon Johnson laid a substantial foundation upon which significant progress could have been made in rebuilding cities, tying physi-cal and social needs programs together, and meeting the housing requirements of the nation. And HUD was a key element in that foundation.

Although the Johnson administration's approach to urban development housing suffered from underfunding, I believe the principal reason HUD failed to attain stature within the federal government is that the ambitious new urban and housing programs of the Johnson years were never given a chance to settle into place or to make adjustments as they went along—a normal process in large-scale innova-tions. That is partly because these programs were exposed early on (beginning in 1969) to a hostile Nixon administration, which rejected the philosophy and approach they embodied, and partly because new HUD Secretary George W. Romney (1969–1973) pushed some programs too fast. In the Section 235 home-ownership program, for instance, Romney failed to take time to correct fraud, dis-honest appraisals, abuses by speculators, and shoddy construction, then abruptly terminated the program. In the area of racial integration Romney pushed so hard as to create a congressional backlash, then was forced to retreat from that effort. This pattern of rapid program change would continue as subsequent administrations fre-quently changed the emphases and directions of key programs. In my opinion, this type of stop and go, taking off in one direction and then changing quickly to anoth-er, is largely responsible for the department's poor public image and its failure to fulfill its originators' hopes and expectations. Moreover, past and present efforts to reduce expenditures and cut programs have seriously hurt HUD and neutralized its advocacy of constructive approaches.

In this article I trace the evolution of HUD's policies, programs, and perfor-mance, setting forth the major legislative developments over the past two decades. My main thesis is stated in the preceding paragraph; what follows will support that proposition, with emphasis on the indifference of the Reagan administration toward cities and shelter for the less advantaged. The article discusses what we

have learned, the achievements and the deficiencies of HUD, and several unresolved issues. It concludes with an analysis of the future of federal housing and
urban development activities and of HUD, treating the costs of current neglect of
urban and shelter needs.

EVOLUTION AND HUD'S POLICIES AND PROGRAMS

The roots of HUD's early policies and programs reach back to the New Deal, but
their most important precedents lie in the department's precursor, the Housing and
Home Finance Agency. In fact, the goals, emphases, and programs of HHFA during the Kennedy and early Johnson years were carried over directly into HUD, to
be supplemented soon thereafter by new activities. The most important elements
HUD inherited from HHFA were the department's continued emphasis on housing
production, with a newly deepened concern for lower-income households; a federal executive order of extremely limited application that addressed racial discrimination in housing, and subsequent legislation that expanded that application somewhat; a growing number of categorical grants for community development; and
increasing concern for the people directly affected by urban renewal.

Model Cities, 1966

The first major legislation proposed for HUD was the Demonstration Cities and
Metropolitan Development Act of 1966. Title I authorized what came to be known
as Model Cities.[2] The concept of "demonstration cities" was conceived and developed by the 1965 Presidential Task Force on Urban Problems, chaired by Robert
C. Wood.[3] It became the first prominent HUD program to have the undisputed
imprimatur of the new administration and the Great Society. The original proposal envisioned coordination of multiple programs of several federal departments and
agencies in comprehensive physical, social, and economic redevelopment of a limited number of target neighborhoods. It was intended to demonstrate what could be
achieved if all available federal resources were focused on a community and it was
assumed that HUD would be able to coordinate those resources. By the time the
concept was translated into law, it had been converted from a demonstration
involving some sixty cities, into a quasi-operational program in some 150 cities,
with woefully inadequate funding.

Both the proposal and the program had a number of weaknesses. For example,
HUD—as a junior federal department—lacked the capacity to coordinate the programs of its more mature peers; at the same time, the crucial role the states would
play in the allocation of federal grants was not recognized. When its inability to
coordinate became clear, HUD appealed to the White House for assistance in
securing interdepartmental and intra-agency cooperation, but the response was
"less than dramatic," reflecting White House reluctance to play a coordinating role
in urban affairs (Frieden and Kaplan 1975, 110).[4] Although both the task force
report and HUD relied heavily on comprehensive planning, the political institutions to implement planning, the state of the art of planning, and the clarity of HUD

regulations were not sufficient to produce the expected dramatic improvements in target neighborhoods.

The classic evaluation of Model Cities—that it did not live up to its promises (Frieden and Kaplan 1975, 234)—is valid. As just discussed, that was partly because the 1966 Model Cities legislation increased the number of eligible cities without proportionately increasing funding for the program. Had the number of model city neighborhoods been kept proportional to the availability of financial resources, the program might have achieved much more. It still would have suffered (although perhaps to a lesser degree) from coordination and planning problems. But decreasing the number of participants could have reduced the confusion and complexity in HUD's regulations; it certainly would have permitted HUD to render greater technical assistance to each target area and allowed it to concentrate the efforts of the limited pool of gifted planners among fewer target neighborhoods. That might have produced more imaginative and creative approaches, and the promises made for the program might have been less exaggerated.

Even as implemented, however, Model Cities demonstrated substantial achievements, some of which have had lasting effects. It opened numerous job opportunities for the poor and minorities. In the process it accelerated upward job mobility, especially in public employment, and did much to energize ghetto residents to political activity. Model Cities provided performance standards for citizens participation without destroying the role of the mayor and demonstrated how federal benefits could be concentrated in areas of greatest need (Frieden and Kaplan 1977, 286–87, 310–11). In the final analysis, I believe the principal objective of Model Cities—to provide decent community services and rehabilitate the neighborhoods where the poor are concentrated—was a valid goal in 1965 and remains so today.

1968: A Watershed Year in Housing Policy

A top HUD official in the Nixon and Ford administrations described the Housing and Urban Development Act of 1968 as one of two basic elements in a watershed year for national housing policy (Orlebeke 1975, 142). Among the act's features were numerical production goals for housing designed to serve a broad spectrum of income groups. The Federal National Mortgage Administration was transformed from a federal agency into a government-sponsored private corporation so that budget limits could be lifted from its secondary market activities (buying and selling of mortgages). The newly created Government National Mortgage Association was designed to tap additional sources of funds for housing credit (such as endowment and pension funds and individual investors). The act set up two new programs to provide FHA interest subsidies to construction and major rehabilitation of moderate-income housing, Section 235 for ownership and Section 236 for rental. It relaxed restrictions on where subsidized housing could be located, and it increased the authorized limit on spending to build public housing. In response to a recommendation of the President's Committee on Urban Housing (known as the Kaiser Committee, 1967–68), Title IX of the act established the

National Housing Partnership as a tool to attract private industry's involvement in reconstructing and rehabilitating slums. And an expanded program for developing new communities, introduced as Title IV of the act, authorized federal guarantees of bonds issued by private developers to help them finance land acquisition for large-scale projects that incorporated a balance of housing, industrial, and commercial development.

Title VIII of the Civil Rights Act of 1968 was the second major housing policy initiative in that year. It vastly extended the prohibition of racial discrimination in housing, including individual housing transactions and credit institutions, so that within three years of enactment, the prohibition would cover 80 percent of the nation's housing supply. It also provided some enforcement powers and charged the secretary to administer HUD's programs so that they advanced the nondiscrimination policy.

These two milestone 1968 laws showed the government's recognition that an adequate supply of decent, affordable shelter and unrestricted access to that shelter were complementary benefits. In securing passage of these laws, President Johnson had brought both commitment and legislative skills into play. The legislative process took place against a background of urban crisis. At times that crisis encouraged opposition to or delay of the legislation. At other times it provided an impetus toward passage of civil rights legislation; in the case of the open occupancy housing bill, for instance, President Johnson capitalized on the outrage that arose upon the assassination of Martin Luther King, Jr., to wrest the legislation out of the House Rules Committee, securing passage and signing the bill within a week.

Forging a Coalition for HUD Legislation

In HHFA congressional relations had been under the jurisdiction of the agency's general counsel, who had left a congressional staff position to join HHFA. He had successfully cultivated the congressional committees while neglecting actual and potential lobbying groups. With the establishment of HUD, this function was transferred to a new congressional liaison director who took the leadership in developing for HUD a clientele of constituents to support its legislative proposals and programs, initially based on social issues. The effect of the constituent lobby was felt first in the struggle for Model Cities. By the time the 1968 Housing and Urban Development Act was being formulated, HUD had assumed leadership in organizing and supporting an extremely diverse coalition of some seventy-five groups under the aegis of the U.S. Conference of Mayors. The coalition's membership ranged from the National Association of Home Builders through organized labor to national welfare and civil rights organizations. Its most notable characteristics, aside from its wide diversity, were its unprecedented commitment to housing for the disadvantaged and the novel participation of the politically influential home builders in such an effort.

THE NIXON AND FORD YEARS, 1969–1976

During the early years of the Nixon administration, HUD continued its established directions and goals. In the face of presidential indifference, ambivalence, and hostility, the department leadership fought successfully to keep Model Cities alive, albeit with some dilution (Frieden and Kaplan 1975, 119 et seq.). During Nixon's presidency HUD built on the 1968 Housing and Urban Development Act, extending the New Communities program and pushing it into implementation. The department initially embraced the housing production goals set in the 1968 legislation, as well as the section 235 and 236 programs for subsidized housing (U.S. HUD 1972, 8–9); the result was an unprecedented volume of housing construction. No less enthusiastic was HUD's initial enforcement of the 1968 Civil Rights Act's program of affirmative action to eliminate racial discrimination in housing. To the application review process for all HUD grant programs, including the popular water and sewer grants for suburbs, HUD added the requirement that localities provide subsidized housing—an effort to disperse racial minorities geographically throughout metropolitan areas. The action caused an immediate backlash in Congress, leading the White House to oppose it. HUD Secretary Romney was forced to modify the regulation (Danielson 1976, 213–242).

HUD Backtracks

In early 1973 HUD abruptly reversed its policies and goals, placing a moratorium on construction of subsidized housing.[5] The controversy spurred by the moratorium (e.g., see U.S. Congress 1973) intensified in reaction to the release, some eight months later, of HUD's rationale for it. Among other things, the report—later to be published under the title *Housing in the Seventies* (U.S. HUD 1974)—asserted that housing subsidies were costly and failed to offer equal treatment to everyone in the same economic bracket (horizontal equity) and that sections 235 and 236 were inherently flawed and unworkable. Subsequent research has corroborated the cost criticism; that is not surprising, since the statute and its legislative history specifically and repeatedly show the lawmakers' recognition that they were high-risk (and, therefore, high-cost) efforts (Semer and Zimmerman 1974). Like most new administrations, however, the leaders under Nixon demonstrated a penchant for ignoring the lessons their predecessors had learned (Downs 1974, 135).

Housing in the Seventies prompted discussion about whether sections 235 and 236 were inherently flawed and unworkable.[6] As in any new approach of such magnitude, the subsidized housing programs had some design defects. Careful analyses of administrative actions and problems in HUD under Nixon revealed, however, that program operation, rather than structure and design, was the basic cause of problems in the housing subsidy programs. Continual reorganizations of the department, decimation of FHA, and HUD's excessive pressure to produce large numbers of new housing units at any cost had weakened the operation of both programs. Cutbacks in federal spending and the Nixon administration's tight monetary policy had constrained mortgage credit, thereby pushing thousands of builders toward the new subsidized programs, where financing was available.

FHA's efficiency and professional competency had reached new lows, occasioned also by that agency's (and HUD's) questionable recruitment practices, involving many violations of the merit system and the lack of effective training programs. There were widespread criminal activities in the programs, too (Downs 1974; McFarland 1978; Schechter 1974).[7]

The programs of the 1968 Housing and Urban Development Act went far toward achieving the act's goals. The General Accounting Office's analysis, for example, found that Section 236 was "the foremost example of Government assistance for privately developed rental housing. . . . [It] was intended to primarily serve moderate income families, and it does" (U.S. GAO 1978a, 1, 4). There are questions, however, about some of the assumptions behind those programs. Was it utopian to aim to eradicate substandard housing in a single decade (Downs 1974, 142)? Regardless of the answer, I was and remain convinced that without such a spectacular goal, what Downs described as "a dramatic rise in the status of housing and housing-related problems on the nation's priority list" would not have been attainable (1974, 134). On the one hand, unanticipated economic changes, such as rapid inflation and the 1976 energy crisis, led to unexpected increases in operating costs. Those increases joined high rates of unemployment in threatening the economic viability of some subsidized housing. On the other hand, some feared that the home building industry was incapable of achieving such ambitious production goals. By the early 1970s that fear had been proved baseless.

The great expansion of production may have contributed to, but certainly was not primarily responsible for, the increasing abandonment of housing in the central city in the early 1970s (Orlebeke 1975, 149). It is somewhat ironic that progress toward the goal of eradicating substandard housing made housing allowances appear more feasible. Sections 235 and 236 significantly increased the volume of standard lower-income housing. Where this occurred, tightness in this segment of the housing market was reduced, filtering became more effective, and reasonably modest demand-oriented subsidies were rendered operative (see footnote 17).

The Housing and Community Development Act of 1974

The Housing and Community Development Act of 1974 was the result of a compromise between three bills proposed in 1973 by the Nixon administration, the House, and the Senate. The administration's Better Communities bill proposed to make Community Development Block Grants to cities to fund urban development projects at 100 percent of their cost; it required no matching local funds. The administration's bill did not provide for strict federal oversight of the grant-funded projects. It also proposed housing allowances (handing out payments to low-income families to assist them with rental of units of their own choice) as a tool for housing assistance and horizontal equity, but the funding it proposed for that program fell far short of what would have been needed.

The House version of the bill linked Community Development Block Grants to a requirement that cities provide for an adequate supply of low- and moderate-income housing. The Senate version differed from the administration version in that it provided for considerably more stringent oversight of grant-funded projects. Both congressional versions insisted on either extending the existing moderate-income housing programs, setting up a substitute program, or both.

As ultimately enacted, the 1974 statute linked block grants to adequate local supplies of low- and moderate-income housing; funded projects at 100 percent of cost; and struck a compromise on the strength of oversight requirements. Its Section 8 program was a compromise between the administration's and Congress's versions of housing assistance. This subsidy program, embracing both new construction and existing housing, had some weaknesses: it restored a requirement for local approval (which had been removed by the 1968 legislation) that had proved to be a major impediment to the goal of dispersing lower-income and minority groups; it lacked a mechanism for financing new construction; and it essentially cut off subsidies to units that had been vacant for sixty days or more.

One distinct and outstanding strength of the 1974 act, however, was its requirement that any applicant for a Community Development Block Grant submit a Housing Assistance Plan. The the HAP, in turn, required a comprehensive assessment of the housing needs of low- and moderate-income households, spelling out plans for meeting those needs, including target locations for subsidized housing. HAPs were intended to significantly accelerate provision of lower-income housing at scattered sites. But the effectiveness of HAP requirement in area planning and dispersal of economic groups depended on the availability of federal housing assistance and was limited by its citywide (rather than metropolitan) scale. Its effectiveness also depended on how vigorously HUD administered it. That vigor was lacking until a federal court intervened in 1976 to require it and the more sympathetic Carter administration took office.

Although the conference report (U.S. House 1974, 147) clearly authorized financing Section 8 projects with FHA mortgages, Romney's successor, James T. Lynn (1973–75) was reluctant to use them. Nor did HUD reactivate section 236 to take up the slack, despite authority in the 1974 act to do so. Instead it relied on state housing agencies, which, after the serious difficulties of the New York State Urban Development Corporation, experienced greatly reduced capacity to finance construction. The bottom line was little lower-income new construction or major rehabilitation. The pipeline of starts for assisted housing, already drying up because of the 1973 moratorium, had its volume further reduced, and that also prevented realization of the expectations for the HAPs (U.S. House 1977, 28).

The 1974 Community Development Block Grant program, despite its glowing language, further weakened HUD's leverage to encourage planning on a metropolitan scale, mainly because it distributed most of the grant funds to individual urban governments on an automatic formula basis. There is persuasive evidence, too, that during its early years, the CDBG program did not give priority to activities benefiting low- or moderate-income families (U.S. GAO 1976, 11; U.S. House 1977, 22, 23, 27; Ginsburg 1977, 80–83). The program did less than it could have, and much less than Model Cities did, to reach poor people (Frieden and Kaplan 1977, 308).

Secretary Lynn carried out Nixon's policies of cutting HUD's budget, impounding program funds, killing programs, and ignoring the 1974 act and the congressional intent behind it. Secretary Carla A. Hills, who succeeded Lynn in March 1975 and inherited confusion, low morale, and retirement of many of HUD's best staff members, attempted to correct the deficiencies in the administration of the 1974 Housing and Community Development Act set forth above. Yet the success of that effort was limited, no doubt by the Ford administration's acceptance of New Federalism and its attempts to make targeting federal community development funds to the more affluent appear legitimate. Moreover, Lynn, who had moved on to the strategic position of director of the Office of Management and Budget, had a continuing negative influence on HUD's effectiveness. In Hills's last year in office, however, the federal government's financial commitment to housing assistance increased significantly.

THE CARTER YEARS AND SOME NEW DIRECTIONS

The election of President Carter and the designation of Patricia Roberts Harris as secretary of HUD (1977–79) ushered in a second period of significantly changed emphasis in policies and program direction, as well as in program content. Although the new emphases and directions were readily apparent, their impact was not as great as that of changes in the two preceding administrations and in the one that followed.

During the Carter administration HUD attempted to unscramble the confused organization it inherited and to make the HAPs more effective in dispersing racial and economic groups throughout the metropolitan areas. The 1977 Housing and Community Development Act broadened the 1974 legislation, releasing Section 236 operating subsidies to cover increases in real estate taxes and utility costs (authorized in the 1974 act but never activated). It also strengthened the Section 8 construction and rehabilitation program by allowing units to continue receiving subsidies for up to a year after being vacated. While the 1977 act extended the general trend—begun with the 1974 housing act—toward using block grants for community development projects, several of its new programs encouraged greater involvement of neighborhoods as partners in community development and called specifically for citizen participation in project decisions.[8] The act also added the Urban Development Action Grants program, which awarded competitive grants to local governments to leverage private investments in enterprises that provide central city jobs. UDAG funds were intended to promote economic development of distressed areas (like Model Cities), but the program did not attempt to coordinate grant-funded projects with other housing and community development activities (Struyk, Tuccillo, and Zais 1982, 399).

Under Harris, HUD revived the pre-1973 importance of supply-oriented housing assistance programs but permitted the Section 8 program to play an important demand-side role. The department also issued regulations stipulating that 75 percent of each block grant go to support the projects in low- and moderate-income neighborhoods and requiring citizen participation in local decisions about what projects should be undertaken.

The department published a comprehensive national survey of the incidence of racial discrimination in housing (U.S. HUD 1979), and it sponsored greater cooperation with local fair housing groups. Throughout the Nixon-Ford years champions of fair housing had complained vociferously of HUD's failure to issue comprehensive Title VIII regulations. In December 1980, just before the Carter administration's demise, Moon Landrieu, who had succeeded Harris in 1979, promulgated such regulations.[9]

The policy and program redirections in HUD during the Carter years were a refreshing break from the Nixon-Ford period. Program achievements, however, were less impressive, as proposals to increase federal aid to cities and the disadvantaged collided with the fiscal policies that dominated the President and Congress, especially in the latter years of the Carter administration (Harney 1977). Even as a mix involving more new construction was initiated, the commitment to expansion in assisted housing during the last Carter year was less than during the final year of the Ford administration (Struyk, Tuccillo, and Zais 1982, 398; Turner and Struyk 1984, 38–40). Expenditures for aid to urban neighborhoods, although greater than in the Nixon and Ford years, were never more than modest in comparison to those of the middle and late 1960s (Clarke 1984, 499). These developments provided precedents for much greater dilution of the programs when deeper budgetary constraints were initiated.

THE REAGAN ADMINISTRATION

Priority for urban development and housing as well as the image and credibility of HUD reached their nadir with the advent of the Reagan administration and the tenure of Secretary Samuel R. Pierce. The Reagan administration reversed most of the Carter deviations from the policies of the Nixon and Ford years, so that by 1982 it could be said that Reagan had proposed a fundamental redirection in U.S. housing policy. Government priorities were shifting away from the poor at the same time that the building industry and the thrift institutions were becoming more dependent on the operation of the market (Struyk, Tuccillo, and Zais 1982, 417). Federal involvement in mortgage credit was greatly reduced, and the administration now seems intent on eliminating FHA and GNMA (Struyk, Tuccillo, and Zais 1982, 405–406). In fiscal 1977 the federal government brought 388,000 housing units into the assistance programs; 52 percent of those either were newly built or had undergone substantial rehabilitation. By fiscal 1982 that number was down to 52,000 and only 12 percent were newly built or had undergone substantial rehabilitation (Turner and Struyk 1984, 38).[10] And nowhere has HUD's performance in the 1980s been as disappointing as in the field of fair housing. This is but one phase of the widely recognized insensitivity and, indeed, often hostility of the administration toward effective enforcement of civil rights legislation.

Reagan's HUD eliminated some project grant programs and consolidated others into block grants. Those actions, when combined with general cutbacks in HUD funding, reduced federal expenditures on urban development. As a result of legislation and administrative actions of HUD, the Community Development Block

Grant program—which remained the department's main instrument for community development—became essentially a revenue sharing program (Struyk, Tuccillo, and Zais 1982, 412). The Reagan administration diluted efforts HUD had made under Carter to target community development programs toward the needy as well as the efforts to render HAPs more effective. Reagan's HUD cut spending on spatially targeted programs and it withdrew direct funding in neighborhood development activities (Clarke 1984). The department began to champion a new program—urban enterprise zones—based on the notion that market forces will cure the ills of inner city areas if only the barriers to economic growth are removed.[11]

At the time this article was written (June 1985), the Reagan administration's budget for fiscal 1986 proposed to reduce spending on HUD programs by almost 47 percent, the highest percentage cut proposed for any federal department. The following were among the specific cuts proposed:

• a two-year moratorium on additional housing assistance (including housing assistance for the elderly);
• limiting the touted housing voucher program to 3,500 additional units;
• terminating the UDAG program;
• subjecting the 1983 Rental Housing Development Rehabilitation Grants program—which provided grants to make rehabilitation of rental housing feasible for lower-income tenants, and which a recent departmental study (U.S. HUD 1984) declared a success—to a two-year funding moratorium;
• cutting the CDBG program by 10 percent and altering the grant formula so that cities of 50,000 or more would face a potential 24 percent reduction in block grant funds;
• freezing rent ceilings in both the Section 8 existing housing and the voucher programs at their fiscal 1985 levels;
• discounting aid for the homeless;
• imposing a two-year moratorium on funding for construction of new public housing; and
• imposing a one-year partial moratorium on funding for modernization of existing public housing (U.S. HUD 1985).

Other urban-related activities outside HUD were subjected to similar treatment in the proposed 1986 budget, demonstrating further the administration's lack of commitment to urban development and housing.[12] The budget proposal would provide no funds for General Revenue Sharing and no operating subsidies for urban mass transit or Amtrak. In addition, it would hurt cities through proposed cuts in job training, food stamps, and Aid to Families with Dependent Children as well as freezes and cuts in Medicaid and Medicare and associated social programs.

LESSONS FROM THE FIRST TWENTY YEARS OF HUD

Several lessons can be drawn from the way various factors have influenced HUD's performance during the past two decades. First, the government's difficulty in setting clear goals for the department has permitted continual sudden shifts in priorities and vacillation in program direction. When goals are not stated clearly, it is often because complex problems or diverse concerns are involved. Clearly stated goals characterized (and strengthened) the 1930s housing programs, which came at a time when the nation's primary concerns—shoring up the mortgage and credit systems and revitalizing the economy through stimulation of residential construction—were compatible with providing low-income housing. By the early 1950s, however, urban renewal had become a complicated activity typified by conflicting goals (Weaver 1965, 76). For another example, the Federal Housing Authority, the federal highway program, and federal tax policy supported suburban growth, whereas other programs, beginning with urban renewal, were designed to strengthen the core cities.

A second and equally basic lesson is that assumptions that shape goals and mold programs can adversely affect those programs if they are erroneous or unrealistic. The discussion above the Model Cities program shows an example of that. Another example is in the unrealistic assumption underlying urban renewal that public investment would stimulate private construction worth four to six times the public expenditure involved (Weaver 1965, 75).

A third lesson is the importance of including people with expertise and experience in the area in groups appointed to design programs and policies—witness the absence from the Model Cities task force of people with first-hand experience in federal program management (see footnote 3). A fourth lesson is the value of a strong commitment by HUD to the objectives set forth in program legislation—whether of its own initiative or in response to White House policy or pressure. A lack of such commitment was a critical factor in the Nixon and Ford years, when Congress and the President differed sharply on policy and programs. Often legislative provisions or administrative actions have militated against achievement of announced program goals, belying rhetoric in support of those goals. In his recent treatment of urban development and housing programs both inside and outside HUD, President Reagan has retreated even from rhetoric in support of program goals. Having undermined commitment within HUD, and detecting the lack of a strong coalition to press for urban development and housing programs in general, the current administration has considered such activities an easy target for drastic spending cuts. In contrast, the Johnson years demonstrated that the commitment of the President to program goals and to allocation of resources, along with leadership by HUD in developing programs and building a coalition of support, can produce good legislative results and program funding. Lack of commitment to the legislation guiding HUD programs has resulted in the start-stop environment in which HUD programs have been carried out. As suggested above, amid sudden switches in policy, those programs often have not been given a chance to benefit from experience. Instead, when programs such as Section 235, Section 236, or Model Cities have encountered problems, they have been discarded wholesale.

Achievements

HUD's actions have seldom, if ever, solved the problems they addressed. Their shortcomings often have resulted from limited financial resources (Schussheim

1974). But HUD has recorded several general achievements beyond the specific ones detailed in preceding sections.

First, the department developed a somewhat unusual structure, grouping programs so that related problems would be addressed in a coordinated way, conferring both line and staff functions on assistant secretaries, and creating strong regional administrator posts that had authority to make case-by-case decisions (Weaver 1968b, Tape 1, 42; Tape 2, 3).[13] It also redirected the mission of the Federal Housing Administration so that FHA became an integral part of HUD and functioned as an instrument for producing lower-income housing (McFarland 1978, 44–45, 226–27). Another achievement was that sections 235 and 236 were able to draw private industry into the task of providing lower-income housing (*Professional Builder* 1968, 28), thereby also drawing home builders into the coalition supporting the 1968 Housing and Urban Development Act while increasing the volume of lower-cost housing.

Other significant achievements by HUD include the great expansion of federal funding for research into urban and housing problems; use of scattered sites for assisted housing, which increased public acceptance of public housing; turnkey approaches to public housing, which sped up construction and neutralized the objections of home builders (McFarland 1978, 132, 228); the initiation of a modernization program for existing public housing; development of the concept of the potentially significant Housing Assistance Plan; use of neighborhood groups as instruments for inner-city rehabilitation, largely through Model Cities and UDAG; successful establishment of a fully funded experimental program of housing allowances and vouchers[14]; and development of Section 8 to use the existing housing supply more effectively.

Deficiencies

As suggested above, a list of HUD's deficiencies must include its failure to develop the capacity to consistently build effective coalitions in support of comprehensive urban development and housing legislation during the 1970s and 1980s. This failure weakened any role HUD could expect to play as the focal point for national urban policy. It resulted, however, mainly from various administrations' lack of commitment to HUD's legislated goals. Other deficiencies include the unnecessary limitations and problems of the massive 1967 Boston Urban Redevelopment Project (BURP), which resulted from faulty and inadequate planning[15]; HUD's inability to develop an urban land policy involving advance acquisition (Weaver 1968a, 9–10; 1980, 69–72)[16]; and the freeze, disintegration, and eventual abandonment of the New Communities program in the 1970s.

Some HUD deficiencies reflect apparent internal conflict between the desire to champion small target areas to achieve certain goals (such as more meaningful citizen participation) and the need to address problems on a larger geographical scale to deal with such topics as metropolitan areawide planning, mass transit, and dispersal of lower-income housing and open occupancy. Other allegedly incompatible approaches to be found within HUD itself include spatial dispersal of racial minorities versus upgrading of ghettos; and new construction versus use of existing units for housing subsidies. In each instance both approaches are needed, because in each of these areas, the conflicting goals are both desirable and hence must be pursued simultaneously. Related to the latter illusory dilemma is HUD officials' frequent failure to recognize that there must be a mix between demand- and supply-oriented housing assistance programs, depending on the availability of lower-cost shelter in the local housing market.[17] HUD also has been reluctant to acknowledge that horizontal equity in assisted housing requires an entitlement program, and it has been late in recognizing that preferential tax treatment for affluent homeowners is actually a housing subsidy—indeed, a very expensive entitlement.

Two Unresolved Issues

HUD inherited an active concern for planning from HHFA, which had promoted a program of direct assistance for developing plans at all levels of government and had made financial support available for training planners. Subsequently, categorical grants for certain purposes required that the grant-funded projects be consistent with an areawide plan. HUD continued those approaches and added legislation providing both for better coordination of federal programs and for supplementary grants if states and localities made comprehensive planning effective. Throughout those and associated efforts, it became apparent that for planning to become effective on a metropolitan or area scale, government had to provide a mechanism for carrying out the plan. For a time the concept of metropolitan government was attractive to governmental reformers, but it proved infeasible. HUD turned to another device, the requirement that certain applications for federal aid be reviewed and critiqued by a metropolitan area planning body. That helped, but it fell far short of assuring compliance with an areawide plan.

One of the problems is the complexity of the issue. But it has been rendered more intractable by the pervasive stop-and-go (and sometimes stop again) character of HUD programs in the past two decades. Relevant events are the 1973 moratorium on New Communities, their restoration and subsequent abandonment; another is the abrupt withdrawal of 701 planning assistance. Whatever the resolution may be, a consistent, straightforward, and uncomplicated approach is essential. Here, as was the case in Model Cities, I would advocate development of performance standards designed to target attention on problems that defy localized treatment. A possible instrument is modest incentive matching grants to states. They are the most likely instruments for providing a mechanism to implement metropolitan plans.

A second unresolved issue lies in the enduring conflict between providing more assisted housing in ghetto neighborhoods and promoting residential racial integration. The issue is closely related, or course, to the matter of site selection and is especially troublesome in public housing (Weaver 1965, 87–95). The situation is complicated further because a larger volume of assisted housing is a prerequisite for open occupancy, since without it there will be little if any affordable shelter available to blacks in much of suburbia. Yet, paradoxically, while blacks were achieving greater freedom of residential location, were moving more into the suburbs, and were improving the quality of their housing, residential racial segregation declined only slightly (Weaver 1984). We have not yet solved this dilemma, nor have we recognized the extent and tenacity of residential racial segregation.

THE FUTURE

It is difficult to be optimistic about the immediate future of federal housing and urban development activities or of HUD. The established philosophical and ideological commitments of the Reagan administration, its economic policies, the resulting effects of unprecedented and growing budget deficits, and the conservative mood of the nation[18] do not augur well for improved targeting of programs to the benefit of lower-income people or even for sustained (let alone increased) federal support for housing community development. The proposed 1986 federal budget is even more discouraging and foreboding.

In light of this immediately pessimistic outlook, those concerned about urban development and housing might well ponder and articulate the cost of continuing neglect. At the same time, it is prudent to examine the philosophical and economic assumptions of the Reagan administration (Weaver 1981, 86–90; 1985). The false propaganda that the Great Society was a failure is based on the assertion that it did not eradicate the ills it addressed. Conceding its frequently inflated promises and defects in the structure and operation of some of its innovations, we still need to challenge what has become conventional wisdom in evaluating the social programs of the 1960s. We must take a closer and more objective look at the complexity of the problems and the results achieved by those programs. For example, both public housing and housing assistance programs have had intricate missions, but each has provided only a single tool to solve multifaceted problems. Their ability to improve the availability and quality of shelter has been significantly affected by the state of the economy, federal budget deficits, and general borrowing costs. Equally important, public housing has had to deal with a small but extremely disruptive group of troubled individuals and households among its clientele. Yet for all the problems and criticism, public housing still inspires a long waiting list. Urban renewal, although unable to achieve its multiple, often conflicting goals and fulfill its unrealistic promises, has made a positive contribution to revitalizing downtown America and has left a legacy of technical expertise in land clearance, assembly, and redevelopment. Model Cities delivered enduring political power to the low-income neighborhoods it targeted. Many HUD programs have produced cadres of experts in housing development and rehabilitation. Those benefits will remain even when the federal programs that produced them are phased out or seriously cut back.

Programs that achieved less than promised often involved bold experiments, many of which, as in the case of Model Cities and BURP, provided lessons for the future. I agree with Keyes, who observed, "The success of such future efforts will be in many ways a function of the degree to which BURP is interpreted not as a success or failure in its own terms but rather as a major exploratory step in the complex and frustrating process of learning how to rehabilitate old neighborhoods"

(1970, 173). This evaluation lends credence to current suggestions that HUD should increase its efforts to encourage innovations at the local level and disseminate information about those innovations.

We may not be able soon to overcome the current inclination to neglect urban and shelter needs. But we can and should emphasize the unique role of cities in our society and the high priority American families accord adequate and attractive housing. That priority suggests the danger a democracy confronts when it fails to supply even the minimum standard of housing to a significant segment of the population. Nor can we afford to neglect further the existing urban infrastructure, the cultural facilities cities traditionally have provided, or the economic and social ills that beset cities. To do so would substantially degrade the quality of life for many Americans of varied economic and social levels. As is true of the effect of the Reagan administration's policies and programs, the least advantaged would suffer most.

AUTHOR'S NOTE

Three of my former colleagues at HHFA and/or HUD—Henry B. Schechter, Morton J. Schussheim, and Robert C. Wood—as well as a current associate, Martin E. Sloane, read an earlier draft of this paper and made significant comments. I appreciate deeply their assistance. A grant from the Ford Foundation covered expenses incident to the preparation of this paper.

NOTES

1 When President Nixon proposed broad executive reorganization plans to strengthen HUD's authority and coordination capability, Veterans Administration housing functions were not included; nor was the executive reorganization carried out. President Carter's similar proposal suffered the same fate.

2 Demonstration Cities became Model Cities when, during hearings before the Banking and Currency Subcommittee of the House of Representatives, a sympathetic southern congressman observed that there were enough demonstrations in cities without proposing a program so designated.

3 Extragovernmental task forces, as well as interdepartmental ones, can contribute significantly to the development of new programs. The early HUD experience suggests that the most productive pattern is one that provides full and continuing interchange between governmental and nongovernmental bodies. President Johnson used extragovernmental task forces to develop new approaches to housing and urban development by looking beyond the bureaucracy and officials inherited from the Kennedy administration. Whereas the HHFA had participated in the 1964 presidential task force, the more important 1965 Presidential Task Force on Urban Problems was instructed to avoid contacts with the agency. Thus, the task force that developed what became the Model Cities

program operated with little input from me, the official who would be charged with steering it through Congress and administering it. That was unfortunate; had I, as the subsequent lead administration witness, been part of the discussions that led to formulation of the proposal, I could have defended it more effectively when it came before Congress and could have implemented it more effectively. I had anticipated the problems of coordination that were to plague Model Cities and also had witnessed the reluctance of the White House and the Bureau of the Budget to intervene to coordinate water and sewer grants administered by several departments. If I could have shared with the group this experience and my concept of structural hindrances to coordination, it might have modified the task force's overoptimism about interdepartmental and interagency coordination.

The next significant presidential task force, however—the President's Committee on Urban Housing (1967–68)—maintained continuing communications with HUD. In the fall of 1967 an interdepartmental task force was established to develop proposals for the 1968 legislation, with the secretary of HUD as chairman and top HUD personnel acting as staff members. The task force shared its recommendations with the committee (Bohen 1967), which testified in favor of those recommendations. Both groups were committed to numerical housing production goals and ultimately agreed on figures, which were incorporated in the statute.

4 Although HUD's youth was an impediment to coordination in 1966, the more permanent barrier was the structure of the federal government itself. As long as programs affecting urban development and housing are dispersed in many departments and agencies of the federal government, the varying primary concerns of the departments and agencies involved (as well as of their supporting lobbies) remain an impediment to a tightly unified federal approach and dictate that only White House intervention can effect coordination. Model Cities demonstrated, however, that more than jurisdictional rivalries between departments and agencies are involved. The U.S. Department of Health, Education, and Welfare, for example, was the most cooperative with HUD, but many of its grants went to the states rather than directly to the cities, thereby limiting its ability to deliver program support. The Department of Labor cited similar impediments as rationale for lack of effective cooperation.

5 New communities were among the casualties of the 1973 moratorium. On the basis of assertions of mismanagement and abuses, they were frozen at a time when thirteen projects were in various stages of development (Boyd 1982, 107, footnote 7).

6 Several requirements are fundamental in evaluation of housing and urban development programs. First, evaluation of goals must be carefully delineated and differentiated from evaluation of results; otherwise the evaluator is prone to set his or her own program objectives and judge performance on the basis of them rather than the announced aims (Weaver 1972, 44–48). Another requirement is recognition of the complexity of evaluation in the sphere of housing and urban development. As Frieden and Kaplan wrote, "There is need for a thorough examination of the still-marginal nature of evaluation technology" (1975, 186). Peter Rossi wisely observed (1978, 591) that human services are "highly operational dependent." Thus, there is a constant possibility that the treatment may deviate from the program design, the mode of delivery may add some unintended treatment to the basic act, and a treatment may not be capable of delivery "in a reasonable way at all by the typical human services organizations."

7 For example, in its 1972 year-end report the Department of Justice said 180 indictments had been returned implicating 137 people charged with fraud in HUD inner-city programs. Of those, 119 defendants had been convicted. In May 1972 an assistant attorney

general had testified to Congress that more than 750 criminal cases involving federal housing fraud were pending (Schechter 1974, 46). This evidence that mode of delivery added some unintended treatment to the basic act was complemented by the administration's three-year failure to request funds for counseling services to the universe of new homeowners, even though the 1968 act authorized such action.

8 For an analysis of these Carter administration programs, see Clarke (1984).

9 The delayed issuance of these regulations fostered a suspicion that it reflected a half-hearted commitment. At the least it signaled a reluctance to act in what was a highly controversial area. As could be expected, the Reagan administration promptly rescinded the regulations, promising to issue revised ones. To date it has failed to do so.

The most impressive action of the Carter administration in the area of fair housing was that of the Department of Justice when, in 1978, it abandoned emphasis on bringing as many legal challenges as possible and concentrated on pursuing fair housing cases that would have broader impact (Sloane 1984, 139–140).

10 Besides increased cutbacks in volume of assisted housing and changes in the mix between existing and newly constructed units, the Reagan administration quickly changed the ground rules as well. For example, the rents upon which subsidies are based were lowered, the value assigned to food stamps as a component of income was increased, the proportion of income tenants are required to pay for rent was increased from 25 percent to 30 percent, and the proportion of lower-income families among those receiving housing assistance was increased. The first three of those changes clearly reduced the benefits of the program; the greatest adverse impact was upon poor households (Struyk, Tuccillo, and Zais 1982, 410–11). The change in income mix will significantly increase the already perplexing management problems in public housing (Wood 1982) and throughout assisted housing programs (Struyk, Tuccillo, and Zais 1982, 408).

11 For a succinct description and evaluation of urban enterprise zones, see Glickman (1984, 474).

12 A recent article in *JAPA* on the urban posture of the Reagan administration accurately stated that "it is crucial to understand that most of the important public-sector effects in cities result from actions of agencies that have little or no specifically urban focus" (Glickman 1984, 471).

13 For a detailed description and evaluation of the organization of HUD, see Redford and Blissett (1981, 30–45).

14 This, in contrast to Model Cities, was restricted to a few localities and thus met a basic requirement for an experiment (Weaver 1972, 48). There is, however, disagreement about the choice of cities for testing one of the four phases of the experiment (U.S. GAO 1978b, 1, 15–30, 74, 100–101, 121–22).

15 The Boston Urban Rehabilitation Project was located in a predominantly black area. Its unnecessary limitations stemmed from officials' lack of understanding of the ghetto and their disregard for the indigenous population. Despite my explicit direction that the FHA pay special attention to relocation, FHA depended on sponsors to handle the matter. In addition, the indigenous population and the larger black community were not involved in the planning or initial execution of the undertaking, and communication with these groups was woefully inadequate. These and related developments spelled confrontation with a large and vocal segment of black Boston. This generated adversary relationships that not only hindered the economics of the undertaking but encouraged vandalism to the project and, at times, threatened its physical survival. At the same time, however, FHA did a remarkable job in streamlining its existing rehabilitation process.

This was a notable achievement because it reversed years of bureaucratic buildup, and more so because it signified FHA commitment to housing for lower-income recipients.

Despite continuing adverse publicity, troubling increases in construction and operating costs (ultimately reflected in rents) and the need to divert HUD funds earmarked for other functions in order to train black construction workers, neither President Johnson nor the new department abandoned BURP or their commitments to housing rehabilitation in urban core areas. But although adjustments were made throughout 1968 to upgrade the relocation procedure, to increase participation by blacks as sponsors and construction workers, and to improve communications with the black community, BURP never recovered from its earlier mistakes (Keyes 1970).

16 There is far from universal agreement as to the potential effectiveness of such an urban land policy; see, for example, de Leeuw, Schnare, and Struyk (1976, 143).

17 A recent study that seems to exaggerate the efficacy of filtering, especially for the poor and discriminated-against, concedes that it is less effective in very tight housing markets (Turner and Struyk 1984, 67). That implies that in such markets there is need for new construction or substantially rehabilitated housing for the disadvantaged.

18 The Reagan administration has reduced taxes and expanded the defense budget. As a consequence there has been an increase in the deficit of such magnitude as to present serious long-term economic dangers. Recognition of this greatly restricts spending on domestic programs unless there are tax increases and cuts in defense budgets. The conservative mood of the nation, responding to the rhetoric of the present administration and its supporters, resists tax increases, supports defense spending, and lacks enthusiasm for support of domestic social programs.

REFERENCES

Bohen, Fred. 1967. Memorandum to Joseph Califano, October 24. Austin: Lyndon B. Johnson Library, University of Texas.

Boyd, Eugene. 1982. Urban growth, demographic projections, and legislative action: The Title VII example. In *Strategic Issues: Historical Experience, Institutional Structures, and Conceptual Framework*, report of the Committee on Energy and Commerce, U.S. House of Representatives (C. Print H243-17). Washington: U.S. Government Printing Office.

Clarke, Susan E. 1984. Neighborhood policy options: The Reagan agenda. *Journal of the American Planning Association* 50, 4 (Autumn): 493–501.

Danielson, Michael N. 1976. *The politics of exclusion.* New York: Columbia University Press.

de Leeuw, Frank, Anne B. Schnare, and Raymond J. Struyk. 1976. Housing. In *The Urban Predicament*, edited by William Gorham and Nathan Glazer. Washington: The Urban Institute.

Downs, Anthony. 1974. The successes and failures of federal housing policy. *The Public Interest* 34 (Winter): 124–145.

Frieden, Bernard J., and Marshall Kaplan. 1975. The politics of neglect: Urban aid from Model Cities to Revenue Sharing. Cambridge: MIT Press.

———. 1977. Community development and the Model Cities legacy. In *Toward New Human Rights: The Social Policies of the Kennedy and Johnson Administrations*, edited by David C. Warner. Austin: University of Texas.

Ginsburg, Robert L. 1977. Second year: Community Development Block Grant experience: A summary of NAHRO community monitoring project (January 1977). *Journal of Housing* 34 (February): 80–83.

Glickman, Norman J. 1984. Economic policy and the cities: In search of Reagan's real urban policy. *Journal of the American Planning Association* 50, 4 (Autumn): 470–78.

Harney, Kenneth R. 1977. Harris pressed in HUD-OMB budget dispute. *Washington Post* December 3: D-1.

Keyes, Langley C., Jr. 1970. *The Boston rehabilitation program: An independent analysis.* Cambridge: Joint Center for Urban Studies of MIT and Harvard University.

McFarland, M. Carter. 1978. *Federal government and urban problems: HUD: Successes, failures, and the fate of our cities.* Boulder, Colo.: Westview Press.

Orlebeke, Charles J. 1975. A framework for housing policy. In *Agenda for the New Urban Era*, edited by Harvey S. Perloff. Chicago: American Society of Planning Officials.

Professional Builder. 1968. Did Bob Weaver give builders a fair shake at HUD? And vice-versa? *Professional Builder* (October): 28.

Redford, Emmette S., and Marlan Blissett. 1981. Housing and urban development: A new commitment to urban problems. In *Organizing the Executive Branch: The Johnson Presidency.* Chicago: University of Chicago Press.

Rossi, Peter. 1978. Issues in the evaluation of human services delivery. *Evaluation Quarterly* 2: 273–299.

Schechter, Henry B. 1974. *Critique of Housing in the Seventies.* Prepared for Housing and Urban Affairs Subcommittee, Senate Committee on Banking, Housing, and Urban Affairs (Print S242-4). Washington: U.S. Government Printing Office.

Schussheim, Morton J. 1974. *The modest commitment to cities.* Lexington, Mass.: Lexington Books.

Semer, Milton P., and Julian Zimmerman. 1974. FHA mortgage insurance programs during the 1960s. Unpublished report prepared for the Office of the Assistant Secretary for Policy and Research, U.S. Department of Housing and Urban Development. Washington, D.C. October.

Sloane, Martin E. 1984. Overview of federal housing policy: Past and present. In *A Sheltered Crisis: The State of Fair Housing in the Eighties.* Presentations at a consultation sponsored by the U.S. Commission on Civil Rights, Washington, D.C., 26–27 September 1983. Washington: U.S. Government Printing Office.

Struyk, Raymond J., John A. Tuccillo, and James P. Zais. 1982. Housing and community development. In *The Reagan Experiment*, edited by John L. Palmer and Isabel V. Sawhill. Washington: The Urban Institute Press.

Turner, Margery Austin, and Raymond J. Struyk. 1984. *Urban housing in the 1980s: Markets and policies.* Washington: The Urban Institute Press.

U.S. Congress. Joint Economic Committee. 1973. *Housing subsidies and housing policy.* Report of the Subcommittee on Priorities and Economy in Government. March 5. Washington: U.S. Government Printing Office.

U.S. Department of Housing and Urban Development. 1972. *Fourth annual report on national housing goals* (H. Doc. 92-319). Washington: U.S. Government and Printing Office.

———. 1974. *Housing in the seventies.* Washington: U.S. Government Printing Office.

————. 1979. *Measuring discrimination in American housing markets: The housing market practices survey*, USGPO HH1:2:D6319. Washington: U.S. Government Printing Office.

————. 1984. *Rehabilitating rental housing: The benefits and costs of alternative approaches*. Washington: U.S. Department of Housing and Urban Development.

————. 1985. *FY 1986 budget: Summary*. February. Washington: U.S. Department of Housing and Urban Development (photocopied).

U.S. General Accounting Office. 1976. *Meeting application and review requirements for block grants under Title I of the Housing and Community Development Act of 1974*. Washington: U.S. General Accounting Office.

————. 1978a. *Section 236 rental housing—An evaluation with lessons for the future*. Washington: U.S. General Accounting Office.

————. 1978b. *An assessment of the Department of Housing and Urban Development's Experimental Housing Allowance programs*. Washington: U.S. General Accounting Office.

U.S. House. 1974. *Housing and Community Development Act of 1974*. Conference report (H.Rpt. 93-1279). Washington: U.S. Government Printing Office.

————. Committee on Banking, Finance, and Urban Affairs. 1977. *Community Development Block Grant program*. Report of Subcommittee on Housing and Community Development. Washington: U.S. Government Printing Office.

Weaver, Robert C. 1964. Memorandum to Bill Moyers, December 3. Legislative Proposals, 1965 folder, book 4, box 100, files of Bill Moyers. Austin: Lyndon B. Johnson Library, University of Texas.

————. 1965. *Dilemmas of urban America*. Cambridge: Harvard University Press.

————. 1968a. *Looking back—and ahead* (SPP/MP-73). Washington: U.S. Government Printing Office.

————. 1968b. Transcript of oral history interview. November. Austin: Lyndon B. Johnson Library, University of Texas.

————. 1972. Management of urban programs. In *Improving Management for More Effective Government*, 50th Anniversary Lectures of the U.S. General Accounting Office. Washington: U.S. Government Printing Office.

————. 1980. Coordinating rural and land policy. In *The Farm and the City: Rivals or Allies?* edited by A. M. Woodruff. Englewood Cliffs, N.J.: Prentice Hall.

————. 1981. Black Americans and neoconservatism. In *The Social Welfare Forum, 1980*. New York: Columbia University Press.

————. 1984. Housing discrimination: An overview. In *A Sheltered Crisis: The State of Fair Housing in the Eighties*. Presentations at a consultation sponsored by the U.S. Commission on Civil Rights, Washington, D.C., 26–27 September 1983. Washington: U.S. Government Printing Office.

————. 1985. Fair housing: The federal retreat. *Journal of Housing* 42, 3 (May/June): 85–87.

Wood, Elizabeth. 1982. *The beautiful beginnings, the failure to learn: Fifty years of public housing in America*. Washington: National Center for Housing Management.

Comment: HUD—A Study in Power and Piety

George Sternlieb
Center for Urban Policy Research, Rutgers University

In "Comment: HUD—A Study in Power and Piety," George Sternlieb attempts to answer the question: "What has caused HUD, despite its enormously important province, to be relegated to the backwaters of the power hierarchy?" (p. 422) He offers a three-part explanation: race, leadership, and the failure of HUD to define its mission as central to *all* of housing.

The formation of HUD was painful, its infant years disrupted by the siren call of the urban riots and Great Society promises. The department is now twenty years old—and has yet to find a solid place in the Washington firmament. To secure the latter requires power as well as piety.

The rise and fall of HUD deserves much more study than it has received. It is important both as a study of *real politik* and as a microcosm of an era. But for perspective we must step back in time.

Ten years before HUD was launched, William C. Wheaton was writing his belated doctoral thesis about the potential of a federal department of *urban affairs* ("The Evolution of Federal Housing Programs," University of Chicago, 1954). The postwar euphoria about cities had abated; it would be reignited (literally) only by the urban fires of the 1960s. Clearly, new impetus was required if the federal government's role in urban affairs was to be formalized at the Cabinet level.

Wheaton, one of the most prescient thinkers of our time, was deeply aroused by the plight of cities. He believed, however, that the urban dilemma by itself was not a strong enough issue to provide the basis for a new department that could compete effectively among the power baronies of Washington. It would have to be linked to another issue that was politically attractive enough to generate a broad and powerful constituency. Public works was Wheaton's first choice as a partner issue, but it was spread among a variety of departments and was too crucial and too basic to their patronage (and their clout) to be considered. Instead he proposed housing, an area that would provide the leverage, the trading counters, with which to secure legislation for the urban domain.

Housing had undisputed priority in America's political calculus: its patrons and clients were powerhouses of Capitol Hill. The thrift institutions were thriving; the homebuilders were national heroes, although the shadow of the scandals attached to earlier shelter programs lurked just behind the fence. The mortgage bankers certainly were not unenthusiastic, even though that industry was a mere seed of its later maturity. Tract suburbia was in full flower, and Congress could not do enough for the returning war heroes—the World War II tide had been augmented by veterans of Korea, and the Vietnam anomie would not develop for another generation. Housing would be the blocking back, Wheaton thought, and urban redevelopment would follow in its powerhouse wake.

But even then Wheaton had some misgivings. Pleased as he was with this potential coupling, he still closed his thesis with the admonition that if the urgency of Americans' need for shelter ever abated perceptibly, there might well be substantial friction about the federal role in providing housing—and with it, a decline in the potency of housing as the draft horse for the reformulation of the aging city.

If anything, he was overly optimistic! The new department had a stormy birth. President Johnson hopelessly contaminated its launching by making it evident that Robert C. Weaver was not his choice for HUD secretary but rather was being forced upon him. The housing lobbies were accustomed to doing business with the monied ends of the regrouping that became HUD, particularly the Federal Housing Administration, and succeeded—at least initially—in keeping those functions somewhat segregated from the balance of the department. The Farmers Home Administration was carefully kept out of the department, further weakening HUD's patronage capacity.

The frail entity called HUD was barely afloat before the urban riots unfolded. There was not time to develop an institutional/patronage power base. As the department's urban mission was broadened in response to crisis, its link to housing in general (as against social housing) atrophied. The half-life of fear and indignation generated by burning cities—and the consequent interest in the trauma of the central city—lasted only a couple of years. Its most substantial bureaucratic monument was a thin residue of legislation, such as the Model Cities program, that soon shriveled on the urban vine.

When President Nixon imposed the moratorium on subsidized housing in 1973, the mourners were few. Conspicuous by their absence were the really heavy political hitters—the thrift institutions and the mortgage bankers.

By that time, nearly two-thirds of all Americans owned their homes. They had become much more concerned with preserving and elevating their financial worth than with the problems of the less fortunate. America was changing from a shelter society into a post-shelter society; capital gains had become far more important to most Americans than sound roofs and good plumbing alone. "Housing," that enormously potent seven-letter word that had had a premier place in the politician's lexicon just a few years before, suddenly became far more limited: it meant social housing for the poor, it meant "those people living next to me," it meant the potential for high tax rates and fear of change. Americans would continue to plow ever-increasing proportions of their income into houses—but that concept was a long way from "housing."

The main thrust of federal involvement in housing in general had been moved out of HUD's domain. The Federal Housing Administration's share of the market had shrunk drastically, the former professionalism of its staff drastically watered down by high-ranking, inexperienced newcomers fleeing from jobs in the shrinking Model Cities program.

The HUD of Secretary George W. Romney, who had performed forcefully to enlarge the department despite a conservative governmental frame, was disemboweled by the new urban reality: the department's image had been transformed from the savior of cities into the principal slumlord of Detroit, from a rejuvenator of housing into a hapless financier of phony housing rehabilitation projects. And that image change came on the edge of the "stagflation" that was to dominate the 1970s, when real family incomes in America were to shrink drastically for the first time since the Depression. HUD represented charity; HUD represented waste; HUD was not central to the thinking of middle America.

Under President Carter HUD was the vehicle—the container—for social activism. It shared that role with the Department of Health, Education, and Welfare, but the latter had far more potent weapons in its armory. HUD, by comparison, was relatively patronless. It had become, and still is, an easy target.

One easily could view the peregrinations of the department as comical; but that would be a very sad mistake. There are functions of great importance within HUD's potential domain, including all the elements of the built environment. In order to secure fulfillment of them, however, we need to take a harder look at what went wrong in the past, and we need to conceive a thorough restructuring with which HUD can face the future.

In the search for a new structure for HUD, however, we must distinguish carefully between what was and was not important in HUD's identity crisis, based on its mixed history. The Department of Agriculture, after all—with a far smaller constituency—has enjoyed an incredible level of success over the years (though its aura now may be wearing thin). All the waste at HUD is trivial compared to any major weapons system; yet the Department of Defense seems to have a built-in dynamic of its own. Scandal leads to slaps on the wrist and nominal fines, not to the obliteration of programs. And one could go on in this vein.

The issue is this: What has caused HUD, despite its enormously important province, to be relegated to the backwaters of the power hierarchy? None of the several answers to that somewhat rhetorical question is appetizing, but I think they must be faced.

First and foremost is the issue of race. While President Johnson's hesitation in accepting the political necessity of appointing Weaver as HUD secretary may have had a number of antecedents—and, in the light of my own knowledge of Robert Weaver, all of them wrong!—it dramatized HUD, just as it was being launched, as a department that had, in the view of white America, a skew toward minority groups.

Second, with the exception of Romney the leadership of the department has never been in the hands of someone who came from Capitol Hill—or, alternatively, directly from a position of high confidence with the Chief Executive. That may be of relatively small importance in departments whose functions are well defined and whose role has powerful flywheels built into it. It is of overwhelming importance, however, when a department's domain must be marked out.

Third, and most important from a power-base point of view, is the necessity for the department to become more central to *all* of housing, to have lines of patronage, that feed into the nation's jugular, rather than the attenuated sectors of specialized low-income groups. America's flirtation with painful social justice came to an end a decade ago.

The lines of force laid out by William Wheaton some thirty years ago still must be reckoned with. Americans are too spasmodic in their guilt and the levels of financial contribution they will make to assuage it too erratic to be depended on. And the city is fading from the central focus. If HUD is to help the poor, it must have a far broader constituency. HUD's program spectrum also must be broadened if it is to be central to urban development. Putting together a meaningful, powerful constituency will require a change of course that undoubtedly will outrage many of HUD's traditional clients—and, indeed, those who have suffered along with HUD through the years. But in the Washington of today—and, I would suggest, of tomorrow as well—the department must do well in order to do good!

EIGHT. HOUSING, SOCIAL AND COMMUNITY PLANNING— SUGGESTED READINGS

Bratt, Rachel, ed. 1986. *Critical Perspectives on Housing*. Philadelphia: Temple University Press.

Checkoway, Barry. 1986. *Strategic Perspectives on Planning Practice*. Lexington, MA: Heath.

Feiss, Carl. 1985. "The Foundations of Federal Planning Assistance: A Personal Account of the 701 Program." *Journal of the American Planning Association* 51, 2:175–84.

Franck, Karen, and Sherry Ahrentzen. 1989. *New Households, New Housing*. New York: Van Nostrand Reinhold.

Gans, Herbert J. 1982. *The Urban Villages: Group and Class in the Life of Italian Americans*. New York: Free Press.

Hayden, Dolores. 1984. *Redesigning the American Dream: The Future of Housing, Work, and Family Life*. New York: Norton.

Lake, Robert. 1981. *The New Suburbanites: Race and Housing in the Suburbs*. New Brunswick, NJ: Center for Urban Policy Research, Rutgers University.

Jencks, Christopher, and Paul E. Peterson. 1992. *The Urban Underclass*. Washington, DC: The Brookings Institution.

Mair, Andrew. 1986. "The Homeless and the Post-Industrial Society." *Political Geography* 5, 4:351–368.

Marris, Peter, and Martin Rein. 1967, 1973. *Dilemmas of Social Reform: Poverty and Community Action in the United States*. Chicago: Aldine.

Orfield, Gary, and Carole Ashkinaze. 1991. *The Closing Door: Conservative Policy and Black Opportunity*. Chicago: The University of Chicago Press.

Rohe, W., and L. Gates. 1985. *Planning with Neighborhoods*. Chapel Hill: The University of North Carolina Press.

Rohe, W., and Scott Mouw. "The Politics of Relocation: The Moving of the Crest Street Community." *Journal of the American Planning Association* 57, 1.

Schorr, Lisbeth B. 1988, 1989. *Within Our Reach*. New York: Anchor Books, Doubleday & Company, Inc.

Spain, Daphne. 1992. *Gendered Spaces*. Chapel Hill: The University of North Carolina Press.

9

POLITICS OF PLANNING

Looking Back

Allen B. Jacobs
Professor of City and Regional Planning, University of California

In *Making City Planning Work*, Allen B. Jacobs combines a personal account of his eight-year experience as planning director of San Francisco with six case studies of typical issues faced by a city planning department. In "Looking Back," he reflects on the experiences—rewards, frustrations, battles, and professional skills—of a planner. He notes that "you never win all the contests and it is unpleasant to lose for whatever reason. But when you win because of your professional skills alone or even in combination with your political abilities, the victory is sweeter" (p. 433). The chapter offers important insights into the politics of planning.

Comprehensive, citywide, long-range physical planning is important and can work. The idea of a comprehensive plan that contains policies, principles, and visions of what a community wants to be in relation to its physical development, to serve as the basis for both immediate and long-range actions and for legislation geared to its achievement—the idea of such a plan as a foundation of city planning is valid, and it is borne out by much of the work that was done in San Francisco.

Measured against a demanding model of what a comprehensive plan should be, as best set forth in Jack Kent's *Urban General Plan*, our San Francisco efforts may be found wanting in some respects.[1] But failure to reach an ideal in its entirety does not make it less than worthy. It would be hard to say that the master plan documents adopted between 1971 and 1974 constituted what Kent describes as a "unified general physical design for the community." There was no single, overall, published, comprehensive framework or idea about the city to which all of the separate plan elements related. If pressed, I could verbalize such a plan. It would call for respect for and maintenance and improvement of the existing physical character of the city. It would respond to important social and economic issues within that framework. It would not be a plan that called for major, citywide physical change. But we never published such a document. We simply never got to it, although we had the matter on our agenda.

On the other hand, the master plan elements for residence, transportation, urban design, and recreation and open space go a long way toward meeting that part of Kent's definition. Moreover, the elements are consistent with each other or were made so as each new element was adopted. Further, the plans were based in large measure on an assessment of the social needs of the residents, particularly those for whom public support seemed most in order.

Long-range, citywide plans of the kind that have been discussed here can, of course, be responsive to social and economic issues. Maintaining existing residential areas and adapting them to contemporary living standards instead of tearing them down, addressing housing needs of low- and moderate-income people, providing recreation and open space facilities in high-need areas, emphasizing the use of mass transit, keeping automobiles out of neighborhoods, protecting and enhancing views and the physical scale and character of the city—these are a few of the kinds of people-felt issues that the master plan elements responded to. They were real. In addressing them I do not recall making major compromises with long-range objectives or visions.

Each of the master plan elements was accompanied by a set of recommendations for programs and actions to carry it out. The programs were successful in varying degrees. We have seen that the programs that were most directly under the control of the planning department, especially those that could be achieved through legislative action, had a higher success rate than those that required actions on the part of others. It was not always possible to get the mayor, the Board of Supervisors, or other departments to endorse our policies or to pursue the programs intended to carry them out. And the capital improvement program was never the priority-setting and coordinating tool that it might have been. It suffered from a dearth of funds, and I was never able to get the commission to assert itself strongly in the process. I could not effectively orchestrate the capital budgeting process with all the actors involved around city hall.

Nevertheless, the plans and programs were there. Their purposes were clear when they were followed, and their mere existence in print provided information and a starting point for those citizens who were concerned about the future of their city.

As time passed and with a growing and more solidly based set of plans to rely upon, individual short-range proposals—both public and private—could be viewed in the light of long-range considerations. As a result, we had fewer Transamericas and U.S. Steels. We could review the location of a subsidized housing development in the context of the housing plan element. We could measure a neighborhood rezoning proposal against the housing and urban design elements. When a piece of public land was to be sold or leased, we could check it against a policy of the plan, as we could the vacation or widening of a street. We could relate a small renewal project in Chinatown to both the citywide and neighborhood plans that we had prepared, and we could advocate such a project. City planning was especially pleasing when the projects and programs were clearly the outcome of our plans. We were exhilarated when all our research, meetings, presentations, reconsiderations, confrontations, and responses to demands led to concrete actions, or even when all we knew was that the ideas had a fighting chance of becoming reality.

We were not always effective, nor did we win all our battles. Often, our mouths were too big for our stomachs in that we simply proposed much more than we, or anyone else, could implement. And the dictates of our plans were not adhered to in every case where we had discretion. I was furious when the planning commission or the Board of Supervisors overruled my staff on an issue—a major development proposal for instance—about which I felt the plans were clear. We could at least do battle. As the plans became clearer, it became harder for the commissioners to overrule the planners, especially if the commission had voted for the plans. Increasingly, too, people became aware of what was in the plans, and they used them to advocate or oppose projects. And they demanded changes in the plan as well.

In some cases, the mere existence of a plan or a proposal for a plan stimulated debate over issues that would ultimately have to be decided; for example, the location of public facilities such as police stations, the distribution of low-income housing, and the height of buildings in outlying neighborhoods. That, too, is comprehensive planning at work.

In *Land and the Environment: Planning in California Today*, Paul Sedway and Thomas Cooke list six functions of local planning.[2] The first is "long-range goal and policy making," which I assume includes the kind of citywide physical planning I have been addressing. Another possible function is "middle range programming and assessment of alternatives," which I think relates to planning and assessing more detailed programs involving immediate community issues, physical and otherwise (perhaps our neighborhood plans and our involvement with the FACE and RAP programs fall into this category). Sedway and Cooke also refer to the function of coordinating the programs of other agencies; the function of compiling and conveying information; incremental decision making on particular issues as they arise; and a line function that includes such things as zoning administration, subdivision approval, design review, and master plan referral. If we add the design and implementation of large-scale urban development projects, we have a reasonably inclusive list of the kinds of activities that might normally engage city planners. All of these activities are important, but all but one—conveying information—are found wanting without some framework within which to function and make recommendations. That framework is the general or master plan. Without it city planners have a much harder time explaining why their ideas and their proposals are preferable to anyone else's. There were times when I might have argued otherwise, most notably in the early San Francisco months when I was impatient to get on with the action, to respond to the burning issues. But then, that has so often been our way, and we continue to have the same burning issues. Taking the time to decide what we want our communities to be and then acting to achieve those goals seemed more and more worthwhile in San Francisco as time passed. It was a route that proved more practical as well.

The emphasis of city planning upon the physical nature of the city is perfectly reasonable, although no one would deny for a moment that the man-made physical environment should be responsive to people and to social and economic issues and aspirations. Of course, economic well-being and social relationships and services are at least as important as the physical settings within which they get acted out. It is more than reasonable, too, that those concerned with planning the physical environment should have their marching orders determined by social and economic policies that they may not have planned. But this does not make a fundamental orientation to planning the physical environment unimportant or less than socially relevant if it is not so comprehensive as to include within its realm planning for all related matters.

Planning for the physical environment can be responsive to social issues without taking direct, formal responsibility for social planning. It seems to me that when city planners have not planned as well as they might—especially when they have not considered social imperatives and economic realities adequately (to their own everlasting criticism and guilt)—they have too often responded to their failings by extending the scope of their planning.[3] It would have been better to have been more systematic and rigorous in the first place, including as many relevant factors as possible but still focusing on planning for the urban physical environment—in short, to do better what city planning started out to do.

Ever since I was awarded a degree in city planning from a school that stressed, I thought, the worthiness of comprehensive, long-range physical planning for urban areas, I have heard that whole notion criticized. Repeatedly, I have heard the quality, content, usefulness, and effectiveness of the comprehensive plan challenged, as often as not by those who teach city planning. The critics say that the comprehensive plan is too vague, too subjective, too biased, too specific. It is elitist and divorced from the people, they add, full of end-state visions that are unrelated to the real issues of a dynamic world. Besides, it is impossible to achieve, "pie in the sky."

There are certainly elements of truth in these assertions. But, in general, they coincide neither with my sense of reality nor with the centrality of the idea. Comprehensive plans have always been policy documents, even if they have not been read that way. They have become less and less end-state, static pictures of the future. They regularly deal with pressing current issues: housing, transportation, jobs, public services, open space, urban design. Often they are prepared concurrently with programs that are geared to their achievement, and some of these are quite innovative. Far from being divorced from the people, comprehensive plans dealing with land use are required and demanded by citizens and elected officials alike. There is no reason that plans cannot be responsive to felt issues in any case. Any planning efforts are remarkable in a society that could never be accused of having a bias toward city planning in the first place, a society that has tended to look at land and urban environments as little more than high-priced consumable commodities. And isn't it grand that plans are visionary! Why shouldn't a community have a view, a vision of what it wants to be, and then try to achieve it?

For many years now, since Robert Walker wrote *The Planning Function in Urban Government* in 1941, a growing body of practical wisdom has been calling for city planning to be located in the office of the chief executive: the mayor or the city manager.[4] The federal establishment, increasingly involved in the nuts and bolts of local government, including its city planning, prefers to have city planning located centrally. But I would be very cautious about giving up the semi-autonomous planning commissions. If the objective of city planning is to be able to prepare plans and then to have them carried out, then it is not at all clear to me that such an objective can be most easily achieved by working from within the office of a mayor of a large city.

Most big city mayors are not oriented to planning, especially to long-range city planning. Furthermore, the business and labor interests that are most influential in electing and supporting big city mayors will not necessarily share the concerns of the planners, particularly when the latter are not hell-bent for maximizing development. Big city mayors and the interests that elect them are more often attuned to quantity of urban development than to quality or to moderation. In the best of circumstances, it is difficult for a mayor to be concerned with the "long run," especially when he holds office for four years and is besieged with problems that require immediate answers. There may, of course, be nothing wrong with that state of affairs. City planners should be expected to work with chief executives, as well as with legislators and others, on all kinds of physical development issues. But that need not be done from within the office of the executive. It might even be more difficult from within than from outside. It is possible to advocate a city planning position to the mayor from within that office, but that may be the end of the line if the mayor disagrees. Besides, what is there to lead to a conclusion that city planners will be given critical positions or listened to any more if they are in chief executives' offices than if they are not? Independence is required if city planning recommendations are to be made public as a matter of course.

Considering the always-present demands of the moment that occupied the mayor's office in San Francisco, I cannot imagine that we could have devoted adequate time to long-range plan making had we been a part of that office, certainly not to the extent we did. There would always have been more urgent things to do. Nor can I imagine that the plan elements addressed to housing, urban design, and recreation and open space would have come out the way they did. Long-range plans would have been milder, less far-reaching, more oriented to executive discretion. It would also have been more difficult to advocate their implementation as strongly as we did.

City planning under a commission need not be out of the mainstream of decision making if the commission and the staff choose not to be. There is little to stop them from being involved and responsive to the needs of the city. City planners under a commission can have considerable freedom to innovate and to work for their own plans and those causes they conclude to be consistent with their city planning charge. They can explore ways of implementing plans on their own, yet within the framework of the government that establishes the planning department in the first place. In the beginning, I looked at the commission as a somewhat unnecessary appendage to the city planning staff, as a barrier that prevented us from working directly with the mayor and the Board of Supervisors, with other departments, and with the people themselves. In time, I changed my mind, even when we disagreed most violently and when the commission failed to support the staff on what I felt were critical matters. Commissioners know things about a community that a staff will never know. Their views are not necessarily elitist, even when they come from the ranks of wealth and power. A commissioner can provide a buffer from the demands of the moment. Perhaps most important, as I have noted elsewhere, city planners under a commission have the freedom to respond to and build a citywide planning constituency as well as separate, issue-oriented coalitions. That can be pretty heady business. Ultimately, it means that the planners' proposals can come before elected officials with considerable force and that they can achieve strong backing, assuming of course that what the planners produce is worthy.

Mayor Alioto was not particularly oriented to city planning. Still, a lot of city planning was accomplished while he was in office. At least I would like to think so. Sometimes, the city planning position held sway, even over the mayor's opposition. As it was, he could have rendered city planning less effective had he wished to. If city planning did well under Mayor Alioto, it can be argued that its achievements were his. Fine. The mayor was benevolent in this regard and tolerated many points of view he did not necessarily share. As a person, I think he should be honored for that. My point, however, is that the opportunity to push strong, controversial points of view is greater—the chance for planning to be effective is greater—if city planning is located out of the mayor's office rather than in it.

Alan Altshuler, speaking of the place of the city planning function in government, said that he had "no doubt that any city can find a timid planning director if it wants, one who will be awed by the barrier that veto-group politics poses to the initiation of new ideas. The difficult problem is to give a bold planning director room in which to maneuver, to encourage him to take the risks of initiating. No administrative set-up can make the role of the initiator easy; all that can be done is to make the risks more bearable to bold men."[5] The words "city planners" might have been substituted for "planning director." I believe the risks are more easily and better taken outside of the mayor's office than in and that the planning commission is as good a place as any other.

Risk taking and effectiveness aside, there is a more compelling reason to have city planning located outside of a chief executive's offices. It has to do with the whole nature of centrality in government. People ought to have more than one place to go in government to get what they want, to have their grievances redressed, to complain, and to propose ideas. If a mayor won't listen, or won't start or stop something, then perhaps the city council will. Or the courts. The same should hold true at the departmental level. If the department of public works refuses to consider methods to restrict traffic in a residential area, then other arms of government, elected and appointed, ought to be available to people. In San Francisco, the planning department and its commission served that function. It acted as a sounding board, an advocate, an initiator within government, another place for people to go, including a place to complain about bad planning. By the same token, the city planners could be stopped from getting their way. They might be compelled by others to do things they might not wish to do. But that is a reality they should be willing to live with, while at the same time trying to gain more responsibility and to bring about changes in legislation and in the administrative processes of government that will make planning more effective.

If the San Francisco planning department had been in the mayor's office, people would have had one less avenue through which to pursue their concerns. We would have been forever associated with the chief executive. The people at the federal level who were associated with urban affairs never seemed to understand the beauty and health of decentralized government as they used their considerable leverage to encourage communities to copy their favorite model. It is true that government, and perhaps city planning and development, might have been more efficient if it had been centralized, but I do not believe that the main objective of government is to be efficient. Rather it is to respond to the democratically determined needs of its citizens. Responsiveness is more important than efficiency, and I believe that responsiveness is more easily achieved if the planning department is not part of another office. Moreover, the San Francisco experience shows that city planning and plan implementation can indeed take place without centralized leadership and control.

Throughout this volume, I have stressed the importance of having a highly qualified, trained, and dedicated professional staff with expertise in a number of areas of city planning. That notion bears repeating.

My initial, generally unkind, assessment of the quality of the staff I found was probably overdone. It is all too easy for a new boy in town to forget that people and institutions were there before his arrival (they may not even have been awaiting his arrival) and that they had made important contributions to planning and to urban problem solving. Nonetheless, it was necessary to improve that staff. And it was possible to do so. Despite a perfectly terrible civil service system, we could attract bright, energetic, and skilled professionals, mostly young people. They came—as people like that usually do—because there was a challenge, a feeling that there would be a no-nonsense attack on problems. They saw that they would have a chance to direct their skills and enthusiasm to matters that they considered important. Existing staff, too, can and will respond to new challenges.

It is critical, however, to have some professional skills and knowledge. In the early San Francisco years, there were too many people, fresh from some of the best graduate schools, who responded to questions about their abilities by speaking of their understanding of the problems of the poor and of the minorities, of their desire to "work with the people." That was not enough. Those qualities should be everyone's.

As our abilities increased, our successes increased. Our most notable successes—with the master plan elements and the legislation prepared to help carry them out; with the various public programs that were prepared, particularly in housing and open space; and with the day-to-day zoning issues—grew from a systematic approach to the work at hand. We did best when we had staff members with the professional skills we needed. To some extent the specific skills of the staff determined the substantive areas we pursued. But even when the expertise was not at hand—in the areas of seismic safety and noise, for instance—we could still do well, with the aid of consultants. However, we could only work well with consultants if we had people on the staff who could relate the subject in question to land-use planning. We did not do as well as I would have liked in dealing with some ad hoc development proposals, with planning for the northern waterfront, and with planning for industry, because we did not have people with sophisticated knowledge about the economic analysis and fiscal management aspects of city planning. And we were never very good at traffic engineering.

I have always felt somewhat lacking as a professional for not having learned better the "nuts and bolts" of my art and craft. I wished I knew more about analytic techniques, land and market economics, utilities engineering, housing analysis, fiscal management—that I had worked enough with those areas so that they were more a part of me. A city planning director does not get to do very much city planning personally and directly, although that is where the fun is. Still, he ought to know in detail, in regard to a number of substantive areas, what is required. He ought to be able to show the way.

These misgivings notwithstanding, we did well in any area involving land-use law and in city planning matters that were related to housing, urban design, recreation and open space, neighborhood planning, information collection and analysis, and graphic communication. In time, our professional expertise was noticed and respected, even if our advice was not always followed. I have no way of knowing for certain, but I suspect that Mayor Alioto's continued tolerance of a city planning staff that often disagreed with him came out of his recognition of its professional quality.

I learned many times how important the dissemination of understandable, untampered with, factual information can be. I am sure, for example, that a major reason for our continuing role in housing was the information that we continually collected and published on that subject. During this same period, the Redevelopment Agency was putting out materials that people often found suspect. People tend to assign more responsibilities to an agency that gives them reliable information.

So many of the issues that city planners are involved in are like battles. Sometimes we won because of our professional skills, and sometimes we won because of our political acumen. We might not have been in favor of street widenings or turning a two-way street into a one-way street, but in a given situation we ought to have had the analytical skills to determine whether or not such proposals were necessary to move traffic or desirable in terms of their impacts on the lives of people and on activities that bordered the street. Traffic engineering is not so difficult, and analysts like Donald Appleyard have shown how to assess people's responses to traffic.[6] With or without those professional skills, we might also call upon friendly residents to help support our positions.

You never win all the contests and it is unpleasant to lose for whatever reason. But when you win because of your professional skills alone or even in combination with your political abilities, the victory is sweeter. When the *only* thing that stops the street from getting widened is your ability to "call out the troops," that is, your political skills, that is not a very good victory. It is a little bit shameful. The planning commission, the mayor, or the city council could as well hire anyone else; they don't need a city planner.

Certainly I was involved in the politics of city planning. Every city planner is. Overall, however, the best "politics" is top professional work, forcefully presented and defended.

It will come as no surprise that I believe city planners ought to have points of view and that they should be prepared to go to bat for them. They ought to have something to say about the quality of the urban environments they are involved in shaping. Being top-notch technicians is important, but it is not enough.

City planners should not be neutral, and I do not believe their clients, at the level of local government, expect them to be without values or opinions. After they have arrived at some position, some point of view, some desired direction, one would hope to see it reflected in both public plans and day-to-day recommendations. Why hide it? Further, city planners should be willing to stand up for their points of view if they want to be effective. They should be prepared to "mix it up." They must do more than recommend. Within a democratic process they should advocate and search for ways to carry out their plans. I believe, too, that they should value and nurture their utopian predilections. They are nothing to be ashamed of. I do not believe we have done these things enough. We have tended to be meek.

I am not suggesting for one minute that city planners do battle with every person with whom they disagree or with every interest that is different than theirs. Nor am I suggesting that *every* matter that comes up has a right and wrong side for the planners. Some matters have reasonable alternatives, not just one answer. Some will come out all right no matter what point of view prevails. In any event, the planners must do an honest job of evaluating various courses of action, and they must make their evaluations public. However, I am suggesting that there are many matters that do have right and wrong sides for planners and that when this is the case they should be prepared for conflicts, even with those interests they might wish most to serve. My experience with city planning in San Francisco indicates that everyone—elected and appointed officials, interest groups, and residents—appreciates, respects, and responds positively to strong advocacy, even if there is not always agreement with what is being proposed. I doubt that people in other places are that much different from San Franciscans in this respect.

The client, that is whoever literally or figuratively signs the city planner's paycheck, should have the right to fire the planner. The city planner would do well to have his or her bags packed. The worst losses are in battles that were never fought. We have points of view related to the way cities should be built and about the ways they should function. We might as well state them.

Planning cities can be a frustrating business. I do not think that Americans like cities very much. Planning them may be alien to our predispositions and to our habits. In the past, we could always move away from what we didn't like. Since we were a land of plenty, we did not have to plan. We have been more concerned with quantity than with quality. My observation is that when "how much" is in conflict with "what kind," the quantity bag men usually win. We see a continuous rush to bigness, but it may be a losing bargain. Private property rights and a growth-for-its-own-sake mentality have, for so many major American cities, produced a development cycle that results in ever-increasing intensities of land use—from rural to urban, urban to more urban—until we leave these cities or tear down large sections and start over.

Our patience for solving urban problems is short, and we get new problems before we have a chance to solve the old ones. Nothing, it seems, will stand still long enough for us to get a handle on it or to find a lasting solution. Victory today, over the wrong thing in the wrong place, does not ensure that the same battle will not have to be fought tomorrow or the next day.

Many of the problems that cities and their planners are asked to deal with require larger than local solutions. They have to be resolved at a metropolitan, regional, or larger scale, we think. Alfred Heller, long-time president of the conservationist and planning-oriented California Tomorrow, has said that for big cities like San Francisco, "all the major development decisions were made decades ago; and that all that is left today is to tinker with the remains by making 'urban design' rules."[7] But if he is right, then what are so many local people concerned about, and wouldn't the same thing be true at the state and regional level? In any case, the governmental structure to do effective city planning at a larger than city scale rarely exists. Besides, are the city planners (like the local people they represent) really sure they want to give planning powers to some super government? Can those fellows really be trusted? At the same time, people at the neighborhood or district scale think that theirs is the level at which to do city planning and to guide and control urban development. The city planner may have a hard time meshing neighborhood concerns with citywide plans and regional interests.

There is seldom enough time, or people, or information, or tools at the city planners' disposal to prepare the kinds of plans and implementing programs they would like. Often the tools and programs they do devise, such as zoning or urban redevelopment, get misused. There is never enough money (and the city planners rarely control its use in any case). City planners don't usually build things or run programs by themselves. They are always trying to get others to do what they want, and people are reluctant, if not ornery. More and more, it seems that someone from the federal or state government knows your business better than you and is telling you how to do it. (And will they cop out on you when the going gets tough? Better not to depend on them.) Just when you think you know your craft, your art, and what it will take to solve a problem and to plan for the future, there is yet another hurdle.

City planners may have a hard time knowing when they have been successful. It is hard to know what constitutes a good batting average. Very seldom does all of a plan get carried out. In many cities, success is measured by what happens, by what gets done, by what is accomplished. We are accustomed to thinking that way, but sometimes it is better to measure success by what does not happen. Any number of variations are possible and city planners, as well as their clients, may have a hard time identifying success when they see it. Success depends upon many variables—timing, people, laws, economics, you name it—and few of them are controlled by the city planner.

Nevertheless, the city is where the action is. It is the first line of government for most people. They feel their problems and frustrations where they live and work, and it is in their communities where people state their expectations and lodge their complaints. It is possible to do planning in cities within a context of specific faces and names as well as of places and things. It is possible to relate abstract policies and plans and programs to tangible experiences. The city planner can feel and experience what he is dealing with.

Even if city planners rarely design or build anything directly or operate a program, they can, working at the city level, have an impact on the environment. They can help a community decide what it wants to be and then help to achieve that future. They can see their successes and their failures, even those successes that are represented by something that did not happen.

The impact of local city planning may be more than local. When the solutions that are developed are truly innovative, they may be adopted and used elsewhere. But perhaps the most satisfying plans are the ones that respond purely to local needs and circumstances, those not required or mandated by any other level of government. Similarly, the best programs are the ones that are developed locally and carried out with local resources—because the community wants and endorses them for their own sake—not because of the availability of funds or aid programs, often illusory anyway, from some other level of government.

Certainly, there are frustrations. But if after many years you end up with one small park that might not have existed otherwise, one major piece of legislation, or one program that allows people to fix up their homes or live in sound and fairly priced housing in neighborhoods they enjoy, then the satisfactions can be very great. Such achievements will always be small in relation to the need. But there is always the chance of ending up with many parks and open spaces, a full transit system, a whole city of neighborhoods of well-maintained housing at prices that people can afford, and a host of facilities and services that together make a city what it can be. Those are very high stakes indeed.

NOTES

1 T. J. Kent, Jr., *The Urban General Plan* (San Francisco: Chandler Publishing Co., 1964).

2 Paul Sedway and Thomas Cooke, *Land and the Environment: Planning in California Today* (Los Altos, California: William Kaufmann, Inc., 1975), p. 139.

3 For an example of where city planning has gone and is going, see "National Policies for Planning," American Institute of Planners, revised draft, June 15, 1977, part I, pp. 1–3, on "The Role of Planning." This document, in its definition of planning, leaves considerable doubt as to whether planning has any roots at all in the physical environment or any particular relationship to urban areas. It is more concerned with government and "the planning process" than with the substance or focus of planning. Its only reference to the planning commission is in a historical sense, not as a desirable place to do city planning. A skeptic, observing the direction city planning has taken in the late 1970s, might say that since the definition of the field has become so broad that it includes all planning, for everyone, and that since everyone plans in one way or another, then everyone is a planner. That skeptic might well ask why a special planning organization or society should exist at all. (The final version of this document was adopted in October 1977 and released in 1978 under the title *AIP Planning Policies*.)

4 Robert A. Walker, *The Planning Function in Urban Government* (Chicago: University of Chicago Press, 1941).

5 Alan A. Altshuler, *The City Planning Process; A Political Analysis* (Ithaca: Cornell University Press, 1965), pp. 390–91.

6 For example, see Donald Appleyard and Mark Lintell, "The Environmental Quality of City Streets: The Residents' Viewpoint," *Journal of the American Institute of Planners*, March 1972. Also see San Francisco Department of City Planning (Donald Appleyard, consultant), *Street Livability Study*, June 1970.

7 Alfred Heller, "To Plan or Not to Plan," *San Francisco Bay Guardian*, April 14, 1977.

Planning in the Face of Power

John Forester
Professor of City and Regional Planning, Cornell University

John Forester's book is about "the vulnerabilities of democracy, about power and professional responsibility, about political action and ideology, inequality, domination, and resistance, illegitimate authority, and democratizing practices" (p. *xi* of the original). The author combines an analysis of social and political theory with his own empirical investigations to examine what planners do in the face of concentrated economic and political power. In this chapter, he tries to demonstrate that planners can make choices about their exercise of political power in the planning process. He argues that information is an important source of a planner's power and, if used strategically, can be a means of empowering citizens.

If planners ignore those in power, they assure their own powerlessness. Alternatively, if planners understand how relations of power shape the planning process, they can improve the quality of their analyses and empower citizen and community action. By focusing on the practical issues of information control, mis-information, and distorted communications more generally, this chapter will elaborate a pragmatic and progressive planning role for all those planning in the face of power.

Whether or not power corrupts, the lack of power surely frustrates. Planners know this only too well. They often feel overwhelmed by the exercise of private economic power, or by politics, or by both.[1] In health planning, for example, as in local land-use planning, planners must often react defensively to the initiatives of established, usually private medical care "providers" or project developers. Those providers have time, money, expertise, information, and control of capital; the countervailing consumers, in contrast, have few such resources. Nevertheless, planners in many areas are legally mandated to make democratic citizen participation in the planning process a reality rather than a romantic promise.

Furthermore, planners often have had little influence on the implementation of their plans. Those painstaking plans have too often ended up on the shelf or have been used to further political purposes they were never intended to serve. Given these conditions of work and the intensely political nature of planning practice, how then can planners work to fulfill their legal mandate to foster a genuinely democratic planning process? What power can planners have? In a time of retrenchment, these questions become more important than ever.

Once-and-for-all solutions in planning practice should not be expected, however, because the object of planning, future action, routinely involves the unique and novel. Even when planning serves to rationalize economic decisions, it must be attentive to the special problems presented by the case at hand. Even technical problems that can be solved with standard methods exist amid conflicting interpretations and interests, established power, and excluded segments of the population—all of which inevitably limit the efficacy of purely technical solutions. But despite the fact that planners have little influence on the structure of ownership and power in this society, they can influence the conditions that render citizens able (or unable) to participate, act, and organize effectively regarding issues that affect their lives.

This chapter seeks to demonstrate that by choosing to address or ignore the exercise of political power in the planning process, planners can make that process more democratic or less, more technocratic or less, still more dominated by the established wielders of power or less so. For instance, planners shape not only documents but also participation: who is contacted, who participates in informal design-review meetings, who persuades whom of which options for project development. Planners do so not only by shaping which facts certain citizens may have, but also by shaping the trust and expectations of those citizens. Planners organize cooperation, or acquiescence, in addition to data and sketches. They are often not authoritative problem-solvers, as stereotypical engineers may be, but, instead, they are organizers (or disorganizers) of public attention: selectively shaping attention to options for action, particular costs and benefits, or particular arguments for and against proposals.[2] A key source of the planner's power to exert such influence is the control of information.[3]

This chapter therefore argues that (1) information is a complex source of power in the planning process; (2) misinformation of several distinct types—some inevitable, some avoidable, some systematic, some ad hoc—can be anticipated and counteracted by astute planners; (3) such misinformation undermines well-informed planning and citizen action by manipulating citizens' beliefs, consent, trust, and sense of relevant problems, and planners can counteract these influences; (4) planners themselves sometimes participate in distorting communications and, in special cases, may be justified in doing so; and (5) because planners can expect misinformation to influence processes of decision making, agenda setting, and political argument more generally, they can counteract it in several ways to foster a well-informed, democratic planning process, thereby empowering affected citizens as well.

INFORMATION AS A SOURCE OF POWER

How can information be a source of power for planners? Four ways of answering this question are rather common, but we will also consider a fifth. These reflect the perspectives of the technician, the incrementalist or pragmatist, the liberal-advocate, the structuralist, and what I will call the progressive.[4] Each perspective suggests a different basis of power that planners may cultivate in their practice. We will discuss below how the different approaches to the control and management of information can make a practical difference in planning and in broader political processes. Although each of these perspectives will be discussed separately, in actual practice planners might combine several of them in any given case. For example, a transportation planner might strategically combine the attitudes of the technician and the progressive,[5] or a health planner might utilize approaches of both the pragmatist and the liberal-advocate.[6]

The technician. The technician supposes that power lies in technical information: knowing where the data can be found, which questions to ask, how to perform the relevant data analysis. Here, because information supplies solutions to technical problems, it is a source of power. This view reflects at once the most traditional problem-solving notion of planning and one of the profession's most criticized ideals—for it avoids, or pretends it need not concern itself directly with, politics. The technician supposes that political judgments can be avoided, that the political context at hand can be ignored. Adopting a benign view of politics, the technician believes that sound technical work will prevail on its own merits. But many planners and critics alike have been skeptical of this technocratic attitude.[7]

The incrementalist. The organizationally pragmatic incrementalist holds that information is a source of power because it responds to organizational needs. People need to know where to get information, how to get a project approved with minimum delay, and what sorts of design problems to avoid. Here, knowing the ropes is a source of power: informal networks, steady contacts, and regular communication keep planners informed. This is a social problem-solving view in which "social" is narrowly construed to mean "organizational." Planners do, of course, work in organizational networks in which different actors depend on one another for key information. Ironically, when others depend on the planners' information, that information is a source of power—despite the fact that incrementalist planners (as Lindblom suggested thirty years ago) may not know what good such power may serve beyond its impact on narrow organizational politics.[8]

The liberal-advocate. The liberal-advocate views information as a source of power because it responds to a need created by a pluralist political system; information can be used by underrepresented or relatively unorganized groups to enable them to participate more effectively in the planning process. This is the traditional advocacy planning perspective.[9] It seeks to redress inequalities of participation and distribution by bringing excluded groups into political processes with an equal chance, equal information, and equal technical resources. Traditional technical-assistance projects also fall within this view, aiming to provide technical skills and expertise so that community groups, among others, can compete on an equal footing with developers. The liberal-advocate focuses on the information needs of a particular client, i.e., the disenfranchised, the underrepresented, the poor, and the powerless.[10]

The structuralist. The structuralist paradoxically supposes that the planner's information is a source of power because it serves necessarily, first, to legitimize the maintenance of existing structures of power and ownership and, second, to perpetuate public inattention to such fundamental issues as the incompatibility of democratic political processes with a capitalist political-economy. The structuralist view, ironically, is reminiscent of the conservative functionalism of several decades ago, but now the argument takes a political-economic turn: The actions of the state, and the planners who work within it, inevitably function to prop up capitalism. The structuralist perspective suggests that planners have power but, despite their best intentions, keep people in their place and protect existing power. The planners' power cannot serve freedom.[11]

The progressive. Finally, the progressive approaches information as a source of power because it can enable the participation of citizens and avoid the legitimizing functions of which the structuralist warns. The planner's information can also call attention to the structural, organizational, and political barriers that needlessly distort the information citizens rely on to act.[12] The progressive perspective thus combines the insights of the liberal and the structuralist views and goes one step further. It recognizes that political-economic power may function systematically to misinform affected publics, by misrepresenting risk or costs and benefits, for instance. The progressive view anticipates such regular, structurally rooted misinformation and organizes information to counteract this "noise" (or "ideologizing," as some would call it).[13]

Each of these planning perspectives points to a different source of the need for information, and thus defines a different basis of power: technical problems, organizational needs, political inequality, system legitimation, or citizen action.

Since the progressive view builds on the other positions, it is particularly important to consider it in more detail. Emphasizing popular participation and planners' organizing practices, the progressive view also recognizes the obstacles to such participation. We will first compare the other views; then we will examine the progressive's position.

Limitations of Common Views

The technician is not wrong so much as intentionally neglectful. Politics is thought to "get in the way" of rigorous work. The political context of planning is understood as a threat, not as an opportunity.[14] Yet it was a political process that created not only the set of problems to be addressed but the technician's job as well. Therefore one cannot choose between being technical or being political. The technician is necessarily a political actor; the crucial questions are: In what way? How covertly? Serving whom? Excluding whom?

Following the publication of Lindblom's classic article "The Science of Muddling Through," the incrementalist view first found great favor for being practical, but then inspired no end of criticism for being unprincipled, apolitical, or, in a phrase, for admonishing us to "make do."[15] In its rejection of the rational-comprehensive call to get all the facts, the incrementalist position serves as an important antidote, but it says little about the improvement of planning practice, about what planners should be doing and how they might do it.

The liberal-advocate's view gained a more explicitly ethical following, in part for addressing issues of inequality, but it has been correctly criticized for failing to address the historical and structural character of these issues.[16] The liberal-advocate has been characterized as a nurse, ministering to the sick yet unable to prevent their illnesses from occurring in the first place.

The structuralist's position is as tragic as the liberal-advocate's: pure in intention, yet frustrating in practice. Finding all planning practice to be a legitimation of the status quo, the structuralist systematically fails to address real opportunities in planning.[17] The structuralist view may fail even to identify and exploit what might be called "internal contradictions" in the structure of the political economy and the planning process in particular. The irony of the liberal-advocates' position is that their best intentions may be betrayed by their ignorance of the structural effects of political-economic organization—for example, private control of investment, or the fact that an increased number of environmental-impact reports will not prevent environmental destruction. The tragedy of the structuralist view is that its apparently comprehensive position may be wholly undialectical in that it supposes the power planners face (or serve) to be monolithic and without internal contradictions.[18]

The Progressive Analysis of Power

The progressives have problems, too. Like the more strictly technical planners, they need good information. Like liberal-advocates, they need to supply information to citizens, communities, and labor groups in order to aid their organizing and democratic efforts. Yet the progressives need to act on the basis of a political analysis that tells them how the political system in which they work will function regularly to misinform both participants in the planning process and affected citizens more generally.[19] The progressive planner needs to anticipate, for example, that developers may withhold information or misrepresent likely project consequences, such as revenues; that consultants may be used less for analysis than for legitimation; that agency meeting schedules may favor private entrepreneurs while excluding affected working people whose business is their own daily employment; that documentation provided by a project's planners for public review is not likely to discuss project flaws or alternatives as candidly as project virtues; and so on.

Unlike the incrementalist or liberal-advocate, the progressive believes that misinformation is often not an accidental problem in planning: It may well be a systemic problem to be addressed and counteracted on that basis.[20] The practical tasks facing the progressive planner, then, are like those that community organizers and political actors have traditionally performed. Health planners, for example, increasingly recognize the need for educative and organizing skills to address the problems of daily planning practice.[21] Still, developing such educative, organizing responses to expectable misinformation requires planners to address several crucial, practical questions of political and organizational analysis.

What types of misinformation can be anticipated? Are some distortions inevitable while others are avoidable? Are some distortions socially systematic while others are not? How does misinformation affect planning and citizen action? What practical responses are possible? Might planners themselves be sources of distortion? Can this be justified? How can planners expect misinformation to flow through the relations of power that structure the planning process? Finally, in the face of expectable misinformation and distortion threatening well-informed planning and citizen action, what can progressive planners do in practice? The remainder of this chapter addresses these questions and the larger question of what this analysis means for an effective, progressive planning practice.

TYPES OF MISINFORMATION

We should distinguish several types of misinformation (see Table 1). Some misinformation will be ad hoc, random, or spontaneous. For example, in a public hearing a developer's consultant may speak too quickly or unwittingly use technical terms that the audience fails to understand. As a result, communication suffers, but hardly as the result of any systematic cause. Other instances of misinformation, though, will reflect actors' political-economic roles. Consider the remarks of James C. Miller III, executive director of a presidential task force on regulatory relief, indicating that industry representatives can be expected to exaggerate likely costs of proposed regulations, while government representatives (i.e., the regulators) can be expected to inflate the benefits of the same proposed regulations.[22] Such misrepresentations are clearly not ad hoc; they are rather structural products of political-economic relationships.

If planners can anticipate both types of misinformation (systematic and ad hoc), they can vary their practical responses accordingly. For example, impromptu and informal measures might suffice in response to nonsystematic distortions of information, because such distortions may merely be matters of blind habit. Clarifications can be requested; time for questions and cross-examination can be

TABLE 1 BOUNDED RATIONALITY REFINED: COMMUNICATIVE DISTORTIONS AS BOUNDS TO THE RATIONALITY OF ACTION

Contingency of distortion	Autonomy of the source of distortion	
	Socially ad hoc	**Socially systematic structural**
	1	2
Inevitable distortions	Idiosyncratic personal traits affecting communication	Information inequalities resulting from legitimate division of labor
	Random noise	Transmission/content losses across organizational boundaries
	(cognitive limits)	(division of labor)
	3	4
Socially unnecessary distortions	Willful unresponsiveness	Monopolistic distortions of exchange
	Interpersonal deception	Monopolistic creation of needs
	Interpersonal bargaining behavior; e.g., bluffing	Ideological rationalization of class or power structure
	(interpersonal manipulation)	(structural legitimation)

allotted in hearings, reviews, or commission meetings; a sensitive chairperson can intervene to suggest that a speaker speak more slowly, more directly into the microphone, less technically, and so forth.

In contrast, responses to systematic misinformation must be more strategic, based on the planner's analysis of the power structure at hand. As Steven Lukes argues, systematic misinformation is rooted in the political-economic structures that define who initiates and who reacts; who invokes authority or expertise and who is mystified or defers; who appeals to trust and who chooses to trust or be skeptical; and who defines agendas of need and who is thus defined.[23]

Some instances of misinformation might be socially necessary (that is, unavoidable), whereas still others are not. That there is some division of expertise and knowledge in society seems to be a socially, if not a biologically, necessary matter, not in the particulars of distribution (that being a political question), but in the fact of any unequal distribution at all. Some people will have developed skills for graphic arts, others for community organization, others for music composition; some might be mechanics, others painters, others farmers, and still others teachers. How the division of labor is structured in a given society is a political question— but that there must be *a* division of labor in capitalist, socialist, or future societies seems to be necessary in social life. Thus, some misinformation will be unavoidable; it will flow from *some* division of labor and thus of knowledge, expertise, and access to information. Other misinformation, such as capricious propaganda, will be socially unnecessary and thus avoidable.

This analysis of misinformation and communicative distortion provides the basis for a powerful reformulation of Herbert Simon's notion of the "boundedness" of the rationality of social action.[24] The rationality of action is bounded, to be sure; but how? How inevitably? How politically? We turn to these questions below.

Some constraints on social action may be necessary, but other bounds may just be social or political artifacts—constraints that are contingent on mere relations of custom, status, or power that are hardly inevitable or immutable. Working to alter the *necessary* boundedness of rational action may be foolishness, but working to alter the *unnecessary* constraints that distort rational action may be liberating.

In addition, some constraints on social action will be the result of random disturbances, but still others will be systematic, rooted in the political-economic structures that provide the context for any action. Treating random distortions as though they were systematic is a sign of paranoia; treating systematic distortions as though they were merely ad hoc phenomena is to be ethically and politically blind, assuring only repeated surprise, disappointment, and, most likely, failure.

HOW MISINFORMATION CAN MANIPULATE ACTION

How can information and communication, always potentially distorted, shape the actions of the people with whom planners work?[25] How can a politician's promise, a developer's project proposal, or a planner's report influence the actions of city residents? Informed and unmanipulated citizen action depends on four practical criteria in social interaction.[26] In every interaction, a speaker may speak more or less (1) comprehensibly, (2) sincerely, (3) appropriately or legitimately in the context at hand, and (4) accurately. In every interaction, too, a listener's subsequent action depends in part on how these same four criteria are satisfied. Consider each briefly in turn.

First, depending on the terms in which issues are discussed, citizens may find the issues clear or barely comprehensible, relevant to their own concerns or not, framed in ordinary language or in bureaucratese. Planners may, for example, either pinpoint key issues or bury them in data, verbiage, computer printouts, or irrelevant details—and what citizens understand, their *comprehension*, will grow or suffer as a result.

Second, depending on the intentions with which issues are presented, citizens may find their trust deserved or not. Citizens may be misled by false assurances of self-protecting agency staff, by technicians who claim to be neutral, or by established interests who deceptively claim to serve the greater public good. Thus public *trust*, always precarious, may be honored or manipulated.

Third, depending on what justifications are used as issues are presented, citizens may find their consent manipulated or not. Agency staff may claim legitimacy because the proper procedures have been followed; rivals within the community may claim legitimacy because they are acting in the public interest, acting to right wrongs, or acting as representatives of populations in need. In each case, the claim to legitimacy is an attempt to shape citizens' action through the mobilization of their *consent*.

Fourth, depending on the use of evidence and data, citizens may find issues either misrepresented or reported accurately. Politicians and project proponents and opponents alike may exaggerate or fabricate estimates of costs, benefits, risks, and opportunities. Whether or not the truth sets anyone free, systematic misrepresentation in the planning process is likely to breed cynicism, cripple action, and manipulate citizens' *beliefs* as well.[27]

There is no guarantee against the presence of manipulation in planning. Informed planning and citizen action are vulnerable to the mismanagement (whether ad hoc or systematic) of planners' and citizens' comprehension, trust, consent, and beliefs. Tables 2 and 3 show how such mismanagement can occur as the exercise of power through the processes of decision making, agenda setting, or the shaping of people's felt needs.

Responses to Misinformation

Each of the four criteria suggests how different types of misinformation can influence participation in the planning process.[28] More important, each type of misinformation calls for a different type of response from planners. The progressive planner may counter the manipulation of a neighborhood organization's trust by revealing previous instances of such misinformation presented to other neighborhoods—in the case of a developer's suspicious promise, for example. By weeding jargon out of communications and by calling attention to important planning issues that might otherwise be obscured by the sheer volume of data in consultants' reports or proposals, planners may avoid the assault on comprehension that can paralyze citizen action. A hospital administrator's inflated claim to expertise to gain the consent of consumers in a health-planning agency may be countered by marshaling dissenting expertise or by exploring the issue to clarify just what expertise is appropriate in the case at hand. Finally, planners may counteract the management of citizens' beliefs or knowledge by promoting project-review criticism and debate and by further politicizing planning processes. "Politicizing" here means more democratically structured, publicly aired political argument, not more covert wheeling and dealing.

In land-use and health-planning processes, such corrective actions are variants of organizing strategies in communities and bureaucracies. They seek to enable informed participation that recognizes the rights of others but is skeptical of the purported benevolence of established interests that stand to reap substantial private gains from proposed projects.[29] Informing the "affected but unorganized" earlier rather than later in the planning process is one simple rule of thumb that helps to counter the varieties of misinformation: commonplace acts of checking, double-checking, testing, consulting experts, seeking third-party counsel, clarifying issues, exposing assumptions, reviewing and citing the record, appealing to precedent, invoking traditional values (democratic participation, for example), spreading questions about unexplored work of Allan Jacobs in San Francisco and of Norman Krumholz in Cleveland.[30]

Yet what is crucial here is not any new progressive social technology or political gimmickry. Planners already have a vast repertoire of practical responses with which they can counteract misinformation: commonplace acts of checking, double-checking, testing, consulting experts, seeking third-party counsel, clarifying issues, exposing assumptions, reviewing and citing the record, appealing to precedent, invoking traditional values (democratic participation, for example), spreading questions about unexplored possibilities, spotlighting jargon and revealing meaning, negotiating for clearly specified outcomes and values, working through informal networks to get information, bargaining for information, holding others to public commitments, and so on.[31]

Progressive planners, therefore, must learn to anticipate misinformation before the fact, when something may still be done to counteract it. The more traditional perspectives treat information problems as either inevitable or ad hoc (see Table 1), and as a result, planners often respond too late. The practical problem, then, is not to invent new strategies in response to misinformation—such strategies abound. Instead, the planner must be able, as the progressive view suggests, to anticipate and counteract the practical misinformation likely to arise in various organizational and political processes (see Table 2).

With such vision, progressive planners can then draw on a repertoire of responses to counteract the disabling effects of misinformation in the planning process. Only if planners anticipate these problems can they counteract misrepresentation with checking and testing of data. Only then can they defend against false appeals to trust by checking the record of past promises. Only by anticipating misinforma-

TABLE 2   POWER, INFORMATION, AND MISINFORMATION: THE MANAGEMENT OF COMPREHENSION, TRUST, CONSENT, AND KNOWLEDGE

Modes through which power may be exercised	Forms of misinformation			
	Managing comprehension (problem framing)	Managing trust (false assurance)	Managing consent (illegitimacy)	Managing knowledge (misrepresentation)
Decision making	Resolutions passed with deliberate ambiguity; confusing rhetoric, e.g., "the truly needy"	"Symbolic" decisions (false promises)	Decisions reached without legitimate representation of public interests but appealing to public consent as if this were not the case	Decisions that misrepresent actual possibilities to the public (e.g., the effectiveness of insufficiently tested medications)
Agenda setting	Obfuscating issues through jargon or quantity of "information"	Marshaling respectable personages to gain trust (independent of substance)	Arguing, e.g., that a political issue is actually a technical issue best left to experts	Before decisions are made, misrepresenting costs, benefits, risks, true options
Shaping felt needs	Diagnosis, definition of problem or solution through ideological language	Ritualistic appeals to "openness," "public interest," and "responsiveness"; encouraging dependence on benign apolitical others	Appeals to the adequacy and efficacy of formal "participatory" processes or market mechanisms without addressing their systematic failures	Ideological or deceptive presentation of needs, requirements, or sources of satisfaction (false advertising, "analysis for hire")

tion can planners resist obfuscation with clear and powerful writing. Only then can they address the manipulation of consent by invoking shared tradition, precedent, or established rights. The progressive approach thus draws on the vast store of strategies that planners and citizens already possess; it also suggests that planners and citizens can anticipate misinformation in time to *use* those strategies effectively, rather than looking back regretfully and saying, "Well, what we should have done was . . ."

These responses involve risks to planners that depend both on the internal support for planners in planning departments and on the external support planners receive from other agencies, community groups, or established figures.[32] How much risk is involved should be neither minimized nor exaggerated, but further assessed in theory and in practice.[33]

PLANNERS AS SOURCES OF MISINFORMATION

Planners themselves can produce misinformation. They often work within pressing time constraints, with limited data. In addition, they often face organizational and

TABLE 3 POWER AND MISINFORMATION IN HEALTH PLANNING: AN ILLUSTRATION OF THE MANAGEMENT OF COMPREHENSION, TRUST, CONSENT, AND KNOWLEDGE

Modes through which power may be exercised	Forms of misinformation			
	Managing compre-hension (problem framing)	Managing trust (false assurance)	Managing consent (illegitimacy)	Managing knowledge (misrepresentation)
Decision making	Mute and suppress disagreements, dif-ferences of opinion, and conflicts within the board	Appear "demo-cratic"; claim to be "representative," "objective"	Control committee nominations and official appointments	Focus on task only; ignore process, hide omissions
Agenda setting	Overwhelm the board with data	Ensure that sympa-thetic professionals chair the board and key committees	Selectively schedule and time announce-ments; use profes-sional language	Avoid sensitive issues of current relevance to the agency
Shaping felt needs	Claim that the best kind of training pro-gram is one where the information flows one way, from an expert to the board members	Avoid group-process type training and training in conflict and negotiation skills	Avoid staff who are trained in community organizing	Provide information so consumers believe they need what you already think they need

Source: Adapted from Steckler and Herzog (1979).

political pressures to legitimate existing processes, to mitigate or avoid conflict, and to gain consensus and consent from potentially warring factions (developers, community groups, labor representatives) whenever possible. Under such condi-tions, planners can sometimes exacerbate the problems caused by misinformation: misrepresentation of facts, improper appeals to expertise or precedent, misleading statements of intentions, or the obfuscation of significant issues. Moreover, the production of misinformation by planners often does not occur just by happen-stance; rather, it may be encouraged by the very structure of the bureaucracies in which the planners work.

There can be no guarantee that planners will not produce misinformation. Yet two questions are crucial for planning practice: First, when can misinformation be ethically justified or rejected?[34] Second, if misinformation cannot be prevented, what good comes from an analysis of these problems?

The ethics regarding misinformation from planners (and from professionals more generally) has been a neglected topic in the planning profession until recent-ly. In the last several years, a number of studies have begun to address these issues, and they provide guidance for the isolated justification—but more frequently for the rejection—of planning actions that distort communications; for instance, with-holding information, or exaggerating risks or uncertainties.[35] Acts depend on par-ticular contexts for their sense and meaning; so must any ethical justification or rejection, seeking to protect human integrity, autonomy, and welfare, be interpreted and applied anew in particular historical contexts. If general ethical principles are not applied to specific cases, planners risk becoming dogmatists, blind to the requirements of specific cases, or sheer relativists, thinking that whatever seems right in the situation will suffice. Rigid adherence to formal principle, then, may callously substitute ready-made solutions for discriminating and sensitive ethical judgments. Situational relativism, in contrast, actually provides an ethics of convenience for the powerful. When the situation decides, then those with the power to define the situation really decide, and "right" is reduced to "might." Thus, at either extreme, questions of genuine justification in practice become meaningless.[36] How then are planners to apply general principles protecting integrity, autonomy, and welfare to concrete cases?

We might ordinarily wish to discourage lying, for example, because of the corrosive effect it has on social trust, but in some special circumstances we might justify it: such as deceiving a violent assailant about the whereabouts of his or her victim who has taken refuge in our house.[37] Similarly, misinforming actions by planners may at special times be justified, too, but only under particular and rare conditions, and hardly as often as might be supposed: when reasonable alternatives (as judged by a diverse, informed public) are not available; when the informed consent of others may be available (a client requests a rough summary of issues, not a more precise technical analysis); or when substantial and serious harm may be done otherwise. Each of these conditions is quite "soft" and open to a range of interpretations, but each may nevertheless be useful for the evaluation of planners' possible misinforming actions.

In the face of ever-changing historical circumstances that demand practical action, any general ethical analysis must be largely indeterminate. Yet the analysis of misinformation still can serve a politically critical function. Only after the types of misinformation that may be produced by planners are distinguished can concrete alternatives in specific circumstances be examined—and only then can we turn to the questions of justification or rejection. This chapter cannot offer ethical judgments independent of all practical cases, but it can and does serve, first, to identify the types of misinformation (whether produced or faced by planners, or both); second, to identify a repertoire of responses to misinformation; and third, to suggest how ethically to evaluate practical strategies for presenting, withholding, checking, or challenging information in the planning process. How, then, can planners work in the face of power?

THE STRUCTURAL SOURCES OF MISINFORMATION

In practice, how planners respond to misinformation will depend in part on their view of the sources of that misinformation. If they perceive misinformation to be accidental or unique to particular communities or types of projects, they are likely to work in a more ad hoc manner than if they view it as structural, to be routinely expected and countered. Questions about the sources of misinformation therefore become immediately practical. What types and mechanisms of power are faced by planners and by citizens affected by the planning process, and how influential are these modes of power? How does such power work, and how is it limited or vulnerable?

Extending Steven Lukes's cogent analysis, we can explore three answers to these questions.[38] Each answer will suggest different strategies for progressive planners to employ. One exercise of power can be understood by focusing—as the pluralists do—on decision making. Decision-makers can inform or misinform citizens effectively by virtue of their ability to prevail in formal decision-making situations.

A subtler exercise of power occurs in the setting of agendas—controlling which citizens find out what and when, about which projects, which options, and what they might be able to do as a result. Such power is immediately reminiscent of the information-brokering roles often attributed to planners: Shaping who finds out what and when often shapes action (and inaction).[39]

Yet another, still more insidious, exercise of power exists in the ability of major actors to shape the self-conceptions, the sense of legitimate expectations, and finally the needs of citizens: for example, the conceptions that citizens must acquiesce in the face of big government and big business; that socialism for poor and middle-income people is perverse, but appropriate for the wealthy who control investment; that individual market consumption will fulfill all needs; and that collective action is not a public responsibility but a nuisance.[40] Difficult to measure, this form of power nevertheless seems undeniable.

Each of these three modes of power can thwart the efforts of planners and informed citizens who seek to participate in a democratic planning process. Each of these modes—control of decision making, agenda setting, and needs shaping—can create misinformation that not only subverts informed and articulate citizen participation, but also weakens working relationships between planners and citizens. In health planning, for example, hospitals that propose expansion often utilize the pomp and circumstance of their medical staff to manipulate the trust and consent of consumer members of health-planning boards.[41] Consumer participation may then become characterized by passivity and deference, and progressive planning staff who question the need for expansion may come to be viewed with suspicion by the consumers. In such a case, the hospital staff members exert power not through decision making, but through their ability to shape agendas of discussion and citizens' perceived needs. But how are these agendas and self-perceptions shaped? Why do the consumer board members listen?

Power as Political Communication

Hospital staff members in the above example are able to exert power because the information they present—and the way they communicate—is highly political.[42] They very selectively inform and misinform citizens. They may call attention to particular apparent needs and obscure others, whatever the resources available to meet those needs. Appealing to the public trust in their reputation and their record of community service, hospitals may stress pressing community problems and their devotion and commitment to addressing them. They may appear to welcome legitimate, open discussion and public education while simultaneously ignoring the inability of significantly affected populations to join in those discussions. They may omit a careful analysis of public-serving alternatives to the proposed expansion and thus misrepresent the actual planning options faced by the health-planning body. In each of these cases—and they are all common enough, as any review of public participation in planning reveals—the established and often private "developer" can exert power through the control of information.

By informing or misinforming citizens, power works through the management of comprehension, or obfuscation; of trust, or false assurance; of consent, or manipulated agreement; and of knowledge, or misrepresentation.[43] Each of the three modes of power works in this way, either to thwart democratic participation and encourage passivity, or to encourage articulate political action and the realization of a democratic planning process (see Tables 2 and 3).[44]

Anticipating Misinformation: Progressive Planning Responses

The progressive planner seeks to anticipate and counteract misinformation that hampers publicly accessible, informed, and participatory planning. Each mode of power (decision making, agenda setting, and needs shaping) and each dimension of misinformation (obfuscation, false assurance, pretension to legitimacy, or misrepresentation of facts) may present distinct obstacles to progressive planning practice, and each obstacle calls for a distinct response.[45] As discussed here, planners can prepare participants in the planning process to face such misinformation— sometimes preparing them with facts, sometimes with questions and arguments, sometimes with expertise, and at other times just with an early warning.

Planners can respond to decision-making power by anticipating political pressures and mobilizing countervailing support.[46] Anticipating the agenda-setting attempts of established interests, planners can respond through a variety of informal, information-brokering roles, keenly attuned to the timing of the planning process, its stages and procedures, and the interests and perceptions of the participants all along the way. In addition, planners may work to include or seek ties to those traditionally excluded, encouraging attention to alternatives that dominant interests might otherwise suppress. As presented here, then, progressive planning practice represents a refinement of traditional advocacy planning, a refinement based on the practical recognition of systematic sources of misinformation. Finally, planners who anticipate the attempts of established interests to shape the perceived needs of citizens may not only work against such needs-shaping rhetoric, but they may also encourage, or ally themselves with, progressive, local organizing efforts. In the face of these modes of power, no single type of planning response will be sufficient. No doubt many strategies will be necessary if planning practitioners are to respond to, and indeed empower, citizens who hope to have an effective voice regarding the issues that affect their lives.

CONCLUSION

The power available to progressive planners encompasses the information strategies of the technician, the incrementalist, and the liberal-advocate, but it is more extensive still. Recognizing structural, routine sources of misinformation, the progressive planner seeks to anticipate and counter the efforts of interests that threaten to make a mockery of a democratic planning process by misrepresenting cases, improperly invoking authority, making false promises, or distracting attention from key issues. In environmental planning this means beginning with the demand that impact reports be intelligible to the public and not simply commented on at public hearings once they are written. It means countering corporate misrepresentations of costs, risks, and available alternatives, too. In health planning this means attending to preventive health care as well as to curative medical care, to workplace threats as well as to medical responses. In neighborhood planning it means tempering the exaggerated claims of developers and demystifying the planning process—and the rest of local government—itself. In each area, progressive planners can encourage and inform the mobilization and action of affected citizens.

Just as each form of misinformation is a barrier to informed public participation (see Table 2), so might an analysis of these barriers help citizens and planners alike to identify, anticipate, and overcome such obstacles to a democratic planning process. Planners can work to distinguish inevitable from avoidable distortions, ad hoc from structural distortions, and they may respond to these accordingly, so protecting reasonably informed planning and empowering citizen action as well.[47] Indeed, in a political world, any rationality in planning and administrative practice can be maintained only if analysts carefully assess the institutional contexts in which they work—as we will see in the next chapter. Anticipating and working to counteract distortions of communication that weaken democratic planning, then, progressive planning—structurally critical yet hardly fatalistic—is at once a democratizing and a practical organizing process.

NOTES

1 See Altshuler (1965), Balkas (1979), Baum (1980a, 1980b), Bradley (1979), Howe and Kaufman (1979), Page (1977), and Roche (1981).

2 Cf. Forester (1981b).

3 See, e.g., Marris and Rein (1984), Krumholz, Cogger, and Linner (1975), Benveniste (1977), Rabinowitz (1969), Kaufman (1974), and Needleman and Needleman (1974).

4 The term "progressive" is used because "radical" has been discredited as not pragmatic, "advocate" is overly narrow, "ethical" is conventionally misunderstood to be simply idealistic, and "professional" has been reduced, colloquially, from implying a "calling" to denoting merely the possession of expertise and socioeconomic status. Our use of "progressive" appropriates those elements of the Progressive Era that called into question the structural relations of nondemocratic control of capital and investment; this use rejects, however, those elements of the same era that sought instead to rationalize, objectify, manage, and quiet the conflicts and exploitation inherent in the political-economy. In sociological terms, the problem of this chapter, and the book as a whole, is to clarify the diverse possibilities of counter-hegemonic practices.

5 E.g., Rabin (1980).

6 E.g., Bradley (1979).

7 See, e.g., Altshuler (1965), Benveniste (1977), Bradley (1979), Jacobs (1978), Krumholz, Cogger, and Linner (1975), Meltsner (1976), and Roche (1981).

8 Cf. Benveniste (1977), Kravitz (1970), Lindblom (1959), Meltsner (1976), Nilson (1979), Thompson (1967), and Wildavsky (1979).

9 The classic analysis is Davidoff (1965).

10 Cf. Davidoff (1965) and Mazziotti (1974).

11 Cf. Harvey (1978), Piven and Cloward (1971), and Saunders (1979). Like that of the other perspectives, the brief description of the structuralist perspective here is ideal-typical. Structuralist perspectives have been both forcefully presented (Poulantzas 1973) and criticized (Thompson 1980). The intention here is not to delineate substantially a structuralist position but rather to characterize it briefly, if necessarily too simply; a fuller treatment is a task for critical accounts of the way planning theory draws on the broader fields of social and political theory and political-economy. The structuralist position is sketched here to indicate that problems of local effectiveness versus system determinism (or the philosophical "problem" of voluntarism versus determinism) are always present in planning practice, as shown in the familiar question planners ask: "Am I really making a difference here, or is everything I'm doing getting washed out by the larger political and economic system?" Depending on how this question is asked, it may lead to paralysis or, alternatively, to sharper strategic thinking. In any case, the structuralist view of information as power is presented here not to represent Marxist structuralist work in general (nor to represent all work that simply takes into account social, political, or economic structures), but instead to indicate how a view of systems-determinism might be manifest, and have extremely undialectical consequences, in practice. There are, of course, other Marxist positions, in theory and in practice, besides that of the structuralist perspective briefly presented here (Tabb and Sawers 1978).

12 Necessary and unnecessary distortions, as well as structural and nonstructural distortions, are discussed and distinguished in the next section of this chapter. These distinctions are presented schematically in Table 1 (p. 34).

13 E.g., Burlage and Kennedy (1980), Burton and Murphy (1980), Bradley (1979), Forester (1981a), Freire (1970), Friedmann (1980), Gorz (1967), Hartman (1978), Kemp (1980), Kraushaar (1979), Needleman and Needleman (1974), and Schroyer (1973). Cf. Krumholz (1982).

14 Cf. Szanton (1981) and Meltsner (1976).

15 See Lindblom (1959).

16 Two fascinating discussions of the liberal attitude described so briefly here may be found in the work of John Schaar (1967) and Isaac Kramnick (1981); their essays discuss the inegalitarian ironies of traditional liberal arguments for equal opportunity. Kramnick's historical analysis suggests that the liberal doctrine of equal opportunity arose as an argument against the claims of eighteenth-century English aristocracy. Although the resulting promotion of meritocracy can be seen as an emancipatory movement in the context of aristocracy, the same doctrine of equal opportunity today, leading to the same results, meritocracy, can hardly be appreciated as emancipatory any longer.

17 See Saunders (1979).

18 It might be conjectured that planners holding such a view do not last long as planners or, alternatively, that this perspective provides an all-encompassing rationalization for planning inefficacy, if not also for finding cynical satisfaction in meeting lower expectations, Herbert Simon's "satisficing."

19 As we will see, *how* the misinformation confronting planners comes about is a matter of the specific institutional settings in which planners work. In a capitalist political-economy in which the state functions both productively, to protect and foster capital accumulation, and reproductively, to promote and gain legitimation, the actual content of the misinformation faced by planners and citizens generally will, of course, differ in specific ways from that faced by members of bureaucratic socialist or other political-economic systems. Nevertheless, misinformation and systematic distortions of communication may be anticipated in a variety of political-economies, and our analysis here attempts only to provide a framework for research that suggests the dimensions in which hegemonic misinformation and communicative distortion can be expected to occur. It remains for analysts of planning in capitalist, bureaucratic socialist, and other political-economies to specify the contents of expectable misinformation generated in those institutional settings.

20 For the purposes of this discussion, "systemic," "systematic," and "structural" will be used virtually synonymously. Further analyses of misinformation must distinguish between distortions of communication that are rooted in (Weberian) status structures and those distortions that are rooted in (Marxist) class structures. What substantive theory of social and political-economic structure planners assume or employ will determine what sorts of structural distortions they may be able to anticipate in practice. Social and political theory, thus, informs planners' abilities to anticipate problems of practice, problems calling for preemptive response on the one hand, and threatening failure on the other (Forester 1987). See Clegg's work (1975, 1979), for example, for a critical discussion of power and structure; see also Stone (1980).

21 E.g., Bolan and Nuttal (1975), Burlage (1979), Burlage and Kennedy (1980), Checkoway (1981), Lancourt (1979), and Roche (1981).

22 See Brownstein (1981).

23 Cf. Lukes (1974), Gaventa (1980), and Forester (1982a, 1982b).

24 The next chapter develops this analysis at length. Table 1 (p. 34) presents a reformulation of the meaning of the "boundedness" of rational action. These categories (necessary versus unnecessary, ad hoc versus systematic) may provide an initial, graphic representation of the meaning of Richard Bernstein's claim that Habermas's critical communications theory of society is essentially an attempt to reformulate a comprehensive social and political theory of rationality (Bernstein 1976). See also McCarthy (1978) and note 47, below. The task of any critical social and political theory is to be able to distinguish carefully the necessary from the unnecessary, and the ad hoc from the systematic constraints on social action (whether involving planners, citizens, decision-makers, or others) so that appropriate responses (enabling what social and political rationality there may be) will be possible. The analysis of misinformation and communicative distortion provides the basis for ethically and politically refined assessment of both (i) the problematic rationality of social and political action; and (ii) the practical responses and actions possible to counteract the threats to—and especially the systematic distortions of—socially and politically rational interaction. The paradigmatic types of systematic distortions of social action are social-psychological neurosis and political-economic ideology. In each case systematic distortions produce domination rather than emancipation (Held 1980). By providing an analysis of communicative distortions that allows actors to anticipate and then respond practically to misinforming or distorting communicative influences, a critical social theory joins an account of power relations to an account of emancipatory, politically informed and guided practice. This analysis thus suggests research to clarify, first, those bounds or constraints on rationality (types of communicative distortions) and, second, those actions and practices required to counteract or avoid those distortions mapped schematically in Table 1.

25 Table 2 (p. 442) arrays the effects of misinformation against the various levels of the exercise of power through which such misinformation may be communicated. These dimensions of Table 2 are based on recent analyses of political power (Lukes 1974; Gaventa 1980) and of the pragmatic structure of communicative interaction (Habermas 1979; Held 1980; Shapiro 1976; McCarthy 1978; and Forester 1981c); cf. Chapter Nine. The problem of political misinformation might be approached in two ways: either by cataloguing the types of "symbolic" power that political acts may manifest (Edelman 1964, 1971, 1977) or by assessing the vulnerability of political action to distorted communications (Habermas 1970a, 1975, 1979; Bernstein 1976; Shapiro 1976). The former approach illuminates the functions of "symbolic politics," but it fails to ground those functions in an account of practical interaction, a theory of social action. Thus, the argument of this chapter complements the analysis of communicative action in planning practice (Chapters Five and Nine, for example) to consider problems of practice and relations of power directly. On parallels to Foucalt's analysis of power and discourse, see Ingram (1986).

26 Habermas (1979), Forester (1981c). See Chapter Nine for a more detailed exposition.

27 In the field of transportation planning, Yale Rabin, for example, writes: "Some believe that central city decline, minority isolation, and gasoline dependent dispersal have merely evolved from the incremental effects of millions of free choices and independent transactions in the metropolitan marketplace and that these conditions therefore simply reflect the mainstream values of a pluralistic society. The evidence, however, strongly suggests that these choices and transactions and the values which motivated them have been profoundly influenced by the systematic withholding by public officials of essential information about the fundamental nature and foreseeable impacts of highway policies and projects" (1980, 35).

28 Again, we can expect vulnerabilities of social action (to the structural management of attention, trust, consent, and knowledge) to be present whether that action (negotiating, bargaining, covering up, arguing, appealing, promising, threatening, and so on) is situated historically in capitalist or noncapitalist political-economies. But *how* actors actually face particular structural influences managing their knowledge, consent, trust, and framing of problems will vary, and must therefore be specified concretely (and strategic and practical anticipation and resistance must therefore also vary and likewise be specified) across differing political economic systems. The analysis of misinformation and response, then, may provide a framework for comparative analysis of planning practices. For work in this direction, cf. Adler (1986).

29 E.g., Checkoway (1981), Needleman and Needleman (1974), and Forester (1982b).

30 See Benveniste (1977), Jacobs (1978), Krumholz, Cogger, and Linner (1975), Lancourt (1979), Meltsner (1976), Needleman and Needleman (1974), and Roche (1981).

31 See, e.g., Goffman (1981), Lyman and Scott (1970), Needleman and Needleman (1974), Susskind and Cruickshank (1987), and Wilensky (1967).

32 See Needleman and Needleman (1974), Fainstein and Fainsten (1972), and Gondim (1986).

33 See Krumholz, Cogger, and Linner (1975); also Hoch and Cibulskis (1987).

34 Answering this question analytically will prevent unjustified acts in planning no more than distinguishing perjury from truth-telling will prevent perjury. Still, without the analytical distinctions, confusion and mystification are guaranteed, for one could never then distinguish perjury from truth-telling or outright lies from honest claims.

35 See Rohr (1978), Bok (1978), Howe and Kaufman (1979), Marcuse (1976), Euben (1981), Fleischman and Payne (1980), Forester (1980, 1981b), and Wachs (1985).

36 This analysis reflects the help of Stephen Blum. For a related analysis, see Anderson (1985).

37 See, e.g., Bok (1978).

38 See Lukes (1974), Gaventa (1980), and Roche (1981).

39 See, e.g., Meltsner (1976), Benveniste (1977), Kemp (1980), Rabinowitz (1969), Needleman and Needleman (1974), Marris and Rein (1984), and Checkoway (1986).

40 See Lukes (1974).

41 See, e.g., Clark (1977) and Checkoway (1981).

42 I.e., sociologists refer to such power as "hegemony." Cf. Thompson (1984).

43 To argue that power works as communication, in several dimensions, is not to argue that power and force are unrelated. Even dictatorial power may work far more often through the communication of the threat of force than through the application of force itself. Legitimate power, while retaining its potential use of force, appeals to and depends on consent rather than on the threat of violence. See, for example, Habermas's (1977a) discussion of Arendt's concept of power, and Pitkin's (1972) discussion of the distinction between legitimate power (authority) and illegitimate power (domination); cf. Forester (1986). As applied here, and presented schematically in Chapter Nine, critical theory is an analysis of contingent, hegemonic power (cf. Giroux 1983; Marris 1982 [discussion of metaphors of power]).

44 Forester (1982b) argues that these dimensions of misinformation provide a powerful reformulation of the notions of agenda setting and mobilization of bias in discussion of political power. That essay emphasizes variations in the content of agenda setting and needs shaping; the present chapter emphasizes the types of misinformation (necessary or avoidable, ad hoc or systematic) that may be anticipated and counteracted by progressive planning practitioners. See also Chapter Five below.

45 Thus, further research should identify in detail the appropriate strategies to respond to the particular types of misinformation (see Tables 2 and 3).

46 See, e.g., Fisher and Foster (1978), Forester (1981b), Gaventa (1980), Hartman (1978), Kraushaar (1979), Lancourt (1979), Needleman and Needleman (1974), Roche (1981), and Scott (1985).

47 Table I (p. 438) also allows us to locate the differences in outlook that separate several conventional planning perspectives and political sensibilities more generally. For example, incrementalists and pragmatists seem to assume a world where the significant distortions are inevitable; their typical question, then, is "What can we do, given that distortions will always haunt whatever planning we attempt?" Incrementalists, pragmatists, and technicians seem to spend little time separating socially unnecessary distortions from apparently necessary ones. While technicians hope that more powerful methods will mitigate the effects of distortion, incrementalists and pragmatists retreat to a "satisficing" position. Liberals, in contrast, find inequalities of access, knowledge, expertise, and information to be socially unnecessary and hardly inevitable, so they work to provide compensatory or remedial programs designed to overcome and eliminate those socially unnecessary distortions of human action. The liberal, though, seems generally unconcerned with distinguishing ad hoc distortions from socially systematic or structural ones. Here is the crux of the difference between the liberal and the progressive: the progressive seeks to isolate the ad hoc from the more structurally rooted distortions and then respond to each accordingly.

In terms of Table I, technicians may treat all information problems as if they are located in quadrant 1; incrementalists and pragmatists treat distortions as if they are located in quadrant 1 or 2. Liberals, in contrast, worry less about inevitable distortions than about politically contingent ones; thus, lacking a theory of the reproduction of social structures, they concentrate their attention in quadrant 3. Progressives, in contrast, distinguish the four quadrants and concentrate their attention on those avoidable distortions they can anticipate regularly (because these are structurally rooted) and then work to counteract, i.e., those in quadrant 4. If planners fail to distinguish the distortions in quadrant 4 from those in the other quadrants, they risk either mistaking recurring and expectable distortions for ad hoc and transient ones, or accepting avoidable distortions as if they were inevitable. In the former case, the error produces recurring surprise and avoidable distortion; in the latter case, the error produces fatalism while opportunities to improve the quality of practical work in the planning process remain unappreciated. The next chapter develops these arguments at length.

To Be Professionally Effective, Be Politically Articulate

Norman Krumholz
Professor of Urban Planning, Design, and Development, Cleveland State University

John Forester
Professor of City and Regional Planning, Cornell University

Making Equity Planning Work records and analyzes the great Cleveland experiment from late 1969 to 1979 in the practice of equity planning. At a time when the national tide had turned against issues of equality and racial justice, Norman Krumholz and his staff of professional planners persevered in their pursuit of progressive programs and policies. Their efforts resulted in changes in Ohio's property law, improvements in public-service delivery, protection of transit services for the most transit-dependent, and the rescue of city parklands and beaches (p. *xvii* of the original). How was this accomplished? In this chapter, "To Be Professionally Effective, Be Politically Articulate," the authors review the Cleveland political experience and suggest ways for planners in other localities to have similar successes. Krumholz and John Forester state that "to play an effective role in the messy world of urban politics, planners have to be professionally able, organizationally astute, and, most of all, politically articulate" (p. 456).

The promise of [innovative planning is] to keep curiosity and open-mindedness alive throughout the government and . . . produce a flow of valuable new ideas, of which every government has a chronic shortage. . . . The important thing in each jurisdiction will be the systematic search for ideas already in the public domain but likely to be ignored by existing operating agencies. Competence for the invention-oriented planning practitioner will consist largely of a taste for reading and conversing widely (though with discipline), and a capacity to show imagination in applying the ideas he finds to the setting of his own jurisdiction. The plain fact is that, except within certain narrow specialties, no one else seems to do this in most American state and local governments.

Alan A. Altshuler
The City Planning Process (1965)

To play an effective role in the messy world of urban politics, planners have to be professionally able, organizationally astute, and, most of all, politically articulate. In Cleveland, developing that professionally sound and politically articulate planning voice did not mean back-room deal making. It meant actively anticipating and counteracting threats to Cleveland's vulnerable populations. It meant articulating a vision of a better Cleveland, a city of more services and less poverty, a city of greater choice and less dependency, a city of adequate shelter not only downtown but all across town. Being politically articulate planners meant defining issues and setting agendas, working on problems before being invited to do so. It meant knowing ahead of time that politicians and city department staff would often be too busy, too uncertain, too self-interested, to get involved in some issues—and that this would produce opportunities for the planners to make a difference. Developing an articulate equity-oriented planning voice in Cleveland meant negotiating to serve the interests of the poor, but it meant much more than that, too: building trust and the planners' reputation, providing technical assistance, developing strong ties to the media to inform public opinion, at times leaking information to oppositional figures, drafting legislation, again and again bringing technical analysis to bear on issues of public costs, benefits, and well-being.

The Cleveland cases suggest that planners in other localities too can nurture and inform public debate, expect and respect differences, listen carefully, build cooperation, and work both aggressively and professionally to defend the interests of those least organized in our society. But they need not deny or regret political debate, dread or mystify political and economic conflict, or long for an apolitical society wiped clean of conflicts of interests and values. For if the truism that "planning is political" means anything, it means that planners will inevitably work within a web of political relationships. If they ignore those relationships, planners will virtually assure their own ineffectiveness.

ANTICIPATING PROBLEMS AND ORGANIZING SUPPORT

Many of the "new staff" Krumholz hired came to Cleveland to do equity-oriented work. Once on the job, they seemed painfully aware of the costs of their own inaction in the face of the city's business as usual. All around them, politicians pressed typically narrow agendas, developers lobbied for political support and favors, agencies suffered the effects of political pressures and patronage appointments, and city policies were shaped by the influence of local business elites.

Had the planners been less interventionist than they were, absentee landlords who had abandoned buildings would have held the city hostage all the more. Local construction interests might have procured contracts for white elephants like the

Downtown People Mover and enriched themselves at public expense. Illegal dumpers might still be using the lakefront as a dump.

But the planners did take initiative and act. They did not wait for someone to bring a full-blown problem to the Planning Commission before they went to work. The staff anticipated problems, studied them, typically took their results to the mayor, and argued for various strategies of response. A passage in a letter from Krumholz to Forester makes the point best. Asked to speculate about how a random day during his tenure as planning director might have differed from another city planning director's day, Krumholz began:

> I might begin my day with a breakfast meeting with some of my staff to review things or just because it's fun. J. Doe might begin with a breakfast with the Chamber of Commerce for exactly the same reasons. If there's a hot item on the local agenda I might be invited to breakfast with the Chamber's people, but as a potential adversary. For example, if their hot proposal is a domed stadium (it is, in Cleveland), I would have prepared studies challenging the financing (because it's going to take much public subsidy) and the site location (because it will displace a local market used extensively by the black community). They would want to quiet down my noisy questioning. J. Doe would take a supportively quiet position and adopt the public posture that there's nothing to comment on until legislation is formally placed before the Planning Commission. Of course, by that time, it's all over. I would try to stop or reshape the issue (and others) long before it came up in the form of legislation.

"Of course, by that time, it's all over." That simple line could serve as the epigraph for this entire book. It captures a view of professional action set in a real-time political context.

Amplifying Krumholz's point, Mayor Perk's law director, James B. Davis, provides us with a City Hall insider's account of the Cleveland planners' influence in local government. Asked how Krumholz and the planning staff fit into the daily operations of City Hall, Davis said:

> He didn't fit into it at all; he was not on anybody's game plan; he was not on anybody's chart. The city planning director had no role [in City Hall's decision-making processes] on paper, but Norm managed to have a major role anyhow. . . . [He] was a pretty good politician. He made himself enormously useful on a host of issues to whichever mayor it was. He could assemble more information, faster, and more tightly compressed on paper, than anybody else.
>
> And whenever a mayor needed some help, some immediate guidance, some policy paper on something, and had the wit to ask for it, Norm would be there the next day, with the thing all done. I'm overstating a little bit, but his turn-around time was fantastically fast and they knew that. And in many cases he had anticipated what they were going to be doing anyway, and he had something all ready for them. He could do things for them that nobody else in City Hall could; that was his political way of getting his foot in the mayor's office. . . .
>
> He could see things coming up over the horizon that would be major issues for the city . . . be it a stadium contract, whatever . . . those were not things that he needed to be given any special invitation about. He could see them coming. He had a host of ways of knowing these things were coming up, and he would start to investigate.

In the same interview (October 31, 1987), Davis spoke of the scope of planning under Krumholz's tenure: "Norm's perception was that . . . [a physical planning agenda] was important, . . . but he was vastly more concerned with the absolutely critical issues of running the city, which were financial, and [with] the financial impact on the city of anything that moved. . . . He was concerned with all the big new projects that would come floating through the city of Cleveland, and this was where he was not only a think tank but sort of an OMB [Office of Management and Budget] for City Hall. He probably better than anybody had a sense of what meaningful things could be done with a city budget, and he went through it with a fine-tooth comb, . . . trying to get the most bang for the city out of the buck. Now, he was not part of the [budget process] in any formal way, but he had his own involvement with it."

SHAPING THE NEW AGENDA

Arriving in Cleveland, Krumholz asked for his planners' analysis of the Euclid Beach rezoning proposal.[1] His staff's analysis was terse: The Council's for it, the mayor's been noncommittal, and, the implication seemed to be, "the merits" are unfortunately beside the point. When past experience has convinced a staff that their opposition to a project would be futile, the planners might reasonably limit their resistance to the proposal so they can work productively on more promising issues. Yet this reasonable and practical judgment has a deeper political significance. For here the experience of past powerlessness recreates future powerlessness—even if, ironically, this happens without any *present* exercise of influence, without any explicit threats, deals, pressure, or warnings.[2] In the Euclid Beach case, the planners' accommodation to the politics of zoning not only pre-empted their analysis but reflected a more pervasive professional malaise and cynicism that Krumholz and the new staff would soon work hard to change.

Krumholz's history in Pittsburgh had been instructive. He saw how strong directors with differing senses of the planning agency's mission achieved substantially different results. Cal Hamilton appeared to pay less attention to politics and decision making than to getting the models right; John Mauro apparently did just the opposite. Krumholz had been impressed by Mauro's engaged style of work, if not always by his particular objectives.

Krumholz tried to assemble a planning staff that fit professional analysis into political contexts, that brought analysis to bear upon political decisions, that worked aggressively within, through, and around the decision-making processes of the city by using competent analyses at every possible step. Together, Krumholz and Bonner developed a new style in the Planning Commission. Knowing that analysis or politics alone could lead to the staff's undoing, they believed that professional analysis articulated cogently and persistently in the political process could enhance the planning staff's credibility, respect, and practical influence. It *is* necessary, Krumholz argues, to keep saying the same thing over and over if you want anyone to notice. This includes talking at local meetings, in county and state testimony, in speeches to the profession, in op-ed pieces, in interviews with local reporters, in speeches written for the mayor, and so on.

Struck by Mauro's patience in press briefings, Krumholz echoes Mauro's practical point: "You can have the best ideas in the world; you can do the most careful analysis of an issue; you can write it up in the most brilliant style possible; but if you don't get it in the papers, no one will know it has been done. And if no one knows about it, you might as well not have done it." Krumholz came to Cleveland with the clear sense, based on his work under Mauro, that planners could play important educational roles in the public realm.

Yet the planning staff that Krumholz inherited in 1969 was hardly prepared to launch a politically engaged, equity-oriented, interventionist planning strategy. Only by choosing projects in the planners' new work program, and by hiring new staff when he could do so, could Krumholz begin to change the posture of city planning in Cleveland. Building on the best of his inherited staff and adding new professionals, Krumholz moved to redefine the political direction, raise the public profile, and improve the professional reputation of the whole planning operation.[3]

The Cleveland planners' production of the equity-oriented *Policy Planning Report* was the most visible sign of the new agenda. With the *Report*, the planners formally and publicly expressed their commitments to equity concerns and identified problems they hoped to tackle. The months of passionate and searching arguments that went into it also reaffirmed the staff's commitments—not just to the equity agenda, but to one another too. Publicizing the *Report* through official channels and the media also helped the planners find like-minded allies in the city.

BUILDING A REPUTATION FOR PRACTICAL, EQUITY-ORIENTED ANALYSIS

To influence action in City Hall, the Cleveland planners had to raise their profile, to show what they could do. They needed to complement their principled focus—on the vulnerability of those Cleveland citizens "with few choices"—with an articulate and public planning voice that could express the concerns of those citizens. Bonner, Cogger, Wright, and Krumholz worked, accordingly, to make their professional planning analyses increasingly public. Krumholz puts the problem this way:

> It is important to gain and hold the confidence of political and business leaders. If you alienate enough powerful people, you jeopardize your recommendations, the reputation of the planning agency, and your job. At the same time, it seemed to me that we had the responsibility to represent the best interests of the people of Cleveland as we saw them. We went about doing that in a cordial but nondeferential way, without compromising the facts of a case or our professional integrity. A good way to do this was to project an air of professional and technical competence and an apolitical, conservative, even skeptical public stance. The stance was built by always speaking soberly, using numbers when we had them to describe and quantify the issue, and wearing conservative suits and ties.

Articulate staff analysis served the mayors, other agencies, and community organizations alike.[4]

Krumholz's staff needed not just to calculate correctly, but to inspire confidence. With Charlie Volz as the trusted link to the Solid Waste Division, the planners could analyze the division's financial and service-delivery problems. With Layton Washburn as the old friend of Parks Commissioner Nagy, the planners could pursue the lakefront parks proposal. That a politics of personal networks mattered here did not make the technical merits of proposals irrelevant—far from it. But confidence in the staff was crucial. Without it, no report or memo, presentation, argument, or telephone call can be trusted, and without trust, the real merits of a planner's analysis will never get the attention they deserve.[5]

The Cleveland staff knew that every day's work would not only address a given project, this site or that parcel or that proposal, but that it would also strengthen or weaken their own reputation because of its timeliness, acuity, and style. Participating in the daily round of meetings and telephone conversations, planners recreate their agency's reputation as they speak articulately or not, provide relevant data or do not, appreciate the pressures on others or ignore them, and so on. In any given presentation, staff need both to present a cogent analysis of "the facts" and to present themselves in a way that will get them a hearing tomorrow, that will build trust and credibility, that will establish their own potential influence and competence. This is simple common sense, but too often that sense is neither so common nor so simple.[6]

Planners must balance tomorrow's continuing need for cooperation, coalition building, and information gathering with today's need to support or oppose a particular project. Working today with community residents, agency staff, politicians, and developers who may be passionately focused on a given project, the planners nevertheless have to try not just to get results in the short term, but to build long-term relationships too. In each day's work, planners face the challenge of maintaining what we may call their "strategic position." Meeting that challenge, the Cleveland cases suggest, takes time, sensitivity, political judgment, and negotiating skill as well. The Police Department's rejection of the planners' assistance, for example, provides a warning. When planners focus on issues but ignore the working relationships that will make their work consequential, they are likely to guarantee their own uselessness.

PRACTICAL RHETORIC AND PUBLICITY

The Cleveland experience should persuade us that professional planning is far more political craft than laboratory science. No matter how rigorous a project analysis, no matter how brilliant the results or recommendations, the planner's inevitable work of *articulating* that analysis—gauging when, how, to whom, and to what ends to express the issues—is an activity that is simultaneously professional and political.

Heard in a highly political world, the planners' words mattered. Krumholz has argued that a city planner who believes that solutions lie in comprehensive "central planning" of our national economy would be wise to avoid publicly stating that in so many words. Those words in our society are so nearly taboo that they are almost undiscussable; the ideas at stake would be "dragged down" by the words. But, he suggests, the discussion *can* proceed if conveyed in different words. Muny Light, then, is not to be saved because it represents a triumph of public power over the private sector, but because it is a city asset that should be retained because it makes good business sense. Krumholz has speculated that Mayor Kucinich's downfall was triggered in part by his refusal to modify his political style and language. To have implied that Brock Weir, the CEO of the Cleveland Trust Bank was a vampire sucking the blood of the people of Cleveland was somewhat imprudent, especially since Weir was key to the decision by local banks to call or roll over the city's notes.

Choosing one's words carefully, Krumholz argues, is just as important inside as outside government. In advice giving, argument, not deference, is needed inside the mayor's cabinet as well as inside the planning agency. But the terms of the arguments "must not preclude future agreements." To develop trust with other city agencies, criticisms of those agencies' policies must be "gentle but revealing," Krumholz says, giving the mayor an opportunity to resolve a disagreement among "competent old friends"—both agency directors.

Professional posture had direct political benefits in Cleveland: an aura of publicly recognized legitimacy that strengthened the planners' hand. Confronted by a glowering Jim Stanton upset about public housing hearings or attacked in the press for their positions on development projects, the planners' appeal to professional principles appeared both to shield them and to refocus public attention on the equity issues at hand. What better political protection for planners than their appeal, not to expertise, but to their public and professional mandate, their traditional public-serving mission?

The planners' concern with their own practical voice reached down to the most rudimentary reports they wrote for Planning Commission meetings. In those reports the staff wrote for the broader public and the press as well as for commission members and the files. To begin building an aura of professional competence, Krumholz points out, the planners adopted, beginning with the Euclid Beach issue, "a standard reporting format for issue review, analysis, and recommendation. This written document clearly set out the facts of each case under review, the staff's evaluation and discussion, a recommended course of action for the commission, and the reasons for the recommendation. The format was simple, straightforward, and consistent. It provided a clear history of the issue for incorporation into the official commission minutes as well as a convenient handout to newspaper and television reporters." Presenting the facts of the case, the staff's evaluation, and recommendations for action, these previously mundane reports now enabled professional analysis to serve a broader political function: public education through the mass media.[7] Planning Commission hearings served the planners less as havens from the political world than as settings in which to put pressing issues on the public agenda.

The reports to the Planning Commission, Krumholz notes, "did not emphasize any conflicts that arose within staff discussions. If views conflicted, and they frequently did, we tried to iron them out within our staff discussions and present a unified position to the world. We tried to avoid qualifying statements or uncertainty, preferring instead simple and straightforward themes." The Cleveland staff hoped to make themselves heard in an arena characterized by complexity, little time, poor data, and much conflict. In such settings, they sought to present professional recommendations as cogently as possible, as a prelude to, rather than as a substitute for, further debate.

The issue here is a poorly appreciated yet crucial problem of rhetoric. Planners who hope to pursue an equity agenda must speak and write as well as think and calculate. They must develop an articulate voice, organizing attention to issues and maintaining credibility even when data are inadequate and tempers are short. They must face the challenge of being persuasive without being manipulative. They must face uncertainty without being paralyzed by it. Faced with the real complexity of housing or transit or service delivery problems, they must select which issues to focus upon and which to put aside. They must be articulate organizers as well as clear-thinking analysts. Gauging what to say and what not to say, when and how to speak to be understood, whether to be challenging or not, encouraging or not—all these are practical problems of rhetoric, of speech and writing, that call for subtle political judgments, for a working political literacy, in daily planning practice.[8]

RELATIONS WITH THE MEDIA

In part, of course, the Cleveland planners' ability to call attention to equity issues depended on the mutually beneficial relationships they nurtured with the local media. The planners could give local journalists and reporters timely information, data, and analysis as only insiders could. In turn, those journalists and reporters provided a broad forum for issues the planners wanted to place on the public agenda and a growing measure of credibility for the staff as well. Without ensuring victories on particular issues, good relations with the media allowed a politically literate planning staff to educate the public about urban issues in a more general way—and perhaps also to set the context for future debates about projects. In a setting where lucrative private deals were likely to be made by construction interests, law firms, and politicians, the Cleveland planners bet that cooperation with the media would generally tend to be boondoggle-exposing and public-protecting, whereas secrecy would protect the already powerful. They hoped, too, that media attention would dignify the planning staff as serious professional actors simply by covering their actions and reporting their analyses as newsworthy.

We should ask, then, what would happen if planners across the country took public education seriously as they presented their analyses of the issues of the day before planning boards and commissions? The pedagogic quality of planning analyses would surely improve under the pressure of public scrutiny. The visibility and status of planning staff would most likely increase too—as would, we suspect, the overall difficulty of private raids on the public purse.

Nevertheless, relationships with the media are always politically complex and risky. Krumholz relates several cases in which he gave information to the press at some personal risk. In the People Mover case, to take the most striking example, Krumholz gave information to journalists in the hope of bringing the inflated promises of the project to public attention—even though he felt he could not do this publicly in his official capacity.

If planners can at times exert influence through the media, though, so too can the press create public expectations of planners. The planners can come to be seen as haughty and distant or as down-to-earth and pragmatic, as in the pocket of local politicians or as speaking consistently to broader interests within the city.

Press and television coverage of planning issues increasingly has a political significance of its own. For if we hope for a civic life richer than one dictated by deals made in smoke-filled back rooms, we can appreciate that city planners' pursuit of visibility and publicity is a political good in itself. In a democratic culture particularly, public discussion of projects and decisions can educate and empower the citizens of the political community we call the city. Such "political talk," Benjamin Barber writes, "is not talk *about* the world; it is talk that makes and remakes the world."[9]

In the freeway case, press coverage and attention contributed to a political climate in which senatorial candidate (and governor) Rhodes came to pledge that he would never force a highway on a community that did not want it. The media's coverage of downtown development disputes brought the planners' analyses of tax abatement strategies to the public's attention. The media's exposure of CEI's strategies to buy out Muny Light also enabled the planners' work to enrich public debate. Had Krumholz and his staff not carefully worked with local journalists and reporters, they would have missed, if not squandered, important opportunities that lay before them.

Yet access to the media will hardly help if the planners have nothing to say. When issues pressed, budgets were limited, and too little staff time was available, the Cleveland planners sought help at times from outside expertise. How they did that in the case of the freeway fight raises provocative practical and ethical questions.

STRENGTHENING PLANNING ANALYSES BY USING OUTSIDE EXPERTISE

In the freeway case, the planners built alliances with the staff of the very organization whose highway proposals they were trying to stop. Krumholz recalls his strategy:

> We wanted to deepen [the division between the NOACA board and its planning staff] and use the NOACA planning staff for our own purposes—in effect, to supplement our own staff at City Hall. That was not as difficult as it may sound. Many members of the NOACA staff had already quietly indicated that they were on the city's side in the controversy. . . . They had already prepared and recommended other courses of action that the board had rejected. Many were idealistic and liberal professional planners; I wanted them as allies.

The NOACA planning staff had no decision-making authority, and Krumholz did not try to undermine or subvert NOACA from the inside by lobbying its staff. But NOACA's planners had equity concerns of their own.[10] They offered information and expertise to help Krumholz improve the quality of his staff's alternative route proposal. This political alliance between planners in contending agencies allowed the city planning staff more ably and publicly to press the facts of the case, to assess viable alternatives, and to show the costs and impacts of proposed routes.

What might have happened had Krumholz's staff only assessed the implications of the I-290 proposal? Without the expertise to explore real alternatives, they could have done little planning. Had they paid attention only to the likely consequences of the proposed route, the planners might have chronicled a story of urban displacement instead of acting effectively to prevent it.

Wishing to explore freeway alternatives that were less socially damaging, Krumholz organized a planning team composed of public planners and private engineers. His staff's reputation had enabled sympathetic professionals throughout the city and county to identify themselves as allies—and Krumholz used their help and protected their confidentiality. He recalls, "I have found through the years and on many different issues that it is often possible to get excellent professional assistance from staff members of outside agencies who are angry about or disappointed by their own agency's decisions. If you are visible and publicly identified with a position these professionals favor, they may be very helpful, but always on a *sub rosa* basis, because to be identified in this work might cost them their jobs."

Krumholz had also obtained the *pro bono* services of transportation engineers from a local firm. To supplement a city staff's capabilities in this way is unconventional, no doubt, yet still principled (since the planners were seeking to protect the welfare of the city against suburban power)—whether or not it was indeed justified.[11] Krumholz had to make an ethical judgment that would have supremely practical effects: in the interests of calling public attention to the I-290 proposal and workable alternatives, should he welcome, and work to organize, professional support, even if it came from a private firm or NOACA itself?

Krumholz does not spell out his ethical reasoning, but two possibilities come easily to mind. The first, generally utilitarian, argument might take an expected increase in welfare due to stopping the freeway (preventing massive displacement) to outweigh the possible harm to social trust brought about by cooperation with the engineering firm. The second argument might recognize a conflict of obligations between two public trusts, with the obligation to avoid *sub rosa* work giving way here to the obligation to protect the interests of populations who are relatively unorganized, underrepresented, and otherwise inadequately protected by existing decision-making processes. Each of these arguments could, of course, be contested. Here we wish not so much to defend the decision as to make another point: the necessity for planners to make deeply practical, ethical judgments seems inescapable. If that weak claim is true, then planning education hamstrings students of planning if it does not prepare them to think through the challenges such judgments and choices present.[12]

CONCLUSION

The model of apolitical planning dies hard, in part because we have too few examples of exemplary equity-oriented planning that weaves together professional work, political vision, and organizational pragmatism. The Cleveland planners provide us with such examples, warts and all. Committed to serving those poor and vulnerable citizens whom "business as usual" promised to neglect, the Cleveland planners anticipated the play of private power, sweetheart deals, and bids for costly public subsidies.

As they worked with community leaders or mayoral advisors, with agency staff or specially created single-issue task forces, the Cleveland planners were able to develop an articulate, largely public, equity-oriented voice that integrated professional analysis and political initiative. They did not sacrifice professional integrity to political pressure. Instead, their work teaches us that had they not given voice to the equity-planning agenda, had they not pinpointed the vulnerability of the transit-dependent, had they not actively protected tax-payers facing ill-conceived infrastructure projects, the planners would have had far less to show for their professional work. The Cleveland planning experience demonstrates the possibilities of a politically astute, articulate, and effective equity-planning practice.

NOTES

1 For another account of the problems associated with "getting going," see Allan B. Jacobs, *Making City Planning Work* (Chicago: American Society of Planning Officials, 1978).

2 For an extended analysis, see Steven Lukes, *Power: A Radical View* (New York: Macmillan, 1974). See also John Gaventa, *Power and Powerlessness* (Urbana: University of Illinois Press, 1980). In an interview (October 31, 1987), journalist Roldo Bartimole pointed to the self-censorship of planning staffs and the challenge of an equity-planning leadership to end this by setting the context for the staff to do their work and to speak articulately to equity concerns.

3 For analyses of psychological and social-psychological aspects of professional interactions and self-limiting strategies of information suppression, unilateral control, self-fulfilling projection, and defensive behavior, among others, see Howell Baum, *The Invisible Bureaucracy* (New York: Oxford University Press, 1987); and the work of Donald Schon and Chris Argyris: for example, *Theory in Practice: Increasing a Professional Effectiveness* (San Francisco: Jossey Bass, 1974). On the influence of race, see Thomas Kochman, *Black and White Styles in Conflict* (Chicago: University of Chicago Press, 1981).

4 The transit negotiations, suggests Michael J. Hoffman (then working for Cuyahoga County), showed "how a hard-working, knowledgeable bureaucracy, with a steadfast director, can affect policy decisions in the public sector. . . . Only city planning had a plan; it backed that plan with sound data; then it fought off assaults with the accuracy of its figures that others were unable to refute. . ., . What was achieved was substantial, and would not otherwise have occurred, because the poor had no other advocates" (letter to Forester, June 6, 1988).

5 Compare Krumholz's strategic advice to equity planners: Frame "recommendations in data, analysis, and written hand-outs so everybody (especially the media) gets it straight. Become the *professional* and maintain that image. . . . While everybody else in City Hall was *political*, we were *professional*. As a result, we were considered the neutral experts in many areas, aiding our influence and providing protection against political threats" (letter to Forester, June 13, 1986). Howell Baum writes: "Unless [planners] respond to the political environment, they are unlikely to have influence. However, if they appear overtly political, they will be indistinguishable from other, explicitly political actors and will be unlikely to have any special influence" (letter to Forester, April 4, 1988).

6 As planners produce whatever results they do today, they simultaneously reproduce, strengthening or weakening, the social relationships necessary to produce anything else tomorrow. For analysis of the simultaneously productive and reproductive character of

planning practice, see John Forester, *Planning in the Face of Power* (Berkeley: University of California Press, 1989). For a closely related account dealing with recent European theories of hegemony and discourse, see Maarten Hajer, *City Politics: Hegemonic Projects and Discourse* (Brookfield, Vt.: Avebury, 1989).

7 For an early view of planning as an instrument of civic education, see Thomas Schlereth, "Burnham's *Plan* and Moody's Manual: City Planning as Progressive Reform," in Donald Krueckeberg, ed., *The American Planner* (New York: Methuen, 1983).

8 These issues of rhetoric extend far beyond matters of simple persuasion, "communication," or clarity, for they involve deeply political choices about the ways problems and strategies of response are to be seen, if they are to be seen at all. For analyses of the rhetorical character of work in law and economics respectively, see J. B. White, "Rhetoric and Law: The Arts of Cultural and Communal Life," in his *Heracles' Bow: Essays on the Rhetoric and Poetics of Law* (Madison: University of Wisconsin Press, 1985); and Donald N. McCloskey, *The Rhetoric of Economics* (Madison: University of Wisconsin Press, 1986). For a discussion of policy and planning analysis, see Giandomenico Majone, *Evidence, Argument and Persuasion in the Policy Process* (New Haven: Yale University Press, 1989) chs. 1 and 2. For three very different analyses of political talk, see Joseph Gusfield, *The Culture of Public Problems* (Chicago: University of Chicago Press, 1981); Murray Edelman, *Political Language* (New York: Academic Press, 1977); and Benjamin Barber, *Strong Democracy* (Berkeley: University of California Press, 1984). For applications to planning, see Forester, *Planning in the Face of Power.*

9 Barber, *Strong Democracy*, p. 177 (italics in original).

10 Recall that the NOACA board had minimal representation of Cleveland residents, the freeway proposals threatened to have an extensive impact upon poor residents of the city, and some NOACA board members had said openly that they were not even familiar with the areas through which the proposed route ran. Is it surprising that NOACA staff members (or outsiders) questioned the soundness of the routes adopted by the NOACA board or the board's very legitimacy?

11 For a sustained analysis of a "democratic" conception of bureaucratic responsibility and an assessment of information leaking by public servants, see John Burke's instructive and nuanced *Bureaucratic Responsibility* (Baltimore: Johns Hopkins University Press, 1986). Burke writes, for example: "If superiors in the organizational hierarchy or legislators were blocking access to information necessary for informed political choice, then bureaucratic action to remedy this situation would be in order" (p. 113). Yet "a democratic approach does not propose some abstract or unqualified demand for information disclosure. . . . In addition to recognizing obligations to aid the process of political choice, a responsible official must always consider his normal duties—his promise to fulfill his official tasks and those of the broader hierarchical order in which they are set—in determining what he can do by way of remedy. By following this institutionally cognizant course, the bureaucrat will generally find that the legitimate need of the agency or organization for non-disclosure enters into his judgment about whether to act. Balancing these respective demands is necessary because the claims for non-disclosure made by superiors may be spurious or self-serving or, in contrast, the interests served by disclosure may be relatively weak" (p. 68).

12 For detailed treatments of these problems, see Burke, *Bureaucratic Responsibility*, and Dennis Thompson, *Political Ethics and Public Office* (Cambridge: Harvard University Press, 1987).

NINE. POLITICS OF PLANNING—SUGGESTED READINGS

Banfield, Edward C., and James Q. Wilson. 1963. *City Politics*. New York: Vintage Books.

Barber, Benjamin. 1984. *Strong Democracy: Participatory Politics for a New Age*. Berkeley: University of California Press.

Benveniste, Guy. 1989. *Mastering the Politics of Planning*. San Francisco: Jossey-Bass Publishers.

Braybrooke, David, and Charles Lindblom. 1963. *A Strategy of Decision*. New York: Free Press.

Caro, Robert A. 1974. *The Power Broker*. New York: Random House/Knopf.

Catanese, Anthony James. 1984. *The Politics of Planning and Development*. Beverly Hills, CA: Sage Publications.

Clavel, Pierre. 1986. *The Progressive City: Planning and Participation*. New Brunswick, NJ: Rutgers.

Fisher, Robert, and William Ury. 1983. *Getting to Yes*. New York: Penguin.

Hall, Peter. 1980. *Great Planning Disasters*. London: Weidenfeld & Nicolson.

Molotch, Harvey. 1993. "The Political Economy of Growth Machines." *Journal of Urban Affairs* 15, 1:29–53.

10

ENVIRONMENTAL PLANNING

The Obligation to Endure

Rachel Carson

Rachel Carson focused worldwide attention on the dangers of chemical pesticides to our environment. Commenting on humanity's frightening assault on the
environment, Carson asks, "All this has been risked—for what? Future historians may well be amazed by our distorted sense of proportion" (p. 472). The
direct relevance of this selection to planning is its reminder of the fragility of the
natural world and our need to be wise in protecting it.

The history of life on earth has been a history of interaction between living things
and their surroundings. To a large extent, the physical form and the habits of the
earth's vegetation and its animal life have been molded by the environment.
Considering the whole span of earthly time, the opposite effect, in which life actually modifies its surroundings, has been relatively slight. Only within the moment
of time represented by the present century has one species—man—acquired significant power to alter the nature of his world.

During the past quarter century this power has not only increased to one of disturbing magnitude but it has changed in character. The most alarming of all man's
assaults upon the environment is the contamination of air, earth, rivers, and sea
with dangerous and even lethal materials. This pollution is for the most part
irrecoverable; the chain of evil it initiates not only in the world that must support
life but in living tissues is for the most part irreversible. In this now universal contamination of the environment, chemicals are the sinister and little-recognized partners of radiation in changing the very nature of the world—the very nature of its
life. Strontium 90, released through nuclear explosions into the air, comes to earth
in rain or drifts down as fallout, lodges in soil, enters into the grass or corn or wheat
grown there, and in time takes up its abode in the bones of a human being, there to
remain until his death. Similarly, chemicals sprayed on croplands or forests or gardens lie long in soil, entering into living organisms, passing from one to another in
a chain of poisoning and death. Or they pass mysteriously by underground streams
until they emerge and, through the alchemy of air and sunlight, combine into new
forms that kill vegetation, sicken cattle, and work unknown harm on those who
drink from once pure wells. As Albert Schweitzer has said, "Man can hardly even
recognize the devils of his own creation."

It took hundreds of millions of years to produce the life that now inhabits the
earth—eons of time in which that developing and evolving and diversifying life
reached a state of adjustment and balance with its surroundings. The environment,
rigorously shaping and directing the life it supported, contained elements that were

hostile as well as supporting. Certain rocks gave out dangerous radiation; even within the light of the sun, from which all life draws its energy, there were short-wave radiations with power to injure. Given time—time not in years but in millennia—life adjusts, and a balance has been reached. For time is the essential ingredient; but in the modern world there is no time.

The rapidity of change and the speed with which new situations are created follow the impetuous and heedless pace of man rather than the deliberate pace of nature. Radiation is no longer merely the background radiation of rocks, the bombardment of cosmic rays, the ultraviolet of the sun that have existed before there was any life on earth; radiation is now the unnatural creation of man's tampering with the atom. The chemicals to which life is asked to make its adjustment are no longer merely the calcium and silica and copper and all the rest of the minerals washed out of the rocks and carried in rivers to the sea; they are the synthetic creations of man's inventive mind, brewed in his laboratories, and having no counterparts in nature.

To adjust to these chemicals would require time on the scale that is nature's; it would require not merely the years of a man's life but the life of generations. And even this, were it by some miracle possible, would be futile, for the new chemicals come from our laboratories in an endless stream; almost five hundred annually find their way into actual use in the United States alone. The figure is staggering and its implications are not easily grasped—500 new chemicals to which the bodies of men and animals are required somehow to adapt each year, chemicals totally outside the limits of biologic experience.

Among them are many that are used in man's war against nature. Since the mid-1940's over 200 basic chemicals have been created for use in killing insects, weeds, rodents, and other organisms described in the modern vernacular as "pests"; and they are sold under several thousand different brand names.

These sprays, dusts, and aerosols are now applied almost universally to farms, gardens, forests, and homes—nonselective chemicals that have the power to kill every insect, the "good" and the "bad," to still the song of birds and the leaping of fish in the streams, to coat the leaves with a deadly film, and to linger on in soil—all this though the intended target may be only a few weeds or insects. Can anyone believe it is possible to lay down such a barrage of poisons on the surface of the earth without making it unfit for all life? They should not be called "insecticides," but "biocides."

The whole process of spraying seems caught up in an endless spiral. Since DDT was released for civilian use, a process of escalation has been going on in which ever more toxic materials must be found. This has happened because insects, in a triumphant vindication of Darwin's principle of the survival of the fittest, have evolved super races immune to the particular insecticide used, hence a deadlier one has always to be developed—and then a deadlier one than that. It has happened also because, for reasons to be described later, destructive insects often undergo a "flareback," or resurgence, after spraying, in numbers greater than before. Thus the chemical war is never won, and all life is caught in its violent crossfire.

Along with the possibility of the extinction of mankind by nuclear war, the central problem of our age has therefore become the contamination of man's total environment with such substances of incredible potential for harm—substances that accumulate in the tissues of plants and animals and even penetrate the germ cells to shatter or alter the very material of heredity upon which the shape of the future depends.

Some would-be architects of our future look toward a time when it will be possible to alter the human germ plasm by design. But we may easily be doing so now by inadvertence, for many chemicals, like radiation, bring about gene mutations. It is ironic to think that man might determine his own future by something so seemingly trivial as the choice of an insect spray.

All this has been risked—for what? Future historians may well be amazed by our distorted sense of proportion. How could intelligent beings seek to control a few unwanted species by a method that contaminated the entire environment and brought the threat of disease and death even to their own kind? Yet this is precisely what we have done. We have done it, moreover, for reasons that collapse the moment we examine them. We are told that the enormous and expanding use of pesticides is necessary to maintain farm production. Yet is our real problem not one of *overproduction*? Our farms, despite measures to remove acreages from production and to pay farmers *not* to produce, have yielded such a staggering excess of crops that the American taxpayer in 1962 is paying out more than one billion dollars a year as the total carrying cost of the surplus-food storage program. And is the situation helped when one branch of the Agriculture Department tries to reduce production while another states, as it did in 1958, "It is believed generally that reduction of crop acreages under provisions of the Soil Bank will stimulate interest in use of chemicals to obtain maximum production on the land retained in crops."

All this is not to say there is no insect problem and no need of control. I am saying, rather, that control must be geared to realities, not to mythical situations, and that the methods employed must be such that they do not destroy us along with the insects.

The problem whose attempted solution has brought such a train of disaster in its wake is an accompaniment of our modern way of life. Long before the age of man, insects inhabited the earth—a group of extraordinarily varied and adaptable beings. Over the course of time since man's advent, a small percentage of the more than half a million species of insects have come into conflict with human welfare in two principal ways: as competitors for the food supply and as carriers of human disease.

Disease-carrying insects become important where human beings are crowded together, especially under conditions where sanitation is poor, as in time of natural disaster or war or in situations of extreme poverty and deprivation. Then control of some sort becomes necessary. It is a sobering fact, however, as we shall presently see, that the method of massive chemical control has had only limited success, and also threatens to worsen the very conditions it is intended to curb.

Under primitive agricultural conditions the farmer had few insect problems. These arose with the intensification of agriculture—the devotion of immense acreages to a single crop. Such a system set the stage for explosive increases in specific insect populations. Single-crop farming does not take advantage of the principles by which nature works; it is agriculture as an engineer might conceive it to be. Nature has introduced great variety into the landscape, but man has displayed a passion for simplifying it. Thus he undoes the built-in checks and balances by which nature holds the species within bounds. One important natural check is a limit on the amount of suitable habitat for each species. Obviously then, an insect that lives on wheat can build up its population to much higher levels on a farm devoted to wheat than on one in which wheat is intermingled with other crops to which the insect is not adapted.

The same thing happens in other situations. A generation or more ago, the towns of large areas of the United States lined their streets with the noble elm tree. Now the beauty they hopefully created is threatened with complete destruction as disease sweeps through the elms, carried by a beetle that would have only limited chance to build up large populations and to spread from tree to tree if the elms were only occasional trees in a richly diversified planting.

Another factor in the modern insect problem is one that must be viewed against a background of geologic and human history: the spreading of thousands of different kinds of organisms from their native homes to invade new territories. This worldwide migration has been studied and graphically described by the British ecologist Charles Elton in his recent book *The Ecology of Invasions*. During the Cretaceous Period, some hundred million years ago, flooding seas cut many land bridges between continents and living things found themselves confined in what Elton calls "colossal separate nature reserves." There, isolated from others of their kind, they developed many new species. When some of the land masses were joined again, about 15 million years ago, these species began to move out into new territories—a movement that is not only still in progress but is now receiving considerable assistance from man.

The importation of plants is the primary agent in the modern spread of species, for animals have almost invariably gone along with the plants, quarantine being a comparatively recent and not completely effective innovation. The United States Office of Plant Introduction alone has introduced almost 200,000 species and varieties of plants from all over the world. Nearly half of the 180 or so major insect enemies of plants in the United States are accidental imports from abroad, and most of them have come as hitchhikers on plants.

In new territory, out of reach of the restraining hand of the natural enemies that kept down its numbers in its native land, an invading plant or animal is able to become enormously abundant. Thus it is no accident that our most troublesome insects are introduced species.

These invasions, both the naturally occurring and those dependent on human assistance, are likely to continue indefinitely. Quarantine and massive chemical campaigns are only extremely expensive ways of buying time. We are faced, according to Dr. Elton, "with a life-and-death need not just to find new technological means of suppressing this plant or that animal"; instead we need the basic knowledge of animal populations and their relations to their surroundings that will "promote an even balance and damp down the explosive power of outbreaks and new invasions."

Much of the necessary knowledge is now available but we do not use it. We train ecologists in our universities and even employ them in our governmental agencies but we seldom take their advice. We allow the chemical death rain to fall as though there were no alternative, whereas in fact there are many, and our ingenuity could soon discover many more if given opportunity.

Have we fallen into a mesmerized state that makes us accept as inevitable that which is inferior or detrimental, as though having lost the will or the vision to demand that which is good? Such thinking, in the words of the ecologist Paul Shepard, "idealizes life with only its head out of water, inches above the limits of toleration of the corruption of its own environment . . . Why should we tolerate a diet of weak poisons, a home in insipid surroundings, a circle of acquaintances who are not quite our enemies, the noise of motors with just enough relief to prevent insanity? Who would want to live in a world which is just not quite fatal?"

Yet such a world is pressed upon us. The crusade to create a chemically sterile, insect-free world seems to have engendered a fanatic zeal on the part of many specialists and most of the so-called control agencies. On every hand there is evidence that those engaged in spraying operations exercise a ruthless power. "The regulatory entomologists . . . function as prosecutor, judge and jury, tax assessor and collector and sheriff to enforce their own orders," said Connecticut entomologist Neely Turner. The most flagrant abuses go unchecked in both state and federal agencies.

It is not my contention that chemical insecticides must never be used. I do contend that we have put poisonous and biologically potent chemicals indiscriminately into the hands of persons largely or wholly ignorant of their potentials for harm. We have subjected enormous numbers of people to contact with these poisons, without their consent and often without their knowledge. If the Bill of Rights contains no guarantee that a citizen shall be secure against lethal poisons distributed either by private individuals or by public officials, it is surely only because our forefathers, despite their considerable wisdom and foresight, could conceive of no such problem.

I contend, furthermore, that we have allowed these chemicals to be used with little or no advance investigation of their effect on soil, water, wildlife, and man himself. Future generations are unlikely to condone our lack of prudent concern for the integrity of the natural world that supports all life.

There is still very limited awareness of the nature of the threat. This is an era of specialists, each of whom sees his own problem and is unaware of or intolerant of the larger frame into which it fits. It is also an era dominated by industry, in which the right to make a dollar at whatever cost is seldom challenged. When the public protests, confronted with some obvious evidence of damaging results of pesticide applications, it is fed little tranquilizing pills of half truth. We urgently need an end to these false assurances, to the sugar coating of unpalatable facts. It is the public that is being asked to assume the risks that the insect controllers calculate. The public must decide whether it wishes to continue on the present road, and it can do so only when in full possession of the facts. In the words of Jean Rostand, "The obligation to endure gives us the right to know."

Urban Nature and Human Design: Renewing the Great Tradition

Anne Whiston Spirn
Professor of Landscape Architecture, University of Pennsylvania

This article calls attention to the importance of nature in city design. Anne Whiston Spirn asserts that most planners and designers have viewed natural forces as apart from, rather than as an integral part of, the city. Thus, with few exceptions, cities have failed to use the full potential of nature in creating healthy, economical, and beautiful urban environments. Spirn states that "existing knowledge about urban nature would be sufficient to produce profound changes in the form of the city, if only it were applied" (p. 485).

"Once we can accept that the city is as natural as the farm and as susceptible of conservation and improvement, we work free of those false dichotomies of city and country, artificial and natural, man versus other living things."

Kevin Lynch (1981)

INTRODUCTION

Nature pervades the city, forging bonds between the city and the air, earth, water, and life within and around it. Urban nature consists of air, the materials suspended within it, and the light and heat transmitted through it. It is the landforms upon which the city rests and the minerals embedded in the earth beneath it; the water in rivers and reservoirs, pipes and soil; and the organisms that live within the urban habitat. But urban nature is more than a collection of individual features like wind, hills, rivers, and trees. It is the consequence of a complex interaction between the multiple purposes and activities of human beings and the natural processes that govern the movement of air, the erosion of the earth, the hydrologic cycle, and the birth and death of living organisms.

The city is part of nature. Recognition of that basic fact has powerful implications for how the city is designed, built, and maintained, and for the health, safety, and welfare of every resident. For the past century, however, consideration of nature has been viewed as pertinent mainly to the design of parks and new suburbs. But cultivation of nature is as relevant to planning transportation and sewage systems as it is to planning open space; as applicable to downtown reconstruction as to land development at the city's edge; as germane to comprehensive planning as to project design. There is an historic tradition for such a field, a foundation of knowledge to support it, and projects that illustrate the beneficial application of that knowledge. This paper represents an initial effort to elucidate this tradition and is part of a larger project to trace its roots and sketch a theoretical framework.

In themselves, the forces of nature are neither benign nor hostile. Acknowledged and harnessed, they represent a powerful resource for shaping a hospitable urban habitat. Ignored or subverted, they magnify problems that have plagued cities for centuries: poisoned air and water; more frequent or more destructive natural hazards; depleted or inaccessible resources; increased energy demands and high construction and maintenance costs; and now, in many cities across the globe, a boring sameness.

Unfortunately, especially in this century, planners and designers have mostly neglected and rarely exploited natural forces within cities. The belief that the city is apart from, and even antithetical to, nature has dominated the way in which the city is perceived and continues to affect how it is built. Issues such as energy conservation, waste disposal, flood control, and water supply are treated as isolated problems, rather than as related phenomena arising from common human activities, exacerbated by a disregard for the processes of nature. Urban environmental planning has most often been a reaction to these specific problems, rather than a considered proposal for managing the relationships among them, or for seizing opportunities to solve several problems with a single solution. Solutions to narrowly defined problems are costly and inefficient and frequently precipitate other, unanticipated problems. The focus on specific problems in isolation from their broader context has characterized the environmental planning literature (Galloway and Huelster 1971) and has dominated the curriculum (Deknatal 1984). This fragmented approach undermines the exploration of potential multi-purpose solutions.

More is known about urban nature today than ever before. Over the past three decades, natural scientists have amassed an impressive body of knowledge about nature in the city. Yet little of this information has been applied directly to molding the form of the city—the shape of its buildings and parks, the course of its roads, and the pattern of the whole. A small fraction of that knowledge has been employed in establishing regulations to improve environmental quality; but these have commonly been perceived as restrictive and punitive, rather than as posing opportunities for new urban forms. Regulations and their enforcement have also proven vulnerable to shifts in public policy, at the mercy of the political concerns of the moment, whereas the physical form of the city endures through generation after generation of politicians. Regulations controlling the emission of air pollutants may be altered or unenforced, for example, but urban form designed to disperse those pollutants will continue to do so regardless of changes in policy.

A few cities, however, have exploited nature ingeniously to shape an urban habitat that is safe, healthy, economical to build and maintain, beautiful, and memorable. Although such cities are not common today, they are part of an abiding tradition in city design. An overview of that tradition is outlined here, along with an assessment of existing knowledge and prospects for city design.

NATURE, HUMAN PURPOSE, AND CITY DESIGN: THE TRADITION[1]

For centuries city designers have exploited nature to promote human purposes. The roots of this tradition are as diverse as the many ways in which nature contributes to environmental quality. For example, concern for health motivated Hippocrates' observations on "airs, waters, and places" in the 5th century B.C., John Evelyn's proposals for dissipating "the Inconvenience of the Aer and Smoke of London" in the 17th century, and the sanitary reform movement in the 19th century. The desire to protect the city from hazards, both human and natural, provoked Aristotle's advice for exploiting defensible topography and securing a reliable water supply, and underlies the current interest in hazard planning. Authors through the ages have described the delights of urban groves and gardens, and contemporary social scientists have attempted to measure the pleasure that urban residents derive from plants and parks.

Nature has not meant the same thing to all people in all ages. Yet similar questions have been posed repeatedly: Does nature influence human development, or is man the sole architect of the environment in which he lives? Should man seek to coexist with nature or to dominate nature? Does man exist within nature or apart from it? Answers to these questions have profound consequences for how cities are perceived, designed, and built. To the ancient Greeks, for example, air, water, and fire were powerful elements that could determine the development and character of human cultures. The form of Greek cities was often adapted to the climate, topography, and natural hazards of their locale.

In contrast is the modern view of man as dominant and nature as fragile. This concept has spawned varied reactions; two views—the arcadian and the imperialist—represent the extremes.[2] The arcadians would protect nature, whose "harmony" they perceive as threatened by human actions.[3] The imperialists, on the other hand, would consolidate man's dominion over nature "to multiply and subdue the earth." To both arcadians and imperialists, the city has obliterated nature. Neither attitude has served the city well. Those city designers of the past century who have made important contributions to the field of urban nature and human design—Olmsted, Geddes, Mumford, McHarg, and Lynch, among them—have trod a middle ground between the arcadians and the imperialists. In so doing, they have sought to forge a consonance between natural processes and human purpose.

More than two thousand years ago, Hippocrates described the effects of "airs, waters, and places" upon human society, including the health of both individuals and the community at large. He contrasted the ill health plaguing cities that occupy damp, marshy ground or windy slopes with the benefits enjoyed by cities located to exploit sun and breezes (Hippocrates, ca. 5th century B.C.).[4] Subsequent writers suggested how cities might be sited and designed to avoid such problems.

The Roman architect Vitruvius, for example, specified how the layout of streets and the orientation and arrangement of buildings should respond to seasonal patterns of sun and wind (Vitruvius, ca. 1st century B.C.).

In the 15th century, the Italian architect Alberti distilled the knowledge of ancient Greeks and Romans on the subject and added observations of his own. Alberti advocated that the siting of cities and the design of streets, squares, and buildings within them should be adapted to the character of their environment so that cities might promote health, safety, convenience, dignity, and pleasure (Alberti 1485). To Alberti, the forces of nature were powerful and deserved respect:

> We ought never to undertake any Thing that is not exactly agreeable to Nature . . . for Nature, if you force or wrest her out of her Way, whatever Strength you may do it with, will yet in the End overcome and break thro' all Opposition and Hindrance; and the most obstinate Violence . . . will at last be forced to yield to her daily and continual Perseverence assisted by Length of Time. (Alberti 1485)

Alberti underscored this warning by cataloguing the disasters incurred by cities that had disregarded the power of nature. He also discussed landscape management techniques, including drainage, embankment, and channel improvements and forest plantation. Alberti was one of the last architects to take such a broad view. In later centuries, this tradition was continued mainly by landscape architects and engineers.[5]

When Francis Bacon stated that "nature is only to be commanded by obeying her," he represented an important change in attitude (Bacon 1624). Implicit in Bacon's statement is the conviction that nature can be understood, and through that understanding, cultivated and controlled for human benefit. John Evelyn's proposed plan to solve the air pollution of 17th century London evidenced a similar confidence. Evelyn based his plan on an understanding of the source of London's pollution and the climatic forces that acted to concentrate or disperse it. The plan is remarkable for its comprehensive scope. His recommendations, outlined in *Fumifugium: Or the Inconvenience of the Aer and Smoake of London Dissipated* (1661), included the prohibition of high-sulfur coal, the relocation of polluting land uses like tanneries from central London to outlying areas downwind of the city, and the plantation of entire blocks with trees and flowers to sweeten the air. Evelyn was also the author of *Sylva* (1664), a work on trees and their cultivation. Later, when Louden,[6] Paxton, and Olmsted applied their experience in landscape gardening and "scientific agriculture" to the environmental problems of the 19th century city, they followed Evelyn's precedent.

By the nineteenth century, rapid urban and industrial growth produced alarming changes in both city and countryside. Many observers perceived these changes as evidence that human impact on nature was out of control, especially in large, industrial cities. George Perkins Marsh summed up that mood of disquiet in 1864:

> Man is everywhere a disturbing agent. Wherever he plants his foot, the harmonies of nature are turned to discords . . . the earth is fast becoming an unfit home for its noblest inhabitant, and another era of equal human crime and human improvidence . . . would

reduce it to such a condition of impoverished productiveness, of shattered surface, of climatic excess, asto threaten the deprivation, barbarism, and perhaps even extinction of the species (Marsh 1864).

With the publication of *Man and Nature*, a book influential in its own time and since, Marsh became the "fountainhead of the conservation movement" (Mumford 1931). But Marsh did more than sound a warning. He proposed that man's economy be designed to work in concert with nature's: "in reclaiming and reoccupying lands laid waste by human improvidence or malice . . . the task . . . is to become a co-worker with nature in the reconstruction of the damaged fabric" (Marsh 1864).

This was an approach embraced by Marsh's contemporary, Frederick Law Olmsted. Olmsted designed parks, parkways, and residential neighborhoods as part of a broader program to promote the health and welfare of urban citizens by improving the quality of their environment. To achieve these ends, he often harnessed nature's processes in "reclaiming lands laid waste by human improvidence." For example, Olmsted's design for Boston's Back Bay transformed "the filthiest marsh and mud flats to be found anywhere in Massachusetts . . . a body of water so foul that even clams and eels cannot live in it"[7] into a constructed salt marsh—an attractive landscape that accepted the daily and seasonal flux of tides and floods. Olmsted argued that the employment of a "natural" water body, rather than a masonry flood storage basin, would be more effective and attractive; an amenity rather than an eyesore. His primary objective here was to improve water quality and prevent floods; enhancement of adjacent land values and provision for recreation and transportation were important, but secondary, objectives.[8] Despite the scope of Olmsted's vision, however, he still perceived the city itself as artificial, and the urban park and parkway as oases of nature in an otherwise bleak environment.

Olmsted and the sanitary engineers with whom he collaborated were part of a movement for preventative sanitation provoked by environmental health problems.[9] This sanitary reform movement had a fundamental influence on the shape of American cities, and city design was essential to their programs:

A city, most sanitarians would have agreed, should be arranged as an airy, verdant setting, free from the excessive crowding and physical congestion then common in major urban centers. Its site should be dry and readily drained of storm water. Parks and trees should be abundant enough to refresh the air. There should be ample opportunities for outdoor exercise. A pure water supply should be available as well as a water-carriage sewer system. Nuisance trades, such as slaughter-houses, should not operate within built-up districts. Sunless, ill-ventilated tenements, dark, moist, cellar dwellings, and backyard privies and cesspools should be avoided (Peterson 1979).

The introduction of public water and sewer systems and projects such as The Fens and The Riverway in Boston produced dramatic improvement in urban public health by the end of the century. During the four decades of practice, Olmsted forged new functions for urban open space that embraced concerns for health and safety, as well as beautification. Today, a century later, many prized urban amenities are the result of those efforts. Yet their broad, original purpose and the ways in which nature was exploited in their design are often forgotten. Within the field of urban nature and human design, modern practitioners have rarely advanced the impressive accomplishments of landscape architects like Olmsted and their colleagues in engineering who, together, founded the American city planning movement at the turn of the century.[10]

Soon after the turn of the century, most city designers who wished to integrate nature and city turned to new towns and suburbs; only a few remained dedicated to the reconstruction of existing city centers. Two British planners, Ebenezer Howard and Patrick Geddes, represent these divergent approaches. Ebenezer Howard rejected the old city and proposed new "garden cities," where the advantages of town and country might be combined; where industry and commerce could be integrated with homes, gardens, and farms (Howard 1902). The garden city and the new towns and "greenbelt" suburbs it inspired had as their goal the integration of nature and human settlement; but most merely incorporated the trappings of nature, like trees, lawns, and lakes, and were built with as little regard for the processes of nature as were the old cities. With few exceptions, they have utilized the same techniques of land development and building. As they have grown older and as urbanization has spread around them, they have come to exhibit many of the same environmental problems as older cities.

Patrick Geddes argued for the realization of the ideal city latent in every town. "Here or nowhere is our utopia," was his response to proponents of the new garden city movement (Geddes 1915). From his perspective as a biologist and geographer, Geddes viewed the city and its surrounding countryside as an organic whole. He advocated that city design be based upon an understanding of the natural and social history of each city and region and the needs of its current residents. To attain such an understanding, Geddes undertook "regional surveys" and displayed the results in exhibits and reports. These formed the basis for proposals that were "consistent with the unique individuality of the particular city" (Goist 1974). Geddes' regional approach has had an enduring influence upon city design through the work of Lewis Mumford.

Mumford, like his mentor Geddes, advocates that solutions to the problems facing both city and countryside depend upon perceiving both as part of a region: "Once a more organic understanding is achieved of the complex interrelations of the city and its region, the urban and the rural aspects of environment, the small-scale unit and the large-scale unit, a new sense of form will spread through both architecture and city design" (Mumford 1968). To Mumford this new urban form "must include the form-shaping contributions of nature, of river, bay, hill, forest, vegetation, climate, as well as those of human history and culture, with the complex interplay of groups, corporations, organizations, institutions, personalities" (1968). Yet Mumford's attitude to the central city is problematic. Although he speaks of integrating nature and city and the need not to "widen the retreat from the city, but to return to the original core, with a new method of containing and distributing its great numbers" (1961), nevertheless much of his work has been in support of the new town movement.

Mumford's recommendations for integrating urban nature and human purpose to produce a new city form remain very general. The importance of his contribution lies not in specific prescriptions, but in his analysis of the shortcomings of city design as it has been practiced in this century—shortcomings that include the neglect of nature. Mumford has also influenced important theorists and practitioners, among them Ian McHarg and Kevin Lynch. McHarg and Lynch share the conviction that the city must be viewed in its regional context and that urban form is an expression of the natural and cultural history of a region. To both, nature has a social value to be cultivated and incorporated into city design. From that common ground, they diverge.

An emphasis on natural processes is central to McHarg's approach: "Let us accept the proposition that nature is process, that it is interacting, that it responds to laws, representing values and opportunities for human use with certain limitations and even prohibitions" (McHarg 1968). McHarg's emphasis upon processes rather than upon features like floodplains or fault lines yields a holistic appreciation for nature and fosters designs that transcend narrow temporal and spatial limits.[11] McHarg employs a checklist of natural factors—to be addressed regardless of location, scale, or land use—which is comprehensive and ordinal: climate, geology, hydrology, soils, vegetation, and wildlife. Like Mumford, McHarg's attitude to the city is ambivalent; his greatest success has been with designs for newly urbanizing areas. His general approach, however, is equally relevant to the inner city. Balanced with other concerns, the social, economic, and aesthetic implications of nature are as important in the center of the city as they are at its edge.

Lynch's *A Theory of Good City Form* (1981) is a clearly expounded statement of what constitutes environmental quality in cities and how urban form can promote or undermine that quality. This framework incorporates all the varied ways that nature contributes to environmental quality, as well as the contribution of other social and economic factors. Good city form, as defined by Lynch, can be judged by how well it sustains life ("vitality"), by how clearly it is perceived in space and time ("sense"), how well environment and behavior "fit," and by whether these elements are provided in a manner that provides "access," "control," "efficiency," and "justice." The profound significance of urban nature for city design and the quality of human life is evident when viewed through this lens.

Lynch, in particular, stressed the importance of how people perceive the city and explored the role that nature plays in enhancing the identity, legibility, coherence, and immediacy of urban form. City form that exploits distinctive natural features enhances and intensifies a city's sense of place. City form that respects and reflects natural features and the social values they acquire has a coherent and legible structure, one that embodies shared values. City form that increases the visibility of natural processes (the passing of the seasons, the movement of water, the birth and death of living organisms), creates an environment that has both a sense of immediacy and of evolution over time. "The mental sense of connection with nature is a basic human satisfaction, the most profound aspect of sensibility. . . . The movements of sun and tides, the cycles of weeds and insects and men, can also be celebrated along the city pavements" (Lynch 1981).

Although Lynch's dimensions of environmental quality integrate the value of nature with other social and economic concerns, they fragment natural features and systems into categories that relate more to human needs than to the modes in which nature operates.[12] Exclusive reliance on such a framework obscures potential connections among features and activities and militates against city design that serves multiple environmental functions. The results of such an approach are already evident in the planning profession's focus on special areas like energy conservation and hazard planning to the exclusion of other related issues.[13]

If urban nature is to be wholly integrated into city design and its value fully realized, a new framework is needed: one that recognizes both the integrity and interconnectedness of the natural world and the importance of all human concerns, one that relates to all elements of urban form at all scales. Scientific knowledge exists to inform such a framework, and there are models that demonstrate the benefits such an approach would yield.

NATURE AND THE CITY: AN OVERVIEW OF THE LITERATURE

Cities do not obliterate nature, they transform it, producing a characteristically urban natural environment. All cities, by virtue of density of people and buildings and the combustion of fuel, the excavation and filling of land, the pavement of ground surface, importation of water and disposal of wastes, and the introduction of new plant and animal communities, alter the character of their original environments in similar ways. These interactions between human activities and the natural environment produce an ecosystem very different from the one that existed prior to the city. It is a system sustained by massive importation of energy and materials, a system in which human cultural processes have created a place quite different from undisturbed nature, yet united to it through the common flow of natural processes. These changes are generated not only by human activities, but also by the form of the urban fabric in which they take place. Changes in the form of the city can therefore modify many of the attributes of urban nature.

A growing literature has traced the interactions between natural processes, human purpose, and urban form. Fueled by the environmental movement and the energy crises of the 1970s, this literature on urban nature has matured in the past two decades. While the bulk of the literature deals with the description and measurement of specific natural phenomena, there is a body of work that applies that knowledge to city design. Although the literature within individual scientific disciplines is rich, cross-disciplinary studies and investigations by city designers are comparatively rare. The following paragraphs provide a brief overview of the applied literature.[14] This overview is organized by the various compartments of the physical and biological environment—air, land, water, life, and ecosystems—since this framework most closely reflects the disciplines concerned with urban nature, the natural processes involved, and the interrelationships among issues.

Urban Air

There are excellent reviews of the scientific literature on climate and air quality, including its implications for city design (Chandler 1976; Landsberg 1981), and of more specialized subjects such as air quality and urban form (Rydell and Schwartz 1968; Spirn and Batchelor 1985). These and other studies demonstrate how urban form can promote or undermine air quality, comfort, and energy conservation through its influence on air circulation and the urban heat island. Intense pedestrian-level winds, pockets of stagnant air where pollutants concentrate, and ventilating breezes, for example, can all be initiated, eliminated, or ameliorated by altering urban form. These phenomena have been observed and compared in wind tunnel tests of single buildings and building complexes, (Gandemer and Guyot 1976; Durgin and Chock 1982), of street canyons (Cermak 1975; Wedding et al. 1977), and even of entire downtown areas (Spirn 1984a; and Spirn 1984b). It is also possible to moderate or intensify the urban heat island effect at the microscale (Landsberg 1968; Hutchinson et al. 1982) and at neighborhood and city-wide scales (Landsberg 1981).

Urban Land

There are comprehensive texts on urban geology and city design (Legget 1973; Leveson 1980) and on specific problem areas like geological hazards (Bolt et al. 1975; Schuster and Krizek 1978). The U.S. government has published many case studies that demonstrate the application of geological information to city planning (Nichols and Campbell 1969; Robinson and Spieker 1978). To date, however, attention has been focused mainly on the prevention of geological hazards and the reduction of losses incurred from them. Other important issues have received less attention: how to rebuild cities following a future disaster, for example, or how to design cities that conserve and exploit mineral resources. The absence of a plan for reconstruction after a disaster has resulted, time and time again, in the repetition of past mistakes despite widespread public support for "doing it right" (Bolt et al. 1975). Existing projects demonstrate the advantages of sequential use of mineral deposits, including coordination of extraction with site preparation for anticipated future land uses (Bates 1978; Stauffer 1978).

Urban soil is an important mineral and biological resource that has received little attention. The first urban soil survey in the United States was published in 1976, and there have been few since (U.S. Soil Conservation Service 1976). A small, but growing literature documents the characteristics of urban soils and how they might be managed to support the city's landscape and help assimilate the city's wastes (Patterson 1975; Craul 1982).

Urban Water

Water is by far the city's largest import and export (Wolman 1965); in coming years the management of water resources will pose the city's greatest challenge.

There are excellent sources on urban storm drainage and flood control (Dunne and Leopold 1978; Sheaffer et al. 1982; Whipple et al. 1983) and reviews of conventional and innovative sewage and water treatment methods (Barnes et al. 1981; Bastian 1981). There are projects that demonstrate the aesthetic and economic benefits of using naturally-occurring or constructed wetlands, ponds, and flood plains to prevent floods, treat waste water, protect water quality, and manage water supply resources (Poertner 1973; Wright and Taggart 1976; Notardonato and Doyle 1979; Bastian and Benforado 1983). To date, however, there is no text that incorporates storm drainage and flood control, water supply, water quality, and wastewater treatment as they relate to city design. Given the importance of water for the city and the close interrelationships among these issues, this gap in the literature is a serious one.

Urban Life

There is no single source that adequately surveys the city's many plant communities and the functions they serve. Plants, especially trees, can transform the appearance of a city, but the benefits they provide extend far beyond beautification. At the local scale, vegetation modifies microclimate (Hutchinson et al. 1982), captures particulate air pollutants (Smith and Staskawicz 1977), prevents erosion, and provides wildlife habitat (Gill and Bonnett 1973). At the city-wide scale, the cumulative effect of trees can moderate the intensity and extent of the urban heat island and can mitigate pedestrian-level wind problems (Spirn 1984b). Urban forests can be designed and managed for timber production as well as for aesthetics and recreation (Osband 1984); wetland and floodplain plant communities can be managed to improve the quality of surface waters, conserve groundwater resources, and prevent flooding (Spirn 1984a). Urban vegetation can even affect the psychological health of city residents (Lewis 1979; Francis et al. 1984) and their attitudes to the environment in which they live (Rapoport 1977).

There is a small body of literature on urban wildlife and habitats, including an overview of the field (Gill and Bonnett 1973) and reviews of specific issues, such as pest control and habitat management to attract amenity wildlife (Leedy et al. 1978). Few cities would consider the creation of wildlife habitat as a primary objective. If habitat requirements are considered when planning for other functions, however, amenity wildlife can be increased within the city and many pest problems averted. There are guidelines for such habitat design, both local and regional (Goldstein et al. 1980/81; Godron and Forman 1985).

Urban Ecosystems

Literature on urban ecosystems is scanty, but promising. The potential contribution of ecologists to urban planning and the identification of future research needs has been summarized (Holling and Orians 1971; Cooper and Vlasen 1973).

Environmental models, especially in relation to air and water quality, have evolved significantly in the past two decades, and "ecological" approaches to resource and waste management have been explored (Morris 1982; Spirn 1984a). Recent developments in landscape ecology (Godron and Forman 1985; and Forman 1981) yield new insights into spatial patterns in the urban ecosystem.

However imperfect current models are, the view of the city as an ecosystem, composed of many smaller ecosystems, is a useful strategy for city designers. Natural processes link the air, land, and water of the city and the organisms that live within it. The pathways along which energy and materials flow through the urban ecosystem are also the routes along which pollutants disseminate and where energy is stored and expended. Such an approach is as relevant to the design of a building or park as it is to the planning of a neighborhood or region. It permits a more comprehensive assessment of the costs and benefits of alternate actions than is otherwise possible.

Existing knowledge about urban nature would be sufficient to produce profound changes in the form of the city, if only it were applied. Several barriers to applying that knowledge lie within the literature itself: the fact that much material is sequestered in specialized scientific journals, conference proceedings, and technical reports; the bewildering profusion of information, often unintelligible to the lay person and sometimes contradictory; and the relative scarcity of work that assesses and synthesizes existing knowledge. Most interdisciplinary works that attempt to be comprehensive consist of books by multiple authors. While such volumes have made an important contribution, they often lack consistency, treating some subjects in great detail while others are neglected (Detwyler and Marcus 1972; Laurie 1979).[15] Rarely do they make explicit recommendations for city design; and when they do, most treat environmental planning issues at the city-wide scale only. Fortunately, there are existing projects that demonstrate the benefits of this approach.

URBAN NATURE AND CITY DESIGN: THREE CASES[16]

An emphasis upon natural processes, rather than upon the individual features that arise from them, yields a framework for city design that is dynamic rather than static, that highlights the interrelation of issues, actions, and locations, and that facilitates the integration of work at local and regional scales. Multiple benefits may be gained when storm drainage, flood control, sewage treatment, and water supply are seen as related issues that require an integrated solution, as they were in Woodlands, Texas, described below. Long-term, economical solutions are possible when depleted energy and material resources, on the one hand, and waste disposal, resulting in contamination of air, earth, and water, on the other, are perceived as a single problem with several faces. Stuttgart, in the Federal Republic of Germany, has implemented an energy conservation, air quality, and waste disposal program that recognizes these connections.

Woodlands, Texas

Woodlands, a new town now being built on 20,000 acres of pine-oak forest north of Houston will eventually be a city of 150,000 people. Water emerged as a critical factor early in the planning process. Much of Woodlands is very flat, with poorly-drained soil. The construction of a conventional storm drainage system would have entailed extensive clearance of woods and loss of much of the remainder over the long run, due to a lowered water table. It would also have increased the severity and frequency of floods downstream. In addition, since Woodlands lies atop the recharge area for an aquifer that underlies Houston, a conventional storm drainage system would have decreased the water entering the aquifer and thus contributed to ground subsidence under Houston. (Houston has already subsided ten feet in some areas due to oil and water extraction.)

The proposed solution—a "natural" drainage system—comprises ponds, wooded floodplains, and well-drained soils instead of concrete ditches. In this system, the larger floodplain network drains runoff from major storms, while well-drained soils and ponds absorb and store the rainfall from lesser storms in parks, street rights-of-way, and private yards. When compared to the cost of a more traditional system, it was estimated that the natural drainage system would save the developer over $14 million. The retention of the beautiful, wooded setting and the acquisition of a town-wide open space system are additional benefits.

The natural drainage system has structured the design of the new town. Major roads and commercial development are sited on ridgelines and higher elevations, while floodplains and recharge soils are preserved in parks and public rights-of-way. Roads, golf courses, and parks impound stormwater over sandy soils to enhance its absorption. Use of the floodplain and well-drained soils as open space works well from both ecological and social standpoints. Much of the hydrologic system is wooded; it not only soaks up and carries off rainfall, but also assimilates urban runoff and treated wastewater. Where understory is left uncleared, the woods are self-regenerating, requiring no fertilization, no new planting, no pruning, and no raking. The floodplains harbor a spectacular plant community—including large evergreen magnolias, water and willow oaks, and towering pines and a diverse, abundant native wildlife, including white-tailed deer, opossum, armadillo, and many birds—making the whole town a vast nature reserve. A continuous system of hiking, bicycle, and bridle paths runs within the drainage network, linking all parts of the town.

The quantity and quality of stormwater flowing out of the new town has been monitored since before construction began over a decade ago. Increased runoff is only one third the amount generated by a typical suburban development in Houston, and the quality of that runoff is substantially better. In April 1979, a record storm hit Houston. Nine inches of rain fell within five hours, and no house within Woodlands flooded, though adjacent subdivisions were awash (Juneja and Veltman 1979).

The plan for Woodlands thus does more than protect the health and safety of its residents. Well fitted to the hydrologic system that existed prior to its construction, it has a built-in resilience to flood or drought. The town's overall structure is coherent and meaningful; it reflects and reinforces the landforms, waterbodies, and plant communities within it and makes visible the movement of water through it. Since the drainage system must be linked, open space is accessible to every home and business. It is an efficient system, not only in its ability to drain and store stormwater, but also in its conservation of water resources, its assimilation of wastes, and its provision of low maintenance parkland that costs far less to maintain than the conventional suburban landscape of lawns and trees.

Denver

A drainage system like Woodlands' is most easily implemented in a new town, but it is practicable even in the dense cores of existing cities. For example, Denver has also implemented storm drainage and flood control plans that are based upon the hydrologic cycle. These plans tie regional flood planning to the design of specific drainage projects and reconcile the need to drain local streets and plazas with the need to protect downstream areas from increased floods. Denver's Urban Drainage and Flood Control District, formed in 1969, coordinates the adoption and implementation of adequate and consistent floodplain regulations among local governments and undertakes master plans for individual watersheds that straddle municipal boundaries.

Rooftops, plazas, and parking lots in downtown Denver are now as much a part of these regional flood control plans as suburban creeks and the urban floodplain. The city requires new and renovated buildings in the Skyline Urban Renewal District to detain stormwater on site. The alternative, upgrading the existing storm sewer system to accommodate increased runoff, would have been an expensive burden for the city and would have increased flooding in the nearby South Platte River (Poertner 1973). The principle applied here is the same as that employed at Woodlands; developers in Denver have used rooftops, plazas, and parking lots to detain stormwater instead of ponds and soil. These fulfill their function with minimal inconvenience to pedestrians and drain gradually after a rainstorm peaks.

The riverbed, banks, and floodplain of the South Platte River have been redesigned and reshaped, not only to contain floodwaters, but also to permit their overflow into designated areas (Wright and Taggart 1976). The design of riverside amphitheatres, plazas, and sportsfields was based upon flood hydraulics, built to resist flood damage and provide flood storage. But the benefits have extended beyond public safety. The central channel of the river was dredged and refashioned not only to accommodate floodwaters, but also to create a white-water slalom run for boats. The Platte River Greenway, comprising 450 acres in eighteen parks and fifteen miles of riverside trails, is now Denver's largest park. With increased use of the river for walking, bicycling, and boating has come a heightened awareness of the river's water quality and a strong constituency for improving that quality. Many sources of water pollution have been removed from the riverbanks as a consequence: an old dump has been converted to a nature preserve; a highway maintenance yard piled with salt and sand became a park after those materials were moved to a less vulnerable spot. Citizens have brought pressure upon the city to cease dumping street sweepings and salt-laden snow in the river. Districts bordering the South Platte, among them several of Denver's lowest-income neighborhoods, have gained new parks and riverbanks free from former hazards and nuisances.

Stuttgart

Stuttgart, an industrial city of 630,000 in The Federal Republic of Germany, provides yet another model of city design that exploits natural processes. For the past several decades Stuttgart has attempted to improve air quality and reduce the energy required to heat and cool buildings. Stuttgart lies in a valley and is plagued by persistent inversions two days out of three, a situation that resulted in frequent, unhealthy concentrations of air pollutants before the current program was implemented.

Climatologists in Stuttgart have plotted the patterns of air circulation through and around the city and continue to survey air quality to pinpoint critical areas (Franke 1976; Robel et al. 1978). These studies identified the fresh, cool air that flows through the city down canyons and along the valley bottom on calm, clear nights as a resource which ventilates and cools the city. During frequent calm periods this hill-to-valley air movement provides the only ventilation in downtown Stuttgart. Land use within these fresh air channels is therefore regulated, and many are landscaped. Together, they form a radial open space system that extends from forests at the city's outskirts to parks and pedestrian streets in the downtown. As fresh air flows down into the valley, it is funneled into a linear park several miles long that runs through the heart of the city, bordered by institutions and businesses.

As a citywide system, these open spaces do more than promote air quality and a comfortable local climate. The forested park at the city's edge is managed for timber and for the protection of the city's water resources, including the recharge areas for its many mineral springs. The landscaped terraces and steps that tumble down the fresh air canyons create short-cuts with intermittent views of the city below. The large, downtown park is filled with sitting areas, playgrounds, flower gardens, and cafes.

Stuttgart has also decreased the emission of air pollutants through a program to reduce the energy required to heat and cool buildings. The summer heat load on downtown buildings has been reduced by converting parking lots from asphalt to turf block, and by introducing roof gardens and "wet roofs" with an inch or two of ponded water. In sections of the city where air circulation is poor, the burning of oil and coal is prohibited. Steam, produced by burning garbage in municipal incinerators, is now piped to heat individual homes and businesses in these areas; and the byproducts of cinders and ash are used in construction roadbeds.

Woodlands, Denver, and Stuttgart illustrate the benefits of applying an understanding of natural processes to city design. All three examples address the prevention of hazards, the conservation of resources, the disposal of wastes, and the protection of critical areas. But the result is more than the sum of the parts. In each case, concern for all these issues is synthesized in a single program that links city-wide planning to the design of local projects. Although the impetus for each lay in concern for a single overriding problem—water in Woodlands, floods in Denver, and air pollution in Stuttgart—in each case the solution incorporated other concerns besides the primary one.

Woodlands, Denver, and Stuttgart are not isolated examples, nor do they represent revolutionary ideas. The germ of Stuttgart lay in ancient Greek city planning, and the principles upon which Woodland's and Denver's drainage systems are based were applied a century earlier by Olmsted. In these examples and the historic tradition to which they belong lies an important direction for future city design.

URBAN NATURE AND CITY DESIGN: PROSPECTS

How to integrate the diverse elements of nature with one another and with other issues facing the city? How to synthesize all this into a coherent structure that provides equitable access to the city's resources and that remains responsive to changing human needs? How to accomplish this in the dense, inner city as well as in new towns and in expanding settlements at the edge of the metropolis?

Answers will vary from city to city depending upon the overriding problems of their natural and socio-economic environments, the institutional framework within which those problems must be addressed, and the legacy of the past, as embodied in the urban fabric and in cultural traditions. Each city should first focus on those problems that are of primary importance and then, in creating solutions to those problems, find ways to accommodate other concerns. Some cities, such as Denver, must contend with recurrent natural disasters; others, such as Stuttgart, are prone to serious, prolonged air pollution episodes. Some cities occupy ground that contains valuable mineral resources; others face growing problems of waste disposal that threaten their water supplies. Many American cities, however, share two major problems: the deterioration of urban infrastructure, including water supply and sewage treatment systems, and the decline of inner city neighborhoods. A comprehensive view of urban nature could contribute to the restoration of both.[17]

The introduction of public water supplies, storm and sanitary sewers, and public park and transportation systems in the 19th century transformed the shape of the American city. When these diverse public improvements were coordinated, they formed a coherent framework within which the growing city evolved. Many of the great urban parks and parkways built during that period, for instance, served not only to beautify the city and to provide recreation space, but also to eliminate environmental hazards and nuisances and facilitate transportation within the city. In many cities that infrastructure is now a century old and must soon be renovated or reconstructed.

In the past few decades there have also been dramatic changes in the demographics of inner cities, shifts often accompanied by a proliferation of abandoned buildings and land and a decline in public services. In some cities vacant land now comprises ten percent of the total land area, and some neighborhoods are more than half vacant. Together, the need for reinvestment in urban infrastructure and the resource of vacant lands represent an opportunity for harnessing nature to reshape the city and, in the process, to address many other urban problems as well.

Most cities, for example, face the prospect of increased water demand and floods, accompanied by depleted water supplies and continued water contamination. Vacant lands, many of which occur in low-lying parts of the urban landscape, afford an opportunity to explore alternative solutions to these problems that might not otherwise be feasible. These include the reduction of flooding and combined sewer overflows during and following rainstorms, the exploration of alternative wastewater treatment methods, the implementation of decentralized treatment systems, and the exploitation of the residual resources in waste that would otherwise pose a disposal problem.

The development of some vacant lands to accomplish such objectives could, if designed to do so, provide recreational and aesthetic amenities, promote investment in inner city neighborhoods, and yield new funding sources for maintaining public parkland. Stormwater detention areas have been landscaped and managed as parks. Woodlands, meadows, and constructed wetlands have been used for treating wastewater, with portions also used as parkland and wildlife habitats (Bastian and Benforado 1983; Spirn 1984a). Sewage sludge poses a major disposal problem for most cities; yet sludge is extremely high in nutrients and forms an ideal soil amendment. Large-scale reclamation of urban vacant lands, whether for housing, for commerce, or for open space, will require enormous quantities of soil. Sewage sludge composted with woodchips is relatively inexpensive and has been used for such purposes in Washington, D.C., and Philadelphia (Patterson 1975; Marrazzo 1981).

The opportunities afforded by vacant land are not limited to issues of water management. In Dayton, Ohio, for example, open land (currently parking lots) surrounding the central business district has been linked to wind problems at the base of tall downtown buildings. Wind tunnel studies have suggested that these wind problems could be mitigated by adding trees or buildings to open lands upwind (Spirn 1984a).

Vacant lands are extraordinarily diverse in their physical character and social context as well as in the constellations that they form collectively. Perceived as part of the city's greater land and open space resource, and viewed together with the social and economic needs of the neighborhoods in which they occur, vacant lands represent an opportunity to integrate nature and city in new ways. In the process they can transform the city and the way people live within it.

The integration of nature and city design is now possible on a scale that was previously unimaginable. Modern science has given us a view of the natural world in which the human organism has an important but not omnipotent role and ecology has yielded a systems framework that elucidates the interactions between humans and their habitats. Information technology provides a tool for storing and correlating a complex array of data in a manner that would have been impossible even a few decades ago. If we are to realize the potential of these advances for city design, however, a means must be found to bring together those from many disciplines now working on urban nature and its implications for city design, to assemble and assess the knowledge they produce, and to stimulate the construction of projects that incorporate that information.[18]

Neither the arcadian nor the imperialist view of nature will serve to advance this field, but rather the middle ground that aspires to a beneficial meshing of the cultural processes of society and the physical and biological processes of the natural world. Such an approach could yield a new form for the city, one that would "have the biological advantages of the suburb, the social advantages of the city, and new aesthetic delights that will do justice to both modes" (Mumford 1961).

NOTES

1 This article focuses on the role of nature in city design in Europe and North America, primarily in the United States and Great Britain. There are important traditions in other parts of the world, especially in East Asia, but their inclusion here is outside the scope of this initial article. The figures discussed here are only a few of those who have applied an understanding of nature to city design; many others have also made important contributions.

2 The terms "arcadian" and "imperialist" are used by Donald Worster in *Nature's Economy: The Roots of Ecology (1977).* Worster demonstrates that both attitudes have been influential in ecological thought since the 18th century. The management and conservation of nature for human benefit represents a middle ground between these two poles. The distinction between preservation and conservation has split American environmentalists ever since 1897, when John Muir and Gifford Pinchot clashed bitterly over the management of Yosemite Valley. This split has permitted imperialist view to prevail.

3 Implicit in the arcadian view is a romanticization of nature and a nostalgia for a simpler, pastoral life. This nostalgia, however, may be for a way of life that never existed, or one that has been enjoyed only by a privileged few. See Raymond Williams, *The Country and the City* (New York: Oxford University Press, 1973), and Leo Marx, *The Machine in the Garden* (New York: Oxford University Press, 1964), for a discussion of the pastoral image in literature and society.

4 The writings attributed to Hippocrates were probably not written by a single individual, but they do provide a summary of medical thought in the late 5th century, B.C. See Clarence J. Glacken, *Traces on the Rhodian Shore* (Berkeley: University of California Press, 1967).

5 Most architects since Alberti have been concerned exclusively with the aesthetic or sociological aspects of city design and have shown little interest in nature, except for its decorative qualities. There is, however, a long-standing tradition that has addressed the relationship between architecture and climate, particularly sun and wind (Unwin 1911; Atkinson 1912; Rey 1915; Aronin 1953; Olgyay 1963; Knowles 1981).

6 See J.C. Loudon (1829) "Hints for Breathing Places . . ." *Gardener's Magazine* V:686–90 and M. Simo (1981) "John C. Loudon's London: On Planning and Design for the Garden Metropolis." *Garden History* 9: 184–201. Loudon presented a plan for greater London, including green "belts" and "wedges" in 1829.

7 E.W. Howe. (1881). "The Back Bay Park, Boston." Speech read before the Boston Society of Civil Engineers in March 1881. Washington, D.C.: Library of Congress, Olmsted Papers.

8 This was the first time, to this author's knowledge, that anyone had deliberately created a salt marsh (as opposed to a lake or pond) for such a purpose. Olmsted discussed both his rationale and the difficulties he encountered in a speech to the Boston Society of Architects on April 2, 1886. See Olmsted Papers, Washington, D.C.: Library of Congress.

9 Olmsted had studied civil engineering himself and was a close friend of George E. Waring, Jr., a pioneering sanitary engineer. His frequent collaboration with Waring and other sanitary engineers produced innovative designs for drainage and transportation systems in parks, parkways, and entire cities. See Schultz and McShane 1978.

10 The National Conference on City Planning, inaugurated in 1909, created the American City Planning Institute in 1917 "to study the science and advance the art of city planning." All 75 members of the ACPI were originally trained in other fields; most presidents through 1942, as well as more than half the original members, were trained as landscape architects or engineers. See John L. Hancock, "Planners in the Changing American City, 1900–1940," *AIP Journal* 33:290–304.

11 See, for example, his work on Woodlands New Community (described in this article) in which the water supply, flooding, and subsidence of Houston, over twenty miles away, were seen as related to the new town project and a solution proposed that addressed both local and regional problems. The author served as project director on two phases of this project.

12 Lynch himself does not make an explicit connection between nature and his dimensions of environmental quality, except as represented by individual natural factors. McHarg, in his own professional work and that of his associates, has increasingly incorporated social and economic concerns but in a different manner than Lynch. Narendra Juneja, a partner of McHarg's, was explicit in the assignment of social values to natural processes, distinguishing between their value to society as a whole, to specific interest groups, and to individuals. See, for example, *Medford: Performance Requirements for the Maintenance of Social Values Represented by the Natural Environment of Medford Township, New Jersey* (Philadelphia: Center for Ecological Research in Planning and Design, University of Pennsylvania, 1974) and *Environmental Resources of the Toronto Central Waterfront* (Philadelphia: Wallace McHarg Roberts and Todd, 1976). Many of the social values defined by Juneja in these reports are comparable to those utilized by Lynch, and the emphasis on performance requirements rather than environmental determinants represents a shift from McHarg's earlier writings.

13 Specialization may be desirable and even necessary, but when planning students' sole exposure to environmental factors consists of a single specialized course in water resources, energy conservation, or waste management, those students may never gain an appreciation for the urban natural environment as a whole. See Charles Y. Deknatal, "Choices of Orientation in Teaching Environmental Planning," *Journal of Planning Education and Research* 1984 (3):118–125, for a review of environmental planning curriculum. Such an approach may also lead to artificial distinctions between subject areas, obscuring the connections between them. The conservation of energy and mineral resources and environmental pollution, for example, are closely related problems which demand integrated solutions.

14 Space does not permit a comprehensive review of this literature and the promise it holds for city design. A more extensive review and bibliography is provided by the author in *The Granite Garden: Urban Nature and Human Design* (New York: Basic Books, 1984).

15 Recently the profession of forestry has provided a forum for researchers and practitioners with an interest in urban nature (U.S. Forest Service 1977; Hopkins 1980), and has coined the term "urban forestry" to describe the field. Although "urban forestry" aptly captures the applied nature of the field, nevertheless, it reflects neither its breadth nor its applicability to non-forest biomes.

16 The case studies of Woodlands, Denver, and Stuttgart, as well as the introduction to this article have been adapted from my book, *The Granite Garden: Urban Nature and Human Design* (Basic Books, 1984). Copyright © by Anne Whiston Spirn.

17 The author has explored this subject in greater detail, using the example of Boston, in "Reclaiming Common Ground: The Future Shape of Boston," a paper sponsored by the American Institute of Architects and McGraw-Hill Publications, delivered to the Boston Society of Architects on April 30, 1985.

18 The author is currently concluding a study of the open space potential of vacant urban lands, funded by a grant from the National Endowment for the Arts. This study defines potential open space uses broadly, including not only recreation, but also functions related to agriculture, forestry, air quality and climate, the conservation of mineral and water resources, flood control, and storm drainage, among others. The objective of the study is to enable city planners and neighborhood groups alike to evaluate the open space potential of vacant land and to weigh the benefits of open space uses with other uses, such as housing.

REFERENCES

Alberti, L.B. 1485. In *Ten Books on Architecture*, ed., J. Rykwert. New York: Transatlantic Arts, 1966.

Aristotle. 1959. *Politics and Poetics.* Translated by B. Jowett and T. Twining. New York: Viking Press.

Aronin, J.E. 1953. *Climate and Architecture.* New York: Reinhold.

Atkinson, W. 1912. *The Orientation of Buildings, or Planning for Sunlight.* New York: Wiley.

Bacon, F. *New Atlantis.* 1624. In *The Complete Essays of Francis Bacon.* New York: Washington Square Press, 1963.

Barnes, D.; Bliss, P.J.; Gould, B.W.; and Vallentine, H.R. 1981. *Water and Wastewater Engineering Systems.* Bath: Pitman.

Bastian, R.K. 1981. *Natural Systems in Wastewater Treatment and Sludge Management: An Overview.* Washington, D.C.: U.S. Environmental Protection Agency.

——— and Benforado, J. 1983. Waste Treatment: Doing What Comes Naturally. *Technology Review.* Feb./Mar., 59–69.

Bates, R.L. 1978. Mineral Resources for a New Town. In *Geology in the Urban Environment*, eds., R.O. Urgard, G.D. McKenzie, and D. Foley. Minneapolis: Burgess.

Bolt, B.A.; Horn, W.L.; MacDonald, G.A.; and Scott, R.F. 1975. *Geological Hazards.* New York: Springer-Verlag.

Cermak, J.E. 1975. Applications of Fluid Mechanics to Wind Engineering—A Freeman Scholar Lecture. *Journal of Fluids Engineering.* 97:9–38.

Chandler, T.J. 1976. *Urban Climatology and its Relevance to Urban Design.* Technical Note 149. Geneva: World Meteorological Organization.

Cooper, W.E. and Vlasen, R.D. 1973. Ecological Concepts and Applications to Planning.

In *Environment: A New Focus for Land-Use Planning*, ed., D.M. McAllister. Washington, D.C.: National Science Foundation.

Craul, P.J., ed. 1982. *Urban Forest Soils: A Reference Workbook.* Syracuse, NY: U.S. Forest Service and State University of New York.

Deknatal, C.Y. 1984. Choices of Orientation in Teaching Environmental Planning. *Journal of Planning Education and Research.* 3:118–125.

Detwyler, T.R. and Marcus, M.G. eds. 1972. *Urbanization and Environment: The Physical Geography of the City.* Belmont, CA: Duxbury Press.

Dunne, T. and Leopold, L.B. 1978. *Water and Environmental Planning.* San Francisco: W.H. Freeman.

Durgin, F.H. and Chock, A.W. 1982. Pedestrian Level Winds: A Brief Review. *Journal of the Structural Division, Proceedings of the American Society of Civil Engineers.* 108:1751–1767.

Evelyn, Sir John. 1661. *Fumifugium: Or The Inconvenience of the Aer and Smoake of London Dissipated.* Oxford: Old Ashmolean Reprint, 1930.

———1664. *Sylva.* London: Martyn and Allestry.

Forman, R.T.T. 1981. Interaction Among Landscape Elements: A Core of Landscape Ecology. In *Regional Landscape Planning: Proceedings of Educational Sessions, American Society of Landscape Architects.*

Francis, M.; Cashdan, L.; and Paxton, L. 1984. *Community Open Spaces.* Washington, D.C.: Island Press.

Franke, E., ed. 1976. *Climate: Data and Aspects for City Planning.* Translated for EPA by Literature Research Company, TR-79-0795. FBW—A Publication of Research, Building, and Living, No. 108. Stuttgart, W. Germany: Karl Kramer.

Galloway, T.D. and Huelster, R.J. 1971. Planning Literature and the Environmental Crisis: A Content Analysis. *American Institute of Planners Journal.* 37:269–274.

Gandemer, J. and Guyot, A. 1976. Integration du phenomene vent dans la conception du milieu bati. Paris: Ministere de la Qualite de la Vie.

Geddes, P. 1915. *Cities in Evolution.* London: Williams and Norgate.

Gill, D. and Bonnett, P. 1973. *Nature in the Urban Landscape: A Study of Urban Ecosystems.* Baltimore: York Press.

Glacken, C.J. 1967. *Traces on the Rhodian Shore.* Berkeley, CA: University of California Press.

Godin, G.; Wright, G.; and Shepard, R.J. 1972. Urban Exposure to Carbon Monoxide. *Archives of Environmental Health.* 25:305–313.

Godron, M. and Forman, R.T.T. 1985. *Landscape Ecology.* New York: Wiley. In Press.

Goist, P.D. 1974. Patrick Geddes and the City. *Journal of the American Institute of Planners.* 40:31–37.

Goldstein, E.L.; Gross, M.; and DeGraaf, R.M. 1980/1981. Explorations in Bird-Land Geometry. *Urban Ecology.* 5:113–124.

Grandjean, J. and Gilgen, A. 1976. *Environmental Factors in Urban Planning.* London: Taylor & Francis.

Hancock, J.L. 1967. Planners in the Changing American City, 1900–1940. *Journal of the American Institute of Planners.* 33:290–304.

Hippocrates. Ca. 5th century B.C. Airs, Waters, Places. In *Hippocrates*, Vol 1. The Loeb Classical Library, ed., T.E. Page. Cambridge, MA: Harvard University Press, 1962.

Holling, C.S. and Orians, G. 1971. Toward an Urban Ecology. *Ecological Society of America Bulletin.* 52:2–6.

Hopkins, G., ed. 1980. *Proceedings of the National Urban Forestry Conference, Nov. 13–16, 1978.* 2 vols. Syracuse, NY: State University of New York.

Howard, E. 1902. *Garden Cities of To-Morrow*, ed., F.J. Osborne. Cambridge, MA: MIT Press.

Howe, E.W. 1881. The Back Bay Park, Boston. Speech read before the Boston Society of Civil Engineers in March 1881. Washington, D.C.: Library of Congress, Olmsted Papers.

Hutchinson, B.A.; Taylor, F.G.; Wendt, R.L.; and the Critical Review Panel. 1982. *Use of Vegetation to Ameliorate Building Microclimate: An Assessment of Energy Conservation Potentials.* Environmental Sciences Division Publication No. 19103. Oak Ridge, TN: Oak Ridge National Laboratory.

Juneja, N. 1974. *Medford: Performance Requirements for the Maintenance of Social Values Represented in the Natural Environment of Medford Township, N.J.* Philadelphia: University of Pennsylvania.

———— and Veltman, J. 1979. Natural Drainage in the Woodlands. *Environmental Comment.* Nov., 7–14.

Knowles, R. 1981. *Sun, Rhythm, Form.* Cambridge, MA: MIT Press.

Landsberg, H.E. 1968. Micrometeorological Temperature Differentiation Through Urbanization. In *Urban Climates*, Technical Note 108. Brussels: World Meteorological Organization.

———— 1981. *The Urban Climate.* New York: Academic Press.

Laurie, I.C., ed. 1979. *Nature in Cities: The Natural Environment in the Design and Development of Urban Green Space.* Chicester, England: Wiley.

Leedy, D.L.; Maestro, R.M.; and Franklin, T.M. 1978. *Planning for Wildlife in Cities and Suburbs.* Washington, D.C.: U.S. Fish and Wildlife Service, Office of Biological Services.

Legget, R.F. 1973. *Cities and Geology.* New York: McGraw-Hill.

Leveson, D. 1980. *Geology and the Urban Environment.* New York: Oxford University Press.

Lewis, C.A. 1979. Healing in the Urban Environment: A Person/Plant Viewpoint. *American Planning Association Journal.* 45:330–338.

Loudon, J.C. 1829. Hints for Breathing Places. . . . *Gardener's Magazine.* V:686–690.

Lynch, K. 1960. *The Image of the City.* Cambridge, MA: MIT Press.

———— 1972. *What Time is this Place?* Cambridge, MA: MIT Press.

———— 1976. *Managing the Sense of a Region.* Cambridge, MA: MIT Press.

———— 1981. IA Theory of Good City Form. Cambridge, MA: MIT Press.

McHarg, I. 1964. The Place of Nature in the City of Man. *Annals of the American Academy of Political and Social Science.* 352(March):1–12.

———— 1968. Values, Process, and Form. In Smithsonian Annual II. *The Fitness of Man's Environment.* 207–227.

———— and Wallace, D.A., eds. 1970. *Metropolitan Open Space and Natural Process.* Philadelphia: University of Pennsylvania Press.

Marrazzo, W.J. 1981. The Selling of Waste. *EPA Journal.* 7:26–27.

Marsh, G.P. *Man and Nature.* 1864. Cambridge, MA: Harvard University Press, Belknap Press, 1974.

Morris, D. 1982. *Self-Reliant Cities: Energy and the Transformation of Urban America.* San Francisco: Sierra Club Books.

Mumford, L. 1931. *The Brown Decades.* New York: Harcourt, Brace.

———— 1961. *The City in History.* New York: Harcourt Brace Jovanovich.

———— 1968. *The Urban Prospect.* New York: Harcourt Brace Jovanovich.

Nichols, D.R. and Campbell, C.C., eds. 1969. *Environmental Planning and Geology: Proceedings of the Symposium on Engineering Geology in the Urban Environment.* Washington, D.C.: U.S. Geological Survey and U.S. Department of Housing and Urban Development.

Notardonato, F. and Doyle, A.F. 1979. Corps Takes New Approach to Flood Control. *Civil Engineering.* June, 65–68.

Olgyay, V. 1963. *Design with Climate: Biclimatic Approach to Architectural Regionalism.* Princeton, NJ: Princeton University Press.

Olmsted, F.L. 1886. The Problem and the Solution. Speech to the Boston Society of Architects. April 2, 1886. Washington, D.C.: Library of Congress, Olmsted Papers.

Osband, G. 1984. Managing Urban Forests. Cambridge, MA: Harvard Graduate School of Design, Dept. of Landscape Architecture. Student report.

Patterson, J.C. 1975. Enrichment of Urban Soil with Composted Sludge and Leaf Mold: Constitution Gardens. *Compost Science.* 16:18–22.

Peterson, J.A. 1979. The Impact of Sanitary Reform upon American Urban Planning, 1840–1890. *Journal of Social History.* 13:83–103.

Poertner, H.G. 1973. Better Storm Drainage Facilities at Lower Cost. *Civil Engineering.* Oct., 67–70.

Rapoport, A. 1977. *Human Aspects of Urban Form.* Oxford: Pergamon Press.

Rey, A.A. 1915. The Healthy City of the Future: Scientific Principles of Orientation for Public Roads and Dwelling. *Town Planning Review.* 6:2–9.

Robel, F.; Hoffman, U.; and Riekert, A. 1978. *Daten und Aussagen zum Stadtklima von Stuttgart auf der Grundlage der Infrarot—Thermographie.* Stuttgart, W. Germany: Chemisches Untersuchungs amt der Landeshauptstadt Stuttgart.

Robinson, G.D. and Spieker, A.M. 1978. Nature to be Commanded. . . . Professional Paper 950. Washington, D.C.: U.S. Geological Survey.

Rydell, C.P. and Schwartz, G. 1968. Air Pollution and Urban Form: A Review of Current Literature. *American Institute of Planners Journal.* 34:115–120.

Schultz, S.K. and McShane, C. 1978. To Engineer the Metropolis: Sewers, Sanitation, and Planning in Late Nineteenth Century America. *Journal of American History.* 65:389–411.

Schuster, R.L. and Krizek, R.J., eds. 1978. Landslides: Analysis and Control. Special Report 176. Washington, D.C.: National Academy of Sciences.

Sheaffer, J.R.; Wright, K.; Taggart, W.; and Wright, R. 1982. *Urban Storm Drainage Management.* New York: Marcel Dekker.

Simo, M. 1981. John Claudius Loudon: On Planning and Design for the Garden Metropolis. *Garden History.* 9:184–201.

Smith, W.H. and Staskawicz, B.J. 1977. Removal of Atmospheric Particles by Leaves and Twigs of Urban Trees: Some Preliminary Observations and Assessment of Research Needs. *Environmental Management.* 1:317–330.

Southworth, M. and Southworth, S. 1973. Environmental Quality Analysis and Management for Cities and Regions: A Review of Work in the United States. *Town Planning Review.* 44:231–253.

Spirn, A.W. 1984a. *The Granite Garden: Urban Nature and Human Design.* New York: Basic Books.

———— 1984b. Designing for Pedestrian-level Winds: The Integration of Wind Engineering Technology and Urban Design. In *Proceedings of the Conference of Educators in Landscape Architecture.* Guelph, Canada: University of Guelph.

———— 1985. Reclaiming Common Ground: The Future Shape of Boston. Paper sponsored by the American Institute of Architects and McGraw-Hill Publications as part of a national lecture series on *The Future Shape of the City.* Presented to the Boston Society of Architects, April 30, 1985.

———— and Batchelor, W.G. 1985. Street-level Air Pollution and Urban Form: A Review of Recent Literature. Prepared for the Boston Redevelopment Authority. Cambridge, MA: Harvard Graduate School of Design.

Stauffer, T.P. 1978. Kansas City: A Center for Secondary Use of Mined Out Space. In *Geology in the Urban Environment,* eds., R.O. Utgard, G.D. McKenzie, and D. Foley. Minneapolis: Burgess.

U.S. Soil Conservation Service. 1976. *Soil Survey of District of Columbia.* Washington, D.C.: U.S. Department of Agriculture and U.S. Department of the Interior.

Unwin, R. 1911. *Town Planning in Practice.* London: T. Fisher Unwin.

Vitruvius. Ca. 1st century B.C. In *The Ten Books on Architecture.* Cambridge, MA: Harvard University Press, 1914.

Wallace McKay Roberts and Todd. 1976. *Environmental Resources of the Toronto Central Waterfront.* Philadelphia: Wallace McKay Roberts and Todd.

Wedding, J.B.; Lombardi, D.J.; and Cermak, J.E. 1977. A Wind Tunnel Study of Gaseous Pollutants in City Street Canyons. *Journal of the Air Pollution Control Association.* 27:557–566.

Whipple, W.; Tucker, S.; Grigg, N.; Grizzard, T.; Randall, C.; and Shubinski, R. 1983. *Stormwater Management in Urbanizing Areas.* Englewood Cliffs, NJ: Prentice-Hall.

Williams, R. 1973. *The Country and the City.* New York: Oxford University Press.

Wolman, A. 1965. The Metabolism of Cities. *Scientific American.* March, 178–190.

Worster, D. 1977. *Nature's Economy: The Roots of Ecology.* Garden City, NY: Anchor Books.

Wright, K. and Taggart, W.C. 1976. The Recycling of a River. *Civil Engineering.* Nov., 42–46.

Carrying Capacity: A Key to Environmental Planning?

David R. Godschalk

Professor of Urban and Regional Planning, University of North Carolina

Francis H. Parker

Professor of Urban Planning, Ball State University

Planners are engaged in a perennial search to find scientifically acceptable criteria that will solve their complex, wicked problems. Levels-of-service standards, as used in Florida and other states' growth-management legislation, are the current manifestation of "carrying capacity." In this article, David R. Godschalk and Francis H. Parker examine definitional, measurement, and methodological issues in operationalizing the carrying-capacity concept. As the authors observed: "Ideally, environmental planners need a Mother Nature model" (p. 507). Almost twenty years later, we still await the creation of a model that will comprehensively measure all the important variables and interactions in the environment that result from growth and development.

The environmental movement has generated many efforts to develop new planning and impact assessment methods. One of the most appealing of these new approaches draws on the carrying capacity concept.

To its advocates, environmental policy based on carrying capacity seems to promise a *scientific certainty* not previously available in the planning field. Especially when some states and localities are attempting to impose limits on development and growth, the appeal of using objective environmental determinants as the basis for managing growth is strong. If a moratorium, a lowered density standard, or a population limit can be supported by hard scientific data on carrying capacity, then governmental decision-makers can justify their policies, not only to disappointed entrepreneurs, but to skeptical courts as well.

Many federal planning requirements implicitly recognize the validity of a carrying capacity approach to planning. The Coastal Zone Management Act of 1972 requires that states inventory and designate "areas of particular concern." While carrying capacity is not directly mentioned in the act, it obviously is one way to identify areas, such as vulnerable habitats, aquifer recharge zones, and storm-prone beaches, where there appear to be inherent limits to use. Air and water quality standards established by the Environmental Protection Agency define the legal capacities of the air and water for carrying effluent or emissions. The National Environmental Policy Act of 1969 requires statements on the environmental impact of proposed public projects prior to their authorization. And the House

Reprinted by permission of the *Journal of Soil and Water Conservation*, 30 (July-August 1975), Soil and Water Conservation Society.

Committee on Public Works has examined the feasibility of a national public works investment policy based on carrying capacity (2).

States also have begun to think about how their future development may be constrained by carrying capacity. Florida's legislature debated but did not pass a state growth policy that declared, "The desired kind, rate and extent of growth shall be determined by the carrying capacity of natural and man-made systems of an area" (12).

Hawaii's legislature has taken more definite steps, requesting that the governor's office develop "criteria for defining the state's optimum carrying capacity as relates to its environmental systems," to include consideration of "population, air quality, water quality and supply, energy supplies, transportation systems, and land use capabilities" (13). The Hawaii legislature also asked the governor to submit to it criteria and a mechanism for "officially declaring areas or systems at environmental overload or in danger of environmental overload, and to recommend related steps and procedures to prevent such overload" (14).

Maine's Site Location Law of 1970 sets up carrying capacity criteria for reviewing large-scale development projects, and Vermont's Act 250 extends the concept beyond the environment to include the financial capacity of governments to provide public services.

Several carrying capacity studies have been carried out at the regional level. Among the notable ones are the Lake Tahoe regional planning agency's land capability map, based on the physical capacity of the land to tolerate development without undue damage, and the Colorado River Basin study of future capacity for food production, environmental quality maintenance, and water development (3). The results of these studies have been suggestive but not yet conclusive, especially in dealing with social and economic factors as well as ecological factors.

PITFALLS OF CARRYING CAPACITY

When planners try to come to grips with building workable criteria and planning processes around the carrying capacity concept, they run into some discouraging pitfalls. Beneath the surface appeal of the concept lie dilemmas of definition, measurement, and methodology.

Constructing a straightforward definition of carrying capacity is not as simple as it might seem. It is easy to say that carrying capacity means the ability of natural and man-made systems to support the demands of various uses and that it refers to inherent limits in the systems beyond which change cannot be absorbed without producing instability, degradation, or irreversible damage. On closer inspection, however, carrying capacity not only includes an environmental definition but also institutional and perceptual definitions. It is not one but three concepts, each of which has different applications, draws on different bodies of theory, and uses different methods of implementation. Some of the present confusion surrounding carrying capacity could be eliminated if these differences were recognized.

ENVIRONMENTAL CARRYING CAPACITY

Environmental carrying capacity, briefly, is the limit at which human activity will lead to undesirable changes in the environment. The concept rests on an assumption that there are certain limits the environment itself imposes on development. In examining these environmental limits, however, it becomes apparent that they are not all of one type. Any serious attempt to use environmental carrying capacity must begin by explicitly defining the term.

The first notion of environmental carrying capacity and probably the most appealing is that if an absolute physical limit that can be violated, if at all, only at exorbitant expense or the risk of inordinate health or safety hazards. Development can and does take place in potential avalanche zones but on a very limited and specialized basis. Cites under the sea are theoretically possible but raise so many difficulties that they are relegated to science fiction.

Probably the most basic example of an absolute carrying capacity limit is the earth's finite ability to produce food for a burgeoning population. While a real threat, worthy of global attention, this type of limit cannot be of much use in planning at the local or regional level.

Most examples of apparently absolute physical environmental limits are based in part on certain assumptions. If the assumptions can be altered, then the physical limit itself can be pushed back.

The critical assumptions have to do with technology, economics, and acceptable life-styles (9). The carrying capacity limit, as set, frequently assumes that all of these will remain constant in the foreseeable future. This being the case, we can then predict, on the basis of present knowledge, when a region's carrying capacity will be reached.

One example of this is Von Wodtke's analysis of carrying capacity in the Los Angeles basin (15). Assuming that exhaust emission control technology does not change radically and people continue to rely on automobile transportation, Van Wodtke can prove that the basin's carrying capacity is a population of 14 million people, well below the official planning target of 20 million. Above this population, air pollution will be unacceptable by present standards.

Von Wodtke's assumptions are probably realistic, but they illustrate that most relevant examples of carrying capacity must be based on a set of assumptions. If there are technological breakthroughs, if we are willing to forego certain conveniences such as individual automobiles, or if we are willing to invest enough money in ameliorative measures, we can move the carrying capacity upward. Environmental carrying capacity is not fixed once and for all but depends on the conditions of human society at any specific time and place.

Environmental Applications

There are at least three different ways environmental carrying capacity has been applied. These differ by the amount of environmental change that is considered acceptable in a particular situation.

In the first case, environmental carrying capacity is set at the minimum level of new activity that can be accommodated before any significant alterations result in the existing environment. In this case the environment can accept only a small loading of new activity before changes start to occur in ecosystems, in variety of plant and animal life, etc. High value is placed on maintaining the overall integrity of an existing natural environment. Often, this not only precludes urban development but most forms of agriculture, timber management, and even recreation, all of which can substantially alter the natural environment.

The second application deals with cases where change per se is acceptable, but where the level of environmental loading is limited to that level that will not degrade certain aspects of the environment below pre-determined standards. This application is probably the largest and most relevant. It will become increasingly feasible as more standards are set on ambient air and water resources. Working backward from the standards, it will be possible to determine how much unused capacity there is in an area. This carrying capacity, which historically has been treated as a free good, will be increasingly subject to allocation through licensing (for example, permits for waste discharge up to the assimilative capacity of a body of water) or negotiation (as with the transfer of development rights).

The third application, sometimes used in resource management, deals with the capacity of the environment to accept a new activity before the activity becomes self-limiting. Examples are rangeland management, where the introduction of too many cattle may deplete the resource base and lead to sarvation. In this case, massive environmental changes will be tolerated, and the limit of acceptable degradation will be that point at which the basic resource system collapses, whether irreversibly or temporarily. This application may not be suitable for most types of urban development, but it may be relevant in the case of widespread drainage of wetlands for agriculture. Not enough is known about the effects of such drainage on certain kinds of peat soils, but there are indications that it may lead in some cases to irreversible changes through fire or other destruction of the soil resource itself.

Environmental Theory

The theoretical base for environmental carrying capacity is drawn largely from ecology and the natural sciences with a strong emphasis on the integrity of natural systems. There is a search for natural principles, such as the species diversity in an area or a system's total energy use, that can serve as objective measures of the environment's "health."

Paradoxically, this objective theoretical base is most useful in those categories of carrying capacity analysis that are least likely to be used. As noted, ecological studies can clearly be the basis for the first level of carrying capacity (that of maintaining the natural system intact), and they can be applied to the third category (that of system collapse under overloading). They are less helpful in the large middle ground, the area of carrying capacity relative to some man-made standard of environmental quality. In this area, such studies can and must be done to establish cause and effect relationships, but they cannot themselves establish the objective level at which standards must be set. The great temptation with environmental carrying capacity is to claim some inherent natural rightness in it. In fact, after all the objective evaluation has been done, the establishment of target levels is an exercise in human value judgment.

Environmental Planning Methods

Planning methods for environmental carrying capacity analysis begin with traditional resource inventories, increasingly supplemented by aerial data collection via satellite, high-altitude photography, and conventional airplane. With the use of multiband photography, increasing quantities of information can be interpreted without extensive ground surveys.

Beyond the simple inventory, the next stage is to define the relationships between each resource and its expected or potential uses. Expected values of water use, waste production, etc., need to be developed (or modified to suit local conditions if adopted from elsewhere). Methodologically this is similar to environmental impact analysis, except that it is done for a range of potential uses and activity levels rather than for a specific project. Ideally the output at this stage is a series of graphs indicating the load on each resource for each increment of population and activity.

During this stage, there also is an attempt to define and focus on the most critical resource. There will almost always be a particular resource that is the limiting factor in growth, thereby defining the carrying capacity. Early stages of the resource inventory should concentrate on identifying these critical resources and their relationships.

The most critical problem, obviously, is determining the relationship between the resource and the loads on it accurately enough to predict the carrying capacity limit in advance. If this can be done, the next step is to study the remaining resources to see if they impose additional carrying capacity limits of their own.

The picture that emerges from this analysis will not be that of a single, fixed carrying capacity limit, but rather a series of limits imposed by different critical resources. Each one defines the carrying capacity of a particular resource in light of certain assumptions about technology and economics. In some cases these limits may coincide. In most cases they will not. Instead they will define a series of thresholds for growth. Many of these thresholds can be crossed if there is an accompanying investment in technology or management. Where the threshold can be crossed, it frequently will not be feasible to do so incrementally because the technology for doing so will demand large investments (e.g. going from individual waste disposal to central collection and treatment).

Whether it is desirable to make the necessary investment to cross one threshold may well depend on the proximity of other threshold limits imposed by other resources. The extent to which carrying capacity is an absolute limit on growth may well depend on whether there is such a conjunction of limits.

Critical research needs focus on determining cause and effect relationships between human activity and the rate of consequent environmental degradation. Failing in our ability to define such relationships over a broad range, the next focus must be on identifying those limits or thresholds that are about to be reached. We need a variety of early warning systems based on observable environmental changes to inform us when major thresholds are approaching. We also need research to distinguish the human value elements of environmental carrying capacity from the objective natural facts, though this may tend to weaken the concept's appeal.

PERCEPTUAL CARRYING CAPACITY

In some cases the critical factor is not the objective physical capacity of the environment but rather our perception of the environment's character. These are not always the same. The physical environment may appear "natural" but be badly degraded. Conversely, the environment may be degraded visually but still function adequately as a natural system.

Perceptual carrying capacity is the amount of activity or degree of change that can occur before we perceive the environment to be different than before. This subjective concept is applicable only where a high value is placed on the visual or psychological quality of the environment.

Perceptual Capacity Applications

Perceptual carrying capacity is most applicable in cases where the environment is valued for a particular experience, such as recreation. It has been applied, for example, to determine the capacity of wilderness areas to support hiking, where too many hikers will destroy the experience of wilderness that all are seeking.

Perceptual carrying capacity can also apply to different levels of urbanism. There are differences in visual feeling among forestland, rural settlement, small-town, and urban environments. To maintain variety and visual quality in the environment, it may be important to maintain these differences and to determine how much development can be permitted in an area before it becomes a different environment perceptually. Issues of perceptual character underlie many efforts by smaller suburban communities to control their growth (2).

Perceptual Capacity Theory

The theoretical base for perceptual carrying capacity is essentially that of environmental psychology. The theory posits ways of discovering and analyzing the mental image of the environment in people's minds. This image may not always coincide directly with reality, and it may differ among individuals, economic classes, and cultural and ethnic groups.

It appears likely that perceptions of the environment do not always change at the same rate as the environment itself. Instead, there are certain threshold levels at which an environmental alteration is suddenly recognized. For example, although development occurs at a uniform rate, there may be discrete points where a change from rural agriculture to rural settlement or from rural settlement to small town is suddenly perceived. If this is true (and it is largely untested), this could be an important way of determining what levels of development are compatible with citizen desires for their environment. Carrying capacity would be based on expressed public attitudes and, in turn, would serve as the basis for planning policies.

Perceptual Planning Methods

The methods necessary to use perceptual capacity merge with the research necessary to evaluate its usefulness. The basic research question is whether the concept of perceptual thresholds actually holds true and, if so, whether there is sufficient agreement on where the thresholds occur to make them useful guides for planning. Such work is being conducted in New England (*16*). It needs to be done in other settings also.

One method of perceptual planning uses a citizen survey based on cognitive mapping. The survey employs a series of photographs to determine how respondents define different levels of development, after which respondents are asked to apply these definitions to areas with which they are familiar. The result is a map of residents' perceptions of their environment, together with a compilation of their attitudes toward what they perceived. The planner gains an understanding of how much value is placed by citizens on different areas of the environment and how much development that area could carry before becoming an environment that residents value less.

INSTITUTIONAL CARRYING CAPACITY

Institutional carrying capacity is the ability of organizations in an area to guide development toward public goals. It involves the limitations imposed by governmental structure, budgets, and personnel as well as the more general economic and cultural limits of the area on environmental decision-making.

Hahn (*5*) noted that there are stages of institutional development that areas pass through as they move from rural to urban and that "planning programs in rural areas often fail to respond to the informal nature of rural government, the slower pace of change and smaller number of perceived crises, and special problems of meeting costs and demands for professional personnel in rural communities." Institutional capacity involves both objective facts, such as the size of the planning staff and the presence of land use controls, and subjective attitudes, such as reluctance to depend on government for problem solving, unwillingness to pay high taxes, and resistance to professional advice. The growth management controls that can be used in an urban metropolitan county are inappropriate for a rural agricultural county.

Certain thresholds of institutional capacity to guide development can be visual-ized. For example, a major threshold for a rural government may simply be its ability to draft and pass basic land use regulations, such as zoning. Other thresholds might include the ability to enter into intergovernmental cooperation efforts (such as regional or statewide programs), the ability to objectively analyze the impacts of a difficult land use decision, the ability to adopt advanced land use regulations (such as timed development or transfer of development rights), or the ability to change community attitudes toward growth (such as changing the way land is perceived—from a saleable commodity to a conservable resource). Most state and federal officials recognize the need to consider institutional capacity thresholds in the programs they administer in cooperation with local areas, and many of these programs are aimed at increasing local capacity.

Institutional Capacity Applications

Many federal grant programs contain an institutional development component as well as a substantive objective. The Coastal Zone Management Act declares that present state and local institutional arrangements for planning and regulating land and water uses in coastal areas are inadequate and creates a program to encourage governments to develop unified policies and criteria for dealing with land and water use decisions of more than local significance. Air and water quality programs encourage the establishment of regional programs to coordinate and strengthen planning and management at the local level. In many cases, the main result of these types of programs has been to raise the threshold of institutional capacity, including more coordination and planning among governments.

Clearly, the so-called quiet revolution in land use control demands a quantum jump in institutional capacity. The increased loading resulting from the need to introduce new forms of land use planning and control (not only to decision-makers, but also to citizens, interest groups, and courts) has severely stressed the abilities of even experienced planning agencies. For example, the Florida state planning officer reported that it took some 3,500 hours of staff time to designate the state's first area of critical concern (*11*). Public agencies under pressure to implement new growth management approaches may suffer stress and overload from unfamiliar and complex demands.

Institutional Capacity Theory

Relevant theory for understanding institutional capacity comes from several disciplines. Among the important sources are communications theory, organization theory, innovation theory, and community theory. Recently, a synthetic theory, drawing together a number of these sources, has emerged in the form of "guidance theory" for land use and environmental planning (*7*).

Elements of a theory of institutional capacity range from the role of the individual in the organization, to the role of the organization in a field of other organizations, to the function of a community of several organizational fields within a state or federal system. Not only the structural and functional aspects but also the motivational and value aspects of these elements are important.

Theoretical measures need to be developed around the capacity of an institution to innovate, to manage conflict, and to make and carry out plans. In each of these general areas thresholds need to be identified and related to particular functions, such as land and water use, service delivery, and environmental quality.

Institutional Planning Methods

The field of institutional development is only beginning to produce a systematic body of planning methods (4). Much of the needed research should be aimed at learning about effective methods of assessing institutional capacity and carrying out institutional development.

One of the first steps should be careful case studies of recent efforts to manage growth at the state and local levels in order to demonstrate the type and amount of resources necessary for effectiveness under varying circumstances, to identify the critical organizational constraints and thresholds, and to describe the direct and indirect effects of applying new methods.

For instance, in a coastal county of a given population and economic base, what level of institutional capacity is needed to make the proper judgments about which areas are of public concern, how they should be regulated, and how local government needs to be changed to manage them? In fact, is the local government capable of making these decisions, or does the job need to be done by a state or regional organization?

A second research need is for a comparative study of a representative sample of environmental planning and management institutions. This study would test findings from case studies and attempt to produce knowledge about the general types of institutions, the resources needed for various functions, and the comparative efficiency and effectiveness of different strategies. It would be an evaluative analysis as well as a descriptive study. One output might be a validated conceptual model of the institutional development process as it relates to environmental planning and management.

CARRYING CAPACITY METHODS

Carrying capacity has a way to go before it becomes an operational planning tool. Since the concept is a complex mix of three separate types of capacity—environmental, perceptual, and institutional—the appropriate methods come from a variety of disciplines.

Measurement of the separate types of carrying capacity presents some difficult challenges. Carrying capacity is not a static quantity. Rarely can one find an absolute limit—one that cannot be changed or expanded by additional investment of resources. Measurement techniques thus must be dynamic rather than static. They are akin to monitoring, in which continuous readings are taken on critical indicators, and where the concern is for variation within a range rather than around a fixed point. In addition, the important measurements and values themselves will be subject to change as new technology emerges.

The methodology associated with carrying capacity raises issues familiar to the planning field from experience with large-scale transportation systems' modeling. It is tempting to try to describe the entire environmental or institutional system under consideration in terms of a mathematical computer model in which the critical levels, rates, and relationships are specified. Not only can the system's limits be studied, but the effects of different interventions can be tested on the model. However, modeling methods for environmental systems are still being developed. They are expensive and complex, and they tend to focus on only one element of carrying capacity rather than all three. Perhaps they will prove to be the planning tools of tomorrow, or perhaps they will be found too cumbersome or error-prone to be useful in actual decision-making. Meanwhile, those who want to make plans based on carrying capacity will find that their traditional demand-based methods are inadequate and that the necessary supply-based methods have yet to be proved.

Ideally, environmental planners need a Mother Nature model. That is, they should have a quantitative model that comprehensively accounts for all the important elements and the dynamics of their inter-relationships within an environmental system. The closest approach to such a model that we know of is the energy-based model of Thomas Odum, which has been assembled at the University of Florida (*10*). However, this model is not widely available, contains parameters and equations particular to Florida's regions, is expensive to program, and is subject to problems of accuracy and credibility. Hopefully, these drawbacks will be overcome in time. But the problems of this type of large-scale system simulation may take a long time to solve (*8*).

What can planners do while waiting for the model builders to finish their Mother Nature models? An interim learning approach would be to do a first-cut analysis of the obviously critical environmental factors, enact some experimental controls on these factors, and learn from the resulting experience about the effects on carrying capacities. In Florida the critical factor appears to be water supply, especially in the rapidly growing urban areas of the southern part of the state. To cope with this problem, regional water management agencies have been created to referee allocation and distribution of the scarce resource. On the North Carolina Coast the critical factors may turn out to be combinations of fragile natural environments, limited institutional abilities to manage growth in rural counties, and assimilative waste capacity, as large-scale recreational developments begin to pre-empt the coastal waterfronts.

A more useful approach for the long run would be to start to define thresholds for the elements of environmental, institutional, and perceptual systems beyond which a qualitative change occurs. That is, the threshold beyond which a different order of public investment is needed to prevent degradation (such as the population density per acre requiring a change from septic tanks to sanitary sewers), or a different type of experience results (such as a natural wilderness being perceived as a crowded recreation area when the number of users per day passes a certain range), or an institutional agency fails to adequately perform its function (as when a building inspection department of a given staff size has so many jobs to inspect that it is unable to cover all aspects of the building code requirements for each structure). These thresholds would be like "tipping points," which, when passed, result in a series of changes in other parts of the system. Thus, even though the different elements were not all fitted into a comprehensive model, they could be dealt with individually with some assurance that their effects on the system could be discerned.

Many of the critical environmental subsystem models already have been developed, including models of soil loss, air quality, and runoff. Linking these subsystem models to empirically determined, dynamic threshold values can provide a method of monitoring the status of an area's environmental capacity (6). In the process, field research can be carried out on the relationships between environmental capacity and perceptual and institutional capacity.

CONCLUSIONS

There is a dearth of planning methods for dealing with the separate types of carrying capacity, and the validity of trying to incorporate all of them in a single comprehensive Mother Nature model remains questionable (1).

Nevertheless, if its limitations are recognized, the carrying capacity concept can be a valuable planning tool. In almost every planning case there will be some resource in critical supply that imposes limits on development. Often these limits can be overcome through added investments or increased regulations.

The merit of carrying capacity is that it highlights thresholds beyond which growth can be tolerated only if paired with major public investments or new institutional arrangements. These thresholds can help to focus public debate on the desirability of accommodating the new development, providing a cost-benefit calculus for those affected by the proposed change. Carrying capacity does not replace judgment but it can help to inform it, just as it does not replace scientific research on environmental cause and effect relationships but it can help to focus that research on concrete policy issues. These advantages alone justify serious consideration of the carrying capacity concept by the planning profession.

REFERENCES

1 Bishop, A. B., and other authors. 1974. *Carrying capacity in regional environmental management*. U. S. Environ. Protection Agency, Washington, D. C.

2 Brewer, Michael F., and Patrick Petersilia. 1974. *Carrying capacity as a potential guide for community growth and regional development*. In *A National Public Works Investment Policy*, background papers prepared for the Committee on Public Works, U. S. House of Representatives. U. S. Govt. Print. Office, Washington, D. C.

3 Conservation Foundation. 1974. *Carrying capacity analysis is useful—but limited*. CF Letter (June, 1974).

4 Eaton, Joseph W. 1972. *Institution building and development: from concepts to application*. Sage Publ., Beverly Hills, Calif.

5 Hahn, Alan J. 1970. *Planning in rural areas*. AIP Journal (Jan.): 44–49.

6 Hawaii Environmental Simulation Laboratory. 1975. *Carrying capacity analysis in*

context: application to growth management in Hawaii. Rpt. to the 8th Legislature. Univ. Hawaii, Honolulu.

7 Kaiser, Edward J., and other authors. 1973. *Promoting environmental quality through urban planning and controls.* U. S. Environ. Protection Agency, Washington, D. C.

8 Lee, Douglas B., Jr. 1973. *Requiem for large-scale models.* AIP Journal (May): 163–178.

9 Peterson, E. K., and other authors. 1973. *Ecology and the economy.* Pac. N. W. River Basins Comm., Vancouver, Wash.

10 Shadix, Jerry A. 1974. *Interface four: urban design studio report four.* Dept. Arch., Univ. Florida, Gainesville.

11 Starnes, Earl M. 1974. *State planning in Florida.* Proc., Council of State Govt's. Land Use Task Force, Lexington, Ky.

12 State of Florida. 1974. *House concurrent resolution 2800.* Reg. Sess., Tallahassee. (Was not passed)

13 State of Hawaii. 1974. *Senate concurrent resolution no. 26.* Honolulu.

14 State of Hawaii. 1974. *Senate concurrent resolution no. 27.* Honolulu.

15 Von Wodtke, Mark. 1970. *The carrying capacity of the Los Angeles Basin.* Cry California 5: 22–26.

16 Zube, Ervin. 1974. *Strategies for land use planning.* In Proc., Soc. Am. For., Appalachian Sec. Mtg., Jan. 31–Feb. 1, Greensboro, N. C.

TEN. ENVIRONMENTAL PLANNING—SUGGESTED READINGS

Brown, Lester, Christopher Flavin, and Sandra Postel. 1991. *Saving the Planet: How to Shape an Environmentally Sustainable Global Economy*. New York: Norton.

Hardin, Warren. 1988. *Tragedy of the Commons*. Monticello, IL: Vance Biographies.

Leopold, Aldo. 1987. *Sand County Almanac and Sketches*. New York: Oxford University Press.

Ortolano, Leonard R. 1984. *Environmental Planning and Decision Making*. New York: Wiley.

Pahlke, Robert. 1989. *Environmentalism and the Future of Progressive Politics*. New Haven: Yale.

Sagoff, Mark. 1988. *The Economy of the Earth*. Cambridge: Cambridge University Press.

Strong, Ann. 1975. *Private Property and the Public Interest*. Baltimore: Johns Hopkins.

11

INTERNATIONAL PLANNING

A Planned City

Lisa Peattie

In *Planning: Rethinking Ciudad Guayana*, Lisa Peattie revisits an area that she first studied twenty-five years ago and described in *The View From the Barrio* (Ann Arbor: University of Michigan Press, 1968). The current book is an important, eloquently written case study of both a culture and of the development planning process. Peattie is a keen observer, and her case study serves as an important source for her ideas about the practice of planning and urban design. "A Planned City," the first chapter in the book, introduces the history and context of Ciudad Guayana and then briefly addresses the question of why the planning for the city that began twenty years ago was not successful. Peattie considers three possible explanations and then observes that the most important reason was that the planners had been unable to include local businessmen and residents in the process. Unfortunately, planning had been used to shift even more power and resources to the large corporate bodies.

While we often speak of the need for planning, we know at the same time that a number of planned cities are just awful. Indeed, there is a group of very well known planned cities that, although widely separated in space and produced by nations with sharply differing cultures and politics, share certain strikingly unappealing characteristics. Brasília, Chandigarh, and Islamabad are particularly notable instances of the genre: cities of monumental buildings rendered sterile in effect because of the antiseptically orderly character of their setting; cities of the most rigorous separation of classes, which typically extends to excluding the poor altogether from the areas covered by planning controls; cities that seem unadapted to pedestrians, small enterprises, the modest, and the domestic.

Brazilians used to like to tell a story about a visitor to Brasília whose belt breaks. He is depicted going desperately from place to place holding up his pants in a city that offers no convenient shopping facilities at the local or neighborhood level.

In addition to such stories, there is by now a literature of criticism on these cities, of which Epstein's *Brasília: Myth and Reality* and Madhu Sarin's book on Chandigarh are two notable examples.[1] But so far as I know, these critiques always center around a concept of flawed planning. The planners misjudged; the planners were unsympathetic to the needs of the masses. I propose here to explore another way of thinking about the similar obnoxiousness of these planned cities: that it results from the nature and functions of central planning itself. I propose to explore this possibility via the story of another well-known planned city in Venezuela with which I myself had some years of involvement in its early days.

Ciudad Guayana, the city of this story, differs sharply from Brasília, Chandigarh, and Islamabad in not being a government capital. It was proposed not as a seat of and monument to government, but as an industrial growth pole. In Brasília or Chandigarh, the city's business is government; in Ciudad Guayana, government's business was industry. The announced purpose of the city was economic growth and the decentralization of development away from the capital. Nevertheless, there are certain similarities between this city and the three capitals mentioned earlier. Like them, it is characterized by strikingly large buildings in an otherwise sparsely developed area. Like them, it excludes the poor from the area of planning controls. Like them, it has an awkward, inhuman quality as a place to live.

Can it be that planning is not the way to a better environment after all?

If planning is the way to better cities, Ciudad Guayana should have turned out splendidly. It was not only located at a dramatic natural site, with a rich collection of natural resources, it was planned by an international team of experts under a powerful independent agency with extensive legal powers and ample funding.

In a national magazine article on the planning of Ciudad Guayana, one of those most involved in organizing the project wrote in 1965:

> In the lower Orinoco Valley of Venezuela, a new city is rising. Called Ciudad Guayana, this city is more than just another urban settlement; it is the focal point of an effort to establish the national economy of Venezuela on a broader and more stable basis than its present heavy dependence on petroleum. As such the city of Guayana is perhaps one of the most ambitious and significant enterprises of its kind in the world today.[2]

In 1961, when Ciudad Guayana was founded, Venezuela was completing its third decade of petroleum-driven economic growth. A nation two-thirds rural in 1936 had become two-thirds urban and was still urbanizing rapidly. Oil—still in the hands of U.S. companies—accounted for 22 percent of the Venezuelan gross national product (GNP), two-thirds of Venezuelan government revenue, and 90 percent of foreign exchange. The democratically elected Betancourt government that came to power after the years of dictatorship announced as its major strategy that of "sowing the oil"—of using the oil royalties to build a permanent economic base. The Ciudad Guayana project was part of the national planning strategy that was the outcome of the oil boom, and it was financed by the oil revenues.

The new city was to be at the junction of the Orinoco and Caroní rivers in the south of Venezuela. Eight degrees off the equator, sea level, the area was hot and dry. The existing urban settlements there lacked a phone system, a public library, a theater or a university, and even, to a great extent, piped running water! More important, in many ways, it was an airline journey or a twelve-hour drive from Caracas, the glittering city where money and power and the contacts to get more of them were concentrated. But it had a dramatic natural site (two rivers, and a spectacular waterfall) and a rich collection of natural resources (hydroelectric power, iron, bauxite). Two U.S. companies, subsidiaries of U.S. Steel and Bethlehem Steel, were already mining iron in the area and shipping it out from company towns in the area of the proposed city. The Orinoco River provided access to cheap water transport for the heavy ore. The Venezuelan government owned and managed a dam and hydroelectric plant and was completing a steel mill. There were thus ore, energy, transportation, and the beginning of basic industry.

The program for developing these resources was backed up with both money and power. The development of the region and the planning of the new city were under the charge of a powerful development agency, the Corporación Venezolana de Guayana (CVG), responsible only to the president of Venezuela. Its head, Colonel Alfonzo Ravard, was a military officer, an engineer with an already-established reputation as an administrator in the region. The agency's control over land—not only to regulate use but to allocate through sale or lease—superseded the powers of the local municipal government.

Furthermore, in 1961 the CVG signed an agreement with the Joint Center for Urban Studies of the Massachusetts Institute of Technology and Harvard University for research and technical assistance in regional development and in planning the city, which made available a great deal of high-powered professional expertise. The contract provided for a total of $883,700 worth of professional services over three years.[3] In July of 1964, a two-year extension was signed providing for an additional $1,081,200.[4] The CVG also funded a large staff of Venezuelan counterparts in the planning enterprise.

Twenty years later, there is a city of around 350,000 people where the planners drew plans for one—but one rather different from the planners' dream.

On the eastern side of the Caroní River there had been in 1962 the rather raggle-taggle municipal center of San Félix with its plaza and market. Now there is a vast proliferation of shantytown settlements spreading south and east of the plaza, once a comfortably shabby shaded space, now an expanse of concrete.

On the west side of the Caroní, the location of the steel mill and the modern U.S. Steel company town called Puerto Ordaz, there are commercial office blocks in several scattered groupings and the development agency's own monumental building. There are also a number of residential developments for the middle- and higher-income groups. Many of these consist of high-rise apartment buildings standing scattered about the vast sunbaked spaces. Because during the oil boom the developers overbuilt for a very small high-income market, when I visited in 1982 I was told there were eight thousand vacant apartments. A particularly luxurious development, built to house the staff of the steel mill, was too expensive even for those rather well-paid persons and was one of the empty projects.

One problem is that the major industries that were to make the city an economic growth pole are in terrible trouble: a source not of industrial dynamism and of national income but of debt and managerial concern. When oil prices suddenly soared in 1973, more than ten billion dollars of Venezuela's new OPEC riches went into Guayana,[5] largely into a fourfold expansion of the steel mill and the enlargement of productive capacity in electricity and aluminum. But the implementing agencies turned out to lack the managerial capacity to execute the ambitious projects. While the city's facilities were strained to the point of crisis, the industrial projects brought accusations of patronage and mismanagement. Meanwhile, even as oil revenues fell, the world markets for steel and aluminum dropped sharply.

But the problems of the city are not simply those of running out of money. This is not the city that the planners intended, even at reduced scale. In 1986, I am told, the vacant apartments have been filled and the city is growing. But what kind of a city is it? The planners had concerned themselves with issues of economic efficiency, amenity, social equity, and community. The city as it has evolved is conspicuously lacking on all four counts.

It lacks efficiency. Three-quarters of the population live at one end of a lineal city, and the major industries and two-thirds of the jobs are located at the other end; thus, the majority of the working population must commute daily the length of the city. They must make the commute across a classic bottleneck: a double bridge over the river that separates the two sections. This distribution of population is not at all that which was planned. Although specific predictions varied, all the planners, whether calculating by hand or by computer, proposed that "in the long run . . . residential growth would move westward from Puerto Ordaz in a broad band toward the steel mill, leaving only a minority of the population in San Félix."[6] The situation is at present reversed, since nearly three-quarters of the population live to the east in San Félix.

Both halves of the city lack amenity. The eastern part of the city, in which the working class lives, consists of a series of shantytown settlements. Streets are cheaply paved, if at all, and lack adequate drainage. In 1983 a study found that only a third of households in this sector were connected to the city water system.[7] Only 60 percent of the elementary school age population and 12 percent of the older youth were enrolled in school; although all schools were functioning on double shifts, the system simply lacked capacity.[8]

Puerto Ordaz, on the other side of the river where the privileged classes live, in contrast to the shantytowns of the east, is characterized by an awkward and unpleasant luxury: high-rise apartment buildings scattered widely apart, without pedestrian access, without trees and gardens, and with a deficiency of places for meeting and collective amusement.

The city lacks equity. Per capita, the development agency in 1977 had invested in the privileged Puerto Ordaz part thirty-nine times what it had invested in the working-class part[9]—and it is apparent to any casual glance.

The city lacks community. A 1983 report from the urban development agency points to the numerous factors which create a strong social segregation within the urban area: (1) natural barriers, especially the river, (2) the sharp segregation of use brought about by zoning, (3) the socioeconomic homogeneity of each residential area, and (4) the relative autonomy of the state-owned industrial enterprises. "Ciudad Guayana," the study says, "more than any other city, may be conceived of as a group of communities and a stratification of social groups."[10]

It is not only that there is no single center that serves as a point of identification for all the citizens (or more accurately in this case, the inhabitants). More striking is the fact that after twenty years, no one but the planners themselves still think of it as a single city. Ciudad Guayana as an entity exists only in the publicity flyers of the development agency. If one is to purchase a ticket at the Caracas airport, the airline will not know what you are talking about if you ask for Ciudad Guayana; you may get a ticket to Puerto Ordaz, the iron-mining company town that existed before planning began. The telephone directory has a section for Puerto Ordaz, the west side of the river, and another, linked only by the same area code, for San Félix on the east side. Some think of three settlements, adding to San Félix and Puerto Ordaz an industrial district called Matanzas.[11]

Of those who were involved in the planning effort back in the sixties, most have left the scene; the Americans, of course, have mainly returned to the States. Many have not even been back to visit. The chief economist of the project, while based in Boston, is an exception, for he was brought back by the development agency in the mid-seventies to work on the expansion made possible by the oil boom.

His view of the outcome of the project centers on the role of the city for national economic objectives:

> The Guayana program has achieved its basic goals. An urban-industrial hydro-power center has been established and is thriving and expanding, albeit with growing pains, rough edges and missteps. Population of Ciudad Guayana has risen from 4,000 in 1960 to 300,000 plus in the 1980s and is growing. The industrial base continues to expand; a new bauxite mine and ore processing plant are currently being brought on stream and the Guayana is again proving useful. In this time of declining oil revenues, devaluation and import restrictions, the Guayana region is serving the national economy well.[12]

The chief urban designer of the Joint Center team, Wilhelm von Moltke, visited the city for a few days in February of 1981 and even more briefly in early 1984. On both occasions he was delighted by the good results of at least one of the design team's ideas: that of laying out urbanizations in a cul-de-sac pattern with loop access roads surrounding central open spaces. Proposed by the designers as a way of creating green spaces and of building community at the neighborhood level, the scheme was subsequently abandoned in the face of criticism of its complexity and cost relative to more standard blocks. But in the experimental prototypes were the green areas and in at least one case a small community building! In other respects, however, the city was to von Moltke rather distressing. In 1981 he drafted a memorandum with his impressions for the CVG. He commended the "vitality of the city" but declared himself:

> . . . very disappointed in the environmental quality of the Alta Vista Center, the absence of human scale, the lack of visual structure, the lack of integration of the many large elements, the lack of concern for the pedestrian, the lack of landscaping, street furniture and other amenities.

He saw the "miscellaneous high-rise apartment buildings . . . in most inappropriate locations" and the "continued development of residential areas east and south-east of San Félix [which] extends the journey-to-work." He felt strongly that a height limit on buildings should have been imposed.[13]

Lloyd Rodwin revisited the city in 1977 with his wife. In the course of his trip he noted the "disastrous" decision on the part of the agency to sell off the land in the center of the city. "The values and the rents from this land," he wrote in a letter to the president of the CVG, "are essential for recapturing a reasonable share of the infrastructure investments."[14] In a more philosophical mood, a few years later, he observed:

> It turned out to be a tougher job than we thought. It was harder to find the right people. People who looked good would turn out to be disasters. There were constraints which the planning team didn't recognize.[15]

The city did not turn out as planned. One problem, of course, was the disappearance of the resource base when oil prices dropped. But this is not the whole story. There would not have been eight thousand vacant apartments in 1981 if the oil boom had continued—although it seems likely that even with the oil boom not all that building would have found a market. But the inefficiency, inequity, and lack of community characterizing the city were there before the oil boom and during the boom as they are now. Even during the boom, oil wealth did not seem to be producing a city that was agreeable to live in; on the contrary, there were protests from both the planners and the citizens as to the "crisis" produced for the city by oil-supported industrial expansion.

No, we must see the present problematic city not simply as the outcome of resource shifts; it is also the outcome of planning. The planners, their way of working, and the way that working process interacted with the other things that were going on in the city and in Venezuela constitute the roots of the present. The city was not planned as it is, but the city is the outcome of planning. The planning process helped make it what it is.

One way of explaining the undesirable outcome of the city is as planning messed up; people and institutions failed to obey the plan. The planners were unable to enforce their plans and thus to realize their dream. Rodwin's 1965 paper warned about the difficulties in implementing planning controls:

> Attracted by the prospect of jobs, poor migrants invade the area, put up makeshift shelters and exacerbate the problem of organizing land uses and public services. Most costs tend to be high, almost no amenities exist and living conditions are bleak. Understandably enough, the inhabitants become impatient with "fancy" long-range plans and delays; they grumble about the neglect of their immediate needs and care little if these needs do not fit the priorities or the plans. Up to a point their views can be slighted or ignored, but this is always dangerous. It is hardly surprising that the new city rarely measures up to the original dreams of its planners.[16]

A simpler version of this argument was provided by a Venezuelan economist with the project whom I met again, after twenty years, when I revisited the development agency's offices in January 1982. I asked him how he thought the city had turned out. "Well," he said, "no matter how well they plan it, people keep moving in and messing it up."

This way of looking at the problem was clearly present from the beginning of the planning process. Indeed, the desire to keep people from moving in and messing up the planned city was, it will be seen, a basic reason for the separation between rich and poor, and the contrast between the settlements on the east and west of the river.

A second explanation also departs from the failure of the planners to control the actual processes of urban growth, but this time puts the blame on the planners. The planning process was too rigid. What was wanted, it is argued, was not so much a plan or final design, but a program for directing and channeling urban growth. This way of viewing the issue, like the preceding one, was also present from the beginning, put forward in a succession of consultant memoranda from the early days.

> The more fundamental problem is to view the plan not as a static design but as a path of growth.[17]

> Accept the idea that we should be making a plan for the nature, rate, quantity and quality of urban change and a plan for the development process rather than a plan for some static future state (which will never occur in just that form).[18]

> Any expectation that the ultimate appearance of the city will be like the planning team's initial blueprint will be doomed to disappointment. . . . One of the main factors that will control the city's future pattern will not be what is put into the blueprint as much as what will be imposed by rancho (i.e., squatter settlement) movements.[19]

The comments are surely justified; the production of a plan, in the sense of a set of visually displayed decisions as to the locations of various activities in some future state of the city, was not sufficient to direct the activities to those places. Nor could the planners stop various institutional and personal actors from doing what they wanted to do, rather than what the planners wanted them to do. Even in the early days, when the development agency had decreed a freeze on all construction until such time as the plan should have been developed, squatters continued to put up their shacks and commercial developers continued to construct buildings counter to plan; Sears was building a six-story office building while the planners debated the nature of the commercial center elsewhere in which Sears was to be the prime tenant. A focus on the plan as locational map did little to organize a process which could have negotiated such decisions.

A third view is that the planners were snobs. They were unable to plan realistically for the development of the city, since to do so would have been to recognize and provide for the needs of a mass of poor and low-status people with whom they did not wish to be identified. Snobbery identified the proper outcome of planning with the urban settings appropriate for high-income people, the "modern" with the expensive. Snobbery kept the workers at one end of the city, away from both the industrial jobs to which they would have to commute and the urbanizations of the elite.

Again, there is evidence for an endemic snobbery, both among the planners and among others of the citizenry. When I revisited the city twenty years after my first arrival and asked my cab driver what he thought of the planning, he compared San Félix, the working-class side of the river, to Puerto Ordaz, the upper-income part of the city: "San Félix is terribly planned—all shantytowns; Puerto Ordaz—that's well planned."

These three perspectives are not mutually exclusive. Indeed, I believe that they are all in various ways true. The planning process was one that focused on formal order and on the production of a somewhat statically conceived spatial plan. There was little use of the planning process as one of interacting with, and thus coming to mobilize and direct, the actions of local people. The plan was indeed altered by the initiatives of private actors, not only the squatters whom Abrams saw as shaping the urbanization pattern but also some large corporate investors who put their buildings where they chose, rather than where the plans had proposed. And indeed a strain of unrecognized, perhaps even unconscious, social snobbery in the planners responded to the demand outside the planning office for "nice" neighborhoods and a "high standard" city.

Furthermore, the three interpretations are interrelated. The social separation of the planners from the people of the site, the institutional basis of the attitudes we call snobbery, helped to drive the planning process toward formalism. The formalism, in turn, made for a process that left "implementation" for a second stage of consideration, rather than using planning to develop the social supports for a proposed development path. This process certainly left an opening for unplanned actors to develop counter to the plan.

I wish to propose, here, a fourth interpretation. This, too, does not exclude the others. It constitutes, rather, a way of thinking about the relationships between the others and between the social roots of the planning enterprise. Here, planning will be thought of as a kind of social ritual, the function of which is to legitimize government activities that, if frankly described, would arouse conflict and dissent. The so-called mistakes in planning Ciudad Guayana may be understood as the working out of certain irreducible conflicts in the real unstated goals of the project, issues that were fuzzed over by the way in which the objectives of the city were described and the way in which the planning was carried out. Planning a growth pole meant reorganizing the environment for large corporations. The planners could not have taken the local businessmen and residents into the process without diluting the overriding objective. Therefore, they left them outside. Planning was a way of shifting power and resources toward large corporate bodies. But to make this explicit would have been to threaten the political legitimacy of the government that executed the policy, and which depended on voter support. If planning had been thought of in terms of process, all this would have been quite visible. Thought of as urban design and economic targets, it became a collective product: The City Plan and The Planned City.

The planners were very idealistic people. They believed in what they were doing. One of the functions of the planning process was to construct the planning activity in a form that enabled the planners themselves to feel they were serving an essentially noble purpose. The design focus served to convert the city into a kind of monument to the idea of progress, an ideological construction within which private gain could be thought of as social progress and the general good. The attention to "good design" and values of "amenity," thought of as there for the general enjoyment, made it possible to think of an undivided community interest in the outcome of the planning process. Underlying uneasiness about class divisions and income contrasts was addressed through a focus on physical centers: neighborhood centers, the city center as "the heart of the city." Finally, the organization of an interdisciplinary team, including an anthropologist, made it possible to think of planning as addressing social issues and, indeed, as a technique of liberal reform.

NOTES

1 David G. Epstein, *Brasília—Plan and Reality: A Study of Planned and Spontaneous Urban Development* (Berkeley: University of California Press, 1983); Madhu Sarin, *Urban Planning in the Third World: The Chandigarh Experience* (New York: Mansell Publishing, 1982).

2 Lloyd Rodwin, "Ciudad Guayana: A New City," *Scientific American*, September 1965, 122–23.

3 "Memorandum of Agreement between the Corporación Venezolana de Fomento hereinafter Sometimes Referred to as the 'Corporación' and the Massachusetts Institute of Technology hereinafter Sometimes Referred to as 'M.I.T.' " (1961, Mimeographed).

4 "Memorandum of Agreement between the Corporación Venezolana de Guayana and the Massachusetts Institute of Technology, March 1964" (Mimeographed).

5 Jackson Diehl, "Venezuela's Force-Fed Industrial Center Goes on a Crash Diet," *Washington Post*, March 4, 1983, sec. A.

6 Anthony Penfold, "Urban Transporation," in *Planning Urban Growth and Regional Development: The Experience of the Guayana Program of Venezuela*, by Lloyd Rodwin et al. (Cambridge: MIT Press, 1969), 187–88.

7 CVG, Ministerio del Desarrollo Urbano, *Ciudad Guayana XXI: Logros, problemas y oportunidades, una sintesis del diagnostico* (Caracas: CVG, 1983), 9.

8 Ibid., 14.

9 Claude Brun M., *Ciudad Guayana más allá de 1980* (Caracas: CVG, División de Ingeniería y Construcción, Departamento de Planeamiento Urbano, 1979), 9.

10 CVG, Ministerio del Desarrollo Urbano, *Ciudad Guayana XXI*, 7.

11 Ibid., 9.

12 Alexander Ganz, letter to author, May 26, 1986.

13 "Impressions of Ciudad Guayana from a Visit on February 25, 1981" (Typed memorandum from Willo von Moltke to General Alfonzo Ravard).

14 Lloyd Rodwin, letter to Dr. Argenis Gamboa, president of the CVG, February 2, 1977.

15 Lloyd Rodwin, interview with author, April 5, 1983.

16 Rodwin, "Ciudad Guayana," 122.

17 William Alonso, "Report Concerning Some Aspects of the Projected Guayana City" (Joint Center Guayana Project, Memorandum A-6, July 1962), 28.

18 Robert B. Mitchell, "Observations and Recommendations after Visit to Caracas, January 28–February 3, 1962" (Joint Center Guayana Project, Memorandum A-4, February 1962), 15.

19 Charles Abrams, "Report on the Development of Ciudad Guayana in Venezuela" (Joint Center Guayana Project, Memorandum A-5, January 1962), 26.

Housing Policies for the Urban Poor in Developing Countries

Gill-Chin Lim
Dean of Architectural Studies and Programs, Michigan State University

This article provides an overview of housing problems in developing countries, presents a model of housing markets, and suggests important new policy directions. The author discusses the distinctive features of housing in developing countries—the occupation of land without due permit, the variety of building materials and structures, and multiple occupancy—as opposed to developed countries. Gill-Chin Lim concludes that because of the dynamic and fragmented nature of the housing market, new plans should be developed that are consistent with the behavior of individuals and recognize the several stages of housing development for different submarkets.

The current world population of five billion will probably increase to 6.4 billion toward the year 2000, roughly two billion of whom will reside in the cities of developing countries.[1] A large proportion of these urban dwellers will lack adequate means to meet their needs for housing and other daily sustenance. Furthermore, the cities in which they live, ill-prepared to support their needs, will suffer from a chronic shortage of resources to provide necessary services. Many of these urbanites will sleep on streets, build shacks illegally, or double up in the existing squatter settlements.

The essential features of the housing problem of the urban poor in developing countries have been fairly well recognized among policymakers and researchers (Dunkerley et al. 1978; Oberlander 1985). Policymakers employ a mixture of traditional regulatory measures along with a few relatively new programs such as sites and services,[2] the combined effects of which are poorly understood. The countries sometimes also receive conflicting advice from the international donor agencies that provide financial assistance for their housing programs.

Several underlying norms are shared by both traditional and more recent housing policies: unique occupancy, minimum physical requirements for housing units, and one-step regularization of the housing market. They shape the crucial elements of housing programs such as type and size of housing, and investment targets. These norms originated in developed countries, however, and have been applied to developing countries with varying success. Their validity in the context of developing countries has not been seriously questioned. This paper examines traditional and more recent housing policies and proposes new directions for housing policies for the urban poor in developing countries.

The paper begins with a review of the nature of the housing problems in developing countries, emphasizing three distinctive features: the large proportion of

Reprinted by permission of the *Journal of the American Planning Association* 53, 2, Spring 1987.

illegal settlers, heterogeneous physical stock, and diverse tenure arrangements. Second, a model of housing markets defines various housing submarkets and explains the behaviors of individual consumers in the housing market. Third, the paper describes traditional government policies and evaluates evidence that they have not succeeded in alleviating housing problems. Fourth, it summarizes some notable recent shifts in shelter policies and their effects, with attention to the activities of major international donor agencies and to policy changes in developing countries. Fifth, the paper analyzes the underlying norms of housing policies universally shared by the traditional and more recent approaches—unique occupancy, minimum physical standards, and one-step regularization. Theoretical and empirical evidence indicates that these norms lead to misallocation of resources for housing. Finally, new directions in housing policies are discussed. In particular the paper proposes a shift away from traditional regulatory measures, increased investment in adaptable shared housing for multiple occupancy, and the establishment of policies to facilitate multistep transition in the housing market.

NATURE OF THE PROBLEM

Between 1970 and 1982 the average annual rate of urban population growth was 4.4 percent for low-income developing countries and 4.2 percent for middle-income countries (World Bank 1984). The population in cities over 100,000 in developing countries reached 480 million in 1975 and is likely to rise to 1.4 billion by 2000 (Council on Environmental Quality and Department of State 1980). As Table 1 illustrates, toward the beginning of the next century, many cities in devel-

TABLE 1   ESTIMATES AND ROUGH PROJECTIONS OF
SELECTED URBAN AGGLOMERATIONS IN
DEVELOPING COUNTRIES

City	Population (millions)			
	1960	1970	1975	2000
Calcutta, India	5.5	6.9	8.1	19.7
Mexico City, Mexico	4.9	8.6	10.9	31.6
Greater Bombay, India	4.1	5.8	7.1	19.1
Greater Cairo, Egypt	3.7	5.7	6.9	16.4
Jakarta, Indonesia	2.7	4.3	5.6	16.9
Seoul, Korea	2.4	5.4	7.3	18.7
Delhi, India	2.3	3.5	4.5	13.2
Manila, Philippines	2.2	3.5	4.4	12.7
Tehran, Iran	1.9	3.4	4.4	13.8
Karachi, Pakistan	1.8	3.3	4.5	15.9
Bogotá, Colombia	1.7	2.6	3.4	9.5
Lagos, Nigeria	0.8	1.4	2.1	9.4

Source: Council on Environmental Quality and Department of
State (1980), p. 242

oping countries will have more than doubled their current size, becoming super-agglomerations.

During the last two decades the economies of developing countries have also grown substantially. Between 1960 and 1982, low-income developing countries recorded an average annual growth rate of 3.0 percent in GNP per capita. The rate was 3.6 percent for lower middle-income countries, and 4.1 percent for upper middle-income countries (World Bank 1984).

An important aspect of economic growth in developing countries that should not be overshadowed by the achievement of the overall growth rate is income distribution. Income distribution becomes more unequal as a poor nation moves toward the middle-income bracket (Kuznetz 1955) and, in fact, the share of household income in the lowest two quintiles of poor nations remains significantly smaller than that of the comparable segments of rich nations (World Bank 1984). Consequently, despite the general increase in per capita income, a large proportion of the population in developing countries lives in severe poverty (Linn 1979). The World Bank (1980) estimates that more than 200 million people in cities in developing countries lived below the absolute poverty line in 1980. The great majority of poor people simply cannot afford to purchase through market mechanisms a quantity and quality of housing adequate to sustain a decent standard of living.

The inability to afford a regular housing unit leads the poor to find unconventional solutions to their housing problems, and some of these solutions are even illegal in certain contexts. In particular, three distinctive features of housing for low-income population in developing countries deserve a special note. These features are not common in housing markets in developed countries. First, many people occupy land without due permit of the owner or due process of subdivision. The proportion of such informal settlements in large cities of developing countries is extremely high—ranging from 32 percent in São Paulo to 85 percent in Addis Ababa (Table 2; U.N. Center for Human Settlements [U.N. CHS] 1984).[3]

The second distinctive feature is the variety of building materials and physical structures the poor adapt to housing. In industrialized countries, construction material for housing is fairly standardized. However, in developing nations, the very poor who cannot purchase regular housing units rely heavily on temporary materials. For example, poor inhabitants of Bombay, India, may use gunny sacks and wooden boxes (Municipal Corporation of Greater Bombay 1984). In other countries, flattened cans, mud bricks, and cardboard are also used. Dwelling units built with temporary materials usually violate three central elements of building codes: minimum required standards for construction material, minimum lot size, and minimum floor area.

Renting and multiple occupancy are the third important aspect of accommodation for the poor.[4] The low level of income and the lack of financing mechanisms prevent many people from owning a home as a unique occupant.[5] The proportion of renter occupants was 75.7 percent in Hong Kong in 1971, 30.0 percent in the Republic of China in 1975, 66.9 percent in Malaysia in 1975, 34.0 percent in Mexico in 1970, and 36.5 percent in Korea in 1975 (Korea Research Institute for Human Settlements [KRIHS] 1981).[6] The extent of multiple occupancy is clearly

TABLE 2   ESTIMATES OF THE PERCENTAGE OF CITY POPULATIONS
RESIDING IN INFORMAL SETTLEMENTS

City	Population in 1980 (thousands)	Estimated population in informal settlements	
		Number (thousands)	Per-centage
Addis Ababa, Ethiopia	1668	1418	85
Luanda, Angola	959	671	70
Dar es Salaam, Tanzania	1075	645	60
Bogotá, Colombia	5493	3241	59
Ankara, Turkey	2164	1104	51
Lusaka, Zambia	791	396	50
Tunis, Tunisia	1046	471	45
Manila, Philippines	5664	2266	40
Mexico City, Mexico	15032	6013	40
Karachi, Pakistan	5005	1852	37
Caracas, Venezuela	3093	1052	34
Nairobi, Kenya	1275	421	33
Lima, Peru	4682	1545	33
Sao Paulo, Brazil	13541	4333	32

Source: U.N. CHS (1984), p. 9

demonstrated by the data on housing supply ratio—the number of housing units divided by the number of households in a country. The ratio was 73.6 percent in Hong Kong in 1973, 78.2 percent in the Philippines in 1977, 68.5 percent in Korea in 1980, and 85.1 percent in Colombia in 1973 (KRIHS 1981; Lim, Follain, and Renaud 1984).[7]

In sum, cities in the developing world contain a large number of poor living in accommodations that do not meet the conventional Western definition of home— a housing unit that meets all legal requirements and is occupied by a single household. This is an imposed definition, and in many cultures, occupation by several generations is the norm, not necessarily a problem.

A MODEL OF HOUSING MARKETS[8]

The three main features of low-income housing markets described above suggest that the housing market in developing countries should not be discussed only in terms of formal production and consumption. A more appropriate model can be developed by translating these features into basic criteria by which to classify housing submarkets.[9] The model serves two important functions: to define various housing submarkets and to gain clearer theoretical insights into the behavior of consumers.

Submarket Structure and Definitions

The first classification criterion is the legality of land occupancy. Legal occupants use land in accordance with legal provisions concerning property rights and development, while illegal occupants do not have legal title or have violated subdivision regulations. The second criterion concerns the legality of physical characteristics of the individual units—whether or not they meet the minimum government standards for building material, lot size, and floor area. The third criterion is the status of tenure. Some households are owners with unique or multiple occupancy, while others are renters with unique or multiple occupancy.[10] The classification system generates eight types of housing submarkets (Figure 1).

Box A in Figure 1 represents the *regular* or *formal* housing market. A housing unit in this submarket is owned or rented by a household with legal title to the land and building, and the unit meets the building codes and other government specifications for a legal dwelling unit. Box B is the *slum* housing market, which consists of units built on legally owned or rented land but which do not meet the legal minimum standard for physical characteristics. Some units of *gecekondu* in Turkey and *panjachon* in Korea fall under this submarket. Box C is the *invasion* housing market in which dwellers occupy land illegally or live in illegal subdivisions. Their units, however, conform to the minimum physical standards. Some invaders may occupy land as if they were owners and rent spaces to tenants.[11] *Barrios piratas* in

FIGURE 1 Structure of submarkets for housing.

Physical Characteristics of Land and Structure \ Occupancy of Land	LEGAL		ILLEGAL	
LEGAL	A Regular Housing Market		C Invasion Housing Market	
	Owners	Renters	Owners	Renters
ILLEGAL	B Slum Housing Market		D Squatter Housing Market	
	Owners	Renters	Owners	Renters

Colombia and *colonia ilegal* in El Salvador are examples of the invasion housing market. Box D represents the *squatter* housing market, where housing violates both the legality of land occupancy and physical standards. *Favelas* in Brazil and *tugurios* in El Salvador are squatter settlements. Boxes B, C, and D can be called the *nonregular* or *informal* housing market as opposed to the regular or formal housing market.[12]

Long-Term Multistep Transition Model

The submarket structure can be used to develop theoretical insights into the behavior of consumers in the housing market. First, it suggests that the poor normally have to make a multistep transition through different submarkets to improve their housing condition (Figure 2). Individuals may make this transition either by moving to different locations or by changing their housing characteristics at a fixed location. A household can skip some stages or move in either an upward or a downward direction during the transition. A person who arrives in a city as a street sleeper may move through different submarkets step by step with the possibility of eventually becoming an owner of a regular housing unit. A squatter on a piece of land without legal title and in violation of building codes may in the end pay for the legal title and also have his structure improved to meet the code requirements. A one-step transition from the squatter to the regular housing market would be possible but it is unlikely among the poor.

Second, in the submarket structure, it would usually take considerable time for the poor to move from the informal to the regular housing market. Rarely can a street sleeper afford to turn into an owner of a regular housing unit within a short

FIGURE 2 An example of a multistep transition in a housing market.

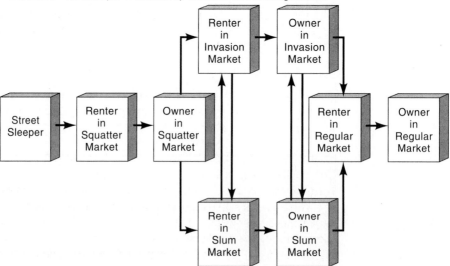

time. Some may stay in one submarket for a long time, because their demand or need does not change.[13]

TRADITIONAL HOUSING POLICIES

Key Housing Policies

Until recently governments in developing countries dealt with the problems of housing primarily by regulatory measures. One of the most popular policies is control of land and housing prices. The rationale is that land or housing is too expensive for the poor, and therefore freezing the prices will make land and housing more accessible to them. The second pervasive regulatory measure is to set minimum physical standards for individual land and structure, in the hope that they will prevent people from building low-quality housing that the governments believe to be unsafe and unhealthy.

Third, some governments have attempted to eradicate informal settlements—particularly those occupied by squatters—only sometimes providing a site for relocation. The logic behind the eradication policy is that physical removal of squatter or other informal settlements would reduce their number in urban areas. Although not as widely practiced as it used to be, it is still employed in some cities, and supported by the courts.[14] In most developing countries, however, squatter and other informal settlements are generally tolerated, if not recognized by law.

The fourth regulatory measure that developing countries sometimes adopt is large-scale development restriction. The best-known measure of this type is the greenbelt. Supporters of the greenbelt argue that the delineation of the boundary of a city by a greenbelt will limit urban growth, effectively putting a ceiling on invasion and squatter settlements.

Fifth, there have been overall attempts at the national level to encourage population decentralization. These attempts are based on the notion that balanced distribution of population among regions would reduce the demand for housing in large metropolitan areas, and thus alleviate urban housing problems.

Negative Impacts of the Traditional Housing Policies

Given the critical shortage of housing, the housing policies in developing countries should focus on facilitating the supply of housing and increasing effective demand at stable prices. Traditional housing policies, however, run counter to these objectives.

All five measures described here exert harmful influence on the housing condition of the poor. Because price control discourages suppliers of housing from entering the market or expanding their output as the demand increases, housing shortages also increase. A black market for housing may develop. In addition, the government must decide how to allocate housing among individuals who want more than what is available. A high minimum physical standard raises the price of regular housing units, making them even less affordable to the poor, who therefore remain in the nonregular housing market.

Eradication of squatter housing destroys units that the poor have built with little public expenditure.[15] Removal of squatters from specific areas, however, does not decrease the demand; it simply creates new squatter areas somewhere else. The greenbelt and other forms of development restrictions limit the supply of land in a city. As the population and income of the city increase, the physical constraints on development will cause the price of housing to rise sharply, particularly near the growth control areas. Decentralization, if implemented successfully by incentives, can reduce the demand for housing in large cities. But, if decentralization is accompanied by restrictive measures such as building permit control, it will increase the price of housing.[16]

To summarize, there are strong theoretical reasons to question the effectiveness of traditional urban housing policies. They tend to limit the supply significantly and drive up prices.[17] Many experts on housing problems agree on the counterproductive effects of many traditional policies such as price control (Mayo, Malpezzi, and Gross 1986; Mills 1980), minimum physical standards, eradication of squatter housing, development controls (Doebele 1983; William Lim 1983; Mayo, Malpezzi, and Gross 1986), and greenbelts (William Lim 1983; Mills 1980). Studies that examine the effects of specific policy measures also support the main theoretical argument proposed here. For example, Wheaton (1981), in his study of Egyptian housing policy, explains that any system of price and quantity controls is likely to be circumvented through a form of black marketing that may result in sectoral distortion, inflation, and regressivity. Kim, Mills, and Song (1986) demonstrate the undesirable effect of greenbelts on housing markets.

RECENT SHIFTS: INTERNATIONAL AGENCIES AND COUNTRY EXPERIENCES

Criticism of traditional urban housing policies over the last few decades (Cohen 1983; Doebele 1983; Mills 1980; Turner 1977) has been accompanied by a gradual shift in orientation. For example, sites and services projects are now widely accepted as a viable means to provide housing for the low-income population. International donor agencies have played an important role in initiating this shift (U.N. CHS 1983; 1984; U.S. AID 1985; World Bank 1975; 1980).

Consensus and Conflict in Recommendations

The most important consensus reached among major international donor organizations such as the United Nations, the U.S. AID and the World Bank is that new housing policies must acknowledge and emphasize the positive contribution of the informal housing sector. This emphasis has been translated into programs such as squatter and slum upgrading, self-help housing, and sites and services projects.

Donor agencies have also recommended changes in minimum physical standards of housing and use of the affordability concept in designing programs. Traditionally, developing countries invested primarily in housing units with very high physical standards, but these have been beyond the reach of the poor. To make new housing programs available to more poor people, it has been recommended that the minimum physical standard be substantially lowered. Currently, the design of residential development projects that receive assistance from the international donor agencies is based on affordability—the ability of the household to pay for housing.

An area that lacks consensus among international agencies is the role of the public sector in land development. The United Nations, on the one hand, recently stressed the need to increase public intervention in the process of land development for housing (U.N. CHS 1983; 1984). Specific policy suggestions include public land acquisition and disposal through preemption, appropriation, readjustment, and nationalization.

In contrast, the World Bank's policies in recent years have underscored the importance of the private sector in the development process (World Bank 1981). Because the Bank believes that the current public policies are major barriers to the supply of shelter it does not advocate the public land development approach (World Bank 1980). In fact, the results of research conducted at the Bank strongly favor a reduction of public intervention. Its research proposes the lifting of various regulations and recommends policies based on consumer behavior in the free market (Mayo, Malpezzi, and Gross 1986). Specifically, it warns against policies that result in counterproductive outcomes. These policies include, according to the Bank, unrealistic building codes and zoning regulations, slum removal, public housing, and unfocused systems of subsidy for shelter and infrastructure.

Country Experiences

The acute shortage of housing and the widespread occupation of land without legitimate tenure are perceived as potential sources of political instability and social unrest. These internal political circumstances and pressure from the international community have been responsible for several important changes in housing policies in developing countries. Most notable among these changes is a gradual acceptance of squatter and slum upgrading, self-help housing, and sites and services projects as key housing programs. Such projects are typically aimed at low-income populations that cannot afford to buy housing in the regular housing market, and they feature revised minimum physical standards that are lower than traditional minimum standards. For example, in a housing project for Madras, India, financed by the World Bank, the minimum plots were reduced from 40 square meters to 35 square meters (World Bank 1985). In Bogotá, Colombia, the revised physical standard was adopted to deal with illegal settlements in the entire city (Kingsley 1982).

During the last decade, a number of countries have also increased their land or housing development activities through their public land or housing development agencies.[18] Although the creation or expansion of these development agencies is not necessarily a result of recommendations by international organizations, many receive technical advice or financial assistance from them. These housing development agencies are given special legal power—eminent domain, expropriation, preemption, and tax credits—to carry out large scale housing development.

In an increasing number of countries, housing development is shepherded along by a long-range national housing development plan ultimately intended to provide a separate unit to every household in the nation. A typical long-range national housing development plan can be described by the following steps: First, policy-makers define the minimum physical standards for land and structure. These standards are not necessarily derived from an affordability analysis. In fact, they are frequently based on a needs concept that exceeds the affordability standard. Then, using population projections, the number of existing housing units, the attrition rate of housing, and the target housing supply ratio, the development agency calculates the amount of new housing needed for the projected population. In the third step, this gross housing and land development target is allocated over a span of years, yielding annual housing and land development needs. Sometimes, the agency also calculates the total financial requirements for reaching the target.

For example, in Korea a long-range land development plan estimates that a total of 958.7 square km will be needed by 1995 to achieve the housing supply ratio of 84.4 percent. This long-range plan adopts a minimum land size of 264.5 square meters for large units and 82.6 square meters for small units (Korean Land Development Corporation [KLDC] 1981). The World Bank (1980), using a similar method to estimate the investment required to satisfy the housing need for the world, suggests that about $160 billion (in 1975 value) will be needed to provide a basic unit of shelter for each household living in poverty in the year 2000.

Impacts of Recent Policy Shifts

The recent shifts in housing policies mark a significant advance beyond the traditional approaches and reflect the enhanced priorities for the housing sector in the national development planning process. For instance, during the 1970s and 1980s, Indonesia, Malaysia, and Korea incorporated sectoral plans for housing as a major element in their national development plans (Yeung 1983; Lim 1985a).

These shifts have affected institution building in developing countries. Changes in legal standards for housing programs and efforts to implement large scale projects through direct public sector involvement have compelled the public sector to undertake various institutional changes. Unified housing agencies (Yeung 1983)[19] and financing institutions were created (Renaud 1984). New administrative divisions of housing and regional planning were set up in national planning agencies. These experiences have enlarged the institutional capacities of developing countries to deal with public projects.

Overall, the new programs based on lower minimum standards and affordability to consumers have embraced a large number of the urban poor who previously were not able to participate in regular housing programs. Most notable have been the World Bank's shelter projects. Through 1982 the World Bank started 90 projects in 50 nations—in the form of either upgrading or sites and services. Between 1975 and 1980 it spent $1.3 billion with an estimated 10 million beneficiaries (World Bank 1980). The Housing Guaranty Program of U.S. AID authorized

$1.395 billion for 146 projects in 39 countries as of September 1985 (U.S. AID 1985).

CRITICAL EXAMINATION OF UNDERLYING NORMS OF HOUSING POLICIES

As the achievements of recent housing programs become more widely publicized, it is likely that they will be recommended by experts and international agencies as superior to traditional programs. Several underlying norms shared by both traditional and recent programs, however, need to be examined critically for their effectiveness in providing housing for the poor in the long run.

Probably the most important of these norms is that of unique occupancy, which indicates that each household must have a single dwelling unit.[20] Traditional housing projects, new programs such as sites and services, and long-range plans all purport to allocate one dwelling unit to one household. This goal is based on a crucial assumption about the behavior of consumers in housing markets: that they prefer unique occupancy. However, as the discussion of the submarket structure indicates, it is quite possible that individuals will opt for multiple occupancy—that is, to share housing with others—perhaps to qualify for more space or other attributes of housing, or because of cultural traditions.

An empirical study for Korea shows that as income grows, individuals spend more to enjoy their physical space than to move to separate occupancy dwellings (Lim, Follain, and Renaud 1984). People may want to enjoy larger housing space while sharing a house with others. The popularity of *mesones* in El Salvador is further evidence of consumer preference for multiple occupancy. The *mesón* is a group of 5 to 50 rooms built around one or more central patios. The traditional *mesones* are converted from middle class houses, but the new ones are being built because of increasing demand. The main reason for the high demand for *mesones* is their convenient location in the center of the city. Most families rent a single room, which is shared, on average, by 2.8 persons (Fernandez-Palacios and Bamberger 1984). The norm of unique occupancy thus may impose an allocation decision contrary to consumer preference and cause misallocation of resources for housing.

International donor agencies have begun to recognize the limits of effectiveness of the unique occupancy approach. A proposed housing project designed by U.S. AID incorporates rental rooms as a basic element of a housing unit to allow multiple occupancy.[21] The World Bank also notes the possible benefit of renting a part of a housing unit to other households (World Bank 1980; Mayo and Gross 1985; Bamberger, Gonzalez-Polio, and Sae-Hau 1982). This recognition notwithstanding, use of rental systems for multiple occupancy by low-income people is not an important element of recent housing programs, and the majority of current housing projects in developing countries are still guided by the norm of unique occupancy.

The second norm shared by housing policies is the minimum physical standard prescribed by the government. This is what the government believes to be the desirable physical structure and minimum size of a housing unit. The concept of a minimum standard is arbitrary in the sense that its determination depends on the economy as well as the culture of a particular society. The acceptable minimum standard varies across societies and changes over time. When a high physical standard is enforced along with the norm of unique occupancy for reasons of safety and general welfare, the proportion of the population able to join the regular housing market is greatly reduced. It creates an impediment for a large number of people in entering the regular housing market.

Traditional housing policies have set unrealistically high minimum standards, making a large quantity of housing illegal. Even new programs planned with the affordability analysis and lower physical standards are beyond the financial capabilities of many poor people. Ayres (1983) and Payer (1982) criticize the World Bank's affordability standards as too high for the poor. The Bank's own finding indicates upward bias in affordability and physical design standards (Mayo and Gross 1985).[22]

The third norm is one-step regularization of the entire housing market—the effort to transfer households from the slum, invasion, and squatter housing markets to the regular housing market in single step. While traditional housing strategies try to regularize all housing market operations by enforcing building codes and other rules or by removing informal units, recent approaches instead change the definition of regular housing, lowering the legal minimum standard.

The norm disregards an important dynamic aspect of the housing market structure described earlier (see Figure 2)—the long-term multistep transition by households from the squatter housing market to the regular housing market. Certainly the long-run policy objective is to provide regular housing units for all members of the society. But hastening the transition—forcing squatters to skip intermediate steps of housing improvement or not giving them enough time to make transitions—lays undue financial burdens on them or governments. It is dysfunctional, because it is not in line with the intertemporal consumer behavior.

The World Bank's experience with sites and services projects provides important empirical evidence to support this point. Many poor people in developing countries cannot buy or rent housing units designed according to affordability assumptions—usually substantially reduced from the conventional standard. Only some can do so, with a large subsidy from the government. Some initial participants in such sites and services projects sell or sublet their units, relinquishing the status of single owners in the regular market (Keare and Parris 1982; Mayo and Gross 1985).

SUGGESTIONS FOR NEW DIRECTIONS

To provide better and more low-income housing without undue burden on the poor and on the governments, new housing policies must address not only the recognized problems inherent in traditional policies but also the potential sources of misallocation embedded in recent policies. Several key policy recommendations can be drawn from the analysis in this paper.

First, traditional regulatory measures that limit the supply and increase the costs of housing should be abandoned or significantly modified. This is not to argue against supporting public land or housing development agencies that address the imperfections of housing markets. The critical issue is not so much whether developing countries should have public development institutions as what functions these institutions should perform. They can redefine their role as providers of land and housing information, advocates of regulatory relief, assessors of development impacts, inducers of private investment, and mediators of development conflicts.[23] Second, eradication of informal settlements should be stopped, and national plans for granting legal status should be prepared. Allowing the poor to have security of tenure is the first step toward upgrading. Third, national housing policies should emphasize expanding the amount of housing space while maintaining flexible tenure arrangements for the poor. The norms of unique occupancy and minimum physical standards should be relaxed to accommodate those who have strong preference for space or other attributes over unique occupancy. Builders should be encouraged to consider construction of adaptable shared housing that can be remodeled easily for unique occupancy as income increases or needs and preferences change.[24] Offering incentives to builders and occupants of shared housing should be examined. Fourth, housing programs should be developed in the multiple stages of the transition process shown in Figure 2, allowing participants to make the transition from informal to regular housing over time. Although the ultimate long-term goal is to provide regular housing units to all dwellers, an effective policy should support gradual improvement toward the regular housing market, not one-step regularization. Fifth, housing policies in developing countries need to be flexibly designed with attention to segmented housing markets. The distinct needs, affordability, and consumption behavior of families in each submarket should be accounted for in designing appropriate policies.[25]

In sum, long-range national housing plans need to be based on different norms and strategies than we use now. New plans should pay attention to the dynamic and fragmented nature of the housing market and should be consistent with the behavior of individuals. A plan with several stages of housing development for different submarkets would be much more effective than current plans formulated by one-step regularization and unique occupancy.

Author's note: I have benefited tremendously from comments made by Howard Sumka, Edward Kaiser, Stephen Malpezzi, Bertrand Renaud, Al Guttenberg, Leonard Heumann, Lewis Hopkins, Ronald Pushchak, Peter Schaeffer, Sid Sen, and three anonymous referees. I am indebted to Man-Soo Joo for his valuable research assistance. This work was supported by the Research Board, University of Illinois, Urbana-Champaign.

NOTES

1 Sources of statistical information used in this paper include: Council on Environmental Quality and Department of State 1980; Linn 1979; World Bank 1980; 1984. Some of the data presented here do not pertain to all developing countries; the paper focuses on developing countries with market or mixed economies.

2 Sites and services projects refer to the provision of land with essential services to meet

the basic housing needs of low-income populations. Allottees of sites and services projects normally build the physical structures through self-help construction (World Bank 1974). The earliest such projects began in the 1940s and 1950s and were implemented without external assistance. Large-scale projects with assistance from international donor agencies started in the late 1960s and early 1970s (Mayo and Gross 1985).

3 The literature on housing in developing countries uses various terms—squatters, slums, and informal settlements—to describe different types of housing submarkets. These terms have been used without a systematic classification scheme, and the definitions are not exact. U.N. CHS (1984), which presents the data cited here, defines "informal settlements" as follows: settlements that are developed by the process "outside the legal framework and regulations that prescribe the way land ought to be developed and buildings ought to be erected" (pp. 8–9).

4 Multiple occupancy is defined as the occupancy of a dwelling unit by two or more households. On the other hand, unique occupancy refers to the occupancy of a dwelling unit by a single household.

5 See Renaud (1984) for issues related to housing finance in developing countries.

6 The renter statistics are for the entire population. Large cities usually have a higher ratio of renters than rural areas. The proportion of renters in developed countries are as follows: 35.3 percent in the United States in 1976, 38.2 percent in Canada in 1976, and 46.5 percent in the United Kingdom in 1977 (KRIHS 1981).

7 In sharp contrast to developing countries, many developed countries have more than 100 percent of housing supply ratio—111.7 percent in the United States in 1979, 102.8 percent in Canada in 1976, 107.9 percent in Japan in 1978, and 117.4 percent in France in 1975 (Lim, Follain, and Renaud 1984).

8 Conceptual difficulties may arise in discussing housing markets and housing policies because of the impact of other policy areas on decisions in housing. For example, interest rate policies, which are in a large measure concerned with the performance of the macro economy, affect the housing sector. This paper focuses on explicit housing policy issues, and therefore the model presented here deals with the internal structure of the housing market. See Lim (1985a; 1985b) for a study of the impact of implicit land policies on land markets.

9 Other criteria can be used to classify submarkets; for example, a land market can be divided between public and private submarkets, or classified by conformance to locational requirements such as zoning. This paper, however, does not use the other criteria because the main features of the land market in developing countries can be described satisfactorily by the three criteria discussed.

10 Unique or multiple occupancy could have been used as a separate classification criterion, resulting in sixteen submarkets. But for the convenience of discussion it is incorporated in the third criterion.

11 Occupants in this group do not own their housing in the legal sense. They may own the physical structure but not the land, although they often claim the right to it. Occasionally, they rent all or some of their unit.

12 Some of the examples here do not fall exclusively under one submarket. For example, some *panjachon* units are slums while others are squatter settlements. For the purpose of policymaking, further distinction beyond popular description may be necessary.

13 The long-term multistep model has not been subject to a full empirical test. Some relevant empirical evidence is presented later in the paper. The model is used to conduct a conceptual analysis of key policy issues in housing.

14 Squatters in Bombay, India, were removed as recently as 1985. The removal was upheld by the Indian Supreme Court (Gibney 1986).

15 Jimenez (1982) shows that squatter dwellings have economic value in the market.

16 For a discussion of decentralization in developing countries, see Lee (1983).

17 However, it should be noted that some regulations could serve useful functions. For example, zoning can be used to deal with negative externalities.

18 Such agencies include: Housing Land Agency, Tunisia, established in 1973; Chilean Urban Development Corporation, established in 1964; Korea Land Development Corporation, established in 1979; National Housing Authority, Thailand, established in 1973; National Housing Board, Ecuador, established in 1973 (Kitay 1985).

19 Unified housing agencies combine a wide range of roles essential in housing development. Their roles may cover land acquisition, project financing, planning, construction, sales, and management for housing.

20 Provision of one dwelling unit for every household has been the prime objective of housing policy in most countries. Developed countries have pursued this objective for several decades. The 1945 Housing White Paper of the United Kingdom stated, "The government's first objective is to afford a separate dwelling for every family which desires to have one." In the United States, the Housing Act of 1949 declared "a decent home and a suitable living environment for every American family" as a national goal (Lim, Follain, and Renaud 1984).

21 Pamela Hussey U.S. AID, April 1986, personal communication; Howard Sumka U.S. AID August 1986, personal communication.

22 Alternatively, it is possible to increase the participation of the poor in the regular housing market by drastically lowering the physical standards. In the short run, this approach can achieve a big improvement in the housing supply ratio. In the long run, however, a very low minimum physical standard based on what the poor can currently afford may not be adequate. Recent studies suggest that income elasticity of demand for housing in developing countries is about .70 (Follain, Lim, and Renaud 1980; Ingram 1984; Malpezzi and Mayo 1985). That is, if household income doubles, demand for housing will increase by 70 percent. The dwelling units built now with a very low standard will become substandard housing in the long run. They may prove to be a public investment for large scale ghettoization. Such housing units would not be demanded and would have to be demolished, if income of the poor increases steadily.

23 KLDC (Korea Land Development Corporation) is a good example. It maintains comprehensive information on land availability, has suggested relaxation of greenbelts, and has conducted environmental impact assessments for large scale housing developments.

24 The total size of an adaptable shared housing unit should be based on minimum standards acceptable for unique occupancy in the future.

25 To design effective submarket policies, the policymaking capacities of local governments must be carefully examined. This raises a difficult question about political decentralization and local-autonomy in developing countries.

REFERENCES

Ayres, Robert L. 1983. *Banking on the poor.* Cambridge, MA: The MIT Press.

Bamberger, Michael, E. Gonzalez-Polio, and U. Sae-Hau. 1982. *Evaluation of sites and services projects. The evidence from El Salvador.* World Bank Staff Working Paper No. 549. Washington: World Bank.

Cohen, Michael A. 1983. The challenge of replicability: Toward a new paradigm for urban shelter in developing countries. *Regional Development Dialogue* 4, 1: 90–99.

Council on Environmental Quality and Department of State. 1980. *The global 2000 report to the President. Vol. 2, The technical report.* Washington: U.S. Government Printing Office.

Doebele, William A. 1983. The provision of land for the urban poor: Concepts, instruments and prospects. In *Land for housing the poor,* edited by Shlomo Angel, R. W. Archer, S. Tanphiphat, and E. A. Wegelin. Singapore: Select Books.

Dunkerley, Harold B., et al., eds. 1978. *Urban land policy issues and opportunities.* Vols. 1 and 2. World Bank Staff Working Paper No. 283. Washington: World Bank.

Fernandez-Palacios, Marisa, and M. Bamberger. 1984. *An economic analysis of low-cost housing options in El Salvador.* Discussion Paper No. UDD-55. Washington: World Bank.

Follain, J., Gill-Chin Lim, and B. Renaud. 1980. Demand for housing in developing countries: The case of Korea. *Journal of Urban Economics* 7: 315–36.

Gibney, Frank, Jr. 1986. Down or out in Bombay. *Newsweek* (January 13): 27.

Ingram, Gregory. 1984. *Housing demand in the developing metropolis: Estimates from Bogota and Cali, Colombia.* World Bank Staff Working Paper No. 663. Washington: World Bank.

Jimenez, Emmanuel. 1982. The value of squatter dwellings in developing countries. *Economic Development and Cultural Change* 30: 739–52.

Keare, Douglas, and S. Parris. 1982. *Evaluation of shelter programs for the urban poor: Principal findings.* World Bank Staff Working Paper No. 547. Washington: World Bank.

Kim, Kyung-Hwan, E. S. Mills, and Byung-Nak Song. 1986. Korean government policies toward Seoul's greenbelt. Mimeo.

Kingsley, Gordon F., Jr. 1982. Political constraints on housing provision: The *normas minimas* program in Bogota, Colombia. Bachelors thesis, Princeton University.

Kitay, Michael G. 1985. *Land acquisition in developing countries.* Boston, MA: Oelgeschlager, Gunn and Hain.

Korean Land Development Corporation (KLDC). 1981. *Long-range land supply plan.* Seoul, Korea: KLDC.

Korea Research Institute for Human Settlements (KRIHS). 1981. *Housing statistics handbook.* Seoul, Korea: KRIHS.

Kuznetz, S. 1955. Economic growth and income inequality. *American Economic Review* 45: 1–28.

Lee, Kyu Sik. 1983. *Decentralization trends of employment location and spatial policies in LDC cities.* Urban Development Discussion Paper No. 20. Washington: World Bank.

Lim, Gill-Chin. 1985a. Land markets and public policy: A Korean case study. Planning Paper No. 85-6. Urbana, IL: Department of Urban and Regional Planning, University of Illinois at Urbana-Champaign.

———. 1985b. Land markets and public policy: A conceptual framework. Planning Paper No. 85-5. Urbana, IL: Department of Urban and Regional Planning, University of Illinois at Urbana-Champaign.

———, J. Follain, and B. Renaud. 1984. Economics of residential crowding in developing countries. *Journal of Urban Economics* 16: 173–86.

Lim, William S. W. 1983. Land acquisition for housing with Singapore as a case study. In *Land for housing the poor,* edited by Shlomo Angel, R. W. Archer, S. Tanphiphat, and E. A. Wegelin. Singapore: Select Books.

Linn, Johannes F. 1979. *Policies for efficient and equitable growth of cities in developing countries.* World Bank Staff Working Paper No. 342. Washington: World Bank.

Malpezzi, Stephen, and S. Mayo. 1985. *Housing demand in developing countries.* World Bank Staff Working Paper No. 733. Washington: World Bank.

Mayo, Stephen K., and D. Gross. 1985. *Sites and services—and subsidies: The economics of low-cost housing in developing countries.* Discussion Paper No. UDD-83. Washington: World Bank.

Mayo, Stephen K., S. Malpezzi, and D. Gross. 1986. Shelter strategies for the urban poor in developing countries. *Research Observer* 1: 183–203.

Mills, Edwin S. 1980. *Procedures for allocating land in Korea.* Korea Development Institute Consultant Paper Series No. 6. Seoul, Korea: Korea Development Institute.

Municipal Corporation of Greater Bombay. 1984. *Report on the revised draft development plan for greater Bombay, 1981–2001.* Bombay, India: Municipal Corporation of Greater Bombay.

Oberlander, H. Peter. 1985. *Land: The central human settlement issue.* Vancouver, Canada: University of British Columbia Press.

Payer, Cheryl. 1982. *The World Bank: A critical analysis.* New York: Monthly Review Press.

Renaud, Bertrand. 1984. *Housing and financial institutions in developing countries.* World Bank Staff Working Paper No. 648. Washington: World Bank.

Turner, John F. C. 1977. *Housing by people: Towards autonomy in building environments.* New York: Pantheon Books.

United Nations Center for Human Settlements (U.N. CHS). 1982. *Survey of slum and squatter settlements.* Nairobi, Kenya: U.N. CHS.

———. 1983. *Land for housing the poor.* Nairobi, Kenya: U.N. CHS.

———. 1984. *Land for human settlements.* Nairobi, Kenya: U.N. CHS.

U.S. Agency for International Development (U.S. AID). 1985. *Annual report; Fiscal year 1985.* Washington: Office of Housing and Urban Programs, Agency for International Development.

Wheaton, William C. 1981. Housing policies and urban "market" in developing countries: The Egyptian experiences. *Journal of Urban Economics* 9: 242–56.

World Bank. 1974. *Sites and services projects.* Washington: World Bank.

———. 1975. *Housing: Sector policy paper.* Washington: World Bank.

———. 1980. *Shelter.* Washington: World Bank.

———. 1981. *Economic development and the private sector.* Washington: World Bank.

———. 1984. *World development report 1984.* New York: Oxford University Press.

———. 1985. The Madras experience: Hard-won successes in sites and services, upgrading projects. *Urban Edge* 9 (December): 8–10.

Yeung, Yue Man, ed. 1983. *A place to live: More effective low-cost housing in Asia.* Ottawa, Canada: International Development Research Center.

ELEVEN. INTERNATIONAL PLANNING—SUGGESTED READINGS

Babcock, Blair. 1984. *Unfairly Structured Cities.* Oxford: Blackwell.

Gomez-Ibanez, Jose A., and John R. Meyer. 1990. "Privatizing and Deregulating Local Public Services: Lessons from Britain's Buses." *Journal of the American Planning Association* 56, 1.

Myrdal, Gunnar. 1957. *Rich Lands and Poor.* New York: Harper.

Peattie, Lisa. 1987. *The View from the Barrio.* Ann Arbor: The University of Michigan Press.

Sanyal, Bishwapriya, ed. 1990. *Breaking the Boundaries.* New York: Plenum.

Sowell, Thomas. 1987. *A Conflict of Visions.* New York: Morrow.

Todoro, Michael. 1989. *Economic Development in the Third World.* New York: Longman.

Waterson, Albert. 1969. *Development Planning: Lesson of Experience.* Baltimore: Johns Hopkins.

12

THE PROFESSION OF PLANNING

Three Crises of American Planning

John W. Dyckman

The three crises described by John W. Dyckman involve the legitimacy and credibility of the planning profession and still persist today. According to Dyckman, the first crisis is the incongruity between planning education and planning practice. He states: "To the extent that they have internalized the conception of planning taught in the schools in which they prepared, they are likely to fall victim to feelings of malaise, or the 'what-is-planning-all-about blues'" (p. 544). New graduates of planning schools are particularly disappointed to find little opportunity to apply, in their entry-level professional positions, the theories and skills they learned in universities. Thus, Dyckman's second crisis involves the curriculum of planning schools. He asserts that although worldly circumstances change, the core of planning—a common culture, a shared ideology, an attitude toward the use of information, and an ethic of rational action—persists. Finally, the third crisis is planning's relationship to the American state. Here, Dyckman argues that "planning is *in* politics, and cannot escape politics, but it is not politics" (p. 551). Effective and legitimate planning must be institutionalized by either governmental or nongovernmental entities.

PLANNING, PROFESSIONALISM AND THE UNIVERSITY

All professions periodically engage in stock-taking, but of the American professions none does so more regularly and searchingly than the planning profession. There are many reasons for this. While all professions tend to be continuously changing as their scientific foundations develop and their technical apparatus is modified, planning changes for even more volatile political and social reasons. Programs change, public demands take new forms, and the place of the profession in the society shifts. Planners caught up in these changes are confused, and call for a review of their situation.

In the American case, moreover, there are certain peculiarities in the status of the activity of planning which impose strains on the persons who call themselves planners, and give rise to self-doubts. Meetings such as this are intended, in part at least, to assuage those doubts. In particular, American planning is beset by paradoxes which torment the practitioners of this art. Many of these will come to mind, of which a few seem to me particularly important.

First and foremost, of course, is American ambivalence about public planning itself. Unlike planners in some countries, where planning is honored ideologically, if not in execution, American planners are unsure of the degree of national commitment to their work. Not only do we lack a public ideology committed to planning, but actual support of planning activity fluctuates from administration to administration, and with national political currents.

Thus the flurry of planning proposals, spurred by the bite of the Depression, which surfaced in the New Deal in 1933 extended hopes which were to founder, but which left a residue of experience that is cherished by the planning memory. (And which are often idealized, both in respect of their social purpose and in the revision of their stumbling execution. As John Kenneth Galbraith has observed, there has rarely been a period of such fuzzy semanticism, but the very fuzziness has left openings for subsequent historians to glamorize the experience.) The stringencies of war added to the planning impulse, and erased some of the bitterness of New Deal frustration in the forties. This made it possible for an early and insistent advocate of planning, Charles E. Merriam, who had himself been a New Deal planning advocate in the National Resource Planning Board, to say in 1945: "The fear that planning will interfere with the development of free industrial society is groundless. The very purpose of planning is to release human abilities, to broaden the field of opportunity, and to enlarge human liberty. We plan primarily for freedom; the ways and means and instruments are secondary to the main purpose. The right kind of planning—democratic planning—is a guaranty of liberty and the only real assurance in our times that men can be free and make a wide range of choices."[1]

On the other hand, an equally early proponent of planning, Rexford Tugwell, speaking in the fifties, observed that, "Some twenty or thirty years ago some of us believed that planning as a profession, and particularly as part of government, was at the beginning of an exciting expansion. Our optimism originated in two identifiable sources: the acceptance of flow and progression as a theory of social change; and accelerating demand for directed betterment of the human condition; the other led us to believe that a series of managerial devices would allow us to satisfy this demand . . . We were too optimistic. The unfortunate fact is that we are not much better off today than we were then. It is true that there are many more individuals who are called planners and many more planning agencies or departments in city and state governments. But neither these officials nor political scientists generally seem to understand how far short they are of the usefulness we foresaw for them a generation ago. They are busy; they produce maps, statistics and reports; they draft zoning ordinances; they rather apologetically identify trends; but they are mere adjuncts to the more important government agencies. They are regarded as a convenience, but they are not responsible and independent contributors. In the Federal government they exist only as minors in a Bureau whose business is the making of the annual budget. In other governments they have even lower status."[2]

The story is well-known. The fortunes of planning fluctuate, but the planners are not significant actors in the American scene. They have certain local powers, but no generalized influence. Their advisory role is treated as backroom drudge work. Our electoral system elevates men and women who are not much bothered by the facts or details. The machinery of planning at their disposal is treated as confirmatory and symbolic, not as relevant to the actual decisions made, which depend on political sensitivity.

Tugwell's comments point to one of the more troubling paradoxes of contemporary American planning. As the functions of planning become more institutionalized in the American scene, the powers of planning seem to decline. There are perhaps important structural reasons for this. The institutionalization of planning observed by Tugwell is largely at the state and local level, and at this level in the American Federal system, less and less of importance is decided. Or, because the environment of state and local governments is open to the Federal sphere of action, the environment is turbulent, unpredictable, and dependent, and the "plans" of locals are highly contingent, and vulnerable to national action.[3] At the same time that the planners have highly localized powers, they deal with issues less and less concordant with the ideological "grand design" of planning.

And, as Tugwell notes, in the Federal government the planning, such as it is, is not done by the "planners." Despite the emergence in recent times of the Humphrey-Javits bill for the creation of National Economic Planning, planning advocates are suspicious of the prospects. Two examples illustrate this climate of misgivings. In his closing address to the March, 1976 meeting of the American Institute of Planners and the American Society of Planning Officials, Martin Meyerson found a number of obstacles to national planning: doubts about leaders, inexact forecasting devices, and reluctance to experiment. Meyerson found a weakening of government legitimacy, deficiency of planning tools, and deepening cleavage of values as likely impediments.[4]

Another, more recent, paper has argued that the core of the difficulty of achieving meaningful national planning is to be found in the ignorance of the planners. In this paper, Peter Schuck contends that, "The state of the art of social engineering is, to put the very best face on it, rudimentary and underdeveloped. Reasonable persons may differ as to whether this ignorance about the workings of social process is an inescapable consequence of their inherent complexity, or whether our social scientists and policy analysts simply have not yet had enough practice. My own conviction is that the ignorance can be dispelled only marginally at best, and that the kinds of propositions about social causality explicit or implicit in any national plan worthy of the name will be exceedingly problematical."[5] To emphasize this point Schuck points to the failures of urban renewal, national transportation policy, and welfare programs, judged by their stated objectives. He disputes the claims that these failures are due to inadequate coordination or to underfunding, or to the sabotage of hostile bureaucracies. He concludes that, "It seems far more plausible to conclude, however, that we simply do not know how to build urban communities, fashion a national transportation system, or eliminate social disintegration, much less accomplish all of these objectives simultaneously through an integrated strategy or plan."[6]

Reasonable persons, among them planners, may also conclude that we are not prepared to allow an adequate test of these social experiments. In social planning we have too often broken off the exercise before such a test could be made. We are partly to blame for promising too much too quickly. There is no doubt that programs are oversold and that we leap from program to program promising new panaceas. But the fact remains that knowledge of incentives, motivation, and social mobilization is primitive in our planning. The California Transportation Agency's recent experience with a reserved traffic lane on freeways for multiple occupancy vehicles—a device long recommended by planners—suggests that we know too little about individual driver behavior and about the transaction costs and social planning preparation necessary to effect changes in even this small part of a total urban behavior system.[7] We learn only too slowly that intervention in complex interdependent systems of action cannot be predicated on simple conceptions of "system efficiency" and on a one-sided reading of motivation.

Contemporary planning activity in America, spurred by the discovery of social science by academic planners, has shown a disposition to apply social science. Where in physical sciences one can normally go from insufficiently critical and sensitive in its handling of these generalizations, researchers have been largely unaware of the dangers of such generalization in social science. Where in physical sciences one can normally go from general theory to less general ones, so that the general supersedes the particular, the same is not true of social sciences. We cannot go from general theories of behavior to specific models that encompass individual cases, the more so when the environment of action, controlled or neutralized in physical science, is both exogenous to the models and decisive in the behavior. If in fact planning is to be rooted in the specific political environment in which it acts, and is to take its meaning from that environment, much of our generalization will be futile unless we can have a general theory of such environments.

Implied in this criticism is the charge that there is imperfect communication between academic planning study and the practice of planning. Further, there is an implication of a symmetry in the flow of information. The flows from the academy to the practice are more abundant than the reverse flows from practice to our learning institutions. In American city planning we are burdened with an unfortunately deep distinction between the ideas of academic students of planning and the actions of the working planners. In particular, we suffer from an unhappy distinction between "professionalism" and "theory." Professionalization has spread rapidly and extensively over city and regional planning activities in America, and at the same time the teaching of city planning has become widely diffused in the academy. But in the course of this expansion, the ties between the two types of activity have become increasingly strained. In my view, this is explicable, but unnecessary.

The gulf between the sets of actors is not hard to explain. To begin with, the reward systems of the different spheres of activity are very different. Individual members of the university must conserve their positions in the university and try to rise in that system. They cannot do so unless they meet the expectations of the university community for publication, and this means the construction of generalizations and ultimately of theoretical systems of explanation. Every professor of planning appreciates the extent of his disadvantage if he has no "theory" to call his own. This obligation is not wholly relieved by the location of planning education in "professional schools." The canons of academic judgment pursue the individual, and determine his success.

Very different criteria are determining for the working professional. That planner may be judged by his fellow professionals, or by the community which he serves, but the criteria will be very different from those of the academic community. Fellow professionals may judge him for the size of the budget or quality of staff he has been able to wrest from the political system, or for the scale of the undertakings he is able to generate, or the innovative methods of analysis and programming he mounts, or even from the publicity he obtains from the media. The community may judge him for his political skills, for his ability to articulate his programs, for his skill in compromising interests, or for his ability to inspire visions of the future. As a recent study by Donald Schon and associates conducted on M.I.T. planning graduates shows, communication skills are valued very highly by working planners, but in the profession such skills may be employed for the most part in the service of persuasion.

Professionalization, moreover, has grown within a framework of bureaucratization of planning. The establishment of planning offices, the qualification of planners in the context of civil service, the integration of planning into local and state governments, and the growth of legal and administrative requirements for planning approvals have powerful implications for the conduct of planners and their intellectual tasks. As Max Weber long ago established, bureaucracy emphasizes and demands "formal," or procedural rationality. Substantive rationality, or what planning is about, takes second place to procedural efficiency in this environment. Any planner preparing environmental impact studies knows that these will be judged more for how they are done than for what they imply. And while universities may be bureaucratic in their practices, different skills are required for advancement in a government bureaucracy and in a university.

Academic planners would warmly endorse the dictum of Charles De Gaulle, who wrote, "The power of the mind implies a diversity that is not to be found in the exclusive practice of a profession, for the same reason that home life is rarely very entertaining."[8]

So the school explores the powers of the mind to stretch our understandings of planning, and the professional planners tend to its home life. A price that planners pay for the bureaucratization of their profession is the inevitable tedium of bureaucratic life. Ensconced in the offices of the state or local government they take on some of the powers of the state apparatus, but they are constrained by all the rules and requirements of the office. To the extent that they have internalized the conception of planning taught in the schools in which they prepared, they are likely to fall victim to feelings of malaise, or the "what-is-planning-all-about blues." The feelings of recent planning graduates on entering the job market are described by one of them as follows: "If he or she is lucky (?) enough to find a job as a planner, he will seldom use his knowledge of economics, sociology, psychology, et al., because he will promptly be put to work coloring maps, making models, or talking with business representatives about the refusal of their petition for a zoning variance. For, speculate as we will about the future of planning, its present is largely made up of mundane tasks for the new professional."[9]

Of course, this is partly the nature of life in organizations. The junior officer rarely has the opportunity to exercise his training in tactics, strategy and combat logistics. Much of his time is spent in routines, in barrack inspection, enforcement of regulations, and parade. The newly minted graduate planner, stuffed with social science and armed with the image of planning as "societal guidance," is likely to experience stunning culture shock in the environment of bureaucratic life. The most perceptive of the planning students recognize this prospect, and shy away from that commitment. Many drift into research organizations, consulting firms, think tanks, or strive to remain in the protective cocoon of the university. Since they cannot start in the bureaucratic game at the top, they no longer aspire to enter official planning offices and to directly influence local environments. The growing incongruity of planning education with planning practice constitutes the first of our planning "crises."

THE DEVELOPMENT OF PLANNING THEORIES AND THE CRISIS OF PLANNING EDUCATION

The second "crisis" which I wish to address is to be found in the teaching of planning in the universities. In the environment of the university, planning curricula grow rapidly and spread in many directions. Both the American Institute of Planners and the Association of Collegiate Schools of Planning are presently engaged in strenuous efforts to codify the course contents and to specify a required educational content. We may view these actions as responses to perceived, threatening disorder. In general, these efforts represent the desire to "bound" the field, so that it is not preempted by other disciplines and so that it is not so diluted as to lose respectability. A recent summary report of a committee of the Association of Collegiate Schools of Planning addresses this issue in the following terms: ". . . if there is a working consensus on an explicit definition of planning we can invite attention to the differences between planning and such related fields as urban studies and operations research at a level that is intellectually defensible. Rather than drawing boundaries around planning education on the basis of "proper" or "conventional" academic labels, credentials and professional socialization, we may distinguish between planning schools and other academic enterprises by the presence or absence of specific curricular objectives."[10]

The need to be "intellectually defensible" is felt keenly throughout the profession, but it is most acute in the universities. Largely for this reason, planning education created a demand for planning theory. In the institutional environment of the university, pressures for generality, explanation, and rigorous argument are paramount. Within the walls of the academy, planning teachers would be second-class citizens without their own theory or theories. At a trivial level, intra-university struggles for status would account for a certain amount of the grasping for theory in planning.

At a more important level, however, ideas of planning need guiding theories for the important *organizing function* which they can provide. Put simply, if we had a theory of planning, it ought to help organize the core knowledge in the field. For a theory is a point of reference and a means of validating knowledge. Economic theory, for example, is rigorously organized so as to say what economics deals with and what it excludes. Theory is always changing so as to include additional elements, but at any moment it is *coherent*. Further, relations that are observed, as in regression analysis, are interpreted and *validated* by reference to the theory. Finally, theory is largely the construct of professional scholars. Writing of economic theory, George Stigler saw this as a temporal process, observing that "a basic distinction must be drawn between the period in which a field of study is dominated by controversies over policy (applications) and the period in which it is a discipline pursued by professional scholars."[11] At the same time that theory is the creature of the scholar, it must have application to the work of men of affairs. This requirement is especially strong in the case of theory designed to affect the conduct of a profession, such as planning.

The problem of planning theory, moreover, is that it tends to be pulled apart by these requirements. In the era when applications were stressed and controversies raged principally over policy, theory could be close to the profession, but the theory was itself embryonic at best. As it began to be developed in the academy, theory encountered increasing demands for explanatory power and for rigor. Efforts to develop these characteristics were achieved, if at all, only at the expense of relevance. As Nicki King notes, "There are built-in tensions which, in providing *rigor*, pull theorists too far into the world of abstraction and unreality. Their theories about guidance are impressive intellectual statements that bear no relation to the operation of social systems in a modern world. By the same token, attempts at providing *relevance* often reduce concepts of societal guidance to the level of the case study, which limits their generalizability and usefulness in providing insights into the true nature of the larger system."[12]

These tensions have been with us since the maturing of planning curricula in our universities. The same tensions echo throughout the introduction that I wrote in 1969 to the special issue of the *Journal of the American Institute of Planners* on planning theory.[13] The purpose of that issue was, the introduction said, "to dissect the uses of planning theory through exploration and demonstration of theories of planning that are especially appropriate to professional planners."[14] In other words, it represented an effort to relate theory to the practice of a well-defined group. It was designed to help bridge a gulf that even then was widening between the academics and the professionals. The difficulties that effort encountered are still with us. Not all these obstacles are the result of difficulties in theorizing about planning. Some result from the difficulty of classifying the professional practice to which the theory is supposed to relate.

For the planning "profession" in America is insecure about its professionalism. If we accept the commonly asserted argument that a profession is characterized, at a minimum, by the "exclusive possession of competence in a specified area"[15] and by the acceptance of a common ethic, we confront the reality that the technical arts of planning are shared with a host of other professions, among them architecture, engineering, and politics, and that the substantive area in which the planners work is not their exclusive domain, but is shared with economists, sociologists, lawyers, journalists, and businessmen. What is more distinctive of the profession of planning is a common culture, with a core of shared ideology. That culture, just as the theories of the scholars of planning, is in flux. But it retains a common core. This core persists, and guides the orientations of planners, when professional tasks change, and when the public interpretation of the planning role is modified by events. To quote my 1969 position: "The rules of the game in public planning are a source of much disagreement between planners, politicians and bureaucrats. This is the point at which planners plead for rational procedures, for giving weight to "technical" information inputs, for consistency and avoidance of contradiction, and for conduct of decisionmaking greatly at variance with prevailing practices."[16] In short, the core has a set of procedures, an attitude towards the use of information, and above all for a commitment to rationality. Further, the "ethic," or normative guidance, of planning is the ethic of rational action.

The presence of this professional orientation of planning does not imply, however, that the appropriate theory for planning is that of rational decision. Academic critics, in and out of planning, have pointed to the difficulties, limitations, and lack of relevance of rational planning. The difficulties are well known to theorists in economics, business, and public administration. Rational planning models require the processing of enormous amounts of information, require an arbitrary limitation of the levels of repercussions to be considered, and encounter severe problems in the aggregation of individual values. Critics such as Simon, March, Braybrooke and Lindblom have attempted to devise models of "limited rationality" which would be more practical for administrators and other public actors. These have been highly pragmatic, "incrementalist" models, which emphasize problem decomposition, and a series of small adjustments and pragmatic trials. Incrementalism is a popular idea with planners, which is more and more appealing as planners find themselves working in structured governmental situations, as administrators rather than as social critics or "agents of change." For it is the nature of incrementalism that, while starting out to economize on the high cost of information and to achieve a practical "rule," it ends with a model that is uncritical of existing structures and excludes the important large scale changes that are most interesting to planning.

The institutionalization of planning in America, and its absorption into state and local government practice, coincided with the academic critique of thoroughgoing rationalism (which had been based largely on utilitarian economics and on statistical decision theory). The convergence of practical tasks and academic views sounded a retreat from big systems to little systems. Planning theorists were not far behind the administrative theorists in modifying their perspectives. Melvin Webber, for example, was one of the early proponents of the ideas of planning as a "process" of thought and action, separated from the idea of the "plan." Later he refined his views of this process, and incorporated a learning model into his view of planning.[17] John Friedmann, in a succession of papers, also incorporated elements of the process view and the theory of learning systems, eventually adding the ideas of "societal guidance" drawn from Mannheim and Etzioni.[18] It is not my purpose to review this literature; it is in any event familiar to those who read the journals in which academic planners publish. What is important for this paper is that these views do not so much dispense with rationalism, or at least with reason, as they restrict and modify it.

These modifications of planning theory marked the effort to make planning thought more congruent with observed planning behavior, on the one hand, and with modified normative rules on the other. But they leave many questions unresolved. Webber's view leans heavily on the means of making the procedures of planning more effective within relatively strict limits to action. As a guide to procedures it expands the conception of "adaptive" planning by providing a model of purposive adaptation. It is weaker on the subject of the norms which are the substantive ends of the process, and for which efficiency and effectiveness are servants. The norm of reducing error is a very general one. In an overtly interventionist activity one needs more specific substance for his purpose if he is to defend the action. It is difficult to discern, in Webber's model, who is ultimately guiding the action.

John Friedmann has made the question of leadership central in his theory of *transactive planning*. In his view, the convergence of certain social and historical ideological movements has produced the conditions for a learning exchange between the planner and his client, a dialogue through which a self-activating society can be realized.[19] The model of guidance is close to that advocated by Etzioni. Like Etzioni, Friedmann seems to take the expert class as given; there are planners and there are clients. How each got to his role, or how they might be exchanged, is not clear. As King put it, "The role outlined . . . is shadowy, and the author shies completely away from issues of equity (one suspects that a true democracy is not being advocated here); trust (how the planner becomes accepted enough that his clients believe he will act in their best interests); and power (which is crucial to implementation)."[20]

While his theory may appear elitist to some, Friedmann has the virtue of rooting it in real society. It is not an argument by analogy with organizational or biological systems. Friedmann's planner is respectful of the "other," and enters openly in dialogue with him. But he doesn't offer to change places with him. There are those who have one kind of knowledge and those who have another. Thus he appears to protect professionalism—if the professional is a wise man. The planner in this formulation does not have to defend his legitimacy—it is somehow conferred upon him. (King calls this "trust.") His power to implement is presumably based on persuasion. The theory rests on a partial and questionable theory of the state (the emergent self-activating society), and on an unsubstantiated legitimation of planning.

The "advocate planners" challenge both of these. In their view, the state is the creature of dominant interests and the planner is the servant of those interests. Therefore, countervailing plans which represent the interests of the underrepresented are needed. These plans become the embodiment of the interests of the voiceless. In its interpretation by practicing planners this position becomes cloudy.

Sometimes it resembles the adversary model of truth-seeking espoused by Paul Davidoff.[21] This model rests implicitly on analogy with the representation of interests in the Law. At other times it takes on radical overtones of class interests. Still others interpret it as raw activism. The need for counter-planning is an obvious response to the bureaucratization of city and regional planning. But the sources of legitimacy of the advocate planners are uncertain. Lisa Peattie and other critics have demonstrated that the advocate planners, as intellectuals and professionals, may be suspect in communities they seek to represent, whose members are neither of those.[22] Such communities, moreover, may have no more consensus on plans than the society as a whole. Clearly, the great weakness of the advocacy planning movement is that it lacks a view of the whole social system. Without that view, its very rationality comes into question. It is difficult to relate the partial actions of the advocates with broader social objectives, except in the case of those whose view is based on the role of classes in the society. And even there the case is hard to make that communities are equivalent to classes. Davidoff thought that the advocacy model would improve rationality in a pluralistic society by allowing for a fuller representation of interests, but his idea of the pluralist society is not fully fleshed-out.

The culture of planning cannot dispense with the need for rationality. The German social philosopher Jurgen Habermas asserts flatly: "The choice of a concept of rationality is decisive for the structure of a planning theory."[23] Habermas, who seeks to synthesize Max Weber, Marx, the neo-Hegelians and some strands of Existentialism in his works, has the most ambitious classification of the uses of rationality that I have encountered. Habermas has classified three major modes of rationality. I will take up his argument in some detail because it offers one organizational frame for the struggles for a planning theory.

The three modes are *purposive rationality, systems rationality,* and *practical rationality*. In the first, "The model of rational action is suited to theories of rational choice and to planning techniques in areas of strategic action. The limits of the model can be seen, however, in the attempt to develop empirically substantive theories of social systems. The theoretical strategy of choosing the concept of subjective rationality of action means a prior decision for normativistic approaches and for methodological individualism."[24] In this class one would lump both the traditional optimizing models of economics and the modified bureaucratic models of the incrementalists. It would also include much of the public choice theorizing (e.g., in Downs, Buchanan and Tullock, and Mancur Olson) which has emerged since Arrow played Pandora and let the Genie out of the box. For these theories preserve the individual as the point of reference (even when he is the politician) and focus on his strategic actions.

In the second mode, "Planning theories laid out in *systems theoretic*" terms are based on a concept of objective rationality that is taken from the paradigm of self-regulated systems. The pattern of *systems rationality* is suited for empirically substantive theories about object domains in which unities that are clearly demarcated from their environment can be identified. Then (but only then) stability or instability can be determined on the basis of a systems maintenance accessible to experience.[25] In this class belong many of the planning models of the systems era. In this spirit we find the work of Churchman, Emery and Trist, Dror, Etzioni and others. As Churchman has often stressed, an essence of the system is a need to postulate the objective teleology of the system. This is a critical point of difference among the writers, but is recognized by all. Thus, for example, Etzioni, in his work *The Active Society* postulates a set of "fundamental needs" of the social system. Others, following the early work of Merton and Parsons, have a "structural" model of the system in which the "functions" or roles depend upon and reinforce the structure. Emery and Trist describe this view as follows: "They have found their main business to be in the analysis of a specific bureaucracy as a complex social system, concerned less with the individual differences of the actors than with the situationally shaped roles they perform."[26] Some studies of the planning profession have combined this role view with the sociology of profession's tradition of Everet Hughes, notably those of Altshuler and Rabinovitz.[27]

Habermas concludes, in his third mode, "Finally, planning theories laid out in *communications-theoretic* terms are based on a concept of practical rationality that can be gained from the paradigm of will-forming discourse (and which can be developed in the form of a consensus theory of truth) . . . It is suited to the critical investigation of constellations of interest that are at the basis of normative structures. This procedure of normative genesis must, of course, be connected to the systems-theoretic approach if it is to contribute to a suitable theory of social evolution."[28] In this formulation, *purposive rationality* leads to diverse strategic planning techniques; *systems rationality* yields bio- or organizational cybernetics, the theory of planning as a political process, and universal functionalism; and *practical rationality* gives us a critical theory of society.

We should note that the keystone of the Habermas *practical rationality* is a "communicative planning." This issue is most explicitly addressed in the work of John Friedmann on "transactive planning." The difference between the works of Habermas and Friedmann is that the end of the Habermas type of planning is the critical examination of society and its ultimate restructuring on the basis of the critical findings. The bulk of the *Legitimation Crisis* is devoted to a critique of the modern state, which Habermas sees to be in a crisis of legitimacy. This is the most important aspect of that work. And it is this emphasis which I wish to address in the final section of the paper.

PLANNING AND THE STATE

The third major crisis of American planning is that of its relations to the American state. We have seen that the advocate planners have posed critical questions about the present political orientation of planning, but lacked complete view of the sociopolitical system in which they operated. In short, they suffered from an imprecise view about the kind of state they envisaged. Other theories either had romantic visions of power and implementation, or took the legitimacy and the authority of planners for granted. And many others simply do not know what kind of state they are talking about.

American planning thought has suffered from more or less unconscious elitism. The guidance theory of Etzioni and Friedmann is unconscious of the implications of assignment of leadership to the "guides." Dror (admittedly an Israeli) has stressed the validity of utopian rationality in administrative planning. These intellectuals of planning, along with the practicing bureaucrats of planning, have been the targets of a barrage of criticism emanating from conservative quarters. Irving Kristol and Nathan Glazer have published a stream of articles in the *Public Interest* pointing to the futility or the presumptions of specific planning proposals. Aaron Wildavsky, in a series of papers, has berated planners for their lack of understanding of *realpolitik*. The presumption of power by planners has provoked a counter-elitism of political savants.

Planning is nothing without politics, we are told, and the rationalism of planning avails naught against the realities of politicians. Is it because planning is utopian in its vision of rational or scientific politics, or because planners are so unworldly? Do they not understand the workings of the political system? In particular, do they not understand power?

Certainly American planners, particularly city planners, have contributed little to the study of their own situation or to the ideas about American government. It is no accident that the best studies of American city planning have been done by political scientists such as Altshuler and Rabinovitz. The only important views on the crucial place of the organization of the state for planning have been those—admittedly somewhat utopian and elitist, but creative—of Rexford Tugwell.[29] At times ideas from abroad have entered our planning literature, as in Dror's views of the "metasystem" of planning. Planners have ignored Daniel Bell's emphasis on the theory of the "public household."[30]

The condition of planning *vis-à-vis* the state in which it is to be located is not confused so much as it is insentient. Planning is *in* politics, and cannot escape politics, but it is not politics. If it is to be effective it will be more or less institutionalized—either as government planning or as counter-planning. Once institutionalized it must face a set of problems of the most intractable sort. These include the dynamic conservatism observed in institutions by Donald Schon;[31] the ubiquity of ill-defined and therefore "wicked" problems first described by Churchman[32] and applied to planning by Rittel and Webber;[33] the powerful incentives to politics to be couched in ambiguous statements, demonstrated by Downs;[34] the obduracy of individual interests; the gaps in our sciences of social and individual behavior; and its lack of understanding of the political system in which it is situated.

At best the planner does not retreat to the precision of technical competence at the cost of social relevance. But he faces technical and political problems which require ideological guidance. And he lives in a political world whose characteristics are often at odds with his ideology of reason. This is true whatever his world: in the states of capitalist electoral democracies he faces organized interests, the power of capital, and the deliberate obfuscations of the politicians; in the socialist states he faces the fundamental confusion of socialist ideology about planning, the conservatism of bureaucracies, and uncertainties about his professionalism in the socialist system.

Martin Meyerson, in the speech cited earlier, spoke of the obstacles facing planning in America. He noted: doubts about leaders; inexact forecasting devices; and a reluctance to experiment. We could freely add to this list, but it is worth noting that the first obstacle is a political one, the second is technical, and the third combines the political and the technical. This division can stand as a paradigm for the types of problems encountered by planning in our society. Some difficulties are political, some technical, some both. They pertain to both capitalist and socialist societies. I have not discussed the technical difficulties—they are well known to the planners. The political ones are less well known. Yet they are pressing in any modern state.

For the modes of politics and the ideologies of planning are not the same. Some confusion on this point was contributed by incomplete Marxism. In a relatively undeveloped argument, Marxists argued that they were going to replace an organization of society by market (Marx said "commodity") relations by an organization of society by means of planned relations. That is, many Marxists saw planning as integral to political ideology and a basis for organizing the state. In fact, we have learned, it is no more integral to the idea of realizing the socialist state than the capitalist one, and in any event, it smacks of statism to many younger socialists. At best, it has left many socialists confused. For example, Vladimir Bakarić, in a recent article, complains: "Actually, I was not referring to lectures and the teachings of Marx's works. What I wanted to say was that all of this has not provided the necessary concrete background for the changes which should be carried out in the socioeconomic system. In a word, the active element was missing."[35] At worst, some socialists feel planning will have to disappear before the state itself can disappear; others believe it will be necessary to secure the dissolution of the oppressing state by planning.

In fact, I believe that planning is an instrument of the state, and where the state exists cannot be separated from the environment of that state, but is nonetheless an independent intellectual creation whose ideology has grown up in a variety of states, and whose uses have been turned to the advantage of many, states and non-states. In this light, I view the connection of planning with socialism as unformulated and incomplete. Were I to be a free interpreter of history, I would identify it closely with the desire of Marx for a more humane allocative system, and with the fundamental rationalism to which Marx adhered all his life. Marx and Engels viewed communism as the abolition of the state, which Marx saw as a form of oppression, through an intervening period in which planning would supersede the capitalist relations. But what was to be the role of planning was never precise.

This at least had the virtue of a clear conception of the state. We have learned— sometimes to our regret—that the independent development of planning can be used in the service not only of the state, but for the maintenance of the most oppressive states. Indeed, the strength of planning is sometimes in proportion to the conservatism of the state, as Stephen Cohen has shown in his study of French capitalist planning. In American planning we lack the vision of what kind of state and what kind of politics we want. We indulge this ignorance at our peril, both as planners and as citizens. Certainly this is a most pressing challenge to creative planning thinking.

Planning and politics are not the same, but it is true that what we do as public actors is always political, especially since when planning is effective it makes allocations of property rights, and every allocation is in some sense a political one. Moreover, as Engels made clear, property is at the heart of state organization. Every land use decision, every transportation decision, every economic strategy has a political content in the sense that the distribution of benefits and costs of that action falls unequally on people. We can have no illusions about our work in this regard. In this light it is all the more remarkable that American planning has largely ignored the organization of the state. Planning can make itself useful to the state without regard to the nature of the state. In that direction lies the dangers pointed out by Bertram Gross, Irving Horowitz and others. But it can also draw on the independence of its intellectual resources to mount a major criticism of the modern state. Only by performing this critical function can it achieve ultimate substantive rationality and be true to its intellectual charge.

NOTES

1 Charles E. Merriam, *Systematic Politics* (Chicago: University of Chicago Press, 1945): 336.

2 Salvador Padilla, ed., *Tugwell's Thoughts on Planning* (University of Puerto Rico Press, 1974): 27–28.

3 In a paper published ten years ago I observed that "the social democracy which is a precondition to collective social planning in a political democracy depends on social gains which will be engineered, for the most part, from Washington. The achievement of economic democracy, the securing of equality in civil rights, the abolition of gross regional differences in education, and other major social gains will be forged by federal power, or not at all." (J. W. Dyckman, "Social Planning, Social Planners and Planned Society," *Journal of the American Institute of Planners* 32 (1966): 66–76. This quote is cited in Andreas Faludi, *Planning Theory* (Oxford: Pergamon Press, 1973): 193. Faludi feels that the built-in atomism of American society is responsible for the inclination of American writers to "advocate a certain amount of centralization as a pre-condition of effective implementation of social policy."

4 Martin Meyerson, "The Next Challenge for the Urban Planner," *Journal of the American Institute of Planners* (Oct. 1976).

5 Peter H. Schuck, "National Economic Planning: A Slogan Without Substance," *The Public Interest* (Fall 1976): 68.

6 Ibid., p. 9.

7 See, for example, Peter Gordon, "A Note on Political Ambiguity," Peter Gordon and James D. Hess, mimeographed paper, Department of Economics, University of Southern California.

8 From *Vers l'armee de metier*, p. 200, quoted in Nathan Leites, *The Rules of the Game in Paris* (University of Chicago Press, 1969): 41.

9 Nicki King, "Planning Theory: An Examination of the Linkages Between

Implementation, Knowledge and Action," Rand Corporation Paper P5161 (Jan. 1974): 14.

10 Henry Hightower, "Toward a Definition of Square One: The ASCP School Review Committee and Procedural Planning Theory," paper presented at the western regional meeting of the Association of Collegiate Schools of Planning, Port Ludlow, Washington, October 18, 1976, p. 1 of report.

11 George Stigler, "Economic Theory and Economic Planning," *American Economic Review* 1 (May 1960), reprinted in Stigler, *Essays in the History of Economics* (University of Chicago Press, 1965): 19.

12 King, "Planning Theory," pp. 1–2.

13 John W. Dyckman, "The Practical Uses of Planning Theory," *Journal of the American Institute of Planners* (Sept. 1969).

14 Ibid., p. 298.

15 See, for example, Harold L. Wilensky and Charles N. Lebeaux, *Industrial Society and Social Welfare* (New York: The Free Press, 1965): 284.

16 Dyckman, "The Practical Uses of Planning," p. 299.

17 Melvin Webber, "Planning in an Environment of Change," Parts I & II, *The Town Planning Review* (Oct. 1968 & Jan. 1969).

18 See, for example, John Friedmann, "Note on Societal Guidance," *Journal of American Institute of Planners* (Sept. 1969).

19 See "Transactive Planning," Chapter 6 in *Retracking America* by John Friedmann (Garden City, New York: Anchor Press/Doubleday, 1973).

20 King, "Planning Theory," p. 7.

21 Paul Davidoff, "Advocacy and Pluralism in Planning," *Journal of the American Institute of Planners* (Nov. 1965): 331–38.

22 See Lisa Peattie, "Reflections on Advocacy Planning," *Journal of the American Institute of Planners* 34, 2 (1968): 80–88.

23 Jurgen Habermas, *Legitimation Crisis* (Boston: Beacon Press, 1973): 139.

24 Ibid.

25 Ibid.

26 The quote is actually from A. W. Gouldner, *Patterns of Industrial Bureaucracy* (London: Routledge, Kegan-Paul, 1955), and appears in F. E. Emery and E. L. Trist, "Socio-technical Systems," in C. W. Churchman and M. Verhulst, eds., *Management Science*, Models and Techniques, vol. 2 (London: Pergamon, 1960): 83–97.

27 Alan Altshuler, *The City Planning Process* (Ithaca: Cornell Univ. Press, 1965), and Francine Rabinovitz, *City Politics and Planning* (Chicago: Aldine, 1970).

28 Ibid., p. 140.

29 See, for example, his papers on "The Place of Planning in Society," Puerto Rican Planning Board, San Juan, 1958; "The Fourth Power," in Planning and Civic Comment (Apr.-June 1939), and his important emphases on constitutional revision.

30 Daniel Bell, "The Public Household," *The Public Interest* (Fall 1974) n.37.

31 Donald Schon, *Beyond the Stable State* (New York: W. W. Norton, 1971).

32 C. West Churchman, "Wicked Problems," *Management Science* 14, 4 (Dec. 1967): B141–142.

33 Horst Rittel and Melvin Webber, "Dilemmas in a General Theory of Planning," *Policy Sciences* 4 (1973): 155–169.

34 Anthony Downs, *An Economic Theory of Democracy* (New York: Harper and Row, 1957).

35 Vladimir Bakaric, "Why Have We 'Returned' to Marx," *Socialist Thought and Practice*, A Yugoslav Monthly, Belgrade (July-August 1976): 67.

Four Critical Junctures in the History of the Urban Planning Profession: An Exercise in Hindsight

Michael P. Brooks

Professor of Urban Studies and Planning, Virginia Commonwealth University

Michael Brooks examines four critical junctures, or "forks in the road," that the planning profession has faced. These junctures involve quests for increased political efficacy, federal government support and sanction, academic respectability, and private-sector validation. In Brooks's opinion, "the paths that *were* chosen . . . led to some seriously dysfunctional outcomes" (p. 557). The cumulative impact of these decisions has been, according to Brooks, to put the "soul of the profession"—its utopian, visionary, reformist tradition—at risk.

The urban planning profession in America faces challenges that pose serious questions about its future roles and functions. While all professions undergo change over time, urban planning today is characterized by trends that threaten to alter its fundamental nature. Today's practitioners frequently find themselves engaged in activities that are far removed from the reformist, visionary, future-oriented spirit that initially attracted them to urban planning. It is possible for a profession to change its norms and behaviors so drastically that it ceases to be recognizable in the context of its historical antecedents; in time it evolves into an altogether different enterprise. Urban planning in the United States is moving in that direction. Should the transformation become complete, something of great value will have been lost.

This article focuses on the urban planning profession per se—that collectivity of individuals who identify their work as "planning" for a particular jurisdiction or sphere of activity and who consider themselves members of the "planning profession," a community of shared interests and activities. (It would be inappropriate, of course, to define the planning profession in terms of membership in the American Planning Association or the American Institute of Certified Planners; nor can we apply the test, as might be done in other professions, of the possession of a university degree in planning. Either criterion would exclude many people who perceive themselves—and indeed who function—as members of the planning profession.)

Planners have long recognized that much of the planning of American cities is carried out by individuals—developers, business leaders, elected officials, bureaucrats in other disciplines—who are not members of the planning profession. I will not focus here on "planning as a process that occurs in cities"; indeed, cities will continue to develop and change regardless of whether persons called "planners" are on the scene (Mandelbaum 1985). For much of the 20th century, however, planners *have* been on the scene, attempting to guide that development and change in

Reprinted by permission of the *Journal of the American Planning Association* 54, 2, Spring 1988.

a manner consistent with the values most important to the profession at the time (aesthetics, the public interest, comprehensiveness, technical efficiency, equity, and so on). The concern underlying this paper is the threatened disappearance of the special perspectives that professional planners have brought to the urban development arena.

The major vehicle for enactment of that perspective—and the most common source of employment for professional planners—has been the public planning agency (municipal, county, or regional). Unfortunately, the problems experienced by many such agencies illustrate the profession's troubled condition. Local planning agencies typically do not enjoy much public recognition of their activities. Many large cities have planning or development directors who have little identification with the planning profession.[1] The planning office in many communities does little more than administer the local zoning process. It is increasingly difficult to identify cities in which professional planners play strong roles in shaping the physical—much less the social and economic—structure of the community. It is a rare planning agency that has sufficient clout to significantly influence the activities of major developers.[2]

Indeed, there continues to be widespread disagreement concerning just what planning agencies should be doing. "End-state" planning—the preparation of a comprehensive plan intended to guide the community's future development—is no longer fashionable within the profession, but no consensus has developed regarding appropriate roles to replace it (Banfield and Wilson 1963: 203; Birch 1980: 43; Krueckeberg 1983: 31–32).

The seminal thinkers of the profession are now largely historical figures; few "heroes" have emerged to replace them. (How many major breakthroughs have occurred in planning thought and practice in recent years?) Increasingly, the profession's agenda appears to be shaped by external, and constantly changing, forces beyond its control.

Concern is widespread among planning educators that the nation's "best and brightest" are no longer attracted to the profession. Indeed, many university planning departments are struggling to survive; some have lowered their admission standards to maintain viable levels of operation. And many of the stronger schools, accreditation standards notwithstanding, have solidified their standing within the academy by adopting scholarly stances that bear little relationship to the workaday world of planning practice.

Some who read those words will find them "alarmist" and will argue that the profession is doing just fine. To be sure, there is little hard data available to support my contentions; I base them on my own observations of trends in planning practice, and others may read those trends differently. Some will suggest that the urban planning profession's problems, while real, are merely the result of a temporary aberration in the nation's political climate; hence we should simply be patient as we await the return of a national mood more sympathetic to the problems of cities and the virtues of planning. Still others will argue that the "problems" I identify here are not problems at all, but rather reflections of changes the profession has made consciously and wisely as it adapts to profound and permanent transformations in the nation itself during the past decade.

This paper is based on a point of view that differs from those in the preceding paragraph. The analysis that follows builds upon an assumption that historical conceptions of the urban planner's role are still valid in today's cities, and that those conceptions are severely threatened. The analysis consists, in effect, of a set of hypotheses regarding the reasons for some of the profession's most serious problems, in the hope that a better understanding of the causes of those problems will in turn contain the seeds of amelioration. Above all, my intent is to stimulate discussion and debate, a willingness to engage in critical introspection being an essential characteristic of any mature profession.

In their thoughtful introduction to a recently-published collection of papers on planning history, David A. Johnson and Daniel Schaffer note the importance of historical analysis in helping us "to uncover and understand those truly historic moments—those critical junctures when influential choices are available to planners and policymakers . . ." (Johnson and Schaffer 1985: 132). This paper will examine four such junctures. I have selected them because I consider them to have been important turning points in the history of the planning profession—and to have worked to the profession's ultimate detriment.

These junctures are not "events" that occurred at a finite point in time, nor are they directly attributable to specific individuals. They do, however, constitute collective choices that the profession has made over time in response to situations featuring two or more alternate paths. They reflect forks in the road traveled by the planning profession through its history. In each case, other choices could have been made. Certainly we cannot identify the consequences—positive or negative—that would have resulted from the selection of other paths. I suggest that the paths that *were* chosen, however, led to some seriously dysfunctional outcomes. Those paths involved the collective quests of the planning profession for increased political efficacy, sanction and financial support from the federal government, academic respectability, and validation by the private sector.

THE QUEST FOR INCREASED POLITICAL EFFICACY

From the establishment of the nation's first city planning commission (in Hartford, Connecticut, in 1907) through the 1930s and 1940s, responsibility for municipal planning was vested primarily in the hands of independent "blue ribbon" lay citizen boards (Spencer 1979: 65–68). Manifesting the precepts of the "good government" movement—a response to the widespread corruption and bossism that had characterized many major cities early in the century—those commissions were intended to protect planning "from evil politicians by having planners work for a righteous group of public-spirited individuals. . . ." (Catanese 1978: 186). The relationships between planners and elected officials were minimal, a situation quite satisfactory to politicians so long as planners focused on long-range concerns and remained aloof from the day-to-day workings of the city (Spencer 1979: 65).

By the 1940s, however, concern over the profession's perceived lack of efficacy was leading to alternative ideas about the appropriate mode of organization (Wilson 1983: 102). The lay planning commissions were increasingly seen as "elitist," and as too far removed from the corridors wherein key development decisions were being made. The solution: shift the planning function to the executive branch, where the planner would have the ear of the mayor (or city manager) and could thus influence decisions more directly. Hence there emerged, as Catanese suggests, a "power behind the throne" conception of planning (1984: 23). The spread of that idea was spurred by the publication of Robert Walker's influential book, *The Planning Function in Urban Government*, in 1941. Indeed, Spencer cites data that the International City Management Association collected: in 1948 more than 50 percent of all planning directors in reporting cities with populations over 25,000 were appointed by planning commissions; by 1971 only 18 percent were appointed by such commissions, most being appointed instead by chief executives (Spencer 1979: 73).

It is reasonable to characterize that shift as a quest by the planning profession for increased political efficacy. Far too many plans had been prepared only to be blithely ignored; too many carefully-formulated recommendations had fallen on deaf ears. It is not difficult to understand the motivations of a profession that desired to see its proposals implemented more frequently. Closer alliance with the city's chief executive was a highly seductive concept.

Did that shift in the organizational context of local planning yield the desired results? No. On the contrary, the major effect, in my view, was to render planning the handmaiden of electoral politics.

To be sure, some writers—Catanese (1984: 18–20) is a major example—have applauded the emergence of an "executive dominance model" of planning.[3] Others, however, have noted the extent to which planners and politicians march to different drummers. Most elected officials, writes Branch (1981: 53–54), "avoid comprehensive planning because they believe that it interferes with the practical requirements for reelection." Undoubtedly some planners have been fortunate enough to serve under "planning-oriented" mayors. Such instances are rare, however. One searches the literature in vain for a list of cities in which planners have played critical and long term roles in influencing the developmental stances of elected officials.[4]

Ultimately, the critical flaw in the "executive dominance model" is its tendency to subjugate the planning process to the political agendas of elected officials. Under that circumstance, planners, no more eager to be fired than are members of any other profession, tend to play their professional roles in a safe and cautious manner. Based on an extensive study of planning agencies in the 1970s, Jerome L. Kaufman concluded that "most planning agencies consciously choose the soft line, with survival—more positively stated as seeking legitimacy—an ever-present consideration. Without much statutory authority, planning agencies generally have preferred egg-walking to making waves . . ." (Kaufman 1974: 127). Moving "closer to the center of government" had not, in Kaufman's view (1974: 127), enhanced the security of planning.[5]

I must conclude that the shift to staff status, and hence the politicization of the planner's role, did little or nothing to solve the inefficacy problem that had spawned the change in the first place. Indeed, the more lasting effects were those of rendering the planner's role suspect, of making that role subservient to larger political imperatives, and hence of diminishing the profession's aura of independent creativity. Those effects weigh heavily upon the profession today. They are not, however, impervious to amelioration.

THE QUEST FOR SANCTION AND FINANCIAL SUPPORT FROM THE FEDERAL GOVERNMENT

Although modest levels of federal assistance to local planning operations had been initiated a few years earlier, the era of major federal support was ushered in with the Housing Act of 1954. Section 701 of that act "energized" the planning profession, as literally thousands of small communities undertook the preparation of comprehensive physical development plans (Kaufman 1974: 113). During the 27 years of the program's existence, annual federal appropriations for local planning assistance increased from $1 million to $100 million; by the time the program terminated in 1981, it had allocated more than $1 billion to local planning (Feiss 1985: 175). It also produced unprecedented levels of demand for planning skills, which in turn fueled the growth of the planning education enterprise.

Nor did the Section 701 program constitute the only manna from heaven. The Housing Act of 1959 provided federal support for the preparation of community renewal plans; matching funds were made available for the preparation of comprehensive plans at the metropolitan, regional, state, and interstate levels. By 1960, "half of the costs of comprehensive planning in America were subsidized by the federal government as an inducement to all levels of government to participate in this activity" (Gerckens 1979: 48).

Also important was the Intergovernmental Cooperation Act of 1968, which led to the issuance of Circular A-95 by the U.S. Office of Management and Budget in 1969. Circular A-95 required review by area-wide regional planning agencies of all proposals for local participation in federal development programs. That led to the creation of a network of regional clearinghouses, and "helped establish the administrative base for the regional planning and coordination thrust of the 1970s" (Gerckens 1979: 51).

Urban renewal, the Community Action Programs, Model Cities, Comprehensive Health Planning, and federal grant programs for planning in the realms of transportation, housing, open space, and environmental quality all provided jobs for planners and enhanced the profession's visibility and growth. With regard to employment opportunities, 1960 to 1980 was truly the golden age of American urban planning.

Even as the profession enjoyed rapid expansion, however, troubling signs could be observed. The federal largesse was accompanied by constant deadlines, unprecedented volumes of guidelines, requirements for data and annual reports, and review processes; for many planners, the preparation of proposals for local participation in this or that federal program—always "due next week"—became a way of life. It was only logical, moreover, to focus the work of one's agency primarily on activities that were currently fundable.

As the planning profession came to rely increasingly on federal funding, it rendered itself highly vulnerable to a reversal of the national mood—as has indeed occurred in the 1980s. As planners increasingly allowed the federal government to determine local agendas, the profession's ability to set its own course, to define its own *raison d'être*, was placed in serious jeopardy (Catanese 1984: 196–200).

Drastic cutbacks in federal funding have had a pronounced negative impact on the demand for planners. (Beauregard [1985: 11] presents data on that demand between 1960 and 1980). The relationship between the number of jobs available and the number of planners seeking employment has become a matter of concern to the profession. It is little wonder, then, that planners have been seeking new outlets for the employment of planning skills. It is also not surprising that those who have jobs want to keep them. How best to do so? By not making waves.

The net result of having the bottom drop out of the profession's funding base, then, has been similar to that discussed in the preceding section—rendering planners more cautious in their professional behavior. Again, this can only serve to sap the spirit of a profession rooted in creativity, idealism, and a willingness to take risks in the pursuit of more humane, attractive, and functional communities.

Could we have perceived in advance the extent to which we were selling our professional souls to the federal treasury? Perhaps not; when euphoria reigns, it is easy to believe that it will last forever. (Indeed, one looks in vain for significant writings in the planning literature, between 1960 and 1975, in which the authors counseled restraint.) That does not mean, however, that we cannot take steps to repair the damage.

THE QUEST FOR ACADEMIC RESPECTABILITY

The rapid growth of the planning profession during the 1960s and 1970s had a dramatic impact on planning education as well. An accurate count of the number of planning programs at any given time has always been difficult, there being some thorny problems of definition. One author pegs the number at 21 in 1954; by 1978 there were 10 bachelor's degree programs, 83 at the master's level, and 21 Ph.D. programs in planning (Branch 1981: 32). Whether those numbers are precise does not matter here; the important phenomenon is the explosion in the number of planning schools that occurred in a period of two dozen years. In the mid-1950s, the would-be planner had a limited array of universities from which to choose; by 1980, most major universities offered some form of planning education. The increase in the number of planning students was even more dramatic; according to Krueckeberg, master's degrees awarded in city, community, and regional planning "increased from barely more than 100 per year in 1955 to nearly 15 times that number in 1975 . . ." (Krueckeberg 1984: 79).

Did that rapid growth have an impact upon the nature of planning education itself? I suggest it did, in the following manner.

Universities are highly competitive with one another, and strongly desire to manifest "academic quality" in the scholarly credentials and accomplishments of their faculty members. Competition also occurs within the academy, of course, as departments vie with one another for students, resources, and academic status. Prior to the 1960s, however, the planning profession had little tradition of academic scholarship; indeed, the best-known teachers in the early planning schools were typically "master practitioners"—in the tradition of architecture education—rather than persons who had distinguished themselves in research and scholarly publication. Thus, few "planning scholars" were available to staff the numerous planning schools that emerged in the 1960s.

How did universities fill the gap? First, they frequently hired urban scholars from related disciplines—geography, economics, sociology, civil engineering, and other fields. (Significantly, that was also the era in which large sums of money were being spent on elaborate exercises in mathematical modeling—the Chicago Area Transportation Study and the Penn-Jersey study are examples—and such modeling was quickly seized upon by university planning programs as academically respectable subject matter.) Second, a number of doctoral programs in planning were established; these were typically oriented, however, to regional science, regional economic analysis, and other approaches that emphasized quantitative analysis and sophisticated theory building. The teachers of doctoral students frequently had been trained in other fields, which in turn strongly influenced the orientations of successive generations of planning educators.

The inevitable result was a sizable body of educators, teaching in planning departments, who had little sense of identity with the planning profession per se, and whose primary reference group was their fellow academicians (Isserman 1985: 489).[6] It is not surprising, then, that the gulf between the education and practice wings of the profession has become so wide. (Leaders of the Association of Collegiate Schools of Planning decided, a few years ago, to hold that organization's annual conference separately from that of the American Planning Association—a move that has greatly enhanced attendance of ACSP conferences, but at the expense of further isolation from the practitioner community.)

Some observers have suggested that the educator–practitioner gap in planning is typical of all "minor professions," and that such conflicts are inevitable and unresolvable (Teitz 1984: 75). While the patterns manifested in planning may indeed occur in other disciplines as well, it is not necessary to concede their immutability; there is no "iron-clad law of professions" that dictates such an outcome. We can narrow the gap significantly if we choose to do so.

The solution does not lie, as some are wont to profess, in "replacing all the Ph.D.'s with practitioners." Having practiced does not ensure that one will do a good job of conveying current practice skills. Just as there have been scholars who stopped doing significant work after acquiring tenure, there have also been practitioners who joined university faculties and thereafter ceased growing professionally, focusing for years on the last set of agency activities with which they had been involved.

What the profession sorely needs is a larger cadre of educators who deeply care about, and relate to, the practice of planning. Whether those educators have their formal schooling in planning or in other disciplines is not at issue here; indeed, the planning profession has been enriched significantly by the insights of those trained in cognate fields. The issue is how, and to what, that training is applied. As Kaufman notes (1974: 132), planning faculty "should be encouraged to undertake more research on the nettling question of how to make planning agencies more effective." In the same vein, Judith Innes de Neufville urges planning educators "to explain the profession to itself, to make explicit the nature of practice, to develop theories about how and why certain modes of practice tend to produce one or another type of result. Our theories should provide a framework to understand the logic of planning action and discourse, and to create a new exemplar for practice" (de Neufville 1983: 38).

At present there appears to be cause for cautious optimism on this matter. An informal network of planning educators interested in research on practice-relevant issues has recently emerged (the University of Maryland's Howell Baum has played the chief catalytic role), and several significant practice-oriented works have lately appeared (see, for example, the collection of papers in Checkoway 1986; Forester 1987; the symposium on impact fees that appeared in *JAPA*, 54, 1, 1988). It remains to be seen whether those developments will help to bridge the communications gap between planning educators and practitioners. I fervently hope so; the profession needs the analysis and insights that can only be provided by a strong tradition of independent scholarship, while scholars in turn need the reality-grounding of the world of practice. The quest for academic respectability should not, and cannot, be abandoned. We should transform it, however, into a force that breathes new life into our troubled profession.

THE QUEST FOR PRIVATE-SECTOR VALIDATION

As I noted earlier, it is not surprising that the current dearth of jobs in traditional planning agencies has led to a search for new employment avenues. Nor is it surprising that the search has tended to focus on the private sector, given that sector's embodiment of the current national mood. Pointing to the failures of the urban renewal program and other efforts to solve social and economic problems through large-scale government action, the Reagan administration has consistently sought—at least in its rhetoric—to minimize the role of government in the development process. The planning profession has been swept along with that movement.

The increased emphasis on private-sector planning has taken several forms. One is the growing volume of advice to planners to shift to private employment (Catanese 1984: 22; Knack 1984). Another is the argument that the future of local planning lies with the facilitation of public–private cooperation (Catanese 1984: 151–94; see also the *JAPA* symposium on public–private partnerships in the Pittsburgh region, 1987). Still another is the suggestion that planning education should focus increasingly on financial management, marketing, and related skills (Hodges 1985). Given a planning education and "other specialized skills," writes

Hodges, individuals have moved "into allied fields such as real estate development, mortgage finance, and expansion planning for private industries and public utilities. Some have even moved into nonallied fields, such as manufacturing, retail marketing, and the restaurant and lodging industry. . . ." (Hodges 1985: 4; see also Isserman 1985: 488–89). Finally, several university-based planning programs have introduced curriculums, even new degree programs, in real estate development.

Is this urban planning? Must we totally transform the profession to save it? And if we do, will it be worth saving?

The powerful role of the private sector in the development and redevelopment of America's cities cannot be questioned. Nor can one doubt the value of public–private cooperation in that process. The accomplishments of the Urban Development Action Grant (UDAG) program are real and frequently (but not always) commendable.

We must question, however, whether the public sector (and, by extension, urban planners as key representatives of that sector) is being granted a truly efficacious role in the public–private partnership. There is growing cause for concern in that regard (e.g., Boyer 1986). Today most American cities, fearful of economic decline and stagnation, afford the large-scale developer a red carpet reception. Planners are valued primarily to the extent that they "facilitate" the development process. Attempts to inject other values into that process—values of justice and equity, of fairness to all groups, of conservation, of aesthetics—are tolerated only until such values get in the way of private entrepreneurship. The planning becomes dispensable.

In short, the current weakness of the planning profession is that Planners would like to think that they are full partners with the private sector; in reality, such is rarely the case.[7] That, too, bodes ill for the future of the planning profession. I do not suggest that planners should adopt a pervasively hostile stance toward the private sector, but rather that they should retain sufficient independence from it to allow the advocacy of values and interests other than those reflected in the quest for private profit.

When the last planner becomes primarily a "facilitator" in service to the activities of the private sector, we will have lost a profession. Strong forces impel us in that direction at present. One hopes that we will have sufficient strength of professional character to resist those forces.

CONCLUSION

The planning profession in America has been nothing if not flexible. It has adapted readily, throughout its history, to an ever-changing set of political and economic forces. It is entirely possible that this adaptability has enabled the profession to survive. Would there still be a planning profession if planning agencies had remained responsible to citizen planning commissions, rather than aligning themselves with elected officials? One cannot say. Can we survive in the future without becoming handmaidens of the quest for financial profit? Again, the answer is elusive.

Ultimately, however, we must confront and deal with the soul of the profession.[8] It is a soul enriched by the works of creative and dedicated figures in our history—Frederick Law Olmsted, Daniel Burnham, Henry Wright, Clarence Stein, Clarence Perry, Rexford Guy Tugwell, and many others. It is a soul influenced immeasurably by those—Paul Davidoff comes quickly to mind—who have reminded us of the critical responsibilities we bear for the well-being of all who reside in the communities we purport to serve. And fortunately, it is a soul that still receives nourishment from many planners who strive to serve the underlying values of the profession. As I have attempted to demonstrate in this article, we have on occasion taken paths that have proven injurious to the soul of planning. To date, however, none of those injuries have been fatal—or irreversible.

Donald Krueckeberg recently cited two book reviews, one by Richard Bolan and the other by Allen Jacobs, in which each praised the book he had reviewed for helping him to remember why he had chosen to become a planner: "to pursue 'a humanistic vision' and 'a worthwhile utopia'" (Krueckeberg 1983: 1). That perspective contrasts sharply with Krumholz's pessimistic conclusion, at one point in his reflections, that most planners are "ordinary bureaucrats seeking a secure career, some status, and regular increases in salary" (Krumholz 1983: 275). Implicit in that contrast is, perhaps, the field on which the battle for the profession's soul will take place.

In my view, we sorely need to return to the utopian tradition in planning. The urban planning profession needs a new generation of visionaries, people who dream of a better world, and who are capable of designing the means to attain it. That, after all, is the essence of planning: to visualize the ideal future community, and to work toward its realization. It is a much-needed role in our cities, and young men and women continue to enter the profession because they want to perform that role. Let us nurture their instincts, and thereby restore the urban planning profession to its historic mission.

Who will employ such visionaries? Universities, for one; what better base of operations can there be for a planner who desires the freedom to design a better future? Local nonprofit organizations and citizen groups offer similar opportunities. Consulting firms remain a viable option for creative dreamers who are adept at translating their ideas into concrete and implementable plans. In some parts of the nation, state governments are showing signs of willingness to carry out important functions from which the federal government has withdrawn. And finally, city administrations and even private corporations will continue, in some instances, to underwrite the process of thinking about, and planning for, the community's long-range future.

Meanwhile, of course, many people with the word "planner" in their titles will continue to work closely with political and economic leaders in carrying out the day-to-day business of the city. Theirs is an important role too, and it is not my intent to denigrate it. But it would be tragic—for the planning profession and for the nation—if those individuals were to become the sole survivors of the planning movement in the United States.

NOTES

1 In 1983, of the 105 U.S. cities with populations of 150,000 or more, 25 (23.8 percent) had planning directors who were members of AICP. Earlier, in 1974, 54 (51.4 percent) of those same 105 cities had had planning directors who were AIP members (D. S. Sawicki, unpublished).

2 A recent headline in the *Buffalo News* read, "Planning Board Approves Project Already Started" (September 24, 1985: 3). Branch (1981: 5–6, 23–24) is one of several writers who have expressed concern about the inability of planning agencies to influence critical development decisions in their communities.

3 Catanese (1974: 141–42) was somewhat less sanguine about that model ten years earlier, when he cited a "growing realization that the planner cannot remain as the isolated eunuch of the chief executive's office."

4 In describing his relatively good working relationship with San Francisco's then-Mayor Alioto, Allen Jacobs writes, "To be sure, I was not kidding myself about Alioto's being a planner's mayor. He was not. My initial sense was that he was highly development-oriented, even when development might be ill-placed, and that he would not be terribly concerned with long-range views. . . . But then, how many mayors are planners' mayors? One could wait a long time for that happy situation." Jacobs reports that he came, with time, to feel more positive about the helpful and supportive role of the planning commission (Jacobs 1983: 238, 249).

5 "I suspect," wrote Kaufman (1974: 129), "that risk-takers, people inclined to be more receptive to some of the new directions in the planning field, do not as often reach the top staff positions in planning agencies." Also see Krumholz (1983: 274–75).

6 Clearly the planning profession is not alone in that regard. In a recent analysis of the nation's schools of education, Derek Bok writes:

> Because they have neither a strong profession nor a distinctive body of knowledge to impart, education faculties have no firm anchor for their programs and curricula. Instead, external forces push them first in one direction and then in another. Lacking an affluent alumni body to provide a strong financial base, education schools are continually pressed to alter their teaching and research activities to adjust to the constantly changing priorities of foundations and government agencies. Unable to find enough able students interested in public school teaching, professors tend to shift their interest from teacher training to specialized programs that will attract more talented applicants. Uncertain about their status in the university and anxious to win the respect of their arts and sciences colleagues, education faculties often appoint professors with strong scholarly reputations who have little interest in public schools and carry on research only tenuously related to education (Bok 1987: 49).

7 M. Christine Boyer (1983) argues that American planners have always toiled in the service of capitalism. If she is correct, then the only change in recent years is the extent to which that service has become explicit.

8 One respondent to an earlier draft of this paper took issue with its reference to a professional "soul," arguing that such a concept is vague, overlaid with mystic or religious connotations, and therefore flawed as a vehicle for expressing a concrete idea. Certainly other terms could be employed instead—heart, essence, spirit, ethos, guiding principles. I decided to stick with "soul," however; it does seem to communicate the desired idea in a parsimonious fashion. I imply no mysticism or spirituality by that usage.

REFERENCES

Banfield, Edward C., and James Q. Wilson. 1963. *City Politics*. New York: Vintage Books.

Beauregard, Robert A. 1985. Occupational Transformations in Urban and Regional Planning, 1960 to 1980. *Journal of Planning Education and Research* 5, 1: 10–16.

Birch, Eugenie Ladner. 1980. Advancing the Art and Science of Planning: Planners and Their Organizations. *Journal of the American Planning Association* 46, 1: 22–49.

Bok, Derek. 1987. The Challenge to Schools of Education. *Harvard Magazine* 89, 5: 47–80.

Boyer, M. Christine. 1983. *Dreaming the Rational City: The Myth of American City Planning*. Cambridge, MA: MIT Press.

———. 1986. The Tragedy of City Planning. *Crit* 17: 41–48.

Branch, Melville C. 1981. *Continuous City Planning: Integrating Municipal Management and City Planning*. New York: John Wiley and Sons.

Catanese, Anthony James. 1974. *Planners and Local Politics: Impossible Dreams*. Beverly Hills, CA: Sage Publications.

———. 1978. Learning by Comparison: Lessons from Experiences. Pp. 179–207 in *Personality, Politics, and Planning: How City Planners Work*, edited by Anthony James Catanese and W. Paul Farmer. Beverly Hills, CA: Sage Publications.

———. 1984. *The Politics of Planning and Development*. Beverly Hills, CA: Sage Publications.

Checkoway, Barry, ed. 1986. *Strategic Perspectives on Planning Practice*. Lexington, MA: Lexington Books.

de Neufville, Judith Innes. 1983. Planning Theory and Practice: Bridging the Gap. *Journal of Planning Education and Research* 3, 1: 36–45.

Feiss, Carl. 1985. The Foundations of Federal Planning Assistance: A Personal Account of the 701 Program. *Journal of the American Planning Association* 51, 2: 175–84.

Forester, John. 1987. Planning in the Face of Conflict: Negotiation and Mediation Strategies in Local Land Use Regulation. *Journal of the American Planning Association* 53, 3: 303–14.

Gerckens, Lawrence Conway. 1979. Historical Development of American City Planning. In *The Practice of Local Government Planning*, edited by Frank S. So, Israel Stollman, and Frank Beal. Washington: International City Management Association.

Hodges, Allan A. 1985. Career Advancement in Spite of a Planning Education. *Journal of the American Planning Association* 51, 1: 4–5.

Isserman, Andrew M. 1985. Dare to Plan: An Essay on the Role of the Future in Planning Practice and Education. *Town Planning Review* 56, 4: 483–91.

Jacobs, Allen B. 1983. 1968: Getting Going, Staffing Up, Responding to Issues. In *Introduction to Planning History in the United States*, edited by Donald A. Krueckeberg. New Brunswick, NJ: Center for Urban Policy Research, Rutgers University.

Johnson, David A., and Daniel Schaffer. 1985. Learning from the Past—the History of Planning: Introduction. *Journal of the American Planning Association* 51, 2: 131–33.

Journal of the American Planning Association. 1987. Symposium: Public-Private Partnerships for Economic Development in the Pittsburgh Region. *Journal of the American Planning Association* 53, 4: 430–477.

————. 1988. Symposium: Development Impact Fees. *Journal of the American Planning Association* 54, 1: 3–78.

Kaufman, Jerome L. 1974. Contemporary Planning Practice: State of the Art. In *Planning in America: Learning from Turbulence*, edited by David R. Godschalk. Washington: American Institute of Planners.

Knack, Ruth Eckdish. 1984. Moving Into the Fast Lane. *Planning* 50, 7: 24–29.

Krueckeberg, Donald A., ed. 1983. *The American Planner: Biographies and Recollections.* New York: Methuen.

————. 1984. Planning and the New Depression in the Social Sciences. *Journal of Planning Education and Research* 3, 2: 78–86.

Krumholz, Norman. 1983. A Retrospective View of Equity Planning: Cleveland 1969–1979. Pp. 258–302 in *Introduction to Planning History in the United States*, edited by Donald A. Krueckeberg. New Brunswick, NJ: Center for Urban Policy Research, Rutgers University.

Mandelbaum, Seymour J. 1985. Historians and Planners: The Construction of Pasts and Futures. *Journal of the American Planning Association* 51, 2: 185–88.

Spencer, James A. 1979. Planning Agency Management. Pp. 61–87 in *The Practice of Local Government Planning*, edited by Frank S. So, Israel Stollman, and Frank Beal. Washington: International City Management Association.

Teitz, Michael B. 1984. Planning Education and the Planning Profession. *Journal of Planning Education and Research* 3, 2: 75–77.

Wilson, William H. 1983. Moles and Skylarks. Pp. 88–121 in *Introduction to Planning History in the United States*, edited by Donald Krueckeberg. New Brunswick, NJ: Center for Urban Policy Research, Rutgers University.

COMMENTS

Michael Brooks expressed the hope that his article would provoke debate about the profession's future direction: "Above all, my intent is to stimulate discussion and debate, a willingness to engage in critical introspection being an essential characteristic of any mature profession" (p. 557). As the following commentaries by Cisneros, Marcuse, Teitz, and Weiss indicate, Brooks certainly succeeded in this goal.

Have Planners Taken Their Eye off the Ball?

Henry G. Cisneros
Secretary, U.S. Dept. of Housing and Urban Development

I was impressed and even moved by the article by Michael Brooks in the *Journal* in which he talked about how the planning profession in recent years has taken its

Reprinted by permission of the *Journal of the American Planning Association* 55, 1, Winter 1989.

eye off the ball. He outlined four critical junctures that have shaped the profession as it exists today. First, the planner's changed relationship to the executive branch and the political process has resulted in a loss of independence in thinking in public ways. Second, the search for professional identity led planners to seek jobs in the private sector and become appendages of business too often. Third, the emergence of the large government programs of the 1960s and 1970s redefined planners' jobs in terms of what was available—701 funds, Model City dollars, urban renewal monies and others—and the profession became a subset of the money available. Fourth, the search for academic legitimacy had planners trying to adapt to preexisting academic definitions of economics or geography or other fields in the early years. He closed the article by saying that, despite these developments, the profession ought to keep first and foremost its public obligations and responsibilities. I'd like to suggest that this role for planning is going to be more and more important. There must exist in each of us who calls himself or herself a planner that tension between how to get things done in the practical world of services delivery and a vision and a sense of idealism founded in public values.

It is important to reinvigorate and revitalize and think in terms of the planning profession's public responsibilities at this time because the problems we face as a nation demand it. Although I have read the discussion in Washington about the prosperity of the economy and the longest recovery in the postwar years, I also know that we're a country in transition economically. In 1950 we employed about 60 percent of our people in manufacturing, and today we employ about 17 percent in that sector. The result is a qualitative change in the distribution of opportunity and income. Additionally, we are creating a frightening, growing underclass in our society. In 1985 the top one-fifth of Americans earned 43 percent of the national income. That was the largest figure to be earned by the top 20 percent since the end of World War II. The bottom one-fifth earned only 4.7 percent of the national income, the smallest percentage earned by the bottom 20 percent in twenty-five years. These changes in the economy are not pathological, not political, not partisan. We're not talking about a governmental shift from domestic responsibilities but a fundamental change that is occurring in our country.

A second dimension of what is happening that will have an equal significance to the current economic profile is the change in American demographics. Traditional populations are growing older and not replacing themselves. They are juxtaposed against ethnic minorities, born in the U.S. at faster rates of growth or immigrating from other nations. It's not an accident that cities like Philadelphia, Chicago, Baltimore, Atlanta, and Los Angeles have mayors who are black; or that Miami and Denver have mayors who are Hispanic; or that women have been able to put together coalitions of ethnic minorities and progressives in cities like Houston, Dallas, and until recently, San Francisco. These developments reflect a changing demographic pattern that is sweeping across the cities, the states and, indeed, the whole country.

Now match these two dynamics—the changing economic base and the increasing diversity of population—with the role the federal government has chosen for itself in recent years, one that I contend is likely not to change no matter who is president in 1988 or in 1992. The fact of the matter is that the deficit is large and the return to categorical programs on the Lyndon Johnson scale is just not going to happen. The initiative is going to come at the local level. We are in an era of decentralization in which a great deal of the responsibility falls to people who have jobs, titles, responsibilities, and professional backgrounds such as those of planners.

In short, we need the skills of planners in rebuilding the basic infrastructure and institutions of the country in an era when the nation is in fundamental transformation. Planners are prepared to deal with these issues. I am absolutely convinced that there must be that constant tension, discipline, and unforgiving relentless pressure upon them as professionals to share some sense of vision—which they are uniquely trained to do—with the larger society.

Who/What Decides What Planners Do?

Peter Marcuse
Professor of Urban Planning, Columbia University

Michael Brooks's article "Four Critical Junctures in the Planning Profession" is right on target in its conclusions: ". . . we sorely need to return to the utopian tradition in planning. . . . the profession needs a new generation of visionaries, people who dream of a better world, and who are capable of designing the means to attain it." But in my opinion he goes far enough off in the history he recites to explain our departure from that tradition so that the signposts he puts up will hardly help turn us in the direction he (and I) think we should go.

The question is, what are those "truly historic moments," those "turning points in the history of the planning profession" that have made us forget that we entered planning "to pursue 'a humanistic vision' and 'a worthwhile' utopia," and have turned us instead into "ordinary bureaucrats seeking a secure career . . ."?[1] If we can find out where things went wrong, we can better seek a remedy, or at least avoid going astray the same way again. So in what historic events does Brooks see our errors? He points to the following:

• The shift to the "executive dominance model" of planning, with planners, seeking political efficacy, preferring appointment by chief executives to appointments by planning commissions

• The reliance on federal funding, as in the Section 701 program, to support local planning

• The quest for academic respectability, as witnessed by the "explosion in the number of planning schools"

Reprinted by permission of the *Journal of the American Planning Association* 55, 1, Winter 1989.

• The increased emphasis on private sector planning and the facilitation of public–private cooperation

Really? Are *those* the "historic moments" in planning, "critical junctures" where we could have avoided changing from "visionaries" to "bureaucrats"?

Let me suggest some alternates:

• The split between city planning as a professional activity, at the time of the founding of the American City Planning Institute (later the American Institute of Planners, now the APA/AICP), from the housing movement about 1907 (Marcuse 1980); also the broader disassociation of the largely physical and business/commercial-based planning approaches of the city beautiful and the city scientific movements from the social reform movements of the Progressive era

• The embrace of zoning as a key tool of planning without condemning and rejecting its use to exclude the poor, blacks, or unconventional households, from entrenched residential communities, which made zoning more a tool to protect real estate values than to improve the quality of life in democratic communities

• The capture of the New Deal beginnings of national planning by the major national business and trade industry groups, and the failure to link either national or local planning to the upsurge of path-breaking (for the U.S.) social legislation and progressive local actions of the 1930s

• The retreat of planning in the face of the McCarthyite onslaught of the immediate post-World War II period, surrendering in the interests of professional security the right to press actively for any planning measures that one might label "socialistic"[2]

• The support and implementation of urban renewal as a device to "renew" communities by displacing lower income residents from desirable locations to introduce "higher and better uses," with its concomitant conversion of public housing from a model of how decent housing might be provided for all to a relocation resource of last resort for the hard core displacees—a mistake continued even today in the support of gentrification as "revitalization" (with similar consequences) in many cities

• The failure to build on the widespread discontent and the openings for significant change which the civil rights movement, the ghetto rebellions, and the political unrest of the 1960s produced, to develop any enduring structural bases for sounder and more visionary planning

• The eager and uncritical espousal of the "public–private partnership" concept, as an opportunistic concession to the conservative offensive of the Nixon/Reagan era, and part of the longer-term erosion of the substantive content of planning into mere "problem solving" on assignments that others provide

The differences between the two lists are more than a matter of personal preference; only the last point appears on both. Brooks's list seems to magnify the importance of the planning profession's role per se; it is more planning, not a particular kind of planning, that he sees as desirable. The issues on which he focuses have to do with the prominence of the planning profession, as if that were a good in itself. Yet his examples suggest a picture of a planning profession that is largely a business, out to feather its own nest, selling out now to the federal government, now to the private sector, building its ego and its image however it can. That view is, unfortunately, substantially accurate. But it contradicts the idea that more planning will necessarily produce a more humanistic vision. Brooks's historic moments provide no clue as to how we might change either the vision or the results of planning, other than through moral exhortation and provocative writings such as Brooks's own; nor do they suggest what larger forces dictate the real role that the profession does or could play.

Shifting the focus from events internal to the profession to the external events to which planners respond produces an alternate list of historic moments and different suggestions for actions that will allow the profession to "regain" its vision. In each case on the alternate list a conflict between major social forces was going on. Deep economic, racial, ideological, locational, and political divisions are involved. In none of my cases—nor for that matter in any of Brooks's cases—was the outcome within planners' control, certainly not in the control of planners acting by themselves. Neither Brooks's list nor mine represents "collective choices the profession has made"; they involve, at most, reactions by the profession to external events not of its own making.

The limitation of Brooks's formulation thus is that it does not link the change that he (and I) would like to see within the planning profession to outside events. Brooks wants to "restore the urban profession to its historic mission." I am afraid the profession is, at least in one view, precisely filling its historic mission when it grovels before power and chases after money, when it plans for luxury condominiums or subsidized housing, new skyscrapers or historic preservation, comprehensive plans or waterfront development, exactly as its employers may dictate at this time or that (Boyer 1983; Foglesong 1986). But the profession also has within it the humanistic—indeed utopian—strain that Brooks's article seeks to stimulate. Whether or not that strain becomes its "mission" depends on forces far greater than those of planners. As planners we can ally ourselves with those forces in our society that would support a humanistic vision, and we can participate directly in helping to shape the world in which we ply our trade. Reform within our own profession can be part of that effort, but it will only be a small part.

Brooks sounds a welcome call to clarify our own positions and to take stands in support of our principles. But, in choosing examples that look inward, he runs the risk of downplaying the importance of becoming involved as planners and as citizens in the broader issues of our day. A presidential election needs to be made relevant; discrimination, segregation, racism, and sexism abound in our society; we waste our resources and imperil the world's future with our armament buildups and our intervention in other countries' affairs; we devastate our environment in the name of an economic development that benefits the few more than the many. Unless we link the future of our profession with the resolution of those issues, we will be fighting a losing battle.

There is confusion or contradiction (or both) in our profession on these issues. In the spring issue of this journal (p. 246), Brooks calls for reaffirmation of the "soul of our profession," pointing to the "works of creative and dedicated figures in our history—Frederick Law Olmsted, Daniel Burnham . . . Rexford Tugwell, and many others." On Page 241 of the same issue an ad under the headline, "Make No Big Plans," advertises a book by Melvin Levin, President of the AICP, published by APA Planners' Press, which calls such creativity and dedication (by implication) "a recipe for unhappiness for practicing planners." On page 147 appears a commentary properly pointing out some weaknesses in the APA's newly adopted ethical principles, including the vagueness of the statement that the "primary obligation of planners . . . is to serve the public interest." The remedy proposed: revise or eliminate it. As to the principle calling for supporting citizen participation, that is dealt with better in "analysis and essays" than in a statement of ethical principles. A clear picture of the right road for the profession hardly emerges from the assembly of those statements. The difficulty is inherent in planning in our society. Planning is not a single thing, a homogeneous entity that has a "soul" of its own; it is part and parcel of a divided society, and those who undertake it can and do serve widely different masters. We must decide whom we want to serve before we can establish what will happen to our souls.

NOTES

1 All quotations are from Brooks's article in the Spring 1988 issue of this journal; I have taken some liberties in juxtaposing quotations from different portions of the article—the last two are quotations by Brooks of Don Krueckeberg and Norm Krumholz—but I trust I did not distort Brooks's meaning.
2 I recommend Hans Blumenfeld's autobiography. *Life Begins at 65*, to anyone interested in the story of one courageous planner's reactions to the McCarthyism of the Philadelphia Planning Commission under Ed Bacon in the 1950s.

REFERENCES

Blumenfeld, Hans. 1987. *Life Begins at 65*. Montreal: Harvest House.

Boyer, Christine. 1983. *Dreaming the Rational City: The Myth of American City Planning*. Cambridge: MIT.

Foglesong, Robert. 1986. *Planning the Capitalist City: The Colonial Era to the 1980s*. Princeton, NJ: Princeton University Press.

Marcuse, Peter. 1980. Housing in Early City Planning. *Journal of Urban History* 6, 3.

The Uses and Misuses of History

Michael B. Teitz

Professor of City and Regional Planning, University of California

Earlier this year, at a meeting in Berkeley, I found myself defending Michael Brooks's article "Four Critical Junctures in the History of the Urban Planning Profession" against a sharp critique by Peter Marcuse. The focus of Marcuse's criticism was not the basic premise of the paper. Indeed, he agreed most strongly that the planning profession has lost its soul and needs to return to a utopian vision. Rather, he questioned the significance of the four specific historic shifts in professional behavior that Brooks asserted were critical to planners' loss of their traditional ideology and direction. To Marcuse, the really important reasons were not those that Brooks put forward, but rather a much broader set of concerns turning ultimately on the failure of the planning profession to become, at various moments in history, the vanguard of reform in American cities. Thinking it over afterwards, I realized that this was not the first time that I had been in the uncomfortable position of defending a piece of work that I did not particularly agree with against a criticism that seemed articulate but misdirected. In this instance, both authors used arguments constructed around historical propositions in order to support their advocacy of particular directions for the future development of the planning profession. Such arguments are often compelling, but they are also among the most egregious misuses of history.

For planners who also savor history, this is a good time. The past 30 years have seen more high quality historical scholarship on the profession and on cities than had the preceding century. We are beginning to find our roots, and in many instances they do not bear much resemblance to the stories of urban forms and great designers that have constituted much of conventional urban history. Although planning historians reflect many points of view and are certainly not value free, their work is for the most part careful and painstaking. The picture that emerges is complex, and it is often hard for the rest of us to let go of the comfortable myths with which we were indoctrinated in school. Nonetheless, one of the great virtues of history, for those willing to take the time and make the effort to read, is that it lets us see the past anew and better understand where we are. I believe that this is what Brooks and Marcuse would like to do, but this is not what they are actually doing.

The kind of historical argument used by Brooks and Marcuse takes specific events or groups of events out of context and puts them together in order to explain a particular historical outcome. Commonly, there is an imputation either of blame for choices made or of the historical inevitability of the outcome. In the present case it is the former. Analysis of such arguments calls for at least two questions to be asked. First, did the outcome, in fact occur? Second, does the explanation adequately account for it in terms of historical method and knowledge?

Reprinted by permission of the *Journal of the American Planning Association* 55, 1, Winter 1989.

Whether an outcome occurred appears to be an easy question in the case of a single event such as the Kennedy assassination, but it is much harder for complex social or institutional changes. Neither Brooks nor Marcuse does much more than assert the validity of the claim that the planning profession has fundamentally changed. Indeed, Brooks says, "Today's practitioners frequently find themselves engaged in activities that are far removed from the reformist, visionary, future-oriented spirit that initially attracted them to urban planning." An alternative hypothesis might suggest that what he is describing is the psychological development of aging professionals as much as the evolution of a profession. One certainly hears similar complaints elsewhere. Nonetheless, the question is amenable to research. How far was planning practice motivated by utopian or reformist impulses in the past? How much of that impulse remains today and in what form? Do present students differ in their ideology from those of the past? If so, are they less idealistic? There is some work on these questions and more could be done. Marcuse's view on the historic character and role of the visionary tradition is somewhat ambiguous. On the one hand, planning was and is the tool of capital; on the other, it might have been and might still be something else. Clearly, he does not see planning's past in a golden light of visionary ideals, though he is no less convinced of their value.

My view of this part of the issue is that the case is not made well. Brooks's unease about the state of the profession may have a sound basis, but it is intuitive and not dissimilar from a particular strand of discontent that I have heard from people in the professions for as long as I have been listening to them. Planners do seem to have a peculiar need to flagellate themselves (the obverse of idealism?), but if there is something wrong, we should set about finding what it is and do something about it if we care about our field.

The second question to be addressed to this type of argument is whether the explanation adequately accounts for the outcome. On this score, I have little doubt at all. Two applications of history are especially susceptible to misuse. They are grand syntheses and conspiracy theories. Planning has had its share of both. The Brooks/Marcuse arguments are essentially attempts to synthesize the evolution of the planning profession by reference to events that they select as critical. In neither instance are the events connected to each other and to planning in a coherent argument that is historically documented. The planning profession is treated as though it were a single entity that could somehow "decide" whether to take one or another path at the "critical junctures." The path taken in each case leads to perdition. In short, these are ideological arguments decked out with some suitably selected historical accoutrements. It is Roger Rabbit history, a combination of cartoon and reality that tells a simple story of good versus evil. It is amusing if done well, but should not be taken too seriously.

Is there any useful lesson to be drawn from all this? I think that we should pay more attention to the historical work that has been done and try to bring its findings to the attention of the field more effectively. In teaching, that means examining the content of history courses and assessing them carefully. The history of planning thought, especially, needs to be taught in professional programs in ways that enable students to tell the difference between ideology and analysis, rather than as a vehicle for the propagation of particular beliefs about the nature of planning. In the field at large, I would like to see historians engaging professionals more closely both in their writing and at meetings. They have much to offer to the rest of us, not least, in teaching us how to understand and use our professional past.

Planning History: What Story? What Meaning? What Future?

Marc A. Weiss
Professor of Urban Planning, Columbia University

Michael Teitz has advanced a strong and well-argued critique of the Brooks–Marcuse debate, essentially stating that planning history should not be used to promote pet causes. He suggests instead that planners should examine the historical record, including what historians have written, with an eye toward understanding what actually happened and why. Drawing from *The Rise of the Community Builders* (Weiss 1987) and my other research and writing projects on the history of urban planning and the planning profession, what follows are some thoughts on the Brooks–Marcuse debate from the viewpoint of a planning historian.

The fundamental problems with Michael Brooks's paper are two-fold. First, his argument is not really based in historical research and analysis. He is primarily comparing his personal perspective on the present status of the planning profession to an idealized past that never existed. Second, he confuses attitudes and ideologies with behavior and professional practice. His basic complaint about today's planners is that they no longer have heroic ideas like planning's pioneers from past generations. Brooks insists that the current planning profession is not in as good shape as he thinks it should be. He then asserts, without presenting any evidence to support his position, that the reason for this supposed crisis is that planners no longer espouse visionary or utopian values as did the legendary founders of the profession. The plain fact that the planning profession and organized urban planning activity is far more acceptable, influential, and extensive today than during the age of Daniel Burnham seems to make no difference in Brooks's nostalgic historical portrait.

At no time in the past has the planning profession ever consisted entirely of heroic leaders or seminal thinkers. Further, the issue of how influential planners have been in society is entirely different from how certain planners have affected the ideas of their professional colleagues. As Brooks points out, both public policy makers who control large budgets and private entrepreneurs with assets and investment capital have had more power to plan and shape the urban environment than have professional planners. While it is true that planners have always had their

Reprinted by permission of the *Journal of the American Planning Association* 55, 1, Winter 1989.

own special values, either as consultants or public officials they are constantly constrained by the values of their clients in the larger world of economics and politics. This was no less true in 1920 than it is today. Indeed, Brooks's complaint that the "planning office in many communities does little more than administer the local zoning process" has been a standard lament of planners since zoning was first established. It is probably one of the most consistent aspects of the history of planners' attitudes. Yet the spread of zoning beginning in the 1920s was precisely what created much of the demand for planners' ongoing services. With the rise of environmental movements in the past two decades, many planners today have much more freedom to espouse their personal values on the job than they have ever had before, including during Brooks's golden era of Alfred Bettman and Frederick Law Olmsted, Jr.

Contrary to what Brooks argues, planners have always advocated public–private partnerships and have always been valued for their ability to facilitate the development process. As I demonstrate in my book, the very foundations of modern land-use planning and regulation were rooted in joint efforts by government, business, and citizen groups to promote better residential, commercial, industrial, recreational, and other forms of development. From suburban housing tracts to downtown renewal, planners have played a key role in facilitating new development and redevelopment, and they have strongly believed in their role. Planners' organizations have frequently honored and included major real estate developers, from J. C. Nichols in 1917 to James Rouse in the 1980s. Planners in turn have consistently been active in developers' associations, such as the Urban Land Institute, whose original staff in the 1940s was mostly drawn from the planning profession. Daniel Burnham, after all, was probably America's leading "prodevelopment" architect at the turn of the century, and even Sunnyside and Radburn, the famous model communities designed by Clarence Stein and Henry Wright with encouragement from the Regional Planning Association of America (RPAA), were developed privately as a business proposition by Alexander Bing and the City Housing Corporation. Then as now, the main battle is defining and promoting "good" development while preventing "bad" development, with the values and practices around these issues constantly changing between times and places. To argue otherwise is to ignore the realities of historical experience.

Finally, Brooks contradicts himself by berating planners for being politically weak and professionally ineffective on the one hand, and then attacking them on the other hand for essentially "selling out" by attempting to strengthen their political and professional stature. As planning has become more widespread during the past century, there is no evidence to suggest that the field as a whole is less idealistic in its attitudes today than it was back in the time of John Nolen or Walter Blucher. Most planners are still attracted to this field because they have some type of vision and desire to improve communities. Whatever inspired planners back in 1909 continues to work its magic today. Two years ago the American Planning Association elected Norman Krumholz as its president. In the entire history of the NCCP/ACPI/AIP/ASPO/APA, no officially elected leader has better symbolized planning's idealistic, reformist aspirations than Krumholz and his quest for "equity planning." The fact that his election took place so recently stands as a dramatic refutation of Brooks's assertion that the "soul" of Tugwell and Davidoff has vanished from our profession.

Peter Marcuse is operating from a political agenda entirely different from that of Michael Brooks. Whereas Brooks wants to know why planners today are not more ideologically visionary and professionally esteemed, Marcuse asks why planners have not been and are not more radical—fighting for economic and social redistribution and political and structural change alongside their necessary allies among the working classes, the poor, and the dispossessed. This is a useful and interesting question, and Marcuse points to a series of historical events that in his view represent steps leading in the wrong (i.e., nonradical) direction for the planning profession. His argument is neither explored nor documented in analytical terms, and Marcuse's historical discussion is sparse in content and descriptive in form. His question is never answered, though a very strong normative argument is offered.

While the differences between Marcuse's and Brooks's positions are partly concealed by linguistic ambiguity, the authors appear to disagree quite significantly on the issues of who planners should be, what they should think, and how they should act. I suppose it is inevitable that arguing over the meaning of history will become part of any intense political–professional battle. Nevertheless, perhaps it would be helpful to separate the combatants long enough to take a more detailed and detached look at the past performance of American planners before we decide which lessons are the "correct" ones to be learned from the rich and complex historical legacy of our profession.

REFERENCE

Weiss, Marc A. 1987. *The Rise of the Community Builders: The American Real Estate Industry and Urban Land Planning*. New York: Columbia University Press.

On Ethics, History, and Planning Practice

Peter Marcuse
Professor of Urban Planning, Columbia University

Michael Brooks tried to raise key questions about the principles and goals of planning in his "Four Critical Junctures in the History of the Urban Planning Profession" in the pages of the *Journal* last year (54, 2: 24–48); the debate this commentary engendered, in the Winter 1989 issue (55, 1: 78–84), ended up straying from the points he was trying to make. Since I already have said my piece in that debate, I would not have responded further were it not for several pieces in the Spring 1989 *Journal* (55, 1: 79–81) that illustrate well the questions on which I think we need to focus.

Reprinted by permission of the *Journal of the American Planning Association* 55, 4, Autumn 1989.

The question Brooks raised, and to which I tried to respond, has to do with who planners serve, in the real world, and what goals they pursue, and why. Brooks argued that the profession has deviated from its original "utopian" goals because of choices *it* has made, and called for a return to its original vision. I argued in response that the choices the profession has made have been to serve the goals Brooks and I share. Both Michael Teitz and Marc Weiss responded to the discussion as if it were an academic discourse about planning history. Their points, well taken if that had been the case, miss the central question both Brooks and I tried to address: what *should* the planning profession do, what could it do, if it tries to serve ethical goals? Historical analysis can only furnish examples and lessons, not prescripts.

Examples from the Spring 1989 issue of the *Journal* nicely illustrate the point. Robert Cervero, in an excellent article, "Jobs-Housing Balancing and Regional Mobility," shows the negative effects of the jobs-housing imbalance in the suburbs, and urges planners to "seize the opportunity to use land development as a lever to improve mobility." What are the causes of the imbalance he attacks? "Fiscal and exclusionary zoning" and "growth moratoria," which have "unavoidably increased suburban housing prices." Planners appear as free agents, shaping the contours of suburbia; it is up to us to change them. But planners' actions must take into account "ad hoc market forces," or, to be more blunt, racial bigotry, land speculation, the growing polarization of the metropolitan area that finds its geographical reflection and reinforcement in suburban patterns. Planners need to address these issues, not just zoning questions, and need to address them both within and without their profession.

Look by contrast at Martin Wachs' letter on transit subsidies and user fees for automobiles as a way of alleviating the failures of U.S. public transit to achieve its potential. Wachs is aware of the professional levers available to improve public transit. But, he says, the preference for the automobile is a result of "the opportunity demanded by powerful groups to live, work, and travel in relative isolation from other, less influential groups." Planners can, and should, use more of the available tools to bring about change, but ultimately (is the inevitable conclusion) they must also participate in those broader, nonprofessional activities that address "the ethnic, racial, and economic divisions that are . . . salient in American urban policy-making."

Finally, consider two comments from the book review section: Grady Clay— "The historic function of planning has been to cope with the after-effects of industrialization. . . . covering the body to stop the smell without asking who fired the shot"; and Norman Krumholz—"[P]lanning is political, but planners should see this less as an opportunity to serve the mayor . . . than as an opportunity to . . . convince the mayor of the legitimacy of the planner's agenda."

The question Brooks tried to raise is what that agenda should be. The issue I tried to raise in response was the importance of politics in defining and implementing such an agenda—how the mayor is to be convinced. History can illuminate the alternatives, but not provide the answers. Let's get back to a discussion of what those answers should be.

TWELVE. PROFESSIONAL PLANNING—SUGGESTED READINGS

Argyris, Chris, and Donald A. Schon. 1974. *Theory in Practice: Increasing Professional Effectiveness.* San Francisco: Jossey-Bass.

Beauregard, Robert A. 1985. "Occupational Transformations in Urban and Regional Planning, 1960 to 1980." *Journal of Planning Education and Research* 5, 1:10–16.

Krieger, Martin H. 1975. "What Do Planners Do?" *Journal of the American Institute of Planners* 41, 5.

Michael, Donald N. 1973. *On Learning to Plan—and Planning to Learn.* San Francisco: Jossey-Bass.

Perloff, Harvey S. 1957. *Education for Planning, City, State and Regional.* Baltimore: Johns Hopkins.

Teitz, Michael B. 1984. "Planning Education and the Planning Profession." *Journal of Planning Education and Research* 3, 2:75–77.

13

FUTURE ISSUES

The Search for the Future Inside Ourselves

Joel Garreau

Joel Garreau is not a theoretician but a reporter, and a keen observer of
America. In *Edge City*, he asserts that Americans are in the process of making
the biggest changes in a hundred years in how they live and in their settlement
patterns. "Edge cities" are urban centers in spread-out form, far from downtown
but, according to Garreau, performing all the functions of conventional cities.
This may be the future, yet Americans have mixed feelings about its desirability.
Garreau argues, however, that our ambivalence about edge cities stems from a
deep division in American thought that goes back almost to the discovery and
habitation of the continent. Garreau states: "It comes to this. One vision of
American natural landscape was that it had inherent value and should be treasured for what it already was and had always been. The other saw in the land
nothing but satanic wastes; there could be placed on it no value until it was bent
to man's will—until civilization was forced into bloom" (p. 588).

Americans are creating the biggest change in a hundred years in how we build
cities. Every single American city that *is* growing, is growing in the fashion of Los
Angeles, with multiple urban cores.

These new hearths of our civilization—in which the majority of metropolitan
Americans now work and around which we live[1]—look not at all like our old
downtowns. Buildings rarely rise shoulder to shoulder, as in Chicago's Loop.
Instead, their broad, low outlines dot the landscape like mushrooms, separated by
greensward and parking lots. Their office towers, frequently guarded by trees, gaze
at one another from respectful distances through bands of glass that mirror the sun
in blue or silver or green or gold, like antique drawings of "the city of the future."

The hallmarks of these new urban centers are not the sidewalks of New York of
song and fable, for usually there are few sidewalks. There are jogging trails around
the hills and ponds of their characteristic corporate campuses. But if an American
finds himself tripping the light fantastic today on concrete, social scientists know
where to look for him. He will be amid the crabapples blossoming under glassed-
in skies where America retails its wares. We have quaintly if accurately named
these places after that fashionable tree-lined promenade created in the late 1600s—
the Mall in London's St. James's Park. Back then, its denizens even had a name for
the hour when the throng of promenaders "giggling with their sparks" was at its
height. They called it High Mall.[2] Pity we've not picked up that usage. We have
certainly picked up the practice, because malls usually function as the village
squares of these new urbs.

Our new city centers are tied together not by locomotives and subways, but by
jetways, freeways, and rooftop satellite dishes thirty feet across. Their characteris-

tic monument is not a horse-mounted hero, but the atria reaching for the sun and shielding trees perpetually in leaf at the cores of corporate headquarters, fitness centers, and shopping plazas. These new urban areas are marked not by the penthouses of the old urban rich or the tenements of the old urban poor. Instead, their landmark structure is the celebrated single-family detached dwelling, the suburban home with grass all around that made America the best-housed civilization the world has ever known.[3]

I have come to call these new urban centers Edge Cities. Cities, because they contain all the functions a city ever has, albeit in a spread-out form that few have come to recognize for what it is. Edge, because they are a vigorous world of pioneers and immigrants, rising far from the old downtowns, where little save villages or farmland lay only thirty years before.

Edge Cities represent the third wave of our lives pushing into new frontiers in this half century. First, we moved our homes out past the traditional idea of what constituted a city. This was the suburbanization of America, especially after World War II.

Then we wearied of returning downtown for the necessities of life, so we moved our marketplaces out to where we lived. This was the malling of America, especially in the 1960s and 1970s.

Today, we have moved our means of creating wealth, the essence of urbanism—our jobs—out to where most of us have lived and shopped for two generations. That has led to the rise of Edge City.

Not since more than a century ago, when we took Benjamin Franklin's picturesque mercantile city of Philadelphia and exploded it into a nineteenth-century industrial behemoth, have we made such profound changes in the ways we live, work, and play.

Good examples of our more than two hundred new Edge Cities are:

• The area around Route 128 and the Massachusetts Turnpike in the Boston region that was the birthplace of applied high technology
• The Schaumburg area west of O'Hare Airport, near which Sears moved its corporate headquarters from the 110-story Sears Tower in downtown Chicago
• The Perimeter Center area, at the northern tip of Atlanta's Beltway, that is larger than downtown Atlanta
• Irvine, in Orange County, south of Los Angeles

By any functional urban standard—tall buildings, bright lights, office space that represents white-collar jobs, shopping, entertainment, prestigious hotels, corporate headquarters, hospitals with CAT scans, even population—each Edge City is larger than downtown Portland, Oregon, or Portland, Maine, or Tampa, or Tucson. Already, two thirds of all American office facilities are in Edge Cities, and 80 percent of them have materialized in only the last two decades.[4] By the mid-1980s, there was far more office space in Edge Cities around America's largest metropolis, New York, than there was at its heart—midtown Manhattan.[5] Even before Wall Street faltered in the late 1980s there was less office space there, in New York's downtown, than there was in the Edge Cities of New Jersey alone.

Even the old-fashioned Ozzie and Harriet commute from a conventional suburb to downtown is now very much a minority pattern, U.S. Census figures show. Most of the trips metropolitan Americans take in a day completely skirt the old centers.[6] Their journeys to work, especially, are to Edge Cities. So much of our shopping is done in Edge Cities that a casual glance at most Yellow Pages shows it increasingly difficult in an old downtown to buy such a commodity item as a television set.[7]

These new urban agglomerations are such mavericks that everyone who wrestles them to the ground tries to brand them. Their list of titles by now has become marvelous, rich, diverse, and sometimes unpronounceable. The litany includes: urban villages,[8] technoburbs,[9] suburban downtowns,[10] suburban activity centers,[11] major diversified centers,[12] urban cores,[13] galactic city,[14] pepperoni-pizza cities,[15] a city of realms,[16] superburbia,[17] disurb,[18] service cities, perimeter cities, and even peripheral centers.[19] Sometimes it is not clear that everybody is talking about the same thing. My heart particularly goes out to the San Francisco reporter who just started calling whatever was seething out there, past the sidewalks, Tomorrowland.[20]

The reasons these places are tricky to define is that they rarely have a mayor or a city council, and just about never match boundaries on a map. We're still in the process of giving each Edge City its name—a project, incidentally, that could use more flair. In New Jersey, for example, there is one with only the laconic designation "287 and 78." The reason there are no "Welcome to" signs at Edge City is that it is a judgment call where it begins and ends.

Take the traditional measure of urban size—population. The out-counties where Edge Cities now rise are almost by definition larger than the cores they surround. After all, these places we thought of until recently as suburbs are where the majority of Americans have been living for decades.[21] Fairfax County, Virginia, is more populous than either Washington, D.C., or San Francisco. Ninety-two percent of the people in the New York metropolitan area do not live in Manhattan.[22]

A more narrow, and I think more accurate, comparison is to take Edge City—that acreage where the huge growth in jobs and other truly urban functions is centered—and compare it with the old central business district, the old downtown. Even by that tight measure, Edge City is almost always more populous. How many people in America, after all, live right in the old downtown? Fewer than live within sight of that Edge City landmark—the office monument so huge it would have been unthinkable to build one anywhere but downtown only thirty years ago.

That is why I have adopted the following five-part definition of Edge City that is above all else meant to be functional.

Edge City is any place that:

• *Has five million square feet or more of leasable office space—the workplace of the Information Age.* Five million square feet is more than downtown Memphis. The Edge City called the Galleria area west of downtown Houston—crowned by the sixty-four-story Transco Tower, the tallest building in the world outside an old downtown—is bigger than downtown Minneapolis.

• *Has 600,000 square feet or more of leasable retail space.* That is the equivalent of a fair-sized mall. That mall, remember, probably has at least three nationally famous department stores, and eighty to a hundred shops and boutiques full of merchandise that used to be available only on the finest boulevards of Europe. Even in their heyday, there were not many downtowns with that boast.

• *Has more jobs than bedrooms.* When the workday starts, people head toward this place, not away from it. Like all urban places, the population increases at 9 A.M.

• *Is perceived by the population as one place.* It is a regional end destination for mixed use—not a starting point—that "has it all," from jobs, to shopping, to entertainment.

• *Was nothing like "city" as recently as thirty years ago.* Then, it was just bedrooms, if not cow pastures. This incarnation is brand new.

An example of the authentic, California-like experience of encountering such an Edge City is peeling off a high thruway, like the Pennsylvania Turnpike, onto an arterial, like 202 at King of Prussia, northwest of downtown Philadelphia. Descending into traffic that is bumper to bumper in *both* directions, one swirls through mosaics of lawn and parking, punctuated by office slabs whose designers have taken the curious vow of never placing windows in anything other than horizontal reflective strips. Detours mark the yellow dust of heavy construction that seems a permanent feature of the landscape.

Tasteful signs mark corporations apparently named after Klingon warriors. Who put Captain Kirk in charge of calling companies Imtrex, Avantor, and Synovus?[23] Before that question can settle, you encounter the spoor of—the mother ship. On King of Prussia's Route 202, the mark of that mind-boggling enormity reads MALL NEXT FOUR LEFTS.

For the stranger who is a connoisseur of such places, this Dante-esque vision brings a physical shiver to the spine and a not entirely ironic murmur of recognition to the lips: "Ah! Home!" For that is precisely the significance of Edge Cities. They are the culmination of a generation of individual American value decisions about the best ways to live, work, and play—about how to create "home." That stuff "out there" is where America is being built. That "stuff" is the delicate balance between unlimited opportunity and rippling chaos that works for us so well. We build more of it every chance we get.

If Edge Cities are still a little ragged at the fringes, well, that just places them in the finest traditions of Walt Whitman's "barbaric yawp over the rooftops of the world"[24]—what the social critic Tom Wolfe calls, affectionately, the "hog-stomping Baroque exuberance of American civilization."[25] Edge Cities, after all, are still works in progress.

They have already proven astoundingly efficient, though, by any urban standard that can be quantified. As places to make one's fame and fortune, their corporate offices generate unprecedentedly low unemployment. In fact, their emblem is the hand-lettered sign taped to plate glass begging people to come to work. As real estate markets, they have made an entire generation of homeowners and speculators rich. As bazaars, they are anchored by some of the most luxurious shopping in the world. Edge City acculturates immigrants, provides child care, and offers safety. It is, on average, an *improvement* in per capita fuel efficiency over the old sub-urbia-downtown arrangement, since it moves everything closer to the homes of the middle class.

That is why Edge City is the crucible of America's urban future. Having become the place in which the majority of Americans now live, learn, work, shop, play, pray, and die, Edge City will be the forge of the fabled American way of life well into the twenty-first century.

There are those who find this idea appalling. For some who recognize the future when they see it, but always rather hoped it might look like Paris in the 1920s, the sprawl and apparent chaos of Edge City makes it seem a wild, raw, and alien place. For my sins I once spent a fair chunk of a Christmas season in Tysons Corner, Virginia, stopping people as they hurried about their holiday tasks, asking them what they thought of their brave new world. The words I recorded were searing. They described the area as plastic, a hodgepodge, Disneyland (used as a pejora-tive), and sterile. They said it lacked livability, civilization, community, neighbor-hood, and even a soul.

These responses are frightening, if Edge City is the laboratory of how civilized and livable urban America will be well into the next century. Right now, it is ver-tigo-inducing. It may have all the complexity, diversity, and size of a downtown. But it can cover dozens of square miles, and juxtapose schools and freeways and atria and shimmering parking lots with corporate lawns and Day-Glo-orange heli-copter wind socks. Its logic takes a while to decode.

Will we ever be proud of this place? Will we ever drag our visiting relatives out to show off our Edge City, our shining city on the hill? Will we ever feel—for this generation and the ones that follow—that it's a good place to be young? To be old? To fall in love? To have a Fourth of July parade? Will it ever be the place we want to call home?

Robert Fishman, a Rutgers historian who is one of the few academics success-fully to examine Edge City, thinks he knows that answer. "All new city forms appear in their early stages to be chaotic," he reports. He quotes Charles Dickens on London in 1848: "There were a hundred thousand shapes and substances of incompleteness, wildly mingled out of their places, upside down, burrowing in the earth, aspiring in the earth, moldering in the water, and unintelligible as in any dream."

That is also the best one-sentence description of Edge City extant.

Edge City's problem is history. It has none. If Edge City were a forest, then at maturity it might turn out to be quite splendid, in triple canopy. But who is to know if we are seeing only the first, scraggly growth? I once heard an academic with a French accent ask Fishman, seriously, what the *ideal* of an Edge City was. What a wonderfully French question! Who *knows* what these things look like when they grow up? These critters are likely only in their nymphal, if not larval, forms. We've probably never *seen* an adult one.

If Edge City still gives some people the creeps, it is partially because it con-founds expectations. Traditional-downtown urbanites recoil because a place blown out to automobile scale is not what they think of as "city." They find the swirl of functions intimidating, confusing, maddening. Why are these tall office buildings so far apart? Why are they juxtaposed, apparently higgledy-piggledy, among the malls and strip shopping centers and fast-food joints and self-service gas stations? Both literally and metaphorically, these urbanites always get lost.

At the same time, Edge City often does not meet the expectations of traditional suburbanites, either. Few who bought into the idea of quarter-acre tranquillity ever expected to take a winding turn and suddenly be confronted with a 150-foot colossus looming over the trees, red aircraft-warning beacons flashing, its towering glass reflecting not the moon, but the sodium vapor of the parking lot's lights.

The question is whether this disorienting expectation gap is permanent or simply a phase, a function of how fast we've transformed our world. I discussed this with scholars who had examined the history of Venice. Venice today is venerated by American urban planners as a shrine to livability. What was Venice like when it was new?

"People forget that Venice was built by hook or by crook," replied Dennis Romano, a social historian of the early Renaissance. "Venice was just as mercantilist as Tysons. It was full of land speculators and developers. The merchants' primary concern was the flow of goods, of traffic. Those who now romanticize Venice collapse a thousand years of history. Venice is a monument to a dynamic process, not to great urban planning. It's hard for us to imagine, but the architectural harmony of the Piazza San Marco was an accident. It was built over centuries by people who were constantly worried about whether they had enough money."

In his plan for the urban future that he christened Broadacre City, that most relentlessly American of urban visionaries, Frank Lloyd Wright, anticipated with stunning accuracy many of the features of Edge City.

"Nonsense is talked by our big skyscraperites in the blind alley they have set up, defending urban congestion by obscuring the simple facts of the issue," he trumpeted in the 1950s in *The Living City*. "Their skyscraper-by-skyscraper is . . . the gravestone of . . . centralization."[26]

Wright viewed as interchangeable the concepts of individualism, freedom, and democracy. He saw them as fundamentally in opposition to the despised, exploitative "monarchy" of the old downtowns. He yearned for a system in which all men fled the evils of big capital, big authorities, big cities—troglodytes of every stripe—for a connection with nature, the earth, the ground. He thought an acre per person was about right. He saw individuals newly freed coming back together in totally modern agglomerations, on new terms, stronger, growing together "in adequate space." He saw the automobile and aircraft as the glorious agents of that dispersion and reintegration, and he knew exactly what would happen when, inexorably, we blew Edge City out to their scale:

"After all is said and done, *he*—the citizen—is really the city.[27] The city is going where he goes. He is learning to go where he enjoys all the city ever gave him, plus freedom, security, and beauty of his birthright, the good ground."

How *about* that. We've done it! Just as he said. But are we in our new Edge Cities ever going to reap the benefits of what he knew we'd sow?

"Try to live . . . deep *in* nature," he exhorted us. "Be native as trees to the wood, as grass to the floor of the valley. Only then can the democratic spirit of man, individual, rise out of the confusion of communal life in the city to a creative civilization of the ground."

Edge City has quite clearly released us from the shackles of the nineteenth-century city—out into that valley and wood, just as Wright foresaw. It is common for a first-generation Edge City to arise ten miles from an old downtown, and a next-generation one twenty miles beyond that, only to attract workers from distances forty-five minutes beyond that. At this rate, it is easy to see how a field of Edge Cities can easily cover more than ten thousand square miles. This is why the San Francisco area now statistically is measured as halfway across California, pulling commuters out of Stockton, in the Central Valley, into its Edge Cities east of Silicon Valley.

Whether that spatial liberation leads to Wright's "creative civilization of the ground," however, came to be my main concern, for it is central to the battles being fought in America today over such amorphous essentials as "growth" and "quality of life."

The forces of change whose emblem is the bulldozer, and the forces of preservation whose totem is the tree, are everywhere at war in this country. The raging debate over what we have lost and what we have gained, as we flee the old urban patterns of the nineteenth century for the new ones of the twenty-first, is constant. Are we satisfying our deepest yearnings for the good life with Edge City? Or are we poisoning everything across which we sprawl?

Getting to the bottom of those questions leads directly to issues of national character, of what we value. They come down to who we are, how we got that way, and where we're headed. It is why, when the reeling feeling caused by Edge City finally subsides, I think it is possible to examine the place as the expression of some fundamental values. Nowhere in the American national character, as it turns out, is there as deep a divide as that between our reverence for "unspoiled" nature and our enduring devotion to "progress."

In *The Machine in the Garden*, the cultural historian Leo Marx writes about our complicated attitudes toward utilitarian versus pastoral landscapes. For Americans, he observes,

> Regenerative power is located in the natural terrain: access to undefiled, bountiful, sublime Nature is what accounts for the virtue and special good fortune of Americans. It enables them to design a community in the image of a garden, an ideal fusion of nature with art. The landscape thus becomes the symbolic repository of value of all kinds—economic, political, aesthetic, religious . . .
>
> A strong urge to believe in the rural myth along with an awareness of industrialization as counterforce to the myth—since 1844, this motif appears everywhere in American writing . . . It is a complex distinctively American form.[28]

One springtime, over lunch near his MIT office, Marx observed that Edge City represents "an escape from the negative aspects of civilization. Too much restraint, oppression, hierarchy—you justify building out there in order to start again and have another Garden. You want the best of both worlds. This would be Thomas

Jefferson's Virginia; he very explicitly wanted a land that is midway between too much and too little civilization."

In fact, says Marx, the whole thing goes back to the very dawn of our civilization. Captain Arthur Barlowe, captain of a bark dispatched by Sir Walter Raleigh, described Virginia in 1584 in what became a cardinal image of America: an immense garden of incredible abundance. Virginia is a land of plenty; the soil is "the most plentifull, sweete, fruitfull, and wholsome of all the worlde"; the virgin forest is not at all like the "barren and fruitles" woods of Europe. We "found shole water," Barlowe wrote, "wher we smelt so sweet and so strong a smel, as if we had bene in the midst of some delicate garden abounding with all kinde of odoriferous flowers . . ."[29]

What Barlowe was describing, of course, was Eden. That image inflamed the popular imagination as the first English settlement succeeded in America, in Jamestown, Virginia, 1607. It drove Shakespeare when, three years later, he wrote *The Tempest*.[30]

What is so striking about these reports depicting Virginia as Paradise Regained—tapping a deep and persistent human desire to return to a natural idyll—is how sharply they conflict with the views of the second set of Englishmen to show up in America to stay. Those were the Pilgrims of the Massachusetts Bay. When the *Mayflower* hove to off Cape Cod in November 1620, what William Bradford saw shocked him. He described it as a "hidious and desolate wilderness, full of wild beasts and willd men." Between the Pilgrims and their new home, he saw only "deangerous shoulds and roring breakers."[31]

This wasn't heaven. Quite the opposite.

"Which way soever they turnd their eys (save upward to the heavens) they could have litle solace or content . . . The whole countrie, full of woods and thickets, represented a wild and savage heiw."

His people, said Bradford, had "no friends to wellcome them, nor inns to entertaine or refresh their weatherbeaten bodys, no houses or much less townes to repaire too, to seeke for succoure."

There was, in short, no civilization. Bradford found this void horrifying, hellish.

Here, then, is established the enduring divide in the way Americans have related to their land ever since. The hideous wilderness appears at one end of the spectrum, and the Garden at the other. These are such antithetical ways for man to understand his relation to his environment that Leo Marx calls them "ecological images. Each is a kind of root metaphor, a quite distinct notion of America's destiny." These vastly different systems of value, noted Ralph Waldo Emerson, would "determine all their institutions."

It comes to this. One vision of the American natural landscape was that it had inherent value and should be treasured for what it already was and had always been. The other saw in the land nothing but satanic wastes; there could be placed on it no value until it was bent to man's will—until civilization was forced into bloom.

The history of America is an endless repetition of this battle. We are fighting it to this day, nowhere more so than in our current frontier, Edge City. In the unset-

tled, unsettling environment of Edge City, great wealth may be acquire
out a sense that the place has community, or even a center, much less a
the resolution of these issues goes far beyond architecture and landscap
to the philosophical ground on which we are building our Information Age
It's possible that Edge City is the most purposeful attempt Americans have
since the days of the Founding Fathers to try to create something like a new l

Edge City may be the result of Americans striving once again for a new, rest
tive synthesis. Perhaps Edge City represents Americans taking the functions of t
city (the machine) and bringing them out to the physical edge of the landscape (th
frontier). There, we try once again to merge the two in a newfound union of nature
and art (the garden), albeit one in which the treeline is punctuated incongruously
by office towers.

If that is true, Edge City represents Americans once again trying to create a new
and better world—lighting out for the Territory, in the words of Huckleberry Finn.
If that new world happens to be an unknown and uncharted frontier, well, that's
where we've headed every chance we've had—for four hundred years. Frank Lloyd
Wright genuinely believed that Americans continued to be the sons and daughters
of the pioneers. He called us "the sons of the sons of American Democracy."
Wright saw us as heading out of our old cities, freed from old verities, creating a
new spiritual integrity in community. The enduring, exhilarating, and frightening
themes to be examined in Edge Cities are if, whether, and how we are pulling that
Utopian vision off.

This goes to the ultimate significance of Edge City. The battles we fight today
over our futures do not have echoes only back to 1956, when Dwight D.
Eisenhower changed America forever with the creation of the interstate highway
program. Nor does it go back only to the New Deal of the 1930s, during which
Franklin Delano Roosevelt shaped America into a society of homeowners. It goes
to the core of what makes America America, right back to the beginning, with the
Pilgrims in 1620 and the Virginia Cavaliers of 1607.

It addresses profound questions, the answers to which will reverberate forever.
It addresses the search for Utopia at the center of the American Dream. It reflects
our perpetually unfinished American business of reinventing ourselves, redefining
ourselves, restoring ourselves, announcing that our centuries-old perpetual revolution—our search for the future inside ourselves—still beats strong.

It suggests that the world of the immigrants and pioneers is not dead in America;
it has just moved out to Edge City, where gambles are being lost and won for high
stakes. It adds another level of history to places already filled with ghosts. That is
why one day Edge City, too, may be seen as historic. It is the creation of a new
world, being shaped by the free in a constantly reinvented land.

NOTES

1 the majority of metropolitan Americans now work: Residential and job statistics from
U.S. Bureau of the Census, *Statistical Abstract of the United States, 1990*, 110th ed.
(Washington, D.C., 1990). Office space statistics from Salomon Brothers, Inc., New

York, and the Office Network, Houston. See also Robert Fishman, "Megalopolis Unbound," *Wilson Quarterly* (1990): 24.

2 High Mall: *Oxford English Dictionary*, see "mall."

3 the best-housed civilization: See, for example, Irving Welfeld, *Where We Live: The American Home and the Social, Political, and Economic Landscape, from Slums to Suburbs* (New York: Simon & Schuster, 1988).

4 Already, two thirds of all American office facilities: Peter O. Muller, *Journal of Urban History* 13, no. 3 (May 1987): 352.

5 By the mid-1980s, there was far more office space: Existing prime office space inventory, March 1988: midtown Manhattan, 155.6 million square feet; downtown Manhattan (Wall Street), 78.2 million square feet. Existing prime office space inventory in New York suburbs (Edge Cities), December 1987: 183.7 million square feet (21.1 million on Long Island, 33.5 million in Westchester, 40.1 million in Fairfield, and 89.0 million in northeastern New Jersey). Even by the mid-1980s, more than twice as much space was under construction in the Edge Cities of the New York area than in all of Manhattan, a trend that continues into the 1990s. By 1988, 11.6 million square feet were being absorbed in the Edge Cities, but the Manhattan figure actually turned to a negative 800,000 square feet. See David Shulman et al., *New York Metropolitan Area Office Market* (New York: Salomon Brothers, July 1988); Thérèse E. Byrne, *The Edge City as a Paradigm: Remodeling the I-78 Corridor* (New York: Salomon Brothers, September 1989). Also see "The Office Network Office Market Report" (Houston, various dates); Peter O. Muller, "A Review of *Suburban Gridlock* by Robert Cervero," *Geographical Review* 78, no. 4 (October 1988), 447–48.

6 Most of the trips metropolitan Americans take: "According to the 1980 U.S. Census, there were twice as many suburbanites commuting to suburban jobs in metropolitan areas as there were to jobs in the central cities. Between 1960 and 1980, intrasuburban commuting accounted for 57 percent of the increase in metropolitan commuting. Less than 8 percent of regional workers—ranging from 3 percent in Los Angeles to 10.9 percent in San Francisco—are employed in the 10 largest urbanized areas. For a typical area, the central business district commuter probably represents less than 10 percent of all highway travelers during the heaviest rush hour." *Myths and Facts About Transportation and Growth* (Washington, D.C.: The Urban Land Institute, 1989). Also see Robert Cervero, *Suburban Gridlock* (New Brunswick, N.J.: Rutgers University, Center for Urban Policy Research, 1986); Cervero, *America's Suburban Centers: A Study of the Land Use/Transportation Link* (Washington, D.C.: U.S. Department of Transportation, January 1988); Alan E. Pisarski, *Commuting in America: A National Report on Commuting Patterns and Trends* (Westport, Conn.: Eno Foundation for Transportation, 1987); U.S. Bureau of the Census, *Statistical Abstract of the United States*.

7 a casual glance at most Yellow Pages: In the 1989 Bell Atlantic Yellow Pages for the District of Columbia (not its Maryland or Virginia "suburbs," which are served by separate directories), eighty-five numbers were listed under "Television & Radio—Dealers." Of those, only ten could be construed as being in the area's otherwise large and thriving downtown. Of those ten dealers, more than half were located in neighborhoods that stretched the definition of "downtown"—Georgetown or southwest D.C., for instance.

8 urban villages: Christopher B. Leinberger and Charles Lockwood, "How Business Is Reshaping America," *Atlantic*, October 1986.

9 technoburbs: Robert Fishman, *Bourgeois Utopias: The Rise and Fall of Suburbia* (New York: Basic Books, 1987).

10 suburban downtowns: Truman A. Hartshorn and Peter O. Muller, "Suburban Downtowns and the Transformation of Metropolitan Atlanta's Business Landscape," *Urban Geography* 10, no. 4 (1989).

11 suburban activity centers: Urban Land Institute, Washington, D.C.

12 major diversified centers: Thomas Baerwald, "Major Diversified Centers in Midwestern Metropolises" (Paper presented to the West Lakes Division of the Association of American Geographers, November 1983).

13 urban cores: Robert Charles Lesser & Co., Los Angeles.

14 galactic city: Peirce F. Lewis, "The Galactic Metropolis," in *Beyond the Urban Fringe*, ed. Rutherford H. Platt and George Macinko (Minneapolis: University of Minnesota Press, 1983).

15 pepperoni-pizza cities: Peter O. Muller, University of Miami.

16 a city of realms: James E. Vance, Jr., *This Scene of Man: The Role and Structure of the City in the Geography of Western Civilization* (New York: Harper & Row, 1977), 408–9.

17 superburbia: *Philadelphia* magazine.

18 disurb: Short for "dense, industrial, and self-contained suburban region." Mark Baldassare, University of California, Irvine.

19 service cities, perimeter cities, and even peripheral centers: James Timberlake, Kieran, Timberlake & Harris, Philadelphia.

20 "Tomorrowland": David Beers, "Tomorrowland: We Have Seen the Future, and It Is Pleasanton," *San Francisco Examiner*, Sunday, January 18, 1987, *Image* magazine.

21 majority have been living: The 1970 Census showed that the U.S. population included more suburbanites than city dwellers or farm residents. The 1980 Census showed that in the fifteen largest U.S. metropolitan areas, the majority of residents lived outside the central city in every one except Houston, which had an aggressive policy of annexing former suburbs.

22 Ninety-two percent of the people: U.S. Bureau of the Census, 1987 estimate for New York–northern New Jersey–Long Island, NY-NJ-CT CMSA: 18,053,800. New York County, 1989 update: 1,428,285, or 7.91 percent of the total.

23 Who put Captain Kirk in charge: I am indebted to the *Wall Street Journal* for first addressing this burning question.

24 "barbaric yawp over the rooftops of the world": Walt Whitman, "Song of Myself," *Leaves of Grass* (1892; reprint, New York: New American Library, 1955).

25 "hog-stomping Baroque exuberance": Tom Wolfe, *From Bauhaus to Our House* (New York: Farrar, Straus & Giroux, 1981).

26 "Nonsense is talked by our big skyscraperites": Frank Lloyd Wright, *The Living City* (New York: Horizon Press, 1958), 81. This book incorporates the work published under the title *When Democracy Builds* (1945).

27 "After all is said and done": Ibid., 81–82.

28 "regenerative power is located in the natural terrain": Leo Marx, *The Machine in the Garden: Technology and the Pastoral Ideal in America* (London: Oxford University Press, 1964), 228.

29 "Barlowe": Ibid., 36–37.

30 "Shakespeare": Ibid., 41.

31 "Bradford": Ibid., 41–42.

THIRTEEN. FUTURE ISSUES—SUGGESTED READINGS

Gleick, James. 1987. *Chaos: Making a New Science*. New York: Viking Penguin.

Isserman, Andrew. 1985. "Dare to Plan: An Essay on the Role of the Future in Planning Frontier and Edgetown." *Town Planning Review* 65, 4.

Louv, Richard. 1990. *Children's Future: Listening to the American Family; New Hope for the Next Generation*. Boston: Houghton Mifflin.

Schorr, Lisbeth B. 1988. *Within Our Reach*. New York: Anchor Books, Doubleday & Co., Inc.

Sennett, Richard. 1990. *The Conscience of the Eye*. New York: Knopf.

Shalala, Donna E., and Julia Vitullo-Martin. 1989. "Rethinking the Urban Crisis: Proposals for a National Urban Agenda." *Journal of the American Planning Association* 55, 1.

Van Der Ryn, Sim, and Peter Calthorpe. 1986. *Sustainable Communities: A New Design Synthesis for Cities, Suburbs and Towns*. San Francisco: Sierra Club Books.

Vernon, Raymond, William Alonso, Anthony Downs, Peter Hall, and Lawrence Susskind. 1991. "The Coming Global Metropolis: Symposium Essays." *Journal of the American Planning Association* 57, 1.

Wilson, William Julius. 1987. *The Truly Disadvantaged: The Inner City, the Underclass, and Public Policy*. Chicago: The University of Chicago Press.